THE ROUTLEDGE HANDBOOK OF HALAL HOSPITALITY AND ISLAMIC TOURISM

T0313234

The Routledge Handbook of Halal Hospitality and Islamic Tourism provides a greater understanding of the current debates associated with Islamic tourism and halal hospitality in the context of businesses, communities, destinations, and the wider socio-political context. It therefore sheds substantial light on one of the most significant travel and consumer markets in the world today and the important role of religion in contemporary hospitality and tourism.

The book examines halal hospitality and lodging, Islamic markets, product developments, heritage, certification, and emerging and future trends and issues. It integrates case studies from a range of countries and destinations and in doing so emphasises the significant differences that exist with respect to regulating and commodifying halal, as well as stressing that the Islamic market is not monolithic. Written by highly regarded international academics, it offers a range of perspectives and enables a comprehensive discussion of this integral part of Islam and contemporary society.

This handbook will be of significant interest to upper level students, researchers, and academics in the various disciplines of Tourism, Hospitality, Food Studies, Marketing, Religious Studies, Geography, Sociology, and Islamic Studies.

C. Michael Hall is a Professor in the Business School at the University of Canterbury, New Zealand; Docent in the Department of Geography, University of Oulu, Finland; and a Visiting Professor, Linnaeus University, Kalmar, Sweden. His research interests include tourism, regional development, sustainability, global environmental change, and food.

Girish Prayag is Associate Professor of Marketing in the School of Business at the University of Canterbury, New Zealand. His research interests include place attachment, organisational resilience, disaster management, and tourist emotions.

THE ROUTLEDGE HANDBOOK OF HALAL HOSPITALITY AND ISLAMIC TOURISM

Edited by C. Michael Hall and Girish Prayag

Routledge
Taylor & Francis Group

LONDON AND NEW YORK

First published 2020
by Routledge
2 Park Square, Milton Park, Abingdon, Oxon OX14 4RN

and by Routledge
605 Third Avenue, New York, NY 10017

First issued in paperback 2022

Routledge is an imprint of the Taylor & Francis Group, an informa business

British Library Cataloguing-in-Publication Data
A catalogue record for this book is available from the British Library

Library of Congress Cataloging-in-Publication Data
Names: Hall, Colin Michael, 1961- editor. | Prayag, Girish, editor.
Title: The Routledge handbook of halal hospitality and Islamic
tourism / edited by C. Michael Hall and Girish Prayag.
Other titles: Handbook of halal hospitality and Islamic tourism
Description: Abingdon, Oxon ; New York, NY : Routledge, 2019. |
Includes bibliographical references and index.
Identifiers: LCCN 2019003034 (print) | LCCN 2019016694 (ebook) | ISBN 9781315150604 (eBook) |
ISBN 9781138557055 (hardback : alk. paper) | ISBN 9781315150604 (ebk)
Subjects: LCSH: Tourism--Religious aspects--Islam. | Muslim travelers. |
Hospitality--Religious aspects--Islam. | Hospitality industry--Islamic countries.
Classification: LCC G156.5.R44 (ebook) | LCC G156.5.R44 R68 2019 (print) |
DDC 338.4/791091767--dc23
LC record available at https://lccn.loc.gov/2019003034

ISBN 13: 978-1-138-55705-5 (hbk)
ISBN 13: 978-1-03-240146-1 (pbk)

DOI: 10.4324/9781315150604

Typeset in Bembo
by Integra Software Services Pvt. Ltd.

As-salaam Alaikum. Peace be upon you.

This volume is dedicated to the Muslim community of Christchurch and to the wider Islamic community of New Zealand. You are Us.

and

to the memory of Michele Carboni

CONTENTS

FIGURES

PLATES

TABLES

CONTRIBUTORS

Erin Addison, Wadi Musa, Jordan and Campo, Colorado, USA

Bailey Ashton Adie, School of Business, Law and Communications, Solent University, Southampton, Hampshire, UK

Muhammad Hasmi Abu Hassan Asaari, School of Management, Universiti Sains Malaysia, 11800 USM, Pulau Pinang, Malaysia

Hamed Al-Azri, Department of Marketing, College of Economics and Political Science, Sultan Qaboos University, Muscat, Oman

Paul W. Ballantine, Department of Management, Marketing and Entrepreneurship, University of Canterbury, Christchurch, New Zealand

Michele Carboni, Centre for North South Economic Research (CRENOS), Università degli studi di Cagliari, Via San Giorgio, 12, 09124 Cagliari, Italy

Ning (Chris) Chen, Department of Management, Marketing and Entrepreneurship, University of Canterbury, Christchurch, New Zealand

Ben Debney, Deakin University, Burwood, 221 Burwood Hwy, Burwood, Victoria 3125 Australia

Teoman Duman, Department of Business Administration, Epoka University, Tirana, Albania

Firdaus Ahmad Fauzi, Department of Foodservice Management, Faculty of Hotel and Tourism Management, Universiti Teknologi MARA, Kampus Puncak Alam, Shah Alam, Selangor, Malaysia

Mazuri Abd Ghani, Faculty of Economics and Management Sciences, Universiti Sulan Zainal Abidin, 21300 Kuala Nerus, Terengganu, Malaysia

C. Michael Hall, Department of Management, Marketing and Entrepreneurship, University of Canterbury, Christchurch, New Zealand; Department of Geography, University of Oulu, Oulu, Finland; and Linnaeus University, Kalmar, Sweden

Saman Hassibi, Department of Management, Marketing and Entrepreneurship, University of Canterbury, Christchurch, New Zealand

Kieran Hegarty, Faculty of Arts, Monash University, Clayton, Victoria, Australia

Joan C. Henderson, Lochearnhead, Perthshire, Scotland

Muhammad Azman Ibrahim, Faculty of Business and Management, Universiti Teknologi MARA Puncak Alam, Selangor, Malaysia

Rami K. Isaac, Centre for Sustainability, Tourism & Transport, NHTV Breda University of Applied Sciences, Mgr Hopmansstraat 2, 4817 JT Breda, The Netherlands; Institute of Hotel Management & Tourism, Bethlehem University, Rue des Freres, Bethlehem, Palestine

Noorliza Karia, Operations Section, School of Management, Universiti Sains Malaysia, 11800 USM, Pulau Pinang, Malaysia

Vai Shiem Leong, UBD School of Business and Economics, Universiti Brunei Darussalam, Tungku Link, BE1410 Brunei Darussalam

Sharifah Zannierah Syed Marzuki, Faculty of Business Management, Universiti Teknologi MARA: Shah Alam, Selangor, Malaysia

Masairol Masri, UBD School of Business and Economics, Universiti Brunei Darussalam, Tungku Link, BE1410 Brunei Darussalam

Nazlida Muhamad, UBD School of Business and Economics, Universiti Brunei Darussalam, Tungku Link, BE1410 Brunei Darussalam

Deniz Parlak, European University Viadrina, Frankfurt (Oder), Brandenburg/Icerenkoy, Karsli Ahmet Str. No 80A/37, Atasehir/Istanbul 34752 Turkey

Carlo Perelli, CRENoS, Centre for North South Economic Research, Via San Giorgio, 12, 09124 Cagliari, Italy

Girish Prayag, Department of Management, Marketing and Entrepreneurship, University of Canterbury, Christchurch, New Zealand

Shanshan Qi, Institute for Tourism Studies, Macao, China

Omar Abed Rabo, Department of Humanities, Bethlehem University, Jerusalem

Nor Hidayatun Abdul Razak, Faculty of Business Management, Universiti Teknologi MARA, Kampus Puncak Alam, Shah Alam, Selangor, Malaysia

Mohd. Rizal Razalli, School of Technology Management and Logistics, College of Business, Universiti Utara Malaysia, Sintok, Kedah, Malaysia

Leela Riesz, Florence, Massachusetts, USA

Siti Asma' Mohd Rosdi, Faculty of Management and Economics, Universiti Pendidikan Sultan Idris, Kampus Sultan Azlan Shah, Proton City, Tanjong Malim Perak, Malaysia

Talha Salam, UBD School of Business and Economics, Universiti Brunei Darussalam, Tungku Link, BE1410 Brunei Darussalam

Amir Sayadabdi, Department of Anthropology, University of Canterbury, Christchurch, New Zealand

Shuko Takeshita, Department of Japanese Cultural Studies, Aichi Gakuin University, 12 Araike, Iwasaki-cho, Nisshin, Japan

Bronwyn P. Wood, College of Business and Economics, Department of Business Administration, United Arab Emirates University, Al Ain, Abu Dhabi, United Arab Emirates

PREFACE

Probably at few times in recent history has the movement and mobility of people of the Islamic faith been so significant yet so misunderstood. Islam is simultaneously a major world religion that affects consumption and business practices globally; a market of an estimated 1.8 billion people, including a rapidly growing international tourism market; a major influence on food-ways as a result of specific food requirements; and an area of contested political identity in many countries. In this climate there is therefore a clear need for an improved understanding of the significance of Islamic tourism and hospitality in both Muslim and non-Muslim majority countries and destinations.

To engage in travel and come to understand and engage with the world is an integral part of Islam. International travel by Muslims, what is widely called Islamic tourism, has become a major market targeted by Muslim and non-Muslim majority countries alike. Yet, like many faiths, Islam requires its adherents to follow certain behaviours and practices. Halal, what is lawful under Islam, therefore becomes a major factor in Islamic consumption as well as the capacity to provide services to Muslim customers. Although food is a significant component of the halal concept, the notion of what is permissible and appropriate goes beyond food to cover many aspects of hospitality and tourism. This Handbook has therefore been prepared so as to provide a source book for those interested in gaining a better understanding of different aspects of Islamic tourism and hospitality from a range of different perspectives and contexts.

Despite the size of the Islamic tourism market and its influence on lodging and accommodation design, food provision, and wider entertainment and hospitality provision, knowledge of the market and its requirements by non-Muslims is often extremely limited. The notion of 'halal' being a case in point. The word halal literally means permissible, and in translation it is usually used as lawful. The concept covers all aspects of Islamic life. However, to many non-Muslims the term is often understood only in relation to meat that has been killed in an Islamic fashion. Such a situation is clearly of significance when the notion of halal covers so many dimensions of tourism-related consumption and their appropriateness. Moreover there are differing interpretations of halal and its implementation within the various major Islamic traditions and in different Islamic countries that also necessitate a more sophisticated understanding of the concept than has previously been the case, even including previous works on Islamic tourism. For example, while a number of countries have been moving to formalise halal regulations and certification arrangements there may be negative responses from some businesses to such measures because of their impact on notions of trust and their role in commodifying religion, i.e. potentially changing what is a personal sacred relationship with God to something that is profane and which is embedded in neoliberal ideologies of branding, competitiveness, strategy and marketisation. Indeed, there are significant tensions between Islamic hospitality as derived from the teachings in the Qur'an and the hadith and the demands of contemporary commercial tourism and hospitality enterprises as well as governments and politicians who seek to promote halal and Islamic tourism for economic and political advantage.

Despite religious and other differences many countries are seeking to develop tourism from Islamic markets. Such travel may be overtly religious in purpose, e.g. pilgrimage in its various forms, or may be leisure, business or visiting friends and relations based. Destinations and the businesses within them may need to modify hotel and restaurant designs in order to cater to some Islamic markets while for other markets and businesses changes will be minimal. Even the nature of tourism marketing itself may need to be adapted to the needs of the Islamic market, while the wider business environment will also have significant implications for Islamic tourism and hospitality. Therefore, this book seeks to provide a contribution to improving understanding of a major international tourism market and its implications in the context of businesses, communities, destinations and the wider socio-political context, while also providing a critical account of some of the wider debates and issues surrounding halal hospitality today.

This Handbook is divided into several parts to help provide a greater understanding of the main issues associated with Islamic tourism and halal hospitality. After a comprehensive introduction the book is divided into five major parts on halal hospitality and lodging, halal markets and developments, heritage tourism, emerging issues and relationships in certification, and issues and challenges. The majority of the chapters on halal hospitality and lodging have a Malaysian focus which highlights that country's move to position itself as an international halal hub. Part II on halal markets and development reflects some of the diversity that is to be found in the Islamic tourism market and presents chapters drawing from both market and destination perspectives. Part III consists of three chapters each highlighting some of the issues associated with the potential commodification of Islamic heritage by tourism and the advantages and disadvantages this may bring. The chapters also begin to recognise some of the political issues associated with Islamic heritage. Part IV presents chapters that examine emerging halal certification issues including in relation to non-Muslim countries and logistics. Part V presents chapters that discuss major issues and challenges with respect to halal hospitality and Islam. For example, several chapters examine the way in which halal and Islam has become a part of the politics of identity. However, it is important to recognise that this is not just in Western countries but also applies to Islamic-majority countries as well and how halal certification and the Islamification of the marketplace may be used more for political and economic ends than the promotion of the spiritual values of halal and Islam. The book then concludes with a brief chapter that discusses a research agenda for halal hospitality and Islamic tourism.

Hospitality and by its nature, tourism, is a defining element in bringing different people together in a political, cultural and religious context. It is integral to our humanity and belief system and reflects as to whether our statements with respect to hospitality are more than just words. Importantly, this is reflected in terms of how we welcome others into our own homes, how we welcome them into our public space and our countries, and how we welcome them into our commercial spaces of hospitality and lodging. Tourism, arguably, brings all these different spaces of hospitality into one and sheds substantial light on how we welcome strangers and others. The search for knowledge is intimately connected to the act of travel. How do we then welcome our fellow travellers? Hospitality is therefore a space to reflect on ourselves and our ethical and moral conduct. At a time in which some politicians seek to build walls and fences to keep people out and others either seek to exterminate other voices even when they have been given assurance that they would be held safe or ignore the persecution of their fellow human beings for economic and political gain, then hospitality research provides a space for reflection indeed. We therefore hope that the chapters in this book will provide such a space for critical reflection on tourism and hospitality not only in an Islamic context but beyond.

C. Michael Hall and Girish Prayag

ACKNOWLEDGEMENTS

Michael would like to thank a number of colleagues with whom he has undertaken related research over the years and who have often enacted their own hospitality over the years. In particular, thanks go to Dorothee Bohn, Tim Coles, David Duval, Martin Gren, Stefan Gössling, Johan Hultman, Dieter Müller, Paul Peeters, Yael Ram, Jarkko Saarinen, Dan Scott, Anna Dóra Sæþórsdóttir and Allan Williams for their thoughts, as well as for the stimulation of Agnes Obel, A Long Walk, Ann Brun, Beirut, Paul Buchanan, Nick Cave, Bruce Cockburn, Elvis Costello, Stephen Cummings, Chris Difford and Glenn Tilbrook, David Bowie, Ebba Fosberg, Father John Misty, Mark Hollis, Hoodoo Gurus, Margaret Glaspy, Aimee Mann, Larkin Poe, Vinnie Reilly, Matthew Sweet, David Sylvian, and The Guardian, BBC6 and KCRW—without whom the four walls of a hotel room would be much more confining. Michael would like to thank the many people who have supported his work over the years, and especially the Js and the Cs who stay at home and mind the farm. Girish would like to thank his parents, Ansoomatee and Jayduth, for their continuous love and support and would especially like to offer grateful thanks to Lyndon, Chris and Emma for putting up with him through yet another book.

We are indebted to the support of several people at the University of Canterbury, but particularly Irene Joseph, as well as our various graduate students who have worked on halal-related topics over the years. Jodyne Cowper-James has provided invaluable assistance with proofreading and editing. We would also like to gratefully acknowledge the support of The Federation of Islamic Associations of New Zealand to host a research symposium on halal tourism. Finally, we would like to thank the ongoing support of Emma Travis at Routledge for the book.

C. Michael Hall and Girish Prayag

ABBREVIATIONS

AFIC	Australian Federation of Islamic Councils
CAC	Codex Alimentarius Commission
CIBAL BRAZIL	Central Islamica Brasileira de Alimentos Halal
COMCEC	Standing Committee for Economic and Commercial Cooperation of the Organization of the Islamic Cooperation
DOE	Department of Environment
ETP	Economic Transformation Programme
FIANZ	Federation of Islamic Associations of New Zealand
HDM	Halal Directory Malaysia
HFSAA	Halal Food Standards Alliance of America
HICO	Halal International Certification Organization
HMC	Halal Monitoring Committee
IBH	Islamic-based hospitality
IFANCA	Islamic Food and Nutrition Council of America
IPP	Industry Partner Programme
IQS	Islamic Quality Standard
ISDB	Islamic Development Bank
ISNA	Islamic Society of North America
ISWA	Islamic Society of the Washington Area
JAKIM	Department of Islamic Development of Malaysia/Jabatan Kemajuan Islam Malaysia
JIT	Japan Islamic Trust
MATRADE	Malaysia External Trade Development Corporation
MFT	Muslim-friendly tourism
MHA	Malaysia Hotel Association/Muslim Consumers Association of Malaysia
MOF	Ministry of Finance Malaysia
MOTAC	Ministry of Tourism and Culture
MOTOUR	Ministry of Tourism
MUI	Indonesian Council of Ulama/Majelis Ulama Indonesia
MUIS	Islamic Religious Council of Singapore/Majlis Ugama Islam Singapura
OIC	Organisation of Islamic Cooperation

PEMANDU	Unit Pengurusan Prestasi dan Pelaksanaan
SESRIC	The Statistical, Economic and Social Research and Training Centre for Islamic Countries
TEKUN	National Entrepreneur Group Economic Fund/Tabung Ekonomi Kumpulan Usaha Niaga
UNWTO	United Nations World Tourism Organisation
WTTC	World Travel & Tourism Council

1

INTRODUCTION TO HALAL HOSPITALITY AND ISLAMIC TOURISM

C. Michael Hall, Nor Hidayatun Abdul Razak, and Girish Prayag

Introduction

Halal means permissible in Arabic and the concept is a cornerstone of Islam and is used to refer to what is permissible to Muslims. For many non-Muslims, the idea of halal is often thought to relate only to food and what is allowed to be consumed by Muslims (Regenstein, Chaudry & Regenstein 2003; Riaz & Chaudry 2004; Bonne & Verbeke 2008). However, although important, the notion of halal is much wider than just food and relates to all aspects of life (Wilson & Liu 2011). The source of what constitutes halal and *haram* is derived from the *Quran*, The prophet's *Hadith* (the Prophet Mohammed's teachings), and what Islamic jurists have deemed as haram (forbidden).

In recent years the notion of halal tourism and hospitality has become an increasingly important part of the global tourism and hospitality industry and has also received much greater recognition in the academic literature. Of course, if we are honest, by this we mean that the Islamic market and its hospitality and tourism needs has finally become recognised as economically significant by people, usually from Western countries or companies, who are not of the Islamic faith, although the economic potential of the halal market has also become a focus of Organisation of Islamic Cooperation (OIC) countries. It has become a part of, what Rudnyckyj (2009) terms, "the spiritual economy". But such economic recognition is only part of the story. Certification of halal and the development of specific standards provide new opportunities for international trade and competitiveness, including the positioning of countries within the Islamic world as they vie for political and economic leadership and advantage, as well as positioning of Islam within their own countries. Globalisation and the expansion of international tourism also means that a number of Muslim majority countries have also become important international tourism destinations in their own right, while migration has also meant the growth of significant Muslim minorities in Europe, the Americas, and Australasia. This has meant that there is also now greater cultural recognition of Islam and the need to better understand the implications of the faith for tourism and hospitality by industry, tourists and policy-makers as well as the measures undertaken by businesses and governments to meet the needs of Muslim travellers and visitors.

Telfer (1996: 83) defines hospitality as "the giving of food, drink and sometimes accommodation to people who are not regular members of a household" (see also Telfer 2000). The religious dimensions of tourism and hospitality have been given increased attention in the academic literature. For example, with respect to pilgrimage (Henderson 2011), religious needs (Weidenfeld 2006), religious lodging experience (Hung 2015), religious issues and patterns (Din 1989), religious facilities (Shuriye & Che Daud 2014), certification (Aziz & Chok 2013; Abdul, Ismail, & Mustapha 2013; Marzuki, Hall, & Ballantine 2012a), and religious identity (Eum 2008). However, the religious dimensions of hospitality indicate the potential for tensions between the commercial material and technical dimensions of hospitality and tourism industry services and the social relationship between host and guest which may be highly influenced by religious belief systems and different cultures of hospitality (Aramberri 2001; Carboni & Janati 2016; Siddiqui 2015; Kushimoto 2017; Yarbakhsh 2018).

Seen from the perspective of economic exchange, hospitality can be defined as "the method of production by which the needs of the proposed guest are satisfied to the utmost and that means a supply of goods and services in a quantity and quality desired by the guest and at a price that is acceptable to him [*sic*] so that he [*sic*] feels the product is worth the price" (Tideman 1983: 1). Yet despite the centrality of economic exchange in commercial hospitality relationships, hospitality is also a socio-cultural domain in which there are "requirements to offer shelter to strangers, to provide food and drink and protection from danger. These obligations extended to all, irrespective of status or origins" (Lashley 2008: 71). Both hosts and guests are expected to respect each other in giving and accepting the hospitality. In many countries, these obligations originate from cultural or religious beliefs that function in tandem with economic relationships. Furthermore, any division between hospitality in terms of commercial operations and hospitality in the home is also breaking down or at least becoming more fluid given the growth of operations such as Airbnb and the commercial home (Gössling & Hall 2019; Hall 2009). Indeed, the social dimensions of hospitality are often promoted as a point of differentiation by many commercial providers whether large or small (Lashley 2008).

Nevertheless, commercial hospitality operations emphasise that the hospitality provider "provides, and fulfils" (King 1995: 229) the customer's requirements. According to King, hospitality in the commercial context is

> a specific kind of relationship between individuals—a host and a guest. In this relationship, the host understands what would give pleasure to the guest and enhance his or her comfort and well-being, and delivers it generously and flawlessly in face to face interactions, with deference, tactfulness and the process of social ritual. The objective is to enhance guest satisfaction and develop repeat business.
>
> *(King 1995: 229)*

Yet, if King's statement is considered in relation to the religious beliefs of hospitality suppliers and consumers, it is clear that tensions between commercial and religious understandings of hospitality concept could be difficult to manage both between and within people (Saad, Ali, & Abdel-Ati 2014). Furthermore, not being able to meet religious requirements may have commercial consequences, for example, Muslim customers may not be comfortable with some accommodation services and be dissatisfied or not even purchase them (Laila, Kholidah, & Abdurrahman 2012) while providers may miss the opportunity to penetrate local and global markets (Samori, Ishak, & Kassan 2014). The need to understand the religious requirements of customers should therefore be part of a broader improved cultural understanding strategy in tourism and hospitality education, training, and research programmes for those working in the sector. In the case of the present book this is clearly focused on Islam, but it is readily apparent that in the global tourism and hospitality marketplace other religious beliefs also require greater understanding.

This first introductory chapter introduces the reader to some of the issues surrounding religion, hospitality, and the host–guest relationship in both a general religious context and with respect to Islam. A major theme highlighted in this chapter, and throughout the book, is the apparent tension between religious and commercial needs, including the interpretation of what hospitality actually means. The chapter also provides a brief introduction to Islamic tourism and hospitality before the concept of halal hospitality is discussed in further detail in the following chapter.

Religion, hospitality, and the host–guest relationship

Religion is arguably essential to understanding the development of the host–guest relationship in hospitality. According to Aramberri (2001) host–guest relationships in the pre-modern era of hospitality are based on three features: protection, reciprocity, and duties for both sides (host and guest). Religious teachings are a means to structure and inform such features. For example, Siddiqui (2015) linked the scriptures of the three Abrahamic religions—Christianity, Judaism, and Islam—to the host–guest relationship. She stresses the obligation of hosts to treat the guests well as a reflection of the worship of God based on the story of Prophet Abraham welcoming guests in *Genesis* 18:1–10, and serving food (calf) in Quran 51:24–30 and *Hebrews* 13:2. In fact, generosity and life-giving qualities in hospitality are seen potentially to create the possibility of long-term relationships with others (Burgess 1982). However, Aramberri (2001) argued that pre-modern traditions of host–guest relationships do not work in the modern hospitality industry as it is not a long-term relationship that requires reciprocity if the roles are swapped in the future. In addition, the long-term relationship exists more based on the provider–customer relationship (i.e. a loyal customer relationship) that involves a monetary transaction (Lugosi 2008). Arguably, providers may not be able to be genuine in the commercial context (Lashley & Morrison 2000) as substantial pressures may exist between hospitableness (i.e. generosity) and its costs to the business (Hemmington 2007; Weidenfeld 2006).

Kirillova, Gilmetdinova, and Lehto (2014) also indicate that religion is an important factor in host–guest relationships and suggest that religious differences between host and guest can be a threat to positive hospitality service (see also Wijesinghe 2007). Nevertheless, O'Gorman (2009) notes that commercial hospitality does portray some aspects of humanity and spirituality. He argues that protection and security are still offered to guests in contemporary hospitality practices such as by strictly following security protocols, providing CCTV, and strong linkages with police, fire, and other security personnel in order to increase security (Cowell, McDavid, & Saunders 2012). In such cases the generosity in safeguarding the customers' security is shown through the effort given by the providers.

Studies on hospitality in a religious context are relatively limited (Kirillova et al. 2014; Timothy & Iverson 2006; Weidenfeld 2006). Kirillova et al.'s (2014) study on the interpretation of hospitality across different religions, found that Muslim and Christian participants interpreted hospitality as helping those in need among their own community and then extending it to strangers. Such interpretations emphasise the priority of hospitality towards members of a community instead of to total strangers, as typically occurs in commercial host–guest relations. Kirillova et al. (2014) also claimed that specific teachings associated with each religion possibly influence interpretations of appropriate hospitality behaviours. For example, Christians are expected to love their neighbours as they love themselves, Muslims should be generously hospitable to neighbours, and Buddhists should be hospitable and charitable to friends, relatives, and neighbours. However, these representations are from those who are considered religious in the context of their respective religion rather than the commercial context of hospitality (Chambers 2009).

Hospitality in a religious context can involve rituals or collective acts of worship to religious commitment that contribute to the development of social relationships through the adoption of common religious values and experience (Hassan 2005, 2007). Meeting the requirements or regulations of belief systems can be challenging to business. A study by Cheung and Yeo-chi King (2004) found that devoted Confucian business providers considered that adhering to Confucian moral values slowed their business growth and reduced profit making, as the values prioritise righteousness over profitability in business dealing. Similarly, halal providers in Muslim and non-Muslim countries face difficulties in ensuring that their tourism packages are strictly halal due to their inability to adhere to the halal concept (Eid & El-Gohary 2015; El-Gohary 2016). Difficulties to commit to religious rituals has led to numerous cases of kosher fraud in the United States and influenced some states to implement disclosure laws to force vendors to show evidence that their kosher products were genuine (Tieman & Hassan 2015). Hence, offering hospitality within the context of religious requirements can be a challenge for providers, especially those who cater to global markets (Hassan 2007), while the role of religiosity is also important in understanding hospitality in the context of the religious requirements of guests.

Religious customers are regarded as customers with requirements that are proscribed by their religious beliefs and that are involved with tourism activities other than pilgrimage (Hung 2015). The needs of religious customers may include specific religious requirements that affect staffing, facilities, servicescape, and information services. Studies on the needs of religious customers have grown given the needs of providers in understanding religious customers' expectations in multi-religion destinations (Weidenfeld & Ron 2008). Whilst fulfilling religious needs are necessary for customers to practise their daily religious routine, fulfilling such needs can improve their satisfaction with the hospitality and tourism experience (Weidenfeld 2006).

Customers' religion and religiosity influence consumption habits (Fischer 1998, 2008, 2011; Fischer & Lever 2016; Hanzaee & Ramezani 2011; Jamal 2003), including customers' concerns as to food choices in hospitality service, which is arguably one of the most widely recognised aspects of religion in service provision. Some foods are permitted and others prohibited for religious customers. For example, Jews will look for kosher, Muslims for halal, and Hindus for vegetarian offerings (Mak, Lumbers, Eves, & Chang 2012; Sack 2001). These restrictions require providers to pay attention to the provision of foods in hospitality services including not only the dishes that are served, but also the use of ingredients, the food supply chain, and food preparation procedures (Hanzaee & Ramezani 2011).

Every religion has norms and rules that are shared among the religious communities and those who do not understand may conflict with religious norms and rules (Hung 2015). Religions such as Buddhism, Christianity, Hinduism, Islam, Judaism, and Shinto have teachings that affect food requirements (Table 1.1). Fasting is also often an important matter for religious customers. Customers will consider looking at places that could cater their needs, such as during the Ramadan fasting month when Muslim customers will need providers that serve meals for breaking fast in the evening and breaking-dawn (*sahur*). Buddhists and Hindus will look to accommodation that provides vegetarian foods; and Jews will consider providers that could provide food that strictly prepared according to kosher requirements. Although some followers may not comply due to unavailability of appropriate food or differences in local custom (Dugan 1994), providers should consider religious needs in order to better respond to their customers as well as add value to their hospitality service (Tama & Voon 2014; Weidenfeld & Ron 2008).

Table 1.1 Religious food restrictions

Major religion	Restrictions	Remarks
Buddhism	Prohibition of meat, meat products, or their derivatives in any food intake Prohibition of use on onions, leeks, garlics, scallions, and chives Alcohol use is strongly discouraged	Soybeans and products derived from them are major sources of protein for Buddhists. Follow a lacto–ovo–vegetarian diet (meaning milk, milk products, and eggs are permitted). Fasting is up to individuals.
Christianity	The Methodist Church recommends limiting the use of alcohol. Christian Scientists and members of the United Church of Christ are strongly discouraged from using it. Jehovah's Witnesses do not condone excessive drinking of alcohol. Meat must have the blood completely drained from the carcass before it may be consumed. Kosher meats are acceptable. There is no ritual fasting. Seventh-day Adventists strongly discourage alcohol consumption and strongly encourage a lacto–ovo–vegetarian diet. Meat must be kosher. Caffeine, aged cheeses, and 'hot' spices (peppers) are also discouraged. There is no ritual fasting. Eastern Orthodox Church members prohibit red meat intake on Wednesdays or Fridays during the liturgical year, and the very observant also refrain from eating fish, poultry, and dairy products on these days. During Lent (this church follows the Jewish calendar), red meat, poultry, dairy, and fish are not allowed at any time. From Good Friday until Easter Sunday only small meals and water are allowed. Roman Catholics prohibit red meat or poultry products or their derivatives on Fridays during Lent; however, fish, eggs, and dairy products are allowed. On the two mandatory fast days, Ash Wednesday and Good	African Methodist Episcopalians, Episcopalians (Anglicans), Disciples of Christ, Lutherans, and Presbyterians have no food prohibitions, no fasting period, and no restrictions on alcohol. Alcohol is permitted to all Baptists.

(Continued)

Table 1.1 (Cont).

Major religion	Restrictions	Remarks
	Friday, only small snacks are allowed, no meat is allowed, but drinks are permitted throughout the day. Mormons do not allow alcohol; so-called 'hot' drinks such as coffee and tea; cold caffeinated drinks such as colas; and any chocolate and other food products that contain caffeine. The first Sunday of each month is a voluntary fast day.	
Hinduism	Meat, fish, eggs, garlic, onions, mushrooms, and root vegetables that resemble a head are not allowed. Alcohol use is strongly discouraged.	The Hindu religion recognizes five castes of people. People are born into their caste; they cannot change castes over their lifetime. They only eat food prepared by members of the same caste. Mixed-caste dining is not allowed. A person of the highest caste (a Brahmin) cannot dine with a person of the opposite sex or with a non-Hindu. Before eating, Hindus ritually clean themselves by taking a bath; hands, feet, and mouth are washed before and after eating. Fasting is associated with special events, such as marriages.
Islam	Prohibition of pork and pork-derived foods, including lard and bacon, and flesh and other products from carnivorous animals or from those that eat carrion. Alcohol in all forms is forbidden. No contamination of *halal* (permitted) and *haram* (prohibited) utensils for kitchen use.	During Ramadan, which lasts about a month, Muslims fast from before sunrise until after sunset. During the fast all drinking water and smoking are forbidden.
Judaism	The dietary rules consist of two parts: forbidden foods and the process of cooking foods. Kosher foods (allowed to eat) must follow both parts.	The mashgiach monitor the whole process, including the kosher ingredients that are used; cleaning products used on machines; meat and dairy products are not mixed; and the cleanliness of the kitchen operations. Once it meets all requirements, a kosher symbol can be used on the products.

Meat products must be from animals that have cloven hoofs and chew their cud. For example, beef can be kosher (if butchered properly), while pork can never be kosher. By-products (lard or animal gelatin, for example) from non-kosher animals are forbidden. Only the four quarter cuts from kosher animals are permitted. Animals must be slaughtered in a humane manner and according to a set process with specific equipment by a butcher (approved by Jewish community). The blood is drained, and the cuts are salted to remove all traces of blood. Only fish with fins and scales are permitted, shellfish is forbidden as well as by-products of non-kosher fish. Only domesticated birds are permitted and must come from a certified kosher farm. Meat and dairy products cannot be consumed or served together, for example, beef stroganoff, a turkey and swiss cheese sandwich, or a cheeseburger. Kosher kitchens have two sets of cooking utensils to avoid contamination of meat and dairy items.	Judaism has six fasting days: Yom Kippur, Tisha, Fast of Esther, Tzom Gedaliah, the Tenth of Teves, and the Seventeenth of Tammuz. Given the complexities of Jewish dietary rules there is strong interest in veganism. In 2018 it was reported that Israeli vegans make up 5% of the country's population, a higher percentage than anywhere else in the world. Growing religious zeal for veganism has been fostered by rabbis who question whether the Jewish faithful should eat animals at all, especially under modern farming methods considered inhumane. Animal abuse is explicitly forbidden in the Bible. In September 2017, more than 70 rabbis from around the world signed a declaration urging Jews to choose veganism.	
Shinto	No specific food taboos, however, eating meat is considered to render a person unclean for several days and thus ineligible to enter the shrine.	None.

Source: Adapted from Dugan, 1994; Regenstein, Chaudry, & Regenstein, 2003; Holmes, 2018.

Religious-based food restrictions may affect not only what you eat but how and where one eats, and who with. For example, in Hinduism, members of the Brahman caste do not eat with subordinate castes. Some Muslim customers also appreciate eating-places that are separately reserved for women and men as well as for family members only (Shechter 2011; Sobh, Belk, & Wilson 2013). Issues related to segregation between sexes in a hospitality and tourism setting remain substantially under-researched and, in addition to food, include religious-inspired rules involving spas, swimming pools, and recreational treatments (Oktadiana, Pearce, & Chon 2016). These are significant issues as they may pose very different management and design issues from those set by secular markets, and providers' awareness of these issues may also be lacking, leading to potential issues in managing accommodation and hospitality services for religious customers.

Of course, not only are the religious perspectives of consumers important to understanding the place of religion in the host–guest relationship but also those of providers and suppliers. Through the analysis of relevant texts and in-depth interviews with 30 respondents, including Buddhists, Christians, and Muslims, Kirillova et al. (2014) indicate that irrespective of religious beliefs, hosts have prioritised their own communities first with respect to hospitality, then outsiders. Their study suggests there are differences in the interpretation of hospitality and hospitable behaviour in line with religious values (Table 1.2). Interestingly, the role of religious hospitality in a commercial context was well understood as part of the needs of business ventures. For example, Buddhists saw that friendly behaviour in commercial hospitality can help to retain business and the Christian and Muslim respondents in Kirillova et al.'s (2014) study viewed their behaviour as consistent with financial and business expectations. Moreover, the providers also pointed out that as their relationship with customers of different religions involved financial transactions, the guests were entitled to *claim* hospitality instead of only *accepting* it. This business venture relationship is also consistent with Aramberri's (2001) perspectives on the transformation of the host–guest paradigm in contemporary hospitality, in which it is framed more towards a relationship between a

Table 1.2 Perspectives on commercial hospitality behaviour by Buddhists, Christians, and Muslims

Buddhists	*Christians*	*Muslims*
• Although being a monetary exchange, it should be no different from private hospitality • Donate money and give blessings to others • Consider dietary restrictions, particularly offering vegetarian food	• Being pleasant and welcoming • Genuinely greeting people • Staff should be hospitable • Being and acting with sincerity • Treating everyone equally	• Commercial sphere is seen as less genuine than other domains and is standardised and impersonal • As a business donate to the local community • Treat everyone equally • Hard to balance religious and commercial demands • Interaction with customers is important • Be mindful of dietary needs • Provide place for prayer to allow guests to fulfil their religious duties

Source: Derived from Kirillova et al., 2014.

provider and a customer in a business situation rather than a more personal host and guest relationship.

The study of hospitality in a religious context has opened up discussions about and the need for greater understanding of halal and Islamic hospitality (Yusof & Muhammad 2013). Although halal has become another segment in hospitality and tourism offerings, and is gaining popularity in Muslim and non-Muslim countries alike, there are many areas of debate and contention such as the application of Islamic principles in Islamic hospitality (Laila, Kholidah, & Abdurrahman 2012), halal certification (Marzuki, Hall, & Ballantine 2012b), halal food standards (Razalli, Yusoff, & Roslan 2013), and halal accommodation (Samori & Sabtu 2012). Confusion and lack of understanding of the concept and its requirements affect both the provision of halal hospitality and consumer acceptance (Yusof & Muhammad 2013), as well as making it difficult for destination marketing organisations to appropriately position themselves in the halal tourism market.

The significance of halal tourism

Islamic tourism may be simply defined as tourism by Muslims (Zamani-farahani & Henderson 2010). The terms 'halal hospitality', 'sharia tourism', 'Islamic tourism' or 'Muslim tourism' are often used interchangeably with that of 'halal tourism' although, as will be noted, these terms should be treated slightly differently. In reflecting on the social and relational nature of tourism and religion, halal or Islamic tourism is defined by Razzaq, Hall, and Prayag (2016) as tourism and hospitality that is co-created by consumer and producer in accordance with the teachings of Islam.

Many nations in the Islamic world are capitalising on the rise in demand for Muslim-friendly tourist services. Henderson (2010) argues that the concept of Islamic tourism is a recent one, and one that has been gathering pace in some countries in South East Asia such as Malaysia and Singapore. Although, in some ways, such a perspective is surprising given the significance attached to travel in Islam, both relating to the duties of a Muslim with respect to pilgrimage as well as the importance that the Quran attaches to travel and knowledge of the world. Nevertheless, countries such as Malaysia have been trying to brand themselves as a global halal hub (Bon & Hussain 2010; Syed Marzuki et al. 2012a, 2012b), and are capitalising on catering to Muslim tourists' needs especially the ones from Middle Eastern countries by offering halal tourism products. Similarly, Singapore has also begun to promote itself as a Muslim-friendly country to the Muslim world. Both these countries have seen a significant rise in Muslim tourists arriving at their shores (Henderson 2010).

Industry reports often emphasise the financial significance of the halal market (Euromonitor 2015), and halal travel in particular, for example the Organisation of Islamic Cooperation (OIC 2017) expect halal tourism to be worth $243 billion by 2021. Such promotion of the halal travel market reflects that the Muslim market represents approximately just over 20 per cent of the world population (Isfahani, Pourezzat, Abdolmanafi, & Shahnazari 2013), but, despite the size of the market with its particular characteristics, Islamic tourism has been a relatively minor area of academic interest (Alserhan 2010; Alserhan & Alserhan 2012; Carboni, Perelli, & Sistu 2014; Razalli et al. 2013; Stephenson 2014). Nevertheless, given the growing levels of disposable incomes in some Muslim populations and increased international mobility, Islamic tourism is attracting attention from governments, institutions, and researchers that recognise its potential economic and employment benefits (Haq & Wong 2010; OIC 2017). For example, the Islamic Development Bank (ISDB) sees potential in Islamic tourism stimulating economic and social growth of Muslim countries (Okhovat 2010) and emphasises the socio-economic development and poverty reduction dimensions by encouraging the integration of Islamic values in tourism activities. Similarly, the OIC is actively engaged in tourism capacity building among its members.

> considering the modest share of the OIC region in the world tourism market and the concentration of the tourism activity in only a few OIC countries, it seems that a large part of the tourism potential of the OIC region remains unutilised.
>
> The problems facing tourism and the development of a sustainable international tourism sector in the OIC countries are less trained human resources, poor governance as well as low quality services.
>
> *(OIC 2018)*

The Statistical, Economic and Social Research and Training Centre for Islamic Countries (SESRIC) reported that in 2011 international tourist arrivals in the OIC countries reached 151.6 million, representing a 15.2 per cent share in the total international tourist arrivals worldwide and generating US$135.5 billion of international tourism receipts with a 13.0 per cent share in the world's total tourism receipts (OIC Secretariat 2014). The number of international tourist arrivals in the OIC region fell from 179.4 million in 2014 to 173.4 million in 2015. As a result, international tourism receipts in OIC countries decreased from $167 billion in 2014 to $139 billion in 2015. Overall, the OIC countries' share of total international tourist arrivals was 14.9 per cent in 2015 and the share of total tourism receipts was 10.1 per cent (OIC 2017). Nevertheless, these figures highlight the potential for tourism growth among OIC members. Indeed, the OIC countries are behind the global average with respect to both employment generation from international tourism, estimated at 6.4 per cent of total employment in OIC members in 2018 compared to 9.8 per cent globally, as well as the total contribution of tourism to gross domestic product (GDP), 8.7 per cent in the OIC states compared to 10.3 per cent globally (OIC 2017). Nevertheless, the total contribution of tourism to GDP in the OIC countries has gradually been increasing. Of the 36 OIC countries for which data is available, 22 countries had a surplus in which their international tourism receipts exceeded tourism expenditures with Turkey, Malaysia, and Morocco having the highest surplus. Of the 14 OIC countries with an international tourism trade deficit, Kuwait, Saudi Arabia, and Nigeria had the largest deficits (OIC 2017).

Most of the receipts from international tourism in OIC countries are concentrated in ten destinations: Turkey, Malaysia, Saudi Arabia, Egypt, Morocco, Indonesia, Kuwait, Tunisia, Jordan, and Iran. However, it should be noted that these statistics include travel by non-Muslims to these countries as well as Muslim travellers. Indeed, many predominantly Muslim countries and countries for which Islam is the official state religion also have significant non-Muslim minorities. Middle East countries generated US$83.2 billion in exports by visitors in 2016 and this is forecast to reach US$148.3 billion in 2027 in tourism revenue (World Travel & Tourism Council [WTTC] 2017).

Growth in travel for leisure and business by Muslims has created increased interest in their travel needs, and especially the various products and services they use, including accommodation, food services, transportation, attractions, and other related sectors to the hospitality service (Sahida, Rahman, Awang, & Man 2011). According to the OIC (2017) in a global survey jointly conducted by Dinar Standard and Crescent Rating, 'halal food', 'overall price', and a 'Muslim-friendly experience' were ranked among the top three Muslim tourist market needs. Similarly, a survey reported by the Standing Committee for Economic and Commercial Cooperation of the Organization of the Islamic Cooperation (COMCEC 2016) examined the factors that influence the choice of Muslim tourists regarding destinations and found that the existence of 'Muslim-Friendly Tourism' (MFT) services, the total cost of these services, and the friendliness of locals, were the top three factors affecting the decision of where Muslims travel for leisure (OIC 2017). Nevertheless, COMCEC have also noted a low level of awareness of MFT standards by Muslim tourists in Turkey (OIC 2017).

The need to respond to Islamic values in a commercial tourism and hospitality setting has also generated awareness of the need to ensure that business products and services that cater to, or seek to target, the Islamic market, satisfy requirements of being halal, and avoid that which is haram (forbidden in Arabic). The commercial satisfaction of halal requirements for Muslim travellers is often referred to as halal hospitality, while the demand for halal hospitality services when customers are on a leisure holiday is referred to as halal tourism. Importantly, the concept is not recognised in Islamic majority countries alone and, as a result of changing patterns of international migration and travel, the concept has been introduced to non-Muslim countries such as Canada, Taiwan, Hong Kong, and Australia (Kamali 2011). The commercialisation and commodification of halal as a product and as a brand has also led to increased efforts to regulate and certify halal products in both Muslim and non-Muslim countries given increased international trade in halal products, recognition of consumer rights, and a desire to give confidence in halal brands (Friese 2009; McMillan, O'Gorman, & MacLaren 2011; Zizek 1997).

Interest in the Muslim market is undoubtedly part of the reason why many accommodation and other tourism and hospitality providers offer halal products and services (Wilson et al. 2013; Stephenson 2014). Yet, much of the focus in the existing halal literature has been on halal food certification (Fernando, Zailani, & Mohamed 2010; Zailani et al. 2010; Razalli et al. 2013; Samori et al. 2014), rather than on the larger picture of what constitutes halal in a hospitality and tourism setting (Alserhan et al. 2018). This means that much of the existing work on halal in a hospitality context has been focused on the restaurant sector (Gayatri, Hume, & Mort 2011; Marzuki, Hall, & Ballantine 2014; Prabowo, Abd, & Ab 2012). While the technical aspects of halal are important, as with many religions, hospitality in the Islamic context is more than just a technical or commercial service and is understood as being part of a particular set of social relationships that are imbued with a broader spiritual significance and which potentially affect the broader orientation towards, and relationships with, customers. For example, hospitality is noted in the Quran (*Adz-Dzaariyat* 24–27), where it is about manners in entertaining guests even though they are strangers.

> Has the story reached you, of the honoured guests of Abraham (PBUH)? When they came in to him and said: "Peace be upon you!" He [Abraham] replied: "Peace be upon you," and said: "You are a people unknown to me." Then he turned to his household secretly and brought out a fattened [roasted] calf. Then placed it before them [noticing that they refrained from eating, he said]: "Will you not eat?"
>
> (Adz-Dzaariyat *24–27*)

These verses indicate the way guests should be provided hospitality. The manners and obligations of entertaining guests are further elaborated and the ways in which Muslims are required to understand and implement halal hospitality in their daily lives are discussed.

As noted above, the concept of hospitality has a number of different dimensions. For example, Lashley and Morrison (2000) suggest that it involves social, private, and commercial dimensions. Hospitality in a social dimension represents the obligation to entertain guests genuinely according to culture and religion. The private dimension of hospitality refers to the hospitality offered to guests at home, and a commercial dimension revolves around the relationship of host and guests in a business context in which hospitality services are sold. To these dimensions we can also add a technical dimension of hospitality, which refers to the products and services that are provided by hospitality businesses in order to meet religious and other requirements and which are often subject to regulation and governance by religious and/or governmental authorities. The technical dimension in this book refers primarily to halal certification and other requirements, including the provision of a prayer room, prayer mat, direction to Kiblah, Quran, and prayer timetable (Battour, Ismail, & Battor 2011). Even though the social and commercial dimensions of hospitality in general are discussed in previous research (Marci 2013; McMillan et al. 2011; Mukherjee 2014), there is relatively limited knowledge of these two dimensions in the context of halal hospitality, compared with the interest shown by tourism and hospitality agencies and researchers in the technical dimension.

Nevertheless, there are significant tensions in the provision of halal hospitality and tourism services. From a social perspective, halal hospitality is concerned with the hospitable conduct of the relationship between host and guest (generous and genuine), religious aspects (spiritual and ritual), and trust (commitment) (Ismaeel & Blaim 2012). However, from a technical perspective, halal hospitality is concerned with the material aspects of hospitality provision that meet halal status. This comes not only from the interpreted authority of the Quran and the Sunnah that prescribe the way of life for Muslims, but also from government and religious institutions that can regulate products and services which is sometimes referred to as shariah tourism or hospitality in Islamic societies, meaning that which is lawful in Islam. Yet there is no single global halal standard, whether for food, hospitality, or tourism. Instead, there are a multitude of certifying bodies internationally, with many countries having established a halal authority to address halal issues or recognising different bodies within the country. Examples of these halal authorities include the Department of Islamic Development of Malaysia/Jabatan Kemajuan Islam Malaysia (JAKIM), the Indonesian Council of Ulama/Majelis Ulama Indonesia (MUI), the Japan Islamic Trust (JIT), the Federation of Islamic Associations of New Zealand (FIANZ), the Islamic Religious Council of Singapore/Majlis Ugama Islam Singapore (MUIS), and the Islamic Food and Nutrition Council of America (IFANCA).

From a commercial perspective, hospitality providers treat guests according to their religious needs because of the financial gains that can be made (Kirillova et al. 2014). The use of halal certificates (often provided by third parties and/or government organisations) is part of how providers give assurance to customers with respect to the religious appropriateness of the food that is provided (Hanzaee & Ramezani 2011; Tieman 2011, 2012; Tieman & Ghazali 2014), but a certificate by itself does not necessarily indicate the totality of the religious and/or social basis of hospitality. Muslim-friendly hospitality, for example, is regarded as an 'alternative' service that caters to the need of Islamic religious oriented customers offered by Muslim and non-Muslim providers in order to fulfil market demand (Sahida et al. 2014), including potentially the increased number of Muslims travelling to some non-Islamic countries (Kamali 2011; Razzaq et al. 2016). Nevertheless, there are real tensions and issues with the formalisation and commodification of halal requirements.

As the halal dimension is important for Muslim customers (Abdullah, Zainoren, Abdurrahman, & Hamali 2012), hospitality and tourism providers have to consider the importance of going halal to gain a competitive advantage in the industry (Mohsin, Ramli, & Alkhulayfi 2016). Abdullah et al. (2012) suggest that commitment to implementing halal compliance is evidenced by having halal certification at the premise provided by the authorised authority. Such actions can be important for positive perception and reputation of businesses by Muslim consumers. Yet, the authentic provision of halal hospitality arguably requires the providers' full understanding of the concept beyond a narrow technical appreciation. In reality halal hospitality and tourism providers can be categorised as either being certified, i.e. formally recognised by relevant authorities, or claimant, i.e. providers that claim they provide halal hospitality, for example via their advertising or in response to customer queries, but who do not have any certification. However, in some cases claimant businesses may serve both halal and non-halal foods and drinks, or other combined elements of entertainment, and accommodation, in what may be referred to as mixed hospitality. For example, a restaurant that serves both halal and non-halal dishes.

Analysing halal

It is clearly of interest to the present work as to why businesses are claiming to provide halal hospitality without the authorised halal certificate. There are many reasons given by accommodation providers for not obtaining an official halal certificate. These include: limited knowledge of halal, the concept, cost, problems with the supply chain, consumer demand for non-halal foods, bureaucracy, and that it might not be compulsory (Nur, Rahman, Saleh, Rahman, & Hashim 2011). However, there is little understanding of the implications that this has for service provision and Muslim consumer response (Syazwan, Talib, Remie, & Johan 2012). Indeed, research conducted on halal restaurants in New Zealand noted that in some cases businesses would not display certification for halal foods, even though they may have had it, because they felt that as 'good Muslims' their word should be sufficiently trusted (Wan Hassan, & Hall 2003).

Other significant dimensions of halal provision include whether an Islamic religious affiliation is necessary for businesses or individuals to provide halal hospitality, and the implementation of halal regulations. For example, in Malaysia, both Muslim and non-Muslim providers can be halal hospitality claimants. Under the Malaysian Trade Description Act 2011 a halal certificate is compulsory for those serving Muslim customers regardless of whether the providers are Muslim or not. This halal certificate covers products and services such as food and beverage, cosmetic, chemical, shipping, entertainment, fashion, and banking. "The 2011 Act aims to promote good trade practices by prohibiting false trade descriptions and false or misleading statements, conducts and practices in relation to the supply of goods and services, thereby protecting the interest of consumers" (DagangHalal 2017). Yet, despite the regulatory context, significant problems have been recognised with respect to certification because of the level of understanding of the halal concept. Food safety and the violation of halal processes and supply chains in restaurants (Marzuki et al. 2012a; Said, Hassan, Musa, & Rahman 2014; Hasri, Taib, & Ahmad 2016) can create a problem for the credibility of food providers, while comments from JAKIM suggest that many accommodation providers do not understand the halal procedure (Noordin, Noor, & Samicho 2014). As stated by Nur et al. (2011: 88), "Reports of fraudulent practices by food operators in mass media and the majority of food premises displaying various types of private Halal logo nowadays has confused the consumers and created doubt over the Malaysia's Halal logo validity." The credibility of relevant authorisation authorities, such as the Department of Islamic Development (JAKIM), is also jeopardised (Kamaruddin, Iberahim, & Shabudin 2012) as consumers may blame the authority for not enforcing legislation (Badruldin et al. 2012).

Lack of knowledge of halal procedures may also affect the level of customer trust of hospitality services (Abdullah et al. 2012; Marzuki et al. 2012a). The time and cost involved in solving such trust issues may, of course, be "a valuable asset in a relationship" to sustain the halal market (Rahim & Voon 2012: 176). However, although formal certification and regulation is significant, it does not necessarily provide the larger picture by explaining the perceptions and attitudes of consumers and providers with respect to halal, and their understanding of what constitutes halal hospitality and tourism. Furthermore, in many non-Islamic majority countries it is important to recognise that halal certification and promotion has unfortunately become politically symbolic of identity politics, and anti-migrant and Islam sentiment, even though such countries are often simultaneously seeking to export halal products and attract Islamic tourists. Therefore, in seeking to help develop a better understanding of halal hospitality and Islamic tourism this book aims to engage with the concept of halal not just as a religious term, but also as a commercial, social, cultural, regulatory, technical, and political concept.

References

Abdul, M., Ismail, H. and Mustapha, M. (2013) 'Halal food certification: Case of Malaysian SME entrepreneurs', *China–USA Business Review*, 12 (2): 163–173.

Abdullah, F., Zainoren, A., Abdurahman, A. and Hamali, J. (2012) 'Developing a framework of success for the foodservice industry in Malaysia', *International Journal of Business and Society*, 13 (3): 309–334.

Alserhan, B. A. (2010) 'On Islamic branding: Brands as good deeds', *Journal of Islamic Marketing*, 1 (2): 101–106.

Alserhan, B. A. and Alserhan, Z. A. (2012) 'Researching Muslim consumers: Do they represent the fourth-billion consumer segment?', *Journal of Islamic Marketing*, 3 (2): 121–138.

Alserhan, B. A., Wood, B. P., Rutter, R., Halkias, D., Terzi, H. and Al Serhan, O. (2018) 'The transparency of Islamic hotels: "Nice Islam" and the "self-orientalizing" of Muslims?', *International Journal of Tourism Research*, https://doi.org/10.1002/jtr.2197.

Aramberri, J. (2001) 'Paradigms in the tourism theory', *Annals of Tourism Research*, 28 (3): 738–761.

Aziz, Y. A. and Chok, N. V. (2013) 'The role of halal awareness, halal certification, and marketing components in determining halal purchase intention among non-Muslims in Malaysia: A structural equation modeling approach', *Journal of International Food & Agribusiness Marketing*, 25 (1): 1–23.

Badruldin, B., Mohamed, Z., Sharifuddin, J., Rezai, G., Abdullah, A., Abd Latif, I. and Mohayidin, G. (2012) 'Clients' perception towards JAKIM service quality in halal certification', *Journal of Islamic Marketing*, 3 (1): 59–71.

Battour, M., Ismail, M. N. and Battor, M. (2011) 'The impact of destination attributes on Muslim tourist's choice', *International Journal of Tourism Research*, 13 (6): 527–540.

Bon, M. and Hussain, M. (2010) 'Halal', in N. Scott and J. Jafari (eds.) *Tourism in the Muslim world*. Bingley, West Yorkshire: Emerald, 47–59.

Bonne, K. and Verbeke, W. (2008) 'Religious values informing halal meat production and the control and delivery of halal credence quality', *Agriculture and Human Values*, 25: 35–47.

Burgess, J. (1982) 'Perspectives on gift exchange and hospitable behaviour', *International Journal of Hospitality Management*, 1 (1): 49–57.

Carboni, M. and Janati, M. H. I. (2016) 'Halal tourism de facto: A case from Fez', *Tourism Management Perspectives*, 19: 155–159.

Carboni, M., Perelli, C. and Sistu, G. (2014) 'Is Islamic tourism a viable option for Tunisian tourism? Insights from Djerba', *Tourism Management Perspectives*, 11: 1–9.

Chambers, E. (2009) 'From authenticity to significance: Tourism on the frontier of culture and place', *Futures*, 41 (6): 353–359.

Cheung, T. S. and Yeo-chi King, A. (2004) 'Righteousness and profitableness: The moral choices of contemporary Confucian entrepreneurs', *Journal of Business Ethics*, 54 (3): 243–257.

COMCEC (2016) *Muslim friendly tourism: Developing and marketing MFT products and services in the OIC member countries, August (2016)*, Ankara: COMCEC.

Cowell, N. M., McDavid, H. and Saunders, T. S. (2012) 'Managing guest security in a high violence society', *Worldwide Hospitality and Tourism Themes*, 4 (1): 32–47.

DagangHalal. (2017) *Halal directory*. Retrieved from www.daganghalal.com/Directory/DHDirectory.aspx

Din, K. H. (1982) 'Tourism in Malaysia competing needs in a plural society', *Annals of Tourism Research*, 9 (3): 453–480.

Din, K. H. (1989) 'Islam and tourism patterns, issues, and options', *Annals of Tourism Research*, 16: 542–563.

Dugan, B. (1994) 'Religion and food service', *Cornell Hotel and Restaurant Administration Quarterly*, 35 (6): 80–85.

Eid, R. and El-Gohary, H. (2015) 'The role of Islamic religiosity on the relationship between perceived value and tourist satisfaction', *Tourism Management*, 46: 477–488.

El-Gohary, H. (2016) 'Halal tourism, is it really Halal?', *Tourism Management Perspectives*, 19: 124–130.

Eum, I. (2008) 'A study on current culinary culture and religious identity in the Gulf Region: Focused on the ashura practice among the Shia Muslims of Bahrain and Kuwait', *International Area Studies Review*, 11 (2): 55–73.

Euromonitor International (2015) *Doing business in the Halal Market: Products, trends, and growth opportunities.* Retrieved from http://go.euromonitor.com/white-paper-

Fernando, Y., Zailani, S. and Mohamed, A. (2010) 'Location, star rating and international chain associated with the hoteliers' intention for not applying the halal logo certification', *European Journal of Social Science*, 16 (13): 401–408.

Fischer, J. (1998) *Proper Islamic consumption: Shopping among the Malays in modern Malaysia.* Copenhagen: Nordic Institute of Asian Studies Press.

Fischer, J. (2008) 'Religion, science and markets', *EMBO Reports*, 9 (9): 828–831.

Fischer, J. (2011) *The Halal frontier: Muslim consumers in a globalized market.* New York: Palgrave Macmillan.

Fischer, J., and Lever, J. (2016) *Between religion, regulation and consumption: Globalising kosher and halal markets.* Manchester: Manchester University Press.

Friese, H. (2009) 'The limits of hospitality', *Paragraph*, 32 (1): 51–68.

Gayatri, G., Hume, M. and Mort, G. S. (2011) 'The role of Islamic culture in service quality research', *Asian Journal on Quality*, 12 (1): 35–53.

Gössling, S. and Hall, C. M. (2019) 'Sharing versus collaborative economy: How to align ICT developments and the SDGs in tourism?', *Journal of Sustainable Tourism*, https://doi.org/10.1080/09669582.2018.1560455.

Hall, C. M. (2009) 'Sharing space with visitors: The servicescape of the commercial exurban home', in P. Lynch, A. McIntosh and H. Tucker (eds.) *The commercial homes. An international perspective.* London: Routledge, 60–72.

Hanzaee, K. H. and Ramezani, M. R. (2011) 'Intention to halal products in the world markets', *Interdisciplinary Journal of Research in Business*, 1 (5): 1–7.

Haq, F. and Wong, H. Y. (2010) 'Is spiritual tourism a new strategy for marketing Islam?', *Journal of Islamic Marketing*, 1 (2): 136–148.

Hasri, N. H., Taib, M. Z. M. and Ahmad, S. S. (2016) 'Relevance of regulatory policies in governing adherence to halal concept in the design of food premises in Malaysia', *Procedia—Social and Behavioral Sciences*, 222: 306–314.

Hassan, R. (2005) *On being religious: Religious commitment in Muslim societies.* Singapore: Institute of Defence and Strategic Studies.

Hassan, R. (2007) 'On being religious: Patterns of religious commitment in Muslim societies', *The Muslim World*, 97 (July): 437–478.

Hemmington, N. (2007) 'From service to experience: Understanding and defining the hospitality business', *The Service Industries Journal*, 27 (6): 747–755.

Henderson, J. C. (2010) 'Sharia-compliant hotels', *Tourism and Hospitality Research*, 10 (3): 246–254.

Henderson, J. C. (2011) 'Religious tourism and its management: The hajj in Saudi Arabia', *International Journal of Tourism and Hospitality Research*, 13 (5): 541–552.

Holmes, O. (2018) '"There is no kosher meat": the Israelis full of zeal for going vegan', *The Guardian*, 17 March.

Hung, K. (2015) 'Experiencing Buddhism in Chinese hotels: Toward the construction of a religious lodging experience', *Journal of Travel & Tourism Marketing*, 32 (8): 1081–1098.

Isfahani, A. N., Pourezzat, A. A., Abdolmanafi, S. and Shahnazari, A. (2013) 'To investigate influential factors on halal brand in the global markets', *Journal of Basic and Applied Scientific Research*, 3 (1): 958–963.

Ismaeel, M. and Blaim, K. (2012) 'Toward applied Islamic business ethics: Responsible halal business', *Journal of Management Development*, 31 (10): 1090–1100.

Jamal, A. (2003) 'Marketing in a multicultural world: The interplay of marketing, ethnicity and consumption', *European Journal of Marketing*, 37 (11): 1599–1620.

Kamali, M. H. (2011) 'Tourism and the halal industry: A global shariah perspective', in *World Islamic Tourism Forum 2011.* Kuala Lumpur, Malaysia.

Kamaruddin, R., Iberahim, H. and Shabudin, A. (2012) 'Willingness to pay for halal logistics: The lifestyle choice', *Procedia—Social and Behavioral Sciences*, 50 (July): 722–729.

King, C. A. (1995) 'Viewpoint what is hospitality?' *International Journal of Hospitality Management*, 14 (3/4): 219–234.

Kirillova, K., Gilmetdinova, A. and Lehto, X. (2014) 'Interpretation of hospitality across religions', *International Journal of Hospitality Management*, 43: 23–34.

Kushimoto, H. (2017) 'Religious and cultural foundations of hospitality in the Islamic and Japanese traditions: A preliminary comparison', *Advanced Science Letters*, 23 (7): 6247–6251.

Laila, N., Kholidah, H. and Abdurrahman, D. (2012) 'The role of Islamic principles in Islamic hospitality', in R. S. Raja Kasim, M. A. Mohamed Adil, S. K. Ab Manan and F. Abd Rahman (eds.) *International Halal Conference (InHAC 2012)*. Kuala Lumpur, Malaysia: Elsevier, 216–225.

Lashley, C. (2008) 'Studying hospitality: Insights from social sciences', *Scandinavian Journal of Hospitality and Tourism*, 8 (1): 69–84.

Lashley, C. and Morrison, A. (eds.) (2000) *In search of hospitality: Theoretical perspectives and debates*. Oxford: Butterworth-Heinemann.

Lugosi, P. (2008) 'Hospitality spaces, hospitable moments: Consumer encounters and affective experiences in commercial settings', *Journal of Foodservice*, 19 (2): 139–149.

Mak, A. H. N., Lumbers, M., Eves, A. and Chang, R. C. Y. (2012) 'Factors influencing tourist food consumption', *International Journal of Hospitality Management*, 31 (3): 928–936.

Marci, T. (2013) 'Social inclusion in terms of hospitality', *International Review of Sociology*, 23 (1): 180–200.

Marzuki, S. Z., Hall, C. M. and Ballantine, P. W. (2012a) 'Restaurant manager and halal certification in Malaysia', *Journal of Foodservice Business Research*, 15 (2): 195–214.

Marzuki, S. Z., Hall, C. M. and Ballantine, P. W. (2012b) 'Restaurant manager's perspectives on halal certification', *Journal of Islamic Marketing*, 3 (1): 47–58.

Marzuki, S. Z., Hall, C. M. and Ballantine, P. W. (2014) 'Measurement of restaurant manager expectations toward halal certification using factor and cluster analysis', *Procedia—Social and Behavioral Sciences*, 121: 291–303.

McMillan, C. L., O'Gorman, K. D. and MacLaren, A. C. (2011) 'Commercial hospitality: A vehicle for the sustainable empowerment of Nepali women', *International Journal of Contemporary Hospitality Management*, 23 (2): 189–208.

Mohsin, A., Ramli, N. and Alkhulayfi, B. A. (2016) 'Halal tourism: Emerging opportunities', *Tourism Management Perspectives*, 19: 137–143.

Mukherjee, S. (2014) 'Global halal: Meat, money, and religion', *Religions*, 5 (1): 22–75.

Noordin, N., Noor, N. L. M. and Samicho, Z. (2014) 'Strategic approach to halal certification system: An ecosystem perspective', *Procedia—Social and Behavioral Sciences*, 121: 79–95.

Nur, I., Rahman, A., Saleh, R., Rahman, S. A., and Hashim, D. M. (2011) 'Factors contributing to non-compliance of the halal standard among restaurant operators in Malaysia', in *2nd International Conference on Business, Economics and Tourism Management*, Singapore, 88–92.

O'Gorman, K. D. (2009) 'Origins of the commercial hospitality industry: From the fanciful to factual', *International Journal of Contemporary Hospitality Management*, 21 (7): 777–790.

OIC (2017). *International tourism in the OIC countries: Prospects and challenges 2017*. Ankara: Statistical, Economic and Social Research and Training Centre for Islamic Countries (SESRIC).

OIC (2018). OIC Tourism Capacity Building Programme (Tr-CaB). www.oicvet.org/oic-tourism-cap.php

OIC Secretariat. (2014). *The 1st OIC international forum on Islamic tourism*. Jakarta, Republic of Indonesia.

Okhovat, H. (2010) 'A study on religious tourism industry management case study: Islamic Republic of Iran', *International Journal of Academic Research*, 2 (5): 302–308.

Oktadiana, H., Pearce, P. L. and Chon, K. (2016) 'Muslim travellers' needs: What don't we know?' *Tourism Management Perspectives*, 20: 124–130.

Prabowo, S., Abd, A. and Ab, S. (2012) 'Halal culinary: Opportunity and challenge in Indonesia', in R. S. Raja Kasim, M. A. Mohamed Adil, S. K. Ab Manan and F. Abd Rahman (eds.) *International Halal Conference (InHAC 2012)*. Kuala Lumpur, Malaysia: Elsevier, 1–10.

Rahim, Z. A. and Voon, B. H. (2012) 'Dimensions of contract manufacturing service quality for halal food processing', in R. S. Raja Kasim, M. A. Mohamed Adil, S. K. Ab Manan and F. Abd Rahman (eds.) *International Halal Conference (InHAC 2012)*. Kuala Lumpur, Malaysia: Elsevier, 168–172.

Razalli, M. R., Yusoff, R. Z. and Roslan, M. W. (2013) 'A framework of halal certification practices for hotel industry', *Asian Social Science*, 9(11): 316–326.

Razzaq, S., Hall, C. M. and Prayag, G. (2016) 'The capacity of New Zealand to accommodate the halal tourism market—Or not', *Tourism Management Perspectives*, 18: 92–97.

Regenstein, J. M., Chaudry, M. M., and Regenstein, C. (2003) 'The kosher and halal food laws', *Comprehensive Reviews in Food Science and Food Safety*, 2 (3): 111–127.

Riaz, M. N. and Chaudry, M. M. (2004) *Halal food production*. Florida: CRC Press.

Rudnyckyj, D. (2009) 'Spiritual economies: Islam and neoliberalism in contemporary Indonesia', *Cultural Anthropology*, 24 (1): 104–141.

Saad, H. E., Ali, B. N. and Abdel-Ati, A. M. (2014) 'Sharia-compliant hotels in Egypt: Concept and challenges', *Advances in Hospitality and Tourism Research*, 2 (1): 1–15.

Sack, D. (2001) *Whitebread Protestants: Food and religion in American culture*. New York: Palgrave.

Sahida, W., Rahman, S. A., Awang, K. and Man, Y. C. (2011) 'The implementation of shariah compliance concept hotel: De Palma Hotel, Ampang, Malaysia', in *International Conference on Humanities, Historical and Social Sciences*. Singapore: IACSIT Press: 138–142.

Sahida, W., Zulkifli, W., Rahman, S. A., Awang, K. W. and Man, Y. B. C. (2014) 'Developing the framework for *halal* friendly tourism in Malaysia', *International Business Management*, 5 (6): 295–302.

Said, M., Hassan, F., Musa, R. and Rahman, N. A. (2014) 'Assessing consumers' perception, knowledge and religiosity on Malaysia's halal food products', *Procedia—Social and Behavioral Sciences*, 130: 120–128.

Samori, Z. and Sabtu, N. (2012) 'Developing halal standard for Malaysian hotel industry: An exploratory study', in R. S. Raja Kasim, M. A. Mohamed Adil, S. K. Ab Manan and F. Abd Rahman (eds.) *International Halal Conference (InHAC 2012)*. Kuala Lumpur, Malaysia: Elsevier, 552–569.

Samori, Z., Ishak, A. H. and Kassan, N. H. (2014) 'Understanding the development of halal food standard: Suggestion for future research', *International Journal of Social Science and Humanity*, 4 (6): 482–486.

Shechter, R. (2011) 'Glocal conservatism: How marketing articulated a neotraditional Saudi Arabian society during the first oil boom, c. 1974–1984', *Journal of Macromarketing*, 31 (4): 376–386.

Shuriye, A. O. and Che Daud, M. R. H. (2014) 'Hospitality and leisure between religious maxims and modern facilities', *Mediterranean Journal of Social Sciences*, 5 (27): 1127–1135.

Siddiqui, M. (2015) *Hospitality and Islam: Welcoming in God's name*. New Haven, CT: Yale University Press.

Sobh, R., Belk, R. W. and Wilson, J. A. (2013) 'Islamic Arab hospitality and multiculturalism', *Marketing Theory*, 13 (4): 443–463.

Stephenson, M. L. (2014) 'Deciphering Islamic hospitality: Developments, challenges and opportunities', *Tourism Management*, 40: 155–164.

Syazwan, M., Talib, A., Remie, M. and Johan, M. (2012) 'Issues in *halal* packaging: A conceptual paper', *International Business and Management*, 5 (2): 94–98.

Tama, H. A. and Voon, B. H. (2014) 'Components of customer emotional experience with halal food establishments', *Procedia—Social and Behavioral Sciences*, 121: 272–280.

Telfer, E. (1996) *Food for thought: Philosophy and food*. London: Routledge.

Telfer, E. (2000) 'The philosophy of hospitableness', in C. Lashley and A. Morrison (eds.) *In search of hospitality: Theoretical perspectives and debates*. Oxford. Butterworth-Heinemann, 38–55.

Tideman, M. C. (1983) 'External influences on the hospitality industry', in E. H. Cassee and R. Reuland (eds.) *The management of hospitality*. Oxford: Pergamon, 1–24.

Tieman, M. (2011) 'The application of halal in supply chain management: In-depth interviews', *Journal of Islamic Marketing*, 2 (2): 186–195.

Tieman, M. (2012) 'Principles in halal supply chain management', *Journal of Islamic Marketing*, 3 (3): 217–243.

Tieman, M. and Ghazali, M. C. (2014) 'Halal control activities and assurance activities in halal food logistics', *Procedia—Social and Behavioral Sciences*, 121: 44–57.

Tieman, M. and Hassan, F. H. (2015) 'Convergence of food systems: Kosher, Christian and halal', *British Food Journal*, 117 (9): 2313–2327.

Timothy, D. J. and Iverson, T. (2006) 'Tourism and Islam: Considerations of culture and duty', in D. J. Timothy and D. H. Olsen (eds.) *Religion and spiritual journeys*. New York: Routledge, 186–205.

Wan Hassan, W. M. and Hall, C. M. (2003) 'The demand for *halal* food among Muslim travellers in New Zealand', in C. M. Hall, L. Sharples, R. Mitchell, B. Cambourne and N. Macionis (eds.) *Food tourism around the world: Developments, management and markets*. Oxford: Butterworth-Heinemann, 81–101.

Weidenfeld, A. (2006) 'Religious needs in the hospitality industry', *Tourism and Hospitality Research*, 6 (2): 143–159.

Weidenfeld, A. and Ron, A. S. (2008) 'Religious needs in the tourism industry', *Anatolia*, 19 (2): 357–361.

Wijesinghe, G. T. M. (2007) How may I serve you? Women receptionists' lived experience in the hospitality industry. Unpublished doctoral dissertation, University of South Australia, Adelaide, Australia.

Wilson, J. A. and Liu, J. (2011) 'The challenges of Islamic branding: Navigating emotions and halal', *Journal of Islamic Marketing*, 2 (1): 28–42.

Wilson, J. A. J., Belk, R. W., Bamossy, G. J., Sandikci, Ö., Kartajaya, H., Sobh, R. and Scott, L. (2013) 'Crescent marketing, Muslim geographies and brand Islam: Reflections from the JIMA Senior Advisory Board', *Journal of Islamic Marketing*, 4 (1): 22–50.

World Travel & Tourism Council [WTTC] (2017) *Travel & Tourism Economic Impact 2017: Middle East.* London: WTTC.

Yarbakhsh, E. (2018) 'Reading Derrida in Tehran: Between an open door and an empty Sofreh', *Humanities*, 7 (1): 21.

Yusof, M. F. and Muhammad, M. Z. (2013) 'Introducing shariah compliant hotels as a new tourism product: The case of Malaysia tourism industry', in *Proceedings of the 20th International Business Information Management Association Conference (IBIMA 2013)*, Kuala Lumpur, Malaysia, 1142–1146.

Zailani, S., Arrifin, Z., Wahid, N. A., Othman, R. and Fernando, Y. (2010) 'Halal traceability and halal tracking systems in strengthening halal food supply chain for food industry in Malaysia (A review)', *Journal of Food Technology*, 8 (3): 74–81.

Zamani-farahani, H. and Henderson, J. C. (2010) 'Islamic tourism and managing tourism development in Islamic societies: The cases of Iran and Saudi Arabia', *International Journal of Tourism Research*, 12 (1): 79–89.

Zizek, S. (1997) 'Multiculturalism, or, the cultural logic of multinational capitalism', *New Left Review*, 225 (September–October): 28–51.

PART I

Halal hospitality and lodging

2

UNDERSTANDING HALAL HOSPITALITY

Nor Hidayatun Abdul Razak, C. Michael Hall, and Girish Prayag

Introduction

This chapter first discusses the relationship between *halal* and *Shariah* law in general, followed by an account of how the halal rules and regulations affect the commercial aspect of hospitality requirements. Differences in perspectives among different Islamic traditions as well as issues on halal hospitality practices are also examined. A final section then highlights the understanding of the concept and the action taken to overcome some of the difficulties with codifying halal hospitality and tourism.

Halal and Shariah law

Al-Qaradawi (1992) indicates that halal and haram are integral to Shariah law (also known as Shariah principles or Islamic law). The main goal of Shariah law is to protect humankind from harm in all aspects of life, including superstition and evil as well as bring benefits to humankind in their daily activities, including business, entertainment, and travel. Halal (the lawful) refers to anything that is permitted and haram (unlawful) is anything that is prohibited as per Shariah law. Ahmat, Ridzuan and Zahari (2012) note that Shariah law refers to 'the path' that guides a Muslim's lifestyle.

The *Quran, Sunnah, Ijma,* and *Qiyas* are central to Shariah law. Din (1982) stated that the concept of halal in the production, transaction, and trade of any products and services must be based on the Quran (which is a revelation from God), *Sunnah* (the traditions and customs of the Prophet Muhammad), *Ijma* (consensus as to the Prophet's teachings), *Qiyas* (that which is assigned to the Prophet's teachings as a result of deduction or analogy), and *Fatwa* (advice from Islamic authorities). Shariah law provides guidance in the aspects of belief (*Aqidah*), law (*fiqh*), and behaviour (*akhlak*) of Muslims, which involve halal and haram of certain acts and behaviours (Kamali 2015). *Aqidah* in Islam is about faith, in which Muslims believe that there is no God except Allah. Anything done by a Muslim is meant to get His blessing. *Fiqh* is about value structures or jurisprudence of Islam. There is guidance in all acts and behaviours as well as rewards and punishment for a right and wrongdoing. *Akhlak* specifically focuses on individual behaviour and how an individual should behave towards Allah and others. The combination of the various elements that comprise Shariah law mean that some areas of Shariah are akin to

Western notions of law and jurisprudence while others reflect teachings as to how to live life in accordance with God's will.

All Muslims follow Shariah law, although they belong to different legal traditions or schools of thought, or *mazhabs*. For example, there are currently four *mazhabs* of *Sunni* jurisprudence, the *Hanafi, Maliki, Shafi'i,* and *Hanbali*; two *Shia* schools, the *Ja'fari* and *Zaidi*; the *Ibadi* school (dominant in Oman); and the *Zahiri* school. The latter sometimes is regarded as a fifth Sunni school. The *mazhabs* are characterised by doctrinal differences with respect to the recognition of Hadith, Islamic history, theology, and jurisprudence, although they may recognise each other's interpretation of Shariah law they have their own principles of thought. Although not well researched or generally appreciated in the English language literature on Islamic tourism, the different *mazhabs* may have implications for hospitality practices with respect to approach towards non-believers, slightly different interpretations of what is halal, as well as the degree of conservatism they exhibit. In addition to religious teachings, the wider cultural context and living conditions also influence the customary practices of Muslims.

Conformity to Shariah law creates restrictions on society, especially in countries in which religion and state are inseparable, such as Iran and Saudi Arabia (Zamani-Farahani & Henderson 2010; Seyfi & Hall 2019). Nevertheless, customary practices have influenced different choices and preferences with respect to what is *halal* in some areas, such as with respect to the eating of sea creatures. For example, in the *Shafi'i* and *Hanbali* traditions it is permissible to eat all kinds of seafood as long as it lives only in the water (e.g. oyster, shrimp, and shark). In the *Maliki* tradition all seafood can be eaten except eel; and in *Hanafi* it is only permitted to eat sea creatures that are in the form of 'fish' (i.e. must have scales and fins), meaning that hagfish, eel, oyster, shrimp, and lobster are not allowed (Eum 2008). The reason for this is that some fish and shellfish are perceived as being unclean (e.g. have sand in shells) and are, therefore, not safe for consumption, while hagfish and eels have no scales.

Differences in definitions of what is halal are also strongly influenced by the school's interpretation of the Quranic verses (Hassan 2005) because different *mazhab* interpret the Quran with reference to different Hadiths. This has led to confusion and misunderstanding in some cases as to what can be consumed and has become a significant challenge for some hospitality providers with the development of global tourism and an international Muslim consumer market. Ideally, the existence of a global halal standard would facilitate under-standing and avoid confusion with dietary regulations (Eum 2008). But, as Hamdan (2007) argues, the existence of different schools of Islamic thought within Muslim societies raises difficulties in standardising halal requirements in a commercial context. Fischer (2008) argues that setting halal standards is further complicated when halal requirements are framed in terms of being marketable products and services, which also involve providers, halal authorities, and Muslim and non-Muslim customers. Nevertheless, despite the absence of a global standard, providers cannot ignore the travel and worship needs of Muslim customers in domestic and international markets.

Travel and worship

Travel is integral to Islam. The Prophet Muhammad (PBUH) encouraged Muslims to travel to gain knowledge and to spread the Islamic religion. Travel in Islam can be divided into several forms, *musafir, rehlah, siyahah, umrah,* and *hajj* (Eickelman & Piscatori 1990; Hasan, Mahyuddin & Mohd Ahsrof Zaki 2010; Taheri 2016; Gannon et al. 2017) (Table 2.1). Travel in Islam can be performed for many reasons, such as to obtain knowledge, education, experience, business, recreation, relationship, and to commit religious ritual (Sahida, Zulkifli,

Table 2.1 Travel in Islam

Term	Use	Origin
Musafr	Means a traveller, but is also used for guest	Originated from the Arabic word *Safara*, meaning going, walking, and wandering Al-Maidah: verse 6
Rihlah	Also rehlah or rihla. Refers to both a journey and the oral, written, and more recently visual, i.e. documentary, account of that journey. In the Middle Ages rihla consisted of three types: *Rihla*—a journey within a region, particularly Morocco, usually to meet other pilgrims before travelling beyond the local area. *Rihla hijaziyya*—a journey to the Hejaz (the western coastal region of the Arabian Peninsula which includes the holy cities of Mecca and Medina). *Rihla sifariyya*—a journey to both Muslim and non-Muslim lands. The most famous rihla based on such a journey is *The Travels of Ibn Battuta (Riḥlat Ibn Baṭūṭah)*.	Originated from the Arabic word *Rahala*, meaning travelling/trading Quraish: verse 6
Ziyarah	A visit to the tomb of a saint or a holy person, including a visit to the tomb of the Prophet Muḥammad in the mosque at Medina. This may occur for reasons of gaining a blessing or cure although the legitimacy of such a visit is debated depending on the perspective of different schools of Islamic thought.	Originated from the Arabic word *Zara*, meaning visiting or paying a visit Al Takathur: verse 2; Al Kahfi: verse 17
Siyahah	Often used as synonymous with travel and tourism. However, it is also connected to gaining knowledge and learning, including travelling to see the wonders of creation.	Originated from the Arabic word *Saha*, meaning wander the earth Al Taubah: verse 112
Umrah and *hajj*	Umrah is an Islamic pilgrimage to Mecca that can be made at any time of year. It is sometimes referred to as the minor pilgrimage. In contrast, the Hajj (also Hadj, Hadji or Haj) is the major pilgrimage that is a required religious duty for Muslims that must be undertaken at least once in the lifetime of all adult Muslims who are financially and physically able to make the journey. The hajj is one of the pillars of Islam that according to Islamic teaching go back to the time of Prophet Abraham. Hajj is performed over five or six days, beginning on the eighth and ending on the thirteenth day of Dhu al-Hijjah, the last month of the Islamic lunar calendar.	Originated from the Arabic word *Saha*, meaning a worshipping obligation for capable Muslims Ayat surah Al Baqarah: 196

Source: Gannon et al., 2017; Hasan et al., 2010; Eickelman & Piscatori, 1990; Taheri, 2016.

Rahman, Awang & Man 2014), and the objective for each reason is similar, to learn the greatness of Allah and to worship Him always. Travelling in Islam is about improving the spiritual aspect of the individual by observing and appreciating the creations of God (Din 1982). Hashim, Murphy and Hashim (2007) indicate that many verses on travelling in the Quran encourage Muslims to see the creations of Allah and feel for His greatness. These verses include *Al-Imran* (The Amramites) 3:137; *Al-An'am* (Livestock) 6:11; *Yunus* (Jonah) 10:22; *Yusuf* (Joseph) 12:109; *Al-Nahl* (The Bee) 16:36; *Al-Hajj* (The Pilgrimage) 22:46; *Al-'Ankaboot* (The Spider) 29:20; *Al-Rum* (The Romans) 30:42/9; *Saba'* (Sheba) 34:18; *Faater* (Initiator) 35:44; *Ghafer* (Forgiver) 40:82/21; *Muhammad* 47:10; and *Al-Mulk* (Kingship) 67:15. In such a context halal hospitality clearly becomes an important means of facilitating Islamic travel (Hayati, Khadijah & Manan 2012).

One of the most famous, and oft-cited, Muslim travellers was Ibn Battuta, who travelled as far as China and India around 1325 and 1354 and who learnt and wrote about the customary practices of the places where he went including the culture and food (Morgan 2004). In this he reflects on the way in which travel within Islamic traditions is meant to be a two-way enrichment between host and guest and in which hospitality is integral to Islamic custom. Islam is therefore imbued with a substantial, and often explicit, focus on the provision of hospitality which also affects the expectations of its adherents (Kamali 2011). In providing halal hospitality, organisations and individuals must therefore consider whether the activities, values, purposes, products, and services offered are compliant with Shariah law (Abdullah & Mukhtar 2014).

The concept of halal hospitality

According to Saad, Ali and Abdel-Ati (2014: 1) halal hospitality is defined as "a hotel that provides services in accordance to the *Shariah* principles". Samori and Rahman (2013: 99) defined halal hospitality in a similar fashion to Saad but extend their definition by adding "it is not only limited to serv[ing] halal food and drink, but more than that, is to ensure the entire operation throughout the hotel would also operate in accordance with the *Shariah* principles." Another definition is provided by Yusuf (2009), in terms of a hotel where the services offered and financial transactions are based on Shariah principles and it is not only limited to serving halal food and beverages but all parameters that have been designed for health, safety, environment, and the economic benefits of all humankind, regardless of race, faith, or cultures. These definitions emphasise adherence to Shariah law in providing halal hospitality. However, Saad et al. (2014) in their definition only note the hospitality services offered, while Samori and Rahman (2013) focus on diet as well as wider hospitality operations. In part, the different approaches to halal hospitality reflect the different interpretation of halal matters in different countries (Al-Qaradawi 1992) and also the different levels of expertise, knowledge, and awareness of the field (Che Omar, Islam & Adaha 2013). Therefore, there is a range of interpretations over what constitutes halal hospitality, with a narrow perspective focusing on food and drink to a much broader approach that covers the many aspects of hospitality, operational management, financial transactions, services provided, economic contribution, and physical and spiritual aspects of providers and customers. Table 2.2 provides some of the characteristics of halal hospitality service as identified by a number of authors.

Stephenson (2014), writing primarily in a Gulf State context, provides additional characteristics of the concept of halal hospitality which he categorises according to human resources, private rooms, dining quarters, other public facilities, and business operations (Table 2.3). Interestingly, Islamic finance, insurance, charity, and *zakat* (alms) are infrequently

Table 2.2 Characteristics of halal hospitality service

Attributes of halal hospitality	Source and location
Prayer mat, Quran, prayer beads, *Qibla* direction, no alcohol, separated kitchen utensils, no unmarried couple to check in together, no drug-dealing activities.	Din (1982) Malaysia
Provide information on mosque and halal food location.	Hashim et al. (2007) Malaysia
No alcohol, halal foods, Quran, prayer mat, arrow indicating the direction of Mecca, bed and toilet positioned not facing the direction of Mecca, bidets in bathroom, prayer room, appropriate entertainment, no nightclub or adult television channels, predominant Muslim staff, conservative staff dress, separate recreational facilities for men and women, all female floor, guest dress code, Islamic funding.	Henderson (2010) Middle East
Serving halal food and beverages, halal management and operation, design, facilities (separate spa, gym, swimming pool, guest and function rooms for male and female customers), Islamic financing in sharing profit and loss, no interest (*riba* or usury), Islamic insurance (*takaful*).	Sahida et al. (2011) Malaysia
Appropriate dress code, hospitality behaviour, physical facilities such as serving halal food, no alcohol, providing separate gymnasium, sauna, swimming pool and comfortable praying area, free interest financing mode, obligation of paying *zakat*, adhere to Islamic business principles.	Hayati et al. (2012) Malaysia
Have halal certificate, halal logo, *Qibla* indicator, prayer mat, prayer room, no living being symbol, Quran, no gambling and prostitution, predominant Muslim workers, appropriate dress code, proper behaviour, *zakat*, prayer time information, toilet facilities, breaking fast and *sahur*, no unmarried couple in a room.	Samori & Sabtu (2012) Malaysia

discussed in many articles related to halal hospitality and Islamic tourism. The reasons for this are unknown but perhaps these attributes emphasise the accommodation providers' responsibility instead of what is requested by customers with respect to halal hospitality offerings. Nevertheless, several authors argue that in order to become a Shariah-compliant hospitality and tourism business, providers should comply with Islamic business principles including the giving of charity and using Islamic finance for capital sources (Nasir & Pereira 2008; Hayati et al. 2012; Samori & Sabtu 2012; Sahida et al. 2014). Saad et al. (2014) in their study on a Shariah-compliant hotel in Egypt present features of operation, design, and finance according to their ranking in importance (Table 2.4). These characteristics complement the characteristics provided by Stephenson (2014) and other researchers as above, with the additional feature of *zakat* being included as part of the financial characteristics of operations.

The rank order of features presented in Table 2.4 is based on hospitality experts' views (i.e. academic staff, industry consultants, and providers) in Egypt. Saad et al. (2014) also indicate that the formal concept of halal hospitality in Egypt is still at the early stage of implementation as there are no formal procedures or rules available for authorisation. However, he noted that the halal concept is used more as a marketing strategy in Egypt in line with high expectations for future demand for halal hospitality service.

Nearly all of the characteristics of halal hospitality presented in the literature emphasise the physical or tangible aspects of customers' needs. Din (1989: 560) even argued that "it is quite difficult to find a Muslim who can provide the services as outlined in Islamic teachings

Table 2.3 Characteristics of Shariah compliance in halal hotels

Human resources	Traditional conservative dress code for hotel staff and especially female staff; prayer time provision for Muslim employees; restricted working hours for Muslim staff during Ramadan; staff (and guest) adherence to Islamic moral codes of conduct; and guest-centric strategies underpinning service delivery.
Private rooms (bedrooms and bathrooms)	Separate floors with rooms solely allocated to women and families; markers (i.e. *Qibla* stickers) indicating the direction of Mecca; prayer mats and copies of the Quran; conservative television channels; geometric and non-figurative patterns of decoration (e.g. calligraphy); beds and toilets positioned away from facing Mecca; toilets fitted with a bidet shower or health faucet; and halal-friendly complementary toiletries.
Dining quarter	Separate provision for women and families, in addition to the communal area provision; art that does not depict human and animal form; and no music expressing sexual and/or controversial messages.
Other public facilities	No casino or gambling; separate leisure facilities (including swimming pools and spas) for both sexes; female and male prayer rooms equipped with the Quran (also available at the front desk); built-in *wudhu* (the ritual ablutions conducted before prayer) facilities located outside prayer rooms; toilets facing away from Mecca; and art that does not depict human and animal form.
Business operation	Corporate social responsibility strategies (linked to Islamic values) and philanthropic donations; ethical practices including marketing and promotion; transactions and investments in accordance to the principles and practices associated with Islamic banking, accounting, and finance.

Source: Adapted from Stephenson, 2014.

Table 2.4 Category and features of a Shariah-compliant hotel in Egypt in rank order of importance

Category	Features in rank order of importance
Operation	Alcohol and pork should not be served
	Female staff for single female floors and male staff for single male floors
	Food products have to be halal
	Quran, prayer mats in each room
	Majority of the staff are Muslim
	Conservative staff dress
	Conservative TV service
Design	Separate facilities for males and females
	Signs indicating the direction of Mecca in every room
	Appropriate entertainment (no nightclubs)
	Beds and toilets placed so as not to face the direction of Mecca
Financial	Hotel financed through Islamic arrangements
	Hotel should follow *zakat* principles

Source: Adapted from Saad et al., 2014.

(Sunnah), which reflect the original intent of travelling purpose, namely spiritual aims". Ahmat et al. (2012) suggested that there is a lack of an 'internal' or 'personal' aspect in the current promotion of halal hospitality services. Indeed, in Kirillova, Gilmetdinova and Lehto (2014), Muslim respondents considered that hospitality services provided in the context of a business are less genuine because they involve monetary exchange. Ahmat et al. (2012) provided an example of De Palma Hotel in Malaysia that claimed to be the pioneer Shariah-compliant hotel in South East Asia (see also Chapter 7, this volume), yet it only emphasised the tangible aspects in its promotion, even though the management of the De Palma Hotel Group believes that the entire management of hospitality must be halal, which includes adopting a 'Muslim personality'. Ghozali and Kamri (2015) argue that personality can only be judged and felt by the effect arising from certain acts or behaviour by staff. For example, in the context of attire, female Muslim employees in De Palma Hotel must wear outfits and a headscarf that symbolise 'Muslim personality'. All Muslim employees must also respect the five-prayer time without compromising their work schedule at the hotel. Therefore, arranging appropriate time for prayer and taking turns for prayer activities are considered as upholding the personality of the hotel operation.

One way of understanding the growth of halal hospitality and tourism in a business context, is the notion of a 'spiritual economy' (Rudnyckyj 2009) that combines religion and capitalism in framing ethical behaviour to enhance corporate productivity and competitiveness. The spiritual economy in Indonesia described by Rudnyckyj (2009: 104), "consists of producing spirituality as an object of intervention, reconfiguring work as a form of religious worship, and inculcating an ethic of individual accountability and entrepreneurial responsibility among workers". From this perspective, management instil understanding of spiritual economies among employees through training. Employees can be trained to understand how their works involve the principle of worship, which is regarded as significant to the spiritual success in life in Islam. For example, practising the ethics of Islam that emphasise both the physical and the spiritual aspects of work life in the forms of work transparency, productivity excellence, personal responsibility, and rationalisation in every action. Such a notion arguably well characterises the commodification of halal in a country such as Malaysia which seeks to position itself as an international hub for halal products and services, including tourism.

Din (1989) notes how Muslims should provide hospitality to non-Muslims. Nevertheless, there are significant challenges faced by halal hospitality providers in targeting Muslim and non-Muslim customers, such as in satisfying customers' needs without having any conflicts with religious beliefs and traditions (Henderson 2010). Prohibition of alcohol and no-smoking policies, for example, are appropriate in Islam but are not favoured by some customers. To complicate matters further the level of understanding by both Muslim and non-Muslim providers on the halal hospitality concept may be inadequate for some members of the halal market (Ahmat et al. 2012). Razalli, Abdullah and Hassan (2009) indicate that Muslim customers will consider using halal hotels based on providers' initiatives in fulfilling halal requirements, although the success of this depends on the extent to which providers understand the foundations of the concept in Islam.

Hospitality in Islam

Islam consists of five pillars. The first pillar is the witness (*syahadah*) as there is no God except Allah, and Muhammad is the last Messenger of Allah. The second pillar is praying five times a day while the third is giving the *zakat* (alms). The fourth is fasting in Ramadan, and the last pillar is performing the *hajj* if one is able to do it. *Iman* is about affirming the existence of

Allah, His angels, His books, His messengers, the Last Day, and believing in good and bad (*qada'* and *qadar*). *Ihsan* is about worshipping God in which all actions are done for His blessing (*ibadah*) (Laderlah, Rahman, Awang & Man 2011). The Quran states that:

> And I (Allah) created not the jinn and humankind except to worship Me (Alone).
>
> *(Adz Dzaariyat, 56)*

This verse clearly states that the creation of humankind is specifically to worship Allah. The obligation to worship Allah is a must in sustaining the spiritual aspect of life. However, worship does not only mean fasting, prayers, giving alms, and pilgrimage, but includes all activities in life including business activities. The Quran states that:

> By men whom neither trade nor business diverts from the remembrance of Allah and performing of prayer and paying of the poor due (Zakat). They fear a day in which hearts and eyes shall be turned about.
>
> *(An Nur, 37)*

This verse emphasises the Muslim obligation to worship Allah even in conducting trade or business. In explaining the concept of worshipping God in a hospitality business, specifically from an Islamic perspective, Che Omar et al. (2014) suggested that the Islamic-based hospitality (IBH) concept emphasises the *Ruh* of *Syahadah* (soul) and *Mardhatillah* (the blessing of Allah). This concept emphasises the spiritual aspect (soul) with the aim of gaining a better life, both in this world and in the afterlife. From this perspective, a Muslim will receive a reward in business if he follows the principles of Islam and *Iman* while conducting business activities. In opening a halal hospitality business, for example, the business owner helps the community to be a better place. In this way the business owner fulfils his communal obligations or *fardhu kifayah*. If there is no hospitality service available at a place, then offering this service must be considered a personal obligation (*fardhu ain*) for a Muslim. However, the activities associated with offering hospitality must be done with a genuine intention to gain a blessing from Allah. The Prophet Muhammad says:

> Actions are (judged) by motives (niyyah), so each man will have what he intended. Thus, he whose migration (hijrah) was to Allah and His Messenger, his migration is to Allah and His Messenger; but he whose migration was for some worldly thing he might gain, or for a wife he might marry, his migration is to that for which he migrated.
>
> *(Al-Bukhari and Muslim)*

Theoretically, this notion of religious-based hospitality emphasises both the physical and the spiritual dimensions of hospitality. Likewise, Mohd Sirajuddin, Sahri, Khalid, Yaakob and Harun (2013) discuss the spiritual and the physical aspects of halal hospitality drawing on a thematic approach to understanding halal in four verses of the Quran that specifically mention the words *halalan tayyiban* (Table 2.5). Mohd Sirajuddin et al. (2013) state that in order to reach *halalan tayyiban* (e.g. pure, clean, and nourishing) in business practices, there should be a holistic combination between the aspects of *tayyib* and the physical dimension. Any action, behaviour, and object involved in the business, e.g. products and services, must not relate to evil. From a religious perspective, avoiding sin, sexual immorality, transgression, and changing the status of haram to halal can help individual Muslims to reach this holistic benefit.

Table 2.5 Halal themes in four verses of the Quran

Extracted theme of the verses			
Spiritual aspect *(Tayyib)*		Physical aspect *(Halal)*	
(al-Baqarah:168–169)	*(al-Ma'idah:87–88)*	*(al-Anfal:67–69)*	*(al-Nahl:114–115)*
• Avoid evil conduct, i.e. *munafiq* (being hypocritical) • Avoid anything in connection to sin *(su')* • Avoid anything connected to sexual exposure *(fahsya')*	• Avoid transgressing in action • Avoid changing status of haram to halal and otherwise	• Avoid taking for granted non-Muslims in a way that will corrupt Muslim society • Avoid fraudulent financial planning	• Process • Sanitation • Ingredients • Transportation and supply chain • Storages • Non-toxic/not harmful • Non-pork and alcoholic *(khamr)*

Source: Adapted from Mohd Sirajuddin et al., 2013.

With respect to halal a Muslim must therefore not be involved in corruption and fraud and must also avoid haram in all aspects of life. It is important for a Muslim to do halal and avoid the haram in order to gain the blessing of Allah. From this perspective it is therefore important to consider what exactly is understood in terms of the halal hospitality concept, and the extent to which providers genuinely provide the service to cater to the needs of their customers and society at large, or whether they are only taking advantage of the business opportunity.

Halal and haram in hospitality services

The principles of halal and haram are integral to halal hospitality and tourism. Providers must have a thorough understanding of what is halal (permissible) and haram (not permissible) in providing Islamic hospitality. This concept of halal and haram covers the entire aspects of hospitality services such as food, facilities, and activities conducted within the business. In Islam, there are four main sources in determining halal and haram: the *Quran, Sunnah, Ijma* (consensus between scholars), and *Qiyas* (analogy). Siddiqui (1997) explains the uses of these sources. If the changes required for a better society can be found in the Quran, then these changes can be approved and serve as guidelines to Muslim society. If there is no indication of the changes in the Quran, then Muslim scholars and jurists must refer to the *Sunnah*. The third source of *Ijma* (consensus) is used to compare a situation to see whether it is approved or disapproved of in Shariah law. In this case, Muslim scholars and jurists will usually look to what has already been adopted with respect to existing norms. Finally, *qiyas* is used for making a decision on something that is not comparable to a teaching or situation in the Quran or Sunnah. Islam prohibits all kinds of intoxicants *(kharms)* from any source (e.g. corn, honey, or barley) (Al-Qaradawi 1992). Using *qiyas*, narcotics are therefore considered as *kharms* because they are regarded as bringing more harm than benefit to people. The Prophet Muhammad said:

> Truly, Allah has cursed kharms and has cursed the one who produces it, the one for whom it is produced, the one who drinks it, the one who serves it, the one who

carries it, the one for whom it is carried, the one who sells it, the one who earns from the sale of it, the one who buys it, and the one for whom it is bought.

(Al-Tirmidhi and Ibn Majah)

For products whose status as halal or haram is unknown because they were not mentioned specifically in the Quran or Sunnah, and/or involve a new means of production, such as energy drinks, such products are categorised as *mubah* or undecided products that require discussion among Muslim scholars to determine whether such a product is halal or not (De Run, Butt, Fam & Jong 2010). Once their status is decided, a *fatwa* will be published. The acceptance of this *fatwa* is up to individual Muslims, for example, the controversial issue surrounding the slaughtering process for animals according to Shariah law (Fischer 2008; Zakaria 2008). In such situations, different interpretations of the status of a product can exist in different locations.

In addition to halal and haram, another important term in Islam is *mashbooh* (doubtful or questionable). *Mashbooh* contributes to the complexities of issues related to halal and haram (Wan Hassan 2008; Marzuki 2012), as again there may be different interpretations in different locations. Nevertheless, despite the existence of some areas of question or debate over status, some researchers have argued that it is the responsibility of the provider to ensure that the hospitality service provided is halal and not haram (Prabowo, Abd & Ab 2012). As a result, Marzuki, Hall and Ballantine (2012a, 2012b) stress that hospitality providers must improve their understanding and acceptance of the halal hospitality services. This means, for example, that providers should confirm that the entire supply chain, including the raw material, handling, processing equipment, processing, storage, transport, preparation, and delivery, is Shariah compliant.

Halal hospitality entails a genuine commitment to providing hospitality by following Shariah principles or rules. Shariah is "the totality of Allah's commands which regulate life for every Muslim in all aspects" (Sahida, Rahman, Awang & Man 2011: 140), and covers all aspects of tourism and hospitality services (Henderson 2010). These rules are becoming increasingly commercialised and commodified in the hospitality industries of Islamic countries as well as some Western countries (Muhamad & Mizerski 2013). According to Che Omar et al. (2014), the hospitality industry overemphasises the extrinsic physical part of halal hospitality, while the intrinsic part is left unattended. The intrinsic part covers the spiritual aspect (soul) with the aim to gain a better life, both in this world and in the afterlife with the God's blessing. Nevertheless, while Muslims undoubtedly regard both the physical and spiritual aspects of halal hospitality as important, the first encounter of many people, whether Muslim or not, with halal hospitality will be in terms of the information provided by operators prior to the decision by consumers to purchase. In Islam hospitality means to welcome in God's name (Siddiqui 2015). Unfortunately, all too often, commercial hospitality means to welcome in the name of profit. This chapter therefore examines how the concepts of halal and haram are conveyed in terms of food, entertainment, and business values by hospitality and tourism businesses.

Food

Global tourism and mobility has led to increased diversity in food offerings by hospitality operators (Eum 2008). International tourism also opens up new opportunities for the hospitality industry to explore diversity in food offerings. However, the increasing number of travellers has put pressure on the demand for foods that can be eaten according to various scriptures and traditions (Tieman & Hassan 2015). Table 2.6 provides a comparison between the three Abrahamic religions with respect to: prohibition of animals for food, prohibition of

Table 2.6 A comparison of religious food law

	Kosher food laws	Christian food laws	Halal food laws
Prohibition of animals for food	According to Leviticus and Deuteronomy, pig, wild birds, sharks, dogfish, catfish, monkfish and similar species, crustacean and molluscan shellfish, other animals from the sea without fins and scales, most insects, rock hyrax, hare, camel, ostrich, emu, rhea are restricted	According to the Old Testament: pig, camel, rock hyrax, hare, animals in the water without fins and scales, eagle, vulture, osprey, kit, falcon, raven, ostrich, nighthawk, sea gull, hawk, owl, cormorant, ibis, water hen, pelican, carrion vulture, stork, heron, hoopoe, bat, most winged insects, swarming things that swarm upon the earth (Leviticus 11); however, very few Christians practise this today	By Quranic verse (Quran 2:173): pig; based on Hadith, wild animals with a canine tooth and any bird with talons are regarded as detestable, but not prohibited
Prohibition of blood	Prohibited and should be as much as possible removed during and after slaughter	According to Genesis 9:3–4	By Quranic verse (Quran 2:173)
Prohibition of alcohol	Not prohibited, but there are strict production requirements on grape-juice-based products such as wine	Not prohibited	Prohibition of intoxicants by Quranic verse (Quran 5:90) and the Hadith
Fasting	Fasting plays a significant role in Jewish religious tradition, including for weddings and events in the Jewish calendar	Christians traditionally fasted during Lent, Advent, and on the eve or day of various saint's days. Abstinence from red meat traditionally occurred on certain days of the week. However, this practice is continued by few Christians today	Fasting is an important obligation for Muslims, which regulates fasting during Ramadan and optional fasting
Animal welfare	Kindness to animals has a strong foundation in the Torah	The Old Testament defines important principles in animal welfare	Part of Shariah (*Fiqh al-Mu'amalah* or *al-adah*) describes the rulings on the relationship between humans and other creatures of Allah
Slaughtering requirements for livestock and poultry	Strictly defined under the laws of *shechita*; prohibition of pre-slaughter stunning	Undefined for meat that is not used as an offering	Strictly defined under Shariah, but the acceptability of certain procedures (like stunning and machine slaughter) depend on the Islamic school of thought

(Continued)

Table 2.6 (Cont).

	Kosher food laws	*Christian food laws*	*Halal food laws*
In case of doubt	Consult Rabbi	Do not eat (*Romans* 14:23)	Avoid
Segregation requirements in the food supply chain	Segregation between meat products, dairy products, and neutral products (*pareve*)	Undefined	Segregation between halal and non-halal.

Source: Regenstein et al., 2003; Riaz & Chaudry, 2004; Al-Mazeedi, Regenstein, & Riaz, 2013; Tieman & Hassan 2015.

blood, prohibition of alcohol, fasting, animal welfare, slaughtering requirements for livestock and poultry, cases of doubt, and segregation requirements in the food supply chain.

In the case of the prohibition of animals for food, for example, animals from the sea without fins and scales are prohibited for Jewish, Christian, and Muslims (from the *Hanafi* school). Blood is prohibited for all three religions, but alcohol is only prohibited for Muslims. However, there is a great deal of diversity within Christianity, with Nicene churches having few, if any, prohibitions as a result of St Peter having a vision in which a voice tells him that it is permissible to eat non-kosher food because God has cleansed them (Ehrman 2006). The New Testament does provide suggestions with respect to eating that some churches have adopted, e.g. Seventh-Day Adventist and Trappist monks avoid eating meat because in *Corinthians*, Paul of Tarsus comments that some Christians may wish to abstain from meat if it causes "my brother to stumble" into idolatry (1 *Corinthians* 8:13).

When it comes to fasting, followers of the three Abrahamic religions will fast according to certain days. During the fasting day, there are foods encouraged to be eaten, for example, the demand for dates will increase during Ramadan as it is customary for Muslims to eat dates when breaking the fast as, according to tradition, Muhammad broke fast with three dates. The three religions have concerns for animal welfare but when it comes to slaughtering requirements, only kosher and halal require animals to be slaughtered according to religious rituals (the Armenian Orthodox Church is one of the few Christian churches that retains a degree of ritual when slaughtering occurs). Jews will separate food according to sections for meat, dairy, and neutral products. There is no issue on food segregation for Christians, but Muslims seek segregation of halal and non-halal foods.

In some jurisdictions, providers can be subject to legal action if caught violating the religious food restrictions especially those that are already gazetted in trade and food safety laws. In the case of Malaysia, providers that violate the halal requirements are subject to legal action as stated in the Trade Description Act 2011. However, in Malaysia, government agencies are perceived as not disseminating information on halal knowledge and education to service providers (Said, Hassan, Musa & Rahman 2014). As a result, some providers appear not willing to seek certification for reasons that include a lack of understanding of halal hospitality; therefore education on halal certification is important for increasing the number of operators that provide halal hospitality (Said et al. 2014), although perhaps even more significant is consumer demand.

A study by Sahida et al. (2011) on halal hospitality in Kuala Lumpur, Malaysia, suggests that one of the reasons for providing halal services is to cater to the needs of Muslim travellers who otherwise have difficulty in finding accommodation to suit their lifestyle. Most hotels in

Malaysia offer conventional hotel services because of the significance of the international tourism market. Therefore, even in a primarily Muslim country such as Malaysia, it can be quite difficult for religious customers to obtain halal hotel services in large urban centres. Interestingly, Wan Hassan and Hall (2003) found the same difficulty for Muslim travellers in obtaining halal food in New Zealand, despite about 98 per cent of lamb and sheep, 60 per cent of cattle, and 85 per cent of deer grown in New Zealand being halal slaughtered every year.

Halal food is defined as being "free from any component that Muslims are prohibited from consuming" (Riaz & Chaudry 2004: 2). Halal food includes milk (from cows, sheep, camels, and goats), honey, fish, legumes, grains, and plants (that do not intoxicate). Haram food includes swine meat, pork-based products and by-products; carrion or dead animals; blood and blood by-products; animals slaughtered or killed without the name of Allah; intoxicants (e.g. alcohol and narcotics); carnivorous animals; birds of prey; and land animals without external ears, e.g. snakes and worms (Riaz & Chaudry 2004). The Quran states that:

> Prohibited to you are dead animals, blood, the flesh of swine, and that which has been dedicated to other than Allah, and (those animals) killed by strangling or by a violent blow or by a head-long fall or by the goring of horns, and those from which a wild animal has eaten, except what you (are able to) slaughter (before its death), and those which are sacrificed on stone altars.
>
> *(Al-Maidah, 3)*

This verse indicates what can be eaten and what cannot. Furthermore, halal food must be food that is clean, safe, and healthy to consume, while haram food is any food that could harm humans as forbidden by Allah (Isfahani, Pourezzat, Abdolmanafi & Shahnazari 2013). The Quran states that:

> You who believe, eat the good things We have provided for you and be grateful to God, if it is Him that you worship. He has only forbidden you carrion, blood, pig's meat, and animals over which any name other than God's has been invoked. But if anyone is forced to eat such things by hunger, rather than desire or excess, he commits no sin: God is Most Merciful and Forgiving.
>
> *(Al-Baqarah, 172–173)*

These verses signify the need to produce halal and *tayyib* foods that are interpreted as permitted and wholesome. *Tayyib* is used to refer to a standard that has been revealed in the books of Allah that come prior to the Quran, i.e. the Torah (the Old Testament) and the *Injil* (the New Testament) (Mohd Sirajuddin, Saad, Sahri & Yaakub 2014). *Tayyib* highlights a universal standard of food consumption amongst Abrahamic believers, as the Quran states that:

> The food of the People of the Book is lawful unto you and yours is lawful unto them.
>
> *(Al-Maidah, 5)*

This verse refers to the slaughtering method used in Judaism, which is similar to the Islamic slaughtering process, and is regarded as consensually permissible to Muslims among most Muslim scholars including Al-Qaradawi (1992). Both of these religions have firm restrictions to ensure that the food provided is truly kosher or halal and stress ritual cleanliness as a means to achieve spiritual goals (e.g. the blessing from God) (Hashim 2008) (Table 2.7). However,

Table 2.7 Comparison of halal and kosher food requirements

Item	Kosher	Halal
Pig, pork, carnivore	Prohibited	Prohibited
Ruminant animals (e.g. buffalo, cattle, goat, and horse) and birds (e.g. chicken, turkey, duck, and goose)	Slaughtered by a trained Jewish *sochet*	Slaughtered by a Muslim adult
Intention. Pronouncement of God's name	Must be done as part of a continuous slaughter process. If the process stops the intention must be repeated	Done to each animal slaughtered
Slaughter by hand	Mandatory	Recommended
Mechanical slaughter	Not allowed	Can be done, i.e. if there is a huge number of chickens, but must be supervised
Stunning before slaughtering	Prohibited. The animal must be conscious when killed	A contested issue among Muslim authorities, but if used the animal must not be killed by the stun
Other requirements on meat	Only the front quarter of the animal is used unless the *sochet* removes sinew and the sciatic nerve; meat is soaked in salt water. *Chelev* (suet) is also prohibited	All the meat can be used except the penis, testicles, vulva, and glands, and it does not need to be soaked in salt water
Animal blood	Must be drained from carcass. Prohibited	Must be drained from carcass. Prohibited
Fish and seafood	Must have scales and fins	Most Muslim schools consider ocean, sea, or lake creatures as halal. Shi'ites consider that only those with scales are halal, but make an exception for some crustacea, shrimps, and prawns
Microbial and biotechnological enzymes	Allowed	Allowed
Animal enzyme	Must come from kosher animal	Must come from a halal animal
Gelatine	Must come from kosher animal or a vegetable source	Must come from halal animal or a vegetable source
Dairy product	Made by kosher enzyme	Made by halal enzyme
Alcohol (wine)	Allowed	Prohibited
Mixing meat and milk products	Not allowed	Allowed
Insect and insect products	Only kosher locust and grasshoppers accepted	All locust halal; only *Maliki* school of Islam permits wider eating of insects
Plant substances	All allowed	Those involving alcohol (e.g. wine) strictly prohibited
Sanitation equipment	Cleaned; require a certain period, ritually cleaned	Cleaned as a whole; no specific period required
Special occasion	Restrictive during Passover	Same requirements year-round

Source: Regenstein et al., 2003; Riaz & Chaudry, 2004; Hisham, 2012; Al-Mazeedi et al., 2013

there are issues with respect to the entire production process of halal food given the potential for toxic contamination and inhumane farming practices (Mohd Sirajuddin et al. 2013). In addition, animal feeding, slaughtering methods, packaging, logistics, and contamination are problems in halal food production (Ab Halim & Mohd Salleh 2012; Nasaruddin, Fuad, Mel, Jaswir & Abd 2012), along with serious concerns as to the applicability of halal logistics in order to support the halal supply chain globally (Mohd Sirajuddin et al. 2014; Tieman & Ghazali 2014).

Halal food must be cleaned from any contamination by prohibited items or ingredients that would change its status of halal to haram. Cleanliness is expected from the beginning of production to the end food product, e.g. "from farm to fork" (Wan Hasan & Hall 2003). There are also potential issues of kitchen design in accommodation, given that it is a site of food preparation, preservation, storage, and packaging that requires appropriate food hygiene procedures (Hasri, Taib & Ahmad 2016). Cleanliness is necessary, both in terms of the physical and spiritual aspects of halal hospitality. Food contamination, for example, occurs when hospitality providers do not have a good knowledge of the haram ingredients (Prabowo et al. 2012). Providers must not claim their food as halal if contaminated with haram ingredients (Harvey 2010; Ismaeel & Blaim 2012), such as in using gelatine produced from pigs (Nasaruddin et al. 2012). To avoid food contamination, providers must find alternative materials or ingredients to replace non-halal products. For example, Karim and Bhat (2008) indicate that there are marine sources of gelatine made from fish bones to replace non-halal bovine gelatine. In addition, accommodation providers may perform ritual cleansing or *samak* if haram contact occurs.

Food contamination can also involve the utensils used during the production processes. Wan Hassan (2008) found that many hospitality providers have misconceptions about the use of kitchen utensils. These providers viewed that the utensils used for non-halal food can be used to cook the halal food after being washed with soap and water, whereas in Islam these utensils must be washed according to Islamic ritual cleansing (use clay and water). According to Kassim, Hashim, Hashim and Jol (2014), a Muslim must go through an Islamic cleansing (*samak*) process if he/she is in contact with impurities. This cleansing process has to be done before religious activities, such as prayers. There are three categories of impurities (Table 2.8). However, only the extreme category is required to be cleaned with water clay (JAKIM 2013; Tieman 2011). *Samak* or *sertu* encompasses the ritual cleansing of transport, containers, truck, machines, utensils, equipment that are used in the preparation, production, and transportation of halal and non-halal products. In order to confirm that the whole process is halal, *samak/sertu* is necessary to achieve *tayyib* standards (Shariff et al. 2017).

Table 2.8 Categories of impurity (*najis*) and its cleansing method

Classification	Example of *najis*	Cleansing method
Light	Urine of boys aged less than 2 years old and fully breastfed.	Remove *najis* and sprinkle water over the contaminated area.
Medium	Vomit, blood, and urine.	Remove *najis* and wash with free flow clean water until achieving absence of appearance/colour, odour, and feel.
Extreme/severe	Dogs and pigs (*khinzir*) including any liquids and objects discharged from their orifices.	Remove *najis* and rinse seven times with clean water; one of which is water that is mixed with soil/clay. This cleansing method is called *samak*.

Source: Adapted from Kassim et al., 2014.

However, issues with *samak/sertu* for some transportation companies include cost, time, energy, and human resources to undertake *samak* (Ab Talib, Lim & Khor 2013). For example, the number of halal products marketed by a company may not be sufficient for the business to focus on halal shipping alone (Ab Talib et al. 2013).

According to Islamic law, halal permitted animals must be slaughtered hygienically before consumption. Wan Hassan (2008) discussed the animal slaughtering process based on aspects of production allowed by halal certification bodies such as Jabatan Kemajuan Islam Malaysia (JAKIM), Central Islamica Brasileira de Alimentos Halal (CIBAL BRAZIL), Islamic Society of North America (ISNA), Halal Monitoring Committee (HMC), Australian Federation of Islamic Councils (AFIC), and the Federation of Islamic Associations of New Zealand (FIANZ). The key aspects mentioned by Wan Hassan (2008) were updated by Razak (2018) and more halal certification bodies added for comparison purposes (Table 2.9).

Table 2.9 Examples of halal certification bodies and aspects of production allowed

	JAKIM	CIBAL BRAZIL	ISNA	HMC	AFIC	FIANZ	MUI	ISWA	HFSAA	HICO
Slaughtering must be undertaken by a Muslim	/	/	/	/	/	/	/	/	/	/
Stunning (water bath, head only— does not kill the animal)	/	x	/	x	x	/	/	/	/	
Mechanical slaughter (conditions applied)	/	x	/	x	x	/		/	x	/
Verbal recitation of *tasmiyah* (not a recording)	/	/	/	/	/	/	/	/	/	/
Ensuring minimum required vessels are severed	/	/	/	/	/	/	/	/	/	/
Sharing halal and non-halal slaughtering plants (certain conditions applied such as no contamination and Islamic cleansing)	x	x	x	x	na	na	/	/	x	/

Source: Razak, 2018.

Notes: na—information is not available on their website. Australian Federation of Islamic Councils (AFIC), Central Islamica Brasileira de Alimentos Halal (CIBAL BRAZIL), Federation of Islamic Associations of New Zealand (FIANZ), Halal Food Standards Alliance of America (HFSAA), Halal International Certification Organization (HICO), Halal Monitoring Committee (HMC), Islamic Society of North America (ISNA), Islamic Society of the Washington Area (ISWA), Department of Islamic Development of Malaysia/Jabatan Agama dan Kemajuan Islam Malaysia (JAKIM), and Indonesian Council of Ulama/ Majelis Ulama Indonesia (MUI).

There is general agreement that the slaughtering staff must be Muslim and that the verbal recitation of *tasmiyah* (pronouncing the name of Allah) is required. However, there are differences over stunning, the machine slaughtering process, and the conduct of both halal and non-halal slaughtering at slaughter plants. The sharing of slaughter plants between halal and non-halal meat was not agreed to by six certification agencies for reasons of contamination avoidance and ritual cleansing. Three certification bodies do not support stunning and four do not support mechanical slaughter, both of which are significant points of debate within Islam (Regenstein, Chaudry & Regenstein 2003; Riaz & Chaudry 2004; Wan Hassan 2008).

The differences in halal processes may also have commercial and marketing implications. HMC, for example, claimed that the production of meat using stunning and machine slaughter is not halal. To discourage the use of stunning and machine slaughter, HMC is promoting a marketing strategy that position 'non-stunned' meat as 'authentic' halal quality (Lever & Miele 2012). In contrast, Abraham Natural Produce, a small company that produce halal organic meat, claims their meat is more authentic even though their slaughtering process involves stunning (Wilson & Liu 2010). The company further claimed that animal care was carried out from the early stage of rearing following 'organic' procedures; therefore, they promote their meat as being more authentic and of a high quality. However, the extent to which Muslim consumers perceive the relative authenticity of the two producers is unknown. In addition, to further complicate the stunning debate, slaughtering without stunning is considered cruel by some animal rights activists (Mukherjee 2014).

The ritual and spiritual aspects of slaughtering are mentioned in the Quran in numerous verses including *Al-Baqarah*, 172–173, *Al-Maidah*, 1, 3, 4, and 5, and *Al-An'nam*, 121, which allow the killing of animals by the most humane method. The Prophet Muhammad also says:

> Verily God has prescribed excellence in all things. Thus, if you kill (an animal), kill well; and if you slaughter, slaughter well. Let each one of you sharpen his blade so to spare suffering to the animal he slaughters.

> *(Muslim)*

The differences in opinions on the Islamic slaughtering process reflect the various interpretations among Muslim scholars. Other services offered in hospitality are also subject to debate, including entertainment, which is usually regarded as adding to the customer experience (Lugosi 2008).

Entertainment and other services

Wolf (1999) suggests that entertainment is a necessity in customer-oriented businesses. Entertainment can provide pleasure, enjoyment, and a sense of belonging. Hospitality providers can use entertainment to create a pleasing experience for customers such as through shows and themed environments (Teng & Chang 2013). Islam does not forbid its believers from fulfilling their needs in terms of leisure and entertainment so long as they do not contradict Islamic teachings (Al-Qaradawi 1992). Ghani (2009) argues that it is a huge challenge to develop Islamic entertainment in terms of halal and haram. Ghani (2009) also indicates that there are conservative and moderate views among Muslim scholars on the issues of whether some forms of entertainment are halal or are completely haram. For example, for some Muslim scholars entertainment is halal if the objectives and performances emphasise intellectual, moral, and spiritual aspects.

Saad et al. (2014) found that appropriate entertainment, which is "no night club", is the third most important feature of halal hotel design after segregated facilities and signs such as the Qibla. The authors indicate that many religious Muslims (*ulama'*) forbid the use of musical instruments, song, dance, and amusement for entertainment purposes because of concerns that they can cause a Muslim to neglect their duty to God. In addition, the behaviour of Muslim artists that are in conflict with Islamic teachings has led to entertainment sometimes being regarded as something negative that harms society (Saad et al. 2014). However, entertainment is about not only songs, dancing, and music, it also involves physical and spiritual aspects of life. For example, religious song, dance, and music is integral to the Sufi traditions of Islam. Similarly, Fikri and Tibek (2014) examined the acceptance of Islamic entertainment (*nasyid*) in north Sumatra, Indonesia, and found that 86.7 per cent (267 out 308) respondents like *nasyid*. The reasons given were the lyrics of the *nasyid* contain advice about life, the attire worn by the *nasyid* group as well as the moderate body movement is also suited to Muslim culture. This is consistent with the concept of entertainment in Islam that is concerned with always remembering God in every act and keeping with *Syariah* law (Al-Qaradawi 1992).

Hospitality providers provide a range of facilities to customers such as television, dining areas, and swimming pools. According to Rejab and Lateh (2012) to be in line with Shariah law, the television channel selection should have an Islamic information channel and other appropriate channels, such as education, and 'unbeneficial' channels should be avoided. In addition, information such as a prayer schedule, list of mosques, and details of halal restaurants near the hotel should be provided for customers. Moll (2010) in her study on halal entertainment details the producers' opinion on what should be aired by the halal satellite channel, which covers programmes for devoted Muslim as well as less devoted Muslim customers (Muslims with less knowledge about Islam or those with a different reading or interpretation of Islam). However, the commercialisation of halal entertainment has created confusion between religious and commercial entertainment (Eum 2008). In selecting suitable television channels for halal hospitality services, the provider may want to consider whether their customers are pious or not. Often providers are bound to the number of channels available and the associated costs to subscribe for channels that are not necessarily part of the normal deal. Different providers may have different views on specific channels to subscribe to given that they have to balance both consumer demand and the cost to supply suitable channels that comply with the provision of halal hospitality.

A study on foreign Muslim tourists in Malaysia by Battour, Ismail and Battor (2011) found that they had a high priority for the gender segregation of beaches, swimming pools, and gymnasiums, and the absence of adult video channels in hotel entertainment. However, it was acknowledged that such Islamic entertainment may not be appropriate for Western or non-Muslim guests, although hotels could enable guests to block services to channels as one means of managing what guests can see.

The closure of gaming rooms, unisex hair salons, and alcohol sales licences substantially affected hospitality providers in Iran (Okhovat 2010). As Okhovat (2010) argued, Islam is not the only religion that is professed by Iranians and international visitors and this poses a dilemma for Muslim countries that want to enact Shariah law yet also want to develop tourism and attract international markets. Some countries may choose to continue to isolate tourists from the wider society, as in the Maldives, while others strive to find a relative balance between pleasing the tourist and gaining benefit for the local economy, while still ensuring that religious requirements are respected, as in the case of Muslim-friendly service practices in Malaysia, Turkey, and UAE (Eid & El-Gohary 2015; Razalli et al. 2013). Din (1989) argued that Malaysia, for example, maintains a strict policy for Muslims and a moderate policy for non-Muslims in terms of tourism activities. Some activities, such as avoidance of gambling, no consumption of pork and alcohol, consumption of halal food, and segregation of services and facilities by gender are strictly imposed only on Muslims. Such policy approaches may be adopted by other countries to meet the requirements of secular and religious values within Muslim societies. However, Din (1989) also argued that changes in business services as a result of religious prohibition will only work if there is effective enforcement by authorities.

Business values and philosophy

Business ethics refers to the ethical rules and principles applied in any business activities. Abuznaid (2009: 280) defines Islamic ethics as "the code of moral principles that are prescribed by the Quran and Sunnah". The basis for Islamic ethics includes: truthfulness, trustworthiness, generosity and leniency, and avoidance of immoral behaviour such as fraud, cheating, and deceit. Rice (1999) suggested that ethical values such as honesty, trustworthiness, and care for the poor are similar under Islam, Judaism, and Christianity, and that there is a common approach within the Abrahamic religions. However, with respect to business, Islamic ethical values cover the entire aspect of business practices and include issues of interest (*riba*), taxation (alms or *zakat*), and accumulation of wealth. These are similar to other Abrahamic religions but also depend on scriptural interpretation, the nature of institutions, and religiosity. Muslims are obliged to earn a living (e.g. by doing business) and, if capable, they are expected to pay *zakat*.. Each Muslim is obligated to use his or her wealth for the sake of fulfilling the values of Islam, such as by fulfilling the needs of the poor. The Quran states that:

> Take, [O, Muhammad], from their wealth a charity by which you purify them and cause them increase, and invoke [Allah's blessings] upon them. Indeed, your invocations are reassurance for them. And Allah is Hearing and Knowing.
>
> *(At-Taubah, 103)*

Complying with Islamic ethical values in obtaining wealth is integral to religious behaviour in Islam, and not complying is therefore a sin. For example, *riba* is haram in Islam as it puts a burden on others to pay more for a loan. The accumulation of wealth for personal interest is also haram as the wealth must be distributed to others in need through *zakat* (Hanzaee & Ramezani 2011). As stated in the verse above, the commitment to *zakat* can purify an individual's spirit. The purpose of the life of a Muslim is to receive mercy from Allah by earnest compliance to all the teachings of Islam. By successfully undertaking all the Islamic requirements one will be blessed in this life and the hereafter. However, in contrast, in a commercial context, the focus is on making money and providing satisfaction to customers. Therefore, the possibility of conflict between Islamic and secular goals of service remains, especially where managers and owners of hospitality and tourism operations have other belief systems outside Islam, and when management philosophy is more commercially oriented. Indeed, such conflicts may occur even between Muslims. Rice (1999) argues that there is a gap between the philosophy and practice of Islamic ethics in some Muslim countries, especially in the area of international trade and banking. She stresses that in any business dealing, business people have to know a culture's ideal set of ethics prior to the actual ethical practice as there are differences between the two. Nevertheless, the differences between the ideal and the reality of Islamic ethics can be very difficult to discuss openly as it may then cross over into broader political, cultural, and institutional debates and conflicts, including what governments or businesses leaders wish to present internationally about their country or organisation, as compared to the actual realities of preferred behaviours.

Another approach to halal in terms of business values and philosophy is that of Mukherjee (2014), who argues that halal is a form of spiritual capital which is disseminated via the aid of halal verification. Mukherjee (2014) highlights the holiness of Islam that encompasses the moral and spiritual aspects of life, yet noted that when it comes to halal and haram matters especially, verification of standards is required given that business practices are often contrary to Islamic teachings. He also argued that halal may be treated as just another product to be exchanged for profit in the global market as some companies are willing to set aside deeper religious requirements in order to achieve substantial profits. Hanzaee and Ramezani (2011) also discuss the participation of business in the halal industry in order to gain profit. They note the profits gained by halal-friendly burgers, tacos, and chicken by companies such as McDonald's, Taco Bell, and KFC, when joining the halal industry, although such measures raise further questions about the way in which halal hospitality is framed and understood. Nevertheless, the use of halal certification is important in order to be accepted by Muslim customers in many non-Islamic countries as well as in some Islamic countries.

Halal standards and certification

Although there is no single global standard for halal there are numerous national standards and certifications and the development of halal standards is a major point of contention in halal trade and services. Indeed, Dolan (2010: 50) argues that the halal industry is excessively concerned as to "who should lead the industry, who gets to create halal standards, and whose standards are best". Because of the history and strength of Islam in the Middle East, certification bodies from the region tend to be trusted more by Muslim consumers than those of Australia and South East Asia (Dolan 2010). Muslim scholars also have stronger influence in the implementation of Islamic law in those countries (Zamani-Farahani & Henderson 2010) compared with other Muslim countries in the world.

Harvey (2010) argues about the importance of having a universal halal standard in order to curb fraud in the halal industry. For example, in the United Kingdom, the sale of non-halal meat that is claimed as being halal clearly creates difficulty for Muslims consumers. The presence of a universal halal standard with rules and regulations and specific definitions of halal could help overcome many issues associated with confidence in supply chains. Similar to Dolan (2010), Harvey (2010) raised concerns about who should set the universal halal standard and the difficulties in taking action on fraudulent halal claims if involving businesses outside of its national jurisdiction. Halim and Salleh (2012) also stress the need for uniformity of the halal standard globally to assist the growth of the halal industry. They argue that the absence of a universal halal standard leads to disagreements in many aspects such as animal feed, slaughtering methods, packaging, and logistics. In addition, confusion and misunderstanding exist as a result of countries having different halal standards. However, to produce a universal halal standard, some countries would need to change some of their own standards and procedures and be more transparent in their operation. Nevertheless, such actions may not benefit some countries, such as Malaysia which has been promoting its own JAKIM's halal standard (Badruldin et al. 2012). Moreover, it is important to note that support for an international standard is not universal, with much less interest, for example, from the European Commission, which already has strong food laws and regulations (Othman, Sungkar & Wan Hussan 2009).

Malaysia has several halal standards that are also used by some other countries to certify their halal products and services. The standards include the MS 1500:2004 which is the most admissible standard for halal food globally; MS 1900:2005 guides the organisation of the

Table 2.10 List of Malaysian halal standards

Malaysian Standards (MS)
MS 2594:2015
Halal chemicals for use in potable water treatment—General guidelines
MS 2610:2015
Muslim-friendly hospitality services—Requirements
MS 2565:2014
Halal packaging—General guidelines
MS 1500:2009
Halal food—Production, preparation, handling and storage—General guidelines (second revision)
MS 2200: Part 1: 2008
Islamic consumer goods—Part 1: Cosmetic and personal care—General guidelines
MS 2200-2: 2012
Islamic consumer goods—Part 2: Usage of animal bone, skin, and hair—General guidelines
MS 1900:2005
Quality management systems—Requirements from Islamic perspectives
MS 2300: 2009
Value-based management system—Requirements from an Islamic perspective
MS 2424: 2012
Halal pharmaceuticals—General Guidelines
MS 2400
Series on Halalan-Tayyiban Assurance Pipeline
MS 2393: 2010 (P)
Islamic and halal principles—Definitions and interpretations on terminology

Source: Adapted from HDC—Halal Standards, 2017.

principles and practice of quality management from Islamic perspectives; and MS 2610:2015 is for the management of tourism facilities, products, and services for Muslims in hospitality accommodation (HDC 2015). Malaysia has also established halal standards covering the areas of chemicals, hospitality service, packaging, food production and preparation, furs, cosmetics, and quality management system (Table 2.10).

Mohd Sirajuddin et al. (2013) argue that the Malaysian standards emphasise the physical aspect of products, and food and beverage in particular. Other aspects such as services, leisure, and entertainment are not included. Samori and Sabtu (2012), for example, stated that it is important to have a halal standard for hospitality services in order to increase the confidence of customers in Shariah-law compliant practices for products, instruments, operations, and management. However, there is currently no legal standard being developed for hospitality providers to enable them to cover all aspects of their facilities and services when applying for halal certification. The basic requirements of the standards cover the aspects of halal and *tayyib* such as safety, cleanliness, and quality with respect to food (Table 2.11). The HDC (2015) regard the introduction of MS 2610:2015 as good guidance for providers in managing hospitality services with the Malaysian Government's Muslim Friendly Hospitality Requirements (MS 2610:2015) using a number of items to represent halal hospitality (Table 2.12).

Che Omar et al. (2014) discuss the notion of an Islamic Quality Standard (IQS) for hospitality service. They present 18 requirements divided into seven ranking criteria (Table 2.13). The first

Table 2.11 Basic requirements for halal food in MS 2610:2015

1	Does not contain any parts or products of animals that are non-halal to Muslims or products of animals which are not slaughtered according to Shariah law
2	Does not contain any ingredients that are najis according to Shariah law
3	Is safe and not harmful
4	Is not prepared, processed, or manufactured using equipment that is contaminated with things that are najis (filth or unclean) according to Shariah law
5	The food or its ingredients do not contain any human parts or its derivatives that are not permitted by Shariah law
6	And during its preparation, processing, packaging, storage, or transportation, the food is physically separated from any other food that does not meet the requirements stated in items 1, 2, 3, 4, or 5, or any other things that have been decreed as najis (filth or unclean) by Shariah law

Source: Adapted from HDC, 2015.

rank (IQS1) offers basic quality requirements and the seventh rank (IQS7) presents the highest quality requirements for halal hospitality. In terms of the level of Shariah-law compliance, IQS1 to IQS2 are categorised as weak, IQS3 to IQS5 are moderate, and IQS6 to IQS7 are the highest standard. The IQS are cumulative.

Mathew, Abdullah and Ismail (2014) indicate that although the halal hospitality concept is complex, some of the requirements are possible to implement within organisations. For example, using the halal logo to promote to customers that the services provided are halal compliant. However, with about 122 halal certifying bodies around the world with different halal standards and logos, there are clear implementation and customer recognition difficulties with such proposals (Halim & Salleh 2012). Many countries have developed their own halal standard, e.g. Brunei, Maldives, and Jordan (Halim & Salleh 2012), although greater formal mutual recognition of halal standards in the development of free trade agreements would assist in halal trade (Aziz & Sulaiman 2014).

Depending on the national jurisdiction, halal certificates can be issued by any individual Muslim, Islamic organisation, or agency. The national legal context frames the capacity to both regulate and issue certificates. Social acceptance of such certificates is up to the consumer. However, it is typically the responsibility of the authorised authorities to check compliance with the requirements of halal certification and associated law so as to ensure the safety of consumers (Aziz & Sulaiman 2014; Abdul, Ismail, Mustapha & Kusuma 2013). For example, in Malaysia, providers are subject to legal action if they use the halal logo to promote products that contravene the principles of Shariah law (Manual procedure for Malaysia halal certification (3rd Revision), 2014). Statutes such as the Trade Description Act 2011, Food Act 1983, and Abattoir Act (Private) 1993 can also be used for enforcement purposes (Halim et al. 2014). Issuing bodies for a halal certificate from other countries must get approval from JAKIM or MUI (Majelis Ulama Indonesia) to export products to Malaysia and Indonesia. This is to confirm that the issuing body of the exporting country is following the guidelines provided by JAKIM or MUI (Hanzaee & Ramezani 2011).

Non-Muslim trading companies may also acknowledge the importance of halal certification (Abdullah, Ishak & Bustamam 2012a; Abdullah, Zainoren, Abdurahman & Hamali 2012b). Abdul et al. (2013) found that most of the small size businesses in Jogjakarta, Indonesia, agreed that having a halal certificate can enhance customer satisfaction, confidence,

Table 2.12 Muslim Friendly Hospitality Requirements (MS 2610:2015)

No.	Items	Explanation
1	Quran	Islamic scripture containing the revealed words of Allah to the Prophet Muhammad (pbuh) through the medium of Angel Jibrail in Arabic as the primary source of Islamic law.
2	Fasting	The third pillar of Islam. Muslims are prohibited from eating, drinking (including water) and must refrain from smoking, sexual activities, and various other desires and be encouraged to temper negative emotions such as anger and addiction during fasting hours (from dawn to dusk) in the month of Ramadan.
3	Ramadan	The holy month in the Hijri calendar when Muslims perform the obligatory practice of fasting from dawn (fajr) to dusk (maghrib).
4	Halal	An act or product that is lawful and permitted in Islam based on the authoritative sources.
5	Iftar	The meal taken by Muslims at dusk to break their fast.
6	Kiblat	Direction of prayer towards the Kaabah in Makkah.
7	Musalla	Place, space, or room that is reserved for solah.
8	Sajada	A mat generally used by Muslims to perform solah.
9	Recreation	Social, cultural, sporting, and other relevant activities undertaken in leisure time.
10	Recreational facilities	Public and private facilities provided for recreational activities.
11	Sahur	The meal consumed by Muslims before dawn when fasting.
12	Solah	The ritual worship in Islam, as one of the five pillars of Islam, to be performed five times a day.
13	Shariah	Overall legal and regulation of Allah pertaining to life and welfare of mankind for the prosperity of life in this world and in the hereafter.
14	Shariah compliance	Conformity to Shariah.
15	Shariah law	Communication from Allah concerning the conduct of the mukallaf (sane person) which consists of a demand (commandments and prohibitions) and option or an enactment.
16	Wudhu	The rite or act to wash or wipe the specific parts of the body with water to be pure and clean for the solah.
17	Wudhu facility	Appropriate or dedicated area for male and female for wudhu.

Source: Adapted from Department of Standards Malaysia, 2015.

and trust. However, in their research, only 60 per cent (102 out of 153) of the businesses studied were halal certified due to the non-compulsory enforcement of halal certification and the preference of businesses to focus on the local market. It is also a common situation for Muslims to assume that many products and services provided in Muslim countries are halal, even if this may not actually be the case, thus reducing the dependency on halal certification in business operations (Nooh, Nawai, Dali & Mohammad 2007). Wan Hassan (2008) found that more than 50 per cent (out of 99) of halal restaurant providers in New Zealand that she interviewed had no interest in applying for halal certification despite having halal food. Some of the reasons given for this include a belief that Muslim customers have to trust them

Table 2.13 Proposed Islamic Quality Standard (IQS) for halal hotels

IQS	Requirements
IQS1	Bedroom (1 queen/2 standard size bed and telephone). Convenient accessibility and staff are on duty 24 hours; Qibla direction, prayer mat, and time schedule for prayer; serve halal breakfast; at least 2 prayer rooms
IQS2	Restaurant serving halal food
IQS3	Serving halal food at all times
IQS4	Scheduling of swimming pool or spa according to gender
IQS5	Spacious bedroom for prayer; prayer rooms available by gender
IQS6	Spa and gymnasium by gender; additional facilities, e.g. separate saloon for male and female, boutique arcade; serving *sahoor* (pre-dawn meal) and *Iftar* (fast breaking) during Ramadan.
IQS7	2 ≥ swimming pool by gender; 2 ≥ spa by gender; 4 prayer rooms made available for hotel guests; more than 2 restaurants of halal international cuisine; entertainment for family and by gender; bathrooms equipped with bidets

Source: Adapted and modified from Che Omar et al., 2014.

because they have similar beliefs, and that they have been in the market for such a long time and are already trusted for providing halal hospitality among the local customers. Marzuki et al. (2012a, 2012b) noted the limited participation of hospitality providers in Malaysia in halal certification, while also highlighting that a number of food service providers show the halal logo even though they are not actually certified.

Samori and Sabtu (2012) believe that the use of a halal logo can assist in identifying a product or service that has been certified halal by certification bodies, for example, JAKIM has introduced a standard halal logo for that purpose in Malaysia. Most commonly around the world, the symbols used are in Arabic lettering with the word halal or simply the word halal. Abdullah et al. (2012a, 2012b) also suggest that Muslim customers are more confident with a halal logo from trusted halal certification bodies. Similarly, Hanzaee and Ramezani (2011) agree a logo authorised by a local authority or recognised halal certification bodies contributes to product acceptance and trust, especially for repeat purchase (Aziz & Chok 2013). However, despite academic, consumer and, often, government support for halal certification, there are often significant barriers to businesses obtaining certification.

In New Zealand, halal hospitality (food service) providers claimed that the Muslim customer market is not sufficiently significant to their business as New Zealand has a minority Muslim population and many also claimed that the cost of halal certification is expensive (Wan Hassan 2008). Nevertheless, 66 per cent (46 of 70) providers interviewed did have the halal sign on their premises (Wan Hassan 2008). The costs involved in the provision of halal hospitality include the certification fee, maintenance and renovation, and labour (Samori & Rahman 2013). In Malaysia the fee for hotels, catering and convention centres is payable to JAKIM for approval purposes, as well as the provision of halal certificates (Marzuki, Hall & Ballantine 2014). For accommodation establishments, maintenance and renovation costs may be expensive because halal certification involves the specific allocation of rooms for males, females, and families. Providers also need to ensure the presence of prayer rooms by gender. Providers argue that the need for such changes for certification purposes will increase costs for existing establishments (Karim, Ahmad & Zainol

2017), although new hotels can be designed accordingly (Salleh, Hamid, Hashim & Omain 2014). Another area of cost is the hiring and training of staff, especially as to be fully halal compliant there is a need to ensure that an appropriate number of staff is available to handle male and female customers. Such staff costs may be especially high in non-Muslim countries.

Hanzaee and Ramezani (2011) suggest that providers need to gain a clear understanding of the costs involved in the application of halal certification in order to assess its benefits and the repercussions for their business. The cost can be expensive if the process of certification needs to be done annually. In some cases, providers may have to change the ingredients in food production. Consideration also needs to be given to the capacity of halal hospitality and tourism providers to meet the needs of both Muslim and non-Muslim markets (Razalli et al. 2009; Salleh et al. 2014), especially if the business is aimed at international and multicultural customers. As a result, and perhaps almost paradoxically, for many tourism businesses, especially in lodging and food and beverage, the acceptance of halal requirements may therefore be more economically significant in terms of the non-Muslim market.

Conclusions

Halal hospitality attributes have been identified in several studies (Battour et al. 2011; Henderson 2010; Rosenberg & Choufany 2009; Saad et al. 2014; Razzaq, Hall & Prayag 2016). However, the concept of halal has yet to be fully explored in the tourism and hospitality literature. Despite substantial interest from some countries in an effort to attract and promote Muslim markets, implementation of halal certification and regulation is often fraught with difficulties. Although providing halal food, international operators of hotels, resorts, and apartment hotels are often hesitant to develop fully Shariah-compliant properties, unless required to by law in the jurisdictions in which they operate, given that they often target Muslim and non-Muslim markets (Samori & Rahman 2013). For example, hotels in Gulf countries provide separate family sections, all-female wedding receptions, and female staff for female customers in order to fulfil local requirements (Sobh, Belk & Gressel 2012). However, such a situation highlights the extent to which the requirements for halal hospitality are different between countries and jurisdictions, even when they are nominally Muslim countries, raising substantial questions not only about the possibilities for global halal standards but also the importance of recognising that there are different Shariah traditions within Islam as well as different approaches to halal.

In seeking to identify key attributes of halal accommodation Razzaq et al. (2016) noted that the attributes of halal accommodation as identified in the literature, and in their own research, could be identified by both positive and negative attributes of accommodation, while a number of accommodation attributes that may be significant for some accommodation ratings are often neutral for halal tourists (Table 2.14). They also suggest that some accommodation attributes may also be more significant for Muslim travellers on the basis of gender or if they were travelling with family or a group more than others given requirements for appropriate modesty. Or, as in some interpretations of Islam, to segregate gender altogether.

One of the interesting issues that emerges from examining the halal tourism and hospitality literature is that it tends to focus on the more conservative ideals of Muslim behaviour. Such a perspective is also reflected in some of the statements of the OIC regarding tourism. For example, the OIC suggest that as a cultural concept

Table 2.14 Value of accommodation attributes for halal tourism among Muslim tourists

	Perception of accommodation attributes		
	Perceived more positively	*Neutral*	*Perceived more negatively*
All Muslim tourists	• Offers halal food • Can cater to specific religious needs • Can provide prayer times • Can provide a prayer mat • Can provide a copy of the Quran • Has a prayer facility on-site • Has a Qibla marker • Able to cater to special dietary needs • Certified halal items • Supports Islamic financial principles	• Multilingual staff • Family-friendly • Provide DVD players • Provide satellite or cable television • Provide multilingual TV channels • Provides movies • Offers off-premises food options • Dairy-free food options • Gluten-free food options • Vegetarian food options • Has room service • Has a dining establishment on-site • Has in-unit cooking facilities	• Pet-friendly • Proximity to 'red light' district • Proximity to gambling venues • Has a mini bar • Has a bar on-site • Alcohol is served on-site
Male Muslim tourists		• Segregated gym on-site • Segregated day spa on-site • Segregated sauna on-site • Segregated spa bath or pool on-site	
Male Muslim tourists with family/group travel	• Segregated gym on-site • Segregated day spa on-site • Segregated sauna on-site • Segregated spa bath or pool on-site		• Non-segregated gym on-site • Non-segregated day spa on-site • Non-segregated sauna on-site • Non-segregated spa bath or pool on-site
Female Muslim tourists with family/group travel	• Gender-segregated female-only floors • Segregated sauna on-site • Segregated day spa on-site		• Non-segregated spa bath or pool on-site • Non-segregated gymnasium on-site • Non-segregated spa bath or pool on-site

Source: After Razzaq et al., 2016.

Islamic tourism includes visions and ideas that outline the inclusion of Islamic religious cultural sites in tourism programs with "pedagogical" and self-confidence building elements. It tries to encourage a reorientation inside the tourist destinations towards less consumption and "western culture" loaded sites towards more Islamic historical, religious and cultural sites.

(OIC 2017: 28)

While visits to Islamic attractions and destinations are undoubtedly important, the OIC (2017) seems to ignore the interests and needs of the large numbers of Muslim travellers to non-Islamic countries and regions as part of their broader interest in the world around them. Similarly, the OIC explicitly describes Islamic tourism as a 'religious conservative' concept

The religious conservative concept for Islamic tourism is based on the conservative interpretation and understanding of Islam. Merging elements of the extremely conservative Islamic lifestyle with the modern tourism industry could indeed present new tourism options, spaces, and spheres. For a growing conservative intra Arab and intra Muslim tourism market, the implementation of a religious conservative concept in tourism planning as an extra option and as an insertion into the existing mainstream tourism could indeed have a positive economic and social effect.

(OIC 2017: 28)

Such statements point to the need for a better understanding of the actual behaviours, motivations, and needs of Islamic tourists as well as their understanding of and engagement with halal tourism and hospitality. Similarly, research on providers also suggests that significant gaps exist between government statements on the positioning of destinations for halal tourism and the on-the-ground realities of what is offered and the barriers and constraints that exist for businesses to meet halal standards. For example, there is no significant difference in the communication of halal attributes on the websites of accommodation providers in Malaysia, which is a Muslim-majority country (Razak 2018), and New Zealand, a country with only a very small Muslim population (Razzaq et al. 2016). Similarly, Alserhan et al. (2018) found "Islamic" hotels to be not transparent to their guests who were seeking an Islamically compliant holiday and also to those seeking a conventional hotel experience. They suggested several reasons as to why hotels misrepresent themselves: "self-orientalisation", a necessity to present "nice Islam", an "ethics gap", and/or a poor understanding of marketing and market positioning.

In some ways providing halal food is one of the easier dimensions of halal services. Far harder is to follow Islamic financial and business principles. Indeed, in her research in Malaysia, Razak (2018) observed that most Muslim accommodation providers understand the provision of hospitality within the context of adherence to the teachings of Islam. However, her respondents often had different interpretations regarding halal between their religious understanding and in relation to the official JAKIM requirements. From a personal religious perspective, her respondents clearly had their own opinions as to when to comply with government halal requirements, with several respondents regarding their sense of religious obligation and social responsibility in hospitality as being more important in obtaining God's blessing than JAKIM's (see also Chapter 4, this volume).

Despite the potential value of halal certification of businesses for customer assurance, there appear to be major issues with certification compliance, in part because of the absence of international standards (Abdullah et al. 2012b; Al-Harran & Low 2008; Marzuki et al. 2012a). However, in the absence of effective self-regulation, responsible government agencies need to enforce codes of conduct and ethical standards on businesses for certification to be effective. Lack of enforcement is regularly debated in many halal studies (e.g. Marzuki et al. 2012a, 2012b; Wan Hassan 2008), while a lack of understanding of halal hospitality requirements can also contribute to fraud and the mixing of halal and haram attributes in hospitality and tourism businesses (Fadzlillah, Man, Jamaludin, Rahman & Al-Kahtani 2011). Importantly, this is an issue in many countries, with the relative security of halal certification arguably being better in those countries that also have strong consumer law.

Finally, halal hospitality and tourism reflect the tension that exist between the sacred and the profane (Siddiqui 2015), and the demands and needs of both Muslim and non-Muslim providers and consumers in welcoming others (Kushimoto 2017; Yarbakhsh 2018). Muhammad and Mizerski (2013: 367) suggest that those "who adopt religion as their way of life differ significantly to those who adopt religious teachings when needed or necessary". There is potentially much truth in this which links strongly to understandings of halal hospitality as an authentic act of personal hospitality in which the guest is cared for and welcomed, rather than an attitude that because it was ensured that there was no pork on the table then halal service requirements were met! But if this is the case then it also needs to be acknowledged that great care of Islamic tourists is also possible from non-Muslims and vice versa and that hospitality should be something that can be shared rather than serve to divide.

References

Ab Halim, M.A. and Mohd Salleh, M.M. (2012) 'The possibility of uniformity on halal standards in Organization of Islamic Countries (OIC) country', *World Applied Sciences Journal*, 17: 6–10.

Ab Talib, M.S., Lim, R. and Khor, V.Z. (2013) 'Qualitative research on critical issues in halal logistics', *Journal of Emerging Economies and Islamic Research*, 1 (2): 1–20.

Abdul, M., Ismail, H., Mustapha, M. and Kusuma, H. (2013) 'Indonesian small medium enterprises (SMEs) and perceptions on halal food certification', *African Journal of Business Management*, 7 (16): 1492–1500.

Abdullah, F.Z., Ishak, N.K. and Bustamam, F.L. (2012a) 'A case study of small budget chalets at East Coast of Malaysia', *International Journal of Business and Social Science*, 3 (1): 275–282.

Abdullah, F., Zainoren, A., Abdurahman, A. and Hamali, J. (2012b) 'Developing a framework of success for the foodservice industry in Malaysia', *International Journal of Business and Society*, 13 (3): 309–334.

Abdullah, N.F. and Mukhtar, M. (2014) 'Konsep pelancongan Islam: Satu pengamatan'. In *Seminar Kebangsaan Penyelidikan dan Pendidikan Islam Politeknik 2014 (SKPI'14)*. Perak, Malaysia, 1–9.

Abuznaid, S.A. (2009) 'Business ethics in Islam: The glaring gap in practice', *International Journal of Islamic and Middle Eastern Finance and Management*, 2 (4): 278–288.

Ahmat, N.C., Ridzuan, A.H.A. and Zahari, M.S.M. (2012) 'Dry hotel and Syariah compliant practices: Concepts, challenges and reality in Malaysia'. In *International Conference on Innovation, Management and Technology Research (ICIMTR 2012)*. Melaka, Malaysia: 107–111.

Al-Harran, S. and Low, K.C.P. (2008) 'Marketing of halal products: The way forward', *The Halal Journal*, January/February: 44–46.

Al-Mazeedi, H.M., Regenstein, J.M. and Riaz, M.N. (2013) 'The issue of undeclared ingredients in halal and kosher food production: A focus on processing aids', *Comprehensive Reviews in Food Science and Food Safety*, 12 (2): 228–233.

Al-Qaradawi, Y. (1992) *The Lawful and Prohibited in Islam*. [pdf] Available at: https://thequranblog.files. wordpress.com/2010/06/the-lawful-and-the-prohibited-in-islam.pdf

Alserhan, B.A., Wood, B.P., Rutter, R., Halkias, D., Terzi, H. and Al Serhan, O. (2018). 'The transparency of Islamic hotels: "Nice Islam" and the "self-orientalizing" of Muslims?', *International Journal of Tourism Research*, https://doi.org/10.1002/jtr.2197.

Aziz, N.A. and Sulaiman, S.S. (2014) 'Role of the local authority in issuing license for halal certified premise in the city of Shah Alam', *Procedia—Social and Behavioral Sciences*, 121: 133–143.

Aziz, Y.A. and Chok, N.V. (2013) 'The role of halal awareness, halal certification, and marketing components in determining halal purchase intention among non-Muslims in Malaysia: A structural equation modeling approach', *Journal of International Food & Agribusiness Marketing*, 25 (1): 1–23.

Badruldin, B., Mohamed, Z., Sharifuddin, J., Rezai, G., Abdullah, A., Abd Latif, I. and Mohayidin, G. (2012) 'Clients' perception towards JAKIM service quality in halal certification', *Journal of Islamic Marketing*, 3 (1): 59–71.

Battour, M., Ismail, M.N. and Battor, M. (2011) 'The impact of destination attributes on Muslim tourist's choice', *International Journal of Tourism Research*, 13 (6): 527–540.

Che Omar, C.M., Islam, M.S. and Adaha, N.M.A. (2013) 'Perspectives on Islamic tourism and Shariah compliance in the hotel management in Malaysia'. In *Proceeding Islamic Economics and Business*. Kuala Lumpur, Malaysia: 1–11.

Che Omar, C.M., Adaha, N.M.A., Ghaffar, H.A. and Ali, A.I.M. (2014) 'Shariah compliance in hotel operations using Islamic tourism product index'. In *International Conference on Tourism and Development 2014*. Chiang Mai, Thailand: 144–151.

De Run, E., Butt, M., Fam, K. and Jong, T. (2010) 'Attitudes towards offensive advertising: Malaysian Muslims' view', *Journal of Islamic Marketing*, 1 (1): 25–36.

Din, K.H. (1982) 'Tourism in Malaysia competing needs in a plural society', *Annals of Tourism Research*, 9 (3): 453–480.

Din, K.H. (1989) 'Islam and tourism patterns, issues, and options', *Annals of Tourism Research*, 16: 542–563.

Dolan, S. (2010) Globalizing Halal: Tracing the Formation of a Social Concept. MA. Northern Illinois University.

Ehrman, B.D. (2006) *Peter, Paul, and Mary Magdalene: The Followers of Jesus in History and Legend*. New York: Oxford University Press

Eickelman, D.F. and Piscatori, J.P. (eds) (1990). *Muslim Travellers: Pilgrimage, Migration and the Religious Imagination*. Berkeley: University of California Press.

Eid, R. and El-Gohary, H. (2015) 'The role of Islamic religiosity on the relationship between perceived value and tourist satisfaction', *Tourism Management*, 46: 477–488.

Eum, I. (2008) 'A study on current culinary culture and religious identity in the Gulf Region: Focused on the Ashura practice among the Shia Muslims of Bahrain and Kuwait', *International Area Studies Review*, 11 (2): 55–73.

Fadzlillah, N.A., Man, Y.B.C., Jamaludin, M.A., Rahman, S.A. and Al-Kahtani, H.A. (2011) 'Halal food issues from Islamic and modern science perspectives'. In *International Conference on Humanities, Historical and Social Sciences*, Vol. 17. Singapore: IACSIT Press: 159–163.

Fikri, S. and Tibek, S.R. (2014) 'Nasyid as an Islamic alternative entertainment', *IOSR Journal of Humanities and Social Science*, 19 (7): 43–48.

Fischer, J. (2008) 'Religion, science and markets', *EMBO Reports*, 9 (9): 828–831.

Gannon, M.J., Baxter, I.W.F., Collinson, E., Curran, R., Farrington, T., Glasgow, S., et al. (2017) 'Travelling for Umrah: Destination attributes, destination image, and post-travel intentions', *Service Industries Journal*, 37 (7–8): 448–465.

Ghani, Z.B.A. (2009) 'Entertainment in Muslim media: Unsettled problem?', *Journal Hadhari*, 2: 53–64.

Ghozali, M. and Kamri, N.A. (2015) 'Keperibadian Islam dan profesionalisme dalam pekerjaan: Satu analisis teoritis', *Jurnal Syariah*, 23 (2): 255–286.

Halim, M.A.A. and Salleh, M.M.M. (2012) 'The possibility of uniformity on halal standards in Organization of Islamic Countries (OIC) country', *World Applied Sciences Journal*, 17: 6–10.

Halim, M.A.B.A., binti Mohd, K.W., Salleh, M.M.M., Yalawae, A., Omar, T.S.M.N.S., Ahmad, A., et al. (2014) 'Consumer protection of halal products in Malaysia: A literature highlight', *Procedia—Social and Behavioral Sciences*, 121: 68–78.

Hamdan, A. (2007) 'A case study of a Muslim client: Incorporating religious beliefs and practices', *Journal of Multicultural Counseling and Development*, 35 (2): 92–100.

Hanzaee, K.H. and Ramezani, M.R. (2011) 'Intention to halal products in the world markets', *Interdisciplinary Journal of Research in Business*, 1 (5): 1–7.

Harvey, R. (2010) *Certification of Halal Meat in the UK*. Cambridge: HRH Prince Alwaleed Bin Talal Centre of Islamic Studies.

Hasan, B., Mahyuddin, K. and Mohd Ahsrof Zaki, Y. (2010) 'Pelancongan dari perspektif Islam: Analisis pendekatan fiqh'. In Y. Mohd Asmadi, I. Huzaimah & I. Takiyuddin (eds) *Prosiding Seminar Pengurusan Perhotelan & Pelancongan Islam 2010*. Shah Alam: Universiti Teknologi Mara: 1–17.

Hashim, N.H. (2008) Investigating Internet Adoption and Implementation by Malaysian Hotels: An Exploratory Study. PhD. University of Western Australia, Perth.

Hashim, N.H., Murphy, J. and Hashim, N.M. (2007) 'Islam and on-line imagery on Malaysian tourist destination websites', *Journal of Computer-Mediated Communication*, 12 (3): 1082–1102.

Hasri, N.H., Taib, M.Z.M. and Ahmad, S.S. (2016) 'Relevance of regulatory policies in governing adherence to halal concept in the design of food premises in Malaysia', *Procedia—Social and Behavioral Sciences*, 222: 306–314.

Hassan, R. (2005) *On Being Religious: Religious Commitment in Muslim Societies*, Singapore: Institute of Defence and Strategic Studies. [pdf] Available at: www.ntu.edu.sg/rsis/publications/WorkingPapers/WP80.pdf

Hayati, A., Khadijah, S. and Manan, A. (2012) 'The economic potential of halal tourism industry on economic growth in Malaysia'. In R.S. Raja Kasim, M.A. Mohamed Adil, S.K. Ab Manan and F. Abd Rahman (eds) *International Halal Conference (InHAC 2012)*. Kuala Lumpur, Malaysia: Elsevier: 244–253.

HDC. (2015) *Manual Prosedur Pensijilan Halal Malaysia (Semakan Ketiga) 2014*. Putrajaya: Jabatan Kemajuan Islam Malaysia.

HDC. (2017) *Halal Standards*. Petaling Jaya, Selangor: Halal Industry Development Corporation.

Henderson, J.C. (2010) 'Sharia-compliant hotels', *Tourism and Hospitality Research*, 10 (3): 246–254.

Hisham, A. (2012) 'Halal dan kosher: Satu analisis perbandingan'. In *The 9th Symposium of the Malay Archipelago*, Penang, Malaysia: 427–440.

Isfahani, A.N., Pourezzat, A.A., Abdolmanafi, S. and Shahnazari, A. (2013) 'To investigate influential factors on halal brand in the global markets', *Journal of Basic and Applied Scientific Research*, 3 (1): 958–963.

Ismaeel, M. and Blaim, K. (2012) 'Toward applied Islamic business ethics: Responsible halal business', *Journal of Management Development*, 31 (10): 1090–1100.

JAKIM. (2013) *Garis panduan sertu menurut perspektif Islam*. Kula Lumpur: JAKIM. Available at: www .halal.gov.my

Kamali, M.H. (2011) 'Tourism and the halal industry: A global Shariah perspective'. In *World Islamic Tourism Forum 2011*. Kuala Lumpur, Malaysia: 12–13.

Kamali, M.H. (2015) *What Everyone Needs to Know About Shariah*. Available at: www.academia.edu /12062029/What_Everyone_Needs_to_Know_about_Shariah

Karim, A.A. and Bhat, R. (2008) 'Gelatin alternatives for the food industry: Recent developments, challenges and prospects', *Trends in Food Science & Technology*, 19 (12): 644–656.

Karim, M.H.A., Ahmad, R. and Zainol, N.A. (2017) 'Differences in hotel attributes: Islamic hotel and Sharia compliant hotel in Malaysia', *Journal of Global Business and Social Entrepreneurship (GBSE)*, 1 (2): 157–169.

Kassim, N., Hashim, P., Hashim, D. M. and Jol, H. (2014) 'New approach of samak clay usage for halal industry requirement', *Procedia—Social and Behavioral Sciences*, 121: 186–192.

Kirillova, K., Gilmetdinova, A. and Lehto, X. (2014) 'Interpretation of hospitality across religions', *International Journal of Hospitality Management*, 43: 23–34.

Kushimoto, H. (2017) 'Religious and cultural foundations of hospitality in the Islamic and Japanese traditions: A preliminary comparison', *Advanced Science Letters*, 23 (7): 6247–6251.

Laderlah, S.A., Rahman, S.A., Awang, K. and Man, Y.C. (2011) 'A study on Islamic tourism: A Malaysian experience'. In *2nd International Conference on Humanities, Historical and Social Science (IPEDR)*, 17: 184–189.

Lever, J. and Miele, M. (2012) 'The growth of halal meat markets in Europe: An exploration of the supply side theory of religion', *Journal of Rural Studies*, 28 (4): 528–537.

Lugosi, P. (2008) 'Hospitality spaces, hospitable moments: Consumer encounters and affective experiences in commercial settings', *Journal of Foodservice*, 19 (2): 139–149.

Marzuki, S.Z. (2012) Understanding the Expectations of Restaurant Managers Toward Halal Certification in Malaysia. PhD. University of Canterbury, Christchurch, New Zealand.

Marzuki, S.Z., Hall, C.M. and Ballantine, P.W. (2012a) 'Restaurant manager and halal certification in Malaysia', *Journal of Foodservice Business Research*, 15 (2): 195–214.

Marzuki, S.Z., Hall, C.M. and Ballantine. P.W. (2012b) 'Restaurant manager's perspectives on halal certification', *Journal of Islamic Marketing*, 3 (1): 47–58.

Marzuki, S.Z., Hall, C.M. and Ballantine, P.W. (2014) 'Measurement of restaurant manager expectations toward halal certification using factor and cluster analysis', *Procedia—Social and Behavioral Sciences*, 121: 291–303.

Mathew, V.N., Abdullah, A.M.R.A. and Ismail, S.N.B.M. (2014) 'Acceptance on halal food among non-Muslim consumers', *Procedia—Social and Behavioral Sciences*, 121: 262–271.

Mohd Sirajuddin, M.D., Sahri, M., Khalid, M.M., Yaakob, M.A.Z. and Harun, H.M.F. (2013) 'Introducing halalan tayyiban concept in global industry practices: An innovative attempt'. In *International Proceedings of Economics Development and Research*: 44–49.

Mohd Sirajuddin, M.D., Saad, M.A., Sahri, M. and Yaakub, M.A.Z. (2014) 'Benchmarking tayyib as the best practice for halal logistic management: The Qur'anic perspective'. In *International Conference on ISO & TQM (18–ICIT)*. Sarawak, Malaysia: 1–8.

Moll, Y. (2010) 'Islamic televangelism: Religion, media and visuality in contemporary Egypt', *Arab Media & Society*, 10: 1–27.

Morgan, M. (2004) 'From production line to drama school: Higher education for the future of tourism', *International Journal of Contemporary Hospitality Management*, 16 (2): 91–99.

Muhamad, N. and Mizerski, D. (2013) 'The effects of following Islam in decisions about taboo products', *Psychology and Marketing*, 30 (4): 357–371.

Mukherjee, S. (2014) 'Global halal: Meat, money, and religion'. *Religions*, 5 (1): 22–75.

Nasaruddin, R.R., Fuad, F., Mel, M., Jaswir, I. and Abd, H. (2012) 'The importance of a standardized Islamic Manufacturing Practice (IMP) for food and pharmaceutical productions', *Advances in Natural and Applied Sciences*, 6 (5): 588–595.

Nasir, K. and Pereira, A.A. (2008) 'Defensive dining: Notes on the public dining experiences in Singapore', *Contemporary Islam*, 2: 61–73.

Nooh, M.N., Nawai, N., Dali, N.M. and Mohammad, H. (2007) 'Halal branding: An exploratory research among consumers in Malaysia'. In *Proceedings of 3rd UNITEN International Business Management Conference Human Capital Optimization Strategies Challenges and Sustainability*. Melaka, Malaysia: 16–18.

OIC. (2017) *International Tourism in the OIC Countries: Prospects and Challenges 2017*. Ankara: The Statistical, Economic and Social Research and Training Centre for Islamic Countries (SESRIC).

Okhovat, H. (2010) 'A study on religious tourism industry management case study: Islamic republic of Iran', *International Journal of Academic Research*, 2 (5): 302–308.

Othman, P., Sungkar, I. and Hussin, W.S.W. (2009) 'Malaysia as an international halal food hub: Competitiveness and potential of meat-based industries', *ASEAN Economic Bulletin*, 26 (3): 306–320.

Prabowo, S., Abd, A. and Ab, S. (2012) 'Halal culinary: Opportunity and challenge in Indonesia'. In R. S. Raja Kasim, M.A. Mohamed Adil, S.K. Ab Manan and F. Abd Rahman (eds) *International Halal Conference (InHAC 2012)*. Kuala Lumpur, Malaysia: Elsevier: 1–10.

Razak, N.H.A. (2018) Malaysian Accommodation Providers' Understanding of Halal Hospitality. PhD. University of Canterbury.

Razalli, M.R., Abdullah, S. and Hassan, M.G. (2009) *Developing a Model for Islamic Hotels: Evaluating Opportunities and Challenges*. Available at: www.academia.edu/2032086/Developing_a_Model_for_Islamic_Hotels_Evaluating_Opportunities_and_Challenges

Razalli, M.R., Yusoff, R.Z. and Mohd Roslan, M.W. (2013) 'A framework of halal certification practices for hotel industry'. *Asian Social Science*, 9 (11): 316–326.

Razzaq, S., Hall, C.M. and Prayag, G. (2016) 'The capacity of New Zealand to accommodate the halal tourism market—Or not'. *Tourism Management Perspectives*, 18: 92–97.

Regenstein, J.M., Chaudry, M.M. and Regenstein, C. (2003) 'The kosher and halal food laws', *Comprehensive Reviews in Food Science and Food Safety*, 2 (3): 111–127.

Rejab, S.N. and Lateh, N. (2012) 'Aspek-aspek penawaran inap secara syariah di hotel De Palma'. In R. S. Raja Kasim, M.A. Mohamed Adil, S.K. Ab Manan and F. Abd Rahman (eds) *International Halal Conference (InHAC 2012)*. Kuala Lumpur, Malaysia: Elsevier: 301–310.

Riaz, M.N. and Chaudry, M.M. (2004) *Halal Food Production*. Florida: CRC Press.

Rice, G. (1999) 'Islamic ethics and the implications for business', *Journal of Business Ethics*, 18 (4): 345–358.

Rosenberg, P. and Choufany, H.M. (2009) *Spiritual Lodging—The Shariah Compliant Hotel Concept*. Available at: www.4hoteliers.com/4hots_fshw.php?mwi=4010

Rudnyckyj, D. (2009) 'Spiritual economies: Islam and neoliberalism in contemporary Indonesia', *Cultural Anthropology*, 24 (1): 104–141.

Saad, H.E., Ali, B.N. and Abdel-Ati, A.M. (2014) 'Sharia-compliant hotels in Egypt: Concept and challenges', *Advances in Hospitality and Tourism Research*, 2 (1): 1–15.

Sahida, W., Rahman, S.A., Awang, K. and Man, Y.C. (2011) 'The implementation of Shariah compliance concept hotel: De Palma Hotel, Ampang, Malaysia'. In *International Conference on Humanities, Historical and Social Sciences*, IACSIT Press, Singapore, *IPEDR*, 17: 138–142.

Sahida, W., Zulkifli, W., Rahman, S.A., Awang, K.W. and Man, Y.B.C. (2014) 'Developing the framework for *halal* friendly tourism in Malaysia', *International Business Management*, 5 (6): 295–302.

Said, M., Hassan, F., Musa, R. and Rahman, N.A. (2014) 'Assessing consumers' perception, knowledge and religiosity on Malaysia's halal food products', *Procedia—Social and Behavioral Sciences*, 130: 120–128.

Salleh, N.Z.M., Hamid, A.B.A., Hashim, N.H. and Omain, S.Z. (2014) 'The practice of Shariah-compliant hotel in Malaysia', *International Journal of Trade, Economics and Finance*, 5 (1): 26–30.

Samori, Z. and Sabtu, N. (2012) 'Developing halal standard for Malaysian hotel industry: An exploratory study'. In R.S. Raja Kasim, M.A. Mohamed Adil, S.K. Ab Manan and F. Abd Rahman (eds) *International Halal Conference (InHAC 2012)*. Kuala Lumpur, Malaysia: Elsevier: 552–569.

Samori, Z. and Rahman, F.A. (2013) 'Establishing Shariah compliant hotels in Malaysia: Identifying opportunities', *West East Journal of Social Science*, 2 (2): 95–108.

Seyfi, S. and Hall, C.M. (eds) (2019) *Tourism in Iran: Challenges, Development and Issues*. Abingdon: Routledge.

Shariff, S.N.F.B.A., Omar, M.B., Sulong, S.N.B., Majid, H.A.B.M.A., Ibrahim, H.B.M., Jaafar, Z.B. and Ideris, M.S.K.B. (2017) 'The influence of service quality and food quality towards customer fulfillment and revisit intention', *Canadian Social Science*, 11 (8): 110–116.

Siddiqui, A. (1997) 'Ethics in Islam: Key concepts and contemporary challenges', *Journal of Moral Education*, 26 (4): 423–431.

Siddiqui, M. (2015) *Hospitality and Islam: Welcoming in God's name*. New Haven, CT: Yale University Press.

Sobh, R., Belk, R. W. and Gressel, J. (2012) 'Modest seductiveness: Reconciling modesty and vanity by reverse assimilation and double resistance', *Journal of Consumer Behaviour*, 11 (5): 357–367.

Stephenson, M.L. (2014) 'Deciphering Islamic hospitality: Developments, challenges and opportunities', *Tourism Management*, 40: 155–164.

Taheri, B. (2016) 'Emotional connection, materialism, and religiosity: An Islamic tourism experience', *Journal of Travel & Tourism Marketing*, 33 (7): 1011–1127.

Teng, C.-C. and Chang, J.-H. (2013) 'Mechanism of customer value in restaurant consumption: Employee hospitality and entertainment cues as boundary conditions', *International Journal of Hospitality Management*, 32: 169–178.

Tieman, M. (2011) 'The application of halal in supply chain management: In-depth interviews', *Journal of Islamic Marketing*, 2 (2): 186–195.

Tieman, M. and Ghazali, M.C. (2014) 'Halal control activities and assurance activities in halal food logistics', *Procedia—Social and Behavioral Sciences*, 121: 44–57.

Tieman, M. and Hassan, F.H. (2015) 'Convergence of food systems: Kosher, Christian and halal', *British Food Journal*, 117 (9): 2313–2327.

Trade Description Act 2011. (2016) *Laws of Malaysia*. [pdf] Available at www.agc.gov.my/agcportal/uploads/files/Publications/LOM/EN/Draf%20bersih%20PPPUU%20Act%20730%20Lulus%20BI.doc.pdf

Wan Hassan, W.M. (2008) Halal Restaurants in New Zealand: Implications for the Hospitality and Tourism Industry. PhD. University of Otago, Dunedin.

Wan Hassan, W.M. and Hall, C.M. (2003) 'The demand for *halal* food among Muslim travellers in New Zealand'. In C.M. Hall, L. Sharples, R. Mitchell, B. Cambourne and N. Macionis (eds) *Food Tourism Around the World: Developments, Management and Markets*. Oxford: Butterworth-Heinemann: 81–101.

Wilson, J.A., and Liu, J. (2010) 'Shaping the halal into a brand?', *Journal of Islamic Marketing*, 1 (2): 107–123.

Wolf, M.J. (1999) *The Entertainment Economy. The Mega-Media Forces That Are Re-shaping Our Lives*. New York: Penguin Putnam.

Yarbakhsh, E. (2018) 'Reading Derrida in Tehran: Between an open door and an empty Sofreh', *Humanities*, 7 (1): 21.

Yusuf, S. (2009) 'The real sense of Shariah hospitality concept'. In *World Halal Forum*. Kuala Lumpur, Malaysia.

Zakaria, Z. (2008) 'Tapping into the world *halal* market: Some discussions on Malaysian laws and standards', *Shariah Journal*, 16: 603–616.

Zamani-Farahani, H. and Henderson, J.C. (2010) 'Islamic tourism and managing tourism development in Islamic societies: The cases of Iran and Saudi Arabia', *International Journal of Tourism Research*, 12 (1): 79–89.

3

ATTRIBUTES OF MUSLIM-FRIENDLY HOSPITALITY SERVICE IN A PROCESS-BASED MODEL

Teoman Duman

Introduction

A major market for all tourism businesses is the "Muslim Consumer" market (Izberk-Bilgin & Nakata 2016). As a category, this market is understudied in tourism academia. Muslim consumers constitute about 24 per cent of the world's population, making them a significant target market for all tourism businesses (Lipka & Hackett 2017). Understanding needs and expectations of faith-based tourism consumers is becoming more important given the growing economic significance of the market (see Chapter 1, this volume).

Muslim-friendly hospitality is a growing research area within the domain of "Islamic tourism". Earlier discussions focused more on describing the nature of the concept (Din 1989; Duman 2011), whereas more recent ones have come out as more market-specific studies (Izberk-Bilgin & Nakata 2016). By definition, Islamic tourism includes "tourism activities by Muslims that originate from Islamic motivations and are realized according to shariah principles" (Duman 2011: 6). With this definition, Duman separated the definition of Islamic tourism from halal tourism and gave a long description of why they differ from each other. Conceptual definitions and boundaries of Islamic and halal tourism have become clearer with recent publications on these topics (Scott & Jafari 2010; El-Gohary & Eid 2014; Battour & Ismail 2016; Ryan 2016). Table 3.1 outlines that Islamic tourism can be considered as a sub-domain of the religious/faith-based tourism where travel is taken for purely religious purposes whereas halal tourism covers the spectrum of all other travel activities acceptable by shariah law and Islamic teachings. For its followers, the religion of Islam is more than a philosophy, but it is a way of life that guides every aspect of personal and social behaviour. Therefore, for Muslims, all aspects of travel activities have to be according to the boundaries of Islamic teachings (i.e. halal). Table 3.1 also details the research agenda for two research streams: Islamic tourism studies focus on religious tourism markets and religiously oriented travel motivations and behaviours; and halal tourism research focuses on Muslim traveller markets and product characteristics toward these markets. Halal tourism is proposed as covering all tourism activities by Muslims that are realised according to shariah principles. As an academic

Table 3.1 Conceptualisations of Islamic and halal tourism

Travel motivation	Type of tourism	Domain	Research agenda	Indicative literature
Hajj, Umrah and all other travel for purely religious purposes	Islamic tourism	Religious/faith-based tourism	**Consumer specific:** Psychology and decision styles of Islamic tourism consumers, Islamic travel motivations, cultural and religious aspects of Islamic travel **Market specific:** Nature and potential of Islamic tourism markets, destination and service characteristics of religious destinations	Din (1989); Timothy and Iverson (2006); Duman (2011); Samori, Salleh and Khalid (2016); Battour and Ismail (2016)
All travel activities actualised for other purposes	Halal tourism	Leisure/business tourism	**Consumer specific:** Psychology and decision styles of Muslim travellers, travel motivations of Muslim travellers **Market-specific:** Nature and potential of Muslim traveller markets, halalness of marketing mix components of tourism products and services, development of halal standards, properties of Muslim-friendly hospitality services	Scott and Jafari (2010); Carboni and Janati (2016); Henderson (2016); Mohsin, Ramli and Alkhulayfi (2016); Razzaq, Hall and Prayag (2016); Stephenson (2014); Izberk-Bilgin and Nakata (2016); Marzuki, Hall and Ballantine (2014); Sumaedi and Yarmen (2015); El-Gohary (2016)

area, halal tourism is a study of Muslim consumer behaviour, Muslim travel markets, and products and services offered to Muslim consumers. The distinction between Islamic tourism and halal tourism was also well identified by Ryan (2016). Ryan (2016: 121) stated that "Islamic tourism appears to primarily refer to travel undertaken for religious and pilgrimage purposes and is associated with acts of faith relating to the Islamic religion" whereas "halal tourism is tourism undertaken for recreational, leisure and social purposes and members of the Islamic faith travel for the same reason that many of us wish to travel". The terms 'halal' and 'Muslim-friendly' are more appropriate for tourism products and services whereas the term 'Islamic' is more appropriate for the domain area (i.e. Islamic tourism) or Muslim traveller motivations, markets, and destinations. The focus of the present chapter is on halal tourism.

The halal concept in Islam and implications for hospitality services

To understand the psychology of Muslim travellers, a brief description of the Islamic belief system and lifestyle is necessary. To start with, it should be noted that Islam is not only a belief system but also a complete way of life. To be considered a Muslim believer, the five pillars of Islam should be adhered to. The five pillars include declaring one's complete faith that Allah (The God) is the only supreme being and Muhammad (Islam's Prophet) is the messenger of Allah; performing five prayers a day; donating 2.5 per cent of annual income through Zakat, a charity tax to help the needy; fasting (which includes no eating, drinking or intimacy during the daytime in Ramadan); and making a pilgrimage to Makkah at least once, if one has the financial capability and is physically able.

(Scott & Jafari 2010: 3–4)

The lifestyle of a Muslim is prescribed by two main sources of Islam: the *Quran* and *Sunnet* (*Hadith*—deeds and sayings of Prophet Muhammad narrated by others who witnessed these deeds and sayings). In situations where a ruling is not identified in these sources, then two other sources of knowledge are referred to: *Ijma* (consensus of scholars and community) and *qiyas* (analogy done by scholars to other similar situations). Islam categorises deeds and utilisation and consumption of things into five groups. These are *fard/wajib* (compulsory/ obligatory), *mustahabb/mandub* (recommended), *mubah* (neutral), *makruh* (disliked/reprehensible), and *haram* (forbidden). Halal deeds cover the first three categories. Judgements about makruh deeds are given depending on necessity and situation. The conduct of behaviour in Islam therefore is named *Shariah* and the study of this conduct is termed *Fiqh* (Mohsin et al. 2016; see also Chapter 1, this volume).

There are many variations in fiqh rulings by different scholars. Therefore, understanding and application of shariah may differ among societies and individuals depending on the accepted source of the ruling. However, there are certain rulings of shariah that almost all Muslims would agree on. Therefore, tourism businesses that serve Muslim travellers can start with understanding these main rulings and try to serve Muslim travellers accordingly. Very often, it is difficult to categorise every single act as halal or haram for Muslims. Therefore, what is suggested is to follow the teachings in the Quran and the footsteps of Prophet Muhammad to understand what is permissible, what is suggested, and what is not. Therefore, the term "Muslim-friendly" seems to be a more appropriate term to use when describing behaviours of Muslims and characteristics of products that show halal nature.

Halal tourism and its implications

Muslims may travel for any purpose as long as these purposes are considered halal in Islam. Any travel activity is halal as long as it is taken for a beneficial purpose and actualised according to shariah principles. These beneficial purposes can be the *Hajj*, the *Umrah, sillaturrahim* (visiting relatives), *fi-Sabilillah* (acting in the cause of God), appreciating the greatness of God (through visiting places to see the natural beauties, cultures, learning about the divine experiences of past civilisations), health, education, and business (Din 1989; Duman 2011). Some travel activities in Islam are considered *fard* (compulsory) (i.e. the Hajj), whereas the others may be acceptable (halal) or unacceptable (haram).

The concept of haram and its implications

Just as a number of deeds and utilisation and consumption of things are considered acceptable, many others are considered makruh (disliked) or haram (forbidden) in Islam. The makruhs are the ones that are not openly ruled out as haram but rather they are disliked and recommended to stay away from. Haram ones, on the other hand, are clearly ruled out and considered definitely unacceptable. For example, deeds and consumption of products that will lead to pure hedonism, permissiveness, lavishness, and servitude are considered haram in Islam (Din 1989). Islam openly "prohibits adultery, gambling, consumption of pork and other haram (forbidden) foods, selling or drinking liquor and dressing inappropriately" (Zamani-Farahani & Henderson 2010: 80–81).

The halalness or haramness of food and beverage and certain behavioural conduct, such as adultery, gambling, and interest, are clearly prescribed by shariah law and easily understood and adhered to by Muslims whereas some others (e.g. cleanliness of water and environment, dress code, gender roles, entertainment, art usage) create controversy. The roots of such controversy can be found in Islamic literature where interpretations of halal and haram conduct by Muslim scholars differ. Sociologically, such controversy is also due to lifestyle differences among Muslims in different parts of the world that are mostly culture based.

Muslims are bound with the commandments prescribed in the Quran and Hadith to sustain their daily lives in an Islamic way and conduct their prayers in a religiously acceptable way. What is acceptable and unacceptable in Islam depends heavily on the source of the ruling (as there may be a lot of differences among sects or mezhebs of Muslim populations) and a focus on the most commonly accepted rulings will be more practical in developing desired hospitality services for Muslim populations. Commonly accepted rulings of Islamic jurisprudence concern those areas that are related to the halalness of food and beverages, cleanliness in prayer areas, modesty in dress code, halalness of earnings and staying away from interest, and modesty in all other behavioural conduct that do not create controversy according to teachings in the Quran and Hadith. A number of tourism scholars have identified services and behavioural conduct that are necessary for acceptable (halal) hospitality and tourism services (Table 3.2). Although not exhaustive, Table 3.2 covers all core elements of acceptable hospitality services to Muslims, although it should be noted that it is difficult to set clear boundaries on the degree of halalness of some of the items identified above (i.e. dress code, presence of pets, consumption of some food and beverage items) due to interpretational differences among scholars of Islam and the cultural practices of different societies. The following section details Muslim-friendly hospitality service in more detail.

Process-based Muslim-friendly hospitality service consumption

In theory, every action of a Muslim should be according to Quranic teachings and hadith compliant. Muslims believe that all aspects of human life are covered by the teachings of Quran and Hadith. However, just like believers of other faiths, strength of devotion of Muslims varies according to personal preferences. Despite this, it can be said that almost every Muslim is raised by learning about the basic principles of his/her religion and knowing that not obeying these basic principles is binding before the God. Accordingly, those hospitality services that are designed according to teachings in Quran and Hadith will be appreciated and preferred more strongly by Muslim consumers. Therefore, the consumption of a typical hotel service can be analysed from this perspective (see also Chapters 1 and 2, this volume).

For this purpose, most prominent properties of a typical hotel service are identified in Table 3.3 and proposed compliance of these properties according to shariah rules and Islamic values are analysed in a decision process model (Figure 3.1). The attributes of hotel services in Table 3.3 were taken from Lai and Hitchcock (2016) and Ramsaran-Fowdar (2007). Four new items were added to the list to make the scale more inclusive for a Muslim-friendly hotel service. The stages of decision making from a Muslim customer perspective are discussed below.

Table 3.2 Halal attributes of hospitality services

Service area/concept	Halal attribute	Source
Management of the facility	– Islamic financial management (i.e. the facility should be run according to Islamic finance principles)	El-Gohary 2016; Razzaq et al. 2016
Physical facility	– Design and interiors (no picture of human part as display—in house religiously allowed figures) – Prayer rooms	El-Gohary 2016; Mohsin et al. 2016; Samori & Sabtu 2014
Room services	– Checking marital status of guests – Male/female staff for single male/female floors – Female staff for women and families – Separate rooms/floors for single males/females – Position of bed and toilet not facing Qiblah – Quran and prayer mats with identification of direction of Mecca in the room – Bidet in the room – Halal toiletries – Pets not allowed in the facility	Din 1989; El-Gohary 2016; Samori & Sabtu 2014; Mohsin et al. 2016; Salleh, Hamid, Hashim & Omain 2014; Razzaq et al. 2016
Food and beverage	– Halal food and beverage (no alcohol; no ham or pork or similar products) – Halal food and beverage (not serving unacceptable food and beverage described in Quran and Hadith; and food and beverage that include chemical substances, food additives and genetically modified foodstuffs) – Iftar and sahoor services during Ramadan – No drug dealing activities	Din 1989; Mohsin et al. 2016; Salleh et al. 2014; El-Gohary 2016; Izberk-Bilgin & Nakata 2016; Razzaq et al. 2016; Marzuki et al. 2014; Samori & Sabtu 2014; Henderson 2016
Dress code	– Islamic dress code for staff and customers	Mohsin et al. 2016; El-Gohary 2016; Omar & Jaafar 2011; Razzaq et al. 2016; Samori & Sabtu 2014
Hospitality	– Hospitality staff maintaining etiquette and morals – Respect and hospitality toward guests – Helping guests with prayer times and identification of mosque location – Organisation of teraweeh prayer during Ramadan	Mohsin et al. 2016; Salleh et al. 2014; Razzaq et al. 2016

(*Continued*)

Table 3.2 (Cont).

Service area/concept	Halal attribute	Source
Recreation and entertainment	– Guest security – Guest privacy – Separate recreation facilities for male and female – No adult entertainment, no night-clubs, acceptable TV channels without adult broadcasting content – Halal tourism packages	Salleh et al. 2014; El-Gohary 2016; Samori & Sabtu 2014; Razzaq et al. 2016;

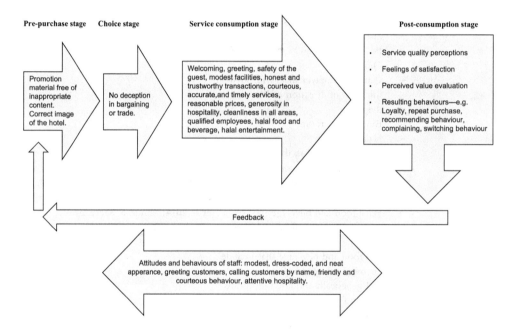

Figure 3.1 Decision-making process towards Muslim-friendly hospitality services

Pre-purchase stage

In this stage, a potential Muslim hotel customer becomes aware of the service (brand), starts searching for information about the service, and develops expectations toward the service. At this point, the Muslim traveller expects to come across promotional material that is free of inappropriate content and a correct image of the hotel should be created. In a hadith, it was stated: "The best of you are those best in conduct. And, the Prophet was not one who was obscene, nor one who uttered obscenities" (Jami` at-Tirmidhi: 27/81). True information should also be given to potential customers without hiding facts or exaggeration. It is well documented in hospitality marketing literature that creating false expectations has adverse effects on customer satisfaction and loyalty (Pizam & Milman 1993). Customer reactions

Table 3.3 A compliance scale of process-based Muslim-friendly hotel service

Item # Process item	Process dimension	Proposed compliance according to shariah rules and Islamic values	Selected sources from Islamic literature
Pre-purchase stage			
1. Awareness, information search—Expectation formation			
Visually appealing brochures, pamphlets, etc.	Tangibles	Visually appealing printed material with appropriate content	Nur/31; Jami` at-Tirmidhi: 27/81
Image of the hotel	Tangibles	Providing a correct image of the hotel	Sahih Al-Bukhari: 34/32/2079
Accurate information about hotel services	Reliability	No deception in bargaining or trade	Ibn Majah: 3/12/2224 Sunan Ibn Majah: 13/48/2355
Advance and accurate information about prices	Reliability	No deception in bargaining or trade	Ibn Majah: 3/12/2224
Choice stage			
2. Evaluation of alternatives and choice			
Service consumption stage			
3. Arrival at the facility—Consumption and evaluation of services			
Arrival at facility			
Availability of transport facilities	Reliability	Welcoming the guest	Sunan Ibn Majah: 33/21/3677
Convenient hotel location	Tangibles	Safe and secure neighbourhoods and arrival areas	Sunan Ibn Majah: 33/21/3677
Security and safety at the hotel	Environment	Safe and secure neighbourhoods and arrival areas	Sunan Ibn Majah: 33/21/3677
Quality of parking—arrival areas	Tangibles	Safe and secure neighbourhoods and arrival areas	Sunan Ibn Majah: 33/21/3677
Appealing interior and exterior hotel decoration	Basic—tangible	Modest decoration and furnishings	An-Nisa/38
Evaluation of reception areas and services			
Attractive lobby/entrance	Basic—tangible	Modest decoration and furnishings	An-Nisa/38
Modern and comfortable furniture	Basic—tangible	Modest decoration and furnishings	An-Nisa/38
Comfortable, relaxed, and welcome feeling	Environment	Greeting someone/a guest to comfort them	An-Nisa/86 Sahih Al-Bukhari: 2/5/12
Accuracy in billing	Reliability	Honest and trustworthy transactions	Ibn Majah: 3/12/2139

(*Continued*)

Table 3.3 (Cont).

Item # Process item	Process dimension	Proposed compliance according to shariah rules and Islamic values	Selected sources from Islamic literature
Reliable message service	Reliability	Accurately informing customers	Sahih Al-Bukhari: 34/ 32/2079
Quick check-in and check-out	Reliability	Providing timely and prompt service	Sahih Muslim: 1/220/ 118
Reasonable room rates	Environment	Reasonable prices and profit levels	Sunan an-Nasa'i: 44/ 57/4505
Hotel technologies (online reservation, email, Internet, fax, international calling facilities, computerised-feedback form, special website promotions, acceptance of credit and debit cards)	Technology	Accurately informing customers	Sahih Al-Bukhari: 34/ 32/2079
Complimentary items	Tangibles	Generosity in hospitality	Sunan Abi Dawud: 43/ 18/4790 Sahih Al-Bukhari: 63/ 131/3905
Settling in rooms			
Cleanliness and comfort of rooms	Basic—tangible	Cleanliness of rooms and prayer areas	Al-Baqara/125 Da'if: 5/41/2799
Spaciousness of rooms	Basic—tangible	Accurately informing customers	Sahih Al-Bukhari: 34/ 32/2079
Hygienic bathrooms and toilets	Basic—tangible	Cleanliness and hygiene of bathrooms and toilets	Hasan: 1/1/355
Timely housekeeping services	Reliability	Providing timely and prompt service	Sahih Muslim: 1/220/ 118
Quietness of room	Environment	Accurately informing customers	Sahih Al-Bukhari: 34/ 32/2079
Room security	Environment	Safe and secure neighbourhoods and arrival areas	Sunan Ibn Majah: 33/ 21/3677
Comfortable and clean mattress, pillow, bed sheets and covers	Environment	Accurately informing customers	Sahih Al-Bukhari: 34/ 32/2079
Variety of basic products and services offered (toothpaste, soap, shampoo, towels, toilet paper, stationery, laundry, ironing, tea, coffee, drinking water)	Environment	Accurately informing customers	Sahih Al-Bukhari: 34/ 32/2079
Room items in working order (kettle, air conditioning, lighting, toilet, fridge, etc.)	Environment	Accurately informing customers	Sahih Al-Bukhari: 34/ 32/2079

(*Continued*)

Table 3.3 (Cont).

Item #	Process item	Process dimension	Proposed compliance according to shariah rules and Islamic values	Selected sources from Islamic literature
	In-room technologies (Wifi, smart TV, telephone, voice mail, on-demand PC, television, Internet plug, meal ordering, email, wake-up system)	Technology	Accurately informing customers	Sahih Al-Bukhari: 34/ 32/2079
	Food and beverage services			
	Quality of food in restaurant(s)	Environment	Providing quality and halal food	Al-Baqara/168/172
	Cleanliness of the food and beverage service areas	Environment	Cleanliness of all areas	Al-Baqara/125 Hadith: Da'if: 5/41/ 2799
	Availability of desired food	Basic—tangible	Availability of halal food options	Al-Baqarah/168/172
	Availability of desired beverages	Basic—tangible	Availability of halal beverage options	Al-Baqarah/168/172
	Accuracy of food order	Reliability	Employment of qualified staff	An-Nisa/58
	Prompt breakfast service	Responsiveness	Providing timely and prompt service	Sahih Muslim: 1/220/ 118
	Availability of room service	Empathy	Availability of halal food and beverage options	Al-Baqarah/168/172
	Entertainment and other services			
	Provision of children's facilities (playground, baby-sitting, swimming pool)	Entertainment	Providing children with adequate facilities	Sunan an-Nasa'i: 31/ 16/3687
	Provision of evening entertainment	Entertainment	Modest and humble entertainment. No gambling, alcohol, drugs (anything harmful to the body). No obscenity or indecency. Gender segregation	Nur/31; Jami` at-Tirmidhi: 27/81
	Casino	Entertainment	Modest and humble entertainment. No gambling, alcohol, drugs (anything harmful to the body). No obscenity or indecency. Gender segregation	Nur/31; Jami` at-Tirmidhi: 27/81
	Variety show (e.g. a concert)	Entertainment	Modest and humble entertainment. No gambling, alcohol, drugs	Nur/31; Jami` at-Tirmidhi: 27/81

(*Continued*)

Table 3.3 (Cont).

Item #	Process item	Process dimension	Proposed compliance according to shariah rules and Islamic values	Selected sources from Islamic literature
			(anything harmful to the body). No obscenity or indecency. Gender segregation	
Recreation and therapy (e.g. a spa)		Entertainment	No obscenity or indecency. Gender segregation	Nur/31; Jami` at-Tirmidhi: 27/81
Shopping		Entertainment	Accurately informing customers	Sahih Al-Bukhari: 34/32/2079
Acrobatic performances		Entertainment	No obscenity or indecency. Gender segregation	Nur/31; Jami` at-Tirmidhi: 27/81
Convention and exhibition centre		Entertainment	Accurately informing customers	Sahih Al-Bukhari: 34/32/2079
Tourist attractions		Entertainment	No obscenity or indecency. Gender segregation	Nur/31; Jami` at-Tirmidhi: 27/81
Availability of swimming pool, sauna, and gym		Tangibles	No obscenity or indecency. Gender segregation	Nur/31; Jami` at-Tirmidhi: 27/81
Variety and quality of sports and recreational facilities		Core hotel benefits	No obscenity or indecency. Gender segregation	Nur/31; Jami` at-Tirmidhi: 27/81

Post-consumption stage

4. Service quality perceptions
5. Satisfaction feelings
6. Perceived value evaluation
7. Resulting behaviours—Loyalty, repeat purchase, recommending behaviour, complaining, switching behaviour

Customer loyalty program		Empathy		

8. Feedback

Attitudes and behaviours of staff

Neat and professional appearance of staff		Tangibles	Modest and neat apperance of staff	Da'if: 5/41/2791
Recognising the hotel customer		Empathy	Greeting someone/a guest to comfort them	An-Nisa/86
Calling the customer by name		Empathy	Calling someone by their preferred name	Al-Adab Al-Mufrad: 34/9/819
Staff performing services right the first time		Reliability	Employment of qualified staff	An-Nisa/58
Performing the services at the time promised		Reliability	Providing timely and prompt service	Sahih Muslim: 1/220/118

(Continued)

Table 3.3 (Cont).

Item #	Process item	Process dimension	Proposed compliance according to shariah rules and Islamic values	Selected sources from Islamic literature
	Well-trained and knowledgeable staff	Reliability	Employment of qualified staff	An-Nisa/58
	Experienced staff	Reliability	Employment of qualified staff	An-Nisa/58
	Staff with good communication skills	Reliability	Employment of qualified staff	An-Nisa/58
	Willingness of staff to provide help promptly	Reliability	Providing timely and prompt service	Sahih Muslim: 1/220/118
	Availability of staff to provide service	Reliability	Providing timely and prompt service	Sahih Muslim: 1/220/118
	Problem-solving abilities of staff	Reliability	Employment of qualified staff	An-Nisa/58
	Friendliness of staff	Assurance	Friendly behaviour to guests	Da'if: 4/11/2494
	Courteous employees	Assurance	Courteous behaviour to guests	Da'if: 4/11/2494
	Ability of staff to instil confidence in customers	Assurance	Providing attentive hospitality to guests	Sahih Muslim: 1/83/48
	Giving special attention to the customer	Empathy	Providing attentive hospitality to guests	Sahih Muslim: 1/83/48
	Understanding the customers' requirements	Empathy	Providing attentive hospitality to guests	Sahih Muslim: 1/83/48
	Listening carefully to complaints	Empathy	Resolving customer complaints by mutual consent	Ibn Majah: 3/12/2185
	Hotel to have customers' best interests at heart	Empathy	Providing attentive hospitality to guests	Sahih Muslim: 1/83/48

towards false advertising have been discussed where hotels have advertised as being completely halal although they were not (Duman 2011). One effect of negative disconfirmation in hotel services for Muslim customers can be the effects on loyalty where repeat business rates can stay at very low levels due to the consequences of false advertising on customer stays.

Evaluation of alternatives and choice stage

At this stage, a Muslim traveller would expect to evaluate alternative hotels that are suitable not only in financial terms but also in terms of halal properties. During choice and transactions, both the seller and the buyer are expected to be honest and not deceive each other. In a hadith, it was stated: "The Messenger of Allah passed by a man who was selling food. He put his hand in it and saw that there was something wrong with it. The Messenger of Allah said, 'He is not one of us who cheats'" (Ibn Majah: 3/12/2224). Additionally, in Islam, the buyer has the right to return the product if he (she) is not happy with the product.

In the hadith, it was stated that: "The seller and the buyer have the right to keep or return goods as long as they have not parted or till they part; and if both the parties spoke the truth and described the defects and qualities (of the goods), then they would be blessed in their transaction, and if they told lies or hid something, then the blessings of their transaction would be lost" (Sahih Al-Bukhari: 34/32/2079). In another hadith, it was stated: "'When you buy something, say: 'There should be no intention of cheating' and for every product you buy, you have the choice for three nights. If you are pleased with it, keep it, and if you are displeased then return it" (Sunan Ibn Majah: 13/48/2355). Choice of hotel property is a significant decision for a Muslim consumer because of the sensitivity of the decision. Typically, Muslim consumers would look for hotels that have halal properties and an atmosphere suited to their belief system. Research shows the importance of affective (e.g. comfortable feeling and entertaining) and sensory (room quality and atmosphere) attributes of hotel choice in addition to cognitive ones (e.g. price, food quality) (Kim & Perdue 2013). It can be expected that Muslim consumers would evaluate all three aspects in their hotel choices and compare hotels on all aspects when they make their decisions.

Service consumption stage

Islamic rulings and traditions encourage service providers to welcome and greet the guests; provide a secure and safe environment; provide modest facilities and avoid extravagance; conduct honest and trustworthy transactions; promote reasonable prices; be generous in hospitality; work with qualified employees to provide courteous, accurate, and timely services; keep all areas clean; provide halal food and beverage with the guests and have acceptable (halal) means of entertainment for the guests. From an Islamic perspective, for a commercial or noncommercial purpose, a traveller coming to the host's facility is a guest and s/he has rights on the hosts. In a hadith, it was stated: "and your guest has a right on you" (Sahih Al-Bukhari: 30/82/1975). Travellers and/or guests are given special status in Islam. In a hadith, it was stated: "Three supplications are accepted, there is no doubt in them (about them being accepted): The supplication of the oppressed, the supplication of the traveller, and the supplication of his father against his son" (Jami` at-Tirmidhi: 27/11). In another hadith, the Prophet said, "Traveling is a kind of torture, as it prevents one from sleeping and eating! So when one has finished his job, he should return quickly to his family" (Sahih al-Bukhari: 70/57/5429), therefore demanding Muslim hosts relieve fellow travellers.

The host should welcome and greet the guest appropriately. As stated in a hadith: "The Messenger of Allah said: Putting up a guest for one night is obligatory. If you find a guest at your door in the morning, then this (hospitality) is (like) a debt that you (the host) owe him. If he (the guest) wants, he may request it, and if he wants, he may leave it" (Sunan Ibn Majah: 33/21/3677). From this perspective, the host is also responsible for the guest's safety. Related to this is a hadith that "It is the Sunnah for a man to go out with his guest to the door of the house" (Maudu: 4/29/3358) indicating that the host is responsible for seeing the guest off from the house.

With respect to greeting, the Quran states: "And when you are greeted with a greeting, greet [in return] with one better than it or [at least] return it [in a like manner]. Indeed, Allah is ever, over all things, an Accountant" (An-Nisa 86). In a hadith, "a man asked the Prophet, 'What sort of deeds or (what qualities of) Islam are good?' The Prophet replied, 'To feed (the poor) and greet those whom you know and those whom you do not Know'" (Sahih Al-Bukhari: 2/5/12). The role of welcoming in hotel services is integral to hospitality service quality. In Islam, welcoming means more than a commercial welcome but rather a welcoming of a guest.

Accordingly, Muslim customers would have high expectations from the hotels they choose in terms of being welcomed.

With respect to physical facilities (building, furnishings, decor), Islam teaches a balance between being nice and beautiful (husn) and modesty. Islam discourages vanity and show-off. In Sura An-Nisa it is stated: "And [also] those who spend of their wealth to be seen by the people and believe not in Allah nor in the Last Day. And he to whom Satan is a companion – then evil is he as a companion" (An-Nisa 38).

All transactions according to Islam have to be honest and trustworthy. Reasonable prices should be promoted because undeserved profits are forbidden in Islam. It was stated in the hadith that "the Prophet forbade artificially inflating prices" (Sunan an-Nasa'i: 44/57/4505). It was stated in another hadith praising the trustworthy merchant that: "The trustworthy, honest Muslim merchant will be with the martyrs on the Day of Resurrection" (Ibn Majah: 3/12/2139). Also, Muslim traders are expected to be generous in their trade dealings. The Prophet said in a hadith: "The believer is simple and generous, but the profligate is deceitful and ignoble" (Sunan Abi Dawud: 43/18/4790). Similarly, it was suggested by the hadith to "entertain guests generously" (Sahih Al-Bukhari: 63/131/3905).

An important element of service transaction process is the provision of services to customers with care. Providing hospitality to the guest is a praised deed in Islam. In a hadith, it was stated: "He who believes in Allah and the Last Day should do good to his neighbour and he who believes in Allah and the Last Day should show hospitality to the guest and he who believes in Allah and the Last Day should either speak good or better remain silent" (Sahih Muslim: 1/83/48). Another hadith on the importance of providing hospitality to the guest stated: "If anyone is a guest of people who provide no hospitality for him, he is entitled to take from them the equivalent of the hospitality due to him" (Abi Dawud: 28/69/3804).

Islam teaches hosts to be courteous to guests. In a hadith, the Prophet stated: "There are three (characteristics) for which whomever has them, Allah will expose His side, and admit him to Paradise: Being courteous to the guest, kind to parents, and doing good for slaves" (Da'if: 4/11/2494). Also, a part of being courteous is calling a guest by their preferred name. In the hadith, it was stated about this issue that: "The Prophet, may Allah bless him and grant him peace, used to like to call a man by the name that he liked best and by his favourite kunya" (Al-Adab Al-Mufrad: 34/9/819). In resolving complaints, hosts are expected to be reasonable and look for acceptable solutions by compromise. In a hadith, it was stated that: "Transactions may only be done by mutual consent" (Ibn Majah: 3/12/2185).

Service providers should also provide services in a prompt and timely manner. It was suggested in a hadith that good deeds should be hastened: "Be prompt in doing good deeds" (Sahih Muslim: 1/220/118). In general, all employees should be competent and appropriate people for their positions. This is a key human resource principle in Islam established by the famous verse in the Quran: "Indeed, Allah commands you to render trusts to whom they are due and when you judge between people to judge with justice. Excellent is that which Allah instructs you. Indeed, Allah is ever Hearing and Seeing" (An-Nisa 58).

The host is also expected to portray a neat and clean appearance. The Prophet was known to wear modest clothes, and be neat and clean all the time. He used fragrance and promoted its use to his followers. In a hadith, the Prophet said: "When one of you is given some fragrance then do not refuse it, for indeed it comes from Paradise" (Da'if: 5/41/2791). Services and products provided by the service providers should be clean and acceptable for consumption according to Islamic standards. Cleanliness is urged and ruled for prayer in many versus in Quran and in hadith. In Al-Baqara 125, it is stated: "Purify My House for those who perform Tawaf and those who are staying [there] for worship and those who bow and prostrate [in prayer]". In one hadith, it was stated that:

> In [the mosque] are men who love to clean and to purify themselves. And Allah loves those who make themselves clean and pure. ... the Messenger of Allah said: "O Ansar! Allah has praised you for your cleanliness". "What is the nature of your cleanliness?" They said: "We perform ablution for prayer and we take bath to cleanse ourselves of impurity due to sexual activity, and we clean ourselves with water (after urinating)". He said: "This is what it is. So adhere to it."
>
> *(Hasan: 1/1/355)*

As mentioned in the hadith, there are clear rules of cleanliness for acceptable prayers in Islam. In another hadith about cleanliness, it was stated that: "Indeed Allah is Tayyib (good) and he loves Tayyib (what is good), and He is Nazif (clean) and He loves cleanliness, He is Karim (kind) and He loves kindness, He is Jawad (generous) and He loves generosity" (Da'if: 5/41/2799).

All that is consumed by Muslims have to be clean and halal. This is stated in a Quranic verse: "O you who have believed, eat from the good things which We have provided for you and be grateful to Allah if it is [indeed] Him that you worship" (Al-Baqarah 172). In another verse it is stated: "O mankind, eat from whatever is on earth [that is] lawful and good and do not follow the footsteps of Satan. Indeed, he is to you a clear enemy" (Al-Baqarah 168). The boundaries of halal food and beverage have been very well identified in the literature (Henderson 2016).

With respect to entertainment services in hospitality facilities, it can be said that all recreation and entertainment services must be designed according to Islamic standards where obscenity and inappropriate behaviours are not allowed. In Surah An-Nur (31), it is stated:

> And tell the believing women to reduce [some] of their vision and guard their private parts and not expose their adornment except that which [necessarily] appears thereof and to wrap [a portion of] their headcovers over their chests and not expose their adornment except to their husbands, their fathers, their husbands' fathers, their sons, their husbands' sons, their brothers, their brothers' sons, their sisters' sons, their women, that which their right hands possess, or those male attendants having no physical desire, or children who are not yet aware of the private aspects of women. And let them not stamp their feet to make known what they conceal of their adornment. And turn to Allah in repentance, all of you, O believers, that you might succeed.

Finally, all services in a hospitality facility should be designed and provided according to the needs of the beneficiaries. Islam recognises every individual in his/her condition and status, and teaches to treat the person according to personal needs of the condition or status. Females, children, disabled, and elderly are given special status and should be treated with care. In a hadith, it is stated: "Treat your children fairly, treat your children fairly" (Sunan an-Nasa'i: 31/16/3687). Furthermore, the family is the building block of Islamic social life (Stephenson 2014) and all halal hospitality services should be designed according to the needs of family.

All the above-mentioned qualities of hospitality services are well researched in services marketing literature. Research on customer segments and the role of customer perceptions based on religious beliefs on service provision is still an emerging area (Jafari & Scott 2014; Oktadiana, Pearce & Chon 2016). Empirical research in this area is still relatively scarce and future research can focus on customer markets to identify the effect of customers' religious beliefs on their hospitality service choice and evaluations. A further under-researched area pertaining to halal hospitality services is the perceptions of non-Muslims on these services. In a number of destinations, hospitality and tourism businesses that are designed to meet Muslim customer needs are increasing. A number of Internet-based travel operators (e.g. halaltrip. com; halalbooking.com; crestentrating.com; luxuryhalaltravel.com) have started operations to sell hospitality and tourism products and services to predominantly Muslim customers, although research on the profile and psychological characteristics of non-Muslim customers who consume such products and services is limited (Wibowo & Ahmad 2016).

Post-consumption stage and feedback

The final stage in the process model is the post-purchase stage and feedback on the consumed services. The resulting behaviours of Muslim customer segment can be expected to be more specific, focusing on evaluations that are based on their religious beliefs. Following the consumption experience, Muslim consumers' summary evaluations of service quality, satisfaction, and value will be based on their expectations which include requirements of their belief system. For example, it can be expected that those hotel services that are weak on properties listed in Table 3.3 will be evaluated as less acceptable and resulting future behaviours of loyalty and recommending behaviour will be less strong. However, this aspect of halal hospitality service consumption suffers from a lack of research.

Conclusion

The purpose of this chapter was to extend the discussion on attributes of Muslim-friendly hospitality services and bring evidence from reliable sources of Islam to clarify expectations of Muslim travellers from hospitality services. In a process model, different attributes of a hotel service were identified and these attributes were associated with shariah rulings and Islamic teachings so as to identify possible expectations of Muslim travellers from hospitality services stemming from the sources of their belief system.

As a sizable consumer market, the Muslim traveller market is still an unexplored market for many businesses. Recent literature indicates that consumer product retailing and food and beverage industries pioneered approaches to Muslim consumer markets and developed products and business strategies to meet the needs of this market (Stephenson 2014; Henderson 2016; Izberk-Bilgin & Nakata 2016). Halal standards are becoming common in many markets (Stephenson 2014; Izberk-Bilgin & Nakata 2016; Henderson 2016; Omar & Jaafar 2011; Marzuki et al. 2014), although services and especially the hospitality and tourism sector, lags behind other sectors (Samori & Sabtu 2014). Studies of the concept of Islamic tourism are still in their infancy and related sectors need guidance to decipher needs and expectations of Muslim travellers.

Future research on Islamic tourism can advance on two research streams. One is the travel taken for religious purposes, which can be called the study of Islamic tourism. Consumers of this type of travel activity are different in their needs and motivations and their demographic and psychographic characteristics should be studied in more detail. A second research stream is all other types of travel taken by Muslims for reasons other than pure religious purposes. Further studies are needed to identify the nature of this market (i.e. the halal tourism market) and the nature of service products that satisfy its needs and expectations. Research that explores the rich travel culture of Muslim populations in the past and present (Stephenson

2014) will also help product development and service advancements for companies that plan to serve Muslim travel markets.

References

Battour, M. and Ismail, M.N. (2016) 'Halal tourism: Concepts, practises, challenges and future', *Tourism Management Perspectives*, 19: 150–154.

Carboni, M. and Janati, M.I. (2016) 'Halal tourism de facto: A case from Fez', *Tourism Management Perspectives*, 19: 155–159.

Din, K.H. (1989) 'Islam and tourism: Patterns, issues, and options', *Annals of Tourism Research*, 16 (4): 542–563.

Duman, T. (2011) 'Value of Islamic tourism offering: Perspectives from the Turkish experience', paper presented at the World Islamic Tourism Forum (WITF 2011), 12–13 July, Kuala Lumpur, Malaysia. Available: https://www.researchgate.net/publication/266285126_Value_of_Islamic_Tourism_Offering_Perspectives_from_the_Turkish_Experience

El-Gohary, H. (2016) 'Halal tourism, is it really Halal?', *Tourism Management Perspectives*, 19 (B): 124–130.

El-Gohary, H. and Eid, R. (2014) *Emerging Research on Islamic Marketing and Tourism in the Global Economy*. Hershey, PA: Business Science Reference, an Imprint of IGI Global.

Henderson, J.C. (2016) 'Halal food, certification and halal tourism: Insights from Malaysia and Singapore', *Tourism Management Perspectives*, 19: 160–164.

Izberk-Bilgin, E. and Nakata, C.C. (2016) 'A new look at faith-based marketing: The global halal market', *Business Horizons*, 59 (3): 285–292.

Jafari, J. and Scott, N. (2014) 'Muslim world and its tourisms', *Annals of Tourism Research*, 44: 1–19.

Kim, D. and Perdue, R.R. (2013) 'The effects of cognitive, affective, and sensory attributes on hotel choice', *International Journal of Hospitality Management*, 35, 246–257.

Lai, I.K.W. and Hitchcock, M. (2016) 'A comparison of service quality attributes for stand-alone and resort-based luxury hotels in Macau: 3-Dimensional importance-performance analysis', *Tourism Management*, 55: 139–159.

Lipka, M. and Hackett, C. (2017) *Why Muslims Are the World's Fastest-growing Religious Group*. Washington, DC: Pew Research Center. Available online at: www.pewresearch.org/fact-tank/2017/04/06/why-muslims-are-the-worlds-fastest-growing-religious-group/

Marzuki, S.Z.S., Hall, C.M. and Ballantine, P.W. (2014) 'Measurement of restaurant manager expectations toward Halal certification using factor and cluster analysis', Procedia—Social and Behavioral Sciences, International Halal Conference InHAC 2012, 121: 291–303.

Mohsin, A., Ramli, N. and Alkhulayfi, B.A. (2016) 'Halal tourism: Emerging opportunities', *Tourism Management Perspectives*, 19: 137–143.

Oktadiana, H., Pearce, P.L. and Chon, K. (2016) 'Muslim travellers' needs: What don't we know?', *Tourism Management Perspectives*, 20: 124–130.

Omar, E.N. and Jaafar, H.S. (2011) 'Halal supply chain in the food industry—A conceptual model'. In Business, Engineering and Industrial Applications (ISBEIA), 2011 IEEE Symposium. IEEE, Langkawi, Malaysia: 384–389.

Pizam, A. and Milman, A. (1993) 'Predicting satisfaction among first time visitors to a destination by using the expectancy disconfirmation theory', *International Journal of Hospitality Management*, 12 (2): 197–209.

Ramsaran-Fowdar, R.R. (2007) 'Developing a service quality questionnaire for the hotel industry in Mauritius', *Journal of Vacation Marketing*, 13 (1): 19–27.

Razzaq, S., Hall, C.M. and Prayag, G. (2016) 'The capacity of New Zealand to accommodate the halal tourism market—Or not', *Tourism Management Perspectives*, 18: 92–97.

Ryan, C. (2016) 'Editorial: Halal tourism', *Tourism Management Perspectives*, 19: 121–123.

Salleh, N.Z.M., Hamid, A.B.A., Hashim, N.H. and Omain, S.Z. (2014) 'The practice of Shariah-compliant hotel in Malaysia', *International Journal of Trade, Economics and Finance*, 5 (1): 26–30.

Samori, Z. and Sabtu, N. (2014) 'Developing Halal standard for Malaysian hotel industry: An exploratory study', Procedia—Social and Behavioral Sciences, International Halal Conference InHAC 2012, 121: 144–157.

Samori, Z., Md Salleh, N.Z. and Khalid, M.M. (2016) 'Current trends on Halal tourism: Cases on selected Asian countries', *Tourism Management Perspectives* 19: 131–136.

Scott, N. and Jafari, J. (eds) (2010) *Tourism in the Muslim World*. Bingley, West Yorkshire: Emerald.

Stephenson, M.L. (2014) 'Deciphering "Islamic hospitality": Developments, challenges and opportunities', *Tourism Management*, 40: 155–164.

Sumaedi, S. and Yarmen, M. (2015) 'Measuring perceived service quality of fast food restaurant in Islamic country: A conceptual framework', Procedia Food Science, The First International Symposium on Food and Agro-biodiversity Conducted by Indonesian Food Technologists Community 2015, 3: 119–131.

Timothy, D.J. and Iverson, T. (2006) 'Tourism and Islam: Considerations of culture and duty'. In D.J. Timothy and D.H. Olsen (eds) *Tourism, Religion and Spiritual Journeys*. Abingdon: Routledge, 186–205.

Wibowo, M.W. and Ahmad, F.S. (2016) 'Non-Muslim consumers' Halal food product acceptance model', paper presented at Procedia Economics and Finance, The Fifth International Conference on Marketing and Retailing (5th INCOMaR) 2015, 37: 276–283.

Zamani-Farahani, H. and Henderson, J.C. (2010) 'Islamic tourism and managing tourism development in Islamic societies: The cases of Iran and Saudi Arabia', *International Journal of Tourism Research*, 12 (1): 79–89.

4

MALAYSIAN ACCOMMODATION PROVIDERS' UNDERSTANDING OF HALAL HOSPITALITY

Nor Hidayatun Abdul Razak, C. Michael Hall, and Girish Prayag

Introduction

Researchers define hospitality in various ways. Telfer (1996: 83) defines hospitality as "the giving of food, drink and sometimes accommodation to people who are not regular members of a household". Being hospitable to strangers or customers involves motives based on a desire to please customers or to fulfil moral obligations (see Chapter 1, this volume). In some situations, providers may combine personal and commercial motivations for hospitality. Tideman (1983: 1) defines hospitality from the perspective of economic exchange that involves "a supply of goods and services in a quantity and quality desired by the guest and at a price that is acceptable to him so that he feels the product is worth the price". In addition to personal motivations and economic exchange, lodging businesses also provide security and protection that "extend to all, irrespective of status or origins" (Lashley 2008: 71).

Relatively few studies acknowledge commercial hospitality in religious contexts. Studies on the provision of hospitality to pilgrims (Cohen 1992; Hill 2002; O'Gorman 2007; Timothy & Iverson 2006), for example, emphasise religious activities and attractions while others focus on religious and spiritual tourism (Cochrane 2009; Haq & Wong 2010; Huntley & Barnes-Reid 2003). Hence, little research exists on an in-depth understanding of hospitality business in a religious context (Din 1989; Weidenfeld 2006; Kirillova, Gilmetdinova & Lehto 2014). Commercial hospitality businesses primarily emphasise monetary transactions although the social and religious aspects of hospitality are still important in some cultures (Chambers 2009) depending on how countries ascribe value to the religious context. Therefore, understanding the religious dimensions of hospitality remains important in enabling providers to understand the current and future needs of customers (O'Connor 2005).

Halal hospitality

Growth in travel for leisure and business by Muslims has created interest in their travel needs, including accommodation, food services, transportation, and attractions (Sahida, Rahman, Awan & Man 2011). The need to respond to Islamic values in a commercial tourism and hospitality setting has generated awareness of halal products and services targeting the Islamic market. The commercial fulfilment of halal requirements for Muslim travellers is referred to as halal hospitality, while the demand for halal hospitality services when customers are on leisure holiday or engaging in business travel, is usually referred to as halal tourism. Importantly, due to changing patterns of international migration, travel flows, and halal hospitality, the concept has also been introduced to non-Muslim countries (Kamali 2011). However, in Muslim countries, the notion of services being halal has long been taken as given.

Due to commercial and religious interest in the Muslim market, many accommodation providers offer halal products and services (Wilson et al. 2013; see also Chapter 2, this volume). Nevertheless, the area is greatly under-researched (Stephenson 2014). Much of the available literature focuses on halal food certification (Zailani, Fernando & Mohamed 2010; Razalli, Yusoff, & Mohd Roslan 2013; Samori, Ishak & Kassan 2014) and the restaurant sector (Gayatri, Hume & Mort 2011; Marzuki, Hall & Ballantine 2014; Prabowo, Abd & Ab 2012) rather than on the larger picture of what constitutes halal in a hospitality setting.

Hospitality in the Islamic context is more than just a technical or commercial service, rather it should be understood as part of a particular set of social relationships embedded within a broader spiritual significance. Although this dimension of halal and hospitality is still limited in the literature, arguably it underpins the services provided to guests by providers who embrace the halal concept, and potentially the broader orientation towards their customers as noted in the Quran.

> Has the story reached you, of the honoured guests [three angels: Jibrael (Gabriel) along with another two] of Ibrahim (Abraham)? When they came in to him, and said, "Salam, (peace be upon you)!" He answered; "Salam, (peace be upon you)," and said: "You are a people unknown to me," Then he turned to his household, so brought out a roasted calf [as the property of Ibrahim (Abraham) was mainly cows]. And placed it before them, (saying): "Will you not eat?"
>
> *(Surah adz-Dzaariyaat, 24–27)*

The concept of hospitality has numerous dimensions. Lashley and Morrison (2000) suggest that it involves social (i.e. obligation according to culture/religion), private (i.e. hospitality offered at home), and commercial (e.g. host–guest relationship) dimensions. In this chapter, we add a technical dimension of hospitality, which refers to the products and services provided by accommodation providers to meet religious requirements. Although the social and commercial dimensions of hospitality are widely discussed in previous studies (Marci 2013; McMillan, O'Gorman & MacLaren 2011), there is relatively limited knowledge of these two dimensions in an Islamic context. The interpretation of halal comes from the authority of the Quran and the *Sunnah* that prescribes the way of life for Muslims, and also from government and religious institutions that can regulate products and services referred to as *Shariah* or halal requirements (Halal Malaysia 2014). Shariah compliance or halal hospitality is characterised according to halal requirements. Razzaq et al. (2016) identified 37 halal attributes for accommodation business (Table 4.1) based on several studies including Stephenson (2014), Battour, Ismail and Battor (2011), and Henderson (2010). These attributes inform

Table 4.1 Halal attributes

No.	Item	19	Gym on-site
1	Mentions halal	20	Proximity to gambling venues
2	Multilingual	21	Serves food on their premises
3	Family-friendly	22	Has in-unit cooking facilities
4	Pet-friendly	23	Has a dining establishment on-site
5	Proximity to 'red light' district	24	Alcohol is served on-site
6	Can cater to specific religious needs	25	Has a bar on-site
7	Can provide prayer time	26	Has room service
8	Can provide a prayer mat	27	Has a mini-bar
9	Can provide a copy of the Quran	28	Certified halal items
10	Provides Sky television (TV service)	29	Vegetarian options
11	Provides DVD players	30	Gluten-free options
12	Provides satellite or cable television	31	Dairy-free options
13	Provides multilingual TV channels	32	Offers off-premises food options
14	Provides movies	33	Able to cater to special dietary needs
15	Pool on-site	34	Has a Qibla marker
16	Spa bath or pool on-site	35	Has a special prayer facility on-site
17	Day spa on-site	36	Female-only floor
18	Sauna on-site	37	Gender-segregated facilities

Source: Adapted from Razzaq et al., 2016: 95.

customers about the halal services offered and are useful for tourism purposes especially for the positioning of Malaysia as a global halal hub.

Halal hospitality in a Malaysian context

Malaysia is actively promoting halal tourism and hospitality as part of its aim to be the world's halal hub (Ministry of Finance, Malaysia 2011). Hence, awareness of halal issues has increased among providers in the accommodation sector (Samori et al. 2014). Income from the tourism industry increased from RM53.4 billion in 2009 to RM65.44 billion in 2013 (Ministry of Tourism and Culture, Malaysia (MOTOUR), 2014), indicating the continuing growth of the industry in terms of tourist arrivals and expenditure. However, there is limited knowledge available on halal in the accommodation context as many halal hospitality studies have emphasised mainly the food dimension (Mohd Shariff & Abd Lah 2014; Bohari, Hin & Fuad 2013; Ratnamaneichat & Rakkarn 2013).

Currently, much of the accommodation in Malaysia, including hotels, resorts, and home-stays, are promoted as providing halal hospitality (Sahida, Zulkifli, Rahman, Awang & Man 2014). In the Malaysian context, websites have proven to be the fastest and cheapest way to become a one-stop centre to offer halal information (Halal Dagang 2013) and can help providers to promote halal hospitality and offer better customer service (Nasution & Mavondo 2008), increase potential customers and sales (Hashim 2008), and provide online booking services (Díaz & Koutra 2013; Tian & Wang 2017). However, accommodation providers do not always fully utilise the advantages provided by a website (De Marsico &

Levialdi 2004). Therefore, it is important to evaluate the extent to which website information satisfies customer needs (Dragulanescu 2002). Razzaq et al. (2016), for example, state that it is important to create awareness and promote halal service offerings to Muslim tourists through accommodation providers' websites. In their study only 3 out of the 367 accommodation providers' websites analysed for Auckland and Rotorua mentioned halal in their hospitality offering. However, so far, no study has been carried out on halal attributes published on the websites of accommodation providers in Malaysia. Using the halal attributes proposed by Razzaq et al. (2016), a similar analysis of providers' websites was conducted in this study.

The provision of halal hospitality involves both Muslim and non-Muslim accommodation providers (Alserhan 2010) as motivations to provide halal products and services may potentially lie beyond religious motivations. Although the potential significance of Islamic tourism and halal hospitality has been recognised in the Malaysian context (Sahida et al. 2014), no specific research has been conducted into Malaysian accommodation providers' understanding of halal hospitality as indicated by the information provided on their websites. Given the growth of academic and industry interest in halal tourism and hospitality, such research may have significant implications for service provisions and providing a deeper understanding of the notion of halal from a supply perspective than has previously been the case. However, there is no detailed research available on how Malaysian accommodation providers understand the concept of halal hospitality, and the implications that this has for service provision (Ab Talib & Mohd Johan 2012). Moreover, in the New Zealand context, it was noted that in some cases businesses would not display certification for halal foods, even though they may have had it because they felt that as 'good Muslims' their words should be sufficiently trusted (Wan Hassan & Hall 2003; Wan Hassan 2008). No research exists to understand whether the same situation may exist in Malaysia. This study therefore aims to examine the understanding of halal hospitality among Malaysian accommodation providers with the aim of furthering our understanding of not only commercial and technical aspects of hospitality and halal services but also social dimensions of hospitality, particularly within an Islamic context.

Data collection

This study uses a sequential mixed-methods approach. Semi-structured interviews were conducted with 16 Muslim and 2 non-Muslim respondents (i.e. from hotels, budget hotels, homestays/lodges, and chalets) to explore their understanding of halal hospitality as influenced by their perceptions, religious beliefs, and experience in commercial hospitality settings (Kirillova et al. 2014). The interviews were guided by a set of open-ended research questions that allowed respondents to elaborate on their perceptions and beliefs. This qualitative phase was followed by a quantitative analysis of the halal hospitality attributes (Razzaq et al. 2016) that could be identified from 781 websites of accommodation providers in Malaysia obtained from the Ministry of Tourism and Culture Malaysia (MOTAC) website at www. motac.gov.my/.

Findings

The interview findings are presented in two themes. First, accommodation providers' understanding of halal hospitality are elaborated upon followed by accommodation providers' own perspectives of halal hospitality business.

The accommodation providers' understanding of halal hospitality

The findings indicated that many Muslim respondents understood halal hospitality as per Islamic teaching and according to their own understanding and interpretation of this teaching. These respondents believed that one must provide halal hospitality as per religious requirements as illustrated in the following two quotes.

> We are Muslims; therefore, we must provide halal services. (Respondent N)

> We are Muslims and we are accountable to provide the right service to the customers. We have to be answerable in the hereafter for all our acts. (Respondent P)

These respondents believed that they must avoid haram activities and be responsible to themselves and others. They believed that it is their responsibility to remind others of religious obligations and thus having signage, giving advice, and preventing haram activities could encourage customers to follow Islamic obligations. They also emphasised that being an accomplice to vices is a sin, hence religious obligations should be presented as part of the business offering as illustrated in the quotes here.

> It is a responsibility of a Muslim to remind other Muslims about religious obliga-tions. Providing halal hospitality is one way of doing *dakwah* (proselytisation) to people. (Respondent B)

> We do not want to be accomplices for anything haram. We monitor the youngsters that come here so that there are no haram activities … we do not want to be accomplices …We have to take care of our responsibilities as Muslims. (Respondent O)

> I do not compromise in letting non-married couples stay together. This is always a problem for any hotel businesses. If we allow them to stay here, then we are also an accomplice to the vice and have to also bear the sin. (Respondent Q)

By affirming that their business practised halal hospitality, respondents expected customers to respect the halal status and cooperate with the Jabatan Agama Kemajuan Islam Malaysia (JAKIM) for inspections to prevent vices at their premises. This is exemplified by the business practices put in place as illustrated in the quotes below. However, it must be noted that businesses cannot fully control the type of haram activities that customers may engage in.

> We do not serve or allow any alcoholic drinks even to non-Muslim foreigners. If the customers bring their own alcoholic drinks without our knowledge, then that is beyond our control. (Respondent R)

> To avoid vices here, we hope that once people know that this is a Shariah compliant hotel, they will stop from doing any vice here. Although we do not allow them, we do not have the authority to stop them. Only the relevant authority can. (Respondent B)

> In Islam, we cannot force people to follow our rules. In my opinion, we only can prevent. We are a business, we need to think of many factors in implementing halal

requirements, for example, where we work, our government, the laws gazetted, and other factors. We can put up signage to remind about Islamic rules but the most important is the individuals themselves, if they want to go against the rules, we cannot do anything … We have many foreigners, we do not know whether they are Muslims or not, we just need to avoid any activities against our practices. (Respondent A)

Muslims respondents believed that they will receive spiritual rewards for good deeds. They will not be rewarded for mixing halal and haram activities in their hospitality service. The respondents thought that it is important to preach to non-Muslims about halal as it is a responsibility to spread the religion to others. Muslim respondents believed that halal means no harm to anybody and Muslims and non-Muslims gain benefits from halal hospitality. These ideas are illustrated in these quotes:

The most important thing is our intention … As a Muslim, you have to believe that when you do good, you are rewarded. (Respondent N)

It is one of our intentions to preach to non-Muslims to get them to understand what is halal and why do the Muslims do it. (Respondent E)

If we carry out our deeds with the intention to do good, this becomes part of worship. (Respondent H)

It is all about the sustenance that Allah SWT provides for me. If we mix the halal with the haram, we won't be rewarded. (Respondent O)

Halal is not necessarily only for Muslims actually, non-Muslims too, great. Things that are halal, means pure right, the way it is clean, the way its handled and all, certainly, there's no doubt. (Respondent G)

Respondents believed that avoiding haram could increase the spiritual feeling (intrinsic value) of being closer to Allah hence they were concerned about the mixing of halal and haram sources. Any contamination requires ritual cleanliness to avoid impurity to one's soul as shown in the quotes below.

Basically, it means not to mix with whatever that is haram. So, our income if possible, should not be mixed with haram sources. (Respondent R)

We cannot eat haram food, it will generate negativity in oneself, soul, and body, and indirectly in the future, until one dies. If one's eat or is involved with many haram things, sin is one part, it is between oneself with God, but if the haram thing is already in one's soul, it will be there, it will always have some influence on one's soul as it has become part of our flesh and blood, and will be very difficult to remove. (Respondent A)

I have my own rules and regulations that I enforce at my accommodation … there is a notice of no beer, no liquor, and no pork. We do not want our place to be unclean. (Respondent M)

For me there is a bit of reservations towards non-Muslims. It is all right for them to stay, but no barbeque as I am not confident and such because they may have non-halal food. That would be a problem to me. (Respondent O)

The respondents also condemned unethical conducts such as misuse of the halal logo and having the halal certificate but not following the requirements, as illustrated in the following quotes.

We have to be more careful about the misuse of halal and the halal logo. The authorities say its halal but in reality, it is not halal, but so many people have eaten or used that thing. They have to answer to that in the hereafter. (Respondent I)

If we can obtain the certificate, but don't follow it, then it's of no use. (Respondent E)

The accommodation providers' own perspectives on halal hospitality business

The respondents mentioned that hospitality in a commercial context requires them to follow Shariah requirements such as halal certification, Islamic funding, facility design, staff training, entertainment, and the management of halal hospitality business. The respondents believed that *riba* (interest) is haram, therefore, conventional financing must be avoided. Some respondents removed entertainment activities and replaced them with Islamic entertainment (see Al Qaradawi 1960). The respondents also believed that top management is responsible for providing halal-related training for staff and the availability of halal advisers to manage halal certification processes. These ideas are illustrated in the quotes below.

Hospitality is a service. If you combine it with halal, then you must adhere to all the requirements. For us here, for halal hospitality, we have to be Shariah compliant. (Respondent A)

It is difficult for me to explain halal hospitality. For halal hospitality, you need certification, and staffs have to be trained on how to handle the preparation, the process, know the suppliers and things like that. (Respondent P)

People are reassured as halal is not just about the food, but it's concerned with the cleanliness, the preparation, the ingredients, even imported ingredients. (Respondent N)

Firstly, if we really want to do halal, the design, for example, the toilet cannot be facing the Qibla. Secondly, when we start, even from financing, we need to find a halal financing. Don't take the conventional financing. Thirdly, we really have to make sure the customers that come to the hotel follow our guidelines. If we really want to be strict, they have to be in hijab to stay at this hotel, but then we are not up that level yet, for halal hospitality. (Respondent E)

Previously, we had an in-house band in the upstairs lounge, we had snooker tables. Now we do not have these anymore. There is a TV in every room, but not with all channels. There are news channels, sports, family and films ... We have eliminated all alcohol, wine. (Respondent C)

We have a panel of Shariah advisors, so any enhancements or changes; we have to inform them first. We have these advisors to make sure we are doing the right thing. (Respondent B)

Many respondents viewed halal hospitality as an opportunity for them to undertake a hospitality-related business; thus their business is designed according to halal principles. The respondents viewed that halal offerings attract businesses in other industries to engage in halal business as illustrated in the quotes below.

If we do non-halal, people won't come. So it is better to orient towards halal hospitality because our main customers are Muslims. (Respondent K)

We don't have many corporate clients. We get more customers from government organisations, so being halal is important. Moreover, one more thing, the majority of our staff here are Malay Muslims. Our guests too are local Muslims. (Respondent C)

It gives us the opportunities to do business with the government. (Respondent N)

Other hotels that have non-Muslims upper management may not be able to do halal hospitality like we do. However, the non-Muslims are also seeing the halal concept as a business opportunity, for example, Rayani Air. It is owned by a non-Muslim but it is Shariah compliant. (Respondent B)

Findings from the analysis of accommodation providers' websites

Given some of the findings of the qualitative research where emphasis on certain attributes and practices were seen as an important indicator of a business offering halal hospitality, the next stage of the analysis was to identify the most common halal attributes presented online by accommodation providers. This provides an insight into how they communicate halal hospitality to their customers. Despite accommodation providers showing some knowledge of halal hospitality and the attributes that customers are searching for to know if a provider is offering halal services, many of the halal attributes identified in this study were not mentioned on the accommodation websites.

The websites of accommodation providers analysed in this study are from businesses located in the Federal Territory of Kuala Lumpur (17 per cent), followed by Sabah (11.8 per cent), Selangor (9.5 per cent), Pahang (8.8 per cent), Johor (8.6 per cent), Melaka (7.7 per cent), Pulau Pinang (6.4 per cent), Perak, Sarawak (5.8 per cent), Kedah (5 per cent), and Terengganu (4.9 per cent), among others. More than 50 per cent of these accommodation providers are hotels, followed by budget hotels (39.7 per cent), chalets (2.4 per cent), and homestay/guesthouse/rest house/hostels (1.4 per cent). In Malaysia, a business with 50 rooms and above is considered to be a large size while one with 10 to 49 rooms is considered to be an accommodation provider of medium size. Based on these criteria, about 70 per cent of the accommodation providers belong to the large size category followed by 29 per cent for medium size.

The halal attributes were ranked from the most frequently mentioned to the least, for easy reference (Table 4.2). The findings from the website analysis showed that the technical dimensions of halal hospitality as proposed by Razzaq et al. (2016) were those most commonly communicated on the websites. Specifically, attributes such as service and security, generally considered important in commercial hospitality (Aramberri 2001; King 1995; Kirillova et al.

Table 4.2 Halal attributes by frequency

No.	Halal attributes	Yes		No		Total
		Frequency	%	Frequency	%	Frequency
1	Room decoration	755	96.7	26	3.3	781
2	Free service	730	93.5	51	6.5	781
3	Satellite/cable TV	648	83.0	133	17.0	781
4	Security system	564	72.2	217	27.8	781
5	Dining outlet on-site	554	70.9	227	29.1	781
6	Mini-bar/mini-fridge/fridge	420	53.8	361	46.2	781
7	Room service	405	51.9	376	48.1	781
8	Pool on-site	344	44.0	437	56.0	781
9	Bar/lounge on-site	336	43.0	445	57.0	781
10	Serve food on premises	327	41.9	454	58.1	781
11	Gym on-site	252	32.3	529	67.7	781
12	Spa and sauna	248	31.8	533	68.2	781
13	Alcohol on-site	213	27.3	568	72.7	781
14	Entertainment	178	22.8	603	77.2	781
15	Recreation/sports facilities	163	20.9	618	79.1	781
16	Family-friendly	133	17.0	648	83.0	781
17	Halal/halal certified/halal logo	105	13.4	676	86.6	781
18	Prayer room and facility	67	8.6	714	91.4	781
19	Sajada/prayer mat	26	3.3	755	96.7	781
20	Vegetarian	20	2.6	761	97.4	781
21	Gender-segregated facilities	15	1.9	766	98.1	781
22	Multilingual staff	10	1.3	771	98.7	781
23	Special dietary needs	8	1.0	773	99.0	781
24	Proximity to gambling venues	8	1.0	773	99.0	781
25	Kiblat direction	4	0.5	777	99.5	781
26	Quran	3	0.4	778	99.6	781
27	Prayer time	3	0.4	778	99.6	781
28	Dairy-free	2	0.3	779	99.7	781
29	Gluten-free	2	0.3	779	99.7	781
30	Female-only floor	1	0.1	780	99.9	781
31	Pet-friendly	0	0.0	781	100.0	781
32	Proximity to 'red light' district	0	0.0	781	100.0	781

2014), were among the most commonly communicated. For example, 72.2 per cent of the websites reported having a security system while 93.5 per cent offered some form of free service. In Islam, generosity is encouraged, thus free or complimentary service can be an important aspect of hospitality. Surprisingly, gender-segregated facilities, which are a hallmark of halal hospitality, were mentioned on only 1.9 per cent of the websites. The halal attributes that communicate halal hospitality are not necessarily the attributes emphasised on these websites.

Other attributes that were among the most frequently mentioned on the websites were room decoration (96.7 per cent), satellite/cable (83 per cent), and dining outlet on-site (70.9 per cent).

Although Malaysia is actively promoting itself as an international halal hub and has its halal certification, only 105 or 13.4 per cent of the 781 websites mentioned halal, being halal certified, or included a halal logo. Other specific halal attributes, such as prayer room, prayer mat, gender-segregated facilities, kiblat direction, Quran, prayer time, and female-only floor, are rarely mentioned on the websites as can be seen in Table 4.2. Although it has been argued that possessing a halal certificate has a commercial value for businesses in attracting demand for halal products and services from local and international customers (Abdullah et al. 2016), the present study found that only 18.4 per cent of accommodation providers were halal certified by JAKIM. There seems to be an important gap between halal attributes communicated to customers and the positioning of these accommodation providers for their customer base.

Discussion and conclusion

This study argues that an understanding of halal hospitality needs to include the broader fulfilment of religious obligations under Islam. Muslim respondents believed that as a sign of faith (Mukhtar & Butt 2012) they must avoid haram and promote halal activities. They also believed in getting rewards and punishments in this world and the world hereafter. While these beliefs underpin the findings from the qualitative research undertaken with accommodation providers, the same cannot be said about how the concept of halal hospitality is communicated on these providers' websites. There are obvious differences between the findings of the qualitative and quantitative phases reported in this study, with the former emphasising the importance of religious beliefs and compliance to rules with few of the attributes depicting these beliefs and compliance reported on websites.

From the qualitative phase, respondents stressed halal attributes that conveyed their practice of halal hospitality included Islamic funding, ritual cleanliness, and acceptable entertainment in conformance to religious teachings. These attributes were perceived as differentiating halal hospitality from conventional hospitality. However, from the quantitative findings, it is clear that attributes depicting conventional hospitality such as free service, satellite/cable TV, and room decoration are some of the most commonly reported attributes on the websites. While the interview participants gave priority to religious obligations to keep their Islamic faith even if they have limited number of customers following Islamic rules, the findings from the website analysis show that little of these religious requirements are communicated.

Islam permits Muslims to enjoy entertainment so long as halal and haram elements, such as intoxication, obscenity, gambling, and inappropriate mixing of men and women, are not combined (Al Qaradawi 1960). In conventional hospitality services, common entertainment activities such as an in-house band, the provision of snooker tables, or karaoke, involve haram elements; hence replacing these with halal entertainments could satisfy Muslim customers' needs (Fikri, Rugayah & Tibek 2014). However, it is clear from the findings of the website analysis that 27.3 per cent served alcohol on-site and 53.8 per cent had a mini-bar or mini-fridge. While the former may be due to a proportion of customers being non-Muslim and therefore the accommodation provider is catering for this market, the latter suggests that there is potentially some mixing of halal and haram. It must be acknowledged that customers will choose goods or services that reflect their taste, social status or religious beliefs (Eum 2009), and price, and the fact that the websites of accommodation providers emphasise more commercial rather than halal hospitality requirements is not necessarily surprising. Striking a balance between commercial and religious interests in managing a hospitality business can be difficult. Though one would expect Muslim providers to understand halal hospitality better than non-Muslim providers, there is no evidence to suggest this based on the analysis of the websites. Without a clear under-standing of the halal hospitality concept, contamination, violation, or misuse of the halal logo will likely occur (Zakaria 2008).

One key recommendation that can be made on the basis of the findings of this study is that an accommodation management that is driven by halal hospitality processes (Ismaeel & Blaim 2012) should include explicit references to halal income, investment, and financing that clearly portray adherence to religious beliefs. Accommodation providers should also provide training to staff with respect to not only commercial and technical dimensions of halal hospitality but also its social dimensions. Mentoring schemes where a panel of halal advisers is made available to accommodation providers to guide halal businesses and the delivery of halal hospitality should be put in place in the accommodation sector of Malaysia. As indicated by interview participants, it is important to provide services that reinforce a positive image of halal hospitality, as suggested in other studies (e.g. Ivanova & Ivanov 2015).

Accommodation providers should also utilise the advantages of online marketing tools and proactively promote the halal hospitality attributes as they are the cheapest and most efficient means available of reaching potential Muslim customers. However, the findings showed that little information is available on halal hospitality attributes even on the websites of halal-certified accommodation providers in Malaysia. For accommodation providers, publishing information on their desirable halal attributes could help them to reach their halal business objectives. Nevertheless, the overall findings from the website analysis in Malaysia are no different from those in New Zealand (Razzaq et al. 2016), raising significant questions about what is stated with respect to halal information and offerings and what is actually offered. These findings may also reflect a concern among providers that mentioning halal explicitly in their business promotion may deter some customers (Razzaq et al. 2016). Alternatively, it may be that there is no perceived need for halal assurance to be provided if most customers are Muslims.

In conclusion, the concept of halal hospitality is claimed to be important in marketing to the Islamic market in both Muslim and non-Muslim countries, but accommodation providers need a better understanding of what halal hospitality and attributes are. Just as significantly a far better understanding is needed of the substantial gap that appears to exist between market information needs and what is provided by accommodation businesses, especially the reasons for non-declaration of halal. It is hoped that improved understandings of halal hospitality concepts can help cater to the perceived demand for halal tourism and hospitality.

References

Ab Talib, S.M. and Mohd Johan, M.R. (2012) 'Issues in halal packaging: A conceptual paper', *International Business and Management*, 5 (2): 94–98.

Abdullah, M., Syed Ager, S.N., Hamid, N.A.A., Wahab, N.A., Saidpudin, W., Miskam, S. and Othman, N. (2016) 'Isu dan cabaran pensijilan halal: Satu kajian perbandingan antara Malaysia dan Thailand'. In *World Academic and Research Congress 2015 (World-AR 2015)*. Jakarta, Indonesia.

Al-Qaradawi, Y. (1960) *The Lawful and Prohibited in Islam*. [ebook]. Available at: https://thequranblog. files.wordpress.com/2010/06/the-lawful-and-the-prohibited-in-islam.pdf (accessed 25 November 2015).

Alserhan, B.A. (2010) 'On Islamic branding: Brands as good deeds', *Journal of Islamic Marketing*, 1 (2): 101–106.

Aramberri, J. (2001) 'Paradigms in the tourism theory', *Annals of Tourism Research*, 28 (3): 738–761.

Battour, M., Ismail, M.N. and Battor, M. (2011) 'The impact of destination attributes on Muslim tourist's choice', *International Journal of Tourism Research*, 13 (6): 527–540.

Bohari, A.M., Hin, C.W. and Fuad, N. (2013) 'The competitiveness of Halal food industry in Malaysia: A SWOT–ICT analysis', *Malaysia Journal of Society and Space*, 1: 1–9.

Chambers, E. (2009) 'From authenticity to significance: Tourism on the frontier of culture and place', *Futures*, 41 (6): 353–359.

Cochrane, J. (2009) 'Spirits, nature and pilgrimage: The "other" dimension in Javanese domestic tourism', *Journal of Management, Spirituality & Religion*, 6 (2): 107–119.

Cohen, E. (1992) 'Pilgrimages and tourism: Convergence and divergence'. In A. Moranis (ed.) *Sacred Journeys: The Anthropology of Pilgrimage.* New York: Greenwood Press, 47–61.

De Marsico, M. and Levialdi, S. (2004) 'Evaluating web sites: Exploiting user's expectations', *International Journal of Human–Computer Studies*, 60 (3): 381–416.

Díaz, E. and Koutra, C. (2013) 'Evaluation of the persuasive features of hotel chains websites: A latent class segmentation analysis', *International Journal of Hospitality Management*, 34: 338–347.

Din, K.H. (1989) 'Islam and tourism: Patterns, issues, and options', *Annals of Tourism Research*, 16 (4): 542–563.

Dragulanescu, N.-G. (2002) 'Website quality evaluations: Criteria and tools', *International Information & Library Review*, 34 (3): 247–254.

Eum, I. (2009) 'A study on Islamic consumerism from a cultural perspective: Intensification of Muslim identity and its impact on the emerging Muslim market', *International Area Studies Review*, 12 (2): 3–19.

Fikri, S., Rugayah, S. and Tibek, H. (2014) 'Nasyid as an Islamic alternative entertainment', *IOSR Journal of Humanities and Social Science*, 19 (7): 43–48.

Gayatri, G., Hume, M. and Mort, S.G. (2011) 'The role of Islamic culture in service quality research', *Asian Journal on Quality*, 12 (1): 35–53.

Halal Dagang. (2013) 'Halal e-market place'. [Online] Available at: www.daganghalal.com/(accessed 20 March 2014).

Halal Malaysia. (2014) 'Manual prosidur pensijilan Halal Malaysia', JAKIM, Putrajaya. [Online] Available at: www.halal.gov.my/v4/index.php?data=bW9kdWxlcy9uZXdzOzs7Ow==&utama=pandua n&ids=gp4 (accessed 20 March 2014).

Haq, F. and Wong, H.Y. (2010) 'Is spiritual tourism a new strategy for marketing Islam?', *Journal of Islamic Marketing*, 1 (2): 136–148.

Hashim, N.H. (2008) Investigating internet adoption and implementation by Malaysian hotels: An exploratory study. PhD. University of Western Australia.

Henderson, J.C. (2010) 'Sharia-compliant hotels', *Tourism and Hospitality Research*, 10 (3): 246–254.

Hill, B. (2002) 'Tourism and religion, by Boris Vukonic', *International Journal of Tourism Research*, 4 (4): 327–328.

Huntley, E. and Barnes-Reid, C. (2003) 'The feasibility of Sabbath-keeping in the Caribbean hospitality industry', *International Journal of Contemporary Hospitality Management*, 15 (3): 172–175.

Ismaeel, M. and Blaim, K. (2012) 'Toward applied Islamic business ethics: Responsible halal business', *Journal of Management Development*, 31 (10): 1090–1100.

Ivanova, M. and Ivanov, S. (2015) 'Affiliation to hotel chains: Hotels' perspective', *Tourism Management Perspectives*, 16: 148–162.

Kamali, M.H. (2011) 'Tourism and the halal industry: A global shariah perspective'. In *World Islamic Tourism Forum 2011.* [Online] Kuala Lumpur, Malaysia, 12–13. Available at: www.iais.org.my/e/attach/ppts/12-13JUL2011-WITF/ppts/Prof%20Dr%20Hashim%20Kamali.pdf (accessed 8 December 2013).

King, C.A. (1995) 'Viewpoint: what is hospitality?', *International Journal of Hospitality Management*, 14 (3/4): 219–234.

Kirillova, K., Gilmetdinova, A. and Lehto, X. (2014) 'Interpretation of hospitality across religions', *International Journal of Hospitality Management*, 43: 23–34.

Lashley, C. (2008) 'Studying hospitality: Insights from social sciences', *Scandinavian Journal of Hospitality and Tourism*, 8 (1): 69–84.

Lashley, C. and Morrison, A. (eds) (2000) *In Search of Hospitality: Theoretical Perspectives and Debates.* Oxford: Butterworth-Heinemann.

Marci, T. (2013) 'Social inclusion in terms of hospitality', *International Review of Sociology*, 23 (1): 180–200.

Marzuki, S.Z., Hall, C.M. and Ballantine, P.W. (2014) 'Measurement of restaurant manager expectations toward halal certification using factor and cluster analysis', *Procedia—Social and Behavioral Sciences*, 121: 291–303.

McMillan, C.L., O'Gorman, K.D. and MacLaren, A.C. (2011) 'Commercial hospitality: A vehicle for the sustainable empowerment of Nepali women', *International Journal of Contemporary Hospitality Management*, 23 (2): 189–208.

Ministry of Finance, Malaysia. (2011) *Economic Management and Prospect.* Kuala Lumpur: Ministry of Finance, Malaysia.

Ministry of Tourism and Culture, Malaysia. (2014) *Rated Tourist Accommodation Premises*. [Online] Available at: www.motac.gov.my/en/check/hotel?h=&n=&v=0 (accessed 15 February 2015).

Mohd Shariff, S. and Abd Lah, N. (2014) 'Halal certification on chocolate products: A case study', *Procedia—Social and Behavioral Sciences*, 121: 104–112.

Mukhtar, A. and Butt, M.M. (2012) 'Intention to choose halal products: The role of religiosity', *Journal of Islamic Marketing*, 3 (2): 108–120.

Nasution, H.N. and Mavondo, F.T. (2008) 'Customer value in the hotel industry: What managers believe they deliver and what customer experience', *International Journal of Hospitality Management*, 27 (2): 204–213.

O'Connor, D. (2005) 'Towards a new interpretation of "hospitality"', *International Journal of Contemporary Hospitality Management*, 17 (3): 267–271.

O'Gorman, K.D. (2007) 'Dimensions of hospitality: Exploring ancient and classical origins'. In C. Lashley, P. Lynch and A. Morrison (eds) *Hospitality: A Social Lens*. Oxford: Elsevier, 17–32.

Prabowo, S., Abd, A. and Ab, S. (2012) 'Halal culinary: Opportunity and challenge in Indonesia'. In *International Halal Conference*. Kuala Lumpur: PWTC, 1–10. Available at: www.sciencedirect.com (accessed 8 December 2013).

Ratanamaneichat, C. and Rakkarn, S. (2013) 'Quality assurance development of halal food products for export to Indonesia'. In *Social and Behavioral Sciences Symposium, 4th International Science, Social Science, Engineering and Energy Conference 2012*. Bangkok, 134–141. Available at: http://doi.org/10.1016/j.sbspro.2013.08.488 (accessed 5 May 2014).

Razalli, M.R., Yusoff, R.Z. and Mohd Roslan, M.W. (2013) 'A framework of halal certification practices for hotel industry', *Asian Social Science*, 9 (11): 316–326.

Razzaq, S., Hall, C.M. and Prayag, G. (2016) 'The capacity of New Zealand to accommodate the halal tourism market—Or not', *Tourism Management Perspective*, 18: 92–97.

Sahida, W., Rahman, S.A., Awan, K. and Man, Y.C. (2011) 'The implementation of Shariah compliance concept hotel: De Palma Hotel Ampang, Malaysia'. In *2nd International Conference on Humanities, Historical and Social Sciences*. Singapore: IPEDR, 138–142.

Sahida, W., Zulkifli, W., Rahman, S.A., Awang, K.W. and Man, Y.B.C. (2014) 'Developing the framework for halal friendly tourism in Malaysia', *International Business Management*, 5 (6): 295–302.

Samori, Z., Ishak, A.H. and Kassan, N.H. (2014) 'Understanding the development of halal food standard: Suggestion for future research', *International Journal of Social Science and Humanity*, 4 (6): 482–486.

Stephenson, M.L. (2014) 'Deciphering "Islamic hospitality": Developments, challenges and opportunities', *Tourism Management*, 40: 155–164.

Telfer, E. (1996) *Food for Thought: Philosophy and Food*. London: Routledge.

The Noble Quran. (2010) *Interpretation of the meanings of the Noble Quran*. [Online] Available at: www.noblequran.com/translation/(accessed 18 November 2014).

Tian, J. and Wang, S. (2017) 'Signaling service quality via website e-crm features more gains for smaller and lesser known hotels', *Journal of Hospitality and Tourism Research*, 41 (2): 211–245.

Tideman, M.C. (1983) 'External influences on the hospitality industry'. In E.H. Cassee and R. Reuland (eds) *The Management of Hospitality*. Oxford: Pergamon, 1–24.

Timothy, D.J. and Iverson, T. (2006) 'Tourism and Islam: Considerations of culture and duty'. In D. J. Timothy and D.H. Olsen (eds) *Religion and Spiritual Journeys*. New York: Routledge, 186–205.

Wan-Hassan, W.M. (2008) Halal Restaurants in New Zealand: Implications for the Hospitality and Tourism Industry. PhD. University of Otago.

Wan-Hassan, W.M. and Hall, C.M. (2003) 'The demand for halal food among Muslim travellers in New Zealand'. In C.M. Hall, L. Sharples, R. Mitchell, B. Cambourne and N. Macionis (eds) *Food Tourism Around the World: Developments, Management and Markets*. Oxford: Butterworth-Heinemann, 81–101.

Weidenfeld, A. (2006) 'Religious needs in the hospitality industry', *Tourism and Hospitality Research*, 6 (2): 143–159.

Wilson, J., Belk, R.W., Bamossy, G.J., Sandikci, Ö., Kartajaya, H., Sobh, R., et al. (2013) 'Crescent marketing, Muslim geographies and brand Islam: Reflections from the JIMA Senior Advisory Board', *Journal of Islamic Marketing*, 4 (1): 22–50.

Zailani, S., Fernando, Y. and Mohamed, A. (2010) 'Location, star rating and international chain associated with the hoteliers intention for not applying the Halal logo certification', *European Journal of Social Sciences*, 16 (3): 401–408.

Zakaria, Z. (2008) 'Tapping into the world halal market: Some discussion on Malaysian laws and standards', *Shariah Journal*, 16: 603–616.

5

EXPLAINING THE COMPETITIVE ADVANTAGE OF ISLAMIC HOTEL CONCEPTS

Insights from Malaysia

Noorliza Karia and Firdaus Ahmad Fauzi

Introduction

An Islamic hotel is a strategic approach for competing in the local and global halal tourism and hospitality industry and fits with the changing market and Muslim tourist demands. A hotel can employ the halal concept in order to achieve competitive advantage by adding value to its products and service portfolios. Halal is the universal concept comprising products and services at premier value to meet the growing demand for halal tourism and hospitality from Muslim consumers. Therefore, the Islamic hotel is an accountable hotel as enshrined in the Quran and trusted by foreign Muslim tourists. It offers innovative services and drives strategic opportunities for enhancing hotel performance. Understanding this issue is vital to provide further empirical evidence and literature for Islamic tourism and hospitality industry, Islamic hotel, halal hotel and strategic management and hotel management.

The tourism and hospitality industry has become the largest and fastest-growing industries in the world, generating 7.6 trillion USD (10.2 per cent of global GDP) (World Travel and Tourism Council (WTTC) 2017), exceeding the global GDPs of the sectors of automotive manufacturing and chemical manufacturing. According to the WTTC, this sector also directly supported more than 108.7 million jobs globally, twice as many jobs as in the financial service sector and five times as many as in the chemicals manufacturing sector. With a projected 4.0 per cent global growth in the next decade, this sector is the 'gold mine' which needs to be explored vigorously to exploit its present opportunities.

In 2016 alone, Malaysia's tourism industry received 26.8 million tourists, providing RM82.1 billion towards the nation's GDP (Tourism Malaysia 2016) (Table 5.1). For the year 2017, total tourist arrivals were expected to be 31.8 million, and the income derived from them were expected to reach RM118 billion. Due to its huge contribution, the tourism industry has been selected as one of the National Key Economic Areas (NKEA) that needs to be continuously improved.

Table 5.1 Tourist arrivals and receipts to Malaysia by year, 2005–2016

Year	Arrivals (millions)	Receipts (RM billion)
2016	26.80	82.1
2015	25.70	69.1
2014	27.44	72.0
2013	25.72	65.4
2012	25.03	60.6
2011	24.71	58.3
2010	24.58	26.5
2009	23.65	46.1
2008	22.05	49.6
2007	20.97	53.4
2006	17.55	36.3
2005	16.43	32.0

Source: Tourism Malaysia, 2016.

Additionally, Malaysia has been named number one destination for Muslim travellers for four consecutive years from 2011 to 2014 (Islamic Tourism Centre of Malaysia (ITC) 2015). It was therefore no surprise that Malaysia was also named as one of the top tourist destinations among the Organisation of Islamic Cooperation (OIC) countries. The Global Muslim Travel Index (GMTI) indicated that Malaysia ranked at number 1 with the highest score among OIC nations, indicating the popularity of Malaysia among Muslim tourists worldwide (ITC 2015). Henderson (2016) mentioned that Malaysia possesses a mature and advanced halal ecosystem, with 6,329 registered mosques and 10,377 Imams dispersed all over the country, 821 total flights from West Asia and OIC countries, and 5,896 food premises of halal-certified kitchens and premises. Moreover, Malaysia also topped the Dubai Islamic Economy Development Centre (DIEDC) Halal Travel Index as the country with the most developed Islamic economy ecosystem for halal travel for the year 2014 to 2015. Tables 5.2 and 5.3 provide details on tourist arrivals in Malaysia from Muslim countries and per capita expenditure of Muslim tourists in Malaysia by

Table 5.2 Top five tourist arrivals from Muslim countries to Malaysia

Rank	Country	Total no. of tourists
1	Indonesia	2,827,533
2	Brunei	1,213,110
3	Bangladesh	204,418
4	Saudi Arabia	113,921
5	Pakistan	97,114

Source: ITC, 2015.

Table 5.3 Top five countries by per capita
expenditure of Muslim tourists in Malaysia

Rank	Country	RM
1	Saudi Arabia	9,459.20
2	Kuwait	8,494.40
3	Oman	7,938.00
4	UAE	7,389.40
5	Iran	5,880.60

Source: ITC, 2015.

country. The latter indicating why Middle East tourists are considered as a 'lucrative market' (Salleh, Hamid, Hashim & Omain 2014).

Malaysia Islamic tourism and hospitality industry

In attempting to cater to more Muslim tourists, Malaysia launched standards for Muslim Friendly Hospitality Services (MS 2610:2015), led by the International Institute for Halal Research and Training of the International Islamic University Malaysia. The standard was drafted cooperatively by the main representatives of Malaysia's tourism industry: (i) Islamic Tourism Centre (ITC), (ii) Tourism Malaysia, (iii) Malaysian Association of Hotel Owners (MAHO), (iv) Malaysian Association of Hotels (MAH), (v) Malaysian Association of Tour and Travel Agents (MATTA), (vi) *Bumiputera* Travel and Tour Agents Association of Malaysia (Bumitra), and (vii) Malaysian Tourist Guides Council (MTGC). Nonetheless, the adoption of the standards is still voluntary.

The definition and conceptualisation of Islamic tourism

The term 'Muslim Friendly Hospitality Services' is defined as products and/or services in the tourism industry guided by Shariah requirements that cater to or provide facilities suitable for Muslim travellers (ITC 2015). The standard incorporates elements of the hospitality industry, tour packages, tourist guides, accommodation segmentation, and travel segmentation. The standard can be used as a benchmark for assessing the integration of Muslim-friendly services in Malaysia, particularly in the hospitality area, and follows the setting of standards for Shariah-compliance practices that have been developed for financial and manufacturing services.

The term 'halal' originated from the Arabic which means permissible, lawful, or allowed. According to the responsible government agency, Jabatan Kemajuan Islam Malaysia (JAKIM), halal is described as things or actions permitted by Shariah law without punishment imposed on the doer. The halal concept is embedded in many aspects of food and beverages, conducts, services, and products which bring benefits and welfare to the universe (*mashlahah*). However, whatever definition is used, the basic parameters of halal are constant: religious requirements, products/services excellence, competitiveness, well-being of humankind and the universe, and the blessing of Allah (Karia & Asaari 2016).

Halal tourism promotes Muslim-friendly travelling experience to its Muslim tourists. The ITC (2015) defines Islamic tourism as "any activity, event and experience undertaken in a state of travel that is in accordance with Islam". In seeking to realise the concept, each year Malaysia plays host to two of the biggest halal events, namely the Malaysia International Halal Showcase (MIHAS) and the World Halal Forum (WHF). Both events have played a pivotal role in seeking to establishing the country's reputation as a global reference and trade centre for the mainstream halal industry (ITC 2015).

However, there is much confusion about the concept of halal tourism. Battour and Ismail (2016) noted that it is hard to decide on the right terminologies and proper clarification of the halal tourism concept. They agreed that terms like 'halal tourism' and 'Islamic tourism' are most commonly used to refer to the subject, however questionable they may be. Regardless of whatever terms are used, one of the main elements in halal tourism is the availability of Muslim-friendly accommodation. The understanding of what constitutes a halal hotel among hoteliers is necessary in order to precisely fulfil Muslim consumers' demand.

Islamic hotel industry

In order to achieve Islamic tourism hub status, the introduction of halal hotels as a form of tourism services is highly important. Being an Islamic country, Malaysia has the capability and ability to cater to the needs of Muslim tourists, especially given shifts in patterns of tourism from Islamic countries following global events. In order to achieve this the Malaysian government established the Islamic Tourism Council in 2009 to strengthen their aspiration towards becoming the Islamic tourism hub. Many rich Islamic countries such as Saudi Arabia, Bahrain, Kuwait, Oman, and Qatar promise huge potential as target markets, with high spending and purchasing power. As of December 2015, 744 halal certificates had been issued by JAKIM to hotels and resorts in Malaysia, with 44 Muslim-friendly hotels in Kuala Lumpur alone (ITC 2015). However, tourists' need for halal hotels are not just for halal foods and restaurants; it goes well beyond major aspects of the hotel operations, such as the employees' and patrons' dress code, the use of halal amenities and cleaning materials and substances, as well as the supply of prayer mats and Al-Quran in each room.

Fundamentally, Shariah is a rule or way of life which came from Allah s.w.t. to mankind through Prophet Muhammad s.a.w. The primary source of Shariah is Al-Quran and Sunnah, and compliance in this context can be defined as adherence and obedience to all that Allah s. w.t. ordered. Consequently, Shariah-compliant hotel can be understood as a hotel which provides services bound with Shariah principles. Thus, a Shariah-compliant hotel is not just about serving halal foods and beverages, but its facilities, amenities, financial, operation, and marketing aspects must also be in line with Shariah principles (Table 5.4). This is of course, parallel with the primary objective of Shariah, which is protecting mankind and preventing harm from and against humans in this world and hereafter.

Halal hotels are different from conventional hotels because they need to provide products and services that are guided by Shariah requirements, in order to cater to Muslim guests, especially with respect to foodservice. As Muslims, they must perform religious obligations that are compulsory, even when they are travelling. As a result, service providers (hoteliers) need to provide conveniences such as a prayer room, halal food and beverages, and halal cutlery, utensils, crockery, equipment, pillows, mattress, and cleaning supplies as part of their responsibilities. Samori and Rahman (2013) suggested that these hotels must use the right Islamic themes, ambience, and architecture to make travellers feel comfortable and that creates value, image, and brand. The differences between halal hotels and conventional hotels in Malaysia are listed in Table 5.5.

Table 5.4 Shariah-compliant hotel requirements

Aspects	Requirements
Operations	• No alcoholic drinks and sell halal foods only • Majority of staff are Muslim • Female staff for single female guest floors, male staff for single male guest floors • Conservative television services • Al-Quran and prayer mats available in each room • Larger function rooms to cater to male and female guests separately • Qiblat sign (direction of Makkah)
Design and interior	• No red-light entertainment • Beds and toilets should not be placed to face the direction of Makkah • Decoration and art should not depict the human and animal form • Separated health and fitness facilities for male and female guests • Separated floors for single male guests, single female guests and families
Financial	• Hotel financed through Islamic financial arrangements • Hotel should follow Zakat principles

Source: After Rosenberg and Choufany, 2009.

Table 5.5 Differences between halal hotels and conventional hotels

Halal hotels	Conventional hotels
Cater to a specific niche market such as orthodox Muslims, business, and families	Open to all categories of customer depending on the hotel type and categories
Decoration much be in keeping with Islamic architectural and design principles	Hotel design is opulent and not limited
Rooms are larger than industry standards to accommodate the need of Muslims to pray inside the room	A standard room ranges from 30 to 40 m^2, junior suite from 55 to 65 m^2, and presidential suite from 200 to 220 m^2
Must serve halal food only	No limitation on food served within the hotel
No alcohol	Alcohol is served throughout the hotel. Alcohol sales bring 80–90% to gross profit in food and beverage sales figures
Gender-specific staff to serve customers and majority should be Muslims	No limitation in staffing requirement
Revenue from room 80–85%	Revenue from room 40–60%
Revenue from food and beverage 10–20%	Revenue from food and beverage 30–40%
Revenue from other departments 5–10%	Revenue from other departments 5–10%
In-room facilities must facilitate Muslims in performing their religious duties such as water bidet and prayer mat	Some hotels provide these facilities upon request
Most Shariah-compliant hotels are small to medium size due to the small niche area and target market	Large size businesses to cater for larger market share

Issues and challenges of Islamic hotel implementation

Though the Malaysian government fully supported the development of Islamic hotels, there are still many challenges. First and foremost, Islamic hotels need to get approval and certifications from JAKIM in order to be recognised as a Shariah-compliant hotel. According to ITC (2015) and JAKIM, 80 per cent of halal certificates were issued to non-Muslim companies in Malaysia raising critical questions about the absence of Muslim entrepreneurs in this area. Regardless of religious denomination, it is essential for hoteliers, especially those who are *Bumiputeras* (a Malaysian term to describe Malays and other indigenous peoples of South East Asia) and/or Muslims to: (i) understand the application of halal knowledge, (ii) raise their interest, and (iii) their capability to acquire halal certification.

The halal certification process comprises aspects of documentation, management responsibility, raw material, location, exterior area, premises, facilities, tools and equipment, staff characteristic, staff policy, pest control, and waste management (Razalli, Yusoff & Roslan 2013). Generally, the activities and behaviours of hotel management in selecting the committees, which includes Muslims who are responsible to ensure the effectiveness in implementation of internal halal control system, falls under management's responsibility. In addition, hotel employees need to have extensive knowledge of halal (in relation to the nature of their work) according to Islamic protocol to be able to comply with the halal certification.

At any time, a hotel will face difficulties in acquiring halal certification, as it requires many procedures and thorough checking. Sometimes even the slightest issue will prevent a hotel from being granted a halal certificate. For instance, each and every ingredient used in the hotel's kitchen must be verified as halal from its source, otherwise it will be categorised as doubtful. If the source of the ingredients cannot be identified and verified, the ingredients must be substituted or obtained from halal-certified suppliers. In the majority of hotel establishments in Malaysia, especially those which are part of large conglomerates such as Marriott International, the term halal habitually covers the kitchen, foods served, and the ingredients. Therefore, only the hotel's kitchen can be certified halal, while the rest of the hotel remains conventional because of the existence of non-Islamic features, such as pubs, the serving of alcoholic beverages, clubs, dance floors, bars, and the hosting of un-Islamic events.

However, there are not yet concrete definitions regarding Islamic hotel concepts such as: (i) Shariah-compliance, (ii) halal hotel, and (iii) Muslim-friendly. Currently, the terms are used interchangeably by hotels and consequently potentially do not really reflect what is really being offered. The question emerges as to whether they are just taking advantage of Muslim guests by offering minimal Muslim-friendly attributes, or are really committed to the core in ensuring that their premises are worthy to be called halal or Shariah-compliant.

On the positive side, it can be argued that being halal-certified brings a competitive advantage to a hotel brand. Providing Shariah-compliant attributes in the accommodation definitely attracts Muslim consumers, while still being able to cater to all non-Muslims guests. Idris and Wahab (2015) conducted a SWOT (strengths, weaknesses, opportunities, and threats) analysis to figure out the competitive advantages gained by a hotel by being halal certified, and identified three main advantages:

Unique Concept: because halal covers a wide area of operations, the rearrangement, refurbishment, and renovation to comply with halal concepts will contribute to a property's uniqueness, as it should differ from existing, conventional hotels. This attribute is critically sought after in an effort to be competitive.

High Margin Expectancy: this is owing to the marketing principles of high demand and low supply. In 2015, Al Jawhara Gardens Hotel of UAE recorded an annual increase of 10 per cent in sales growth after embracing the halal hotel concepts, even without the sales contribution of alcoholic beverages. Interestingly, 80 per cent of their hotel guests were non-Muslims.

Muslim-Friendly Hospitality Services Standards: though the implementation of MS 2610:2015 is voluntary, it will boost Muslim consumers' confidence in using a hotel's products and services. With the existence of such hotels, more Muslims can choose to organise Islamic events with confidence, such as Iftar Ramadhan, Al-Quran recitations, Islamic seminars, Aidilfitri celebrations, Islamic-style weddings and birthdays, and much more.

Ahmat, Ridzuan, Din, Zainol and Razali (2015) raised the issue of consumer awareness regarding the whole concept and practice of the Shariah-compliant hotel. The findings of their research stated that many consumers do not really comprehend the real concept, and blamed it on the lack of consensus between hotels, in addition to the non-existence of a consistent standard, low publicity, and misinterpretation due to lack of awareness. In addition, hotels also face human resource challenges, in the form of high turnover rate and halal training for its employees. Staff turnover is very expensive, and it relates to the training because it would have to be re-done for new staff. Productivity could slow down as new workers need time to adapt and learn how to perform their work in a new environment. Most of the time, hotel management would have to organise training sessions not just for new staff, but also refresher courses for existing staff to keep them up to date with current halal matters. Regular training on halal is very costly, yet crucial to ensure their workers are well informed, motivated, knowledgeable, and maintain their halal integrity.

Even in Malaysia, the number of halal-certified hotels is still small due to the complexities faced by the hoteliers. The first hotel kitchen in Malaysia certified as halal was at the Hotel De Palma Shah Alam, Selangor. The majority of the hotels awarded halal certificates by JAKIM are medium-sized and they are usually owned by independent firms, making it easier for them to make the decision to become halal compliant as they are without big corporate influences and interests. The Adya Hotel Langkawi, Kedah, is one example of a full-fledged, halal-certified hotel in Malaysia.

Case study: Adya Hotel, Langkawi, Malaysia

The Adya Hotel has been embracing the halal concept ever since its inauguration in January 2015. Since then, Adya Hotel has been successful in maintaining the qualification and attributes of a halal hotel. The hotel maintains an internal halal certification committee of seven members, who are responsible for getting the hotel halal-certified every two years. However, the task is less daunting than for older hotels, because the Adya Hotel master plan was to become a halal-certified hotel from the blueprint stage.

The Adya Hotel has been implementing a halal value chain strategy to guide the supply chain operations. This includes the processes of procurement, material movement and storage, and the issuing and handling of halal-certified food products within the establishment. Halal concepts are also being implemented in the processing of non-food materials; overall aspects of their food supply chain; employees' personal hygiene and clothing; utensils; and the working area. The Adya Hotel also applies the Hazard Analysis and Critical Control Point (HACCP) system, a systematic approach to maintain hygienic conditions while minimising and eliminating potential hazards during food handling. The hotel's entire halal food chain operates on several good quality assurance systems: (i) good manufacturing practices, (ii) Hazard Analysis and Critical Control Point (HACCP), (iii) Codex General Principles of Food Hygiene, and (iv) halal certification.

Managing halal in hotel food production is a challenging task because it involves the combination of being both a service and a product. The hotel has to make sure the ingredients, beverages, raw materials, and additives are free of pork, alcohol, and their derivatives. All equipment, tools, and machinery must never have been in contact with haram foods, and halal food ingredients must not be mixed or even come into contact with haram or syubhah ingredients, even in storage facilities before they have been delivered to the hotel. Furthermore, employee training on halal is considered vital to the hotel's operation. All employees are made to understand the core halal concepts and their application. This is done to ensure cleanliness, purity, safety, and hygiene, as well as to fulfil the quality assurance system requirements, including for halal.

The hotel is equipped with Muslim-friendly facilities (see Table 5.6), services, and also provides Islamic activities. As part of their corporate social responsibility programme, the hotel initiated several programmes to show their commitment. There are fund boxes at strategic places in the hotel, so employees and guests can contribute to the deprived. The management also made their commitment towards community service by sharing some amount of their profit into this fund. Adya Hotel encourages staff and guests to join Jama'ah prayer together during working hours, especially during Zohor and Asar prayer. Al-Quran recitation is held weekly, and guests are invited to recite Al-Quran together with the staff. In addition, the Adya Hotel holds Islamic talks and seminars from time to time to which guests are invited.

Adherence to strict halal requirements enables the Adya Hotel to build and gain trust from hotel guests. Islamic concepts can be seen and felt not just in the foodservice operations of the establishment, but also in the building's architecture, as well as embedded within the values and services of every single worker in the hotel. Moreover, there is a positive impact of applying halal concept in food and services quality to non-Muslim hotel guests. From the feedback from non-Muslim guests, they feel the same satisfaction, comfort, and hospitality as everyone else who stays at the hotel, regardless of race or religion.

Conclusion

Malaysia has been recognised as one of the best destinations for Muslim travellers as a result of its strong focus on the Islamic tourism and hospitality industry. Indeed, it was acknowledged as the top country with the most developed Islamic economy ecosystem for halal travel for the years 2014 to 2015 by the Dubai Islamic Economy Development Centre (DIEDC) Halal

Table 5.6 Adya Hotel's facilities and their Muslim-friendly attributes

Facility	Muslim-friendly attributes
Swimming pool	Two separate pools. One for family activities the other for women only
All rooms	Sufficient space for prayer
All rooms	Equipped with *Al-Quran* and *Suratul Yassin* (the 36th surah of the Quran)
Bathroom	Dedicated pipe for ablution
Hotel prayer room	*Jama'ah* congregational prayer for guests and staffs
Hotel speaker system	*Azan* (call to prayer) for each prayer time
Shuttle van	Free transportation to the nearest mosque every Friday prayer

Travel Index. Therefore, the idea of creating an Islamic hotel should be seen as the perfect platform to promote true Islamic concepts. In fact, an Islamic hotel would certainly attract more Muslim tourists and, in turn, generate more return on investment. Hoteliers could take advantage of the situation and join the effort by getting their hotel Shariah-compliant or, at the very least, Muslim-friendly.

The chapter has suggested that an Islamic hotel emphasises the importance of its innovation as a source of its competitive advantage. However, knowledge about the innovation capabilities of Islamic hotels has yet to be explored. The chapter documents the strategies of an Islamic hotel in Malaysia based on the knowledge of halal business prescribed in the Quran. The interview findings of a case study of the Islamic hotel reveal some proactive improvements in handling halal resources and capabilities for achieving competitive advantage.

This chapter is also written to address the prospects of Islamic hotels in Malaysia. Although the potential of expansion and promises of profits are tempting, interested hoteliers and entrepreneurs must consider and prepare for the challenges involved. The government must also provide assistance by setting up clear definitions and specific standards to be used in this sector. There are also many other aspects to be tackled, such as the mechanics of certification for Islamic hotels, logistical services, employees' training, and the tax package, to name a few. The most important thing is that the Islamic hotel concept gives a new commercial value to the hotel brand, as well as representing the good and universal Islamic life environment (Karim, Ahmad & Zainol 2017).

In summary, the idea of creating an Islamic hotel could be seen as one of the perfect platforms to promote true Islamic concepts and their implementation in contemporary lifestyles, especially during emerging issues of 'Islamophobia' and conflicts between and inside religions. While in Malaysia, halal or Islamic identification is seen as a passport for the industry players to cater to the 'so-called' untapped markets of halal hotels. The halal recognition creates trust for the hotel guests, for both Muslims and non-Muslims, domestic or international. Trust, in turn, creates business opportunities and therefore boosts the economy within this sector. Hence, the best way to execute this is by improved synergy between the public and private sectors, all towards the betterment of Malaysia's halal hospitality and tourism industry.

References

Ahmat, N.H.C., Ridzuan, A.H.A., Din, N., Zainol, N. and Razali, M.A. (2015) 'Syariah compliance hotel: The concept and practices', *Journal of Tourism, Hospitality and Culinary Arts*, 7 (2): 52–66.

Battour, M. and Ismail, M.N. (2016) 'Halal tourism: Concepts, practices, challenges and future', *Tourism Management Perspectives*, 19: 150–154.

Henderson, J.C. (2016) 'Halal food, certification and Halal tourism: Insights from Malaysia and Singapore', *Tourism Management Perspectives*, 19: 160–164.

Idris, J. and Wahab, N.A. (2015) 'The competitive advantages of Sharia-compliant hotel concept in Malaysia: SWOT analysis', paper presented at the 2nd International Conference on Management and Muamalah 2015 (2nd ICoMM), Malaysia.

Islamic Tourism Centre of Malaysia (ITC) (2015) 'Malaysia Islamic tourism—facts and figures in brief 2014/2015'. [online] Available at: www.itc.gov.my/document/malaysia-islamic-tourism-facts-and-figures-in-brief/(accessed 8 July 2017).

Karia, N. and Asaari, M.H.A.H. (2016) 'Assessing innovation in Halal service: An Islamic-based view approach'. In S.K.A. Manan, F.A. Rahman and M. Sahri (eds) *Contemporary Issues and Development in the Global Halal Industry: Selected Papers from the International Halal Conference 2014*. Singapore: Springer Science + Business Media, 589–597.

Karim, M.H.A., Ahmad, R. and Zainol, N.A. (2017) 'Differences in hotel attributes: Islamic hotel and Sharia compliant hotel in Malaysia', *Journal of Global Business and Social Entrepreneurship (GBSE)*, 1 (2): 157–169.

Razalli, M.R., Yusoff, R.Z. and Roslan, M.W.M. (2013) 'A framework of Halal certification practices for hotel industry', *Asian Social Science*, 9 (11): 316–326.

Rosenberg, P. and Choufany, H.M. (2009) *Spiritual Lodging—The Sharia-Compliant Hotel Concept.* [pdf] HVS Global Hospitality Services—Dubai. Available at: www.hvs.com/content/2856.pdf

Salleh, N.M., Hamid, A.B.A., Hashim, N.H. and Omain, S.Z. (2014) 'The practice of Shariah-compliant hotel in Malaysia', *International Journal of Trade, Economics and Finance*, 5 (1): 26.

Samori, Z. and Rahman, F.A. (2013) 'Towards the formation of Shariah compliant hotel in Malaysia: An exploratory study on its opportunities and challenges', paper presented at the 2013 WEI International Academic Conference, Istanbul, Turkey.

Tourism Malaysia. (2016) *Tourism Malaysia—Facts and Figures Overview.* [online] Available at: www .tourism.gov.my/statistics (accessed 8 July 2017).

World Travel and Tourism Council (WTTC). (2017) *Travel & Tourism Economic Impact '2017 World.* [pdf] London. Available at: www.wttc.org/-/media/files/reports/economic-impact-research/regions-2017/ world2017.pdf (accessed 8 July 2017).

6

SHARIAH-COMPLIANT HOTEL OPERATIONS PRACTICES (SCHOP)

Mohd. Rizal Razalli

Introduction

The population of Muslims is growing at a faster rate than any other religions. The Pew Research Centre (2011) reported that Muslims constituted about 25 per cent of the world's population. The global population of Muslims is predicted to increase from 1.6 billion in 2010 to 2.2 billion in 2030. If this trend continues, the Muslim population is estimated to grow to 2.76 billion, or 29.7 per cent of the world's population, by 2050. The increase of Muslim population by region from the year 2010 to 2030 is depicted in Table 6.1. These figures indicate that Islam is one of the largest and fastest-growing religions in the world, which in turn will significantly influence the halal industry.

Halal industry

The growth in the number of Muslims worldwide has had a huge positive impact on the global halal food market. The trend shows that the sector has grown progressively over the past decade. The value of the global halal market has been projected at US$547 billion a year (Malaysian-German Chamber of Commerce & Industry 2011). Muslim consumers are creating greater demand for halal food and other consumer goods. This is supported by the statistics shown in Table 6.2. For example, in the years 2004 to 2010, the global halal food market size grew by as much as US$64.3 billion, increasing from US$587.2 to US$651.5 billion (Pew Research Centre 2011). Similar trends can be found in the context of Malaysia as the global market demand for halal products and services also positively influences the growth of the domestic halal food industry. The market size of the halal industry in Malaysia has been estimated at RM1.5 billion. In fact, 90 per cent of this market is derived from the food industry. Meanwhile, other growing halal industries, particularly the cosmetic, pharmaceutical, and halal ingredients are the focus of small to medium-sized enterprises (SMEs) (Seong 2011).

The rapid expansion of the halal food market provides more opportunities in fulfilling the halal market demands, not only to Malaysia but also to other Muslim countries. New market opportunities, such as halal tourism, have emerged and are becoming increasingly popular among contemporary Muslim travellers. Halal tourism has become a new innovative product in the tourism and hospitality industry. Halal tourism promises a holiday destination for

93

Table 6.1 Muslim population by region, 2010–2030

	2010		2030	
	Estimated Muslim population ('000)	*Estimated % of global Muslim population*	*Estimated Muslim population ('000)*	*Estimated % of global Muslim population*
World	1,619,314	100%	2,190,154	100.0%
Asia-Pacific	1,005,507	62.1%	1,295,625	59.2%
Middle East–North Africa	321,869	19.9%	439,453	20.1%
Sub-Saharan Africa	242,544	15.0%	385,936	17.6%
Europe	44,138	2.7%	58,209	2.7%
Americas	5,256	0.3%	10,927	0.5%

Source: Pew Research Center, 2011.

Table 6.2 Global halal market sizes by region (US$ billion)

Region	2004	2005	2009	2010
Global halal food market size	587.2	596.1	634.5	651.5
Africa	136.9	139.5	150.3	153.4
Asian countries	369.6	375.8	400.1	416.1
GCC countries	38.4	39.5	43.8	44.7
Indonesia	72.9	73.9	77.6	78.5
China	18.5	18.9	20.8	21.2
India	21.8	22.1	23.6	24.0
Malaysia	6.6	6.9	8.2	8.4
Europe	64.3	64.4	66.6	67.0
France	16.4	16.5	17.4	17.6
Russian Federation	20.7	20.8	21.7	21.9
United Kingdom	3.4	3.5	4.1	4.2
Australasia	1.1	1.1	1.5	1.6
Americas	15.3	15.5	16.1	16.2
United States	12.3	12.5	12.9	13.1
Canada	1.4	1.5	1.8	1.9

Source: Pew Research Centre, 2011.

Muslims whereby the travellers will be provided services that are aligned with Shariah principles. The main part of halal tourism is concerned with both halal food and accommodation. Halal food is one of the important factors that influences the choice to visit a particular place and affects tourist attitudes, decisions, and behaviour (Henderson 2008). In fact, scholars have indicated that halal food has the potential to enhance the sustainability of tourism destinations and indeed may represent a competitive advantage (Du Rand, Heath & Alberts 2003), while the accommodation sector, which is most likely to provide food to tourists, is also closely interrelated and affected by halal tourism.

Halal tourism and hotel industry in Malaysia

In becoming a high-income nation, Malaysia, through the Economic Transformation Programmes (ETPs), has highlighted the tourism industry as one of the National Key Economic Areas (NKEA) that need to be successfully transformed. One of the 12 entry point projects (EPPs) under the Tourism NKEA is related to the hotel industry. Under the ETP, the hotel industry is classified in the business tourism theme and specifically the objective is to improve rates, mix, and quality of hotels (Performance Management & Delivery Unit (PEMANDU) 2011). In the national plan, the hotel industry is chosen as one of the critical areas that needs improvement in terms of its financial and non-financial performances. These improvement efforts are expected to result in higher quality hotels in terms of products and services that can be provided to local and international customers.

Malaysia has an impressive brand for an Asian tourist destination. Malaysia was one of the three countries in Asia (after Taiwan and Hong Kong) which achieved a double-digit growth in tourism receipts despite the adverse economic downturn in 2009 (Tourism Malaysia 2009). The slogan of "Malaysia is truly Asia" seems to be a success as the number of tourist arrivals increases year on year.

The tourism industry has been one of the main contributors to the national economy (Tourism Malaysia 2011). In 2016, Malaysia received around 26.76 million tourists compared to 24.58 million tourists in 2010, representing an increase of 2.18 million in arrivals. In 2017, the target is 31.8 million and the figure is expected to rise to 36 million in the year 2020 for tourists visiting Malaysia. Meanwhile, in terms of tourist spending, there has been a significant increase from RM56.5 billion in 2010 to RM82.1 billion in 2016.

In the context of the tourism sector, Muslim tourists are seen to be the highest growing area in international tourist arrivals in Malaysia. In 2012, approximately 5.44 million Muslim tourists were registered to visit Malaysia, up 0.22 million tourists from 2011 (Islamic Tourism Centre of Malaysia 2017). The statistics provided by Malaysia Tourism indicated that Muslim tourists spent about RM5,784 billion in 2010 and made up approximately 23.5 per cent of the total tourist arrivals in Malaysia in the same year (BERNAMA 2011). The top five countries for Muslim tourists were Indonesia, Brunei, Bangladesh, Saudi Arabia, and Pakistan (Malaysian Digest 2016). The surge in demand in Islamic tourism has been a blessing for the Malaysian economy. Many Muslim tourists have transferred their holiday vacation destination to Malaysia, particularly after the tragic 9/11 event.

In Malaysia, the development of the hotel sector really commenced in the early 1990s (Aziz 2007). The gradual development of the hotel sector is focused towards luxury hotels as well as the middle and lower class hotels. The hotel sector continues to prosper from year to year. The continued growth in the tourism industry has resulted in the increase in the number of hotels in the country. Newly established hotels have grown due to the increase in tourist arrivals and the increasing demand for accommodation during their trip.

The hospitality industry is the second highest source of income to Malaysia's GDP (Zailani, Omar, & Kopong 2011; Sahida, Rahman, Awang, & Che Man 2011). However, the tourism and hospitality sectors consist of different products and services, but both simultaneously support the industry as a whole (Aziz, Hassan, Hassan & Othman 2009). The hospitality sector consists of several facilities such as rooms, restaurants, health clubs, night clubs, bars and others, such as meeting rooms. According to Samori and Sabtu (2014), the hotel industry provides services such as accommodation, food and drinks to guests or temporary residents who want to stay at the hotel. Hotels are also defined as an operation that provides accommodation and ancillary services to those who are far from home, travelling for work or leisure. Metelka (1990) defined tourism as an "umbrella" term for a variety of products and services offered to and needed by people while away from "home". The different products and services meant that accommodation, food services, transportation, attraction of surroundings and others are related to hospitality activities.

The significant increase in Muslim tourists has resulted in a sudden increase in demand for accommodation. In responding to this growth, a number of initiatives have been launched in the country in order to further boost the tourism sector (Malay Mail 2014). One of the initiatives is the adoption of Muslim-friendly accommodation where Shariah principles apply to the hotel operations and services that will appeal to Muslim travellers. Halal tourism has become an innovative and customised product in the tourism industry, which offers destinations and services for Muslims that comply with the Shariah rules (Razalli, Shuib & Yusoff 2013). This is the main focus of the current chapter.

Halal-based hotel operations

Despite the encouragement and efforts by the Malaysian government to develop the hotel sector, there are still inefficiencies in terms of managing the operations of hotels, particularly on the issues of halal-based operations, better known as Shariah-compliant hotel operations, the term used throughout the chapter.

In order to fill this gap, more research is needed on the Shariah-compliant hotels in Malaysia. The current practices of halal-based hotels are merely limited to halal food production. In other words, hoteliers should also ensure that the halal concept goes beyond the aspect of food. It should include other management aspects as well. Such hotels not only serve halal food and beverages, but also the operations throughout the hotel should be managed based on Shariah principles (Sahida et al. 2011). From this perspective, in addition to the hotel kitchens and food preparation processes, the halal concept will also cover the operations, design, and the financial system of the hotel.

The current general perception that Shariah-compliant hotels are only meant for Muslims should also be shifted. There are also non-Muslim consumers who choose Shariah-compliant hotels for their stay. A Shariah-compliant hotel, Al Jawhara Gardens Hotel Business Development UAE, has an annual 10 per cent increase in growth with 80 per cent of their hotel guests being non-Muslim (Muhammad 2015). Tabung Haji Hotel in Malaysia, for instance, is the choice of many non-Muslim guests due to its excellent services such as a large facility, conducive ambiance, and, more importantly, no liquor (Mohamad Azhari 2015). This means that the Shariah-compliant hotel is certainly applicable to both Muslim as well as non-Muslim consumers.

In addition, Muslim tourists, especially from Islamic countries are very sensitive in their hotel selection. Muslim travellers also have their expectations and demand certain amenities in order to uphold their religious belief while travelling for leisure or business. Rajagopal, Ramanan, Visvanathan and Satapathy (2011) indicated how halal certification can be used as a crucial marketing tool in promoting halal brand/products or services. Hotels with halal certification in their kitchen and premises can give an added competitive advantage to the hotels in attracting not only the foreign tourist but also the local visitor (Zailani et al. 2011).

However, the statistics from the department responsible for halal certification in Malaysia, Jabatan Kemajuan Islam Malaysia (JAKIM), has shown that in 2017 there were only 442 hotels in Malaysia that have obtained the halal certification (JAKIM 2017). In 2016, the total number of hotels in Malaysia was recorded as 4,961 (Tourism Malaysia 2017). Therefore, halal certified establishments represent less than 10 per cent of the hotel industry. Hence, in order to attract more tourists, especially Muslim travelers, to Malaysia, the number of Shariah-compliant hotels should be increased.

Thus, further understanding and transformation of the hotel sector with respect to Shariah-compliant hotels are deemed as timely and necessary. The next section will explain the criteria of the Shariah-Compliant Hotel Operations Practices (SCHOP).

Shariah-Compliant Hotel Operations Practices (SCHOP)

The hotel industry in Malaysia is facing numerous new challenges. One of these challenges is internally driven—its service operations. The increasing number of visitors that come to Malaysia due to halal tourism would result in significant operational challenges to hotels. Currently, there limited research that has investigated operational aspects of hotel management, including Shariah-compliant operations.

Shariah-compliant hotels are those hotels that adopt the Shariah principles in their operational practices. The term Shariah refers to the Islamic law derived from the precepts of Islam, particularly from the Qur'an and the hadith of Prophet Muhammad S.A.W. In Islam, halal and haram principles in a Muslim lifestyle are not only for food and drink, but also cover clothing and accessories, marriage, and work-related activities (Al-Qardhawi 1995) (see also Chapters 1 and 2, this volume). In addition to the requirement to serve halal food and drink, hotel operations should also be implemented based on the Shariah principles (Sahida et al. 2011). From this perspective, the halal concept is not confined to the hotel's kitchen wall, but will also include the operational aspects of the hotel such as human resources, marketing, and the financial system of the hotel as a whole. In other words, the hotel facilities should be comprehensively operated on Shariah principles. However, the concept of Shariah-compliant hotel is still relatively new among hoteliers and generally hotel management still have no clear guidelines how to practise the principles in their work environment. Despite the unavailability of clear guidelines, hotels that introduce the concept of Shariah operations have been gaining an advantage compared to their rivals in the Islamic guest market. This further demonstrates why clear guidelines for Shariah-compliant hotels should be established.

The fact that the Shariah-compliant hotel is still new among hoteliers has resulted in less knowledge and more confusion on the subject matter (Razalli et al. 2013). Even though Muslims are among the largest tourist markets in the world, perceived values of the Shariah-compliant hotel have not been clearly established. Among the general guidelines suggested are those by Rosenberg and Choufany (2009), Henderson (2010), Kana (2011), and Nursanty (2012), but these standards are still not comprehensive enough to cover the scope of the Shariah-compliant hotel as a whole. Current practices of branding hotels in the name of Shariah compliance to accommodate millions of Muslim travellers does not significantly differ from those of normal hotels. In current practice, instead of applying the Shariah principles for the whole operations, the management of the Shariah-compliant hotels only strategise certain parts of their operations to comply with the principles. Hence, this chapter discusses the criteria for Shariah-Compliant Hotel Operations Practices (SCHOP) which have five main dimensions, namely: (1) administrative practices; (2) common areas practices; (3) bedroom practices; (4) service practices; and (5) food and beverage practices.

Criteria for Shariah-Compliant Hotel Operations Practices (SCHOP)

In general, SCHOP consists of five main practices, namely (1) administrative, (2) common areas, (3) bedroom, (4) service, and (5) food and beverage. Figure 6.1 shows the dimensions of SCHOP. These practices are closely related to the structure and operations of most hotels to ensure the practical aspect of the model. All five dimensions have specific attributes that are aligned to Islamic management and Shariah principles. Available frameworks such as the halal certification system by JAKIM, IQS-Islamic Quality Standard for Hotel, Islamic human resource management (Azmi 2009; Khan, Farooq & Hussain 2010), Islamic marketing (Abuznaid 2012; Arham 2010; Hassan, Chachi & Latiff 2008), and Islamic finance (Vejzagic & Smolo 2011) were used as reference points to establish the model. Note that the Qur'an and the hadith are the main sources used for the development of the model. The model is divided into two categories: (1) standard, and (2) advanced. The standard category seeks availability of the practices, while the advanced category measures the degree of implementation of the practices. The following section will discuss the five dimensions in detail.

Administrative practices

Administrative practices refer to the managerial practices in relation to the quality assurance in the hotel. These practices include managerial, financial, and human resources practices. There are 15 specific practices in this dimension. Note that one of the critical requirements is for the hotel to have a group of religious advisers who monitor the compliance of hotel operations to Shariah law (Che Ahmat, Ahmad Ridzuan & Mohd Zahari 2012). Without proper planning, monitoring, and controlling in carrying out halal operations, the main objective to become

Figure 6.1 Shariah-Compliant Hotel Operations Practices (SCHOP)

fully Shariah-compliant hotels cannot be easily achieved. Therefore, in regard to be Shariah-compliant, the management should:

- Establish a Shariah advisory committee to continuously evaluate and monitor the degree of compliance of the hotel to the Shariah law.
- Set Islamic quality principles as the main hotel policy.
- Implement and monitor the internal compliance audit.
- Carry out the improvement programme based on the findings of the internal audit assessment.

The second aspect of administrative practice concerns finance. Note that this aspect is still lacking in many of the current Shariah-compliant hotels. In regards to this aspect, the Shariah-compliant hotel must pay the *Zakah* (for a Muslim owner) or sponsor a social responsibility programme (for a non-Muslim owner) each year. This suggestion, in fact, is in line with Rosenberg and Choufany (2009). *Zakah* is one of the five pillars of Islam and it is compulsory for every Muslim. A hotel should pay a business *Zakah* when it has fulfilled the conditions for *haul* (period of a year) and *nisab* (achieve the required amount of *Zakah*). The purpose of *Zakah* is to purify one's wealth and to ensure equal allocation of wealth to other human beings (Vejzagic & Smolo 2011).

In addition to *Zakah*, other financial aspects of Islamic finance to be adopted by hotel operations relate to salary payment, income saving, and investment. In principle, *Mu'amalat Islam* allows any transactions (*Qawaid Fiqh*) as long as the transactions do not involve any forbidden transactions such as usury (*riba*). Interest in finance is clearly mentioned in the Qur'an as a prohibition to all Muslims as follows:

> Those who consume interest cannot stand [on the Day of Resurrection] except as one stands who is being beaten by Satan into insanity. That is because they say, "Trade is [just] like interest." But Allah has permitted trade and has forbidden interest. So whoever has received an admonition from his Lord and desists may have what is past, and his affair rests with Allah. But whoever returns to [dealing in interest or usury]—those are the companions of the Fire; they will abide eternally therein.
>
> *(Al-Qur'an, Al-Baqarah: 275)*

Mu'amalat Maliyyah in Islam highlights the Shariah principles practised by Muslims since the era of Prophet Muhammad S.A.W and his companions and the progression of hybrid contracts (combination/mixture) that are being used today. Ibn Rusyd and Abu Walid Muhammad b. Ahmad al-Hafid (1981) identified several Shariah contracts that are used in Malaysia's banking industry today based on the guidelines provided by the Shariah Advisory Council of Bank Negara Malaysia (SAC). The contracts that are widely used in the Islamic banking industry would cover the contracts of *Mudarabah* (profit sharing), *Murabahah* (cost increase profit), *Wadiah* (saving), *Musharakah* (joint venture), *al-Bay' Bithaman Ajil* (BBA) (sales with delayed payment), *Wakalah* (Agency), *Qard al-Hassan* (ihsan loan), *Ijarah Thumma al-Bay'* (AITAB—hire purchase), *Hibah* (reward), and several other Shariah-based products. Any business transactions can apply any of these contracts which refer to the guidelines of Shariah in finance by the Bank Islam Malaysia (BIMB Institute of Research and Training 2005), the Shariah Advisory Council of Bank Negara Malaysia (BNM), and the Shariah Advisory Council of Securities Commission (Suruhanjaya Sekuriti 2006). These guidelines can also be used to make financial transactions in accordance to the Syafie *mazhab* used in Malaysia. In the context of the hotel industry, the financial dimensions of major transactions are shown in Table 6.3.

Table 6.3 Transactions and respective contracts

Transactions	Type of contract
Room reservation	*Ijarah* (leasing)
	Bay' al-urbun (deposit/down payment)
Compensation	*Ujrah* (wages)
Savings	*Wadiah/mudarabah*
Retail trade, food & laundry	*Al-bay'* (trade)
Storage services	*Wadiah* (saving)
Supplies materials	*Istijrar* (supply contract)

In the case of the room reservation process, a contract called *ijarah* (leasing or hiring) and *Bay' al-urban* (deposit) are deemed applicable to hoteliers. *Ijarah* refers to a contract between two parties to utilise a lawful benefit against a consideration (Al-Zuhayli 2002). For hotels, *ijarah* is the agreement between the hotel owner who allows possession of his/her assets to be used by the customers, on an agreed rental over a specified period. This implies that the customer has complete freedom to utilise the room after the payment has been made. However, the right is terminated after the agreed period is over. For *Bay' al-urbun*, it is permissible for the hotel to ask for a deposit to secure the rent and protect the property from any damages during the rental period.

With respect to payment of the worker's compensation, a contract called *ujrah* (wages) which is part from *ijarah* seems to be appropriate for hotels. *Ujrah* in Islamic finance is simply defined as a fee. This is the financial fee charged in return for using the services or labour. In this case, the services offered by the employees of the hotels.

All businesses want to be profitable. For the Shariah-compliant hotel, the income generated from its business should be managed according to Shariah principles as well. For savings that yield from the business, hotels can opt for the *wadiah/mudarabah* accounts offered by any of the Islamic banks in the country. *Wadiah* means a deposit. In other words, *al-wadiah* is the act of keeping something from an individual or organisation and will guarantee return of it on the demand of the depositor (Sabiq 1983). *Wadiah* account is an interest-free service offered by the banks and profit will be periodically shared by the bank with the depositor if the bank gains a profit from the money. Meanwhile, *mudarabah* is a deposit in the form of an investment account. It represents an agreement between the capital provider (hotel) and an entrepreneur (bank) under which the provider provides capital to be managed by the bank and any profit or loss will be shared by both parties.

Other services provided by hotels such as store, laundry, and food and beverages should also comply with the Shariah. For any form of retail trade, food, and laundry services, generally *al-bay'* (trade) contract can be applied. For storage services, *wadiah* contract (savings) can be used. For the consistent supply of raw material transactions such as food from the suppliers, the role of the *Istijrar* contract may be highlighted. *Istijrar* is a supply contract in Islam with the terms and conditions agreed between the two parties.

The last practice in the administrative dimension concerns human resources. Human resource management is one of the critical elements that can instil trust among Muslim consumers on the level of Shariah compliance of the hotel. In this regards, a certain percentage of the staff in the hotel should be Muslims. Furthermore, the management should also consider their welfare by providing them apprioprate resources to perform their rights as a Muslim, particularly prayer.

Azmi (2009) has elaborated on the application of Islamic human resource in contemporary organisations. Islamic concepts such as *tanmiyyah* (growth), *jammaah* (teamwork), *taqwa* (fearful), *ibadah* (worship), *tazkiyah al-nafs* (purifying one's soul), *ta'dib* (instilling good manners), *khalifah* (vicegerent) *and al-falah* (success), *taqlid, istidlal, ma'rifah* (degree of faith), *tauhid* (Allah Oneness and Greatness) are all pertinent to organisations. In addition to improving the knowledge and skills of staff in an organisation, human resource development in Islam also plays the role of improving the spiritual soul of the individual in the organisation. Here are the recommendations in terms of human resource management:

- At least 30 per cent of staff should be Muslims.
- Muslim dress code/attire should be imposed.
- Provision of prayer room for staff.
- Provision of gender-specific changing room.
- Time allocation for Friday prayer (men) and also other daily prayers (men and women).
- Provision of training to staff to be friendly and helpful.
- Assurance of safety and security of the staff on the property.

Common area practices

Common area practices refer to those practices in the public areas in the hotel. This particular category is related to the *aurah* or the social interaction between men and women in Islam, Islamic entertainment, and the use of halal products. The following attributes represent specific practices in this category:

- Separate facilities for men and women or at least provision of segregated time slots for men and women. These facilities include the spa, gymnasium, recreational/sport, swimming pool, lounge, lift, toilet, and prayer room for guests.
- Halal products should be used in common areas such as soap in the toilet.
- Assurance of guest safety and security while staying in the hotel.
- Provide Islamic entertainment.
- Absence of magic show.
- Permitted music such as *nasheed*.
- Islamic architecture and design should be used in the property (for example, no picture/ sculpture of living beings).

Bedroom practices

Specific attributes and practices are required in guest bedrooms. For a Shariah-compliant hotel, it is suggested the rooms be provided with certain facilities and amenities such as:

- Qiblat direction
- Qur'an
- Prayer mat
- Prayer schedule
- Bidet
- Halal toiletries
- Halal in-room food
- Islamic in-room entertainment.

Note that in terms of decoration, pictures of living beings should not be part of the room design and alcoholic beverages must not be served in the room. In addition, the hotel needs to provide separate smoking and non-smoking rooms due to smoking being deemed as Haram in Malaysia (JAKIM 1995).

Service practices

As a service organisation, human interactions between a service provider and customers are critical to determine the level of customer satisfaction. The front office department is the heart of the hotel operations where this interaction frequently occurs. Hence the role of receptionists at the front office in dealing with the customer is very important. The fourth category, service practices, is related to those practices in the context of Islamic marketing and Islamic finance. Specifically, these practices should include:

- Islamic greeting
- Notification of the banning of alcoholic drinks
- Information on halal restaurants, mosques, and groceries
- Wake-up call for Subuh prayer
- Available services for additional prayer mat and schedule
- Halal products/services such as:

  - Wedding packages
  - Tours
  - Seminars/conferences

- No gambling products/services
- Halal shopping arcade
- Halal detergent for laundry
- Ethical and fair pricing
- Price display/information on room, meal, and other products
- Absence of price discrimination
- Ethical behaviour
- Proper location
- Absence of unnecessary delay for customer services
- Ethical promotional activities
- Absence of sexual appeal
- Absence of manipulation
- Islamic finance transactions.

Food and beverage practices

The final category is with respect to food and beverages practices. All Muslims must consume halal food and beverages. Even though this category is the focus of many Shariah-compliant hotels, it needs to be further strengthened with halal certification. Hence, it is suggested that the hotel obtain halal certification not only for the kitchen, but also for its restaurant for all meals including the meal provided for room service. The halal certification will help guarantee that the food consumed will be halal for Muslims. It will also ensure that the process of preparation, storage, and handling of the food is being managed properly based on the guidelines of the halal system.

In relation to beverages, it is important that the Shariah-compliant hotel forbids any alcoholic drinks to enter to the hotel property. The prohibition of liquor is clearly mentioned in the Qur'an:

> O you who have believed, indeed, intoxicants, gambling, [sacrificing on] stone alters [to other than Allah], and divining arrows are but defilement from the work of Satan, so avoid it that you may be successful. Satan only wants to cause between you animosity and hatred through intoxicants and gambling and to avert you from the remembrance of Allah and from prayer. So will you not desist?
>
> *(Al-Maidah: 90–91)*

This prohibition also applies to business as the prophet Muhammad S.A.W pointed out in a hadith:

> Allah's Messenger cursed ten people in connection with wine: the wine-presser, the one who has it pressed, the one who drinks it, the one who conveys it, the one to whom it is conveyed, the one who serves it, the one who sells it, the one who benefits from the price paid for it, the one who buys it, and the one for whom it is bought.
>
> *(Termidzi & Ibu Majah)*

Hence, even though liquor is deemed as a major contributor of income to many hotels, it is definitely not permissible for the Shariah-compliant hotel. To Muslims, submission to God's command is paramount and Muslims seek the benefits not only during their lifetime but also in the hereafter.

Table 6.4 summarises all five dimensions and their attributes discussed above. There are five dimensions and a total of 64 attributes for SCHOP.

Conclusion

In conclusion, the Shariah-compliant hotel is a new product in halal tourism that has a huge impact on the national economy. Muslims around the world have special needs and obligations when travelling, and the Shariah-compliant hotel will be able to fulfil some of those needs. Important needs include halal food and beverages, halal products and services, social needs, and the obligation to perform daily prayers. All these needs must be provided by hotels during their guest's stay.

Nevertheless, due to the unavailability of an established standard, the concept has been applied differently by different hoteliers. This also reflects different definitions of what a Shariah-compliant hotel is and, eventually, reflects different practices among the hoteliers. Furthermore, there is no government-linked certification body for the Shariah-compliant hotel. In the case of the hotel industry, the current certification by JAKIM is solely for halal, which is mainly for food and products. It does not cover other Shariah-compliance aspects as mentioned in this chapter.

Therefore, the Shariah-Compliant Hotel Operations Practices (SCHOP) approach has been developed to fill the gap in current practices. SCHOP aims to cover all aspects of Shariah compliance for a hotel. This would include the administration, common areas, bedroom, services, and food and beverages of the hotel. These practices, in fact, reflect the operations of most hotels

Table 6.4 SCHOP dimensions and attributes

1.0	*ADMINISTRATION*
1.1	*Management*
1.1.1	Shariah Advisory Committee
1.1.2	Islamic quality principles in hotel policy
1.1.3	Internal audit
1.1.4	Improvement programme
1.1.5	Zakah/social responsibility payment
1.1.6	*Islamic finance in terms of:*
1.1.6.1	Salary payment
1.1.6.2	Income saving
1.1.6.3	Investment
1.2	*Staff*
1.2.1	*Islamic human resources*
1.2.1.1	30% ratio of Muslim staff
1.2.1.2	Muslim dress code/proper attire
1.2.1.3	Prayer room for staff
1.2.1.4	Separate changing room (men/women) for staff
1.2.1.5	Muslim male staff break for Friday prayer
1.2.1.6	Friendly and helpful staff
1.2.1.7	Safety and security for staff
2.0	*COMMON AREAS*
2.1	*Separate facilities for men and women/time allocation*
2.1.1	Spa
2.1.2	Gym
2.1.3	Recreation/sport
2.1.4	Swimming pool
2.1.5	Lounge
2.1.6	Lift
2.1.7	Toilet
2.2	Halal soap in toilet
2.3	Prayer room for staff and guests
2.4	Attention to guests' safety/security and property
2.5	Islamic entertainment
2.5.1	Absence of magic show
2.5.2	Permitted music
2.6	Islamic architecture and interior design
3.0	*BEDROOM*
3.1	*Islamic room*
3.1.1	Qiblat direction

(*Continued*)

Table 6.4 (Cont).

3.1.2	Quran
3.1.3	Prayer mat
3.1.4	Prayer schedule
3.1.5	Absence of pictures of living beings
3.1.6	Bidet
3.1.7	Halal toiletries
3.1.8	Halal in-room food (creamer, coffee, etc.)
3.1.9	Absence of alcoholic beverages
3.1.10	Islamic in-room entertainment
3.1.11	Smoking vs. non-smoking room
4.0	*SERVICES*
4.1	*Reception/front desk*
4.1.1	Islamic greeting
4.1.2	Notification of the ban on alcoholic drink
4.1.3	Guest safety and security to the room
4.1.4	Information on Halal restaurants, mosques, and halal groceries
4.1.5	Wake-up call for Subuh prayer
4.1.6	Request for additional prayer mat, schedule, etc.
4.2	*Islamic marketing*
4.2.1	*Halal products/services*
4.2.1.1	Islamic packages
4.2.1.1.1	Weddings
4.2.1.1.2	Tours
4.2.1.1.3	Seminars/conferences
4.2.1.1.4	Absence of gambling activities
4.2.1.2	*Halal products*
4.2.1.2.1	Halal shopping arcade
4.2.1.2.2	Halal detergent for laundry
4.2.2	Ethical and fair pricing
4.2.2.1	Price display/information
4.2.2.1.1	Room
4.2.2.1.2	Meal
4.2.2.1.3	Products/packages
4.2.2.2	Absence of price discrimination
4.2.3	Ethical place
4.2.3.1	Proper location
4.2.3.2	Absence of unnecessary delay
4.2.4	Ethical promotion
4.2.4.1	Absence of sexual appeal
4.2.4.2	Absence of manipulation

(*Continued*)

Table 6.4 (Cont).

4.2.5	Islamic finance
4.2.5.1	Islamic finance transactions
5.0	*FOOD and BEVERAGES*
5.1	*Halal-certified restaurant*
5.1.1	Halal breakfasts
5.1.2	Halal meals (lunch/dinner, etc.)
5.1.3	Halal room service meals
5.2	Absence of alcohol

in the world. It is hoped that SCHOP provides proper guidelines for hoteliers to achieve better performance and more importantly to achieve the status of the Shariah-compliant hotel.

References

Abuznaid, S. (2012) 'Islamic marketing: Addressing the Muslim market', *An-Najah University Journal for Research—Humanities*, 26 (6): 1473–1503.

Al-Qardhawi, Y. (1995) *Halal and Haram dalam Islam*. Translated by S.A. Semai. Singapore: Pustaka Islamiyah.

Al-Zuhayli, W. (2002) *Financial Transactions in Islamic Jurisprudence. Vol. 2*. Translated by M.A. El-Gamal. Damascus: Dar Al-Fikr.

Arham, M. (2010) 'Islamic perspectives on marketing', *Journal of Islamic Marketing*, 1 (2): 149–164.

Aziz, Y.A. (2007) Empowerment and Emotional Dissonance: Employee Customer Relationships in the Malaysian Hotel Industry. PhD. University of Nottingham, UK.

Aziz, Y.A., Hassan, H., Hassan, M.W. and Othman, S. (eds) (2009) *Current issues in Tourism & Hospitality Services in Malaysia*. Serdang University: Putra Malaysia Press.

Azmi, I.A.G. (2009) 'Human capital development and organizational performance: A focus on Islamic perspective', *Shariah Journal*, 17(2): 353–372.

BERNAMA. (2011) *Malaysia to be More Aggressive to Dominate Global Halal Market*. [online] Available at: www.halalfocus.com (accessed 7 July 2012).

BIMB Institute of Reseach and Training. (2005) *Konsep Syariah Dalam Sistem Perbankan Islam*. Kuala Lumpur: BIMB BIRT.

Che Ahmat, N.H., Ahmad Ridzuan, A.H. and Mohd Zahari, M.S. (2012) 'Customer awareness towards syariah compliant hotel', paper presented at the International Conference on Innovation Management and Technology Research (ICIMT), Malacca, Malaysia.

Du Rand, G., Heath, E. and Alberts, N. (2003) 'The role of local and regional food in destination marketing: A South African situation analysis'. In C.M. Hall (ed.) *Wine, Food and Tourism Marketing*. New York: Haworth Hospitality Press, 97–112.

Hassan, A., Chachi, A. and Latiff, S.A. (2008) 'Islamic marketing ethics and its impact on customer satisfaction in the Islamic banking industry', *JKAU: Islamic Economy*, 21 (1): 27–46.

Henderson, J.C. (2008) 'Representations of Islam in official tourism promotion', *Tourism Culture and Communication*, 8 (3): 135–146.

Henderson, J.C. (2010) 'Sharia-compliant hotels', *Tourism and Hospitality Research*, 10 (3): 246–254.

Ibn Rusyd and Abu Walid Muhammad b. Ahmad al-Hafid. (1981) *Bidayah al-Mujtahid waNihayah al-Muqtasid. Vol. Juz 2*. Kaherah: Maktabah wa matba'ah Mustafa al-Babi al-Halabi wa Awladih.

Islamic Tourism Centre of Malaysia (ITC). (2017) *Muslim-friendly Tour Highlights*. [online] Available at: www.itc.gov.my/tourists/discover-the-muslim-friendly-malaysia/islamic-tour-highlights/(accessed 25 September 2017).

Jabatan Kemajuan Islam Malaysia (JAKIM). (1995) *E-fatwa*. [online] Available at: www.e-fatwa.gov.my /fatwa-kebangsaan/merokok-dari-pandangan-islam (accessed 2 April 2014).

Jabatan Kemajuan Islam Malaysia (JAKIM). (2017) *Senarai Hotel & Resort Yang Mendapat Sijil Halal Malaysia (Jakim)* [online] Available at: www.halal.gov.my/ehalal/directory_hotel.php (accessed 29 September 2017).

Kana, A.G. (2011) 'Religious tourism in Iraq, 1996–1998: An assessment', *International Journal of Business and Social Science*, 2 (24): 12–20.

Khan, B., Farooq, A. and Hussain, Z. (2010) 'Human resource management: An Islamic perspective', *Asia-Pacific Journal of Business Administration*, 2 (1): 17–34.

Malay Mail. (2014) *Malaysia Plans to Boost Islamic Tourism Sector, Says Ministry*, 4 January. [online] Available at: www.themalaymailonline.com/travel/article/malaysia-plans-to-boost-islamic-tourism-sector-says-ministry#bXSdD42qsAYGY4lw.97 (accessed 29 September 2017).

Malaysian Digest. (2016) *Malaysia Expects to Attract 3.2 million Inbound Muslim Tourist Arrivals*. [online] Available at: www.malaysiandigest.com/frontpage/29-4-tile/603224-malaysia-expects-to-attract -3-2-million-inbound-muslim-tourist-arrivals.html (accessed 28 September 2017).

Malaysian-German Chamber of Commerce & Industry. (2011) *Market Watch Malaysia 2010—The Food Industry*. [online] Available at: http://malaysia.ahk.de/fileadmin/ahk_malaysia/Dokumente/Sektorre ports/Market_Watch_2010/Food_2010__ENG_.pdf

Metelka, C.J. (1990) *The Dictionary of Hospitality, Travel & Tourism*. 3rd ed. Albany, NY: Delmar.

Mohamad Azhari, N.H. (2015) 'Tabung Haji's Syariah compliant hotels expanding', *BERNAMA*, 11 December. [online] Available at: www.bernama.com/en/features/news.php?id=1198350 (accessed 28 September 2017).

Muhammad, R. (2015) 'The global Halal market—stats & trends', *Halal Focus*, 16 January. [online] Available at: http://halalfocus.net/the-global-halal-market-stats-trends/(accessed 12 November 2015).

Nursanty, E. (2012) 'Halal tourism, the new product in Islamic leisure tourism and architecture', Department of Architecture; University of 17 Agustus 1945 (UNTAG) Semarang, Indonesia. [pdf] Available at: www.academia.edu/2218300/Halal_Tourism_The_New_Product_In_Islamic_Leisure_ Tourism_And_Architecture (accessed 24 February 2019).

Performance Management & Delivery Unit(PEMANDU).)2011) *Chapter 10: Revving Up the Tourism Industry*. [pdf] Available at: http://etp.pemandu.gov.my/upload/etp_handbook_chapter_10_tourism .pdf (accessed 27 February 2011).

Pew Research Centre. (2011) 'The future of the global Muslim population', The Pew Forum on Religious and Public Life, 27 January. [online] Available at: www.pewforum.org/The-Future-of-the-Global-Muslim-Population.aspx (accessed 10 September 2017).

Rajagopal, S., Ramanan, S., Visvanathan, R. and Satapathy, S. (2011) 'Halal certification: Implication for marketers in UAE', *Journal of Islamic Marketing*, 2 (2): 138–153.

Razalli, M.R., Shuib, M.S. and Yusoff, R.Z. (2013) 'Shariah compliance Islamic Moon (SCI Moon): Introducing model for hoteliers', paper presented at the Seminar Hasil Penyelidikan Sektor Pengajian Tinggi Kementerian Pendidikan Malaysia, UUM.

Rosenberg, P. and Choufany, H. (2009) 'Spiritual lodging: the Sharia-compliant hotel concept', *HVC-Dubai Office*: 1–6.

Sabiq, S. (1983) *Fiqh Al-Sunnah*. Dar Al-Fikr: Lebanon.

Sahida W., Rahman S.A., Awang, K. and Che Man, Y. (2011) 'The implementation of Shariah compliance concept hotel: De Palma Hotel Ampang, Malaysia', paper presented at the Conference on Humanities, Historical and Social Sciences, Singapore.

Seong, L. K. (2011) 'Halal certification as a spring board for SMEs to access the global market'. *The Star Online*, 28 May. [online] Available at: www.thestar.com.my/business/business-news/2011/05/28/halal-certification-as-a-spring-board-for-smes-to-access-the-global-market/(accessed 28 September 2017).

Samori, Z. and Sabtu, N. (2014) 'Developing hotel standard for Malaysian hotel industry: An exploratory study', *Procedia—Social and Behavioral Sciences*, 121: 144–157.

Suruhanjaya Sekuriti. (2006) *Buku Keputusan Majlis Penasihat Syariah Suruhanjaya Sekuriti*. Kuala Lumpur: Suruhanjaya Sekuriti.

Tourism Malaysia. (2009) 'Malaysia tourism key performance indicators 2009, annual tourism statistical report'. Ministry of Tourism and Culture, Kuala Lumpur, Malaysia.

Tourism Malaysia. (2011) 'Tourism Malaysia—statistics', Ministry of Tourism and Culture, Kuala Lumpur, Malaysia. [online] Available at: http://www.tourism.gov.my/statistics (accessed 23 March 2011).

Tourism Malaysia. (2017) 'Hotel & room supply', Ministry of Tourism and Culture, Kuala Lumpur, Malaysia. [online] Available at: http://mytourismdata.tourism.gov.my/?page_id=348#!from=2015&to=2016 (accessed 29 September 2017).

Vejzagic, M. and Smolo, E. (2011) 'Maqasid Al-Shari'ah in Islamic finance: An overview', paper presented at the 4th Islamic Economic System Conference, Kuala Lumpur.

Zailani, S., Omar, A. and Kopong, S. (2011) 'An exploratory study on the factors influencing the non-compliance to Halal among hoteliers in Malaysia', *Journal of Business Management*, 5 (1): 1–12.

7

ISLAMIC TOURISM

The practices of a Shariah-Compliant Hotel in De Palma Hotel, Malaysia

Sharifah Zannierah Syed Marzuki, C. Michael Hall, and
Paul W. Ballantine

Introduction

Malaysia has retained its primary position among other members of the Organisation of Islamic Cooperation (OIC) as the most halal/Muslim-friendly holiday destination for five consecutive years (Crescent Rating 2016). It took 130 destinations worldwide to generate the destination benchmark index in the Muslim travel market. The notion of Islamic tourism or halal tourism that emerged in recent years showed a phenomenal situation in the tourism industry and it has the potential to grow still further. It is expected that 35 million Muslim travellers from the Middle East will arrive in Malaysia in 2020 (Ariffin & Hasim 2009). Under the Crescent Rating (2016) Index, Malaysia has an index score of 81.9 followed by the United Arab Emirates at 74.7, and Turkey at 73.9.

Looking from a wider perspective, the study by Crescent Rating (2016) also revealed that there were an estimated 117 million Muslim international tourists globally and that figure would grow to 168 million visitors by 2020, which represents 11 per cent of the global market with a market value exceeding US$200 billion. Malaysia's tourism industry should be more proactive in tapping this niche market just as Japan and the Philippines have taken various initiatives to diversify their visitor arrivals. It would therefore be appropriate to understand the needs and preferences of Muslim travellers in order to gain advantage from this fast-growing opportunity.

The basis of Islamic tourism is that the industry must comply with what is stated in the *Quran* and *Hadith*. Muslim travellers are required to fulfil their religious duties, which include prayers five times a day and halal food in order to become a good Muslim. As such, hoteliers are keeping to these needs by having Shariah-compliant offerings. It is reported that there are 344 hotels in Malaysia that are halal certified although this refers to the certification of halal food section (Jabatan Kemajuan Islam Malaysia (JAKIM) 2017). However, there is no universal standard for the Shariah-Compliant Hotel (SCH) concept although there has been a growing focus on this Islamic service with respect to the hospitality industry. This is due to the fact that some hotels claim that they are SCH but some operations do not comply with the Shariah law, e.g. where Muslim female staff fail to fulfil an Islamic way of dress, and/or the facilities and amenities in the hotel room are still inadequate in meeting the demands of Muslim tourists.

Islamic tourism

Islamic tourism is a new trend as the number of Muslim travellers keeps growing at an increasing rate (Battour, Ismail & Battor 2010a, 2010b). This is in line with the overall growth in the number of Muslim followers (Zamani-Farahani & Henderson 2010). This is also an opportunity for Malaysia to promote Islamic tourism to this lucrative market as Islam emphasises that travel can improve health and well-being, reduce stress, and enable Muslims to serve God better (see also Chapters 1 and 2, this volume).

Apart from promoting the goodness of travelling, fulfilling Islamic requirements must also be taken into consideration as far as SCH is concerned. Islamic tourism is defined by three main goals that pertain to economic, cultural, and religious aspects (Neveu 2010). The first goal on economics is to further expand the development of tourism by focusing not only on the Muslim but also on the non-Muslim travellers. Looking at the cultural point of view, Islamic tourism is a means to promoting Islamic heritage and the norms of Islamic practices. As Zamani-Farahani and Henderson (2010: 79) suggest:

> Islam is the foundation of public and private life in Muslim nations and its influence extends to politics, especially in theocracies where the state and religion are indivisible. In these countries, society is ordered in conformity with the principles of the Islamic way, which directly and indirectly affects recreation and travel. Religion thus influences individual host and guest experiences, but also the operation of the industry, tourism policy making and destination development.

Travelling is mentioned in many verses in the Quran that symbolically emphasise that a good Muslim must travel and experience new things in terms of spiritual and social goals as well as the linkages on the purpose of life, environment, people, Islamic religion, and good deeds to be brought to the Hereafter. The lesson gathered from travelling is to prepare the Muslim followers to be ready on the stages in life and after life without ignoring the rules provided in the Quran and Hadiths.

Ye shall surely travel from stage to stage.

(Al-Inshiqaq [The Sundering] verse 19)

Travel through the earth and see what was the end of those who rejected Truth.

(Al-An'Am [The Cattle] verse 11)

Syed Marzuki (2012) defined Islamic tourism as primarily including tourism undertaken mainly by Muslims although it can extend to non-believers motivated to travel by Islam in the Muslim world. In contrast, Zailani, Omar and Kopong (2011) believed that halal tourism is an offering of tour packages and destinations that are particularly designed to cater for Muslim considerations and address Muslim needs. Importantly they note that it is not just applied to food but also includes any Shariah-compliant products ranging from bank dealings and finance to cosmetics and vaccines.

The value of the fast-growing Muslim tourism market is estimated at USD$500 billion annually and the halal market is worth USD$2.1 trillion (Zailani et al. 2011). Not surprisingly, the tourism sector has therefore been identified as one of the key drivers of economic activity in Malaysia (Sahida, Ab Rahman, Awang & Che Man 2011) and a key source of foreign exchange (Md Salleh, Abdul Hamid, Hashim & Omain 2014). The growth of Islamic tourism therefore opens an opportunity to the hospitality industry players to explore and take advantage of this lucrative market which, as well as requiring accommodation, will also increase demand for food and shopping.

Concept and operation of Shariah-Compliant Hotel (SCH)

Previous researchers have defined SCH as a hotel or other lodging that provides services in accordance with Shariah principles (Yusuf 2009; Sahida et al. 2011; Md Salleh et al. 2014; Ab. Halim, Syed Marzuki, Ab. Ghani Hilmi, Ali & Ishak 2016). Md Salleh et al. (2014) identified several factors that have contributed to the growth of SCH:

1 Proactiveness in developing the tourism industry among Organisation of Islamic Conference (OIC) countries including supporting travelling between its members;
2 Travellers from the Middle East have high spending power and they are most likely to stay longer when travelling;
3 Stringent security and difficulty in getting visas to travel to many Western countries have given the opportunity to other countries to gain a competitive advantage in the tourism industry with respect to offering SCH;
4 The growing awareness of Muslim travellers worldwide to search for hotel services that fulfill their religious needs;
5 Investors are increasingly interested in investing in Islamic tourism and SCH given the growth of the market; and
6 The emergence of global halal business valued at USD$500 billion annually and a halal market that is worth USD$2.1 trillion indicates the economic potential for SCH.

Nevertheless, as noted above, as well as various other chapters in this volume (e.g. see Chapter 2), there is no universal standard for a SCH but several attributes have been identified that include: the offering of halal food, separate facilities for women and men like gymnasium and swimming pool, the Islamic room amenities such as prayer mat, prayer clothing for both genders, a copy of Quran, qiblat direction (the direction that should be faced when a Muslim prays during prayer as it is fixed as the direction of the Kaaba in Mecca), Muslim staff working in a SCH, no night club, conservative television channels, and art that does not depict human form (Rosenberg & Choufany 2009; Henderson 2010; Razzaq, Hall & Prayag 2016). Saad, Ali and Abdel-Ati (2014) reiterated that the basis of SCH is to have the design, operations, and financial system that conform to the Shariah rules and principles. However, the concept of SCH about which they wrote in the Egyptian context is not one supported by formal accreditation procedures and is perhaps closer to being a set of guidelines for advertising and promotion.

SCH potentially faces a major challenge with respect to the absence of alcoholic drinks being offered on its premises (Saad et al. 2014). Any hotels that do not provide alcohol are considered as a 'dry' hotel and this may lead to a decrease of guests and number of stays. Henderson (2010), for example, indicated that SCH is taking up the challenge of not offering alcohol to guests although this action will reduce the number of patrons. Nevertheless, SCH may offer other forms of competitive advantage that can balance out any loss of revenue from no alcohol sales. However, as noted above, there is a lack of standards, specifications, and requirements for SCH that can distinguish them from other types of hotels (Rosenberg & Choufany 2009; Henderson 2010) and which may more clearly position the concept in the market.

De Palma—rebranding into Shariah-Compliant Hotel

This case study focuses on the concept of a SCH being operated by De Palma Hotel in Ampang, Selangor, which is a trendsetter of this Islamic concept in the midst of hundreds of conventional hotels in Malaysia. An in-depth interview with the management and observation of the operations were conducted. Semi-structured questions were asked to gather more findings on the uniqueness of the operations and facilities.

The transformation and rebranding to a SCH was launched in 2008 after receiving the support and guidance from a specially set up panel of Shariah Islamic Compliance and the consent of Selangor Islamic Department/Jabatan Agama Islam Selangor (JAIS). The concept was very encouraging and in less than a year people came to accept its existence, with it becoming the catalyst for the philosophy of visitation, worship, missionary values, and comradeship. From its introduction the De Palma Hotel was designed to create a clean and morally healthy image that is conducive to undertaking Islamic worship and facilitating a clear conscience for guests and visitors alike from the hotel experience.

De Palma is the first SCH chain in Asia, and has a range of halal hospitality facilities that can be found in the following locations in Malaysia:

- The flagship De Palma Hotel in Ampang, Kuala Lumpur, which is a four-star hotel designed for a range of Muslim travellers;
- De Palma Hotel in Shah Alam that caters for medium-scale functions and family groups in an academic and industrial setting;
- De Palma Ecoresort, Kuala Selangor, with a coastal setting for the family getaway;
- Palma Café at SACC Mall, Shah Alam
- The Palma Signature Restaurant at Kompleks PKNS in Bangi.

The De Palma Group of Hotels is one of the few in Malaysia that has received halal certification from the Department of Islamic Development Malaysia/Jabatan Kemajuan Islam Malaysia (JAKIM). Halal certification plays an increasingly significant role in the Malaysian hospitality industry (Syed Marzuki, Hall & Ballantine 2012a, 2012b, 2013). Within this context, De Palma provides facilities for Muslim guests to worship while travelling as well as other Muslim-friendly services. The sixth floor of the hotel in Ampang has been designated as an Islamic floor. It contains 29 rooms with special Islamic features such as an ablution tap, prayer mat, prayer clothing, a copy of Quran and hadith. The call of prayer can also be heard in the corridors. Islamic amenities provided by De Palma Hotel include:

- A surau (a worship place for Muslims which is smaller than a mosque) which is a centre for religious classes and lectures for staff and visitors;
- During the month of Ramadhan (fasting month), the hotel organises prayers and religious lectures by international Islamic speakers;
- The hotel also conducts comprehensive religious seminars and programmes on a continuous basis;
- Surau Nurul Hikmah located in the hotel is the first to be given the consent by JAIS to hold Friday prayer.

Apart from the amenities, this Islamic-friendly hotel also provides Islamic snacks such as dates and raisins in the hotel room. Arabic writings and Islamic replicas, such as swords, are also visible in corridors and rooms. A piece of *sarong* (a long piece of cloth) is available in shower rooms to comply with the Shariah rules while bathing. Referring to human resources, female Muslim staff are required to adhere to the Shariah dress code and a prayer is recited to welcome the hotel guests and before they leave. This prayer is for the safe journey of the hotel patrons.

De Palma has faced several challenges in launching their SCH products. Firstly, the public, hotel owners, and hotel guests have been very complacent with respect to changes to conventional hospitality concepts and are not used to religious-based hospitality products although most of the hotel guests are Muslims. Secondly, there is a review of thinking of what is required in providing Shariah-compliant services. Thirdly, this concept is considered to be costly from a business point of view. Finally, there was no precedent in this kind of concept and not taking a risk is regarded by many as a better option. However, the introduction of this SCH has benefited several parties including entrepreneurs, Islamic-based organisations and agencies, and the government, in various ways.

Conclusion

SCH is gaining acceptance among Muslim travellers in particular and it may be an appropriate time for the hospitality industry to adopt this business model. Providing an Islamic concept hotel is appropriate for attracting the Islamic tourism market. Non-Muslim tourists, and especially family markets, may also be attracted to use the facilities offered by hotels that claim to follow the Shariah concept although certain food and beverages are prohibited for consumption on the premises.

The De Palma Hotel, Ampang, has positioned itself as a pioneer in implementing the Shariah concept in its facilities and operations although the provision of the extra Islamic-based facilities has contributed to an increase in the operating budget. However, this has been counterbalanced by high occupancy rates and rising margins. The attributes of this hotel are unique and more comprehensive with respect to Shariah elements of its product if compared to counterparts that offer similar concepts in other countries and within Malaysia.

Of the greatest importance in delivering the SCH services is the competence of staff, cleanliness of facilities, and reasonable pricing. De Palma Hotel is aiming to embark on a new phase which is to introduce the Shariah concept to other states in Malaysia and to take its product internationally. There is a belief in a bright future for this sector in line with the demand from domestic and international Muslim travellers, the strength of Islamic concept, and the improvement in the transportation service for both inbound and outbound tourists. The company expect that the SCH provides a competitive advantage and has the potential to surpass the capability of conventional hotels with offerings to the Islamic market.

References

Ab. Halim, R., Syed Marzuki, S.Z., Ab. Ghani Hilmi, Z., Ali, R. and Ishak, M. (2016) 'Measurement of shariah compliant hotel selection factor using importance-performance analysis', *Journal of Global Business and Society Entrepreneurship*, 1 (2): 82–87.

Ariffin, A.A.M. and Hasim, M.S. (2009) 'Marketing Malaysia to the Middle East tourists: Towards a preferred inter-regional destinations', *International Journal of West Asian Studies*, 1: 39–53.

Battour, M.M., Ismail, M.N. and Battor, M. (2010a) 'Toward a halal tourism market', *Tourism Analysis*, 15 (4): 461–470.

Battour, M.M., Ismail, M.N. and Battor, M. (2010b) 'The impact of destination attributes on Muslim tourist's choice', *International Journal of Tourism Research*, 13 (6): 527–540.

Crescent Rating. (2016) 'Global Muslim Travel Index (GMTI) 2016'. [online] Available at: https://www.crescentrating.com/reports/mastercard-crescentrating-global-muslim-travel-index-gmti-2016.html (accessed 10 March 2017).

Henderson, J.C. (2010) 'Sharia-compliant hotels', *Tourism and Hospitality Research*, 10 (3): 246–254.

Jabatan Kemajuan Islam Malaysia (JAKIM). (2017) 'Halal Malaysia Directory'. [online] Available at: www.halal.gov.my/v4/index.php?data=ZGlyZWN0b3J5L2luZGV4X2RpcmVjdG9yeTs7Ozs=&negeri=&category=&cari=hotel (accessed 2 March 2017).

Md Salleh, N.Z., Abdul Hamid, A.B., Hashim, N.H. and Omain, S.Z. (2014) 'The practice of Shariah-compliant hotel in Malaysia', *International Journal of Trade, Economic and Finance*, 5 (1): 26–30.

Neveu, N. (2010) 'Islamic tourism as an ideological construction: A Jordan study case', *Journal of Tourism and Cultural Change*, 8 (4): 327–337.

Razzaq, S., Hall, C.M. and Prayag, G. (2016) 'The capacity of New Zealand to accommodate the halal tourism market—or not', *Tourism Management Perspectives*, 18: 92–97.

Rosenberg, P. and Choufany, H.M. (2009) *Spiritual Lodging: The Sharia Compliant Hotel Concept*. Dubai: HVS Global Hospitality Services.

Saad, H.E., Ali, B.N. and Abdel-Ati, A.M. (2014) 'Sharia-compliant hotels in Egypt: Concept and challenges', *Advances in Hospitality and Tourism Research*, 2 (1): 1–15.

Sahida, W., Ab Rahman, S., Awang, K. and Che Man, Y. (2011) 'The implementation of Shariah compliance concept hotel: De Palma Hotel Ampang, Malaysia'. In *2nd International Conference on Humanities, Historical and Social Sciences*, 17: 138–142.

Syed Marzuki, S.Z. (2012) Understanding Restaurant Managers' Expectations of Halal Certification in Malaysia. PhD. University of Canterbury.

Syed Marzuki, S.Z., Hall, C.M. and Ballantine, P.W. (2012a) 'Restaurant manager and halal certification in Malaysia, *Journal of Foodservice Business Research*, 15 (2): 195–214.

Syed Marzuki, S.Z., Hall, C.M. and Ballantine, P.W. (2012b) 'Restaurant manager's perspectives on halal certification', *Journal of Islamic Marketing*, 3 (1): 47–58.

Syed Marzuki, S.Z., Hall, C.M. and Ballantine, P.W. (2013) 'Sustaining halal certification at restaurants in Malaysia'. In C.M. Hall and S. Gössling (eds) *Sustainable Culinary Systems: Local Foods, Innovation and Tourism & Hospitality*. New York: Routledge, 256–274.

Yusuf, S. (2009) 'The real sense of Shariah hospitality concept', paper presented at The World Halal Forum, Kuala Lumpur, Malaysia.

Zailani, S., Omar, A. and Kopong, S. (2011) 'An exploratory study on the factors influencing the non-compliance to halal among hoteliers in Malaysia', *International Business Management*, 5 (1): 1–12.

Zamani-Farahani, H. and Henderson, J.C. (2010) 'Islamic tourism and managing tourism development in Islamic societies: The cases of Iran and Saudi Arabia', *International Journal of Tourism Research*, 12 (1): 79–89.

PART II
Halal markets and developments

8

HALAL SERVICE PROVISION— UNDERSTATED, BUT NOT UNDERVALUED

A view from Oman

Bronwyn P. Wood and Hamed Al-Azri

Introduction

This chapter looks at Muslims not so much by how they can be grouped by practice regardless of geography (Boulanouar, Aitken, Boulanouar & Todd 2017), but more how they can be grouped by practice *and* geography. It does this by considering the interest in halal service provision by Omani outbound travellers, particularly in their longer summer holiday travels. Omanis share general characteristics with their geographical neighbours— Yemen, and the GCC countries of United Arab Emirates, Saudi Arabia, Bahrain, Kuwait, Qatar—but also present some distinctions that make their experiences of particular interest. It is hoped that this study, as an exploration of Omanis' travel preferences, will allow the development of a framework which has generalisable characteristics to the wider Gulf, and possibly to the Muslim, travel market. Insights into how to best meet the needs of Muslim tourists in general, and the higher spending GCC travellers, in particular, could interest both academics and hospitality providers, in designing projects, commissioning market research, and developing offerings.

There are certain difficulties in writing about Muslims in English as the English language literature is commonly produced using Western paradigms and or with the underlying assumption that these paradigms are universal (Mukherji & Sengupta 2004; Elmessiri 2006; Venkatesh 1995), in spite of the knowledge that only a small portion of the world is Western or has an individualistic or even Christian heritage. With this in mind, citations from literature can also often fail to provide a comprehensive or complete applicable comparison, and we will try to address all elements relevant to our study in the clearest terms to make these citations relevant.

Oman

Oil was found in Oman in 1964, and Oman is a member country within the group known as the GCC (Gulf Cooperation Council). These are the Arab, Muslim, Middle Eastern countries which have economies centred around oil extraction and export located around the Arabia Gulf. All the countries in this group share common ethnic, religious, and geographic elements, but there are a number of distinctions amongst them as well. Oman is, in fact, the most distinct in a number of ways. Oman is the homeland of Ibadism (Hoffman 2001), a variation on the majority Sunnism of the surrounding countries (Saudi Arabia, United Arab Emirates, Yemen, Qatar, Kuwait) and of Muslims worldwide (~90 per cent) (Pew Research Centre 2009). The majority of the world's Ibadi Muslims live in Oman, and Oman's Sultan, Sultan Qaboos, is an adherent of Ibadism. Oman also has nationals from Sunnism (Peterson 2004) and a small number of Shi'a groups—around 5 per cent of the population, according to the Pew Research Centre (2009). There are also a number of other religious denominations residing side by side in Oman, in the form of the expatriate workforce. Oman is often considered the 'Switzerland' of the Middle East due to its policies of diplomacy and peacemaking in the region. For example, during the embargo from 2017 of Qatar by neighbouring countries, Oman has stood, with Kuwait, in not censuring Qatar.

Amongst the oil producers in the six-country member GCC, Oman is the second smallest producer, before Bahrain. It has a GDP of 26.9B Omani Riyals giving a GDP per capita of 6,456 Omani Riyals ($US16,775) (National Center for Statistics and Information. Sultanate of Oman (NCSI) 2015). Since the current Sultan came to power in 1970, Oman has experienced rapid and extensive growth in terms of infrastructure, education, and all other aspects of life, at times reaching rates as high as 1,370 per cent (1970s). Al-Lamki (2002) highlights this point by noting that pre-1970 there were just three primary schools in Oman, catering to only 900 male students. Today, Oman has a literacy rate of almost 100 per cent in the age group 24 and under, with literacy being lower in older age groups, and lowest in females over 50 at 30 per cent (NCSI 2016).

Oman also differs from its neighbours in that it also has a history of growing and catching food, despite the temperatures being very high and the summers hot and long. The Bedouin (nomadic) population in Oman is very low compared to many other countries in the region, due to the opportunities the landscape provides.

A commonality of Oman with its neighbours is that the government is interested in diversifying the economy and moving away from oil dependency. A further commonality is the large proportion of foreign (expatriate) labour in the workforce. Oman has a 45 per cent expatriate population of over 1.85 million people. Omani nationals total only 1,142,579 males and 1,117,126 females, for a total of 2,259,705 Omani people as at 2014 (European University Institute (EUI) and Gulf Research Centre (GRC) 2014). Omani nationals also make up a relatively small percentage of the workforce—almost 200,000 people in the public sector, and around 218,000 in the private sector as at 2015 (NCSI 2016). If one considers that 30 per cent of the Omani population is under 14 years old, and 35 per cent are women of whom many do not have any intention of seeking work, that proportion looks less stark. Oman has a very diverse linguistic population structure with English commonly spoken in addition to the native Arabic, and Baluchi or Swahili. Large numbers of Omanis who were living abroad returned to Oman when Sultan Qaboos came to power, most settling in the capital, Muscat. A significant number also returned from East Africa where Oman had been a ruling power for several hundred years (Patterson 2013; Valeri 2007). The rich tapestry represented by the many nationalities and languages spoken in addition to the diversity of religion and religious practice and the diplomatic policies of governance make Oman, and particularly Muscat, a varied and colourful environment.

Islam

While Oman hosts several different strands of Islamic practice, the overarching teaching is, in great majority, the same. Islam is a comprehensive way of life, which offers guidance on every aspect of life from food to sleeping (Maududi 1960; Al-Qaradawy 1995; Al Faruqi 1977). There is extensive acknowledgement that Islam embraces all aspects of social and economic life (Alserhan 2015; Bin Yusuf 2010). Bin Yusuf (2010: 220) argues that "the social life of a Muslim is Islam; the economic life of the Muslim is Islam; the political life of the Muslim is Islam". Although Islam is frequently represented as monolithic, legalistic, and rule-bound, it is, in fact, nuanced, synergistic, interlaced, and balanced (Elmessiri 1997) and, as such, gives rise to different cultures of practice.

The shared sources of Islamic law (Shariah) are several. They consist of the Qur'an (the Muslim Holy Book), the hadith (the collected traditions of the Prophet Mohammad), and the rulings of Islamic scholars of two types—analogy and scholarly consensus (as distinct from academics).

This chapter uses Islamic scholars as references for matters of Islamic teaching. Islamic scholars are acknowledged herein as products of a different education system to Western-trained academics. Islamic scholars are required to be experts in Arabic language, to have memorised the Qur'an and fulfil other requirements as well as being accepted as a scholar by other accepted scholars (Roald 2001). A range of scholars is referenced here. "Islamic Studies Academics" cannot issue fatawa (Islamic rulings), are not recognised by Islamic scholars, so they are palatable to other academics but are not regarded as specialists in this field by Islamic scholars, and are not accepted as sources of legislation for Muslims.

In Islamic teaching Muslims (believers) are considered equal in terms of worship—the evaluation of a Muslim's quality being measured on their performance of the requirements of the way of life, and the person's deeds. Muslims are required to demonstrate modesty (haya') in their speech, thought, and action, as modesty is seen as a defining characteristic of the Islamic way of life (Boulanouar 2006). Islam privileges privacy, but characterises privacy as a situation related to the people present, rather than a particular location. This illustrates the twin considerations of a Muslim, which are the vertical, or personal relationship with Allah, and also the horizontal, or societal relationships which make up active adherence to the Islamic model.

All Muslims are required to eat halal (permissible) food, which is almost everything, but does exclude pork and alcohol and their derivatives. For meat to be considered halal, it must be from an animal which has been killed as the name of Allah is mentioned. Any meat killed without that condition being met, cannot be considered halal. The concept of halal is much more than just an idea relating to meat or halal slaughter, it also relates to purity (tayyib) and considers people, products, and process, in a word pairing mentioned many times in the Qur'an.

Gender roles come into play in terms of division of labour and are considered to be related to the natures of each gender, both of which are considered complementary (not equal, not interchangeable). Women are responsible for the internal running of households, which includes educating children and managing décor, but is primarily a role of emotional support to family members; men, on the other hand, have financial imperatives, meaning they usually deal with external matters affecting the family. Motherhood is a very highly regarded role in Islamic teaching. In the majority of schools of Islamic law, the internal portion of the wife and mother's role does not include any responsibility for either cooking or housework. While there is a widespread belief that Islam is a patriarchal teaching, it should be noted that a sexist enactment of Islamic teaching by Muslim followers is not inherent in the framework (Sönmez 2001; Al Mazro'ei 2010).

In Islamic teaching women are free to make and keep their own money. Any money earned from rents or labour is not required to be shared or spent on the upkeep of the family or of the wife—the financial responsibility for the family belongs to the husband. Should the wife wish to contribute to the family, this is a charity from her to her husband (Briegel & Zivkovic 2008).

For Muslim women, there are considerations in terms of travel. Islamic teaching has stated that women must be accompanied by a male relative if travelling. There is a difference of opinion on this point in modern times, depending on whether the Islamic scholar believes the rule to be based on issues of safety, or on more than that—given that travelling is generally safe these days (Khimish 2014). In terms of marriage, Shariah allows women to choose their own spouse and encourages decision-making by consensus (shura), as it does in business and all of life (Weir 2000). All of these aspects of Islamic teaching bear some relationship to travel decision-making, selection of destination, and service requirements.

Omani culture

Ibadism emphasises mu'amalat, which is one of the branches of Shariah, and is the dealings between people (the horizontal worship mentioned above). This may explain the demeanour of the Omanis, which is polite, friendly, and welcoming to visitors and strangers. Omanis pride themselves on this reputation and extend it through their manner of international relations, as mentioned above. The model of relationships between people, especially genders, employed in Oman may not fit into the expected or dominant paradigm in the literature. Employing the wrong paradigm can lead to incomplete, misleading, or meaningless inter-pretations of study findings (Boulanouar & Boulanouar 2013).

Csikszentmihalyi and Rochberg-Halton (1981: 153) note that

> most philosophers and psychologists agree that for a person to develop his or her potentialities fully, it is necessary to take on challenges outside the home. The family, no matter how warm and fulfilling, cannot provide the varied contexts for action that are necessary for the growth of a self. From a societal viewpoint it is equally obvious that a healthy community requires participation in its affairs; excessive investment of attention in the family might in fact drain psychic energy from the pursuit of broader goals and thus decrease the vitality of the community.

In keeping with this viewpoint on (especially) women's development and empowerment, a number of papers in the literature concern Omani women's empowerment through both entrepreneurship (McElwee & Al-Riyami 2003; Ghouse et al. 2017) and specifically tourism (Afifi & Al-Sherif 2014; Mazro'ei & Shaw 2014; Mazro'ei 2017). The idea is that working in tourism could provide both personal empowerment and financial independence, and act as a salve for rural poverty which is widespread.

Varghese (2011: 37), in quoting Keller and Mbewe (1991), defined women's empower-ment as "a process whereby women become able to organize themselves to increase their own self-reliance, to assert their independent right to make choices and to control resources which will assist in challenging and eliminating their own subordination". Despite identifying tourism as a vehicle for women's empowerment, and also as a good economic objective for a country interested in finance diversification, many of the papers are pessimistic about a successful match between local culture and working in the sector. Varghese (2011: 47) concludes that "the women in Oman are empowered, but still her interest towards domesticity affects her empowerment, otherwise women would have been more empowered. In fact, 'social power' plays an important role in generating/sustaining inequalities between men and women".

Amzat et al. (2017: 6) are rather scathing about the attitude of Omani males to females, calling it "traditional … including their chauvinistic bias and stereotyped perception towards the status and roles of women in society". In fact, despite the policy introductions by the current Sultan, Amzat et al. (2017: 6) regard "culture and tradition [as] still hold[ing] them back from becoming equal with men". In their sample of female respondents aged in their twenties, they found that when no financial need exists for women to work, men prefer them to stay at home. They also reported that respondents feel themselves "that from a social point of view, they believe the women's place is in the home" (Amzat et al. 2017: 13). They conclude that "Omani society is a conservative one in which people stick to their traditions and sociocultural stereotypes remain wherein men believe that a woman's place is at home" (Amzat et al. 2017: 16).

Issues of definitions of what constitutes sexism and also where the focus of attention of members of societies should be are reflections of the cultural and religious paradigms one accepts. As mentioned above, believing empowerment to exist only in the paid workforce is just one framework, and seeing education as having an end no more extensive than vocational, a pair for that. The findings of the studies above with regard to Omani samples, may reflect shortsighted conclusions if respondents are not able to answer open-ended questions which unpack the detail of their responses. Goveas and Aslam (2011) identify several factors that encourage women to pursue careers in Oman. Amongst those are "the rights of women as stated in Islam, the role of His Majesty Sultan Qaboos [and] education" (Goveas & Aslam 2011: 233).

Tourism in Oman and the GCC

Although Omanis have been travelling abroad for quite some time, the positive attitude towards inbound tourism is relatively recent. Tourism courses are newcomers to university and college course offerings, and have only been available at all since 2001. Inbound tourism was impossible as late as 1986, with no tourist visas being issued for Oman (Ritter 1986). Several studies of tourism students in Oman show the industry is not well regarded as a career path (Khan & Krishnamurthy 2016), and despite government encouragement into the sector, targets are not met, and tourism courses fail to recruit their maximum capacity of students (Bontenbal & Aziz 2013). In distinct contrast, Alsawafi (2016) found strong support for tourism as a career for both women and men, and reported students found conflicts between culture and roles in both Islam and Omani culture to be insignificant.

Various themes are present in the literature available on the GCC outbound tourism. Young, well-educated travellers like to show off their economic well-being and social status (Observatoire Valaisan de Tourisme 2014) and this permeates their travel behaviour (Michael, Wien & Reisinger 2017). Kester and Carvao (2004) note that international travel is still an activity of the upper-middle and upper-income groups, and these people also tend towards upper-level education, which is a common trend in emerging markets. As far as outbound travel is concerned, GCC nationals spend 260 per cent more on airfares and 430 per cent more on accommodation than the world average (Bundhun 2012).

The Observatoire Valaisan du Tourisme (2014), in their analysis of the Gulf travel market, see Oman as an emerging source market. They note Omanis travel mostly in families for leisure, with the husband as the main travel decision-maker. This makes Oman in the group with Qatar and Saudi Arabia, whereas in UAE, Bahrain, and Kuwait children and wives play a more significant role in travel decision-making.

University students in general are commonly seen as travellers who seek risk-taking and sensation-seeking activities (for example, Mohsin et al. 2017), but many studies also fail to acknowledge that GCC outbound travel is largely family travel (Observatoire Valaisan de Tourisme 2014). Young adult travel also features considerations related to the use and communication properties of social media and photo-sharing sites (Dileep, Sindhu & Ismail 2017; Pengiran-Kahar, Syed-Ahmad, Ismail & Murphy 2010; Hosie 2017) with young men more interested in this than women.

A series of papers has been produced on outbound tourism from Oman by Alsawafi (2013, 2016) and Almuhrzi and Alsawafi (2017). The samples for all of these studies were under-graduate students from Rustaq College of Applied Sciences, which is a public college over 130km inland from the capital city, Muscat. Mohsin and Alsawafi (2011) examined push-and-pull motivations finding that the top ten included safety and security at the destination as the most important pull motivation, followed by natural attractions, availability of mosques, ease of communication (language), local attitudes towards Islamic culture in destination, shopping variety, availability of Arabic and or halal foods, attitudes towards Arabic culture at the destination, prices for goods and services, and a different climate to the one at home. Across these studies halal service provision, particularly access to mosques, language issues, destination attitudes towards Muslims, and availability of halal food were attractive to respondents (Mohsin & Alsawafi 2011).

The current study—results and discussion

For the study's exploratory primary data analysis, a mixed method was used. First, an interview with a local travel agent was conducted to examine their view of the Omani outbound tourism market. This was followed up with a survey of Sultan Qaboos University (SQU) students about their summer holidays in July and August 2017.

Stage One: Interview with a travel agent

An interview was conducted with the two co-founders of a local travel agent in Oman that organises both inbound and outbound packages/tours. The company was established in 2007, and both co-founders have given up their usual, full-time employment to focus on their travel business. The interview was conducted during the agency business hours, so was not recorded, rather, notes were taken. The strongest themes from the interview follow.

Most of the company's revenues (about 70 per cent) come from outbound tourists. The owners believe that inbound travel to Oman is affected by the regional political crises and international terrorism events, even though Oman is not directly involved in any of these. The travel agent has recently started organising business tours to Istanbul and China. While these tours are not yet sufficiently profitable, the travel agent is keen on them because they help build relations and strengthen the brand locally.

In terms of leisure travel, which is more relevant to the study at hand, the travel agent mostly serves honeymooners and families. The most popular destinations for their customers are Turkey, Malaysia, and Thailand. The travel agent believes that these top destinations are perceived by the market to be less risky, and have a good destination brand recognition in the country. Emerging destinations were also identified and included Azerbaijan and Bosnia. Customers usually enquire about general tourism information, safety, halal food, and privacy. However, they do not specifically demand halal services and will adapt whenever it is required, by seeking vegetarian or seafood when halal meat is not available, for example.

They would rather have value meals, than expensively promoted 'halal' food. The customers do not usually ask for alcohol-free accommodation and tours, and are more concerned about the overall experience of the destination.

The co-founders feel that the wives in families are highly influential in travel decision-making. This may be due to their education level, or the fact they are contributing to the financial cost of the trip. As mentioned above, in Islamic teaching Muslim women are not required to offer money they have or earn in support of the family, even if their husband has lesser means than themselves. The travel agent is, consequently, targeting wives in promotions. They report that this strategy seems to be successful in attracting customers.

Stage Two: Survey of university students

Sample demographics

For the second part of the study, a survey was distributed to a sample of Sultan Qaboos University students. A total of 81 students responded to the survey, 54 of which reported travelling in the summer. Consistent with a typical university student population, 81 per cent of the respondents were aged between 21 and 25 years old and 17 per cent aged between 17 and 20. None of the respondents was over 25 years old, or under 17. More than half the sample (58.3 per cent) were females. Family sizes were relatively large with 41.5 per cent having between 6 and 7 members and 30.2 per cent having 10 or more members. Close to 90 per cent of respondents' fathers were in the workforce (46.2 per cent in the government and 23.1 per cent in the private sector). Most mothers (84.3 per cent), on the other hand, were either retired or not employed. Most of respondents' fathers were educated, with 36.5 per cent having a high school/general diploma and 44.3 per cent having a Bachelor's degree or higher. Mothers, on the other hand, were significantly less well educated with only 23 per cent earning a university degree of any kind, 32.7 per cent having high school graduation, and 44.2 per cent had less education than that. As mentioned in the literature covering this region, most travel is family travel—only one of our respondents reported travelling alone. This is consistent with the age group of the respondents, the culture, and also Islamic norms, particularly for women.

Destinations travelled to

The first question asked respondents about their travel in the summer of 2017. Close to half the sample (46.3 per cent) travelled domestically, with Salalah leading the destinations (29.6 per cent of respondents). The UAE was slightly more popular (51.9 per cent among respondents) with Dubai being the most popular UAE—and overall—city destination, at 37 per cent of the sample. Only a few respondents travelled to Middle Eastern (13 per cent) and Asian destinations (7.4 per cent) and this consisted mostly of travel to Mecca and Medina (KSA) and to Malaysia. None of our respondents travelled to Turkey, despite it being identified as a good market for our travel agency. We consider this may reflect the age and life stage of our respondents. Turkey is considered a desirable honeymoon location for Omanis, and most of our sample are still single. Europe attracted 18.5 per cent of respondents, with the UK being the lead destination (11.1 per cent of the overall sample). Just 4 per cent reported travelling to an emerging destination (Azerbaijan). No respondents reported travelling further afield (to the Americas or Oceania).

Upon further investigation, small families (five or less members) were found to be more likely (50 per cent vs 17 per cent) to travel to Europe than larger families (six or more). This may reflect both the cost of a trip like this for many people and/or reflect the income level of the family. For example, it was found that all families that travelled to Asia had fathers with a government or private sector job. In terms of parents' education, there seems to be a clear association between both parents' level of education and travel to Europe; 34.8 per cent of those with highly educated fathers (Bachelor's degree or higher), compared with 10.3 per cent of those with lesser educated fathers; and 46.2 per cent of those with highly educated mothers, compared with 12.5 per cent of those with lesser educated mothers. Also, the data suggest that the lower the level of fathers' education, the higher the likelihood that the family would travel within Oman. This may reflect a lower salary being paid to a less well educated person, but also the recent financial downturn in Oman, and the concomitant response in the population with regard to spending. Value for money is a notable pull factor in this sample, given destination choices.

Major pull factors

Respondents were asked to rank the most important destination aspects they consider in making destination choices. As Table 8.1 shows, the two most important factors reported were destination fame (2.1) (ranked number 1 by 41 per cent of our sample with 1 being most important, and 5 being least important) and value for money (at 2.34 rank). Surprisingly, the provision of halal services was ranked the lowest on average (at 3.44). However, throughout the survey halal considerations were frequently mentioned and emphasised. This point will be discussed more fully below. In terms of the destination appearance, or 'Instagrammability', our finding is consistent with the literature and suggests it is of more interest to males than females.

Preferred types of destinations

Mostly, respondents reported a preference for destinations very similar to Oman (at 28.3 per cent), equalled by no clear preference, and followed at some distance (13.2 per cent) by a preference for destinations very different to Oman (15.1 per cent) (Table 8.2). As would be expected, destination choices in Oman and nearby were favoured for their safety, closeness in terms of both distance and culture, and affordability. The most cited explanations for far-flung choices were, in the majority, seeking new experiences, followed at some distance by the weather. The data suggest that smaller families with highly

Table 8.1 Most important destination aspects respondents consider in making destination choices

Destination aspect	% of respondents who ranked item first
Famous destination	41%
Value for money	31%
Destination distance	31%
Destination offering halal services	26%
The look of the destination (Instagrammability)	24%

Table 8.2 Destination similarity preferences

Destination similarity preference	Frequency	%
Only cities and attractions within Oman	6	11.3%
Very similar to Oman (GCC)	15	28.3%
Somewhat similar to Oman (Arab/Muslim)	7	13.2%
Somewhat different than Oman (Asian/African)	2	3.8%
Very different to Oman (Europe/Americas)	8	15.1%
No clear preference	15	28.3%

educated parents residing in the populous and dense coastal regions (Muscat and Batinah) are more likely to travel to Asia or Europe. These regions are historically more linked to the outside world by seafaring and contact with the Portuguese, the British, and with Africa and are home to a more diverse subcultural society.

Halal services

When asked about how important the provision of halal services is, 83 per cent indicated that they prefer (48 per cent) or would *only* (35 per cent) travel to destinations with halal services. This is not to say that they would not travel to places that did not provide halal services, as travellers were clearly prepared to alter their eating habits (by going vegetarian or eating only seafood) for the duration of the holiday. A further 15 per cent were indifferent, while none (0 per cent) *preferred* destinations not offering halal services. These results suggest that the provision of halal services could encourage Omanis to visit a destination, but absence of such services is not necessarily a hindrance. The most important halal services to respondents were halal food (83.3 per cent), a nearby mosque (48.1 per cent), a prayer mat in the hotel room (44.4 per cent), and a gender-separated gym or pool (40.7 per cent).

A few interesting associations were found in this regard. First, male respondents were more likely to rank halal provision more highly than female respondents (56 per cent male and 44 per cent females, compared to overall 42 per cent male and 58 per cent females). Second, families with highly educated fathers (Bachelor's degree or higher) were more likely to highly rank halal service provision (56 per cent highly educated versus 44 per cent lesser educated, compared to overall 44 per cent highly educated and 56 per cent lesser educated).

In terms of the provision of halal services (mostly food, prayer facility, and separated gym/pool), the survey results are generally supportive of the interview results in that halal services are probably in the minds of Omani travellers, but such services are not necessarily a condition in the choice of travel destinations. This is seen in respondents' lower ranking of halal service provision among important pull factors, and that at least half the respondents would not mind travelling to 'non-halal' destinations. Respondents justify this by saying they could adapt to the absence of halal services by eating vegetarian/seafood meals, by abstaining from drinking alcohol, and by using mobile apps to find out the *Qibla* (direction of Mecca for praying).

That being said, when asked for any further comments, respondents mentioned that halal service provision was appreciated by Muslim travellers, made them feel welcome, and "showed respect for their family". This is very important, because for hotels, these preferences are reasonably simple to incorporate into a guest experience. Just offering a prayer mat at check-in could make all the difference in terms of perceived quality of guest experience for travellers such as these.

Travel decision-making

The most important role in travel decision-making was attributed to fathers (at 56 per cent of respondents), followed by brothers (16 per cent), then mothers (14 per cent). In their explanation, respondents indicated that fathers were 'leaders' of the family, those with more experience in the area of travel or about the destination and the ones mostly financing the trips. Respondents had a very respectful and positive view of this, and were thoughtful about value for money in relation to the trip themselves, even though they were not funding it. This is a less common finding in the literature (Mohsin & Alsawafi 2011). Results also suggested a positive association between mothers' educational level and their role in travel decision-making. Namely, 20 per cent of highly educated mothers (Bachelor's degree or higher) have a greater role in travel decision-making, compared with only 12.5 per cent of less well educated mothers (high school graduation or less).

The survey findings in regard to travel decision-making are in contrast to the findings of the travel agency interview, where mothers/wives were perceived to be the main travel decision-makers. It is important to recall here that the travel agency has reported more honeymooners utilising its services. These couples would generally be younger than the parents of the survey respondents, as well as slightly older than the respondents themselves, and the wives would be expected—given the population demographics—to be more highly educated. This could largely explain the disparity in the finding of travel decision-making between the travel agency interview and the student survey. There was little evidence of shura decision-making between husbands and wives in our student sample. Where there was more mention of shura, it was between siblings or the whole family together, rather than just between parents.

Conclusion

This exploratory study sheds more light onto the emerging area of halal travel by investigating travel preferences, perceived importance of halal service provision, and the role of mothers/wives in travel decision-making amongst Omani nationals. The three main themes which emerged in the travel agent interview have been further investigated through a sample of students reporting on their summer holiday travel. A very clear outcome of this investigation has been the distinct segments reflected in the outcomes. University students, aged 25 and under, clearly reflect the cumulative policies implemented since 1970 and evidenced by the almost 100 per cent literacy of this group. In contrast, the parents of these students fall into the age groups which were less affected by the introduction of extensive schooling for Omanis (particularly women) and from a marketing, and tourism targeting perspective, this is a very valuable finding.

While the travel agent interviewed is targeting younger and more educated urban couples, the student survey conducted gave attention to an older generation. A commonality across our two rather disparate segments was the perceived importance of halal service provision, which was very similar among the two sets within the market. This reflects halal service provision as a 'constant' of consideration, rather than a top of mind consideration. Across all ages and genders, geographical locations and education levels, halal service provision was important. In fact, Islamic considerations were strongly reflected throughout the study, with a noticeable demand indicated for segregated pools and gyms a strong nod in the direction of both privacy and religious norms—albeit one service hotels may find it more difficult to provide. One solution is to ensure the pool and gym are provided with window coverings which can be closed during women's only session times if completely separate facilities are not provided.

The preferred destination selection and the role of wives/mothers in travel decision-making signalled in the travel agency interview were not reflected in the student survey data. It is speculated that this disparity is an indication of a coming generational shift. While the parents, and especially the mothers, of the student respondents were less well educated and less likely to be employed, newer generations are increasingly advancing in their education level and career aspirations. This suggests that the Omani travel market is about to witness an important change in travel preference and travel decision-making. Nevertheless, the opposing force of changing economic conditions must also influence this market. The combined effect could lead to an increase in the preference for domestic and nearby destinations in the Middle East and Asia, although it is expected that Omanis would continue to explore different and new destinations, consistent with their history, culture, and outlook.

This study has indicated findings which bear considerably more scrutiny. An expansion in terms of number of respondents, in terms of depth with the incorporation of interviews, and also in terms of time in seeing if the expectations signalled here are borne out over the next few years—particularly in the area of women's decision-making roles and influence—are warranted. Extending the sample well beyond university students would overcome a limitation of the present study, and we hope will provide useful and useable insights to those interested in this area.

References

Afifi, G. M. and Al-Sherif, N. (2014) 'Women occupational empowerment in the Omani tourism sector', *European Journal of Tourism, Hospitality and Recreation*, 5 (1): 53–84.

Al-Lamki, S.M. (2002) 'Higher education in the Sultanate of Oman: The challenge of access, equity and privatization', *Journal of Higher Education Policy and Management*, 24 (1): 75–86.

Al-Qaradawy, Y. (1995) *Introduction to Islam*. Egypt: Islamic Inc. Publishing and Distribution.

Al Faruqi, I.R. (1977) *Islam: Movement for World Order*. Washington, DC: International Institute of Islamic Thought.

Al Mazro'ei, L. (2010) The Experiences of Muslim Women Employed in the Tourism Industry: The Case of Oman. MA. University of Waterloo.

Almuhrzi, H.M. and Alsawafi, A.M. (2017) 'Muslim perspectives on spiritual and religious travel beyond Hajj: Toward understanding motivations for Umrah travel in Oman', *Tourism Management Perspectives*, 24: 235–242.

Alsawafi, A.M. (2013) Holiday Destinations: Understanding the Perceptions of Omani Outbound Tourists. PhD. University of Waikato.

Alsawafi, A.M. (2016) 'Exploring the challenges and perceptions of Al Rustaq College of Applied Sciences students towards Omani women's empowerment in the tourism sector', *Tourism Management Perspectives*, 20: 246–250.

Alserhan, B.A. (2015) *The Principles of Islamic Marketing*. Farnham, UK: Ashgate.

Amzat, I. H., Al-Ani, W.T.K., Ismail, O.H. and Al Omairi, T. (2017) 'Women's empowerment and its effect on community development in Oman: Predictive model and indicators for best practices', *Community, Work & Family*, 21 (1): 1–19.

Bin Yusuf, J. (2010) 'Ethical implications of sales promotion in Ghana: Islamic perspective', *Journal of Islamic Marketing*, 1 (3): 220–230.

Bontenbal, M. and Aziz, H. (2013) 'Oman's tourism industry: Student career perceptions and attitudes', *Journal of Arabian Studies*, 3 (2): 232–248.

Boulanouar, A.W. (2006) 'The notion of modesty in Muslim women's clothing: An Islamic point of view', *New Zealand Journal of Asian Studies*, 8 (2): 134–156.

Boulanouar, A.W. and Boulanouar, Z. (2013) 'Islamic marketing and conventional marketing theory: A brief case study of marketing what Muslim women wear', *International Journal of Teaching and Case Studies*, 4 (4): 287–295.

Boulanouar, A.W., Aitken, R., Boulanouar, Z. and Todd, S.J. (2017) 'Imperatives for research designs with Muslim women', *Marketing Intelligence & Planning*, 35 (1): 2–17.

Briegel, T. and Zivkovic, J. (2008) 'Financial empowerment of women in the United Arab Emirates', *Journal of Middle East Women's Studies*, 4 (2): 87–99.

Bundhun, R. (2012) 'Emirates airline tour operator sets sights on 25% boost in business'. *The National*, 9 May.

Csikszentmihalyi, M. and Rochberg-Halton, E. (1981) *The Meaning of Things: Domestic Symbols and the Self.* Cambridge: Cambridge University Press.

Dileep, M., Sindhu, S. and Ismail, A.A. (2017) 'Influence of new media on travel decision making', *Atna Journal of Tourism Studies*, 8 (1): 1–16.

Elmessiri, A.M. (1997) 'Features of the new Islamic discourse', *Encounters*, 3: 45–63.

Elmessiri, A.M. (ed.) (2006) *Epistemological Bias in the Physical & Social Sciences.* London: International Institute of Islamic Thought.

European University Institute (EUI) and Gulf Research Centre (GRC). (2014) 'Oman: Population by nationality (Omani/non-Omani), sex and age group (mid-2014)'. *Gulf Labour Markets, Migration and Population (GLMM) Programme.* [online] Available at: http://gulfmigration.eu/tag/foreign-national-populations/

Ghouse, S., McElwee, G., Meaton, J. and Durrah, O. (2017) 'Barriers to rural women entrepreneurs in Oman', *International Journal of Entrepreneurial Behavior & Research*, 23 (6): 998–1016.

Goveas, S. and Aslam, N. (2011) 'A role and contributions of women in the Sultanate of Oman', *International Journal of Business and Management*, 6 (3): 232–239.

Hoffman, V.J. (2001) *Ibadi Islam: An Introduction.* [online] Available at: http://islam.uga.edu/ibadis.html

Hosie, R. (2017) '"Instagrammability" most important factor for millennials on choosing holiday destination'. *The Independent*, 24 March. [online] Available at: https://www.independent.co.uk/travel/instagrammability-holiday-factor-millenials-holiday-destination-choosing-travel-social-media-photos-a7648706.html

Keller, B. and Mbewe, D.C. (1991) 'Policy and planning for the empowerment of Zambia's women farmers', *Canadian Journal of Development Studies/Revue canadienne d'études du développement*, 12 (1): 75–88.

Kester, J.G. and Carvao, S. (2004) 'International tourism in the Middle East; and outbound tourism from Saudi Arabia', *Tourism Economics*, 10 (2): 220–240.

Khan, F.R. and Krishnamurthy, J. (2016) 'Future of Oman tourism: Perception of the students in tourism studies', *International Journal of Tourism & Hospitality Reviews*, 3 (1): 1–11.

Khimish, H.A. (2014) 'The impact of religion on Arab women', *International Journal of Business and Social Science*, 5 (3): 32–42.

Maududi, S.A.A. (1960) *Towards Understanding Islam.* Kuwait: Al Faisal.

Mazro'ei, L.A., & Shaw, S.M. (2013) 'Building Muslim women's resistance through tourism employment', *Tourism Culture & Communication*, 13 (3): 175–189.

Mazro'ei, L.B. (2017) Questioning Women's Empowerment through Tourism Entrepreneurship Opportunities: The Case of Omani Women. PhD thesis, Edinburgh Napier University.

McElwee, G. and Al-Riyami, R. (2003) 'Women entrepreneurs in Oman: Some barriers to success', *Career Development International*, 8 (7): 339–346.

Michael, N., Wien, C. and Reisinger, Y. (2017) 'Push and pull escape travel motivations of Emirati nationals to Australia', *International Journal of Culture, Tourism and Hospitality Research*, 11 (3): 274–296.

Mohsin, A. and Alsawafi, A.M. (2011) 'Exploring attitudes of Omani students towards vacations', *Anatolia—An International Journal of Tourism and Hospitality Research*, 22 (1): 35–46.

Mohsin, A., Lengler, J. and Moyano, C.M. (2017) 'Travel intention of Brazilian students: Are they ready to discover new places and things?', *Tourism Analysis*, 22 (4): 483–496.

Mukherji, P. and Sengupta, C. (eds) (2004) *Indigeneity and Universality in Social Science: A South Asian Response.* New Delhi: Sage.

National Center for Statistics and Information. Sultanate of Oman (NCSI). (2015) *Key Indicators.*

National Center for Statistics and Information. Sultanate of Oman (NCSI). (2016) *Omani Women: Partnership and Development*. [online] Available at: https://www.ncsi.gov.om/Elibrary/Pages/Library ContentDetails.aspx?ItemID=JlAjy2xzgz74YCxg64ZrMQ%3D%3D

Observatoire Valaisan de Tourisme. (2014) *The Gulf Cooperation Council (GCC) Source Market Report*, 2014. [pdf] Available at: https://www.tourobs.ch/media/12508/gcc-source-market-report-ovt-2014.pdf

Patterson, M. (2013) 'The forgotten generation of Muscat: Reconstructing Omani national identity after the Zanzibar revolution of 1964', *The Middle Ground Journal*, 7. [online] Available at: https://www2 .css.edu/app/depts/HIS/historyjournal/index.cfm?name=The-Forgotten-Generation-of-Muscat:-Reconstructing-Omani-National-Identity-After-the-Zanzibar-Revolution-of-1964&cat=5&art=228

Pengiran-Kahar, D.I.N.-F., Syed-Ahmad, S.F., Ismail, S.H.S. and Murphy, J. (2010) 'Shared Arabian Muslim travel photos', Information and Communication Technologies in Tourism 2010: 543–554.

Peterson, J.E. (2004) 'Oman's diverse society: Northern Oman', *The Middle East Journal*, 58 (1): 32–51.

Pew Research Centre. (2009) 'Mapping the global Muslim population', *The Pew Forum on Religious and Public Life*, 7 October. [online] Available at: www.pewforum.org/2009/10/07/mapping-the-global-muslim-population/

Ritter, W. (1986) 'Tourism in the Arabian Gulf Region—Present situation, chances and restraints', *GeoJournal*, 13 (3): 237–244.

Roald, A.S. (2001) *Women in Islam: The Western Experience*. London: Routledge.

Sönmez, S. (2001) 'Tourism behind the veil of Islam: Women and development in the Middle East'. In Y. Apostolopoulos, S.F. Sönmez and D.J. Timothy (eds) *Women as Producers and Consumers of Tourism in Developing Regions*. Westport, CT: Praeger, 113–142.

Valeri, M. (2007) 'Nation-building and communities in Oman since 1970: The Swahili-speaking Omani in search of identity', *African Affairs*, 106 (424): 479–496.

Varghese, T. (2011) 'Women empowerment in Oman: A study based on women empowerment index', *Far East Journal of Psychology and Business*, 2 (2): 37–53.

Venkatesh, A. (1995) 'Ethnoconsumerism: A new paradigm to study cultural and cross-cultural consumer behavior'. In J.A. Costa and G.J. Bamossy (eds) *Marketing in a Multicultural World: Ethnicity, Nationalism and Cultural Identity*. London: Sage, 26–67.

Weir, D. (2000) 'Management in the Arab world: A fourth paradigm?' In A. Al-Shamali and J. Denton (eds) *Arab Business: The Globalisation Imperative*. Kuwait: Arab Research Centre, 60–76.

9

EXPLORING MUSLIM MILLENNIALS' PERCEPTION AND VALUE PLACED ON THE CONCEPT OF 'HALAL' IN THEIR TOURISM PREFERENCES AND BEHAVIOURS

Talha Salam, Nazlida Muhamad, and Mazuri Abd Ghani

Millennials are much more likely to be intrigued about a trip to Thailand rather than the $8,000 Rolex watch that defined affluence for previous generations.

(Swartz 2016)

What makes the millennial Muslim market unique is their cross-cultural background, their love for the internet, and the mastering of social media. It is not an age group that brands should target but a mind-set.

(Salmani 2016)

Muslim tourists and halal tourism are gaining increased recognition as a distinctive tourist segment and area of tourism research respectively. Stakeholders across tourism industry are gearing up to adopt 'halal' tourism, as evident in a number of initiatives across tourism industry (Battour & Ismail 2016). These developments are based on the premise that Muslim consumers value halal products and services. It is irrational to assume Muslim consumers around the globe and across many generational cohorts are uniform in their preferences and behaviours. Therefore, amid the excitement surrounding halal tourism, a pertinent yet unanswered question is the importance of halal in tourism among different segments within the over 1.6 billion Muslim consumer market. This study presented in this chapter explores value of halal among one of the most important Muslim tourist segments—Muslim millennials.

Muslim millennials appear to have a different disposition in the internet-connected world. A 2012 report by PricewaterhouseCoopers (PwC) Malaysia has pointed to different rising incomes and peculiar preferences among the Malaysian millennials. More interest in working flexibly and eyeing international opportunities amid being ardent technology users are some of the defining characteristics for millennials (PwC 2012). Similar observations have been made for Asian millennials in general (Wu 2017). These are among the ever-increasing studies done on millennials. In marketing segmentation research, *millennials* represent the consumers born between 1980 and 2000 and are also known as Generation Y (PwC 2012; Valentine & Powers 2013). Millennials were born in and later grew up in the era of information technology.

At an industry level, there is an increasing interest in studying the preferences of millennials (aged 18–35 years as of 2016–2017) within the overall Muslim consumer market. This increase in interest is particularly visible in the latest edition of the *Global Islamic Economy Report* (Thomson Reuters 2016). This edition dedicated a portion of its research on different sectors of the Islamic economy to understanding the preferences of Muslim millennials. Amid the heightened interest in the industry, academic research on Muslim tourists fell short of particularly investigating the preferences of Muslim millennial tourists. This study is an attempt to fill this research gap.

Literature on tourism points to a number of tourist behaviours and decisions that tourists take during travelling. Tourist behaviours and decisions are influenced by different factors including their personality traits. For Muslim tourists, the decisions like destination selection, place to stay, and what and where to eat can be further influenced by Islamic injunctions. This can be expected of Muslim tourists in general, based on the influence of religion on consumer preferences and behaviours. However, when it comes to Muslim millennials, we do not know the significance of halal in their preferences and decisions.

Therefore, to fill this gap in our comprehension, we are exploring the tourist behaviours and preferences of Muslim millennials. In particular, we are trying to identify what is the value of halal in their preferences and decisions. The term 'halal' is deeply associated with Islam. It literally means permissible and connotes those things that Muslims can consume. In the same vein, the connotation used for halal in this research question is to see the influence of Islamic injunctions on Muslim consumers' decision-making in the area of being a tourist. In other words, value placed on halal relates to the importance given to Islamic injunctions. This is expressed in the main research question of this study: What is the value Muslim millennial tourists place on 'Halal' in destination choice and other tourist preferences?

The primary research question is focused on the halal element alone. To gain a comprehensive understanding of Muslim millennial tourists, we also undertook to explore the associated research question: What are the different factors that influence tourist preferences and behaviours among the Muslim millennial tourists?

To explore these research questions, the rest of this chapter is organised as follows. A literature review covers research on tourist behaviours, Islam and tourism, and Muslim tourists. This leads to the methodology section detailing the research design. Results and findings are presented next and discussed in detail under different sections. Finally, the chapter concludes with a discussion of findings, which also covers the research limitations and future research directions.

Literature review

To better understand the tourist behaviours among Muslim millennials, this literature review covers the extant literature in tourism, halal tourism, and millennial segmentation. First, a review of different forms of tourist behaviours and preferences are discussed. This is followed by a review of current trends in halal tourism and studies on Muslim tourists' behaviours and preferences. Finally, the literature review is complemented by reviewing literature on defining millennials as well as Muslim millennials as distinctive segments. A research agenda is developed and presented from this literature review in the next section.

Tourism and tourist behaviours

An ordinary consumer, living in any part of the world, assumes the role of a traveller when he or she is disinhibited from his home. Yet, for the purpose of compiling information, a tourist or visitor is discerned from a traveller using the length of his/her stay. This distinction is expressed in the definition of a tourist or visitor used by the World Tourist Organization: "A visitor (domestic, inbound or outbound) is classified as a tourist (or overnight visitor), if his/her trip includes an overnight stay, or as a same-day visitor (or excursionist) otherwise" (United Nations World Tourism Organization (UNWTO) 2014). Accordingly, a tourism trip is a trip taken by a tourist or visitor for any reason other than gaining employment (United Nations Department of Economic and Social Affairs Statistics Division (UNSTATS) 2008). In congruence with these widely inclusive definitions of tourist and tourism, the motivations to undertake tourism are also quite diverse—ranging from tourism for casual recreation to health tourism.

Within the diverse forms of tourism, there are a range of activities which are regarded as tourist behaviours. Pizam and Sussmann (1995) enumerated 20 tourist behaviours including activities like taking photographs, bargaining during shopping, and travelling alone or in groups, among others. Using factor analysis, these behaviours were grouped into five categories including: social interactions, commercial transactions, activities preference, bargaining factor, and knowledge of destination. These behaviours define the travelling style of different individuals and were found to be influenced by the nationality of tourists. Manrai and Manrai (2011) listed a number of behaviours divided in the three categories of before, during, and after-travel behaviours. Examples of tourist behaviours in these lists included binary decision of travelling or not (before travel), length of stay (during travel), and destination revisit intention (after travel).

Another important aspect of tourist behaviour is the decision-making process. Based on an extensive review of earlier studies, Cohen, Prayag and Moital (2014) discussed 'decision-making' among the tourists as a key process. They argued that contrary to common belief, tourist decision-making is not an extensive and disciplined process. Among the decisions made by a tourist, selection of destination is a major decision, which has been classified as a tourist behaviour (Manrai & Manrai 2011). Manifested either as a tourist decision or behaviour, destination choice can be attributed to different social, economic, and personality traits. Reviewing literature on tourist behaviours, Lepp and Gibson (2008) talk about the role of sensation-seeking as a distinct personality trait besides novelty-seeking and risk-taking. These traits influence a tourist's style of travelling and tourism-related preferences.

An emerging area in understanding the factors influencing tourist behaviour is the concept of self-image or self-concept of any tourist. Todd (2001) applied self-theory to study self-concept in the case of tourist behaviour. The self-concept model was found to have some applicability in the context of tourism as well. Consequently, it is important to understand that how a tourist perceives himself or herself, then this self-concept will define their style of thinking and even behaviours. Similar application of consumers' self-image has also been done in the context of tourism (Murphy, Benckendorff & Moscardo 2007). This also reifies the importance of a consumers' self-image in his or her tourist behaviour and destination choice.

Islam and tourism: halal tourism

Within the academic and industry research on tourism, halal tourism is a burgeoning area. In successive editions of the *Global Islamic Economy Report* (GIER), there is a continued emphasis on halal travel as a key segment of Islamic economy. According to recent estimates in GIER, the volume of Islamic economy is around USD1.8 Trillion and halal tourism has hovered around USD150 Billion (Thomson Reuters 2016). To understand the growing industry of halal tourism, it is useful to understand the existing research on Islam's perspective on tourism.

According to Din (1989), Islam's views on tourism differ from contemporary, secular views. Seemingly, there is not much encouragement for tourism only for the pleasure of it. Instead, Islam views tourism as a purposeful journey aimed at earning livelihood through trade and even bringing Muslims from different parts of the world together. Such journeys and tourism activity demand perseverance and patience from travellers. Jafari and Scott (2014) have discussed exploring the world as another important facet of travelling (and tourism) in Islam. Their assertion is based on the verses of Holy Quran, which ordain Muslims to engage in travelling for the sake of gaining knowledge and exposure. As a consequence, travelling and tourism has to be an act of consideration and contemplation and should be spiritually 'purposeful'. These reflections imply that tourism for economic, social, cultural, and learning reasons is permitted and even encouraged in Islam.

According to Mohsin, Ramli and Alkhulayfi (2016): "Halal tourism refers to the provision of a tourism product and service that meets the needs of Muslim travelers to facilitate worship and dietary requirement that conform to Islamic teachings." The industry trends and market practices in tourism industry also corroborate this definition of halal tourism. There has been a consistent increase in the number of tourist destinations and organisations keen on accommodating Muslim consumers by being Muslim-friendly (Seth 2016). Japan is one recent example in this regard, where a surge in Muslim tourists mostly from Malaysia and Indonesia led to creating policies and guidelines for making Japan a Muslim-friendly destination (Penn 2015).

Muslim tourists

There are a few studies on finding the preferences of Muslim tourists from different regions. In an unprecedented qualitative research on tourism preferences of Muslim tourists from North America, Shakona et al. (2015) found Islamic injunctions to have a clear influence on Muslim tourist preferences. The study resulted in a list of different considerations of Muslim tourists. These considerations pertained to availability of a mosque to pray, following rules for *hijab* and *Mahram*, eating halal food, and being cautious of their actions during the fasting month of *Ramadan*.

Among Muslim countries, Malaysia has been consistently leading in different indicators that constitute halal travel in the *Global Islamic Economy Report* (Thomson Reuters 2015, 2016). In addition to the strong and positive indicators for inbound tourism, Malaysian tourists are also deemed to be an important consumer segment among Asian tourists. In a competitive analysis, Kim, Im and King (2015) studied the preferences of Malaysian Muslim tourists comparing South Korea, China, and Japan as destination choices. The study found that 'environment' and 'access to Muslim culture' were the two most important factors in destination choice among the Malaysia Muslim tourists. Within 'access to Muslim culture', factors like accessibility of prayer space and halal restaurants were the main concerns. Another study covering Malaysian tourists focused particularly on students or young tourists. The study focused mainly on their activities and preferences like staying at a hotel or relatives, duration of stay, and spending patterns (Chiu, Ramli, Yusof & Ting 2015).

Among different factors studied, religiosity or religiousness of a tourist is expected to have a bearing on Muslim tourists. In part, this proposition is made based on the generic findings that Muslims as consumers exhibit a great influence of their religion. However, there is evidence of influence of religiosity in tourism literature as well. As Shakona et al. (2015) and Kim et al. (2015) showed, Muslim tourists exhibit a strong influence of Islamic injunctions in destination selection and activities during the trip. Such observations have led to a surge in research in the domain of halal tourism.

Despite the visible importance of Muslim millennials in the industry, there is limited academic research on this segment. In the case of tourism literature, this research gap is even more profound. In research on Muslim tourists, Kim et al. (2015) studied Malaysian Muslim consumers and not specifically millennials. On the other hand, Chiu et al. (2015) focused on young consumers but not necessarily Muslims. Thus, there is no specific study exploring the preferences of Muslim millennial tourists and the value this important segment places on the concept of halal in tourism.

Methodology

This study is mainly exploratory in nature aimed at finding the preferences of Muslim millennial tourists. Primary focus was to determine the value of halal in defining the tourism behaviours and preferences of Muslim millennial tourists. To elicit respondents' opinions on their tourism preferences and behaviours, a survey consisting of open-ended questions was used. Use of open-ended questions allows respondents to give their opinions more freely albeit there are concerns as to whether they can give their opinions or not (Geer 1988). Haddock and Zanna (1998) have underscored the usefulness of open-ended questions in eliciting consumers' beliefs, attitudes, and behaviours. They also showed from previous research that respondents do not find it difficult to answer open-ended questions to express their evaluative opinions.

The survey instrument was in two parts. In the first part, open-ended questions for preferences of destination choice, place to stay, and places to eat were asked. In this part, respondents were asked to give their opinions and preferences in open-ended questions, without any mention of halal or Islamic. The second part of the survey contained a mix of open and closed questions. In this part, respondents were specifically asked about their preferences relating to halal in choosing a destination, place to stay, and place to eat. The response options were: not important at all, slightly important, moderately important, very important, and extremely important—later coded on a five-point scale of 1 to 5 respectively. In this way, moderately important at 3.0 was the midpoint response. The last set of questions asked consumers about their self-image on being a Muslim tourist or global tourist. This question was aimed at exploring the self-image of Muslim millennials. Being a global tourist manifested their connectedness, while being a Muslim tourist shows their association with their religion. In this manner, the two parts of the survey were effectively 'unaided' and 'aided' recall for halal in responses. This allowed for exploring and comparing both the unaided and aided recall for halal in different aspects of tourism.

The questionnaire was administered using the online survey platform, *Qualtrics*. The interactive features of *Qualtrics* ensured that in this self-administered survey, respondents had to reply progressively from one section to the other. They were not allowed to navigate back to previous parts. Such an arrangement ensured that respondents could not change their responses in the first part (where no cues for halal were given), after seeing the second part (which was about the importance of halal in tourist activities). If any respondent had gone back to the first part after realising the importance of halal in the second part, the element of unaided recall would be missed. In this way, a mix of pure open-ended, unaided questions in the first part and hybrid of open- and close-ended questions in the second part, allowed deeper exploration of consumers' actual preferences. Here it is important to note that Reja, Manfreda, Hlebec and Vehovar (2003) have shown concerns on data quality of open-ended versus close-ended online questionnaires. These concerns pertain mostly to missing data and possible issues of generic answers. In our case, since the questions were aimed at exploring traits and association with halal or Islamic values, we believe that open-ended questions would not be problematic.

Results and findings

A survey link from *Qualtrics* platform was sent to students in different social networks and personal contact lists of the authors. In all, 77 respondents completed the survey. Around 20 respondents partially completed the survey or their responses were not properly recorded. These were not included in the analysis. Most of the respondents were in the age group 21 to 30 years. They were evenly divided in terms of gender as well as in terms of occupation. The respondents were mostly from South East Asia (Brunei and Malaysia), followed by South Asia (Pakistan) and Middle East (Jordan). South Asian and South East Asian consumers are the largest geographical segments of the global Muslim population, representing 35 per cent and 26 per cent of the 1.6 billion global Muslim population. These important segments are aptly represented in the geographical breakdown of respondents, as shown in Table 9.1.

Tourist preferences

The first part of the questionnaire contained questions which were purely exploratory in the sense that respondents were asked about their preferences and choices in open-ended questions. We wanted to see whether they showed any association with halal or Islamic lifestyle in any way. The first three questions within the first part asked respondents to list five considerations each for destination choice, selecting places to stay, and places to eat. Responses for each of these questions were reviewed to search for those considerations which related in any way with halal or Islamic injunctions. Since the open-ended responses gave liberty to the respondent to use any words or phrases, it was important to scan all responses to search for any association with Islamic values.

For the first question, considerations for destination choices, 77 respondents gave 312 responses. Out of these 312 considerations, only 15 responses could be related in any way with

Table 9.1 Respondents' profile

Gender	Count	Nationality	Count	Age	Count	Occupation	Count
Male	40	Brunei	16	21–25	35	Student	40
Female	37	Malaysia	25	26–30	31	Employed	37
		Jordan	06	31–35	11		
		Pakistan	30				

'halal' or Islamic. These 15 responses by 14 different respondents represented 4.8 per cent of total responses and 18.2 per cent of total respondents. Within these 14 responses, majority included consideration for availability of halal food, followed by consideration that the country should be a Muslim country. In the same manner, the next question asked respondents to list considerations for places to stay. Out of the 323 responses or considerations, only 7 responses by as many respondents were related to halal or Islam in any way. This represented 2.1 per cent of total responses or 9.1 per cent of total respondents showing any consideration for halal. Even though these considerations were for places to stay, availability of halal food dominated again. Five out of these 7 responses were focused on availability of halal food. The other two focused on availability of prayer place. Situation was quite different in the third question in this series, which was about selecting a place to eat. Here, results showed a different picture altogether. Some 43 responses out of a total 319 responses by 43 respondents were for halal food. These responses were 13.4 per cent of total responses by 55.8 per cent of total respondents.

In these three questions, considerations for halal or any Islamic injunctions seemed significant only for selecting places to eat. Respondents seemed to have placed little value on halal or Islamic injunctions in destination choices or places to stay. Regardless how significant or insignificant consideration for halal was across the three tourist decisions or behaviours, the focus remained on availability of halal foods.

Preferred destinations

Within the first part, respondents were also asked for their preferred destinations for travelling. Intention was to understand whether Muslim or non-Muslim destinations are the preference for Muslim millennials. When asked to choose between a foreign or local destination, 58 or 75 per cent of respondents wanted to go to a foreign destination compared to 19 preferring a local destination. This favouring of a foreign over local destination should be seen in the context that the local destination of these respondents was a Muslim country. The nationality-wise breakdown shows that in terms of proportion, Bruneian and Jordanian consumers showed somewhat stronger preference for a foreign destination over a local destination. In terms of gender, the proportion was representative of the overall breakdown, hence no gender differences were observed in the choice for preferred destination. Break-down of responses in terms of nationality and gender is given in Table 9.2.

In further examining the choice between a local or foreign destination, the next question asked respondents to list up to five international destinations they would prefer to go. A total of 376 international destinations were listed. Out of these, 270 or 71.8 per cent were non-Muslim countries and 106 or 28.2 per cent were Muslim countries. The breakdown of these destinations validated the earlier response of a stronger preference for non-Muslim countries over Muslim countries. A review of country-wise breakdown did not show any specific patterns and thus is not presented here.

Importance for halal

While the first part of the survey explored an unaided recall or association with halal, the second part was more of an aided recall for association with Halal. In this part, the questions sought consumers' preferences in destination choice, selecting place to stay, and place to eat—the same areas as of the first part. However, here the questions were deliberately framed to highlight the importance of halal or Muslim-friendliness in these three areas. Respondents were asked about the importance of halal or Muslim-friendliness in their

Table 9.2 Preferred destination—foreign versus local destination

Responses	Foreign destination	Local destination
	Percentage figures in brackets show proportion of total	
Overall (n = 77)	58 (75%)	19 (25%)
Nationality		
Malaysia (25)	16 (64%)	9 (36%)
Brunei (16)	16 (100%)	–
Pakistan (30)	20 (67%)	10 (33%)
Jordan (6)	6 (100%)	–
Gender-wise		
Male (40)	30 (75%)	10 (25%)
Female (37)	28 (76%)	9 (24%)

destination choice, place to stay, or place to eat. In this way, the respondents were answering more specifically about the importance of halal in their tourism preference. In the previous part, we noticed nominal association with issues related to halal or Islam. Surprisingly, in this part, the responses showed a much more pronounced importance of halal across the three decisions—destination choice, place to stay, and place to eat.

Three successive questions asked respondents to rate the importance of halal or Shariah-compliance in choosing destination, place to stay, and place to eat. In the aggregate scores for all respondents, the average score for importance of halal in selecting place to eat was 4.55. On a scale of 1 to 5, this was well above the mid-point value of 3.0. Importance of halal in selecting a place to eat was also much higher than importance of halal in destination selection (3.51) and selecting place to stay (3.36). These responses show that for consumers the concept of halal is most important in the case of places to eat and moderately important in deciding the destination or place to stay. Nationality-wise averages showed that Malaysian consumers gave highest importance to halal compared to consumers from any other country and in any decision. They are followed by Jordan, Pakistan, and Brunei. Gender-wise averages were generally representative of the overall scores. Therefore, no major male–female disparity could be observed. Responses to these questions are tabulated in Table 9.3, showing the importance of halal in three areas.

A subsequent question asked the respondents to select the features they thought were expected to be in a halal or Shariah-compliant tourist destination. Our motivation to ask this question was to explore the consumers' expectations from a tourist destination that brands itself as a halal or Muslim-friendly tourist destination. This question was a hybrid of open-ended and close-ended questions as there were four multiple-choice options in addition to an option of 'other' features. In other features, respondents could list their own preferences. This made this question a mix of close-ended and open-ended. Out of 164 options selected by all respondents, *Offered prayer place* was the leading option selected by 66 respondents and it constituted 40.2 per cent of total responses. This was followed by *Do not serve wine/alcohol* (42 respondents, 25.6 per cent of total responses), *Require modest dressing* (23 respondents, 14.0 per cent of total responses), *Restricts non-family male–female interactions* (17 respondents, 10.4 per cent of total responses). Among the options given by 16 respondents using the *other features* options, half mentioned halal food as a feature they expect from a halal or Shariah-compliant tourist destination.

Table 9.3 Importance of halal in different tourist behaviours

Responses	Importance of halal in destination selection	Importance of halal in selecting place to eat	Importance of halal in selecting place to stay
Overall	3.51	4.55	3.36
Nationality			
Malaysia	4.64	4.80	4.00
Brunei	2.75	3.88	2.88
Pakistan	2.90	4.67	3.07
Jordan	3.83	4.67	3.50
Gender-wise			
Male	3.33	4.73	3.25
Female	3.70	4.35	3.49

Self-image as a Muslim tourist versus global tourist

Based on the self-concept theory or concept of self-image, one important question in the survey sought self-rating as either a Muslim or global tourist. Respondents were also asked to give a rationale for their self-rating. Muslim millennial tourists seemingly have duality of being a Muslim and a globally connected person willing to experience other cultures. Whether they have a self-image of being a 'Muslim tourist' or a 'global tourist' can have implications for their thinking style and tourist behaviours. Thus, in the second part, where responses were already framed in a specific context of halal, the last two questions were aimed at exploring the self-image held by Muslim millennial tourists. Respondents were asked, on a scale of 0 to 10, the extent to which they see themselves as a global tourist or a Muslim tourist. Owing to the interactivity of the online response format, the responses could be given in intervals of 0.5, for a finer gradation.

The responses in this question were highly elucidating, to say the least. Average score for self-image of Muslim tourist (6.99 out of 10) was slightly higher than that of global tourist (6.09). Scores for Muslim tourist and global tourist had a correlation of − 0.31, which means respondents who identify themselves more as a Muslim tourist tend to agree less with being a global tourist. Scores for self-image, both nationality- and gender-wise, are presented in Table 9.4. All scores are out of 10.

There are glaring differences in preferences of respondents from different countries. Malaysian and Jordanian respondents considered themselves more as a Muslim tourist than a global tourist. An opposite scenario was there for the Pakistani tourists. Bruneian consumers showed an intermediate perspective. The correlation data also show diversity among respondents from different countries. Being identified more as a Muslim tourist meant less as a global tourist for Bruneian and Jordanian respondents. However, for Malaysian respondents, there was no correlation in this regard. For Pakistani consumers, the positive relation showed plausibility of being a global tourist while being a Muslim tourist, at the same time.

A related and equally important question followed this self-image rating. After self-rating as global and Muslim tourists, the respondents were asked to give a rationale for their ratings. Beyond the quantified observations, the reasons for holding a particular self-image was also insightful. The reasons for holding the self-image as a Muslim tourist validated a key finding from previous questions in the survey. The results of previous questions showed that concepts

Table 9.4 Self-image as a Muslim tourist versus as a global tourist

Responses	Muslim tourist	Global tourist	Correlation (r)
Overall	6.99	6.09	− 0.31
Nationality			
Malaysia	7.98	5.30	0.02
Brunei	6.69	6.75	− 0.48
Pakistan	6.32	6.80	0.36
Jordan	7.08	4.08	− 0.48
Gender-wise			
Male	7.24	6.08	− 0.29
Female	6.73	6.11	− 0.34

Note: All scores are out of 10.

of halal and Shariah-compliance were mostly related with food. In these self-image questions, similar observations were made as respondents giving high ratings for self-image of being a Muslim tourist did mostly because of concerns for halal food. On the other hand, those who responded highly on self-image of being a global tourist mostly showed interest in experiencing different cultures. These opinions and their diversity can be best expressed in the following four selected responses in which the respondents are rationalising their choice of being a global or Muslim tourist.

> Travelling is all about learning. If you restrict yourself and not be open to new experiences then it is really difficult for you to learn and groom. Personally, for me travelling has taught me more than I've learned from my Bachelor's degree. Being open to new experiences is the key.
>
> *(Male, 24, Pakistani/Muslim tourist: 5.0, Global tourist: 9.5)*

> I would consider myself a Muslim tourist as long as Halal food is available the bathrooms have Muslim showers and clean water. In terms of being a global tourist, it's always exciting to experience different cultures. That is one of my reasons for being fond of travelling.
>
> *(Female, 27, Pakistani/Muslim tourist: 6.0, Global tourist: 6.0)*

> Being a Muslim, I must be conscious about my values as Muslim to make sure I don't comprise my religious values in seeking for worldly pleasure, but at same time taking tourism as avenue for educating oneself, which is also consonant with Islamic religion, so as a global tourist here, I would long to get to learn more to the maximum from that place, being that I am open-minded person.
>
> *(Male, 33, Malaysian/Muslim tourist: 8.0, Global tourist: 5.0)*

> As a Muslim tourist, I would not consider eating non-halal food. As a global tourist, I would have no qualms about observing/trying different traditions as long as I am not required to eat/touch non-halal items, and am provided the facility to pray.
>
> *(Female, 24, Bruneian/Muslim tourist: 10.0, Global tourist: 5.0)*

Discussion and conclusion

This exploratory survey forays into understanding the preferences and behaviours of Muslim millennial consumers in the domain of tourism. The findings and implications of this study are quite insightful. First, it merits mentioning that gender differences were not observed. Male and female respondents were almost equally represented in the sample and their responses were found to be almost similar. In other words, the responses for different questions by male and female respondents were almost the same as aggregate responses. This gender-neutrality of responses contrasts with some previous studies in tourism research, where gender differences were found to be profound and/or females were found to be more active in travelling than males (Tilley & Houston 2016).

The main takeaway from this study are the findings about value accorded to halal by Muslim millennials. Through responses to open-ended and close-ended questions, it was evident that Muslim millennials had much less concern of the importance of halal in selecting the tourist destination and place to stay. Especially in the open-ended, unaided questions on their preferences, there were nominal considerations for halal. Willingness to experience and budget seemed to be more important in selecting a tourist destination and place to stay. In total contrast, the consideration for halal was very high in selecting what and where to eat. Muslim millennials showed a strong concern for access to halal food and that is their key concern in selecting a place to eat, above any other consideration of hygiene and cost. Interestingly, the concern for halal food was so strong that it even influences their tourist destination selection and place to stay within the selected destination.

A related insight gained from the results is that 'experience' rather than 'halal' drives the Muslim millennial tourists and shapes their tourism preferences. Muslim millennial tourists are driven by an urge to experience other cultures, natural scenery, and historical places. They are more outward, keen to explore other cultures. Being experience-oriented is a dominant psychographic trait among millennials or Generation Y, as shown by Valentine and Powers (2013). This study corroborated this observation for Muslim millennials.

There are differences in consumers from different Muslim countries. For instance, Pakistani consumers seem to have a more global outlook compared to Malaysian consumers, who strongly identify as Muslim tourists. Within South East Asia, Malaysian consumers outpace Bruneian consumers in identifying strongly with being a Muslim tourist. A plausible explanation for these differences are the local cultures. Pakistan, the second most populous Muslim country, has more than 95 per cent Muslim population compared to 65 per cent in Malaysia and 70 per cent in Brunei. Both Pakistan and Brunei are conservative societies in their socio-political disposition. Malaysia has over the years grown into a more diversified and globalised society. It can be said that Muslim millennials in the conservative societies are longing for a globalised lifestyle while those living in a globalised lifestyle are bent on being relatively more conservative.

Finally, as for the limitations of this study, it merits mentioning that use of open-ended questions and qualitative approach proved insightful. Still, a small sample size was a limitation that needs to be addressed in future studies. Since there were differences observed among respondents from different countries, it is important that in future studies samples from different Muslim consumers are taken. Even within South East Asia, respondents from Brunei and Malaysia showed diverging responses in some areas. Differences were greater among South Asian, South East Asian, and Middle Eastern consumers. This exploratory study is expected to open up new avenues for research in Muslim tourism, millennial tourism, and of course Muslim millennial consumers and tourists.

References

Battour, M. and Ismail, M.N. (2016) 'Halal tourism: Concepts, practises, challenges and future', *Tourism Management Perspectives*, 19 (B): 150–154.

Chiu, L.K., Ramli, K.I., Yusof, N.S. and Ting, C.S. (2015) 'Examining young Malaysians travel behavior and expenditure patterns in domestic tourism'. In *The* 2015 *International Academic Research Conference*. Paris, France: 47–54.

Cohen, S.A., Prayag, G. and Moital, M. (2014) 'Consumer behaviour in tourism: Concepts, influences and opportunities', *Current Issues in Tourism*, 17 (10): 872–909.

Din, K.H. (1989) 'Islam and tourism', *Annals of Tourism Research*, 16 (4): 542–563.

Geer, J.G. (1988) 'What do open-ended questions measure?', *Public Opinion Quarterly*, 52 (3): 365–371.

Haddock, G. and Zanna, M.P. (1998) 'On the use of open-ended measures to assess attitudinal components', *British Journal of Social Psychology*, 37 (2): 129–149.

Jafari, J. and Scott, N. (2014) 'Muslim world and its tourisms', *Annals of Tourism Research*, 44 (1): 1–19.

Kim, S., Im, H.H. and King, B.E. (2015) 'Muslim travelers in Asia', *Journal of Vacation Marketing*, 21 (1): 3–21.

Lepp, A. and Gibson, H. (2008) 'Sensation seeking and tourism: Tourist role, perception of risk and destination choice', *Tourism Management*, 29 (4): 740–750.

Manrai, L.A. and Manrai, A.K. (2011) 'Hofstede's cultural dimensions and tourist behaviors: A review and conceptual framework', *Journal of Economics, Finance and Administrative Science*, 16 (31): 23–48.

Mohsin, A., Ramli, N. and Alkhulayfi, B.A. (2016) 'Halal tourism: Emerging opportunities', *Tourism Management Perspectives*, 19 (B): 137–143.

Murphy, L., Benckendorff, P. and Moscardo, G. (2007) 'Linking travel motivation, tourist self-image and destination brand personality', *Journal of Travel & Tourism Marketing*, 22 (2): 45–59.

Penn, M. (2015) 'Japan embraces Muslim visitors to bolster tourism', *AlJazeera*, 17 December. [online] Available at: www.aljazeera.com/indepth/features/2015/12/japan-embraces-muslim-visitors-bolster-tourism-151215112245391.html

Pizam, A. and Sussmann, S. (1995) 'Does nationality affect tourist behavior?', *Annals of Tourism Research*, 22 (4): 901–917.

Pricewaterhouse Coopers (PwC). (2012) *Millennials at Work: Reshaping the Workforce*. [pdf] Available at: https://www.pwc.com/my/en/assets/publications/millennials-at-work.pdf

Reja, U., Manfreda, K.L., Hlebec, V. and Vehovar, V. (2003) 'Open-ended vs. close-ended questions in web questionnaires', *Developments in Applied Statistics*, 19 (1): 159–177.

Salmani, S. (2016) 'Introducing the millennial Muslim—and the global market that is worth trillions of dollars', *Mvslim.com*, 7 April. [online] Available at: http://mvslim.com/introducing-the-millennial-muslim-the-global-market-that-is-worth-trillions-of-dollars/

Seth, S. (2016) 'Halal travel morphs as Muslims seek new experiences and destinations', *Global Islamic Economy Gateway*, 6 December. [online] Available at: www.salaamgateway.com/en/story/halal_travel_morphs_as_muslims_seek_new_experiences_and_destinations_-SALAAM06122016084107/

Shakona, M., Backman, K., Backman, S., Norman, W., Luo, Y. and Duffy, L. (2015) 'Understanding the traveling behavior of Muslims in the United States', *International Journal of Culture, Tourism and Hospitality Research*, 9 (1): 22–35.

Swartz, L. (2016) 'What you need to know about millennial travelers', *Millennial Marketing*. [online] Available at: www.millennialmarketing.com/2016/05/what-you-need-to-know-about-millennial-travelers/

Thomson Reuters. (2015) *State of the Global Islamic Economy Report 2015/16*. [pdf] Available at: https://ceif.iba.edu.pk/pdf/ThomsonReuters-StateoftheGlobalIslamicEconomyReport201516.pdf

Thomson Reuters. (2016) *State of the Global Islamic Economy Report 2016/17*. [pdf] Available at: https://ceif.iba.edu.pk/pdf/ThomsonReuters-stateoftheGlobalIslamicEconomyReport201617.pdf

Tilley, S. and Houston, D. (2016) 'The gender turnaround: Young women now travelling more than young men', *Journal of Transport Geography*, 54: 349–358.

Todd, S. (2001) 'Self-concept: A tourism application', *Journal of Consumer Behaviour*, 1 (2): 184–196.

United Nations Department of Economic and Social Affairs Statistics Division (UNSTATS). (2008) *International Recommendations for Tourism Statistics* 2008. [online] Available at: https://unstats.un.org/unsd/publication/Seriesm/SeriesM_83rev1e.pdf#page=21 (accessed 22 September 2017).

United Nations World Tourism Organization (UNWTO). (2014) *Glossary of Tourism Terms*. [pdf] Available at: http://cf.cdn.unwto.org/sites/all/files/Glossary-of-terms.pdf (accessed 22 September 2017).

Valentine, D.B. and Powers, T.L. (2013) 'Generation Y values and lifestyle segments', *Journal of Consumer Marketing*, 30 (7): 597–606.

Wu, S. (2017) *'Reaching Asia's affluent millennials', Asia Research PTE Limited*. [online] Available at: https://asia-research.net/reaching-asias-affluent-millennials/

10

ISLAMIC ZIYĀRA AND HALAL HOSPITALITY IN PALESTINE

Al-Ḳuds 'Jerusalem', al-Khalīl 'Hebron', and Bayt Laḥm 'Bethlehem' between 2011 and 2016

Omar Abed Rabo and Rami K. Isaac

Introduction

Over the past few decades, international tourism activity has shown substantial and sustained growth in terms of both the number of tourists and tourism receipts. While the world tourist arrivals and tourism receipts have been growing substantially over the years, world tourism markets witnessed some important changes in the direction of tourism. This has been clear in the increase observed in the relative share of the developing countries, including the Organisation of Islamic Cooperation (OIC) member countries, in the world tourist arrivals and tourism receipts. As a group, the OIC countries attracted 174.7 million tourists in 2013, compared with 156.4 million in 2009. International tourism receipts in the OIC countries also recorded a significant increase of about $20 billion during the period 2009–2013 and reached $144.1 billion as of 2013 (OIC 2015b). Islam is one of the world's major religions (Esposito 1999) and has an estimated one-and-a-half billion adherents. These are concentrated in the 57 countries belonging to the OIC and there are sizeable Muslim populations in other nations around the world (OIC 2017).

Over the last two decades, the Islamic lifestyle market has been growing as Shariah-compliant products and services (e.g. Ḥalāl food, Islamic tourism, and Islamic finance) have become an important component of the global economy. With an increasing awareness and expanding numbers of Muslim tourists around the world, many tourism industry players have started to offer special products and services, developed and designed in accordance with the Islamic principles, to cater to the needs and demands of these tourists. Nevertheless, despite attracting significant interest across the globe, Islamic tourism is a relatively new concept in both theory and practice. Islamic tourism activity remained highly concentrated in Muslim majority countries of the OIC, which are currently both the major source markets for Islamic tourism expenditures and popular destinations (OIC 2015b).

Nonetheless, several countries around the world and in the Mediterranean region paid attention to this tourism growth, and this interest in the tourism sector attributed to the growing numbers of Muslim tourists to various destinations across the globe. These countries have built a service infrastructure equipped with facilities that provide services to Muslim visitors (restaurants, resorts, accommodation, flights, etc.) in accordance with the principles of the Islamic S̲h̲ariah law. Travel is one of the fastest growing tourism sectors in the world, with an estimated growth rate of 4.8 per cent against the 3.8 per cent industry average (Dinar Standard 2012). In 2015, it was estimated that there were 117 million Muslim international travellers. This is projected to grow to 168 million by 2020, where the travel expenditure by Muslim travellers is expected to exceed 200 billion USD (Crescent Rating 2015).

A United Nations World Tourism Organization (UNWTO) (2016) report revealed the world's fastest growing tourist destinations for 2017, and the results throw up a few surprises. One of the fastest growing destinations is Palestine (Haines 2017). Earlier in 2017 the street artist, Banksy, opened a boutique hotel in Palestine's West Bank, which, in hindsight, appears to have been a sage move: tourism in Palestine is booming. According to the UNWTO, the occupied territories of Palestine witnessed a 57.8 per cent rise in international arrivals so far in this year. Overlooking the Israeli West Bank Segregation Wall, Banksy's politically charged Walled Off Hotel has likely helped raise awareness of tourism in Palestine. However, the numbers of tourists in general and Muslims in particular do not match the religious status of cities, which can receive more than one million Muslim tourists annually. This chapter deals with Islamic and Ḥalāl tourism in three Palestinian cities: al-Ḳuds (Jerusalem), al-K̲h̲alīl (Hebron), and Bayt Laḥm (Bethlehem). This chapter will present the tourism situation in these Palestinian cities and the religious value of visiting the three cities for Muslims according to Islamic teaching (S̲h̲ariah law) and Islamic cultural heritage. In addition, this chapter will raise questions about the forces that affect the tourist situation in these cities, which lead to an increase or decrease in the number of Muslim tourists.

The historical background of Islamic visitors to al-Ḳuds, al-K̲h̲alīl, and Bayt Laḥm

Those who dig into the Arab and Islamic history of Palestine will find great interest in the three major tourism cities of the country, and will join hundreds of companions, some of whom spent their lives in Jerusalem and died there, and the well-known 'ulamā', or intellectuals and religious scientists, referred to traditionally as the faḳīh, muftīun, muḥad-dit̲h̲un, and mutakallimun, who came to Jerusalem to pray in the holy sites and to study in al-Aqsa Mosque (Abed Rabo 2012). From the beginning of the eighth century, Muslim visitors and pilgrims came to al-Ḳuds, al-K̲h̲alīl, and Bayt Laḥm to pray in the holy places. The places visited in al-Ḳuds were concentrated mainly on the al-Aqsa Mosque; in al-K̲h̲alīl the visit focused on al-Masjed al-Ibrahimi; and in Bayt Laḥm, the Church of Nativity. In Islam, al-Ḳuds is the land where Allah took the Prophet Mohammed on a night journey from al-Masjid al-Haram in Mecca to al-Masjid al-Aqsa in al-Ḳuds, which blessed its surroundings, and means the whole land of Palestine is blessed. Based on the night of the Isrā', special traditions were circulated and established, e.g. 'Literature in Praise of Jerusalem' and 'The Faḍā'il literature' (Athaminah 2013), in the Umayyad period in an attempt to encourage pilgrimage to al-Ḳuds and to pray there (Elad 1995).

In his book *Faḍā'il al Bayt al-Muqaddas*, Abū Bakr al-Wāsiṭī (d. after AD 1019) presents an early tradition which dated to the first quarter of the eighth century. He wrote: "He who comes to Bayt al-Muqaddas [Jerusalem] and prays to the right of the rock [on the Haram] and to its north, and prays in the place of the Chain, and gives a little or much charity, his prayers will be answered, and God will remove his sorrows and he will be freed of his sins as on the day his mother gave birth to him" (Al-Wāsiṭī 1979: 23).

During the beginning of the eighth century most of the Muslims who went to Mecca to perform the Ḥadjdj also came to Jerusalem before or after the Ḥadjdj, either to do the ihram from al-Aqsa or to sanctify their pilgrimage. The most frequent Du'ā' (addressed to God) among the Muslims is the sanctity of your Ḥadjdj, which is an indication of the phenomenon of sanctifying the pilgrimage, and is preferred by Muslims to be done in Jerusalem. Those who can perform the Ḥadjdj, visit Jerusalem to sanctify their pilgrimage and if the pilgrim does so, his pilgrimage has been completed. Some pilgrims came to Jerusalem before the season of the Ḥadjdj in order to prepare themselves for Ḥadjdj or the 'umra. This action was called *ihram,* an act of declaring or making sacred or forbidden. The opposite is *ihlāl,* an act of declaring permitted. The word *ihrām* has become a technical term for the state of temporary consecration of someone who is performing the hadjdj or the 'umra; a person in this state is referred to as *muhrim.* The entering into this holy state (also called *ihlāl)* is accomplished, for men and women, by the statement of intention, accompanied by certain rites and, in addition, for men, by the donning of the ritual garment. Famous Muslim scholars like 'Abd Allāh b. 'Umar b. al-Khaṭṭāb (d. in 692–3), the son of the second caliph (r. 13/634–23/644) 'Umar b. al-Khaṭṭāb, came to Jerusalem to perform the *ihram* in al-Aqsa Mosque before the hadjdj (Elad 1995). In the past, entering the state of *ihram* from al-Aqsa Mosque in Jerusalem and specifically from the Rock of Jerusalem was the common tradition of the majority of Muslims who performed the Ḥadjdj or 'umra, for example, Ṣāliḥ b. Yūsuf Abū Shu'ayb (d. in Ramla in AD 895) performed the Ḥadjdj seventy times, and each time he would perform the ihram from the Rock of Jerusalem [min Ṣakhrat Bayt al-Muqaddas] (Elad 1995). In the second half of the tenth century the Jerusalemite geographer al-Muqaddasī who described the people of North Africa, said that there were very few North Africans who did not visit Jerusalem. These huge numbers of Muslims who were visiting Jerusalem in the past are linked to the holiness of Jerusalem and stems from the combining of the pilgrimage to Mecca and al-Medina with the tradition of praying in Jerusalem before and/or after the 'umra or the Ḥadjdj. The Ḥadjdj activities, which Muslims do before or after performing the 'umra or the Ḥadjdj, are based on a very strong Ḥadīth that permits the Ḥadjdj to the three mosques: Mecca, al-Madina, and Jerusalem.

Many commentators explain the verses of the Quran about tourism and there are numerous forms of travel (see also Chapter 2, this volume). The first one is Ḥadjdj that includes pilgrimage and journey to Mecca once in lifetime at least which is obligatory for each healthy adult Muslim except if unable physically. Muslims can make the Ḥadjdj to *al-Aqsa* Mosque in Jerusalem and other Muslim sacred sites in Palestine. The second is visit, in Arabic is *Ziyara,* which is related to visiting holy sites and places. The third one is trip, in Arabic *Rihlah,* which is a trip for other motives for instance learning and work, focusing on a meaningful movement as an element of the spiritual journey in the service of God.

The Prophet said: "Do not set out on a journey (for religious devotion) but for the three mosques—for this mosque of mine (at Medina) the Sacred Mosque (at Mecca), and the Mosque al-Aqsa (Bait al-Maqdis)" (*Sahih Al-Bukhari:* 15/465]). This Ḥadīth (statement) clearly indicates that to complete the Muslim pilgrimage it is highly preferred to do so by visiting all three mosques, which explains the visits of the famous Muslim companions and followers to Jerusalem through Arab and Islamic history of the city, and also this Ḥadīth is agreed upon by all Muslims as a strong Ḥadīth. Muslims used to visit Jerusalem after the hadjdj, for example people from Khurāsān came to Palestine with large groups of pilgrims and visitors in Jerusalem after their pilgrimage in Mecca. In H 414/AD 1024, the pilgrimage convoy passed through Ayla (Elath) and from Ayla to Ramla to the Shamat road to Baghdad. This convoy was described by al-Musabbiḥī who mentioned that it included 200,000 people. In his writing, he declared that the people of Syria gained many economic benefits and that the people of the convoy were happy when they visited Jerusalem (Al-Musabbiḥī 1980).

The phenomenon of visiting Jerusalem, either to sanctify the pilgrimage or to proselytise before the pilgrimage or to visit al-Aqsa and pray there, that existed during the Ottoman rule over Palestine, was limited during the British mandate to the people of Bilad al-Sham until 1948, and after the occupation of Jerusalem in 1967 was confined to the people of Palestine, who are still practising the rite today. This phenomenon has been renewed after the call by Palestinian President Mahmoud Abbas and the activity of the Ministry of Awqaf and Islamic Holy Sites in Palestine and groups of Islamic countries that are encouraging Arabs and Muslims to visit Jerusalem and pray at al-Aqsa Mosque. At the end of Shaʿbān in May 2017, a number of Muslims from South East Asia came to Jerusalem and visited al-Aqsa Mosque to pray and to enter into a state of iḥram there before continuing to Mecca (Ma'an News Agency 2017).

For Muslims, al-Khalīl and Bayt Laḥm are the places where Prophet Mohammed prayed during the night of the Isrā' on his way to al-Ḳuds. On this night the angel Jibril asked him to come down and to pray two rak'ahs, saying to him, "Here is the tomb of your father Abraham" (Ibn al-Murajja 1995: 331) and when Jibril passed by the Prophet Mohammed over Bayt Laḥm, he said to him, "Come down and pray here two rak'ahs. Here is the place where your brother Isa ibn Maryam (peace be upon him) was born" (Ibn al-Murajja, 1995: 252). The traditions in praise of al-Khalīl do not differ in their meaning and structure from the traditions in praise of al-Ḳuds, which also spread from the beginning of the eighth century. These traditions deal with the praises of the tomb of Ibrahim, the rest of the patriarchs and their wives, as well as with al-Khalīl itself. According to tradition, the pilgrimage to Mecca, as is known, was combined with a visit to the Prophet's Tomb. The Muslims of that period combined a visit to Mecca with one to Jerusalem, as well as a visit to the tomb of the Prophet Mohammed with one to the Tomb of Abraham in al-Khalīl (Hebron). The traditions say that all who visit both tombs in a single year are assured acceptance into Paradise. Someone who cannot, or is prevented from, visiting the Tomb of the Prophet, must visit the Tomb of Abraham, to pray and recite Muslim invocations. It is said prayers at Abraham's tomb will be answered.

Concept notes

Most of the scholars who studied this type of tourism as well as the tourism institutions in different countries have used several concepts to define this phenomenon. Some of them used the concept: 'Ḥalāl tourism' (Battour & Ismail 2016). Others used both terms 'Islamic tourism' or 'Ḥalāl tourism' in the same study (Jaelani 2017), with both terms used interchangeably, while some institutions use 'Ḥalāl friendly tourism' to reflect the same meaning for the previous two concepts. We believe that the definition of these concepts should take into account some basic issues, which will affect the accuracy of the use of these concepts, for example: the purpose of the visit, which may determine the destination of the travel. The purpose of the visit leads us to consider whether is it to perform Ḥadjdj (the fifth of the five pillars (*arkān*) of Islam, also called the Great Pilgrimage in contrast to the ʿumra or Little Pilgrimage). Therefore, if the visit is to perform religious obligation, such as Ḥadjdj and ʿumra, the travel destination will be Mecca, al-Madina, al-Ḳuds and al-

Khalīl, the four Islamic cities that Muslims are obliged to visit according to Islamic law and Islamic legacy. In this case, the Muslim cannot fulfil the obligatory duties without performing Ḥadjdj to the cities of Mecca and al-Madina, but before travelling to Mecca, Muslims should prepare themselves [Ihram] by praying at al-Aqsa Mosque in al-Ḳuds and in the Ibrahimi Mosque in al-Khalīl. These activities apply to the concept of 'Islamic tourism', which also includes visits to other religious sites such as shrines (Battour & Ismail 2016). This kind of Islamic religious tourism, of course, includes Ḥalāl activity, where a pilgrim obtains Ḥalāl services in accordance with the Islamic Shariah and its principles and values. Therefore, 'Islamic tourism' indeed encompasses what is now known as 'Ḥalāl tourism' with all its requirements.

The concept of 'Islamic tourism' cannot be applied to all destinations, whether in Arab or Islamic countries because performing Ḥadjdj can be done only in Mecca and the Ihram is preferred to be in al-Ḳuds, and praying in al-Aqsa Mosque, and visiting the Cave of the Patriarchs in al-Khalīl and praying there. While in terms of 'Ḥalāl tourism', it is the concept that applies to the activity of Muslims in Arab or Islamic countries where there are no religious places associated with Ḥadjdj and ʿumra. Therefore, the daily activities of Muslims in these destinations and the services that the Muslims receive there are services based on Islamic law. The third concept that is also used in the Islamic tourism market is 'Ḥalāl friendly tourism' which has appeared in the tourism industry market through non-Muslim countries in order to attract Muslim visitors to visit non-Muslim destinations. 'Ḥalāl friendly tourism' is another form of 'Ḥalāl tourism', but in non-Arab and non-Muslim countries. It aims to Islamise the services provided to Muslim tourists in non-Muslim countries. The common denominator between 'Ḥalāl friendly tourism' and 'Ḥalāl tourism' is the term Ḥalāl, which means that everything permitted in the Islamic Shariah is Ḥalāl.

Islamic and Ḥalāl tourism in al-Ḳuds, al-Khalīl, and Bayt Laḥm

The centre of al-Ḳuds and/or East Jerusalem is the Old City, which is located within the walls of the Ottoman city. While it is just a square kilometre in size, it was and remains a destination for tourists who have come to the city to visit historical and religious places within its walls and explore its rich legacy. Al-Khalīl, located 32 kilometres south of Jerusalem, is similar to al-Ḳuds in that it is a holy city for Palestinians and Muslims. It is the place where Ibraham al-Khalīl dwelt, and it contains his remains, and those of his family, Sara, Isaac, Rebkah, Jacob, and Leah. The location of their tombs was the reason al-Khalīl became a holy place. Between the end of the seventh and the beginning of the eighth centuries the name of the village of Hebron was Habra or Hibra. Muslim geographers of the ninth century called the place the Mosque of Abraham 'Masjid Ibrahim'. In the middle of the tenth century the Jerusalemite geographer al-Muqaddasī (d. around AD 1000), used the names Habra and Masjid Ibrahim in his book *Aḥsan al-taqāsim fī maʿrifat al-aqālīm* (*The Best Divisions in the Knowledge of the Regions*) (Al-Muqaddasī 1906: 172). The name Ibrahim al-Khalīl, meaning Abraham the Friend (of God), was well known during the early Muslim period, and was used in all traditions that related to the area. Only in the thirteenth century does al-Khalīl emerge as the actual name of the city (Elad 1996). Bethlehem 'Bayt Laḥm' is a Palestinian city located 9 kilometres south of Jerusalem, it began to be honoured and visited by Christians from the fourth century until today. It became equally venerated by Muslims as the birthplace of Īsā ben. Maryam (Bayt Laḥm).

Arabs and Muslims lost their access to visit al-Ḳuds and the West Bank after the Israeli government declared occupation in 1967. Even after the signing of the Camp David Accord between Egypt and Israel in 1978, the Egyptian people refused to visit Jerusalem and the West Bank and considered that visiting these cities would be normalising the occupation. Political events developed in Jerusalem and the West Bank when the first Palestinian Intifada began in 1987, which ended with the signing of the 1993 Oslo Agreement between the PLO and Israel. Other Arab countries such as Jordan signed the Jordanian-Israeli peace agreement, but these agreements have not affected the prohibition of Arabs and Muslims from visiting al-Ḳuds and the West Bank under occupation.

Tourism began to flourish after the Oslo Agreement. By 1999 the number of tourists to Israel and al-Ḳuds reached up to 2,923,200 tourists and in 2000 the number was still climbing, reaching around 3,000,000 tourists. In 2001, the outbreak of the al-Aqsa Intifada led to a significant drop in the number of tourists who visited Jerusalem, plummeting from 3,000,000 to 639,300. The drop in tourism was due to the violence that erupted during the Intifada (Jerusalem Institute for Israel Studies (JIIS) 2017). Eventually tourism began to recover as a result of stability, and by 2004 the number of tourists began to increase again. This number is almost unassuming if we compare it with Christian and Jewish tourist arrivals to Jerusalem, and it will be negligible compared to the huge number of Muslim tourist arrivals in other cities in the OIC, which in 2011 reached about 58.7 million Muslim tourists. Palestinian cities have received few Muslim tourists in comparison to other cities in the region. For example, during 2016, Mecca received 6 million pilgrims (this number is not including the Ḥadjdj), who performed the ʿumra (Al-Emarat alyoum 2015). While Jerusalem has received 2,568,300 tourists during 2015, only 440,900 of them stayed overnight in al-Ḳuds hotels, 54,331 of whom were Muslims, which is about 2.5 per cent. The number of visitors from different nationalities and religions increased very slowly during 2016 to reach 2,665,600, only 481,100 of whom stayed overnight in al-Ḳuds (JIIS 2017).

Up until 2011, very few Arab and Muslim tourists visited Palestine. However, since 2011 there has been a new phenomenon in the Palestinian and regional tourism market, namely, Islamic tourism to al-Ḳuds, al-Khalīl, and Bayt Laḥm, despite the controversy among Muslim scholars over the legality of visiting the cities due to the ongoing occupation.

Palestinians in general and the people of the three Palestinian cities, al-Ḳuds, al-Khalīl, and Bayt Laḥm, live in a traditional conservative society, whose traditions are reflected in the social context and in the preservation of traditional principles of socialisation, which are transferred from society to the individual. The conservative traditions stem from the Islamic religion, as well as Arab customs and traditions, which are not separated in Palestinian society. Because Palestinians have kept and preserved the importance of Palestine as a holy land, tourists are able and encouraged to visit Palestine under the concept of Islamic/Ḥalāl tourism. They will pray at al-Aqsa Mosque, which is one of the three holy mosques in Islam, visit the Nativity "*Mahd Isa*" in Bayt Laḥm (the birthplace of Jesus, considered a prophet in Islam), and pray at the Ibrahimi Mosque in al-Khalīl. Because Palestinians have maintained a religious culture, Muslim tourists will receive Ḥalāl services at their hotel accommodation and Ḥalāl food served in Palestinian restaurants. In addition, any tourist in Palestine will find that a mosque is never more than a few blocks away from their accommodation. Muslims visiting al-Ḳuds, al-Khalīl, and Bayt Laḥm will also find that within hotels there are places designated for prayer, while those who wish to pray in local mosques of these cities only need a few minutes to walk through the traditional markets to reach a mosque. The advantage of these sites is their location, where hotels, restaurants, and the aswāk (market/Sūḳ) traditional markets, and shopping centres are located close to religious and historical sites, which is a strong feature to attract Muslim tourists to visit these cities. During their stay, Muslim tourists will also discover the daily lives of Palestinians in the cities and refugee camps nearby.

There are also some Muslim tourists who come individually from non-Islamic countries to Palestine. These Muslim tourists often rent small apartments or rooms from Palestinian families to live in. Some of them rent rooms in refugee camps in Bayt Laḥm and al-Khalīl.

Palestinians in al-Ḳuds, al-Khalīl, and Bayt Laḥm especially, have created many initiatives and organisations to encourage this type of tourism, such as the Jerusalem Tourism Cluster (JTC) in Jerusalem, Visit Palestine, and Volunteer Palestine. Volunteer Palestine, for example, is an awareness-raising travel organisation for international visitors, established by refugees from Bayt Laḥm which runs volunteer placements within refugee camps in Palestine. As part of the volunteering placement, they facilitate homestays, political tours, and cultural activities to ensure the visitors experience the best of Palestine. While the organisation welcomes volunteers and tourists from all over the world, it places a special importance on targeting the Palestinian diaspora and Muslim international communities.

With the success of such programmes in the volunteer-tourism sphere, one could imagine a new concept of Ḥalāl volunteer-tourism flourishing in this market. With many Muslim cultures maintaining a conservative lifestyle around the world, the option of volunteering with an organisation promising a Ḥalāl experience could open up options for youth from conservative communities, particularly young women, to travel with the blessings of conservative family members.

While Palestine offers a plethora of religious sites and institutions for volunteers and tourists, the land also offers visitors an opportunity to go sightseeing at the natural sites and villages of the country, where they will also find all the necessary requirements for Islamic tourism and Ḥalāl services. Muslim tourists can enjoy The Masar Ibrahim al-Khalīl (Abraham's Path, see Isaac 2017), a trail that runs through the West Bank from the Mediterranean olive groves of the highlands of the north to the silence of the deserts in the south, from the area west of Jenin to the area south of al-Haram Al-Ibrahimi in the city of al-Khalīl (Hebron).

In July 2017, the United Nations cultural arm declared the Old City of Hebron a protected heritage site in a secret ballot, an issue that has triggered a new Israeli-Palestinian controversy at the international body. UNESCO voted 12 to 3, with 6 abstentions, to give heritage status to Hebron in the Israeli-occupied West Bank. Hebron is home to more than 200,000 Palestinians and a few hundred Israeli settlers, who live in a heavily fortified enclave near the site known to Muslims as the Ibrahimi Mosque and to Jews as the Tomb of the Patriarchs. The resolution, brought by the Palestinians and which declares Hebron's Old City as an area of outstanding universal value, was fast-tracked on the basis that the site was under threat, with the Palestinians accusing Israel of an 'alarming' number of violations, including vandalism and damage to properties. According to the UNESCO resolution Hebron is one of the oldest cities in the world, dating from the chalcolithic period or more than 3,000 years BC (Al-Jazeera 2017).

Tourist arrivals, hotels, and accommodation

Despite the religious and historical importance of the city in Islam, the number of Muslims who visit al-Ḳuds is small compared to the number of Christians and Jews that visit Jerusalem (Table 10.1), or Muslim tourists visiting other Muslim cities or non-Muslim cities in the world. Table 10.1 shows the percentage of Muslim tourists who visited Jerusalem during the period 2011–2015, compared to other tourists from other religions during the same period (JIIS 2017).

In 2011, 2,142,481 million tourists visited Jerusalem. Only 477,300 of those tourists stayed in East Jerusalem hotels, 29,995 of which were Muslims, making up just 1.4 per cent of the total number of tourists who visited the city that year. The number of Muslim visitors to

Table 10.1 Tourist arrivals

Year	Total	Christians	Jews	Muslims	No affiliation	Others
2011	2,142,481	61.6%	23.2%	1.4%	10.5%	3.2%
2012	2,168,820	63%	19%	3%	11%	3%
2013	2,240,128	63%	19%	3%	11%	3%
2014	2,333,720	58.7%	24.5%	2.2%	12.4%	2.2%
2015	2,173,210	58.6%	24.9%	2.5%	11.8%	2.2%

Jerusalem doubled in 2012. With 3 per cent of all visitors to Jerusalem being Muslim during that year, the number of Muslim tourists in the city increased to about 65,646 out of the 2,168,820 visitors documented. Of those in 2012, 448,200 tourists among them stayed in East Jerusalem. In 2013, the number of Muslim visitors continued to increase, reaching 67,204 Muslim tourists out of 2,240,128 visitors who came to the city. Among them, just 443,300 tourists stayed in East Jerusalem hotels. The number of Muslim tourists who visited Jerusalem decreased slightly in 2014 and 2015. In 2014, 51,342 Muslim tourists visited Jerusalem, representing 2.2 per cent of the total 2,333,720 tourists who visited the city, among them only 510,000 tourists stayed overnight in East Jerusalem hotels.

Although a newspaper report published in the Israeli newspaper *Haaretz* in 2015 indicated that the number of Muslim tourists significantly increased in 2015, official numbers dispute the reported increase. *Haaretz* reported 80,000 Muslim tourists to East Jerusalem in 2015: 26,700 of which were Indonesians, 23,000 Turkish, 17,700 Jordanians, 9,000 Malaysians, and 3,300 Moroccans (Paltoday 2015). These numbers differ from the official numbers given by the JIIS centre in 2015, which documented 54,330 Muslim tourists, about 2.5 per cent of the 2,173,210 total (JIIS 2017), which indicates an increase of 3,000 Muslims tourists between 2014 and 2015.

While the highly respected *Travel and Leisure* (T&L) magazine listed Jerusalem as one of the top ten tourist destinations in the world in 2015 (Lieberman 2015), Jerusalem still experiences low rates of tourism when compared to other international tourism cities due to the instability created by occupation. For example, tourism observers attribute the drop in the number of tourists who visited Israel during 2014 and 2015 to the Israeli war on Gaza (Al-Jazeera 2015). Analysing the statistics, it seems the war in Gaza caused a decrease in the number of Muslim tourists in particular during that period (see Table 10.1) (see also Isaac, Hall & Higgins-Desbiolles 2016).

Between 2011 and 2015, the number of hotels operating in Jerusalem's Old City and surrounding area stood at 30 hotels. In 2016 the number rose to 31. The total number of rooms offered in these hotels ranged between 1,905 in 2011 to 2,052 in 2016 (JIIS 2017). During the period between 2011 and 2015, the restaurants available in al-Ķuds hotels increased from 32 restaurants to 41, creating an increase in potential capacity from more than 3,105 customers to a new capacity of 4,000 customers (Palestinian Central Bureau of Statistics (PCBS) 2016).

Regarding the number of Muslim tourists who visited Bayt Laḥm and al-Khalīl, we do not have official statistics from the Ministry of Tourism or the Palestinian Central Bureau of Statistics (PCBS) for the numbers. The statistics provided by the Ministry of Tourism through the tourism and antiquities police or those provided by the PCBS are statistics according to the country or the regions that tourists came from. The figures and percentages presented in this chapter about the numbers of Muslim tourists who visited East Jerusalem are supposed to apply also to the Muslim tourists who visit the cities of al-Khalīl and Bayt Laḥm because these cities are part of the organised tour for Muslim tourists who visit these three cities (Paltoday 2015).

The number of tourists who visited the cities of al-Khalīl and Bayt Laḥm and stayed overnight between 2011 and 2015, according to the PCBS, ranged between 225,164 and 314,380 tourists, which is half of the total number of tourists visiting East Jerusalem, and less than 1 per cent of the total tourists who visited Jerusalem in general. The number of hotels operating in al-Khalīl and Bayt Laḥm is slightly higher than the hotels in al-Ḳuds. In 2011, there were 28 hotels operating in Bayt Laḥm and al-Khalīl, while in 2015, the number of hotels increased to 37, most of which were located in Bayt Laḥm. The number of rooms in these hotels during the period between 2011 and 2015 ranged from 2,125 rooms to 3,194 rooms in 2015. The number of restaurants operating in these hotels during this period range between 40 restaurants in 2011 with a capacity of 2,125 customers. In 2015 it increased to 56 restaurants, reaching a capacity of 10,899 customers (PCBS 2016). These are restaurants located within hotels, but there are dozens of special tourist restaurants located within the historical markets and in the centres of these cities (Halaika, Nakashian & Dahadha 2016).

Ḥalāl food

All restaurants within hotels or private restaurants in Palestine serve Ḥalāl food to their customers. The meat of poultry or sheep offered in these hotels and restaurants is meat slaughtered in slaughterhouses in al-Ḳuds, al-Khalīl, and Bayt Laḥm. In the process of creating Ḥalāl meat, the name of God is mentioned during the slaughter, based on the rule of the 'good things' or '*ṭayyibāt*' which outlines what is lawful for Muslims to eat, which constitutes an important part of Ḥalāl food according to the Quran: "Eat then of that over which the Name of Allah has been mentioned (when slaughtered), if you truly believe in His verses" (Quran). And Allah Said: "O you who believe, eat of the good things, that are lawful, wherewith We have provided you, and give thanks to God, for what He has made lawful for you, if it be Him that you worship." The Prophet Mohammed (peace be upon him) said: "O people, Allah is ṭayyib (pure and good) and He accepts only what is ṭayyib. Verily, Allah has commanded the believers as He commanded His Messengers. Allah said: O Messengers!, Eat of the Tayyibat and do righteous deeds. Verily, I am well-acquainted with what you do."

Eating Ḥalāl food and living a Ḥalāl lifestyle is a prerequisite for Allah to respond to the prayer of Muslims, and according to Islam, Allah does not respond to the person who lives a Ḥarām (the opposite of Halal) lifestyle and eats Ḥarām food. In the Muslim Hadiths, The Prophet makes "mention of travelers who travel for a long period of time. In the writings, an example is given of a traveler with disheveled hair who is covered in dust. The traveler lifts his hand towards the sky and thus makes the supplication: 'My Rubb! My Rubb!' But his food is unlawful, his drink is unlawful, his clothes are unlawful and his nourishment is unlawful, how can, then his supplication be accepted?"

The vegetables and fruits offered in these restaurants and hotels are produced in the Palestinian land in Al-Khalīl, Bayt Laḥm, Jericho, or the northern Palestinian governorates, which provide the Palestinian market with the freshest vegetables and fruits. The Palestinian farmers in these governorates apply the rules of Ḥalāl agriculture and they are also fighting and controlling their land despite the attacks of Israeli settlers on Palestinian farmers in these provinces (Al-Haq 2017).

Islamic tourism phenomenon in Palestine

The phenomenon of Islamic tourism was not prevalent before 2011, the absence of which may be related to the instability that followed the al-Aqsa Intifada in October 2000, and the Fatwas issued by Muslim scholars forbidding visits to al-Ḳuds, and the West Bank under

Israeli occupation. But since 2011 this phenomenon has become remarkable and the cities in the West Bank are witnessing an influx of tourists from Muslim countries (see the previous section for numbers of Muslim tourists between 2011 and 2015). In an interview conducted by Ma'an News Agency in June 2013 the Palestinian Tourism Minister Rula Maa'yaa said: "Islamic tourism to Palestine began late last year (2012), and was increased day after day, especially with the President's calls and the ministry's contacts with Islamic countries, to encourage its residents to visit the Palestinian cities" (Ma'an New Agency 2013). It seems that the speech of Palestinian President Mahmoud Abbas at the international conference held in Doha, Qatar, on 26–27 February 2012, in which he called upon Arabs, Muslims, and Christians to visit Jerusalem in order to preserve the Arab and Islamic character of the city, has resonated in many Arab and Islamic countries such as Turkey, Malaysia, Indonesia, Jordan, and Morocco. During the conference, Abbas discouraged countries from continuing a boycott of tourism to the area, declaring the importance of:

> encourage[ing] all who can, especially our brothers from the Arab and Islamic countries, as well as our Arab, Muslim and Christian brothers in Europe and the United States to visit al-Ḳuds. This move will have its political, moral, economic and humanitarian repercussions. al-Ḳuds belongs to us and we all have no one to prevent us from reaching it. The influx of crowds and the congestion of its streets and holy sites will strengthen the steadfastness of its citizens and contribute to the protection and consolidation of the identity, history and heritage of the city targeted by the eradication. The occupiers will remember that the issue of al-Ḳuds is the cause of every Arab, every Muslim and every Christian. We confirm here that the visit of the prisoner is a support for him and does not in any way mean normalization with the prisoner.
>
> *(Abbas 2012)*

On 18 April 2012, Prince Ghazi bin Muhammad, the King Abdullah II's personal adviser and head of the Royal āl al-Bayt Society, and the former Egyptian Mufti Ali Gum'a visited Jerusalem together (Al-Jazeera 2012). The call of the Palestinian President Mahmoud Abbas to encourage Arabs, Muslims, and friends to visit al-Ḳuds had led to a debate among Muslim scholars on the issue of Muslims and Arabs visiting al-Ḳuds under Israeli occupation. In opposition to the Palestinian President's call to visit al-Ḳuds, the chairman of the International Union of Muslim Scholars (IUMS), Dr Yusuf Qaradawi, has issued a fatwa prohibiting the visit to al-Ḳuds to non-Palestinians, in order to "not legalize the Israeli occupation in the city" (Donia al-Watan 2012). The Palestinian official position remained constant and called for intensifying visits by Muslims to al-Ḳuds, al-Ḵhalīl, and Bayt Laḥm, as well as the Jordanian position. Therefore, the two sides held a series of activities: On 31 March 2013 King Abdullah II and Palestinian President Mahmoud Abbas signed a "trusteeship and sovereignty" agreement, which continued Jordan's right to "guardianship" and "defense of al-Ḳuds and holy sites" in Palestine (Jordanzad 2013).

Between 28 and 30 April 2014, an international conference concerning Jerusalem was held in Amman, entitled "al-Tariq 'ila al-Ḳuds\The Road to Jerusalem", under the patronage of Jordan's King Abdullah II, the Jerusalem Committee for Jerusalem Affairs, and the Arab Parliament. The subject of the discussion was Israeli violations at al-Aqsa Mosque and ways of assisting Palestinians living in Jerusalem. The conference was attended by Muslim and Christian clerics: the former Egyptian Mufti, Ali Gum'a; Mufti al-Ḳuds, and the Palestinian territories, Sheikh Muhammad Hussein, Palestinian Minister of Religious Affairs Mahmoud al-Habash, Jordanian Minister of Endowments, and others, as well as politicians (Al-wakeel

News 2014). At the end of the conference, the participants issued a fatwa permitting Muslims to visit al-Aqsa, but restricting it only to Palestinian visitors or to Muslim visitors with citizenship from countries outside the Muslim world. The fatwa actually cancels the earlier fatwa issued by al-Qaradhawi. Palestine and Jordan encouraged all Muslims to visit al-Aqsa Mosque, but the fatwa issued in the conference "The Road to Jerusalem" does not permit visits to al-Ḳuds to all Muslims, it is includes "Palestinians … regardless of their nationalities" and "Muslims with passports from countries outside the Muslim World" could visit al-Ḳuds, as long as they didn't financially aid the "occupation" (Al-wakeel News 2014).

During the 22nd season of the International Islamic Fiqh Academy (IIFA) which was held in Kuwait between 22 and 25 March 2015, the IIFA issued a decree stating that visiting al-Ḳuds is a permissible and recommended act and it is obligatory to help the city and its people (OIC 2015a). The Organisation of Islamic Cooperation (OIC) general secretary selected al-Ḳuds as the Capital of Islamic Tourism for 2015 at the eighth conference of Ministers of Tourism held in Banjul, Gambia, between 4 and 6 December 2013. The Ministry of the Awḳaf and Religious Affairs, as well as the Palestinian Ministry of Tourism, continued to coordinate with the Ministries of the Awḳaf in the Islamic countries and also with the OIC to encourage Muslims to visit al-Ḳuds, al-Ḵhalīl, and Bayt Laḥm. Between 14 and 15 June 2015, the Palestinian Ministry of Tourism and Antiquities hosted the United Nation World Tourism Organization (UNWTO) International Conference on Religious Tourism in Bayt Laḥm (Isaac 2015). It was the first time that the UNWTO organised a conference in an observer member state. The attendants of the conference included international ministers, tourism professionals, and tourism academics. At the conference, the Palestinian private sector presented the services it offered through an exhibition alongside the meeting. The conference was very important for Palestine, the audience was aware of the potential of the tourist sector in Palestine, which is witnessing an increase in the number of hotels and a remarkable development in the services provided, which include traditional crafts, transportation and services of tourist offices, tourist police services, and qualified tourist guides from Palestinian universities and colleges.

The places Muslim tourists can visit: al-Ḳuds, al-Ḵhalīl, and Bayt Laḥm

There are many places Muslims can visit in al-Ḳuds especially within the Aqsa Mosque area, e.g. the Dome of the Rock, the Dome of the Prophet, the Dome of Ascension, the Dome of the Chain, the Gate of Mercy, the Gate of the Tribes and the Gate of the Prophet, and also there are places outside the Aqsa Mosque to visit such as the Mount of Olives. Muslims in al-Ḵhalīl can visit Masjid Ibrahim: the Cave of Patriarchs, Bir Haram Ar-Rameh (Ramet Al-khalil\Mamre), the Old City of al-Ḵhalīl, al-Ḵhalīl refugee camps, al Aroub Refugee Camp, and Fawwar. In Bayt Laḥm, Muslims can visit the Church of the Nativity and Omar Mosque, the Old City of Bayt Laḥm, and the refugee camps within the city.

Despite the historical and religious status of the country, Palestine has one of the lowest numbers of visitors in comparison to other countries in the region, which receive millions of tourists every year. Therefore, its regional market has remained extremely low and very weak even amid global increases in the number of tourists. During 2015, about 2,799,397 tourists visited Israel/Palestine (JIIS 2017) out of 53 million tourists who visited the Middle East region (UNWTO 2016). Al-Kuds, al-Ḵhalīl, and Bayt Laḥm are three major holy cities in Palestine. These cities have long been a destination for travellers from all over the world, because of the religious-cultural status of their holy sites. These cities also have the lowest number of both non-Muslim and Muslim tourists in comparison with other cities in the region.

The main obstacles facing tourism in Palestine are the continued Israeli occupation of the Palestinian territories, where Palestinians cannot exploit the abundant amount of tourist resources in their cities, which are under Israeli control, such as Jerusalem and Hebron. For example, in 1997 the al-Khalīl Protocol divided the city of al-Khalīl into two parts. H1, comprising around 80 per cent of the city under full control of the Palestinian Authority, and H2, comprising around 20 per cent and including the Old City and the most affected areas, under the control of Israel. The Palestinian Authority has control over civil affairs, except in the settlement, and Israel controls the security affairs of both H1 and H2 (Clarke 2000; Isaac et al. 2016).

Israel continues to control the tourism sector in general by controlling the crossings and borders and stringently controls the numbers of tourists coming to Palestinian cities. Efforts must be intensified in order to make Palestinian cities independent tourist destinations, which would have a positive impact on the development of these cities economically, due to the likely increase in private sector investments in tourism (Isaac et al. 2016). The lack of Muslim and non-Muslim tourism in Palestinian cities has extreme negative effects on the GDP of these cities, and severely impacts the operational capacity, including employment opportunities, investments, development, and so much more.

Conclusion

This chapter deals with Islamic and Ḥalāl tourism in three Palestinian cities: al-Ḳuds 'Jerusalem', al-Khalīl 'Hebron', and Bayt Laḥm 'Bethlehem'. This chapter presented the tourism situation in these Palestinian cities and the religious value of visiting the three cities for Muslims according to Islamic teaching (Shariah law) and Islamic cultural heritage.

Islamic tourism is an activity, experience, occasion, or purpose to visit historical places, heritage, culture, arts, business, health, education, Islamic history, sports, shopping, or any other human interests but on condition of Shariah compliance. Also, in Islamic tourism, people travel for their vacation and recreation and to be satisfied with Allah. Thus, tourism is a section of human life which does not contradict the main theme of Islam. Islamic and Ḥalāl tourism is indeed a promising market for the tourism industry in Palestine. One of the main opportunities for the tourism sector in Palestine consists of the need of the Muslims conducting the Ḥadjdj rites to visit the al-Aqsa Mosque, in Jerusalem as a complementary part for their Ḥadjdj, which could open the potential for millions of visitors to Palestine per year. Islamic tourism is a recent phenomenon in the theory and practice of global tourism industry. Traditionally Islamic tourism was often associated with Ḥadjdj and ʿumra only. However, recently there has been an influx of products and services designed specifically to cater to the business and leisure-related segments of Muslim tourists across the globe. Islamic tourism remains an emerging niche market with 108 million Muslim travellers, accounting for 10 to 12 per cent of the global tourism sector.

References

Abbas, M. (2012) 'Jerusalem: Palestinian Authority President Mahmoud Abbas speech', International Conference on Jerusalem, 26–27 February, Doha: Qatar. [online] Available at: http://qatarconferences. org/jerusalem/arabic/palestine (accessed 15 June 2017).

Abed Rabo, O. (2012) Jerusalem During the Fāṭimid and Seljūq Periods: Archaeological and Historical Aspects. PhD. Jerusalem: The Hebrew University.

Al-Emarat alyoum. (2015) 'Saudi Arabia: 6 million Muslims perform umrah in 1436 AH'. (Arabic) [online] Available at: www.emaratalyoum.com/life/four-sides/2015-11-23.1.843206 (accessed 20 July 2017).

Al-Haq. (2017) 'Settlements and settler violence'. [online] Available at: www.alhaq.org/advocacy/topics/settlements-and-settler-violence (accessed 10 August 2017).

Al-Jazeera. (2012) 'Alwilayat al'urduniyat a'laa 'awqaf al-quds'. [online] Available at: www.aljazeera.net/news/reportsandinterviews (accessed 22 April 2012].

Al-Jazeera. (2015) 'The number of tourists in Israel decreased by 16%'. [online] Available at: www.aljazeera.net/news/ebusiness (accessed 17 June 2015).

Al-Jazeera. (2017) 'UNESCO declares Hebron old city a World Heritage Site'. [online] Available at: www.aljazeera.com/news/2017/07/unesco-declares-hebron-city-world-heritage-site-170707100548525.html (accessed 30 August 2017).

Al-Muqaddasī, M.b., Aḥmad b. and Al-Bannā' A.B. (1906) *Aḥsan al-taqāsim fī ma'rifat al-aqālīm*, Leiden.

Al-Musabbiḥī, 'Izz al-Mulk Muhammad Ibn Ahmad. (1980) *Akhbar Msr fi sntin (414–415 h.)*, Msr./Egypt.

Al-wakeel News. (2014) 'Final statement of the road to Jerusalem Conference'. (Arabic) [online] Available at: www.alwakeelnews.com/article/95705 (accessed 16 August 2017).

Al-Wāsiṭī, Muhammad b. Ahamad, Abū Bakr al-Wāsiṭī. (1979) *Faḍā'il al Bayt al-Muqaddas* (Ed. I. Hasson), Jerusalem.

Athaminah, K. (2013) *Al-Quds wa-al-Islam: Dirasah fi qadasatiha min al-manzur al-islami*. Beirut: Institute of Palestinian Studies.

Battour, M. and Ismail, M.N. (2016) 'Halal tourism: Concepts, practices, challenges and future', *Tourism Management Perspectives*, 19 (B): 150–154.

Clarke, R. (2000) 'Self-presentation in a contested city: Palestinian and Israeli political tourism in Hebron', *Anthropology Today*, 16 (5): 61–85.

Crescent Rating. (2015) *Muslim/Halal Travel Market: Basic Concepts, Terms and Definitions*. Singapore: Crescent Ratings.

Dinar Standard. (2012) 'Global Muslim lifestyle tourism market: Landscape & consumer needs study'. [online] Available at: https://www.slideshare.net/DinarStandard/global-muslim-lifestyle-tourism (accessed 18 June 2017).

Donia al-Watan. (2012) 'Al-Qaradawi's fatwa raises divisions among scholars'. [online] Available at: https://www.alwatanvoice.com/arabic/content/print/255764.html (accessed 3 June 2012).

Elad, A. (1995) *Medieval Jerusalem and Islamic Worship: Holy Places, Ceremonies, Pilgrimages*. Leiden: E.J. Brill.

Elad, A. (1996) 'Pilgrims and pilgrimage to Hebron (al-Khalīl) during the early Muslim period (6389–1099)'. In B.F. Le Beau and M. Mor (eds) *Pilgrims and Travelers to the Holy Land, Studies in Jewish Civilization*. Omaha, NB: Creighton University Press, 21–61.

Esposito, J. (ed.) (1999) *The Oxford History of Islam*. Oxford: Oxford University Press.

Haines, G. (2017) '10 surprising destinations where tourism is booming in 2017'. *The Telegraph*, 27 September. [online] Available at: www.telegraph.co.uk/travel/news/surprising-countries-where-tourism-is-booming-in-2017/ (accessed 20 August 2017).

Halaika M., Nakashian S. and Dahadha A.I. (2016) *Development of Tourism Sector in East Jerusalem*. Jerusalem and Ramallah: Palestine Economic Policy Research Institute (MAS).

Ibn al-Murajja, Abu 'lMa'ali, al-Musharraf b. al Murajja. (1995) *Faḍā'il Bayt al-Maqdis wa-'I-Sham wa – 'I-Khalil*. (Ed. O. Livne), Shafa-Amro.

Isaac, R.K (2015) 'Understanding religious tourism—motivations and trends', paper presented at the UNWTO International Conference on Religious Tourism: Fostering Sustainable Socio-economic Development in Host Communities, Bethlehem, State of Palestine, 15–16 June 2015.

Isaac, R.K. (2017) 'Taking you home: The Masar Ibrahim Al-khalil in Palestine'. In: C.M. Hall, Y. Ram and N. Shoval (eds) *The Routledge International Handbook of Walking*. London: Routledge, 172–183.

Isaac, R., Hall, C.M. and Higgins-Desbiolles, F. (eds) (2016) *The Politics and Power of Tourism in Palestine*. Abingdon: Routledge.

Jaelani, A. (2017) 'Halal tourism industry in Indonesia: Potential and prospects', *International Review of Management and Marketing*,7 (3). [online] Available at: https://ssrn.com/abstract=2899864

Jerusalem Institute for Israel Studies (JIIS). (2017) *Statistical Yearbook of Jerusalem, No. 31, 2017 Edition. Chapter XI—Tourism*. Jerusalem.

Jordanzad. (2013) 'The Jordanian custodianship of the Alqsa: Return the unity of the two Banks'. (Arabic). [online] Available at: www.jordanzad.com/index.php?page=tag&hashtag=جدس&pn=233 (accessed 6 April 2013).

Lieberman, M. (2015) *World-best-cities*. [online] Available at: www.travelandleisure.com (accessed 4 August 2015).

Ma'an News Agency. (2013) 'Islamic tourism'. (Arabic) [online] Available at: www.maannews.net/Content. aspx?id=603164 (accessed 9 June 2013).

Ma'an News Agency. (2017) 'Muslims from Southeast Asia enter into a state of iḥram in al-Aqsa to perform "Umra"'. (Arabic) [online] Available at: https://maannews.net/Content.aspx?id=909291 (accessed 27 May 2017).

Organisation of Islamic Cooperation (OIC). (2015a) 'Visiting Al-Quds permissible and recommended: International Islamic Fiqh Academy issues decree'. *Organisation of Islamic Cooperation (OIC) Journal*, 29: 45.

Organisation of Islamic Cooperation (OIC). (2015b) *International Tourism in the OIC Countries: Prospects and Challenges*. Ankara: OIC.

Organisation of Islamic Cooperation (OIC). (2017) 'Member states'. [online] Available at: www.oic-oci.org/states/?lan=en (accessed 4 May 2017).

Palestinian Central Bureau of Statistics (PCBS) 2011–2016. Ramallah: MOTA.

Paltoday. (2015) 'Jerusalem tourism gets lifeline from unlikely source: Muslim visitors'. (Arabic) [online] Available at: https://paltoday.ps/ar/post/234292 (accessed 7 June 2015).

United Nations World Tourism Organization (UNWTO). (2016) *UNWTO World Tourism Barometer 2016*. Madrid, Spain: UNWTO.

11

MARKETING EUROPE TO ISLAMIC HERITAGE TOURISTS

Bailey Ashton Adie

Introduction

According to a study undertaken by the Pew Research Center (2012), there were approximately 1.6 billion individuals in the world in 2010 who identified as Muslim, which was 23.2 per cent of the global population of 6.9 billion. Given the enormity of this potential tourism market, it is surprising that there has been so little academic involvement with the subject, and, of the studies that have been published, only a few have touched on cultural or heritage aspects of Islamic tourism (Al-Hamarneh & Steiner 2004; Neveu 2010; Kessler 2015). While one suggested the existence of an Islamic tourism sub-segment focused on mosque visitation (Kessler 2015), this chapter is the first to specifically discuss 'Islamic heritage tourists'. This newly defined tourist segment can be seen as a potentially profitable new market for European destinations with a history of Islamic rule. However, attracting this tourist segment requires not only a presentation of the Islamic heritage on offer but also a respectful marketing strategy in line with Islamic principles as it is crucial to frame heritage tourism appropriately for this market. Currently, there is no state-driven marketing specifically targeting Islamic heritage tourists in Europe and, therefore, it becomes necessary to discuss the ways in which European nations can best market themselves to this new tourist segment.

Framing Islamic heritage tourism

Islam is a holistic religion, wherein 'the holy book *Qur'an* provides guidance in all aspects of human activity' (Jafari & Scott 2014: 2). Therefore, all activities become either *halal* (permissible) or *haram* (forbidden) with restrictions on how they may or not be performed. This is particularly relevant when discussing tourism as it can often involve the relinquishment of control over certain aspects of daily life (i.e. living space, food, lifestyle). Travel, specifically in the form of pilgrimage, is allowed, particularly as pilgrimage to Mecca is one of the five pillars of Islam. However, other forms of travel are also sanctioned, and even encouraged, in the Holy *Qur'an*. This is especially evident in *Surah Al-'Ankabut* verse 20 when Muhammad says 'Travel through the land and observe how He began creation. Then Allah will produce the final creation. Indeed Allah, over all things, is competent.' According to Din (1989: 552) 'the goal of travel is to help instil the realisation of the smallness of man and the greatness of God.' While it is clear that the Holy *Qur'an* permits travel, Sanad, Kassem and Scott (2010: 30) take it one step further by stating that 'one can conclude that tourism is a human right under Islamic law.' Thus, there is religious justification for the discussion of Islamic tourism.

It is important to note that, while Islamic tourism and *halal* tourism are often used interchangeably, this chapter will solely utilise the term Islamic tourism. Henderson (2009) makes a distinction between these two types of tourism, specifically in terms of motivation, with *halal* tourism being expressly religious in nature. In comparison, she defines Islamic tourism as 'travel by Muslims for whom compliance with doctrinal structures when away from home is an important consideration … although primary motives may not be directly connected to religion' (Henderson 2016: 339). Carboni, Perelli and Sistu (2014: 2) provide a slightly diverse understanding of the concept wherein 'Islamic tourism is defined as tourism in accordance with Islam, involving people of the Muslim faith who are interested in keeping with their personal religious habits while traveling. This definition … does not concern exclusively travel to or within Muslim countries.' This is similar to Henderson's but expands on it by emphasising that Islamic tourism can occur anywhere that Muslims travel. In comparison, Jafari and Scott (2014: 9) present a broader conceptualisation with Islamic tourism presented as 'a new "touristic" interpretation of pilgrimage that merges religious and leisure tourism.' While most of these authors are in agreement as to what can be considered Islamic tourism, it is necessary to stress that there is currently no official definition of Islamic tourism.

In addition to these general definitions, several authors have included cultural elements to their descriptions of Islamic tourism. For example, Al-Hamarneh and Steiner (2004) conceptualised Islamic tourism as containing three facets (economic, cultural, and religious/conservative), with the cultural component setting their definition apart. This cultural aspect is echoed in Kessler's (2015: 23) interpretation of the term, for whom Islamic tourism refers to 'Muslims travelling to Muslim friendly destinations offering Halal Tourism options combining religious and cultural Muslim oriented attractions.' Al-Hamarneh and Steiner (2004: 180) highlighted the need to '[reorient] tourist destinations towards less consumption and "western-culture loaded" sites and toward more Islamic historical, religious, and cultural sites.' This aligns with the Jordanian definition of Islamic tourism, which, according to Neveu (2010), emphasises the importance of visiting areas that are important to Islamic history in order to enhance visitor knowledge. While these definitions touch on the importance of heritage visitation, they are too narrow in scope for the term, specifically as there are other non-religious reasons for which Muslims may travel (i.e. visit family or friends, business, for stress relief). This is addressed, in part, by Kessler (2015) who identified a subset of Islamic tourism referred to as 'Mosque Tourism'. This tourism segment is characterised by the targeted visitation of mosques by both Muslims and non-Muslims in Muslim countries for both religious and non-religious purposes. However, while this definition is quite encompassing, it is still very specific to the visitation of one type of Islamic built heritage.

The concept of Islamic heritage tourism presented in this chapter builds on the previously discussed definitions of Islamic tourism, with particular attention paid to the previously mentioned cultural aspects. While all prior descriptions of the Islamic tourism market segment agree on the importance of travel that follows Islamic principles and includes visits to Islamic destinations, it is of interest to further delineate potential Islamic tourists. This is due to the various motivations for travel sanctioned in the Holy *Qur'an*, which are particularly relevant to the discussion of an Islamic heritage tourist segment. For instance, travelling to better understand the history of mankind is highlighted in *Surah Muhammad* verse 10, which states 'Have they not travelled through the land and seen how was the end of those before them?' This sentiment is echoed several times in different *surahs* (i.e. *Surah Al-An'am*: 11, *Surah Yusuf*: 109, *Surah An-Naml*: 69). Muslims are thus encouraged to bear witness to past civilisations in order to learn from them (Timothy & Iverson 2006; Jafari & Scott 2014). Additionally, *Surah Al-Hujurat* verse 13 says 'O mankind, indeed We have created you from male and female and made you peoples and tribes that you may know one another.' This encourages Muslims to travel in order to interact with different cultures (Din 1989; Sanad et al. 2010; Jafari & Scott 2014). As can be seen, heritage tourism is a *halal* form of travel that is supported by the Holy *Qur'an*. Thus, based on the established religious endorsement of travel as well as the previous literature, Islamic heritage tourism is best described as the purposeful visitation of places of historical and cultural import, with a particular emphasis on those sites which pertain to Islamic heritage, while following Islamic tourism principles.

Islamic marketing

Based on the definition of the newly identified Islamic heritage tourist market segment, marketing strategies in line with Islamic ethics will be needed in order to ensure compliance with the segment's religious requirements. It should be noted that while general principles of Islamic marketing exist, the Islamic market is incredibly diverse (El-Fatatry, Lee, Khan & Lehdonvirta 2011; Prokopec & Kurdy 2011; Temporal 2011). However, this does not preclude the usage of general marketing tactics which are based in the tenants of Islam as this is an integral aspect of this market. Prokopec and Kurdy (2011: 212) refer to it as the '"think *sharia* (or *halal*), act local" approach.' This is particularly important as 'advertising that does not take into account the sensitivities of Islamic values and culture, may result in lost sales and perhaps loss of company image' (De Run, Butt, Fam & Jong 2010: 29). Therefore, it is unsurprising that marketing would have 'to be consistent with [Muslim] religious understanding, knowledge, and feelings' (Haque, Ahmed & Jahan 2010: 73).

According to Dean (2013: 25), Islamic marketing is 'the promotion of a product that appeals in any way to the Muslim values of either the producer or the consumer, or both.' Furthermore, according to Ali (2011), Islamic ethics play a strong role in daily life and therefore have an impact on marketing initiatives. This has resulted in the creation of specific, recommended guidelines that align with general ethical considerations related to Islamic business transactions, which are identified by Ali (2011) as effort, competition, transparency, and morally responsible conduct. For Ali (2011), morally responsible conduct is the crux of these four principles. He notes that, without a moral underpinning, transparency, competition, and effort may not be sustainable in the long term. Thus Islamic morality, which greatly impacts on intent and purpose, is woven into the other three ethical principles, which are elaborated in the following paragraphs.

The first of these principles, effort, is best expressed in relation to its purpose, which requires that 'marketing in Islam should be to meet societal demands and be in line with societal goals' (Ali 2011: 21). The emphasis, then, is on societal benefit and not maximising profits (Saeed, Ahmed & Mukhtar 2001; Marinov 2007; Ali 2011; Prokopec & Kurdy 2011). In fact, Temporal (2011: 7–8) stresses that marketing to create demand 'is at odds with Islamic economics, which espouses moderation and a resource-based view of consumption.' Rice and Al-Mossawi (2002: 82–83) referred to this as 'balanced consumption' wherein 'social responsibility is preferred to conspicuous consumption and profit-seeking.' This societal-focused marketing then stresses the importance of the consumer's individual humanity and not just as a source for profit (Arham 2010). However, this does not imply that Islamic marketing must be reactionary. Instead, it should endeavour to forecast the consumers' needs and wants in order to effectively fulfil potential demand (Ali 2011).

This focus on societal benefit is also an important aspect of Ali's (2011) second principle, competition, which is encouraged in Islam. However, competition should be based on the concept of *Adl*, or justice, which emphasises 'the fair treatment of competitors' in advertising (Turnbull, Howe-Walsh & Boulanouar 2016: 8). According to Cader (2015: 181), 'defaming competition is a violation of Islamic etiquette and considered reprehensible behavior.' This extends to comparative advertising, which Rice and Al-Mossawi (2002: 74) indicate should be avoided, 'especially those referring to a competing brand by name.' Therefore, while competition is encouraged, it should be undertaken in a fair and just manner. In continuation of the concept of fair and just treatment of competitors, competition shouldn't lead to the creation of monopolies or price alterations (both increases and decreases) that are not in line with the market. Instead, competition is expected to result in improved quality levels as this is the only permitted method by which to increase prices, apart from an increase in quantity of the product (Marinov 2007). Thus, competition is essential within Islamic markets, but competitors need to be treated in a just manner which benefits all.

Transparency, Ali's (2011) third principle, is one of the most stressed within the literature, specifically in relation to the necessity for truth in advertising. Arham (2010: 159) states that 'products should be communicated within ethical boundaries so that customers do not feel deceived.' Rice and Al-Mossawi (2002: 79) underscore that 'exaggeration is regarded as a form of lying, whether exaggeration is by metaphor or by embellishing a description.' Therefore, there can be no upselling of products. Cader (2015), in his study on Saudi Arabia, elaborated on the necessity of honesty in advertising in relation to ambiguity in marketing, specifically in non-specific pricing and/or lack of clarity in terms of product quantity. Furthermore, 'all defects should be disclosed to the buyer before a sale' (Prokopec & Kurdy 2011: 217). According to Saeed et al. (2001: 134), marketers 'must, under all circumstances, have a regard for the intellectual integrity and a higher degree of consciousness of the consumers to ensure that the hard earned money of customers is not wasted.' As a result, transparency, as with effort and competition, is intrinsically tied to the concept of societal benefit.

As can be seen, Islamic marketing needs to, ultimately, result in the betterment of society, be aware of the demands of the market, and provide honest and fair treatment of the consumer. Saeed et al. (2001: 134) also note that, more specifically, 'stereotyping of women in advertising, excessive use of fantasy, the use of suggestive language and behaviour, and the use of women as objects to lure and attract customers' are forbidden in Islamic marketing. Consequently, it can be assumed that those activities which are specifically *haram* (i.e. drinking alcohol, gambling, eating pork) would also not be permitted for use in advertising aimed at Muslim consumers.

All of these factors need to be taken into account when marketing to Islamic heritage tourists, particularly when developing a marketing plan for a non-Muslim majority location.

Islamic heritage tourism in Europe

While Islamic heritage is predominantly associated with the Middle East and North African regions, large Islamic empires throughout history as well as expansive trade routes have resulted in the existence of a broad array of Islamic heritage sites in various regions around the world. Europe is one of these oft-overlooked regions with a significant history of Islamic rule, which can be tied, predominantly, to two different groups, the Arabs and the Ottoman Turks. Arab rule in Europe was concentrated mainly in the Iberian Peninsula, including much of what is contemporary Spain and Portugal, during the early Middle Ages. In comparison, the Ottoman Empire controlled most of Southeast Europe from the late Middle Ages to the mid-nineteenth century. While Europe is not automatically considered as an Islamic heritage destination, this history has attracted evident Islamic heritage tourist interest in the region, as can be seen in the heritage-specific tours offered by several *halal* and Islamic tourism companies (i.e. Ilimtour, Islamic Travels, Spain Baraka Tours). These companies provide packages to several Islamic heritage destinations, namely Spain, Portugal, Bosnia and Herzegovina (BiH), Russia, Greece, and Italy. Spain is the most popular destination, being offered by all three Islamic tourism companies, with Bosnian, Portuguese, and Italian tours run by two out of the three. Both Spain Baraka Tours and Islamic Travels sell package tours to BiH with an emphasis on the Islamic heritage elements of the tour (Spain Baraka Tours 2016a; Islamic Travels 2017b). Portugal is offered by Ilimtour and Spain Baraka Tours. However, of these two, only Spain Baraka Tours (2016b) stresses the Islamic heritage element in their tour description. Additionally, visits to Italy are offered by Spain Baraka Tours (2016a) and Islamic Travels (2017c), but those provided by Spain Baraka Tours do not have Islamic heritage elements. The tour that will be provided by Islamic Travels (2017c) appears to have a strong Islamic heritage focus, but currently that section of their tour site is still being completed. Only Islamic Travels (2017a, 2017d) provides tours to Russia and Greece, placing particular emphasis on Islamic heritage. Given the existence of these heritage excursions, there appears to be an interest in the general Islamic tourism market for heritage-driven trips outside of what are considered traditionally Muslim countries.

Ottoman Empire

At its peak, the Ottoman Empire stretched across much of Southeast Europe, but only BiH and Greece are currently included in private Islamic heritage tour itineraries. Moreover, out of all the European countries with these tours, BiH is the only one that has a majority Muslim population with a little over 50 per cent of the population identifying as Muslim (Agency for Statistics of Bosnia and Herzegovina 2016). This would appear to make it an ideal European destination for Islamic heritage tourists given its existing practising population. BiH's official tourism website frequently mentions their Islamic heritage, highlighting the impact that the Ottomans had on religion in the country (Tourism Association of Federation of BiH 2005a) and referring to BiH as a 'sacred crossroads' where Islam, Judaism, and both eastern and western Christianity meet (Tourism Association of Federation of BiH 2005b). However, while the BiH tourism website often discusses the Muslim population, there is no information specifically for Muslim tourists, particularly in relation to the accessibility of *halal* amenities. Furthermore, while the images used throughout the website in general are not offensive, one of the banner images across the top of the website depicts two women who are dressed for summer and thus uncovered, which is contrary to Islamic sensibilities (Tourism Association of Federation of BiH 2005c).

Similar to BiH, most of Greece was part of the Ottoman Empire for several hundred years and still contains many remnants from this period, including mosques and fortifications. The Greek tourism website does highlight Islamic sites in their guides on what to do in specific locations. For example, the site suggests visiting the Hamza Bey Mosque, the White Tower (an Ottoman fortification), and the Turkish baths when visiting the city centre of Thessaloniki (Greek National Tourism Organisation (GNTO) 2017e). In Athens, there is a short description of the areas of interest in the historic centre related to the 'Ottoman occupation' (GNTO 2017b). The information provided on Ioannina is almost exclusively dedicated to Islamic heritage structures (GNTO 2017c). Another area of Greece with identified Islamic heritage is Didymoteicho, which lies close to the Turkish border, and was briefly the capital of the Ottoman Empire (GNTO 2017a). Recommended sightseeing locations include two separate Turkish bathhouses as well as a fourteenth-century mosque, which is described as 'the oldest and biggest Muslim sacred precinct on European soil' (GNTO 2017a). In terms of Islamic heritage tourist-specific requirements, Greece's website performs similarly to BiH's with no mention of places wherein to access *halal* food or where to find active mosques. Additionally, as on the Bosnian site, the female subjects of the photos on the tourism site's homepage are often portrayed wearing what would be deemed immodest clothing (GNTO 2017d).

While BiH and Greece both benefit from Islamic heritage tourism, they are not the only countries in Europe with Ottoman heritage. Other parts of Southeast Europe, specifically Albania, Bulgaria, Macedonia, Serbia, Kosovo, and Montenegro, still retain visible elements of their Islamic history. Of these, both Albania and Kosovo have majority Muslim populations, but only Albania maintains an official tourism portal. Based on a 2011 census, Albania's total Muslim community is approximately 59 per cent of the total population (United States Department of State. Bureau of Democracy, Human Rights and Labor 2013), but, as was seen in BiH, there is no mention regarding the accessibility of *halal* food in the country. Also, as with previous national tourism publications, there are multiple images of women dressed immodestly, which is most notable in the Albanian tourist rights document (National Tourism Agency n.d.). However, there is a much stronger emphasis on the country's Ottoman heritage which is notable in that one of its two cultural World Heritage sites is the Historic Centres of Berat and Gjirokastra, 'rare examples of an architectural character typical of the Ottoman period' (UNESCO 2017). When promoting Berat, the Albanian National Tourism Agency (2017a) recommends touring four separate mosques as well as a *tariqa*, a Sufi school. In Gjirokastra, they suggest a visit to the Mosque of Bazaar as well as Ottoman Bazaar neighbourhood (Albanian National Tourism Agency 2017b). In Vlora, the Muradije Mosque is 'highly recommended' (Albanian National Tourism Agency 2017d) while Kuzum Baba, a religious site belonging to a Muslim minority group (*Bektashi*), is also mentioned (Albanian National Tourism Agency 2017c).

In comparison to Albania, the Bulgarian tourism website has less engagement with its Ottoman past. This is apparent in its discussion of Bulgarian history wherein the approximately 400-year period of Ottoman rule is relegated to a mere mention of the conquest before moving directly into a discussion of the development of liberation movements (Ministry of Economy, Energy and Tourism (Bulgaria) n.d.-a). However, this is not to say that there is no presentation of the extant Islamic heritage. Plovdiv is noted as having the Dzhumaya Mosque, a Turkish bathhouse that has been repurposed as a contemporary art centre, and a clock tower built in the sixteenth century (Ministry of Economy, Energy and Tourism (Bulgaria) n.d.-b). The site highlights Banya Bashi, an active sixteenth-century mosque located in the capital city, while also emphasising the need for respectful behaviour when visiting the mosque (Ministry of Economy, Energy and Tourism (Bulgaria) n.d.-d). In Shumen, the Sherif Halil Pasha Mosque is presented as the largest and 'most architecturally significant mosque in Bulgaria' (Ministry of Economy, Energy and Tourism (Bulgaria) n.d.-c). While these mosques are not only promoted but also emphasised as being active places of worship, there is, as with the previously discussed countries' websites, a lack of information regarding *halal* facilities, which are a necessity for Islamic tourists.

As with all the previously discussed national tourism websites, any indication of *halal* amenities is also lacking from Macedonia's official tourism portal, and there are multiple images of women dressed inappropriately for marketing directed at Islamic tourists (Macedonia Timeless n.d.-d). However, in contrast to the previously discussed countries, there is more information available regarding mosques around the country, of which there are approximately 600 (Macedonia Timeless n.d.-b). Nonetheless, while there is a subsection of the website dedicated to mosques in general, only the Decorated Mosque in Tetovo is mentioned, albeit very positively (Macedonia Timeless n.d.-c). Though the section dedicated to mosques is not well populated, there are several mentions of Islamic heritage sites around Macedonia on other parts of the tourism portal. In the South, Bitola, the second largest city in the country, has 'one of the oldest Muslim sacral cultural-historical objects in Macedonia', namely the Isak Mosque (Macedonia Timeless n.d.-a). Skopje, the capital, has multiple remnants of Ottoman rule, including Stone Bridge, referred to as 'the symbol of Skopje', the fifteenth-century Turkish bathhouse Daut-Pasha Hamam, 'an impressive monument of Islamic architecture', the Old Bazaar, the first Ottoman clock tower, and the Mustapha-Pasha Mosque (Macedonia Timeless n.d.-e).

The final three countries with Ottoman heritage, Serbia, Kosovo, and Montenegro, will be discussed together as there is barely any engagement with their extant Islamic heritage and no amenities specifically for Islamic tourists. Additionally, as Kosovo does not have its own official tourism portal, all information regarding Islamic heritage has been taken from the Serbian tourism website. Based on the available information, the only Kosovan Islamic heritage presented is found in the capital city, Priština, and consists of two different mosques, a clock tower, and a private, upper class residence from the nineteenth century (National Tourism Organisation of Serbia 2017c). As this information is derived from the official Serbian tourism portal, it is unsurprising that within Serbia there is almost no acknowledgement of any remaining Islamic heritage, with merely a passing reference to the existence of Turkish additions to Belgrade Fortress (National Tourism Organisation of Serbia 2017a). Additionally, there are only two mosques identified on the website, Bajrakli Mosque in Belgrade and Altun-alem Mosque in Novi Pazar (National Tourism Organisation of Serbia 2017b). The Montenegrin site is also fairly sparse in relation to information regarding Islamic heritage sites. While there is a section dedicated to mosques, it identifies only three, the Hussein Pasa Mosque in Pljevlja, the Tzar's Mosque in Plav, and the Mosque in Petnjica (National Tourism Organisation of Montenegro n.d.-a). The Old Town of Bar is noted as having a clock tower, bath, and powder magazine all dating from the time of Ottoman rule (National Tourism Organisation of Montenegro n.d.-b), and the Old Town Ulcinj is also identified as having an Ottoman powder magazine as well as 'a Turkish drinking fountain from 1749' (National Tourism Organisation of Montenegro n.d.-c). As can be seen, neither Serbia nor Montenegro present much of their Islamic history.

As previously mentioned, all of these countries have Islamic heritage due to their historical ties to the Ottoman Empire. However, they all engage with this heritage in very different ways. Albania and BiH actively promote their Islamic heritage, which is unsurprising given that they both have Muslim majority populations. Greece, Bulgaria, and Macedonia all engage with their Ottoman heritage, but they do not tend to overemphasise it. In comparison, Serbia, and by extension Kosovo, as well as Montenegro barely acknowledge this aspect of their heritage. Nevertheless, regardless of the differences in promotional levels, none of the official tourism portals provide information on *halal* amenities within the countries, which would be an essential part of attracting Islamic heritage tourists.

Arab rule

While the Ottoman Empire extended through much of Southeast Europe, there was, as previously mentioned, an earlier, shorter period of Arab Islamic rule which was concentrated almost exclusively on the Iberian Peninsula. While the heritage of this region will be discussed shortly, there needs to be a brief mention of the Islamic heritage found in Italy, particularly given the ongoing establishment of an organised, private Islamic heritage tour focusing on Sicily. The only mention of Arab influence on the Italian national tourism portal is made in passing in relation to Syracuse (Italian National Tourist Board n.d.-b). Additionally, only one Arab structure, the Norman Palace in Palermo, is discussed on the entirety of the site (Italian National Tourist Board n.d.-a). There is no other acknowledgement of Sicily's brief role as an Arab Emirate nor is there any additional information provided regarding the availability of either *halal* services or active mosques.

Arab rule in the Iberian Peninsula was only marginally longer than that in Sicily, yet both Portugal and Spain underscore their Islamic heritage to a much greater extent. In Portugal, there are multiple noted sites of Arab origin, including Silves which is the former Arab capital of the Algarve Kingdom (Turismo de Portugal 2013f). Mértola is another former Arab capital and home to the Islamic Museum (Turismo de Portugal 2013d) while Faro retains an Arab Gateway as well as undefined archaeological remains (Turismo de Portugal 2013c). Fortifications appear to be the most common Islamic heritage feature in Portugal. The Castelo de Silves is one of the less altered of the Islamic castles from the Almohade period (Turismo de Portugal 2013a), while one of the older Islamic heritage sites is the Castelo dos Mouros near Sintra whose origins can be traced back to the eighth century (Turismo de Portugal 2013b). Although there are still remnants of both military and secular Islamic heritage sites, religious sites from the period of Arab rule are absent in Portugal. In fact, there are multiple examples on the tourism website wherein a church is described as having been constructed on the site of a mosque, physically displaying the Christian re-conquest of the formerly Muslim lands. Additionally, on their page dedicated to religious tourism, there is no mention of the Islamic past (Turismo de Portugal 2013e). Therefore, it is unsurprising that the Portuguese website has no information on active mosques nor on any *halal* services that may exist.

Among the Islamic heritage tours to European countries, Spain appears to be by far the most popular. As a result, it is unsurprising they also have the most developed national tourism website in terms of targeting the Islamic and *halal* tourism markets. Their official tourism portal has a specific section for members of the Gulf Cooperation Council (i.e. Saudi Arabia, Kuwait, UAE, Qatar, Bahrain, and Oman), which is available in Arabic as well as English. The initial welcome page accentuates the Islamic heritage available in Spain, which is notable in the second scrolling banner available wherein the site 'invite[s] you to discover the living legacy of Moorish culture in Spain' (Turespaña 2017c). While this section of the website is designed for general Islamic tourists, there is a strong emphasis on 'Moorish' heritage sites with Andalusia and the Costa del Sol listed as one of the three 'main destinations' on the welcome page (Turespaña 2017c). The page dedicated to Andalusia underscores the influence that Arab culture has had on the region not only in terms of built heritage but also in regards to both gastronomy and bath culture (Turespaña 2017a). Additionally, in contrast to every other national tourism site presented in this chapter, the Gulf Cooperation Council page on the Spanish portal has a specific subsection dedicated to *halal* tourism. This page includes information on *halal* hotels and restaurants, mosques, access to appropriate worship facilities in airports, religious celebrations, and additional links to Islamic organisations in Spain (Turespaña 2017b). Furthermore, on each individual page for the featured destinations, there is information on where to locate the main mosque, if there is one.

In comparison to the Ottoman Empire's control of Southeast Europe, Arab rule in the Iberian Peninsula and Sicily lasted for a relatively short time period. It should be noted, though, that, regardless of the brevity of Arab influence, all three of the countries are visited by private Islamic heritage tours. As Italy experienced the shortest Islamic influence, it is unsurprising that there is little mention on their official tourism portal. However, although both Portugal and Spain were ruled by the same Islamic dynasty, Portugal only lightly touches on the subject. Furthermore, only Spain's official tourism portal has information specifically for Islamic tourists who are searching for *halal* amenities.

Discussion and conclusions

Europe has a rich history of Islamic rule throughout the centuries, and, as has been noted, there exists significant Islamic heritage from these periods. However, most of the countries discussed in this chapter do little to promote their Islamic heritage. While this is, in and of itself, not necessarily problematic, the presence of private Islamic heritage tours indicates that there is an active Islamic heritage tourist segment that is both interested in and willing to visit European Islamic heritage. Furthermore, of those countries that do accent their Islamic heritage, only Spain provides any information on *halal* amenities and highlights active mosques available in each destination. In order to successfully market European destinations to the newly defined Islamic heritage tourist, the national tourism websites would have to follow a similar model to that seen on the Spanish website in terms of content. This would need to include the creation of a page on their portal specifically dedicated to Islamic tourists, which would be expected to follow Ali's (2011) ethical Islamic marketing principles while also removing inappropriate images of women or *haram* activities.

It should be noted that this research is preliminary in nature and thus provides the groundwork for a more in-depth analysis. Moreover, only the English versions of each website were examined due to the language limitations of the researcher, though information regarding *halal* amenities was checked in all languages. While this chapter has defined Islamic heritage tourists, there is no extant empirical evidence definitively identifying this market segment. Thus further research is needed not only to prove its existence but also to determine if it has any specific demographic trends or travelling habits. Additionally, it would be useful to determine the extent to which Islamic heritage tourists are interested in travelling to European Islamic heritage sites as well as their pre-existing knowledge, if any, of Islamic history in Europe. Furthermore, while only countries with Ottoman and Arab heritage have been discussed in this chapter, there have been additional Islamic periods in Europe, notably the Tatars in the Ukraine, Russia, and Poland. More recent Islamic heritage may also exist in other European countries that have a history of Islamic immigration, such as the UK or France. Given the growing Muslim population worldwide, it may be worthwhile for European countries to capitalise on this aspect of their heritage in order to open up their tourism market to a new audience.

References

Agency for Statistics of Bosnia and Herzegovina. (2016) 'Census of population, households and dwellings in Bosnia and Herzegovina, 2013: Final results'. [online] Available at: www.popis.gov.ba/popis2013/doc/RezultatiPopisa_BS.pdf (accessed 28 September 2017).

Al-Hamarneh, A. and Steiner, C. (2004) 'Islamic tourism: Rethinking the strategies of tourism development in the Arab world after September 11, 2001', *Comparative Studies of South Asia, Africa and the Middle East*, 21 (1): 173–182.

Albanian National Tourism Agency. (2017a) 'Berat: 2400 year old museum city'. [online] Available at: http://albania.al/destination/12/berati/(accessed 3 October 2017).

Albanian National Tourism Agency. (2017b) 'Gjirokastra: The city of stone'. [online] Available at: http://albania.al/destination/13/gjirokastra/(accessed 3 October 2017).

Albanian National Tourism Agency. (2017c) 'Trip through history: Vlora—Narta—Orikum—Amantia—Apollonia'. [online] Available at: http://albania.al/tour/2/a_trip_through_history/(accessed 3 October 2017).

Albanian National Tourism Agency. (2017d) 'Vlora: Beach and rocky sand'. [online] Available at: http://albania.al/destination/19/vlora/(accessed 3 October 2017).

Ali, A.J. (2011) 'Islamic ethics and marketing'. In O. Sandıkcı and G. Rice (eds) *Handbook of Islamic Marketing*. Cheltenham: Edward Elgar, 17–34.

Arham, M. (2010) 'Islamic perspectives on marketing', *Journal of Islamic Marketing*, 1 (2): 149–164.

Cader, A.A. (2015) 'Islamic challenges to advertising: A Saudi Arabian perspective', *Journal of Islamic Marketing*, 6 (2): 166–187.

Carboni, M., Perelli, C., and Sistu, G. (2014) 'Is Islamic tourism a viable option for Tunisian tourism? Insights from Djerba', *Tourism Management Perspectives*, 11: 1–9.

De Run, E.C., Butt, M.M., Fam, K.-S., and Jong, H.Y. (2010) 'Attitudes towards offensive advertising: Malaysian Muslims' views', *Journal of Islamic Marketing*, 1 (1): 25–36.

Dean, J. (2013) 'Muslim values and market value: A sociological perspective', *Journal of Islamic Marketing*, 5 (1): 20–32.

Din, K.H. (1989) 'Islam and tourism: Patterns, issues, and options', *Annals of Tourism Research*, 16: 542–563.

El-Fatatry, M., Lee, S., Khan, T., and Lehdonvirta, V. (2011) 'A digital media approach to Islamic marketing'. In O. Sandıkcı and G. Rice (eds) *Handbook of Islamic Marketing*. Cheltenham: Edward Elgar, 338–360.

Greek National Tourism Organisation (GNTO). (2017a) 'Didymoteicho'. [online] Available at: www.visitgreece.gr/en/destinations/didymoteicho (accessed 3 October 2017).

Greek National Tourism Organisation (GNTO). (2017b) 'On foot—Period of Ottoman occupation'. [online] Available at: www.visitgreece.gr/en/touring/on_foot/on_foot_period_of_ottoman_occupation (accessed 28 September 2017).

Greek National Tourism Organisation (GNTO). (2017c) 'The castle town of Ioannina'. [online] Available at: www.visitgreece.gr/en/castles/the_castle_town_of_ioannina (accessed 28 September 2017).

Greek National Tourism Organisation (GNTO). (2017d) 'Greece: All time classic'. [online] Available at: www.visitgreece.gr/(accessed 3 October 2017).

Greek National Tourism Organisation (GNTO). (2017e) 'What to see in the centre of Thessaloniki'. [online] Available at: www.visitgreece.gr/en/main_cities/what_to_see_in_the_centre_of_thessaloniki (accessed 28 September 2017).

Haque, A., Ahmed, K., and Jahan, S.I. (2010) '*Shariah* observation: Advertising practices of Bank Muamalat in Malaysia', *Journal of Islamic Marketing*, 1 (1): 70–77.

Henderson, J.C. (2009) 'Islamic tourism reviewed', *Tourism Recreation Research*, 32 (2): 207–211.

Henderson, J.C. (2016) 'Muslim travellers, tourism industry responses and the case of Japan', *Tourism Recreation Research*, 41 (3): 339–347.

Islamic Travels. (2017a) 'Greece: Ancient to Ottoman Tourkokratia'. [online] Available at: http://islamictravels.com/greece-ancient-to-ottoman/(accessed 28 September 2017).

Islamic Travels. (2017b) 'Islamic tour of Bosnia'. [online] Available at: http://islamictravels.com/islamic-tour-of-bosnia/(accessed 27 September 2017).

Islamic Travels. (2017c) 'Italy: Imperial Rome & the Emirate of Sicily'. [online] Available at: http://islamictravels.com/italy/(accessed 27 September 2017).

Islamic Travels. (2017d) 'Russia: The Golden Horde Tatars & the Volga'. [online] Available at: http://islamictravels.com/russia/(accessed 28 September 2017).

Italian National Tourist Board. (n.d.-a) 'Palermo'. [online] Available at: www.italia.it/en/travel-ideas/art-cities/palermo.html?no_cache=1&h=mosque (accessed 5 October 2017).

Italian National Tourist Board. (n.d.-b) 'Syracuse'. [online] Available at: www.italia.it/en/discover-italy/sicily/syracuse.html?no_cache=1&h=syracuse (accessed 5 October 2017).

Jafari, J. and Scott, N. (2014) 'Muslim world and its tourisms', *Annals of Tourism Research*, 44: 1–19.

Kessler, K. (2015) 'Conceptualizing mosque tourism: A central feature of Islamic and religious tourism', *International Journal of Religious Tourism and Pilgrimage* [online] 3 (2): 11–32. Available at: http://arrow. dit.ie/ijrtp/vol3/iss2/2 (accessed 11 May 2017).

Macedonia Timeless. (n.d.-a) 'Bitola'. [online] Available at: http://macedonia-timeless.com/eng/cities_and_ regions/cities/bitola/(accessed 5 October 2017).

Macedonia Timeless. (n.d.-b) 'Culture and history'. [online] Available at: http://macedonia-timeless. com/eng/about/about/culture_andhistory/(accessed 4 October 2017).

Macedonia Timeless. (n.d.-c) 'ger + Multicolored Mosque'. [online] Available at: http://macedonia-timeless.com/eng/things_to_do/senses/touch/culture_andhistory/mosques/multicolored_mosque/ (accessed 4 October 2017).

Macedonia Timeless. (n.d.-d) 'Photo gallery'. [online] Available at: http://macedonia-timeless.com/eng/ about/about/photo_gallery/(accessed 5 October 2017).

Macedonia Timeless. (n.d.-e) 'Skopje'. [online] Available at: http://macedonia-timeless.com/eng/cities_ and_regions/cities/skopje/(accessed 5 October 2017).

Marinov, M. (2007) 'Marketing challenges in Islamic countries'. In M. Marinov (ed.) *Marketing in the Emerging Markets of Islamic Countries*. Basingstoke: Palgrave Macmillan, 1–13.

Ministry of Economy, Energy and Tourism (Bulgaria). (n.d.-a) 'History'. [online] Available at: www. bulgariatravel.org/en/Article/Details/4076/History (accessed 4 October 2017).

Ministry of Economy, Energy and Tourism (Bulgaria). (n.d.-b) 'Old town architectural-historical reserve —Plovdiv'. [online] Available at: www.bulgariatravel.org/en/article/details/9/Old%20Town% 20Architectural-Historical%20Reserve%20%E2%80%93%20Plovdiv (accessed 4 October 2017).

Ministry of Economy, Energy and Tourism (Bulgaria). (n.d.-c) 'Sherif Halil Pasha Mosque, Shumen'. [online] Available at: www.bulgariatravel.org/en/article/details/64/Sherif%20Halil%20Pasha% 20Mosque%2C%20Shumen (accessed 4 October 2017).

Ministry of Economy, Energy and Tourism (Bulgaria). (n.d.-d) 'Sofia Mosque'. [online] Available at: www.bulgariatravel.org/article/details/379 (accessed 4 October 2017).

National Tourism Agency (Albania). (n.d.) 'Tourist rights'. [pdf] Available at: http://albania.al/getFile/ gho348xr597b991e83703 (accessed 4 October 2017).

National Tourism Organisation of Montenegro. (n.d.-a) 'Mosques'. [online] Available at: https://www. montenegro.travel/en/objects/mosques (accessed 5 October 2017).

National Tourism Organisation of Montenegro. (n.d.-b) 'The old town of Bar'. [online] Available at: https://www.montenegro.travel/en/objects/the-old-town-of-bar- (accessed 5 October 2017).

National Tourism Organisation of Montenegro. (n.d.-c) 'The old town Ulcinj'. [online] Available at: https://www.montenegro.travel/en/objects/the-old-town-ulcinj (accessed 5 October 2017).

National Tourism Organisation of Serbia. (2017a) *Belgrade Fortress*. [online] Available at: www.serbia. travel/destinations/cities-and-municipalities.a-153.692.html (accessed 5 October 2017).

National Tourism Organization of Serbia. (2017b) *Mosques*. [online] Available at: www.serbia.travel/ culture/religious-buildings/mosques.674.html (accessed 5 October 2017).

National Tourism Organisation of Serbia. (2017c) *Priština*. [online] Available at: www.serbia.travel/ destinations/cities-and-municipalities.a-22.692.html (accessed 5 October 2017).

Neveu, N. (2010) 'Islamic tourism in Jordan: Sacred topography and state ambitions'. In N. Scott and J. Jafari (eds) *Tourism in the Muslim World*. Bingley, West Yorkshire: Emerald, 141–157.

Pew Research Center. (2012) *The Global Religious Landscape: A Report on the Size and Distribution of the World's Major Religious Groups as of 2010*. [pdf] Available at: http://assets.pewresearch.org/wp-content/ uploads/sites/11/2014/01/global-religion-full.pdf (accessed 16 October 2017).

Prokopec, S. and Kurdy, M. (2011) 'An international marketing strategy perspective on Islamic marketing'. In O. Sandıkcı and G. Rice (eds) *Handbook of Islamic Marketing*. Cheltenham: Edward Elgar, 208–225.

Rice, G. and Al-Mossawi, M. (2002) 'The implications of Islam for advertising messages: The Middle Eastern context', *Journal of Euromarketing*, 11 (3): 71–96.

Saeed, M., Ahmed, Z.U., and Mukhtar, S.-M. (2001) 'International marketing ethics from an Islamic perspective: A value-maximization approach', *Journal of Business Ethics*, 32 (2): 127–142.

Sanad, H.S., Kassem, A.M., and Scott, N. (2010) 'Tourism and Islamic law'. In N. Scott and J. Jafari (eds) *Tourism in the Muslim World*. Bingley, West Yorkshire: Emerald, 17–30.

Spain Baraka Tours. (2016a) *Gems of Bosnia & Italy*. [online] Available at: http://spainbarakatours.com/ packages/muslim-package-bosnia-italy-bk-g08zami01/(accessed 27 September 2017).

Spain Baraka Tours. (2016b) *Golden Spain & Portugal*. [online] Available at: http://spainbarakatours.com/ packages/bk-g07mali02/(accessed 27 September 2017).

Temporal, P. (2011) *Islamic Branding and Marketing: Creating a Global Islamic Business*. Singapore: John Wiley (Asia).

Timothy, D.J. and Iverson, T. (2006) 'Tourism and Islam: Considerations of culture and duty'. In D.J. Timothy and D.H. Olsen (eds) *Tourism, Religion and Spiritual Journeys*. London: Routledge, 186–205.

Tourism Association of Federation of BIH. (2005a) *Religion of Bosnia and Herzegovina*. [online] Available at: www.bhtourism.ba/eng/religion.wbsp (accessed 28 September 2017).

Tourism Association of Federation of BIH. (2005b) *Sacred Crossroads: The Heart-shaped Land*. [online] Available at: www.bhtourism.ba/eng/sacredcrossroads.wbsp (accessed 28 September 2017).

Tourism Association of Federation of BIH (2005c) *What to do?*. [online] Available at: www.bhtourism.ba/eng/(accessed 3 October 2017).

Turespaña. (2017a) *Andalusia*. [online] Available at: www.spain.info/gcc/en/destinations/andalusia/ (accessed on 12 October 2017).

Turespaña. (2017b) *Halal Tourism*. [online] Available at: www.spain.info/gcc/en/halal/(accessed 16 October 2017).

Turespaña. (2017c) *Welcome to Spain's Official Tourism Portal*. [online] Available at: www.spain.info/gcc/en/(accessed 28 September 2017).

Turismo de Portugal. (2013a) *Castelo de Silves*. [online] Available at: https://www.visitportugal.com/en/NR/exeres/9B1F1776-2CAE-4B07-97E9-64BDF5F9571E (accessed 5 October 2017).

Turismo de Portugal. (2013b) *Castelo dos Mouros—Sintra*. [online] Available at: https://www.visitportugal.com/en/NR/exeres/C796FDC8-4D00-4AB0-88E1-29999C190724 (accessed 5 October 2017).

Turismo de Portugal. (2013c) *Faro*. [online] Available at: https://www.visitportugal.com/en/NR/exeres/DDB6DCA5-D0D1-4870-B49D-8C93BBC83043 (accessed 5 October 2017).

Turismo de Portugal. (2013d) *Mértola*. [online] Available at: https://www.visitportugal.com/en/NR/exeres/D88B64E6-E4BF-4B6C-A793-EA9545732B79 (accessed 5 October 2017).

Turismo de Portugal. (2013e) *Religious Tourism*. [online] Available at: https://www.visitportugal.com/en/experiencias/turismo-religioso (accessed 16 October 2017).

Turismo de Portugal. (2013f) *Silves*. [online] Available at: https://www.visitportugal.com/en/node/73806 (accessed 5 October 2017).

Turnbull, S., Howe-Walsh, L., and Boulanouar, A. (2016) 'The advertising standardisation debate revisited: Implications of Islamic ethics on standardisation/localisation of advertising in Middle East Islamic states', *Journal of Islamic Marketing*, 7 (1): 2–14.

United Nations Educational, Scientific and Cultural Organization (UNESCO). (2017) 'Historic centres of Berat and Gjirokastra', *UNESCO*. [online] Available at: http://whc.unesco.org/en/list/569 (accessed 3 October 2017).

United States Department of State. Bureau of Democracy, Human Rights and Labor. (2013) *Albania 2013 International Religious Freedom Report*. [pdf] Available at: https://al.usembassy.gov/wp-content/uploads/sites/140/2016/10/2013-International-Religious-Freedom-Report-for-Albania.pdf (accessed 3 October 2017).

12

THE MUSLIM-FRIENDLY OPTION

Tunisia's (mass) tourism in times of crisis

Michele Carboni and Carlo Perelli

Introduction

Tunisia was a pioneer for Muslim countries entering the global tourism market. The Tunisian tourism industry was developed during the Bourguiba presidency (1957–1987), according to European demand, and soon became a pillar of the national economy. Tunisia currently specialises in coastal tourism, offering all-inclusive packages at seaside resorts (Klabi 2014; Mansfeld & Winckler 2015). Long before the fall of Ben Ali during the 2011 Tunisian Revolution, however, the industry suffered many disparities in regional tourism development, poor product quality, and loss of competitiveness. More recently, the 2015 terrorist attacks targeted tourists at Bardo National Museum and Sousse resorts, which had a dramatic impact on Tunisia's reputation as a travel destination. Many have observed that beyond the need for regaining notoriety as a safe destination, new initiatives are needed to revitalise the industry. Considering the sector's historical development and current status, as well as the rising global interest in Muslim tourists, the present study discusses the possibility of transforming Tunisia into a Muslim-friendly travel destination, attracting tourists from underexploited markets.

The number of tourist destinations marketed as 'Muslim-friendly' is growing worldwide, and so are the products designed to meet the needs and expectations of Muslim tourists. For example, in several Muslim countries, such as Turkey and the UAE, 'Sharia-compliant' hotels are emerging (Eid & El-Gohary 2015). The popularity of such concepts as Islamic or halal tourism is also steadily growing (Scott & Jafari 2010). Despite the degree of vagueness often surrounding such concepts (Hamza, Chouhoud & Tantawi 2012; Henderson 2010), there is increasing interest towards Muslim tourists for a variety of geopolitical, demographic, and economic reasons (see Stephenson, Russell & Edgar 2010; Prayag & Hosany 2014; Stephenson & Ali 2010). During Ben Ali's regime (1987–2011), most disregarded the potential of the halal market (Sarra 2012), but a debate on halal products (including tourism) emerged after the Revolution (see La Presse 2011, 2012).

Based on field research, the present study discusses and expands upon two previous studies on the tourism of Djerba and Nabeul–Hammamet, authored by Carboni, Perelli and Sistu (2014, 2017). As in the previous studies, the objective of the present research is to investigate the perceptions of key informants in these two areas, crucial to the Tunisian tourism industry, concerning the possibility of developing Muslim-friendly tourism products.

Tunisian tourism: then and now

As a pioneer in exploring the potential of Muslim-friendly tourism development, Tunisia supported its tourism industry through a state initiative based on a clear top-down strategy (Poirier 1995; Bouzahzah & El Menyari 2013; Di Peri 2015). The sector's growth has been remarkable and relatively fast, both in terms of tourist accommodation capacity and arrivals (Table 12.1).

Created in the 1960s, the five-year National Development Plan has described investments, infrastructure development, and quantitative growth objectives for the sector. During the first stages of development, the Tunisian government operated as planner, owner, and manager of the main resorts. As reported by De Kadt (1979), around 40 per cent of Tunisia's tourist accommodation capacity between 1960 and 1965 was created through direct government initiatives. Although private initiatives emerged in the 1970s, the state held large control over the industry. At the end of the 1980s, a series of liberalisation policies were promoted by the national authorities through the 1987–1991 National Development Plan, marking the consolidation of Former President Ben Ali's control over the tourism sector, which lasted until the regime changed in 2011. (For an impressive overview of the role that firms owned by Ben Ali played in the Tunisian economy and their link with market entry regulations, see Rijkers, Freund & Nucifora 2017).

For decades, Tunisia has specialised in providing all-inclusive packages at seaside resorts. Starting in the 1970s, tourism growth in coastal areas planned by the Tunisian State showed dramatic impacts related to regional disparities, water scarcity, adverse working conditions, and economic integration with traditional sectors (Sethom 1979; Poirier 1995; Hazbun 2008; Miossec & Bourgou 2010). Social and cultural disruption caused by tourism development was also reported; in Djerba, for example, a 'moral' lecture on tourism development described it as a product of European hegemony that questioned key Tunisian values and identity issues (Bourgou & Kassah 2008).

In its initial stages, 'Eurocentric' Tunisian tourism became overdependent on a few markets (Poirier 1995), with consequences stemming from international flow variations and tour operator intermediation (Miossec 1999; Di Peri 2015). Several European countries and

Table 12.1 Tunisia: bed capacity and tourist arrivals, 1965–2010

Year	Bed capacity	Tourist arrivals
1965	8,726	165,840
1971	41,252	608,206
1981	75,847	2,150,996
1991	123,188	3,224,015
2001	205,605	5,387,300
2010	241,528	6,902,749

Source: ONTT, Office National du Tourisme Tunisien, 2011.

Tunisia's Maghreb neighbours, specifically Algeria and Libya, have always been the country's core markets for tourism, which were strongly impacted by the events of 2015 (Mansfeld & Winckler 2015). In 2010, before the Revolution, Europeans and Maghrebians accounted for over 55 per cent and 42.5 per cent of tourist arrivals, respectively (ONTT 2012). Over the last few years, due to internal instability, Libyan arrivals have decreased. This reduction in arrivals, which mainly affected southern coastal destinations close to the Libyan border, was partially mitigated by a rise in Algerian tourists.

Maghrebians and Europeans traditionally differ in their travel motivations. Coastal tourism has always been the only reason that Europeans visit Tunisia, while a break from less safe and/ or more restrictive social environments lies at the base of Maghrebians' motivations. Maghreb tourism activities also include shopping or health care, and over the last decade, Tunisia has emerged as a medical tourist destination, especially the central-southern part of the country. Like any stereotypical 'VIP experience' of cosmetic surgery, Tunisia's marketed 'beautyscape' includes a (sometimes uneasy) cohabitation between Western patient–travellers seeking low-cost services—mostly unaware of the geopolitical context—and Libyans escaping from war zones or other Maghreb visitors (Holliday, Bell, Cheung, Jones & Probyn 2015).

Europeans and Maghrebians also differ in their accommodation choices. Europeans account for the vast majority of nights spent in hotels and other registered accommodation. On the contrary, visitors from North African countries traditionally prefer holiday houses and unregistered accommodation. In 2010, for example, only 19 per cent of North African tourists stayed in hotels (ONTT 2012), while 80 per cent of hotel guests in 2000–2009 were Europeans (Institut Arabe des Chefs d'Entreprises (IACE) 2011).

For a long time, Tunisia has enjoyed its reputation as a safe destination. The tourism sector, called a 'developmental miracle' by Ben Ali's regime (Di Peri 2015), supported the discourse surrounding Tunisia's status as a stable, open Muslim country (Hazbun 2008; Hibou 2011). However, after 9/11 and the events that followed, such as the 2002 terrorist attack in Djerba, the country's international reputation began to decline (Al-Hamarneh & Steiner 2004; Steiner 2010). The 2011 regime change coincided with the apex of the stagnation in Tunisia's transition to a mature coastal destination (IACE 2011). Regional instabilities and security bias further impacted the tourism industry, leading to a crisis that is still unresolved as of 2017, despite slow recovery of European visitor flows.

The effects of the Arab Spring uprising on the Tunisian tourism industry have also been investigated. Econometric estimations of international tourist arrivals indicated that the pre-uprising decline in the tourism sector would probably last due to its post-uprising reduction in competitiveness (Perles-Ribes, Ramón-Rodríguez, Moreno-Izquierdo & Torregrosa Martí 2018). In 2010, Tunisia received almost 7 million international tourists, declining to about 4.78 million in 2011. Similarly, overnight stays decreased from 35.5 million in 2010 to 20.6 million in 2011 (ONTT 2012) (Figures 12.1 and 12.2). Although the Tunisian tourism industry slowly recovered during the 2012–2014 seasons, industry performances returned to 2011 levels after the 2015 attacks at Bardo National Museum in Tunis, leaving 20 dead, and Sousse beach, leaving 38 dead. The industry was mostly affected by a mix of national attacks against tourists and international crises (i.e. the arrival of Syrian and Libyan refugees) occurring in 2015. Consequently, as demonstrated by Cirer-Costa (2017), several North Mediterranean markets rose in demand as they were perceived as destinations with relatively reduced risk and decent security.

Security issues are not the only challenges currently affecting Tunisia's tourism. Structural loss of competitiveness, ageing buildings, quality issues, and low availability of capital for indebted hotels represent the consolidated issues plaguing the hotel sector. (For an analysis of

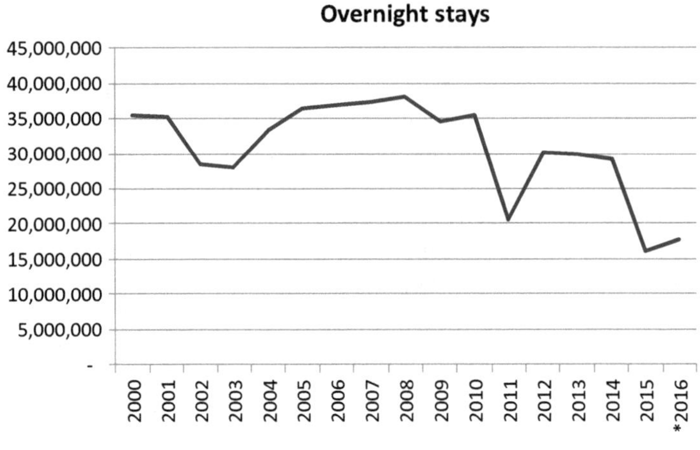

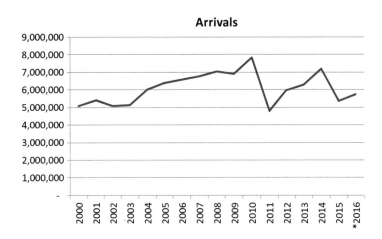

Figure 12.1 Tunisia: overnight stays, 2000–2016
Source: ONTT, 2012, 2017.
Note: ★ Not definitive.

Figure 12.2 Tunisia: tourist arrivals, 2000–2016
Source: ONTT, 2012, 2017.
Note: ★ Not definitive.

Tunisian hotel competitiveness, see Khlif 2006; Errais 2015; Di Peri 2015.) Furthermore, the sector is characterised by an overdependence on a few markets and a single tourism segment: coastal tourism.

Despite efforts made towards diversifying its tourism products, Tunisia has never achieved a strong alternative to coastal tourism. For example, heritage tourism—which commonly occurs in mass coastal tourism—has always been complementary to package vacations, as evidenced by seasonal and inter-annual variations in visitor statistics. Accordingly, the Tunisian tourism industry has participated in the national memory for decades, building, producing, and reproducing a 'mythological heritage' (Perelli & Sistu 2013). The Archaeological Site of Carthage, for example, represents the dominant discourse of a Mediterranean and African identity that overwhelms the Arab-Islamic past. Middle-class Western and Maghreb heritage tourism legitimised the official narrative of national identity, with little to no space left for counter-memories and alternative narratives of the past (Larguèche 2008).

Islam has never played a significant role in developing Tunisia's tourism sector, as Former President Bourguiba imposed a clear separation between religion and the state (Tessler 1980). A slight shift occurred with Ben Ali, who 'reintroduced the idea of Islam as a specific and crucial element of Tunisian culture, history and identity' (Haugbølle 2015: 324). Regardless, no significant changes occurred, and Islam never influenced the sector's development. During Ben Ali's regime, the potential of the halal market was generally ignored (Sarra 2012), and it was not until just after the Revolution that a debate on halal products and tourism emerged (see La Presse 2011, 2012).

Ben Ali's fall—and the unprecedented freedom of speech that Tunisians now enjoy—has allowed for increased public debate on several issues. For example, a debate on 'Tunisianity' entered the marketing domain after 2011, with profound effect (Touzani, Hirschman & Smaoui 2016). Public debate on Tunisian identity at the crossroads of Arab–Muslim, French–Western and other heritages (e.g. Berber, Sub-Saharan and Jewish) is not new (Pouessel 2012), but today's discourse also considers the role of Turkish heritage and, at the same time, its former colonial power (as the Ottoman Empire) and current reference in the Middle East.

This unprecedented debate has also given room to discussion about the potential of the halal market. Post-revolutionary governments have been very careful to reassure mass tourism operators that there is no risk of Islamisation. At the Sixth International Conference of the World Tourism Organization (UNWTO), held in Djerba in April 2012, Former Prime Minister Hamadi Jebali declared that 'there is no halal or haram tourism, there's simply tourism' (Ben Nessir 2012). More recently, during the summer of 2017, Minister of Tourism Selma Elloumi confirmed that halal tourism does not officially exist in Tunisia as a separate niche from existing family tourism products (Krimi 2017).

The Muslim-friendly option

This research focuses on two leading Tunisian destinations, Djerba and Nabeul–Hammamet, which together account for 33 per cent of hotels and over 40 per cent of tourist accommodation capacity across the nation. Djerba is the largest island of North Africa (514 km^2) and, since the 1960s, has been one of the most popular Tunisian destinations for mass coastal tourism. The eastern coast hosts almost all of Djerba's tourism infrastructure. Data on the island show the same trends towards stagnation and decline observable at the national level, for the same reasons mentioned earlier and due to the 2002 bomb attack on the El Ghriba Synagogue. Before the 2011 crisis, European tourists accounted for over 87 per cent of the 980,000 hotel arrivals, while Libyans, who represented the largest portion of non-European visitors, made up only 4.5 per cent (ONTT 2011). With respect to the present research questions, it is important to note that Jewish pilgrimages and related heritage attractions are consolidated tourism products in Djerba. Strategies for bridging the Jewish minority with Tunisia's tourism, heritage, contemporary history, and national identity building are well observable, such as the Ghriba Synagogue pilgrimage. This pilgrimage and the related festival are top tourist attractions and icons of Tunisian religious tolerance (Carboni et al. 2014; Perelli & Sistu 2013; Boussetta 2018).

The Cap Bon Peninsula hosts the Nabeul–Hammamet area, an almost entirely urbanised coastline that is one of the leading tourist destinations in the country. Like everywhere else in the country, the fall of Ben Ali's regime affected Cap Bon: tourist overnight stays decreased from 9.4 million in 2010 to 6.1 million in 2013. Hotel customers are traditionally Europeans, with Algerians and Libyans accounting for less than 5 per cent of total hotel stays.

The present research expands upon two previous studies by Carboni et al. (2014, 2017) conducted in the Djerba and Nabeul–Hammamet areas, applying the same methodology. As such, the present research is based on a qualitative research method that incorporates the consultation of secondary sources and interviews. The primary data (semi-structured interviews) were collected between 2012 and 2017 from 34 men and 13 women across several ages. The interviewees included tourism professionals, non-profit organisation representatives, local administrators, owners of tourist accommodation facilities, local and national tourism-related agencies, and local academics.

The interview structures were the same for both areas. The first section started with the interviewees' opinions about the current state of the destination's tourism sector. The focus then shifted to the relationship between the local population and tourists, with some questions about the impact of tourist presence. Finally, the rising interest in Muslim-friendly tourism was investigated via individual opinions and knowledge of the phenomenon's main characteristics, including questions concerned with the interviewees' opinions on the potential of halal tourism for the Tunisian market. The presentation of the results follows the same structure of the interview questions.

Security issues emerged as one of the main themes, mainly related to the 2011 events. According to several interviewees, European and Gulf State mass media overemphasised the security issues and represented the Revolution in ways that greatly compromised Tunisia's reputation as a safe tourist destination. Some interviewees stated that, according to their personal beliefs, fearful discourses were intended to harm the country. The interviewees did not underestimate the risks related to Islamic terrorism, such as the attacks at Bardo National Museum and the coastal Sousse resorts. However, they did blame international mass media for their excessive emphasis on instability and insecurity within Tunisia.

The interviewees clearly recognised the main problems in the tourism industry, as most of the long-lasting topics of national debate over industry performances emerged during the interviews. Several interviewees mentioned the low quality of services, market positioning, low-cost mass products, high seasonality, and lack of differentiation as the sector's most critical weaknesses. Regarding Djerba, concerns emerged over the environmental and social effects of mass tourism development and the unequal distribution of tourism-related benefits among the local communities. The island's maisons d'hôtes (guest houses) were indicated by many interviewees as a valid solution for increasing the number of structures owned by local entrepreneurs and the interaction between tourists and the local population. Local ownership would also provide greater income to the community. Other interviewees described the potential of the maisons d'hôtes as slightly controversial in terms of quality, health regulations, and safety. Furthermore, the interviewees indicated that the integration of this kind of accommodation with traditional operators, such as travel agencies, is still underdeveloped.

The cohabitation of tourists from different countries and faiths was cited as a well-established fact in Tunisia. The interviewees considered this to be a consequence of Tunisia's history of hospitality, a result of the long-term cohabitation of Arab, Jewish, Berber, and European communities. Regarding Djerba, several interviewees described hospitality as a value that exceeded nationality or religion and a very local cultural trait. The annual Jewish pilgrimage to Ghriba Synagogue is commonly referred to as a symbol of the country's religious tolerance, both by Tunisian residents and the government's discourse on Tunisianity (Perelli & Sistu 2013).

Regarding the cohabitation of tourists with different origins and backgrounds, the interviewees tended to focus on Europeans and Maghrebians, specifically Algerians and Libyans. Tourists from Algeria and Libya, as mentioned earlier, have always been a significant portion of international arrivals. This is surely related to their geographical proximity as well as to a consolidated tradition of transnational mobility between these neighbour countries, as stated by some interviewees. The interviewees also noted that the interactions between Europeans and Maghrebians has always been limited, as the latter tend to stay in unregistered facilities (e.g. vacation homes), whilst the former prefer hotels and other registered accommodation. A small minority of relatively wealthy Maghrebians, mainly Libyans, may share tourism facilities with Western tourists, with no apparent conflicts.

Most disparate were the interviewees' opinions about tourists from the Gulf countries. Despite the low numbers of international arrivals from the Gulf countries (e.g. just 15,000 Gulf tourists visited Tunisia in 2014) (Agence Anadolu 2015), a very strong perception of the differences between Gulf tourists and their Arab neighbours emerged among the interviewees. Nearly every interviewee who mentioned Gulf tourists highlighted that they can be controversial. On the one hand, they tended to have a high spending limit; on the other hand, their interactions with locals are not necessarily positive. Some interviewees reported issues with Gulf tourists' attitudes towards nightlife, prostitution, and respecting local employees.

A sense of caution appeared among the interviewees regarding the possible impacts of the growth of the Muslim tourist market share. According to some interviewees, Maghreb potential as the main component of intra-Arabic tourism has been undervalued; Maghrebians may positively affect local tourism and provide a sound solution for reducing the majority share of European markets. This demonstrates a pragmatic point of view, as the overly simplistic ideal of easy cohabitation was discarded. For example, interviewees who worked with tourists from Iran, a non-Arab Muslim country, perceived them to be a promising niche, and local agencies and tour operators cited that they were generally good customers.

The interviewees were relatively well informed about the worldwide growth of tourism products that considered Muslim religious sensitivities. This awareness appeared to be influenced by the current national debate on halal products. Interviewees more directly involved in marketing declared their interest towards the topic as one that was connected to the need for new markets. Several interviewees suggested a 'technical' approach to this issue, underlining the potential of such products in terms of new markets and product diversification. For example, many hotel managers and tourism professionals indicated Turkey as a successful model for this approach. The main assets of the Turkish model include the variety of tourism services and products, the integration of Western and Muslim tourism, fair prices, and excellent quality. Nevertheless, the interviewees were enthusiastic about and open to Muslim-friendly products, conceiving them as a tool for diversifying Tunisian tourism but not as the only products the country should offer.

The interviewees' perceptions towards the potential of products closer to Muslim religious sensibilities were not unanimous, however. Possibly due to the national debate over the role of Islam in post-revolutionary Tunisia, the interviewees expressed a sensitivity towards differentiating tourists based on religion. Some interviewees were worried about the idea of segregating tourists of different faiths, as such actions would somehow threaten the Tunisian tradition of multicultural cohabitation. The political implications behind the development of halal tourism products and the risk of polarisation in Tunisian destinations were also reported, such as regulations on alcohol consumption or gender segregation. Furthermore, among the interviewees who did not exclude such future developments as a viable tourism niche was recognition that there were several obstacles to its feasibility. The most-mentioned element concerned the very same nature of contemporary Tunisian mass tourism, especially regarding demand. According to the interviewees, today's tourists are not interested in a different product, especially those that are intended to target intra-Arab consumers. In both Nabeul–Hammamet and Djerba, there is a perception that tourists are motivated to take advantage of a more liberal climate in terms of nightlife and tourist behaviour. This is especially the case for Libyan visitors to Djerba.

With respect to supply, the interviewees believed that deeply rooted criticisms of the Tunisian tourism industry would strongly restrict halal tourism development. Lack of financial resources and difficulties in credit access would limit hotels' abilities to alter their facilities according to halal tourism needs (e.g. gender segregation in sports and spa facilities or separate prayer rooms). Due to such restraints, several interviewees remarked that investors should support the improvement and diversification of the existing supply, rather than create and bolster demand for Muslim-friendly tourism.

Finally, the growing attention towards 'local development' emerged during the interviews, and several interviewees stressed the need for reducing social and environmental impacts and increasing the benefit for local communities. Some interviewees described this local turn in existing tourism, including offering real experiences of material and immaterial local heritage to tourists, as the real priority.

Conclusion

An accurate overview of the current Tunisian tourism industry reveals how any fear of Islamisation is unfounded. Despite the regional challenges and the emerging post-revolutionary role of political Islam, Tunisia is still not too keen on religious extremism in any form. Interviewees, especially the younger ones, involved in the post-revolutionary debate on the role of political Islam in Tunisia somehow associated Muslim-friendly tourism with the risk of moving backwards as a society. They feared that emphasis on religious differences in the tourism sector would eventually result in polarisation, but until now, there coexist visions over delicate issues, such as Tunisian gender norms.

On the other hand, tourism professionals expressed their approval of Muslim-friendly tourism as a differentiation tool, which is partly a consequence of the large-scale recognition of the growing presence of Muslim consumers in the international tourism market. As an example, references to Turkey as a model for tourism development is mainly connected to the nation's ability to manage cohabitation of Muslim and non-Muslim tourists. As demonstrated by Elaziz and Kurt (2017), Muslims in Turkey integrate tourism consumption with religious norms, living a hybrid experience, the results of which still need more in-depth research.

Similar degrees of uncertainty have emerged in Tunisia regarding tourism consumption by Maghrebians (2 million Algerian tourists are expected to visit Tunisia in 2017, nearly double the number in 2016) or Tunisians living in Europe. As reported by some interviewees, inter-Arab contact between locals and tourists (e.g. Libyan tourists in southern destinations, like Djerba) is not necessarily easy. The reputation of Tunisia's Maghreb neighbours can be worse than one would expect, stemming from the local perception that their behaviours are just as inappropriate as Westerners'. Domestic tourists also show great variability and diversity in reputation and behaviour. As underlined by Hazbun (2007, 2008, 2010), more research is needed on the role of tourism in producing and consolidating transnational, hybrid knowledge of globalisation in North Africa and the Middle East. An increased understanding of the contribution of local tourist consumption, the role of the government, the development of tour agencies, and the power of local communities in shaping contemporary tourism within the region is needed, including Tunisian development of Muslim-friendly tourism products.

In the interviewees' eyes, the success of Muslim-friendly tourism development in Tunisia seems to be associated with the guarantee of a certain occupancy rate and adequate profits without any adverse effects on consolidated Western demand. In other words, what the present research has revealed is the need for new, local tourism development, as opposed to the moralisation of communities' customs and social lives according to religious tradition. Tourism professionals are aware of the complexity of this issue, such as the national debate on Tunisian identity and new methods for tourism development following the mass tourism crisis. When describing tourism as part of daily life in a coastal community, the interviewees offered a Tunisian approach to Muslim-friendly tourism development. Along with the tour operators' support, other dynamics that can contribute to a new development model for Tunisia's tourism industry include: the integration of new narratives regarding the articulate, multifaceted history and heritage of Tunisia; the consolidation of correlated economic sectors into the tourism value chain; the cooperation between inter-Arab and domestic tourism efforts, with integration of non-Muslim demand; and increased design and diversification of local tourism experiences and products.

References

Agence Anadolu. (2015) 'La Tunisie espère augmenter le nombre de touristes du Golfe de 10% en 2015'. [online] Available at: http://aa.com.tr/fr/economie/la-tunisie-esp%C3%A8re-augmenter-le-nombre-de-touristes-du-golfe-de-10-en-2015/49295.

Al-Hamarneh, A. and Steiner, C. (2004) 'Islamic tourism: Rethinking the strategies of tourism development in the Arab World after September 11, 2011', *Comparative Studies of South Asia, Africa and the Middle East*, 24 (1): 173–182.

Ben Nessir, C. (2012) 'Il n'y a pas de tourisme halal', *La Presse*, 17 April. [online] Available at: www.lapresse.tn/component/nationals/?task=article&id=48453 (accessed 26 October 2017).

Bourgou, M. and Kassah, A. (2008) *L'île de Djerba. Tourisme, Environnement et Patrimoine*. Tunis: Cérès Editions.

Boussetta, M. (2018) 'Reducing barriers: How the Jews of Djerba are using tourism to assert their place in the modern nation state of Tunisia', *Journal of North African Studies*, 23 (1–2): 311–331.

Bouzahzah, M. and El Menyari, Y. (2013) 'International tourism and economic growth: The case of Morocco and Tunisia', *Journal of North African Studies*, 18 (4): 592–607.

Carboni, M., Perelli, C. and Sistu, G. (2014) 'Is Islamic tourism a viable option for Tunisian tourism? Insights from Djerba', *Tourism Management Perspectives*, 11: 1–9.

Carboni, M., Perelli, C. and Sistu, G. (2017) 'Developing tourism products in line with Islamic beliefs: Some insights from Nabeul–Hammamet', *Journal of North African Studies*, 22 (1): 87–108.

Cirer-Costa, J.C. (2017) 'Turbulence in Mediterranean tourism', *Tourism Management Perspectives*, 22: 27–33.

De Kadt, E. (1979) *Tourism: Passport to Development? Perspectives on the Social and Cultural Effects of Tourism in Developing Countries*. Oxford: Oxford University Press.

Di Peri, R. (2015) 'An enduring "touristic miracle" in Tunisia? Coping with old challenges after the revolution', *British Journal of Middle Eastern Studies*, 42 (1): 104–118.

Eid, R. and El-Gohary, H. (2015) 'The role of Islamic religiosity on the relationship between perceived value and tourist satisfaction', *Tourism Management*, 46: 477–488.

Elaziz, M.F. and Kurt, A. (2017) 'Religiosity, consumerism and halal tourism: A study of seaside tourism organizations in Turkey', *Tourism: An International Interdisciplinary Journal*, 65 (1): 115–128.

Errais, E. (2015) 'To invest or not invest in a distressed hospitality sector: The case of Tunisia', *Journal of Private Equity*, 18 (2): 83–100.

Hamza, I.M., Chouhoud, R. and Tantawi P. (2012) 'Islamic tourism: Exploring perceptions & possibilities in Egypt', *African Journal of Business and Economic Research*, 7 (1): 85–98.

Haugbølle, R.H. (2015) 'New expressions of Islam in Tunisia: An ethnographic approach', *Journal of North African Studies*, 20 (3): 319–335.

Hazbun, W. (2007) 'Images of openness, spaces of control: The politics of tourism development in Tunisia', *Arab Studies Journal*, 15/16, (2/1): 10–35.

Hazbun, W. (2008) *Beaches, Ruins, Resorts: The Politics of Tourism in the Arab World*. Chicago, IL: University of Minnesota Press.

Hazbun, W. (2010) 'Modernity on the beach: A postcolonial reading from southern shores', *Tourist Studies*, 9 (3): 203–222.

Henderson, J.C. (2010) 'Sharia-compliant Hotels', *Tourism and Hospitality Research*, 10 (3): 246–254.

Hibou, B. (2011) 'Macroéconomie et domination politique en Tunisie: du "miracle économique" benaliste aux enjeux socio-économiques du moment révolutionnaire', *Politique Africaine*, 124: 127–154.

Holliday, R., Bell, D., Cheung, O., Jones, M. and Probyn, E. (2015) 'Brief encounters: Assembling cosmetic surgery tourism', *Social Science & Medicine*, 124: 298–304.

Institut Arabe des Chefs d'Entreprises (IACE). (2011) *Le tourisme en Tunisie: Constat du secteur, défis et perspectives*. Tunis: IACE.

Khlif, W. (2006) 'L'hôtellerie tunisienne: Radioscopie d'un secteur en crise', *L'Année du Maghreb*, 1: 375–394.

Klabi, F. (2014) 'Forecasting non-residents' monthly entries to Tunisia and accuracy comparison of time-series methods', *Journal of North African Studies*, 19 (5): 770–791.

Krimi, A. (2017) 'Selma Elloumi: le tourisme "Halal" n'existe pas en Tunisie', *l'Economiste Maghrébin*, 7 July. [online] Available at: www.leconomistemaghrebin.com/2017/07/07/selma-elloumi-tourisme-halal-nexiste-tunisie/(accessed 26 October 2017).

La Presse. (2011) 'Vers l'instauration d'un tourisme religieux …', 10 November. [online]. Available at: www.lapresse.tn/26022016/40103/vers-linstauration-dun-tourisme-religieux%E2%80%A6.html.

La Presse. (2012) 'La Tunisie, plateforme des industries halal vers l'Europe et l'Afrique', 16 May. [online]. Available at: www.lapresse.tn/26022016/49882/la-tunisie-plateforme-des-industri es-halal-vers-leurope-et-lafrique.html.

Larguèche, A. (2008) 'L'histoire à l'épreuve du patrimoine', *L'Année du Maghreb*, 4: 191–200.

Mansfeld, Y. and Winckler, O. (2015) 'Can this be Spring? Assessing the impact of the "Arab Spring" on the Arab tourism industry', *Tourism*, 63 (2): 205–223.

Miossec, J.M. (1999) 'Les acteurs de l'amenagement tunisien: les leçon d'une performance'. In M. Berriane and H. Popp (eds) *Le Tourisme au Maghreb: Diversification du produit et développement local et régional*. Rabat: Faculté des Lettres et Sciences Humaines de Rabat, 65–85.

Miossec, J.M. and Bourgou, M. (2010) *Les littoraux: Enjeux et dynamiques*. Paris: PUF.

Office National du Tourisme Tunisien (ONTT). (2011) *Le Tourisme Tunisien en chiffres 2010*. Tunis: ONTT.

Office National du Tourisme Tunisien (ONTT). (2012) *Le Tourisme Tunisien en chiffres 2011*. Tunis: ONTT.

Office National du Tourisme Tunisien (ONTT). (2017) *Le Tourisme Tunisien en chiffres 2016*. Tunis: ONTT.

Perelli, C. and Sistu, G. (2013) 'Jasmines for tourists. Heritage policies in Tunisia over the last decades'. In J. Kaminski, A.M. Benson and D. Arnold (eds) *Contemporary Issues in Cultural Heritage Tourism*. Abingdon: Routledge, 71–87.

Perles-Ribes, J.F., Ramón-Rodríguez, A.B., Moreno-Izquierdo, L. and Torregrosa Martí, M. (2018) 'Winners and losers in the Arab uprisings: A Mediterranean tourism perspective', *Current Issues in Tourism*, 21 (16): 1810–1829.

Poirier, R. (1995) 'Tourism and development in Tunisia', *Annals of Tourism Research*, 22 (1): 157–171.

Pouessel, S. (2012) 'Les marges renaissantes: Amazigh, Juif, Noir. Ce que la révolution a changé dans ce "petit pays homogène par excellence" qu'est la Tunisie', *L'Année du Maghreb*, 8: 143–160.

Prayag, G. and Hosany, S. (2014) 'When Middle East meets West: Understanding the motives and perceptions of young tourists from United Arab Emirates', *Tourism Management*, 40: 35–45.

Rijkers, B., Freund, C. and Nucifora, A. (2017) 'All in the family: State capture in Tunisia', *Journal of Development Economics*, 124: 41–59.

Sarra, A. (2012) *Tunisie—Exportations: Le marché halal … est toujours à notre portée*. [online] Web Manager Center. Available at: www.webmanagercenter.com/management/imprim.php?id=119954&pg=1.

Scott, N. and Jafari, J. (2010) 'Islam and tourism'. In N. Scott and J. Jafari (eds) *Tourism in the Muslim World*. Bingley, West Yorkshire: Emerald, 1–13.

Sethom, H. (1979) 'Les tentatives de remodelage de l'espace tunisien depuis l'indépendance', *Méditerranée*, 35: 119–125.

Steiner, C. (2010) 'Impacts of September 11: A two-sided neighborhood effect'. In N. Scott and J. Jafari (eds) *Tourism in the Muslim World*. Bingley, West Yorkshire: Emerald, 181–204.

Stephenson, M.L. and Ali, N. (2010) 'Tourism and Islamophobia in non-Muslim states'. In N. Scott and J. Jafari (eds) *Tourism in the Muslim World*. Bingley, West Yorkshire: Emerald, 235–251.

Stephenson M.L., Russell, K. and Edgar, D. (2010) 'Islamic hospitality in the UAE: Indigenization of products and human capital', *Journal of Islamic Marketing*, 1 (1): 9–24.

Tessler, M.A. (1980) 'Political change and the Islamic revival in Tunisia', *The Maghreb Review*, 5 (1): 8–19.

Touzani M., Hirschman, E.C. and Smaoui, F. (2016) 'Marketing communications, acculturation in situ, and the legacy of colonialism in revolutionary times', *Journal of Macromarketing*, 36 (2): 215–228.

13

BRUNEI HALAL TOURISM OUTLOOK

Nazlida Muhamad, Vai Shiem Leong, and Masairol Masri

Introduction

Brunei is the last Malay Islamic Monarchy, located on the second largest island in the world. In an effort to diversify its economy, Brunei sees tourism as a highly potential industry to bring more income to the country. The country's cultural and social elements, and its flora and fauna have a lot to offer. As the country is embarking on strengthening the national identity of Malay and Islam, a new opportunity in Halal tourism is seen as a pragmatic strategy to pursue. This chapter introduces Negara Brunei Darussalam, describes tourism and Halal tourism efforts in Brunei and its challenges, and suggests way forward in Halal tourism.

Brunei—the abode of peace

A small oil-rich kingdom, Brunei Darussalam, sits in the heart of Southeast Asia located on the north-west coast of Borneo island. With a land size of 5,765 km^2, the sultanate is enclaved by the east Malaysian state, Sarawak, wherein the country is split into two—the Brunei-Muara, Tutong, and Belait districts located on the west and which also make up the larger land composition, while the Temburong district sits on the eastern side. Human settlement has been recorded on the banks of the Brunei River as early as the sixth century, documenting a Malay trading centre and fishing port, known as Kampung Ayer (Cavendish 2007). This river settlement flourished, expanding trade and becoming the centre of administration; it is now known as Bandar Seri Begawan, the capital of Brunei.

The Arabic word *Darussalam* translates to "the Abode of Peace" and this links the sultanate to around 1,500 years of Islamic history (Mahmud 2014). The population of Brunei stood at 417,500 in 2015, with close to 300,000 (72 per cent) residing in the Brunei-Muara district, while only 9,000 persons live in the Temburong district (Brunei Government 2016). Islam is the official religion of Brunei, and according to the 2011 population census, the majority of the population are Muslims (79 per cent), followed by 9 per cent Christian, 8 per cent Buddhist, and followers of other faiths make up the remainder. In Brunei, a Muslim person is nearly akin to belonging to a Malay racial group, where the Malays are classified as belonging to either one of the following groups: Brunei, Belait, Bisaya, Dusan, Kedayan, Murat, and

Tutong (Young, Muhammad, Baker, O'Leary & Abdalla 2017). The socio-cultural environment of the country is, therefore, heavily influenced by the Brunei Malay culture and Islam, guiding traditions, beliefs, lifestyles, and behaviours of residents in the country.

The date 1 January 1984 marked Brunei's independence from Great Britain after 96 years as a British protectorate state with limited self-governance. Now, Brunei is a sovereign state, and according to Brunei's 1959 constitution, the Sultan of Brunei is the Head of State holding full executive power, including emergency powers since 1962 (Prime Minister's Office, Brunei Darussalam n.d.). The British rule left important implications on the country's administrative and legal framework. The country practises a dual legal system: (1) the English Common Law that covers civil and criminal laws in Brunei and is applicable to all Bruneians, except for Islamic matters, and (2) the Islamic law (*Sharia*) that mostly deals with Muslims' household matters (such as divorce, morality, or sexuality offences). From 1995 onwards, Islamic laws began to a play bigger role in the country's criminal jurisdiction of the Sharia Courts (Lindsey & Steiner 2016), and with some implications on industrial and retail businesses.

The abundant depletable oil and gas resources, coupled with a small population, have propelled the country into one of the richest countries in Southeast Asia. Since independence, Brunei's economic and social standing escalated with most revenue generated from the hydrocarbon industry. The oil and gas sector contributes more than 60 per cent to Brunei's GDP and over 90 per cent of total exports. In 2016, GDP per capita stood at USD26,938.50. However, GDP per capita growth was estimated at −3.8 per cent, which is also the lowest in the Southeast Asia region (World Bank n.d.). Long recognising the need to diversify the country's reliance away from the oil and gas sector, the Government of Brunei issued an alert in 2000 regarding the unsustainable oil and gas resources (Poole 2009). Up to the recent Tenth National Development Plan 2012–2017, the national policies and strategies have been directed at developing the private sector and strengthening the economy. One of the contributors to the national economic development is the tourism sector—recognised for its important role since the Sixth National Development Plan 1991–1996 (Kassim 2003). Potential tourism products included in the country's Tourism Master Plan 2012–2017 leverage on two features: (1) nature, and (2) Islamic cultural heritage (Asia-Pacific Economic Cooperation (APEC) 2012); because both elements fit and complement Brunei's natural and socio-cultural environments.

Islam in Brunei

The first documented evidence of Islam in Brunei is an Islamic law documentation dated back in the seventeenth century (Lindsey & Steiner 2016). At the time, Brunei was a large empire spanning between what is currently the state of Sarawak to the southern part of the Philippines. Islamic religion was the law of the land since then, until the country fell under the British protectorate. Under the British influence, the country adopted the civil law as the main judicial system. The British allowed the practice of Islamic law within a limited scope, handling mostly familial matters such as marriage and divorce (Lindsey & Steiner 2016).

On its Independence Day over 30 years ago, the king announced the nation's main philosophy of MIB (Malay Islam Monarchy). After a long wait, the Sharia code was introduced in 2013. The introduction of the code for the nation is a way forward for an independent Brunei to foster the country's identity and philosophy. Although Sharia law tends to generate negative publicity, Brunei's code stresses the criminal jurisdictions of Sharia law and largely does not affect the daily life of the general public. In fact, the adoption of

Sharia law, for the country, complements the nation's aspiration of being a country with a predominantly Muslim population and a state headed by an absolute Islamic monarchy.

The implementation of Sharia strengthens the country's positioning as an Islamic monarchy government and brings together other piecemeal efforts to inculcate Islamic values and teachings in government and societal activities in the country. The resulting product is a country which presents an appealing Islamic package.

Halal tourism and Brunei

There is a limited discussion on the correct term to use in addressing Islamic influence on the tourism industry or activities. The terms Islamic tourism and Halal tourism are used interchangeably in the tourism literature. Battour and Ismail (2016) argue that the two terms connote different dimensions of Islamic influence on tourism. According to them, instead of Islamic tourism, the term Halal tourism is deemed suitable in this case. While Halal tourism refers to tourism objects—actions, experiences, or events—in the tourism industry that are in line with Islamic teachings and values, and used or engaged in by Muslim tourists, the term 'Islamic' that connotes the high degree of Muslim faith just does not fit to represent the influence of Islam on tourism elements (Battour & Ismail 2016). This chapter adopts the authors' definition of Halal tourism. Generally, adoption of Halal tourism would see destinations offering for instance halal food and eateries and holding halal-friendly events. Effortlessly, Brunei qualifies as a Halal tourism destination.

The Brunei government has placed utmost priority to ensure the running of the country in most aspects complies to Islamic teachings and values. Directly and indirectly, the local tourism industry is highly involved in this process. Realising this opportunity, Halal tourism has become another important initiative undertaken by the sultanate. Upon gaining independence in 1984, this ex-British colonial state introduced the national ideology, *Melayu Islam Beraja* (MIB, Malay Islam Monarchy), which allows the country to uniquely position itself as a tourist destination rich in Malay traditional culture, one that observes and preserves Islamic values, and one founded on a royal Malay monarchical system at the same time.

As Brunei's identity revolves around Muslim Malays, goods and services available in the country (such as food and beverages, accommodation, restaurants, public facilities) would certainly meet halal requirements, and attract potential Muslim visitors to the country. In fact, the recent requirement for food manufacturers and outlets to obtain halal certification is a legal step to ensure halal status of food and eateries in the country. Hotels in the country are halal-friendly as it is not permissible by law to sell alcohol, while leisure activities, products, and services prohibited by Islam such as gambling and television channels for adults are not available in the country.

Tourism in Brunei

The Ministry of Primary Resources and Tourism (MPRT) has initiated a 2016–2020 strategic plan aiming to raise tourist arrivals from 218,000 in 2015 to 450,000 in 2020, which is estimated to generate BND335 million in revenue by 2020 (Bru Direct 2017). Various projects are undertaken to improve tourism infrastructure, public transportation system, aviation and maritime connectivity, upgrade tourist attraction spots, training of staff in the hospitality and tourism industry, amongst others. Notable infrastructure upgrades include expansion of Brunei International Airport in 2015, and construction of the Temburong Bridge due to complete in 2019. The different initiatives are in line with the nation's inspiration to diversify reliance from the hydrocarbon industry, to increase the contribution of the travel industry to Brunei's total GDP. According to the World Travel & Tourism Council (WTTC) (2017), the tourism sector directly contributed 1.4 per cent to total GDP (BND273.5 million) in 2016. Although the figure may seem negligible, the broader impact (including indirect contributions) accounts for 7.2 per cent of GDP (BND1,260.6 million) in the same year.

The country engages in niche tourism, specifically ecotourism and Islamic tourism. The eastern part of Brunei, Temburong district, is mostly covered by pristine rainforest, with a rich ecosystem of flora and fauna; situated in one of the main biodiversity hotspots in the world (Yong & Hasharina 2008). With this rich natural heritage, ecotourism is promoted as one of the main attractions of Brunei with Ulu Temburong National Park accessible only by boat to nature enthusiasts. Other tourist natural resources include Tasek Merimbun, Tasek Lama Recreational Park, certain sites along Brunei River and the Tutong Heritage Drive (Brunei Tourism 2016).

Various activities were initiated and implemented by the Tourism Department in order to achieve the 2016–2020 strategic plan. Three categories of tourism-related services were identified: prime product, emerging product, and activity-based product (MPRT 2017a). Prime products include the main attractions of the country as perceived by potential tourists such as the Ulu-Temburong National Park, Kampong Ayer, and the Mangroves., Emerging products include the potential tourist attractions such as beaches and forest reserves; and activity-based products include diving, birdwatching, Islamic tourism, sport tourism, meetings, and boat cruises.

In the previous Tourism Master Plan 2012–2016, the department placed Islamic tourism as one of its main agendas apart from ecotourism, culture, and heritage (Association of Southeast Asian Nations (ASEAN) 2012; MPRT n.d.). The master plan identified two clusters, i.e. Nature and Culture & Islamic (APEC 2012; Ahmad 2014). According to Ahmad (2015), the products offered are quite similar to the previous 1998 Master Plan that was developed by KPMG with Islamic tourism as an additional niche market. The inclusion of Islamic tourism in the Master Plan 2012–2016 was also initiated by the launching of Islamic Tourism Exhibition at the Sultan Haji Hassanal Bolkiah Islamic Exhibition Gallery in 2011. Consequent to that, in November 2012, the department together with its Malaysian counterpart promoted the 'Brunei–Malaysia Islamic Tour Package' in the United Kingdom at the Islamic Cultural Centre, London Central Mosque (ASEAN 2012).

The 'Brunei Tourism Board' was established in 2005 to develop the tourism sector in the country (Ahmad 2015). It is a platform to be used by MPRT that links tourism initiatives with stakeholders such as hotel operators, tour guides, other government agencies, etc. (MPRT 2016). Brunei plays an important role in supporting tourism within the ASEAN region. Together with other ASEAN member countries, a joint tourism collaboration called 'Visit ASEAN 1992' was launched in Indonesia. Brunei then took its own initiative to boost the tourism sector by declaring 2001 as 'Visit Brunei Year' (Ahmad 2015).

The commitment of MPRT in pushing forward the importance of tourism to the economy is shown by the development of tourism from a unit to a division within the Ministry, later upgraded as a department and eventually to the ministerial level (Oxford Business Group 2016a). Various initiatives and projects were identified, developed, and packaged as tourism products to boost tourism to Brunei, and Islamic tour packages play an important role, as outlined in the following section.

Halal tourism in Brunei

A seminar presentation by Mohamed (2015) at the Regional Seminar on the Contribution of Islamic Culture and its Impact on Asian Tourism Market highlighted Brunei as one of the top ten destinations for the Organisation of Islamic Cooperation (OIC) in 2015 by the Master-Card–Crescent Rating Global Muslim Travel Index (GMTI). Part of the 2012–2016 Brunei Tourism Master Plan included Islamic tourism as one of the three segments of tourism offering by the country.

Besides its MIB philosophy, in 2008, His Majesty the Sultan of Brunei declared the country's inspiration to be 'Negara Zikir' (a country that praises and remembers God) (MPRT n.d.). The word 'Zikir' is an Arabic word that in the context of Islamic teaching generally represents recitation of brief prescribed syllabuses as acts of remembering Allah. The announcement shows the determination and effort to strengthen the perennial values of Islam in the country. It also offers support and motivation to further current Bruneian Muslim society which held various similar events communally throughout the year. In the context of tourism, it prepares the country to further develop a platform for serious efforts in Islamic tourism.

The first visible commitment toward promoting Islamic tourism in the country was in 2011 when the Sultan Haji Hassanal Bolkiah Islamic Exhibition Gallery was opened to the public. The gallery is currently under renovation and expansion, and will house up to 1,000 Islamic manuscripts and artefacts (Oxford Business Group 2016b). Expected to re-open in 2017, it will be a main attraction for both tourists and Islamic researchers. Like any other exhibition galleries in the country, this gallery is not under the jurisdiction of the Tourism Department.

Beside the Sultan Haji Hassanal Bolkiah Islamic Exhibition Gallery at the State Mufti office, another Islamic gallery exhibits the private collection of His Majesty the Sultan's Islamic artefacts at the Brunei Museum located at Kota Batu. The gallery houses a vast collection of Islamic artefacts and manuscripts and has opened its doors to the public for quite some time. However, this was not adequately promoted internationally. As mentioned by the Minister of MPRT

> Ensuring visitors have easy access to information about the Sultanate's Islamic tourism products is one of the foremost priorities of tourism operators. Working toward this goal, the Brunei Islamic Tourism and Grand Mosques app gives visitors accessible, on-the-go information on the country's Islamic heritage, depictions of the most notable grand mosques, a halal food guide and tips on other sites, museums, accommodation and transport.
>
> *(Oxford Business Group 2016b)*

Tourist attractions as part of the Islamic tourism initiative include the Sultan Bolkiah Mausoleum, Sultan Sharif Ali Mausoleum, Brunei History Centre, Omar Ali Saifuddin Mosque, Jame' Asr Hassanil Bolkiah Mosque, Islamic Da'wah Centre, Brunei Museum, and the Darul 'Ifta Building that displays a variety of Islamic artefacts from different parts of the world (MPRT n.d.). Besides promoting Islamic artefacts and sites, the Tourism Department also promotes Islamic activities as part of the Islamic tourism package to Brunei.

The Islamic tourism package was made possible by the full support of the Ministry of Religious Affairs (MORA). MORA supplies the information on religious-related festivals, and liaises with mosques to open Islamic classes such as basic reading of the Quran and workshops to tourist groups. Travel agencies were also involved in developing and promoting these packages to their targeted Muslim tourists. Islamic celebrations, such as Isra' Miraj, the

Prophet's Birthday, Ramadhan and Tarawikh, Hari Raya Aidilfitri, Hari Raya Aidiladha, as well as other Islamic activities organised by mosques and the Islamic Centre, were promoted in their Islamic tourism booklets. An officer in charge of tourism planning at MPRT sees the promotion of Islamic programmes and activities, especially activities run by mosques, as being successful with groups from several countries taking the package.

Current and past tourism initiatives under the Tourism Department

The department received a proposal from a local marketing company to package tourism services in the form of different activities, namely: Shop in Brunei; Golf in Brunei; Dive in Brunei; Birdwatching in Brunei; Dine in Brunei; and Trekking in Brunei. Nonetheless, only Dive in Brunei and Birdwatching in Brunei packages were executed due to a change of management at the Ministry level. Dive in Brunei was launched in 2009 and again in 2017. Meanwhile, Birdwatching in Brunei was launched in 2013.

Diving in Brunei

In July 2017, the Brunei Tourism Department launched the new Brunei diving packages at the Serasa Water Sport Complex. It was a collaboration between the department and the local diving providers in Brunei. Eight diving packages were introduced during the event. According to the local diving operator, 38 per cent of their divers come from overseas from a total of 1,400 divers per year. Nonetheless, the department aimed to increase this number to 5,000 divers per year. This will only be achieved with an increase of international tourist arrivals into Brunei as mentioned by the Ministry (MPRT 2017a).

Birdwatching in Brunei

The package was introduced in 2013 in conjunction with the first Brunei Darussalam Nature Festival. It also coincided with the first Borneo Bird Race 2013, a collaboration with the Sandakan, Sabah Bird Club and Tourism Board. The launching of the birdwatching brochure during the event was a milestone for this segment of activity-based tourism in Brunei (MPRT 2013). To further promote Brunei as a destination for bird enthusiasts, a three-day birdwatching workshop was sponsored by the Tourism Department in collaboration with various local and regional NGOs.

Bandar Seri Begawan and Kampong Ayer tour packages

Bandar Seri Begawan is the capital city of Brunei. It also includes the famous Kampong Ayer, the oldest settlement in Brunei Darussalam. It has existed for more than 500 years and was the centre of business activities during its high time in history. Kg. Ayer comprises many small villages and each has its own craft and expertise. On 7 January 2017, the Tourism Department launched the 'Bandar Seri Begawan and Kampong Ayer' tour packages. They offer eight various combinations of activities that cover the whole of the capital city and Kg. Ayer. The packages were jointly launched by the Ministry of Home Affairs, MPRT, and Ministry of Youth and Sport (MPRT 2017c).

Tutong destination packages

Tutong is one of the four districts in Brunei Darussalam. It is located between Brunei/Muara and Belait district. On 23 August 2017, the Tourism Department in collaboration with

Tutong District Tourism Promotion Coordination Body launched the 'Tutong Destination Packages'. The main aim is to promote various hotspots in the district through eight different packages. Visitors can spend one night and two days or a day visit in Tutong (MPRT 2017d). The packages are considered an emerging tourist attraction that can promote the one village one product (OVOP) initiatives under the Ministry of Home Affairs.

Temburong holiday destination packages, end 2016 promotion

Temburong is another one of the four districts in Brunei. It is mostly covered by the tropical rainforest and separated from the other three districts by Limbang, Malaysia. Visitors can either travel by car via Limbang or take a speed boat ride through Brunei bay. The district is well known for its pristine green rainforest. A major part of the district was declared as the Brunei National Park and is only accessible by the Iban's long boat. On 1 September 2016, the Tourism Department launched the 'Temburong Holiday Destination' tour package (Brunei Tourism 2016)

Brunei December Festival 2017

Another initiative by the department in promoting Brunei as a cultural destination, a nationwide December festival, was launched in August 2017. A total of 30 activities were identified and incorporated into the December festival list. This is an effort to bring together various activities planned by various stakeholders as part of an orchestrated end-of-year celebration. It involved ministries from Home Affairs, Religious Affairs, and the MPRT. The festival was planned in conjunction with Brunei 'Salebration' and school holidays (MPRT 2017b) and will be part of the Brunei Tourism Department's yearly activities.

Discussion

Brunei's unique Malay and Islamic heritage, adoption of Islamic governance, and the exquisite flora and fauna are well suited to position the country's tourism efforts in the Halal tourism industry. Implementation of Sharia and Islamic values in the country may lead to not meeting some common expectations of mainstream conventional tourists. However, positioning the country on the track of Halal tourism offers a sensible platform to inform tourists' expectations prior to visiting Brunei. Explicitly promoting some of the country's tourism products could assist in developing and setting tourists' expectations, and may enable tourism agencies to maximise tourists' satisfaction, and manage their needs while in the country.

The strategy would also help to overcome the problem with positioning Halal tourism, as in the tendency for the strategy to marginalise certain tourist segments. While Muslim tourists are a highly desirable market segment in capitalising the strategic window that is open for Brunei, other segments like the Chinese, Korean, and Japanese markets are strategically profitable and politically viable. Although the Halal tourism literature discusses Muslim tourists being engaged in Halal tourism, perhaps there is room to market the country to non-Muslim tourists who want to experience tourism within the framework of Sharia. Chen, Chen and Okumus (2013) found that young Taiwanese who have never been to Brunei expressed interest in the sultanate's cultural attractions, which include unique heritage, diverse and unique ethnic groups and culture—which demonstrates an opportunity for Brunei to explore the non-Muslim markets.

Brunei is a developing nation. The country is currently building and improving the nation's infrastructure and is on track to achieve Vision 2035. The vision's master plan must be capitalised on by the tourism agencies to craft the nation's tourism industry's way forward.

As Brunei's cultural identity is clearly defined and the country's vision for an environmentally friendly nation becomes apparent, the country's tourism identity and positioning could be derived from these two platforms. The country is developing to become an icon of Islamic governance in the Southeast Asia region. Hence, if current and/or future strategies to enhance Halal tourism by the Brunei Tourism Unit are well executed, they may qualify Brunei as one of the region's top halal destinations.

One of the challenges to Brunei tourism is positioning its uniqueness apart from its neighbouring countries. The country's social, cultural, and natural resources, its flora and fauna, are similar to a certain degree with its neighbouring countries. On top of that, Muslim-majority countries like Malaysia and Indonesia have been drawing Muslim tourists, as Brunei's neighbouring countries have aggressively developed and promoted their Islamic tourism industry (Ahmad 2015). Nonetheless, Brunei is the only Malay Islamic Monarchy in the region. The current Sultan of Brunei is known and respected in the Muslim world for his determination to adopt Sharia law in the country. The Malay Sultan is the symbol of Islam in many Malay nations, including Brunei. In addition to the Sultan of Brunei representing a symbol of Islam, he is also the head of the country and is an iconic figure worldwide. In fact, the Sultan himself becomes one of the main attractions for tourists to visit the country whereby the public and tourists alike are invited to visit the palace once a year during the Eid festival.

In line with its Islamic influence as a nation, Brunei has made significant efforts to develop and maintain galleries and sites to attract Halal tourism as discussed earlier. Setting up a variety of galleries that suit different interests may attract a larger number of tourists into the country. For example, a gallery that highlights integration of modern and classic Islamic arts and cultural artefacts, and Islam and science gallery, would serve both as part of the Halal tourism elements and as a local or Borneo centre of learning for educational institutions. In fact, Brunei can position itself as a hub for Islamic learning through compiling the modern and classic Islamic literature. The galleries and centre would strengthen the nation's identity and philosophy, while offering Halal tourism appealing to tourists.

Its flora and fauna are amongst the main Brunei's tourism attractions. The diversity and uniqueness of flora and fauna are recognised amongst nature lovers and scientists alike. The country has actively participated in many nature heritage and biodiversity programmes, such as the Convention on Biodiversity, which is part of United Nations' efforts to protect the Earth's biological resources. The preservation of nature and appreciation of nature are in line with Islamic values and could be promoted and developed further as part of the Halal tourism efforts to those tourists keen on Islam and natural habitats.

In fact, most of the tourism activities pursued by the Brunei Tourism Board could be augmented to tie in with the Halal tourism theme. For example, the site of the early settlers and the monuments of the earlier kings could be documented to highlight the arrival of Islam in Brunei and the relationship with other Muslim and non-Muslim states. The tour packages that involve Muslim tourists may want to highlight Islamic rituals interspersed with Islamic teachings. Integrating information on other religions in the country not only informs of the country's peaceful integration of multicultural and religious beliefs, at the same time it underlines the core of Islamic teachings that strongly promotes coexistence of a multi-religious society.

Travel agencies are the heart and soul of the tourism industry in Brunei. The agencies play a primary role in promoting the country abroad and facilitating traveller groups in the country. The government could consider creating incentives to reward agents who successfully bring in a certain number of tourists to the country, and develop unique packages. These initiatives may motivate the travel agencies to attract more tourists into the country. While travel agencies are currently focusing on the Chinese, Japanese, Taiwanese, and Korean tourists, Middle Eastern tourists are a large market that is worth pursuing given the popularity of Brunei in the region. The Halal tourism appeal would surely entice some segments from the market to visit Brunei, on the route of visiting neighbouring countries in the region.

Conclusion

Halal tourism is identified by the Brunei government as a potential area to stimulate growth of the tourism sector of the Malay Muslim Monarchical nation. With attention placed on this niche tourism, the country's tourism industry would benefit from a focus on Halal tourism appeal. Not only because Halal tourism is a high growth industry particularly in the Southeast Asia region, but Halal tourism is well suited to Brunei's national identity and ideology. Although contribution to GDP from the tourism industry may be small, Brunei has experienced growth in international visitors over recent years. In 2016, around 54 per cent of the tourists were from ASEAN countries, 24 per cent from the Far Eastern countries, 11 per cent from European and Middle Eastern countries, while the remaining were from Australia and New Zealand (Othman 2017). With the pool of tourists from different regions, Brunei should strategically promote its image according to interests of residents in different regions. Jafari and Scott (2014) explained that other than *hajj* and *umrah* (religious pilgrimage), Muslim tourists may opt for *ziarat* (religiously inspired trips) or for *rihia* (in search of knowledge). Brunei should actively promote local mosques, Islamic galleries and sites to appeal to the large groups of Muslims around the world under the theme of visiting Brunei for *ziarat*, or attract them to learn more about Islamic artefacts and natural heritage for *rihia* purposes. On the other hand, as an attempt to attract tourists from Far Eastern countries, promotions should focus on Brunei's rich Malay traditional and cultural heritage, Islamic festivals, as well as historical and modern Islamic sites. Positioning the country by regions may eventually boost tourism in the country and strengthen Brunei's identity as a Malay Islamic Monarchical state.

References

Ahmad, A. (2014) 'The disengagement of the tourism businesses in ecotourism and environmental practices in Brunei Darussalam', *Tourism Management Perspectives*, 10: 1–6.

Ahmad, A. (2015) 'Brunei tourism at a standstill'. In K.H. Collins (ed.) *Handbook on Tourism Development and Management*. New York: Nova Science, 209–219.

Asia-Pacific Economic Cooperation (APEC). (2012) *Brunei Darussalam Tourism Report*, 40th Tourism Working Group Meeting Taipei, Chinese Taipei 25–26 April. [online] Available at: http://mddb.apec.org/documents/2012/TWG/TWG1/12_twg1_024.pdf (accessed 12 October 2017).

Association of Southeast Asian Nations (ASEAN). (2012) *Brunei Tourism Launched Brunei–Malaysia Islamic Tour Package in the United Kingdom*. [online] Available at: www.aseantourism.travel/countryarticle/detail/brunei-tourism-launched-brunei-malaysia-islamic-tour-package-in-the-united-kingdom (accessed 12 October 2017).

Battour, M. and Ismail, M.N. (2016) 'Halal tourism: Concepts, practices, challenges and future,' *Tourism Management Perspectives*, 19 (B): 150–154.

Bru Direct. (2017) 'MPRT targets increase tourists' arrivals in 2020'. *National*. [online] Available at: www.brudirect.com/news.php?id=21832

Brunei Government. (2016) *Brunei Darussalam Statistical Yearbook 2015*, Prime Minister's Office. Brunei, Darussalam. [pdf] Available at: www.depd.gov.bn/DEPD%20Documents%20Library/DOS/BDSYB/BDSYB_2015.pdf (accessed 15 September 2017).

Brunei Tourism. (2016) 'Temburong Holiday Destination Packages'. *Discoverbruneifeed*. [online] Available at: http://bruneitourism.travel/feeds.php?id=1

Cavendish, M. (2007) *World and its Peoples: Eastern and Southern Asia*. Vol. 9. New York: Marshall Cavendish.

Chen, H.-J., Chen, P.-J. and Okumus, F. (2013) 'The relationship between travel constraints and destination image: A case study of Brunei', *Tourism Management*, 35: 198–208.

Jafari, J. and Scott, N. (2014) 'Muslim world and its tourisms', *Annals of Tourism Research*, 44: 1–19.

Kassim, Y.M.M. (2003) Tourism in Brunei Darussalam: Content and Context. PhD. Loughborough University.

Lindsey, T. and Steiner, K. (2016) 'Islam, the monarchy and criminal law in Brunei: The Syariah Penal Code Order, 2013', *Griffith Law Review*, 25 (4): 552–580.

Mahmud, H.M.H. (2014) Promoting Islamic Tourism in Brunei: Through Customers Understanding Towards the Syariah Compliant Hotel Concepts. MBA. University of Nottingham.

Ministry of Primary Resources and Tourism, Brunei Darussalam (MPRT). (2013) *Opening Ceremony and Launching of 1st Brunei Darussalam Nature Festival.* [online] Available at: www.mprt.gov.bn/Lists/Latest% 20News/NewDisplay.aspx?ID=441&ContentTypeId=0x0100CE966CE70C33234E8D3A6FE5411A 5237 (accessed 6 October 2017).

Ministry of Primary Resources and Tourism, Brunei Darussalam (MPRT). (2016) *First Brunei Darussalam Tourism Board Meeting.* [pdf] Available at: www.mprt.gov.bn/SiteCollectionDocuments/Press% 20Release%202016/NOVEMBER/30.11.2016_MESYUARAT%20PERTAMA%20LEMBAGA% 20PELANCONGAN%20BRUNEI%20DARUSSALAM.pdf (accessed 16 October 2017).

Ministry of Primary Resources and Tourism, Brunei Darussalam (MPRT). (2017a) *Media Release: Promotion of the Brunei Diving Packages* [pdf] Available at: www.tourism.gov.bn/Brochures%20Library/Tourism/ Press%20Release%20-%20Diving%20version%20latest%2011.7.2017%20Final%20version.pdf

Ministry of Primary Resources and Tourism, Brunei Darussalam (MPRT). (2017b) *Media Release: Brunei December Festival.* [pdf] Available at: http://www.mprt.gov.bn/SiteCollectionDocuments/PRESS% 20RELEASE%202017/31.08.2017_Brunei%20December%20Festival.pdf (accessed 12 October 2017).

Ministry of Primary Resources and Tourism, Brunei Darussalam (MPRT). (2017c) *Media Release: Launching of Tourism Packages for Bandar Seri Begawan and Kampong Ayer Warisan Negara Brunei Darussalam.* [pdf] Available at: www.mprt.gov.bn/SiteCollectionDocuments/PRESS%20RELEASE% 202017/JANUARY/7.01.2017_MAJLIS%20PELANCARAN%20PAKEJ%20PELANCONGAN% 20BANDAR%20SERI%20BEGAWAN.pdf (accessed 12 October 2017).

Ministry of Primary Resources and Tourism, Brunei Darussalam (MPRT). (2017d) *Media Release: Launching of Ministry of Primary Resources and Tourism Strategic Plan 2016–2020.* [pdf] Available at: www.mprt.gov.bn/ SiteCollectionDocuments/PRESS%20RELEASE%202017/JANUARY/9.01.2017_MAJLIS%20PELAN CARAN%20PELAN%20STRATEGIK%202016-2020.pdf (accessed 12 October 2017).

Ministry of Primary Resources and Tourism, Brunei Darussalam (MPRT). (n.d.) *Islamic Tourism Brunei Darussalam.* [pdf] Available at: www.bruneitourism.travel/download/islamictourism_booklet.pdf (accessed 19 October 2017).

Mohamed, M. (2015) 'Policy recommendations/marketing of Islamic tourism products'. In *Regional Seminar on the Contribution of Islamic Culture and its Impact on Asian Tourism Market.* [online] 16–17 November, Bandar Seri Begawan, Brunei Darussalam. Available at: http://asiapacific.unwto.org/event/regional-seminar-contribution-islamic-culture-and-its-impact-asian-tourism-market (accessed 19 October 2017).

Othman, A. (2017) '2016 sees rise in tourist arrivals to Brunei', *Borneo Bulletin*, 18 March. [online] Available at: http://borneobulletin.com.bn/2016-sees-rise-tourist-arrivals-brunei/(accessed 16 November 2017).

Oxford Business Group. (2016a) *Focus on Key Niches to Increase Tourism Receipts in Brunei Darussalam.* [online] Available at: www.oxfordbusinessgroup.com/overview/distinct-advantages-focusing-key-niches-increase-tourism-receipts (accessed 14 October 2017).

Oxford Business Group. (2016b) *Brunei Darussalam Builds its Islamic Tourism Offering.* [online] Available at: www.oxfordbusinessgroup.com/analysis/opportunity-awaits-sultanate-building-its-islamic-tourism-offering (accessed 18 October 2017).

Poole, P.A. (2009) *Politics and Society in Southeast Asia.* Jefferson, NC: McFarland.

Prime Minister's Office, Brunei Darussalam. (n.d.) *His Majesty Sultan Haji Hassanal Bolkiah Mu'izzaddin Waddaulah Ibni Al-Marhum Sultan Haji Omar 'Ali Saifuddien Sa'adul Khairi Waddien, Sultan and Yang Di-Pertuan of Negara Brunei Darussalam.* [online] Available at: www.pmo.gov.bn/Pages/Prime-Minister.aspx (accessed 15 September 2017).

World Bank (n.d.) *GDP Per Capita Growth (Annual %).* [online] Available from: https://data.worldbank. org/indicator/NY.GDP.PCAP.KD.ZG?end=2016&locations=SG-BN-HK&name_desc=false& start=1990 (accessed 15 September 2017).

World Travel & Tourism Council (WTTC). (2017) *Travel & Tourism: Economic Impact 2017 Brunei.* [pdf] Available at: https://www.wttc.org/-/media/files/reports/economic-impact-research/countries-2017/brunei2017.pdf (accessed 20 September 2017).

Yong, G.Y.V. and Hasharina, N.H.H. (2008) 'Strategies for ecotourism: Working with globalization', *Southeast Asia: A Multidisciplinary Journal*, 8: 35–52.

Young, A., Muhammad, P.N.P.H., Bakar, O., O'Leary, P. and Abdalla, M. (2017) 'Children in Brunei Darussalam: Their educational, legal and social protections', *International Journal of Islamic Thoughts*, 11: 6–16.

14

MEETING THE NEEDS OF MUSLIM TOURISTS

The case of Singapore

Joan C. Henderson

Introduction

Given the current size and projected expansion of the global Muslim population, there is considerable commercial interest in Muslim travellers. The phenomenon is commonly labelled Islamic or halal tourism, although this obscures the diversity within the overall market. Many destinations outside the Islamic world of the 57 Organisation of Islamic Cooperation (OIC) members are attempting to attract these visitors, but the tourism industry confronts certain challenges arising from defining characteristics related to religious commands. Singapore is an interesting case of a country achieving some success as a Muslim tourist destination whilst it can be argued that potential has still to be realised. This chapter examines the Muslim leisure tourism market and industry responses in the city-state, assessing its strengths and weaknesses as a place for Muslims to visit based on the three central themes of wider national conditions, Muslim-oriented facilities and services, and destination marketing. Attention is also given to future prospects in light of existing trends and rising competition. While distinctive, the Singapore experience affords general lessons about and broader insights into the demands of contemporary Muslim tourists and how these can be addressed.

Muslim tourists

Attention to Muslim consumers is unsurprising in view of the estimated Muslim population of 1.6 billion in 2010 or almost a quarter of the world's total. Over 60 per cent of all Muslims are inhabitants of the Asia Pacific region with Indonesia, Pakistan, India, and Bangladesh having the greatest concentrations. The Middle East and Africa account for around 20 per cent of Muslims and there are large communities in Europe (Pew Research Center 2016). Numbers are growing rapidly with forecasts that one-third of the global population will be Muslims by 2050. They are united by a set of core religious beliefs, yet do not all exhibit the same intensity of religious commitment or acceptance of alternative interpretations of Islam. Tolerance of other sects (and religions) is not uniform and divisions between the two main branches of Shia and Sunni are more pronounced in the Middle East and Africa

(Pew Research Center 2012). There are also economic, social, and cultural differences affecting lifestyles and consumption patterns which are further shaped by age and education so that generalisations about consumer behaviour can be misleading (Temporal 2011).

Islam advocates travelling as a means of acquiring knowledge and understanding of the world and an appreciation of God's work. It also enjoins adherents to welcome strangers and proffer hospitality. There is a long history of Muslim travel (El-Gohary 2016), notably for pilgrimage purposes, but modern flows are unprecedented in their scale and perhaps geographical spread. Muslim travellers have increased in parallel with the population which tends to be younger than the global average and were calculated to number 117 million in 2015. At least 168 million are expected by 2020 who will spend US$200 billion. Expansion can be explained by demographics accompanied by rising disposable incomes and a burgeoning middle class in several majority Muslim countries. Many European and North American Muslims are relatively affluent and all have better access to modern information communication technologies which facilitate travel and the exchange of advice and information. In addition, there have been changes in supply as the tourism and leisure industries pursue opportunities to sell to Muslims and more companies are specialising in the field (MasterCard & CrescentRating 2016a).

Life for Muslims, whether travelling or at home, is governed by Sharia law which is derived from the holy book of the Quran and the Sunnah in the Hadith books depicting the story and teachings of the Prophet Mohammed. Actions which are permissible are classed halal while haram denotes those deemed unacceptable. Rules apply to dress, personal conduct, and social activities in addition to religious duties which include performing prayers five times daily, preceded by ritual washing or wudhu. There are rigid regulations about diet (Chaudry & Riaz 2014) which are commonly explained by a verse from the fifth chapter of the Quran (Bonne & Verbeke 2008). Textual instructions usually call for interpretation by expert religious scholars and an OIC (2009) publication devotes 50 pages to advice about food. Meat is a particular concern and there are specific instructions about slaughtering rites (Harvey 2010). Pork and any related products are forbidden as are alcoholic drinks, but there are no universal standards and any accreditation is usually conducted nationally by Islamic associations which may be independent of government. Authorities do not always agree, but there is broad consensus on what is halal and haram with a third category labelled dubious (syubbah or mashbuh) which it is safer to reject (Marzuki, Hall & Ballantine 2012).

Islam is therefore a critical influence on Muslim tourists and endows them with distinguishing features which set them apart in many ways. However, they may conform to some general patterns whereby certain expectations and experiences transcend religious affiliation. Muslim tourists are not all expecting a familiar environment and interest in discovering new places and exploring different cultures are as powerful a motivator for them as for other leisure travellers. All tourists require transport, accommodation, attractions, amenities, and supporting services. Connectivity is vital, especially by air, for international movement and visa regulations should not be overly restrictive. Affordability is another consideration, linked to currency exchange rates, alongside environmental issues which include climate and natural disasters. Health and safety matter too and places perceived as dangerous will be shunned by most leisure visitors. Finally, all tourists need to be aware of and informed about destinations and marketers strive to persuade them to visit by cultivating favourable images and associations.

The importance attached by Muslim tourists to meeting religious obligations may differ with the individual, yet availability of halal food is often an anxiety (Bon & Hussain 2010). The problem is compounded during the month of Ramadan when Muslims who are physically able must fast during the hours of daylight. Travel is avoided at this time by some, but those on the move (including business travellers who have no option) might be looking for appropriate provision; for example, hotels and restaurants which serve meals known as suhor and iftar before dawn and after dusk respectively. Facilities for worship are also a priority at all seasons and mosques are preferred, but praying can be undertaken at any location judged sufficiently clean. Toilets of a suitable design are welcomed and some Muslims might seek segregation by gender in particular settings and an environment free from proscribed activities such as alcohol consumption and gambling. There is a tendency for Muslims to travel in large family groups so appropriate amenities and entertainments can be a key factor in vacation decisions.

A recent report assesses Muslim travel destination competitiveness on the basis of these considerations. Eleven criteria are cited and organised into three essential elements of 'family-friendly holiday and safe travel destination, Muslim-friendly services and facilities at the destination, and halal awareness and destination marketing' (MasterCard & CrescentRating 2016a: 10). A second exercise (MasterCard & CrescentRating 2016b) evaluates the popularity of destinations at Ramadan using measures of average temperatures during the day, length of fasting, and the above rating. A distinction is made between destinations within and outside the OIC as the former are clearly better positioned to meet specific religious prerequisites. Mecca and Medina are stated to be the first choice for Ramadan tourists (MasterCard & CrescentRating 2016b), but Singapore emerges as third behind Malaysia and Indonesia and above Turkey in a list which excludes the Saudi Arabian holy cities. Malaysia is judged to be the top OIC destination in the broader index followed by the United Arab Emirates (UAE), Turkey, and Indonesia. The most popular non-OIC location is Singapore and reasons for its attractiveness are returned to later in the chapter.

Islamic dictates underlie the demands which define Muslim tourists, but the religion recognises that it is not always possible to comply when travelling. Non-halal food can be eaten and prayers delayed if there is no alternative and the intention to obey is present. The Quran says that 'whoever is driven to necessity, not desiring nor exceeding the limit, then surely Allah is Forgiving, Merciful' (Bonne & Verbeke 2008: 38). Some Muslims may be less orthodox than others and more willing to forgo certain customs depending on individuals, families, and home country environments. There are marked contrasts between austere versions of Islam practised in much of the Middle East, such as Wahhabism in Saudi Arabia where Sharia law is strictly enforced, and more liberal regimes in South East Asia (Zamani-Farahani & Henderson 2010). However, several formerly more secular and moderate countries worldwide are undergoing pressures towards what has been termed Islamisation of state and society which is often driven by political agendas of Muslim and non-Muslim factions. The movement is leading to greater conservatism in both religious and socio-cultural domains as well as igniting tensions with modernisers and religious minorities, illustrated by events in Indonesia and Malaysia (Suryadinata 2017).

Singapore's international arrivals and Muslim tourists

Singapore is constrained by its small size of about 277 square miles (719km^2) and limited natural resources, but has engaged in creative marketing and constant upgrading and product innovation to establish itself as a leading international destination for both business and leisure tourists. The industry is backed by a government prepared to invest heavily and engage in strategic planning. Achievements are reflected in a history of steady growth and recent arrival and receipt increases from 10.3 million and S$14.1 billion in 2007 to 15.2 million and

S$22 billion in 2015 (Singapore Tourism Board (STB) 2016a). There was a record 16.4 million international tourists and expenditure of S$24.8 billion in 2016, but the expansion rate is slowing. The Singapore Tourism Board (STB) is responsible for the sector and has adopted a strategy of quality tourism with the objective of sustaining development through maximising revenue (STB 2013, 2016b).

Asia Pacific currently generates around 80 per cent of Singapore's inbound tourism and primary sources are China, Indonesia, Malaysia, and India. Official figures omit the flows of Malaysian nationals who enter by land using the causeway and bridge which connect the two countries so that their presence is understated in the statistics. Indonesia is another close neighbour and has a population in excess of 237 million, 87 per cent of whom are followers of Islam which makes it home to 13 per cent of the world's total (Pew Research Center 2016). Of Malaysia's 27 million population, 61 per cent are Muslims (United Nations Statistics Division (UNdata) 2017). In terms of tourists from other OIC members, arrivals are relatively low. Only 165,639 out of 14.9 million for January to November 2016 came from West Asia which encompasses states such as the United Arab Emirates and Saudi Arabia (STB 2017a), although average spending is likely to be high by Gulf travellers and their economic significance should not be overlooked.

Quantification of the volume and value of Muslim visitors is, however, difficult because religion is not recorded by Customs and Immigration. Not all citizens of Muslim-majority countries will be of the faith as in the cases of Malaysia and Indonesia while those from non-OIC nations may be, notably Indians whose Muslim community is set to surpass that of Indonesia by 2050 (Pew Research Center 2016). Nevertheless, it can be concluded that Muslims make up a sizeable proportion of Singapore's tourists and the share was calculated to be about 17 per cent or 2.6 million arrivals in 2015 (Lin 2016). It is a market which has the potential to grow alongside the population and mounting prosperity in several Muslim countries, not least Indonesia, yet Singapore is one of many destination options for Muslim tourists.

The wider context

Aspects of conditions in Singapore facilitate its role as a Muslim tourist destination and give it a competitive advantage over some rivals. Malay Muslims comprise 13 per cent of the almost 4 million residents and are the second largest ethnic group behind Chinese (74 per cent) and Indian (9 per cent) (Department of Statistics, Singapore 2016). Malays are the island's indigenous people and were once predominant before colonisation by the British and subsequent transformation into an international trading port which drew migrant workers from around the world. Maintaining racial harmony and averting a recurrence of 1960s race riots has been a preoccupation of the government of the People's Action Party, in power since independence in 1965. It has pursued a policy of meritocracy and sought to avoid the politicisation of race through steps such as banning race-based parties and imposing quotas for public housing to prevent the formation of ghettoes. The 2017 presidential election was reserved for Malay candidates to ensure that the new President, and only the second since independence, is from the minority. The post is largely ceremonial, but the decision is a mark of endeavours to show fairness and foster unity and loyalty amongst the races. There is an official commitment to the elimination of discrimination, creating a climate in which Muslims are less vulnerable to the anti-Islamic sentiment they could be exposed to elsewhere in an era of seemingly increasing Islamophobia (Moufakkir 2015).

It would be misleading to suggest, however, that all Muslims will feel completely at home or comfortable in Singapore in terms of religious and socio-cultural affinity. South East Asian Muslims have their own traits which do not always correspond with Middle Eastern Islamic schools of thought. Interpretations of some social norms and behaviour deviate in a manner apparent in the female dress code which is relatively relaxed in Singapore. Many women choose to wear a headscarf, known locally as a tudung, but often in bright colours coordinated with the outfit and secured by a sparkling pin. Versions of the traditional Malay costume of baju kurung, comprising a loose-fitting tunic and long skirt, are also popular; again these can be brightly coloured and especially on festive occasions when men adopt traditional dress and families tend to don matching clothes. In contrast, some younger women combine a headscarf with jeans. It is very unusual to see face veils or full burkas and there is an official ban on the wearing of the tudung by public service uniformed staff in the professed interests of social harmony. There are no religious or 'morality' police to monitor and enforce observance of rules of clothing and conduct in public places (BBC News 2016).

Muslims are formally represented by Majlis Ugama Islam Singapore (MUIS), the Islamic Religious Council of Singapore, which is a statutory agency with the function of advising the President about Islamic affairs. A key task is halal food accreditation and certification and its approach has been praised for robustness and reliability in international comparisons (Latif, Zainalabidin, Juwaidah, Amin & Ismail 2014). Certification is granted only by MUIS and for categories of eating establishments; endorsements (imported, exported, or re-exported halal-certified products); food preparation areas; poultry abattoirs; products; storage facilities; and whole plants. Chain and franchise businesses must submit separate applications for each outlet and a distinction is made between hotels with a halal-certified restaurant where alcohol is not sold and those selling alcohol, but with a halal-certified kitchen (Henderson 2016a). MUIS also approves foreign schemes and operates a Halal Quality Management System covering the food supply chain which embraces hazard analysis and critical control points (HACCP) and International Organization for Standardization (ISO) standards. The rigorous procedures, involving exhaustive criteria and inspection and auditing for restaurants (MUIS n.d.), makes obtaining a certificate an exacting and expensive undertaking for some enterprises and especially smaller businesses. Nevertheless, the Malay Muslim community and Muslims from other groups, such as Indians, are sufficient in number to be a lucrative pool of customers which is boosted by tourists and commercial returns are believed to justify the investment (Lada, Tanakinjal & Amin 2009).

Over 2,200 eating establishments and 350 caterers/central kitchens were halal certified at the beginning of 2017, allowing them to display the formal mark and be listed in the Singapore Halal Directory (MUIS 2017). At the same time, halal dining can still cause anxiety for Singaporean Muslims and their compatriots. South East Asian Muslims usually follow the Shafii school of Sunni Islam which stresses purity. Sharing food and utensils with non-Muslims may be seen as contaminating (Marranci 2012; Nasir & Pereira 2008) so that there is a preference for eating separately. Singaporeans are united by their love of eating, but food can also be divisive there as elsewhere. Tolerance of difference is, however, evident in communal dining spaces such as traditional hawker centres and modern fast food outlets where both halal and non-halal food are sold and consumed.

Muslims are thus an element of everyday life in Singapore and integral to its society and heritage, although it must be admitted that frictions persist underneath a surface of harmonious multiculturalism due to the numeric dominance of the Chinese and fears of marginalisation amongst some in the minority communities. The part played by Muslims is demonstrated by the availability of halal food and the 71 mosques across the island. Many of the latter are located in residential areas, but they can be found in the more central zones frequented by tourists. Such provision addresses some of the worries of visitors and while circumstances do not accord with those in Middle Eastern theocracies, the divergences may be appealing to even the more conservative. Singapore is a modern and cosmopolitan global city (Cities Research Center & JLL 2016) with a substantial foreign labour force of diverse nationalities and religions. All Muslims can feel comparatively safe in the small republic which is without the political instability endemic in much of South East Asia (Economist Intelligence Unit 2017) and renowned for its order, discipline, and efficiency. The crime rate is one of the lowest in the world and the country is amongst the most corruption-free globally (Overseas Security Advisory Council (OSAC) 2016). The risk of terrorist attack cannot be discounted and is universal, but the administration has a rigorous anti-terrorism policy. The hot and humid tropical climate can be debilitating yet pleasurable and extreme weather and natural disasters are exceptional. Public health and hygiene standards are very high and healthcare is advanced, if expensive (PwC 2016).

Access is critical to global city and tourist destination status and this is supplied by Changi Airport which handled a record 58.7 million passengers in 2016 with over 100 airlines connecting to 380 cities worldwide. It is one of the busiest airports in the world and consistently ranked amongst the best for the user experience. Almost 90 per cent of growth in 2016 came from routes to South and North East Asia and Oceania and the heaviest traffic was on flights to Jakarta and Kuala Lumpur, the capitals of Indonesia and Malaysia respectively. A fourth terminal opened in 2017, increasing capacity from the current 66 million to 82 million, and a fifth is planned whereby 135 million passengers will be able to be accommodated by 2025 (Changi Airport Group 2017b).

Entry to Singapore is strictly controlled in a bid to prevent illegal immigration, but most tourists with valid documents are granted a one-month visit pass on arrival. However, a visa is necessary for nationals of 37 countries, divided into two levels of assessment. The first level group of 17 contains 8 OIC members which are mainly from Central Asia. Of the 20 in the second level category all are OIC members, with the exception of Kosova, and predominantly Middle Eastern and African. Social visit visa applicants must submit a completed form accompanied by a letter of introduction from a Singapore citizen or Permanent Resident who may also be asked for a security deposit of between S$1,000 (US$707) and S$3,000 (US$2,121). The process can be completed online for a fee of S$30 (US$21) and takes one working day for the first assessment level and three for the second (Immigration and Checkpoints Authority, Singapore Government 2017).

Tourist facilities and services for Muslims

Changi Airport is the primary gateway for tourists as a whole and boasts of an 'exciting array of attractions, shopping and dining'. Its online dining guide advertises 22 'halal and vegetarian choices', but there is no reference to other offerings specifically for Muslims. However, each of the three passenger terminals has a 'multi-faith' prayer room (Changi Airport Group 2017a) and another website advises that these have the requisite ablution facilities (Halal Trip 2017). Airport washrooms have a choice of toilet, including the type favoured by Muslims, as do most public lavatories in Singapore.

A total of 208 formally gazetted hotels are catalogued in the 2016 official guide (STB 2016c), 78 of which are described as having 'Muslim-friendly facilities and services'. All of the 78 have a Qibla compass in bedrooms to show the direction of Mecca for purposes of worship, 41 have prayer spaces, and 21 serve halal food, with 18 hotels offering all three amenities. A media report cites instances of more Western international chains introducing iftar menus during Ramadan and prayer rooms with washing facilities (Lin 2016). These properties are not, however, Sharia-compliant which is a label given to hotels conforming to Islamic law. Characteristics such as the prohibition of alcohol and gender segregation in selected areas (Henderson 2010) are unlikely to be commercially viable outside the Islamic world and, indeed, may not be expected by Muslims when abroad.

As stated previously, there are numerous halal-accredited eating establishments in Singapore recognisable by the official certificate on display and which appear in various directories. Food products too are clearly marked with the formal halal logo. Visitors are informed about where to find halal food on the Your Singapore STB website which has links to recommendations by other organisations, but there is no comprehensive list (STB 2017b). MUIS also deals with questions about halal-certified premises and has observed an increase in enquiries from non-Singaporeans (Lin 2016).

Singapore has a mix of attractions, albeit lacking the range of natural and cultural heritage found in bigger and better endowed destination countries. Most of these are not designed for or oriented towards Muslims, but they will still be visited by them according to tourist profiles and inclinations. Online STB promotion categorises 'things to see and do' as neighbourhoods, arts, history, architecture, recreation and leisure, and nature and wildlife. Shopping opportunities, food and festivals, and events are other selling points alongside two integrated casino resorts. While gambling is prohibited by Islam, the complexes contain amenities and entertainments which are acceptable and of family appeal; an example is Universal Studios which is the second such theme park in Asia alongside that in Tokyo. Elsewhere, Singapore Zoo and Night Safari are popular venues for those with children. The STB website suggests three- and seven-day itineraries for families and identifies an assortment of activities and sites of particular interest to them (STB 2017b).

Destination marketing

The latest STB marketing plan outlines three 'strategic thrusts' of 'telling a great Singapore story, attracting the right fans and enhancing our delivery' (STB 2016d). Targets are working millennials, families with young children, active silvers (senior travellers), and BTMICE (business travel, meetings, incentives, conferences, and exhibitions) travellers. Attempts are also being made to diversify in order to reduce reliance on the Asia Pacific region, but the intention is to maintain promotional activity at a high level in core markets of China and India as well as those which are growing such as South Korea and Vietnam.

There is no mention of Muslim tourists as a distinct group in the plan, but secondary Indonesian cities are being targeted because of the perceived continued importance of Singapore's neighbour. The middle class of affluent consumers in the country is forecast to expand from 30 per cent of the population in 2015 to 53 per cent by 2020 and more air routes are being launched by scheduled and budget carriers. Singapore is a preferred destination for Indonesians and an STB (2016e) report acknowledges Muslim travellers from there as worthy of awareness and affinity-building efforts. A Muslim travellers' guide in Bahasa Indonesian was published in 2015 with information about shopping and attractions generally alongside details of halal dining, mosques, and airport prayer facilities. Historic and other sites with connections to Islam are also highlighted (STB 2015).

Singapore is one of the top five destinations for Malaysians who cannot be neglected, but there is an appreciation that it is an unusual market given the cultural similarities and the close (if somewhat tense) relationship between the two neighbours. They have a common history as British colonies and subsequently united for a short period before Singapore was ejected from the federation and became fully independent, leaving a legacy of some political mistrust. Each has a multicultural society made up primarily of Chinese, Malays, and Indians with the first predominant in Singapore and the second in Malaysia. Many Malaysians are familiar with Singapore which is easily accessible and much travel is to see friends and relatives who have settled there. Nevertheless, the STB appreciates that Malaysian Muslim visitors worry about halal food and prayer facilities when in Singapore to which due regard must be given (STB 2014). Another travel guide in the Malay language has been introduced recently in cooperation with a lifestyle magazine, but this stresses fashionable (halal) dining and shopping rather than conveying assurances about religious obligations (Glam Glam n.d.).

Online STB promotion has dedicated sites for Indonesia and Malaysia which contain useful facts for Muslims, but few allusions to Islam. There are no sites for any other Muslim-majority countries, but the global English language website reassures a general audience about halal food and hails the abundance and diversity of cuisines. Attractions linked to the Malay Muslim community are featured in the section devoted to culture and celebrations of Hari Raya Aidilfitri and Hari Raya Hajj appear as examples of festivals and events. The perspective is that of a non-Muslim with explanations of the occasions which are used as illustrations of Singapore's colourful multiculturalism. The approach applies also to the account of the Malay culture and religion which is depicted as one of the 'faces' of Singapore (STB 2017b).

The STB has a network of overseas bureaux dealing with the Americas; Europe; Greater China; North Asia; South East Asia; and South Asia, the Middle East, and Africa collectively. The last has offices in Mumbai (for West and South India and Sri Lanka), Delhi (for North and East India, Bangladesh, Nepal, and Pakistan), and Dubai (with a stated emphasis on Saudi Arabia, the UAE, and Qatar); this compares to five offices in China (STB 2017c). In response to a media query about whether more could be done to entice Muslims, an official from the STB's International Group is quoted as saying that Singapore will remain popular because of a 'sense of familiarity' generated by the availability of food and prayer spaces together with family-friendly attractions. He spoke about working with partners in the Middle East to raise awareness of Singapore as a suitable destination and engaging in marketing which is culturally sensitive and fitting, making greater use of digital and social media (Tay 2016).

Review

Singapore thus possesses several advantages as a destination for Muslim tourists arising from broader conditions prevailing in the country and the nature of its tourism industry. The presence of a sizeable local Muslim community and supporting facilities and services ensures that visitors have access to vital amenities such as mosques and halal food. Muslims are a visible and accepted part of Singapore society and the prosperous and well-managed city-state affords a very high level of safety and security, ameliorating any concerns about threats to well-being. There is an interesting array of attractions, many suited to families, and wide choice of accommodation. Changi Airport provides international air connectivity and the internal transport infrastructure is excellent, facilitating access and mobility. Images of Singapore are generally positive and the Tourism Board is very active in marketing and product innovation. Marketers are also able to communicate reassuring information of specific relevance to Muslims. These favourable attributes perhaps help to explain why Singapore has the top score for non-OIC destinations in the aforementioned Muslim travel index ahead of Thailand, the United Kingdom, and South Africa (MasterCard & CrescentRating 2016a) as well as its strong performance in the Ramadan travel ranking (MasterCard & CrescentRating 2016b).

At the same time, Singapore does exhibit weaknesses as a leisure tourist destination in general related to its size and the extent of urbanisation and industrialisation. There is a reliance on man-made attractions and an absence of natural and cultural heritage, leading to a short length of stay. It has traditionally been seen as rather dull and boring in comparison with more vibrant global cities. While there have been successful attempts to rejuvenate tourism and maintain growth through new developments such as the integrated resorts, there are limits to what can be achieved in the years ahead and some doubts about the future. Regarding Muslims in particular, the visa restrictions which confront nationals of many OIC countries might be discouraging and an obstacle to travel. They may also be disappointed that over 60 per cent of registered hotels reportedly do not make any special provision and only 21 out of 208 serve halal food. There are cost constraints, but measures such as the installation of compasses showing the direction of Mecca are relatively inexpensive. The deficiency could be partly caused by insufficient industry knowledge, suggesting the need for education initiatives. A higher priority to Muslims might also be expected in marketing plans and campaigns, especially to those living outside South East Asia. Tourists from the Middle Eastern Gulf States merit attention because of their affluence and the fact they are not too distant. Flying time is about seven to eight hours and there are direct flights on a variety of routes serviced by several airlines, not least the ambitious and ever-expanding Gulf carriers.

In addition, Singapore faces challenges from destinations within and outside the Islamic world which are actively targeting the Muslim travel market. Japan, for example, has seen a significant increase in South East Asia Muslim arrivals as a consequence of heightened advertising and practical steps such as relaxation of visa rules even though its resident Muslim population is very small (Henderson 2016b). Recommended responses are to extend industry understanding of special requirements, develop more products and services with Muslim appeal, and intensify promotion (MasterCard & CrescentRating 2016b). There are signs of implementation of such proposals in Singapore (and beyond), but there seems scope for additional endeavours. However, it must be recognised that Muslims are only one group of visitors to Singapore and other markets are of equal or greater importance so that over-emphasis on them might be inappropriate. It is unlikely that there will be a major shift in marketing strategy, but Singapore's geographical position between two large and developing Muslim-majority countries and its role as an international civil aviation hub create opportunities to be exploited.

References

BBC News. (2016) 'Who are Islamic "Morality Police"?' [online] Available at: www.bbc.com/news/world-middle-east-36101150 (accessed 13 February 2017).

Bon, M. and Hussain, M. (2010) 'Halal food and tourism'. In N. Scott and J. Jafari (eds) *Tourism in the Muslim World*. Bingley, West Yorkshire: Emerald, 47–59.

Bonne, K. and Verbeke, W. (2008) 'Religious values informing halal meat production and the control and delivery of halal credence quality', *Agriculture and Human Values*, 25 (1): 35–47.

Changi Airport Group. (2017a) 'Changi Airport'. [online] Available at: www.changiairport.com/en (accessed 2 February 2017).

Changi Airport Group. (2017b) *Changi Airport Registers a Record 58.7 Million Passengers in 2016*, Media Release, 30 January.

Chaudry, M.M. and Riaz, M.N. (2014) 'Safety of food and beverages: Halal food requirements', *Encyclopedia of Food Safety*, 3: 486–491.

Cities Research Center and JLL. (2016) 'Benchmarking the future world of cities'. [online] Available at: www.jll.com/research/176/jll_benchmarking-the-future-world-of-cities (accessed 16 November 2016).

Department of Statistics, Singapore. (2016) *Population Trends*. Department of Statistics, Ministry of Trade & Industry, Republic of Singapore.

Economist Intelligence Unit. (2017) *Country Report: Singapore*. London: Economist Intelligence Unit.

El-Gohary, H. (2016) 'Halal tourism, is it really halal?' *Tourism Management Perspectives*, 19 (B): 124–130.

Glam Glam. (n.d.) *Singapura Shiok*. Singapore: Singapore Tourism Board.

Halal Trip. (2017) 'Singapore'. [online] Available at: https://www.halaltrip.com/city-guide-details/275/singapore/#about (accessed 4 February 2017).

Harvey, R. (2010) *Certification of Halal Meat in the UK*. Cambridge: University of Cambridge.

Henderson, J.C. (2010) 'Sharia-compliant hotels', *Tourism and Hospitality Research*, 10 (3): 246–254.

Henderson, J.C. (2016a) 'Halal food, certification and halal tourism: Insights from Malaysia and Singapore', *Tourism Management Perspectives*, 19 (B): 160–164.

Henderson, J.C. (2016b) 'Muslim travellers, tourism industry responses and the case of Japan', *Tourism Recreation Research*, 41 (3): 339–347.

Immigration and Checkpoints Authority, Singapore Government. (2017) 'Countries/regions requiring visa'. [online] Available at: https://www.ica.gov.sg/services_centre_overview.aspx?pageid=252&secid=165/www.ica.gov.sg/services_centre_overview.aspx?pageid=252&secid=165 (accessed 9 February 2017).

Lada, S., Tanakinjal, G.H. and Amin, H. (2009) 'Predicting intention to choose Halal products using theory of reasoned action', *International Journal of Islamic and Middle Eastern Finance and Management*, 21 (1): 66–76.

Latif, I.A., Zainalabidin, M., Juwaidah, S., Amin, M.A. and Ismail, M.M. (2014) 'A comparative analysis of global halal certification requirements', *Journal of Food Products Marketing*, 20 (Sup 1): 85–101.

Lin, M. (2016) 'Hotels catering to growing number of Muslim travellers', *The Straits Times*, 7 July. [online] Available at: www.straitstimes.com/singapore/hotels-catering-to-growing-number-of-muslim-travellers (accessed 5 February 2017).

Majlis Ugama Islam Singapura (MUIS). (2017) 'Halal'. [online] Available at: www.muis.gov.sg/halal (accessed 29 January 2017).

Majlis Ugama Islam Singapura (MUIS). (n.d.) 'Application for halal certification'. Application form. Singapore: MUIS.

Marranci, G. (2012) 'Defensive or offensive dining? Halal dining practices among Malay Muslim Singaporeans and their effects on integration', *Australian Journal of Anthropology*, 23 (1): 84–100.

Marzuki, S., Hall, C.M. and Ballantine, P.W. (2012) 'Restaurant managers' perspectives on halal certification', *Journal of Islamic Marketing*, 3 (1): 47–58.

MasterCard and CrescentRating. (2016a) *Global Muslim Travel Index 2016*. Singapore: MasterCard and CrescentRating.

MasterCard and CrescentRating (2016b) *Ramadan Travel Report*. Singapore: MasterCard and CrescentRating.

Moufakkir, O. (2015) 'The stigmatized tourist', *Annals of Tourism Research*, 53: 17–30.

Nasir, K.M. and Pereira, A.A. (2008) 'Defensive dining: Notes on the public dining experiences in Singapore', *Contemporary Islam*, 2 (1): 61–73.

Organisation of Islamic Cooperation (OIC). (2009) *OIC Standards—General Guidelines on Halal Food*. Jeddah: Organisation of Islamic Cooperation.

Overseas Security Advisory Council (OSAC). (2016) 'Singapore 2016 crime and safety report', *OSAC, United States Department of State, Bureau of Diplomatic Security*. [online] Available at: https://www.osac.gov/pages/ContentReportPDF.aspx?cid=19732 (accessed 4 February 2017).

Pew Research Center. (2012) 'The world's Muslims: Unity and diversity'. [online] Available at: www.pewforum.org/2012/08/09/the-worlds-muslims-unity-and-diversity-executive-summary/(accessed 7 February 2017).

Pew Research Center. (2016) 'Muslims and Islam: Key findings in the US and around the world'. [online] Available at: www.pewresearch.org/fact-tank/2016/07/22 (accessed 28 January 2017).

PwC. (2016) 'Cities of opportunity: The living city'. [online] Available at: www.pwc.com/cities (accessed 10 December 2016).

Singapore Tourism Board (STB). (2013) 'Navigating the next phase of tourism growth', discussion paper presented at Singapore Tourism Board Industry Conference, Singapore, April.

Singapore Tourism Board (STB). (2014) *Malaysia: STB Market Insights*. Singapore: STB.

Singapore Tourism Board (STB). (2015) *Muslim Travellers' Guide to Singapore*. Singapore: STB.

Singapore Tourism Board (STB). (2016a) 'Fact sheet: Tourism performance'. [online] Available at: http://app.stb.sg (accessed 29 January 2017).

Singapore Tourism Board (STB). (2016b) 'Tourism industry conference 2016: Speech by Mr Lionel Yeo, Chief Executive, Singapore Tourism Board'. [online] Available at: https://www.stb.gov.sg/news-and-publications/lists/newsroom/dispform.aspx?ID=654 (accessed 27 April 2016.)

Singapore Tourism Board (STB). (2016c) *Hotel Guide 2016*. Singapore: STB.

Singapore Tourism Board (STB). (2016d) *Marketing Strategy: Of Stories, Fans and Channels*. Singapore: STB.

Singapore Tourism Board (STB). (2016e) 'Emerging market: Indonesia secondary cities', paper presented at Singapore Tourism Board Industry Conference, Singapore, April.

Singapore Tourism Board (STB). (2017a) 'International visitor arrivals'. [online] Available at: https://www.stb.gov.sg/statistics-and-market-insights/Pages/statistics-Visitor-Arrivals.aspx?Aspx (accessed 29 January 2017).

Singapore Tourism Board (STB). (2017b) 'Your Singapore'. [online] Available at: www.yoursingapore.com (accessed 29 January 2017).

Singapore Tourism Board (STB). (2017c) 'About STB'. [online] Available at: https://www.stb.gov.sg/about-stb (accessed 5 February 2017).

Suryadinata, L. (2017) '"Islamization of politics" in Indonesia and Malaysia?', a commentary by Leo Suryadinata, *ISEAS—Yusof Ishak Institute*. [online] Available at: https://www.iseas.edu.sg/medias/, commentaries/item/4721-islamization-of-politics-in-indonesia-and-malaysia-a-commentary-by-leo-suryadinata (accessed 5 February 2017).

Tay, V. (2016) 'Is enough being done to attract Muslim travellers to Singapore?', *Marketing-Interactive.com*. [online] Available at: www.marketing-interactive.com/attracting-muslim-travellers-enough-done/ (accessed 5 February 2017).

Temporal, P. (2011) *Islamic Branding and Marketing: Creating a Global Islamic Business*. Singapore: John Wiley.

United Nations Statistics Division (UNdata). (2017) 'Population by religion, sex and urban/rural residence'. [online] Available at: http://data.un.org/Data.aspx?d=POP&f=tableCode%3A28 (accessed 28 January 2017).

Zamani-Farahini, H. and Henderson, J.C. (2010) 'Islamic tourism and managing tourism development in Islamic societies: The cases of Iran and Saudi Arabia', *International Journal of Tourism Research*, 12 (1): 79–89.

15

STRATEGIES FOR ATTRACTING MUSLIM TOURISTS WITHOUT OBTAINING HALAL CERTIFICATION

A case study of Takayama City in Japan

Shuko Takeshita

Introduction

In recent years, restaurants and accommodation in Japan have focused attention on halal certification as a way to attract foreign Muslim tourists. Academics are showing an interest in this trend as reflected in a sharp increase in the number of Japanese papers that include the term "halal" in the title, growing from a mere six papers in 2010 to 96 papers in 2014, and 47 papers in 2016 (according to the extensive CiNii database of academic articles). However, some of these papers have stressed the fact that halal certification has moved away from its original religious context and today is more likely to be traded as a commodity (Tawada 2012; Namikawa 2014), while other papers have cautioned against over-relying on halal certification (Namikawa 2013; Takeshita 2014; Kawabata 2015).

Food and meals have been viewed as key areas of consumption through which social and cultural boundaries of inclusion and exclusion are defined (Becher 2008), and have also had an enormous impact on shaping and sustaining religious belief and ethnic identity. Food and meals can become a special problem for Muslims travelling or residing in non-Muslim countries, but opinion is divided as to whether the host country should offer halal certification or not.

An increasing number of restaurants and accommodation in Japan have become halal certified to entice Muslim tourists, but Takayama City in Gifu Prefecture is the first Japanese municipality to develop a novel strategy for attracting Muslim tourists without obtaining halal certification. The owners of restaurants and accommodation, as well as city administrators have come together and adopted two basic strategies for attracting Muslim tourists: first they agreed to disclose all ingredients on menus so tourists can make informed decisions as to whether a food item is halal or not, and second they are committed to only serving Japanese food that does not include pork or alcohol.

This chapter will first present an overview of the current status of halal certification in Japan. Then, based on interviews with Muslim tourists in Takayama, it assesses the primary issues faced by Muslims travelling in Japan, and the effectiveness of Takayama's strategies for enticing Muslim travellers without obtaining halal certification.

Status of halal certification in Japan

Halal certification may be obtained in Japan in one of two ways. First, halal certification may be acquired from an organisation that is authorised by Malaysia's JAKIM (Jabatan Kemajuan Islam Malaysia), Indonesia's MUI (Majeris Ulama Indonesia), or Singapore's MUIS (Majlis Ugama Islam Singapura) as a Japanese agency that can confer certification. While this certification is intended primarily for export products, the mark is conferred by a Japanese certification agency and is fundamentally different from marks offered by overseas halal certification agencies (Takeshita 2014). Note too that halal certification does not automatically open doors to overseas Islamic markets. Even after certification is obtained, a company must still find a local distributor, and overcome a host of other obstacles to carve out a market.

The second way in which halal certification may be obtained in Japan is through one of the domestic agencies or non-profit organisations (NPOs) that provide certification based on their own criteria. Essentially, this is halal certification for the domestic Japanese market. It is sought by restaurants and accommodation that wish to attract Muslim tourists. This type of certification agency has mushroomed to several hundreds, and includes for-profit organisations that have no obvious religious affiliation. Among them there are agencies that issue certification to restaurants serving alcohol. An over-reliance on halal certification has led to a tendency to seek certification without careful consideration (Yasuda 2014).

Method

The survey subjects for this study were Muslim tourists planning a trip to Japan who came across the *Hida Takayama Muslim Friendly Project* Facebook page, and agreed to meet with me and be interviewed in Takayama. I interviewed a total of 34 Muslim tourists while we shared a meal at a restaurant in Takayama. The interviews were conducted from November 2015 to July 2016. The subjects came from Singapore, Thailand, Malaysia, and Indonesia, and ranged in age from teenagers to those in their sixties. Furthermore, I interviewed management and service personnel as well as chefs and cooks from the restaurants and accommodation in Takayama during the same survey time frame.

Food-related challenges while staying in Japan

Enjoying the cuisine of another country is one of the pleasures of foreign travel, but eating out presents special problems for Muslims travelling in non-Muslim countries. I interviewed a family of four from Singapore near the end of a 14-day trip in Japan. While in Japan, this family ate most of their meals at ethnic restaurants operated by Muslims and at McDonald's, where they ordered the Filet-O-Fish sandwich. The father in his fifties couldn't eat raw fish, so that eliminated sushi.

On the previous evening in Takayama they had *onigiri* (rice balls) for dinner purchased at a convenience store. The mother in her fifties confided:

We went to a convenience store, but couldn't read the ingredients written in Japanese. I asked the clerk with simple English, "No meat? Fish?" and we ended up buying tuna-filled rice balls.

I should note that there is a possibility that the Filet-O-Fish and the tuna-filled rice balls are not halal compliant since the former may be deep-fat fried in lard or animal-fat shortening, and the latter may contain meat extract or gelatin derived from animal by-products. The one safe option is to dine at a Muslim-operated ethnic restaurant, but a Malaysian male in his thirties commented:

I didn't come all the way to Japan to eat Indian food even if it is halal. I can get plenty of Indian food back in Malaysia. I'm here in Japan, so I want to try Japanese food. Unfortunately, there is a lot of stuff I can't eat because Japanese food uses *mirin* (sweet sake for seasoning). I like sashimi, but I would like to try local cuisine from the different regions of Japan.

Three salient points were revealed by the interview survey. First, Muslim tourists say it would be great if Japan had an official government-led halal-certification system like that in Malaysia, but at the same time, they do not expect a non-Muslim country like Japan to have a perfect certification system all set up. There was a great range of individual views regarding cookware and eating utensils that might come into contact with pork, which varied from "prefer that such utensils not be used" to "using such utensils is fine so long as they have been thoroughly cleaned." Subjects interviewed for this survey did not say that "kitchens should be strictly divided between halal and non-halal areas," as they understood how difficult this would be in a non-Muslim country like Japan.

The second point to emerge from the survey was that the majority of subjects (73.5 per cent) would like to see the ingredients clearly disclosed on food items. According to a questionnaire given to 840 Muslim visitors from Malaysia and Indonesia by the Japan Travel Bureau (JTB), 55 per cent of the subjects stated that they "would like to be able to determine themselves whether a food item is halal based on clear disclosure of the ingredients," as reported by Terue Ishige (JTB) at the Japan Halal Expo 2015 held at Makuhari Messe on 26 November 2015. While staying in Japan, most of the subjects want to experience Japanese food, especially the local cuisine of different parts of Japan. But when they sit down to enjoy a meal, they would like to be able to determine for themselves whether food is halal or not by scrutinising the ingredients, and not have a non-Muslim Japanese waiter or waitress assure them that the food is halal.

The third point revealed by the survey was most Muslim tourists would prefer that the ingredients are disclosed in English, but illustrations might be used as an alternative to Japanese characters.

Takayama's strategy for attracting Muslim tourists

Brief sketch of Takayama

Located in the heart of the Japanese Alps in central Japan, Takayama is a castle town steeped in history and tradition and is a popular tourist destination visited by many foreigners. *TripAdvisor*, the world's largest consumer review travel website, published a ranking of the most popular tourist destinations in Japan in March 2015, and Takayama was placed sixth, the first time the city had made it into the top ten ranking (PR TIMES 2015). The top ten destinations were: Tokyo (first), Kyoto (second), Osaka (third), Nara (fourth), Shari Town in Hokkaido (fifth), Takayama (sixth), Nagasaki (seventh), Miyakojima (eighth), Ishigaki (ninth), and Onna Village, Okinawa (ten) (PR TIMES 2015).

The number of tourists (overnight guests) to Takayama dipped in 2011 in the wake of the Great East Japan Earthquake and the Fukushima Daiichi nuclear disaster like every other tourist destination in Japan. Since then, the overall numbers have started to come back, but a closer look reveals that while the number of Japanese tourists has been approximately 1.7 million and hasn't increased in recent years, the number of foreign tourists has rebounded sharply. In 2016, the number of foreign tourists to Takayama reached 461,253, which is the largest number of foreigners that has ever visited the city, and more than five times as many as the population of the city.

The breakdown of foreign tourists (overnight guests) visiting Takayama in 2016 by country or region of origin reveals that the greatest number of visitors came from Taiwan (89,111), followed by Hong Kong (58,070), and Thailand (35,208). Examining the countries that send more than 1,000 tourists to Takayama every year, the countries showing a striking increase from 2013 to 2016 were Malaysia and Indonesia. The number of tourists from Malaysia soared from 3,359 to 9,965, for a three-fold increase, while the number of tourists from Indonesia sharply increased from 595 to 3,070, for a five-fold increase (Takayama City, Commerce and Tourism Department, Tourism Division 2017). Considering that 60 per cent of Malaysia's population (17.14 million) and 88 per cent of Indonesia's population (200 million) are Muslim, we can anticipate that a growing number of Muslim travellers will be coming to Takayama in the years ahead.

Let us consider some of the background factors contributing to this sharp increase. These include the exemption of Malaysian and Indonesian nationals from having to obtain a visa to visit Japan. The Government of Japan decided that from 1 July 2013, nationals of Malaysia in possession of ordinary identity certificate (IC) passports who wish to enter Japan for a short-term stay (not to exceed three months) shall not be required to obtain a visa (Ministry of Foreign Affairs of Japan 2013). As of 1 December 2014, Indonesian nationals possessing an e-passport with a certificate of visa waiver shall be able to enter Japan for up to 15 days without applying for a new visa or registering for a visa waiver (Ministry of Foreign Affairs of Japan 2014). Economic development of Malaysia and Indonesia has given the middle class more disposable income and created a growing market for overseas travel, greater awareness that tourists are exempt from paying consumption taxes, initiatives by the Japan Tourism Agency (JTA) to attract tourists to Japan (*Visit Japan Campaign*), additional low-cost carriers (LCC) and more flights to Japan. Malaysia and Indonesia are included in a list of 14 countries targeted as priority markets by the JTA. In the case of Malaysia, young Muslim visitors are being targeted for the first time in addition to Muslim families in the past. For Indonesia, well-educated young Muslim visitors are now being targeted in addition to wealthy and upper-middle class visitors targeted in the past (Japan Tourism Agency 2013a, 2013b). The number of tourists coming from Malaysia and Indonesia has been increasing all across Japan (Japan National Tourism Organization 2015).

Takayama initiative

An increasing number of restaurants and accommodation are trying to attract Muslim tourists by obtaining halal certification, but Takayama for the first time in Japan has taken a different approach. Instead of obtaining halal certification, the Takayama project focuses on clear disclosure of ingredients so that Muslim patrons can determine for themselves whether a food item is halal or not. Initially launched as a private initiative, the project is now moving forward as a public–private venture supported by the local government.

The project was established in June 2014 by eight young owners and managers of restaurants, accommodation, and a food wholesaler with the goal of attracting Muslim tourists. The main idea was to set the minds of Muslim tourists at ease regarding dietary issues and religious practices, while at the same time enhancing their satisfaction and enjoyment of time spent in Takayama. A secondary goal of the project was to expand business opportunities for restaurants, accommodation, and food wholesalers.

Before the project got underway, members of the team made several trips to the nearest mosque in Nagoya where they got a basic education regarding halal food rules and Islamic religious practices. This knowledge and information was then passed along to the owners of restaurants and accommodation to entice more Muslim tourists to Takayama.

Two key strategies of the project can be highlighted. First, was the decision not to pursue halal certification, but rather to give individual consumers the information they need to determine whether food is halal or not by clearly disclosing ingredients on menus. Members of the project soon realised:

> Serving up foods that contain no alcohol or pork is really not that difficult. By slightly modifying our recipes, we were able to give Muslim tourists the pleasure and experience of local Takayama cuisine, and dispel the false idea that we couldn't attract Muslim tourists without becoming properly halal certified.

The second strategy was to disseminate information about Takayama's offerings through adroit use of social networking services (SNSs). Muslim tourists who saw the project Facebook page came to Takayama and found they were able to enjoy local cuisine that contained no alcohol or pork. These people then posted photos and spread the word to friends back home and around the world through their own Facebook, Twitter, and Instagram accounts, which created a benevolent cycle bringing in even more Muslim tourists to Takayama. Their strategy was to go with the flow by exploiting social networking services to get the biggest public relations bang for the buck at minimal cost.

Local Takayama cuisine for Muslim tourists

The variety of food items on the menu appropriate for Muslims is gradually increasing. One of the main dinner offerings at *ryokan* (traditional Japanese inns) catering to Muslim guests is *hoba-miso*, which contains halal chicken and non-alcoholic miso. *Hoba-miso* is a local Takayama specialty consisting of grilled meat with miso on a *hoba* leaf, a type of magnolia. Even though they don't obtain halal certification, they need to use halal meat.

The broth used for *Takayama soba* (buckwheat noodles) prepared for Muslims, both in hot noodle soup and for dipping noodles, is made from a non-alcoholic type of soy sauce. The chef at one well-known *Takayama soba* restaurant said, "We were reluctant to change the traditional taste of an item, but we have really tried to make our Muslim customers happy." And it is obvious that these efforts have paid off, because they are seeing increasing numbers of walk-in customers who heard about their place on Facebook.

The *Takayama ramen* (Plate 15.1) made for Muslims is a non-alcoholic and non-pork ramen containing soy-based protein chunks as a substitute for braised pork belly, which is commonly added to ramen. A chef of one *Takayama ramen* restaurant said:

Plate 15.1 Ramen

When we first experimented with cooking without lard or meat, the result was not even close. But through trial and error, we came up with a ramen that really appealed to our Muslim customers.

In fact, their new meatless recipe has been a big hit not only with Muslims but also with their Japanese customers as well, and they are selling more than 100 bowls a month. Plate 15.2 shows a menu of the *Takayama ramen* restaurant. They don't use the words like halal or Muslim. They just say they don't use pork, beef, or alcohol for ramen.

Sukiyaki prepared for Muslims is based on halal chicken and a non-alcoholic type of soy sauce. The consensus among chefs of restaurants and accommodation is that they are able to satisfy halal food rules by simply substituting ingredients that are readily available, and there is almost no difference in price.

The manager of one *ryokan* (where 80–90 per cent of the guests are foreigners) said:

By giving our Muslim guests the dishes they want and request, they are only too happy to come back and visit us again. Moreover, by telling their friends, that brings another wave of tourists. Years of effort have now finally paid off when tourists tell us that they are really glad they came to Takayama.

A growing number of Takayama restaurants have got behind the project and developed halal dishes that Muslims can enjoy. They all fully disclose the ingredients used and provide

Plate 15.2 Global Standard Ramen Noodle menu

information on whether their kitchens are divided between halal and non-halal areas, and whether their cookware and eating utensils might come into contact with pork.

Southeast Asians generally prefer spicy foods, and tend to think that Japanese food is overly sweet. Upon trying the halal chicken-based *sukiyaki*, a 19-year-old Thai male commented, "I was very happy for the chance to try *sukiyaki*. And it was even better after I spiced it up with generous sprinkling of red pepper." Here too, those involved in the project have not cut corners. Especially the restaurant owners are very much aware that they cannot just serve up halal food and think that their job is done. They listen very closely to the opinions of their foreign customers, and do everything they can to match or satisfy their taste preferences. In fact, everyone involved in the project—the owners of restaurants, accommodation, and food wholesale—keep in close contact and discuss how they might improve the experience and satisfaction of Muslim tourists coming to Takayama. It is clear that these relentless efforts have paid off by the growing number of tourists who flock to Takayama every year.

Prayer space

In addition to halal food, providing a designated prayer space is another important way to attract more Muslim tourists. Muslims perform five obligatory prayers a day, but while travelling may combine some prayers and only need to pray three times a day. Morning and evening prayers may be performed in the guest's own hotel room, but Muslims are most appreciative if they can find a convenient place to pray after the midday meal. According to my survey, 91.2 per cent of the subjects indicated that some sort of prayer space or facility is required at tourist destinations.

Several restaurants in Takayama have already set up prayer spaces for Muslim customers. A Thai male in his sixties was very impressed to see prayer rugs laid out in the room next to where they were dining and said:

> I can observe prayer in the corner of a parking lot, in a hallway, or pretty much anywhere. I am not fussy about where I pray, but really appreciated that the restaurant had the forethought to provide a dedicated space for prayer. More than anything, this indicated that the owner really cares about our religious sensibilities.

It is just this type of emotional response that drives word-of-mouth advertising, and attracts increasing numbers of Muslim visitors to Takayama every year.

Conclusion

A false notion has been widespread among owners of restaurants and accommodation in Japan that "without certification, food isn't halal" and thus it cannot be consumed by Muslims. The interview survey revealed that, when travelling, a more troublesome issue than determining whether a restaurant is halal or not is being unable to decipher the ingredients in a food item. This could be remedied by clearly disclosed ingredient information in English or by using self-evident pictograms.

The basic policy of the Takayama project is to show that Takayama wants to please its Muslim tourists by providing them with the information they need to decide on their own whether a food item is halal or not. There are diverse ideas about halal among Muslims, so trying to adjust to the strictest ideas would make it difficult for Takayama to host Muslim tourists. While certainly it is important to make a profit, the goal of the owners of restaurants and accommodation is not to chase after commerce, but to develop a keen understanding of hospitality toward Muslim tourists that goes beyond acquisition of halal certification. Takayama has been making every effort to meet the needs of Muslim tourists rather than merely being satisfied with increasing the number of tourists. This has led to the increase of the number of Muslim tourists to Takayama.

One member of the project team said, "We have been able to make this project work on behalf of our businesses and our community simply because Takayama is a relatively small town and everyone knows everyone else." As I was conducting the interview survey, I observed how quickly the project advanced from initial planning to execution. For example, members came up with the idea of a menu tailored especially for Muslim tourists, and the next day they already had a menu in English replete with illustrations. Or, when the team decided to provide prayer rugs at a prayer space in the restaurant, they were laid at the space a couple of days later. This ability to follow through and get things done has really driven the project forward. The Japan Tourism Agency evaluated the project's activities, and in December 2015 selected Takayama to receive agency support for its initiatives in disseminating information and creating a receptive environment for Muslim tourists.

Considerable interest has focused on creating a congenial environment for foreign tourists coming to Japan in recent years, and the food and dietary practices of the growing number of Muslim tourists have presented thorny issues. A representative of the Takayama project proudly said, "With just a little ingenuity, we were able to provide a much more hospitable environment for Muslims." For the first time ever in Japan, Takayama is making remarkable progress through a public–private initiative in attracting more Muslim tourists without recourse to halal certification.

References

Becher, H. (2008) *Family Practices in South Asian Muslim Families: Parenting in a Multi-faith Britain.* Basingstoke: Palgrave Macmillan.

Japan National Tourism Organization. (2015) *Report on Statistics.* [online] Available at: www.jnto.go.jp /jpn/news/data_info_listing (accessed 15 September 2015).

Japan Tourism Agency. (2013a) *2013 Policy and Business Plan for Promotion in the Malaysian Market.* [pdf] Available at: www.mlit.go.jp/common/000992674.pdf (accessed 21 January 2014).

Japan Tourism Agency. (2013b) *2013 Policy and Business Plan for Promotion in the Indonesian Market.* [pdf] Available at: www.mlit.go.jp/common/000992675.pdf (accessed 21 January 2014).

Kawabata, T. (2015) 'Thriving Halal business in Japan and its problem: As seen in mass media', *Journal of Middle Eastern Studies*, 524: 62–74.

Ministry of Foreign Affairs of Japan. (2013) *Exemption of Visas for Nationals of Malaysia.* [online] Available at: www.mofa.go.jp/mofaj/press/release/press6_000362.html (accessed 17 August 2014).

Ministry of Foreign Affairs of Japan. (2014) *Visa Waiver for Indonesian Nationals Based on a System of E-passport Registration.* [online] Available at: www.mofa.go.jp/mofaj/press/release/press4_001424.html (accessed 29 February 2016).

Namikawa, R. (2013) 'Outlook of Halal food market and procedure to obtain Halal certificate', *Food and Processing*, 48 (6): 62–64.

Namikawa, R. (2014) 'Commentary on the Halal food system in terms of practice. A misunderstanding of Halal system: The difficulty of opening up new markets', *Food and Science*, 56 (4): 14–20.

PR TIMES. (2015) *Trip Advisor's 2012 Ranking: World's Most Popular Destination Cities.* [online] Available at: http://prtimes.jp/main/html/rd/p/000000308.000001853.html (accessed 5 July 2015).

Takayama City, Commerce and Tourism Department, Tourism Division. (2017) *2016 Tourism Statistics.* [online] Available at: www.city.takayama.lg.jp (accessed 1 August 2017).

Takeshita, S. (2014) 'The expansion of Halal certification as business: Focusing on Halal food business', *Bulletin of the Faculty of Letters of Aichi Gakuin University*, 44: 93–100.

Tawada, H. (2012) 'Islam and consumer society: The Halal certification in contemporary Malaysia', *Bulletin of the Faculty of Literature and Human Science of Osaka City University*, 63: 69–85.

Yasuda, S. (2014) 'Muslim tourists in Japan: Current status and problems in adopting Halal certification system in Japanese tourism', *Journal of Middle Eastern Studies*, 520: 49–55.

PART III

Heritage tourism

16

URBAN RENEWAL, CULTURAL TOURISM, AND COMMUNITY DEVELOPMENT

Sharia principles in a non-Islamic state

Bailey Ashton Adie

Introduction

There has been a noted shift in the use of heritage tourism as a development tool. For example, in 2015, the United Nations Educational, Scientific and Cultural Organization (UNESCO) adopted a policy focusing on World Heritage and sustainable development. This emphasises the importance of and potential for World Heritage sites as responsible and sustainable tourism destinations (UNESCO 2015). This is unsurprising given the increasing emphasis on tourism for poverty alleviation, which is one of the main motivations for the work undertaken in the Humayun's Tomb, Hazrat Nizamuddin Basti, and Sundar Nursery Urban Renewal Initiative spearheaded by the Aga Khan Trust for Culture (AKTC) (2014). This project was developed initially to preserve a UNESCO World Heritage Site while simultaneously stimulating the local, predominantly Muslim, community, who lived in a particularly impoverished urban village of New Delhi. Since its inception, this project has expanded to encompass a myriad of socio-economic, environmental, and heritage improvements. As it focuses on the creation of a sustainable urban microcosm, which is bolstered by the surrounding heritage attributes, it can be understood as supporting *Sharia* principles. Most notably, it has created a system through which the local population can earn money in order to improve their quality of life. Furthermore, tourism practices, specifically in terms of the use of local guides, can be understood as a form of *sadaqah*, or charitable giving. This chapter, then, presents a discussion of this New Delhi project in relation to both pro-poor tourism and *Sharia* principles.

Pro-poor tourism and Islam

The emphasis on tourism for poverty alleviation is particularly apparent in the discussion of pro-poor tourism (Hall 2007; Scheyvens 2007; Timothy & Nyaupane 2009; Truong 2014). According to Ashley, Roe and Goodwin (2001: 2) 'pro-poor tourism is defined as tourism that generates net benefits for the poor. Benefits may be economic, but they may also be social, environmental or cultural.' Harrison (2008: 858) expanded on this definition by referring to it as

> an orientation, covering nearly all forms of tourism, that requires commitment to assisting the poor, commercial viability of projects, and co-operation across all stakeholders—national and local authorities, public and private sectors, government, international organisations and NGOs—to achieve the aim of [pro-poor tourism], namely, to ensure that tourism brings net benefits to the poor.

Therefore, pro-poor tourism can be understood as a multifaceted approach which can be applied to any variation of tourism. Furthermore, Basu (2012: 76) states that 'a "pro-poor approach" to slum tourism is the most critical requirement for ensuring its sustainability, wherein "pro-poor tourism" is not an end but a means.' In other words, the goal of pro-poor tourism is the eradication, or at least the lessening, of poverty.

According to Truong, Hall and Garry (2014: 1086) 'for tourism to make a greater contribution to poverty alleviation, local poor people need to be included in decision-making processes, development planning, and project design and implementation.' This means that a concerted effort must be made in order to ensure a bottom-up approach to pro-poor tourism development. However, this does not preclude the input of the non-poor stakeholders.

> In order to generate net benefits for the poor in the South, tourism enterprises and their various linkages have to consider how best to maximise benefits for the local poor. Strategies and processes have to be financially feasible as well as socially, culturally and environmentally beneficial. Such an approach to tourism, however, is dependent on the willingness of the non-poor to bear any attendant costs—economic, social, cultural and environmental.
>
> *(Chok, Macbeth & Warren 2007: 155)*

Therefore, in order for the poor to engage in these activities, there has to be a certain amount of active participation by those who are not direct beneficiaries of the pro-poor initiatives. In addition to the support of the non-poor, Zhao and Ritchie (2007) noted that certain barriers to local participation are structural or cultural in nature and therefore require longer-term projects in order to achieve the desired results. This is emphasised by Schilcher (2007: 184) who notes that 'if tourism development is desired, than it has to be accompanied by uncompromising transfers of assets to "the poor", such as land rights and skills (long-terms training programmes).'

Based on this discussion, it becomes clear that pro-poor tourism needs an ethical underpinning in order to be successful. This harkens back to Hall (2007: 65) when he questioned where does 'the ethical base of ... pro-poor tourism come from?' While not always culturally relevant, Islam can provide a suitable ethical framework for this type of tourism. In Islam, 'the holy book *Qur'an* provides guidance in all aspects of human activity' (Jafari & Scott 2014: 2). Tourism, as discussed in previous chapters in this volume (see especially Chapters 1 and 2), is a permitted activity in Islam as can be seen in multiple verses of the *Qur'an* (i.e. *Surah Al-'Ankabut*: 20, *Surah Muhammad*: 10, *Surah Yusuf*: 109). However, there are additional practices that are based in *Sharia*, which are particularly relevant when discussing pro-poor tourism. In this chapter, *Sharia* is understood as religious law 'which occupies an essential part of the lives of Muslims and therefore its features are agents in determining social order and community life' (Sanad, Kassem & Scott 2010: 19). According to Sanad et al. (2010), there are four sources for *Sharia*: the holy *Qur'an*, the *Sunnah*, general agreement among the Muslim community, and anything derived from the first three sources. Therefore, when using an Islamic ethical framework for pro-poor tourism that is based in *Sharia* principles, it becomes necessary to discuss required behaviour as dictated in the *Qur'an* and the *Sunnah*.

At their core, pro-poor activities require, at minimum, a desire to better the existence of humankind. In Islam, the *Qur'an* has several passages that directly stress this aspect. For example, *Surah An-Nahl* verse 90 states 'indeed, Allah orders justice and good conduct and giving to relatives and forbids immorality and bad conduct and oppression. He admonishes you that perhaps you will be reminded.' This passage charges all Muslims to kindness and fair actions, a sentiment echoed in *Surah Al-Ma'un*. Verses 6 and 7 are particularly noteworthy as non-believers are demarcated as 'those who make show [of their deeds] and withhold [simple] assistance.' The importance of kindness is further stressed in *Surah An-Nisa* verse 36 which entreats followers to

> Worship Allah and associate nothing with Him, and to parents do good, and to relatives, orphans, the needy, the near neighbour, the neighbour farther away, the companion at your side, the traveller, and those whom your right hands possess. Indeed, Allah does not like those who are self-deluding and boastful.

These verses emphasise the importance of fairness and justice as *Sharia* principles that lend themselves to the successful application of pro-poor tourism.

In addition to the themes of justice and kindness, special attention should be paid to the stress on the needy in *Surah An-Nisa* verse 36, highlighting the importance of charity. As one of the five pillars of Islam, charity is a very important theme within Islamic teaching. More specifically, this form of charity, referred to as *zakat*, is the third pillar and is defined as mandatory charity required of all Muslims for whom payment does not cause hardship. *Zakat* is stressed throughout the *Qur'an*, for examples see *Surah Al-Mu'minun* verse 4, *Surah An-Naml* verse 3, *Surah Ar-Rum* verses 38–40, and *Surah Fussilat* verse 7. According to *Surah At-Tawbah* verse 60

> *Zakat* expenditures are only for the poor and for the needy and for those employed to collect [*zakat*] and for bringing hearts together [for Islam] and for freeing captives [or slaves] and for those in debt and for the cause of Allah and for the [stranded] traveller—an obligation [imposed] by Allah. And Allah is Knowing and Wise.

Therefore, there is again a specific emphasis on the charge to assist those who are suffering in poverty. This is further stressed in *Surah Ad-Duhaa* verses 9 and 10 wherein Muslims are admonished to not oppress orphans or reject beggars. While there are many other verses which discuss *zakat* in the *Qur'an*, based on these examples, charity can be said to be extremely important in Islam, and thus tourism and activities designed to alleviate poverty would be strongly in line with an Islamic framework.

It should be noted that the *Qur'an* differentiates between obligatory (*zakat*) and voluntary charity (*sadaqah*). According to *Surah At-Tawbah* verse 103, *sadaqah* is considered a method of purification. However, this charity is better when done quietly as can be seen in *Surah Al-Baqarah* verse 271, which states

> If you disclose your charitable expenditures, they are good; but if you conceal them and give them to the poor, it is better for you, and He will remove from you some of your misdeeds [thereby]. And Allah, with what you do, is [fully] Acquainted.

The importance of humbleness in giving is further underscored in *Surah An-Nisa* verse 114 which is as follows

No good is there in much of their private conversation, except for those who enjoin charity or that which is right or conciliation between people. And whoever does that seeking means to the approval of Allah—then We are going to give him a great reward.

Therefore, those who give *sadaqah* modestly are furthering the Islamic goals of justice and kindness towards humanity. According to *Sunnah Jami at-Tirmidhi*, the Prophet said that

Your smiling in the face of your brother is charity, commanding good and forbidding evil is charity, your giving directions to a man lost in the land is charity for you. Your seeing for a man with bad sight is a charity for you, your removal of a rock, a thorn or a bone from the road is charity for you. Your pouring what remains from your bucket into the bucket of your brother is charity for you.

Sadaqah, then, is essential when discussing the Islamic underpinnings of a pro-poor framework particularly as *sadaqah* can consist of not just financial charity but also general good deeds.

While charitable acts, as defined in Islam, are essential to the motivation and establishment of pro-poor activities, the endeavour cannot be successful or sustainable without the active involvement of the local population. *Surah Al-Baqarah* verse 273 states

[Charity is] for the poor who have been restricted for the cause of Allah, unable to move about in the land. An ignorant [person] would think them self-sufficient because of their restraint, but you will know them by their [characteristic] sign. They do not ask people persistently [or at all]. And whatever you spend of good—indeed, Allah is Knowing of it.

Thus, while charity is designated for those suffering in poverty, there is also an admonition for the poor discouraging begging. This sentiment is echoed in the *Sunnah*. For example, in *Sunan an-Nasa'i*, the Prophet noted that

The poor man is not the one who leaves if you give him a date or two, or a morsel or two. Rather the poor man is the one who refrains from asking. Recite if you wish: "They do not beg of people at all."

Therefore, charity may be given but should not be requested. What then is the best method by which to raise an individual out of poverty?

The *Qur'an* stresses the importance of hard work, as can be seen in *Surah An-Najm* verse 39 which states 'and that there is not for man except that [good] for which he strives.' Therefore, the poor are expected to work hard to raise themselves from poverty. In *Sunan Ibn Majah*, this sentiment is articulated by the Prophet:

If one of you were to take his rope (or ropes) and go to the mountains, and bring a bundle of firewood on his back to sell, and thus become independent of means, that would be better for him than begging from people who may either give him something or not give him anything.

This underscoring of the significance of striving for self-sufficiency in combination with the caution against begging creates a system wherein the most helpful charity would be that which assists the poor in bettering their own circumstances.

Truong, Slabbert and Nguyen (2016: 113) note that '[pro-poor tourism] needs to be underpinned by a philosophy that emphasises participation, representation, and equity.' An Islamic framework, then, is ideal due to the importance of justice, self-sufficiency, and hard work within *Sharia* principles. Additionally, Truong et al. (2016: 113–114) indicated that 'financial support is essential to ensuring that poor people can participate meaningfully in tourism-related activities.' While this interpretation refers to the monetary aspect of support, Chok et al. (2007: 155) stress that 'successful PPT [pro-poor tourism] relies, to a large extent, on the altruism of non-poor tourism stakeholders to drive the industry towards increasing benefits and reducing costs for the poor.' This aligns with the concept of charity within Islam, notably the significance given to the assistance, monetary and otherwise, provided as a method by which to ameliorate the living standards of the poor. Therefore, based on the previous discussion, it is evident that an Islamic framework aligns well with the identified goals and requirements of pro-poor tourism, thus providing an ethical underpinning to the concept.

Nizamuddin Urban Renewal Initiative

In order to illustrate the appropriateness of fit of an Islamic ethical framework for pro-poor tourism activities, a suitable project needed to be selected which not only involved a pro-poor focus on heritage tourism but also was governed by *Sharia* principles. To this end, the Aga Khan Trust for Culture, a wing of the Aga Khan Development Network (AKDN), was the most logical source from which to select a project. The AKDN was formed by his highness the Aga Khan, the 49th hereditary Imam of the Shia Imami Ismaili Muslims, to 'realise the social conscience of Islam through institutional action' (Institute of Ismaili Studies 2000: 1). While the AKDN as a whole is centred around the improvement of humanity in general (Institute of Ismaili Studies 2000; Karim 2014), 'the Aga Khan Trust for Culture's programs address quality of life issues through social, economic, and cultural development primarily in Muslim societies' (Karim 2014: 146). However, while many of the projects run by the AKDN, and by extension, the Aga Khan Trust for Culture (AKTC) are based in Muslim-majority countries, the selected project, the Nizamuddin Urban Renewal Initiative in New Delhi, India, was purposely chosen based on its location in a non-Muslim majority country. This project was selected in order to best demonstrate the functional use of an Islamic ethical framework for pro-poor tourism independent of underlying socio-cultural practices and/or the ethical base of national law.

The Nizamuddin Urban Renewal Initiative came into being in 2007 following the signing of a memorandum of understanding between the AKTC, the Aga Khan Foundation, the Archaeological Survey of India, the Central Public Works Department, and the Municipal Corporation of Delhi (National Institute of Urban Affairs 2015). The Nizamuddin Urban Renewal project was developed 'following the successful restoration of the Humayun's Tomb gardens in 2004' by the AKTC (AKDN 2016d). This came about as, according to the AKTC (2014: 2),

> many of the monuments within the World Heritage Site and its setting were in
> a poor state of preservation. The open space comprising of Sundar Nursery and

neighbourhood parks were in a state of neglect and the historic neighbourhood of Nizamuddin was counted amongst many of the '*slums*' of Delhi that had outgrown available resources; its living culture and historic past struggling for space, sanitation and opportunity.

In order to address these issues, the AKTC developed a holistic, integrated project system, which has three identified areas of focus: Humayun's Tomb complex, Hazrat Nizamuddin Basti, and Sundar Nursery.

The Humayun's Tomb complex is a UNESCO World Heritage Site, added to the list in 1993. According to UNESCO (2017), the tomb stands in an extremely significant archaeological setting, centred at the Shrine of the fourteenth-century Sufi Saint, Hazrat Nizamuddin Auliya. Since it is considered auspicious to be buried near a saint's grave, seven centuries of tomb building led to the area becoming the densest ensemble of medieval Islamic buildings in India.

Both Sundar Nursery and Hazrat Nizamuddin Basti border the World Heritage Site. Sundar Nursery is a large green space that contains additional Mughal-era garden tombs, which are contemporary to Humayun's Tomb, while the nursery itself was developed by the British during the colonial period. The existence of the garden tombs in this area led to the extension of the World Heritage Site's boundaries in 2016 to include much of Sundar Nursery (Archaeological Survey of India 2016).

In comparison to these two areas, Hazrat Nizamuddin Basti is 'one of the city's densest settlements where three- to four-storey modern buildings stand alongside medieval monuments' (Jodidio 2011: 173). It is also 'one of Delhi's oldest settlements with the shrine (Dargah) of the Sufi saint, Hazrat Nizamuddin Auliya, who lived [there] in the early 14th century, and after whom the settlement is named' (National Institute of Urban Affairs 2015). According to research undertaken by the AKTC (AKDN 2009) at the start of the project, only 41 per cent of the Basti's population was actively involved in the workforce with 54 per cent of family units being supported by a single wage earner. Women had very low levels of employment based on a 2008 survey, with a mere 9 per cent having their own income (AKDN 2015). Additionally, 'livelihood opportunities in the Basti were found to be limited in scope and capacity with incomes mostly seasonal and dependent on tourists and pilgrims. Skill deficits were another cause for unemployment in younger residents' (AKDN 2010: 45). This skill deficit was due to the fact that 'less than 1 per cent of the youth had access to vocational education' (AKDN 2015: 124). Overall, it can be seen that this segment of the project area was particularly depressed with, prior to the start of the project, little hope of improvement.

As has been noted, the project is holistic in nature spanning heritage monument conservation, community health interventions, and infrastructure improvements, to name a few. Zhao and Richie (2007: 121) noted that 'due to the multidimensional nature of poverty, understanding any poverty-related issue is always a challenge as a wide range of interwoven factors, such as economic, sociopolitical and cultural forces, need to be taken into account.' Therefore, the broad-reaching purview of the overall project is unsurprising. However, as the scope of this chapter is specifically on pro-poor tourism and heritage, only the elements of the project that are directly connected to these two elements will be discussed. In order to present the planning process and project-assessed impacts, the findings are derived primarily from the annual project reports beginning at the start of the project, 2008, and ending with the most recent accessible report for the year 2015.

Findings and discussion

The Nizamuddin Urban Renewal Initiative falls under the AKTC's Historic Cities Programme whose end goal 'is to create self-sustaining assets that improve the quality of life for the residents of historic quarters' (AKDN 2016c: 3). The projects within this programme focus on a cultural heritage-led urban regeneration with a community focus, referred to as urban rehabilitation (Rashti 2011). According to the literature, in order for a pro-poor tourism project to be successful not only does the local community have to be heavily involved in the planning and implementation process (Truong et al. 2014) but the non-poor stakeholders must also be willing to actively engage (Chok et al. 2007). Additionally, as many pro-poor activities need structural changes (Zhao & Ritchie 2007), political will also plays a role in the planning and implementation process. In order to address the issues, the memorandum of understanding created a public–private partnership, and, to achieve their goals, the AKTC interacts with a myriad of stakeholders (AKTC 2014), including:

- Government agencies
- Local leaders
- Religious heads
- Men and women
- Youth
- Vendors
- Commercial establishments.

By engaging these various stakeholders, the project has been able to enact change, which has had a broad-reaching impact on the whole of the project area. Additionally, due to the continuous community engagement, 'many of the facilities that have been created are effectively managed by the residents themselves' (National Institute of Urban Affairs 2015: 53). Therefore, not only has the community been significantly involved with the whole of the project process, but they also have been made self-sufficient, aligning with the goals of Islamic charitable giving and work ethic.

As two of the three project focus areas are heritage areas, it is unsurprising that there is a strong heritage-focus within the overall project goals. However, these have not been developed externally from the rest of the programme, nor could they be ignored when focusing on heritage tourism. Restoration of Humayun's Tomb and surrounding monuments was a major element of the initial project, with the final work on Humayun's Tomb completed in September 2013 (AKDN 2016b). For example, according to the 2008 Project Report (AKDN 2008), the restoration of tiles on Humayun's Tomb was identified as a necessary part of the conservation process as well as potential income-generator for the local population in Nizamuddin Basti. This resulted in the training of ten youths in traditional Mughal glazed tile making, a skill that had previously been lost in India (AKDN 2013). It has also been suggested that these skills, post-completion, may be used to create tiles specifically for the tourism market (AKDN 2009). In addition to tile making, a six-month long training programme around sandstone craftsmanship was developed for the local youth 'to ensure the availability of high quality of craftsmanship and generate employment opportunities' (AKDN 2008: 100). While these are only two examples, they represent one of the aspects that Schilcher (2007) identified as essential for a successful pro-poor project, namely the development of skills within the impoverished population, in this case via technical training. In relation to Islamic principles, this closely relates to the concept of charity, in this case free skill training, in concert with enabling the poor to better their own living situations.

This training was expressly directed at the male youth of the area, but there was also an emphasis placed upon the improvement of women's lives, particularly due to their extremely low employment rate of 9 per cent, as previously noted. Two self-help groups were developed in order to address this issue, focusing specifically on the female youth population: *Insha* in 2008 and *Noor* in 2009 (AKDN 2009). *Insha* produces and markets mainly fabric-based products, specifically embroidery (*aari* and *zardozi*), crochet, and garment construction (AKDN 2014, 2015). The success of this initiative led to the development of an *Insha* Crafts Centre, which has approximately 65 regular workers with around 200 in total having been trained (AKDN 2015). *Noor* instead develops paper products using a traditional paper-cutting technique referred to as *sanjhi*. According to the 2010 Project Report (AKDN 2010), this paper-cutting technique is used as a method through which to connect the local population with the monuments around them. This is done by using patterns from the buildings as the basis for those in the paper-cutting products. While the products developed by both of these groups are sold in various outlets, they directly sell their own merchandise at a stand located on the grounds near Humayun's Tomb. Based on the data collected in 2015, 'the turnover of the kiosk for the year … was INR. 1,263,575' (AKDN 2015: 142). Because of these interventions, 'family incomes have gone up for 250 families … in an average increase of INR 11,500 per month' (AKDN 2015: 143). This furthers the Islamic principle of the poor man, or woman in this case, raising themselves out of poverty.

Additional exposure for the products produced by *Insha-e-Noor*, as well as the male-specific traditional skills (i.e. tile making), was developed through the creation of an annual event, the *Apni Basti Mela*, first held in 2010 (AKDN 2010). According to the 2015 Annual Project Report (AKDN 2015: 79), 'the Mela helps to instil a sense of pride in the community and generate beneficial cultural and economic opportunities. It also allows many first time visitors to the Basti to recognise the significant heritage value [there].' In 2012, the third year in which it was held, there were an estimated 10,000 to 15,000 visitors over the three-day period (AKDN 2012). While this number includes repeat visitors, the *Mela*'s impact can be considered significant when considering that this event accounted for more than 15,000 visits to the Basti in 2015 (AKDN 2015). Therefore, there is a growing level of interest in the event each year. This, then, becomes a promotional tool from which to springboard additional income-generating activities, notably those that specifically focus on tourism. This is notable given the importance of guided walks during the *Mela* by *Sair e Nizamuddin*, which will be discussed in the following paragraphs.

While all of the previous income-generating interventions are aspects of heritage tourism projects, none are directly focused on tourism activities, with the noted exception of the *Apni Basti Mela*. However, tourism is an important aspect of AKTC projects. His Highness the Aga Khan (2011: 9) states that 'one way that revitalised areas can become economically self-sustained is, of course, through the development of tourism.' Furthermore, tourism is not a new income generator for residents of the Basti, as previously indicated, and, in fact, it is stressed that 'people's livelihoods are heavily dependent on pilgrims/visitors to the Basti' (AKDN 2009: 23). While most of the previous tourist flows could be tied to seasonal pilgrimages, the AKTC project's emphasis is on leveraging cultural assets for the community's benefit (AKTC 2014). Therefore, prior to the commencement of any tourism activities, both the tangible and intangible heritage assets were mapped by youth from Nizamuddin Basti who 'were trained to carry out the inventory based largely on interviews and archival research' (AKDN 2008: 34). This inventory had several suggested uses apart from conservation efforts, including the creation of a guidebook for the Basti (AKDN 2010). As of 2014, there has been a proposal to create tourist markers within the Basti in order to assist visitors to the area (AKDN 2014). However, the most significant outcome of the mapping process, in terms of pro-poor tourism, was the development of an alternative income generator for Basti residents through the development of a heritage tour guide initiative.

This initiative, which would become known as *Sair e Nizamuddin,* was developed in 2008 when it was determined that a tourist guide training programme was necessary in order to allow local youth to benefit economically from the potential growth in tourist visitation to Humayun's Tomb (AKDN 2008). While the heritage tours initially focused on only the Basti (AKDN 2010), they have since expanded to also include visits to Humayun's Tomb (AKDN 2015). When the tour guide training was first offered in 2008, 25 potential candidates were shortlisted with 10 eventually selected for the training (AKDN 2008). This number grew to 15 members in 2011 who conducted walks with more than 450 visitors and over 1,000 students (AKDN 2011). Based on the most recent project report, *Sair e Nizamuddin* led heritage walks for 552 visitors and 2,197 students in 2015 (AKDN 2015). This self-help group has also actively engaged in partnerships with private organisations, with several tour companies placing the Basti tours within their Delhi Itineraries (AKDN 2015). Additionally, as of 2015, *Sair e Nizamuddin* and India City Walks have an official memorandum of understanding wherein India City Walks endorse the group's walks in the Basti, and additional connections have been made with local hotels in order to add the walks to guest itineraries (AKDN 2015). Similar to the other livelihood generating activities, the young tour guides have not only been provided with the education necessary to sustain their activities but have also been allowed a path through which to improve their own circumstances through hard work.

Conclusion

This chapter has illustrated the appropriateness of fit of an Islamic ethical framework, based on *Sharia* principles, for pro-poor tourism. The AKTC has provided the financial support for the project allowing for local participation without monetary constraint, which Truong et al. (2016) and Chok et al. (2007) highlight is essential for successful pro-pour tourism endeavours. However, it is the Islamic elements that strengthen this expansive project. As has been discussed, one of the main goals of the whole programme has been the betterment of the lives of those in Hazrat Nizamuddin Basti. As Islam stresses self-sufficiency and hard work, the individual livelihood projects have striven to ensure that those involved have the skills necessary to not only continue their own work but also to self-manage it in the future. Through the inclusion of the input of multiple stakeholders and a justice-based approach to development, the Nizamuddin Urban Renewal Initiative has shown that Islam can be a suitable ethical framework for pro-poor tourism that emphasises participation, representation, and equity (Truong et al. 2016).

It should be noted that while this chapter has presented several aspects of the Nizamuddin Urban Renewal Initiative, there are many more that have not been discussed which are all integrated into the broader heritage and development initiatives. Additionally, the data have all been derived from the programme's project reports, and primary data collection in the form of interviews, particularly with the local community, may have provided different results. Furthermore, this project is supported by the AKDN, which has an estimated annual budget of 925,000,000 USD (AKDN 2016a). Therefore, it is unclear if this would be feasible on a smaller scale with a less substantial budget. In order to better assess the suitability of an Islamic framework to pro-poor tourism as well as general development activities, smaller scale projects would need to be studied. Finally, it would be of interest to analyse other religiously motivated development projects in order to understand how their ethical frameworks under-pin pro-poor tourism and development projects.

References

Aga Khan Development Network (AKDN). (2008) *Humayun's Tomb—Nizamuddin Basti—Sundar Nursery Urban Renewal Initiative Progress Report*. [pdf] Available at: http://annualreport2015.nizamuddinrenewal. org/docs/Annual_Report_2008.pdf (accessed 25 September 2017).

Aga Khan Development Network (AKDN). (2009) *Humayun's Tomb—Nizamuddin Basti—Sundar Nursery Urban Renewal Initiative Annual Progress Report—2009*. [pdf] Available at: http://annualreport2015. nizamuddinrenewal.org/docs/Annual_Report_2009.pdf (accessed 25 September 2017).

Aga Khan Development Network (AKDN). (2010) *Humayun's Tomb—Nizamuddin Basti—Sundar Nursery Urban Renewal Initiative Annual Progress Report 2010*. [pdf] Available at: http://annualreport2015. nizamuddinrenewal.org/docs/Annual_Report_2010.pdf (accessed 25 September 2017).

Aga Khan Development Network (AKDN). (2011) *Humayun's Tomb—Nizamuddin Basti—Sundar Nursery Urban Renewal Initiative Progress Report 2011*. [pdf] Available at: http://annualreport2015.nizamuddinre newal.org/docs/Annual_Report_2011.pdf (accessed 25 September 2017).

Aga Khan Development Network (AKDN). (2012) *Humayun's Tomb—Nizamuddin Basti—Sundar Nursery Urban Renewal Initiative Annual Report 2012*. [pdf] Available at: http://annualreport2015.nizamuddinre newal.org/docs/Annual_Report_2012.pdf (accessed 25 September 2017).

Aga Khan Development Network (AKDN). (2013) *Humayun's Tomb—Nizamuddin Basti—Sundar Nursery Urban Renewal Initiative Annual Report 2013*. [pdf] Available at: http://annualreport2015.nizamuddinre newal.org/docs/Annual_Report_2013.pdf (accessed 25 September 2017).

Aga Khan Development Network (AKDN). (2014) *Nizamuddin Urban Renewal Initiative Annual Report—2014*. [pdf] Available at: http://annualreport2015.nizamuddinrenewal.org/docs/Annual_Report_2014. pdf (accessed 25 September 2017).

Aga Khan Development Network (AKDN). (2015) *Nizamuddin Urban Renewal Initiative 2015 Annual Report*. [pdf] Available at: http://annualreport2015.nizamuddinrenewal.org/docs/Annual_Report_2015.pdf (accessed 25 September 2017).

Aga Khan Development Network (AKDN). (2016a) *Frequently Asked Questions*. [online] Available at: www.akdn.org/about-us/frequently-asked-questions (accessed 26 September 2017).

Aga Khan Development Network (AKDN). (2016b) *Humayun's Tomb Conservation Completed: The Restoration of the Mughal Emperor Humayun's 16th Century Garden Tomb*. [online] Available at: www. akdn.org/project/humayuns-tomb-conservation-completed (accessed 25 September 2017).

Aga Khan Development Network (AKDN). (2016c) *Improving Lives Through Culture*. [online] Available at: www.akdn.org/publication/improving-lives-through-culture (accessed 23 September 2017).

Aga Khan Development Network (AKDN). (2016d) *India: Cultural Development—Overview*. [online] Available at: www.akdn.org/where-we-work/south-asia/india/cultural-development/cultural-development-overview (accessed 24 September 2017).

Aga Khan Trust for Culture (AKTC). (2014) *Humayun's Tomb—Sundar Nursery—Hazrat Nizamuddin Basti Urban Renewal Initiative: Culture as a Tool for Urban Development*. [online] Available at: www.akdn.org/ publication/humanyuns-tomb-culture-tool-urban-development (accessed 22 September 2017).

Archaeological Survey of India. (2016) *Minor Boundary Modification Humayun's Tomb World Heritage Site*. [online] Available at: http://whc.unesco.org/en/list/232/documents/(accessed 24 September 2017).

Ashley, C., Roe, D. and Goodwin, H. (2001) *Pro-poor Tourism Strategies: Making Tourism Work for the Poor*. Nottingham: ODI.

Basu, K. (2012) 'Slum tourism: For the poor, by the poor'. In F. Frenzel, K. Koens and M. Steinbrink (eds) *Slum Tourism: Poverty, Power and Ethics*. London: Routledge, 66–82.

Chok, S., Macbeth, J. and Warren, C. (2007) 'Tourism as a tool for poverty alleviation: A critical analysis of "pro-poor tourism" and implications for sustainability', *Current Issues in Tourism*, 10 (2&3): 144–165.

Hall, C.M. (2007) 'Pro-poor tourism: Do "Tourism exchanges benefit primarily the countries of the South"?', *Current Issues in Tourism*, 10 (2&3): 111–118.

Harrison, D. (2008) 'Pro-poor tourism: A critique', *Third World Quarterly*, 29 (5): 851–868.

His Highness the Aga Khan. (2011) 'Protecting the past, inspiring the future'. In P. Jodidio (ed.) *Strategies for Urban Regeneration: The Aga Khan Historic Cities Programme*. Munich, Germany: Prestel, 7–21.

The Institute of Ismaili Studies. (2000) *Aga Khan Development Network (AKDN): An Ethical Framework.* [pdf] Available at: www.akdn.org/sites/akdn/files/media/documents/various_pdf_documents/akdn_ethical_framework.pdf. (accessed 21 September 2017).

Jafari, J. and Scott, N. (2014) 'Muslim world and its tourisms', *Annals of Tourism Research*, 44: 1–19.

Jodidio, P. (2011) 'Delhi area programme'. In P. Jodidio (ed.) *Strategies for Urban Regeneration: The Aga Khan Historic Cities Programme*. Munich, Germany: Prestel, 168–189.

Karim, K.H. (2014) 'Aga Khan Development Network: Shia Ismaili Islam'. In S.M. Cherry and H.R. Ebaugh (eds) *Global Religious Movements Across Borders: Sacred Service*. Farnham, Surrey: Ashgate, 143–160.

National Institute of Urban Affairs. (2015) *Urban Heritage in Indian Cities*. New Delhi: India.

Rashti, C. (2011) 'Urban regeneration'. In P. Jodidio (ed.) *Strategies for Urban Regeneration: The Aga Khan Historic Cities Programme*. Munich, Germany: Prestel, 25–31.

Sanad, H.S., Kassem, A.M. and Scott, N. (2010) 'Tourism and Islamic law'. In N. Scott and J. Jafari (eds) *Tourism in the Muslim World*. Bingley, West Yorkshire: Emerald, 17–30.

Scheyvens, R. (2007) 'Exploring the tourism–poverty nexus', *Current Issues in Tourism*, 10 (2&3): 231–254.

Schilcher, D. (2007) 'Growth versus equity: The continuum of pro-poor tourism and neoliberal governance', *Current Issues in Tourism*, 10 (2&3): 166–193.

Timothy, D.J. and Nyaupane, G.P. (2009) 'Introduction: Heritage tourism and the less-developed world'. In D.J. Timothy and G.P. Nyaupane (eds) *Cultural Heritage and Tourism in the Developing World: A Regional Perspective*. London: Routledge, 3–19.

Truong, V.D. (2014) 'Pro-poor tourism: Looking backward as we move forward', *Tourism Planning & Development*, 11 (2): 228–242.

Truong, V.D., Hall, C.M. and Garry, T. (2014) 'Tourism and poverty alleviation: Perceptions and experiences of poor people in Sapa, Vietnam', *Journal of Sustainable Tourism*, 22 (7): 1071–1089.

Truong, V.D., Slabbert, E. and Nguyen, V.M. (2016) 'Poverty in tourist paradise? A review of pro-poor tourism in South and South-East Asia'. In C.M. Hall and S.J. Page (eds) *The Routledge Handbook of Tourism in Asia*. London: Routledge, 101–117.

United Nations Educational, Scientific and Cultural Organization (UNESCO). (2015) *Policy document for the integration of a sustainable development perspective into the processes of the World Heritage Convention*. Paris: UNESCO.

United Nations Educational, Scientific and Cultural Organization (UNESCO). (2017) *Humayun's Tomb, Delhi*. [online] Available at: http://whc.unesco.org/en/list/232/ (accessed 24 September 2017).

Zhao, W. and Ritchie, J.R.B. (2007) 'Tourism and poverty alleviation: An integrative research framework', *Current Issues in Tourism*, 10 (2&3): 119–143.

17

IS THIS SACRED OR WHAT?

The holy place and tourism destination at Jabal Haroun, Petra Region, Jordan

Erin Addison

As she crests the steep trail to the small white shrine an American tourist exclaims in awe, "Is this sacred or what!?" But she isn't talking about the shrine—she's exclaiming over the panoramic mountain view.

Jordan is home to 48 officially designated holy sites. One of the most famous is *Maqaam Nabi Haroun*, the Holy Place of the Prophet Aaron, as much because it is located within Petra Archaeological Park as for its historical and religious significance. The *dhrih*, a tomb or shrine-site, traditionally venerated as the prophet's tomb, is located on the highest peak within Petra. (A key to Arabic transliteration can be found at the end of this chapter). The challenging, 8-kilometre hike to the mountaintop is a favourite with adventure tourism programmes as much for the striking natural scenery as for the cultural significance.

Jabal Haroun ("Aaron's Mountain") has long been associated with the biblical Mount Hor, on which the prophet Aaron (Ar. *haaroun*) died and was buried, according to the *Book of Numbers* 20:23–29. The site is thus a holy place to Jews, Samaritans, Christians, and Muslims alike. On a shelf below the peak there was first a Nabataean temple and then a Byzantine Church, dating to the first and fifth centuries CE, respectively. The Byzantine site was excavated in a series of seasons from 1997 to 2013, revealing that there was once a monastery and lodgings, likely for Christian pilgrims, and a Christian presence on the mountain at least into the eleventh century (Fiema 2002).

The Muslim shrine which stands there today—variously called a *dhrih, maqaam,* or *waly*—was constructed in the fourteenth century (Lahelma & Fiema 2000). *Dhrih* may indicate a tomb or shrine-site; *maqaam* is a holy place (which may or may not include a tomb); *waly* literally refers to the "saint" or guardian himself. It is a small (ca. 8 x 10m) rectangular stone building, much plastered and re-painted, crowned by a conspicuous white dome and metal *hilaal*. Inside there is a simple cross-vaulted chamber with a marble cenotaph just inside the door on the south-west end, beyond which, in the same wall, is the mihrab to orient prayer toward Mecca. The cenotaph bears an Arabic inscription and graffiti in Greek and Hebrew, and between the cenotaph and mihrab is a thick stone pillar, less than a metre high, which

Plate 17.1 Jabal Haroun, Petra Region, Jordan

may have borne sacrifices or offerings (Mietunnen 2013). A short staircase descends from the western end of the room into a sort of grotto, with niches in which people have long placed candles and incense. It is there, beneath thick layers of plaster, that the prophet is believed to have been buried.

The general conformation of the shrine, a small domed building over a cenotaph or tomb, with a mihrab indicated in the wall facing Mecca, is not unusual for locally focused holy places in the Middle East. Incorporating a cave or underground grotto is also common. Nor are such holy places (*maqaamat*) unusual, though they are rapidly becoming forgotten in younger generations. In her very fine dissertation Paivi Miettunen does all of us a service by inventorying and documenting holy places and their associated traditions through much of south Jordan, focusing especially on the "pilgrimage tradition" (*ziyaara*) to Jabal Haroun. The Arabic word *ziyaara* can be used to refer to any kind of visit, including stopping by someone's house for tea. *Ziyaara* used in a sacred context must not confused, however, with the obligatory *hajj* pilgrimage or *'umra* traditions in Islam. I will use the word "pilgrimage" or *ziyaara* throughout to refer to religiously motivated visits to holy places. As for the dispute about whether these are religious or "superstitious" traditions, I refer the reader to Miettunen (2013: 30–32 and 57–61), who reviews the debate sensitively and efficiently.

I first climbed Jabal Haroun as an "adventure tourist" in 1996, innocent of much, including the fact that I would end up moving to Jordan and staying for over 20 years to work on sustainable development projects for rural areas. In 2005 I moved to Wadi Musa, the town that serves the tourist site of Petra and functions as the main hub of the special administrative unit called Petra Region. I was conducting research on deforestation for a Master's thesis in landscape architecture and, eventually, a book on deforestation in the Jibal al-Shara (Addison 2011). I was finding it difficult to document the evident impact of tourism on the environment of Petra Region, so I interned for a successful, locally owned tour operator who was becoming interested in the new market segments of responsible, sustainable, eco- and adventure tourism. We went on to partner in a high-end, luxe eco-adventure tourism endeavour, but he was called by his tribe to stand, successfully as it would turn out, for Parliament in 2010. We both then turned our attention to generating funding for sustainable development projects, including ecotourism development, in Petra Region. In the midst of this (2011–2012) I served as the senior environmental expert on the award-winning *Strategic Master Plan for Petra Region* (American Planning Association (APA) 2012). Thus, much of what I have to say angles from the perspective of an engaged citizen of the community which surrounds Petra and, thus, Jabal Haroun.

I first heard of the pilgrimage tradition in 2005, from an older woman of the `Amariin Bedouin who would have been born in the 1950s. I later heard again a wistful memory of the *ziyaara* from a woman in Wadi Musa who would have been born in the 1930s. Older people in south Jordan often do not know precisely when they were born, because there were few doctors. Often a government medical officer would come to a village and register the birth of every child who had not yet been registered, all as born in the same year. I enquired further from time to time, out of personal curiosity and also for the purposes of guiding tourists. This experience of women as the main bearers of indigenous tradition is supported and explored by Mietunnen (2013), who was researching and writing around the same time I began working in Petra Region. When I asked my local tourism colleagues (all men) about it they were vague, seeming embarrassed or skirting the subject altogether. During the drought winter of 2011–2012, however, I heard from a (young, male) colleague who knew of my interest that there would be a *ziyaara* to the shrine to pray for rain. He would not go, he said, "because these are wrong practices, mistakes, against Islam. We don't do things like this anymore." Evidently 'we' do, however, because a historian and native son of Wadi Musa, Muhammad al-Nasarat, a year or so later published an excellent article on the local tradition, referring in some detail to a *ziyaara* of 2012 (Nasarat 2013), made by members of the community to petition for rain.

Testimonies to the widespread tradition of pilgrimage to the shrine of Nabi Haroun well into the latter half of the twentieth century are collected in Nasarat (2013) and Miettunen (2013). Both authors demonstrate that the tradition had, in the early to mid-twentieth century, gained a "general Islamic significance" to communities well beyond Wadi Musa and the Petra area (Nasarat 2013). But Nasarat (2013: 210) tells us that the last of the "public seasons" was 1985. This is interesting.

One might make a visit, a *ziyaara* to Nabi Haroun anytime, for a variety of reasons, but there was until the late twentieth century a communal pilgrimage season (*mawsim*) in late summer (Miettunen 2013), the season when the grapes ripen (Nasarat 2013). The communal pilgrimage, particularly important to the Layaathna and Bidoul tribes of Wadi Musa and Umm Sayhoun (Nasarat 2013), included the long, steep walk from the floor of the main wadi to the top of Jabal Haroun. Prayers and offerings were made at the top, including some evidence, in the past, of animal sacrifice, and sometimes a meal was cooked there on the mountain. When the "visitors" (*zuwwaar*) returned to their homes in the villages, they hosted special "dinners for Haroun," and before the village was built up as it is today there were celebratory horse races. Songs to "Umm Ghaith" were sung as part of a fertility ritual to bring rain and good harvests, and there is record of local rituals of life cycle transition (fertility, birth, circumcision) (Miettunen 2013), and even records that suggest that at one time local burials faced Jabal Haroun (Crawford 1930). Individuals might go to petition for healing and protection (Nasarat 2013). There are testimonies and photographs of processions amongst the Rwala Bedouin headed by a cross-shaped effigy of Umm Ghaith, made of wood and clothed like a scarecrow (Musil 1927).

Like mine, however, it was Miettunen's (2013) impression that Jabal Haroun is now primarily visited by Westerners, and primarily as a hike, an adventure. Her impressions are less casual than mine had been, because she was specifically studying Jabal Haroun for several years, and she also served with the FJHP (Finnish Jabal Haroun Project) which actually stayed on the mountain for extended periods of time during excavations. After reading her dissertation and Nasarat's (2013) article, I was moved to explore the "marketing" of Jabal Haroun in the tourism industry, and generally how the site is portrayed online to Arabic- and English-language audiences. Jordan tourism is now organised and marketed overwhelmingly online. Print materials are available, but usually disseminated at travel conferences or in-country. I was curious whether Jabal Haroun was ever portrayed as a *ziyaara* destination on Arabic travel sites, whether that significance was acknowledged on English-language sites, and whether or not it figured in adventure tourism promotion to either audience. I analysed the top 50 hits for the search terms "Jabal Haroun Petra" on Google.com and "جبل هارون البتراء" on Google.jo, on three different days over the month of December 2017. A word to the wise: it doesn't work to inventory the top 50 sites on Google.com in Arabic—it mostly displays the same English-language sites with Arabic titles. I wanted to see what an Arab tourist might see, in Arabic, searching Jabal Haroun—and so in Jordan, for example, that would be Google.jo. The same 50 websites remained at the top of each search during that time.

On both the Arabic and English web the assortment of sites was similar—scholarly articles, articles in the travel sections of online newspapers, purely religious sites (Qur'anic, hadith, and Biblical interpretation), a few general interest books on Jordan, tourism, or sacred sites, and, of course, travel and tourism providers and blogs. Some of the latter are sponsored by the Jordanian government, but most were commercial or personal. As I explored the websites, I asked the following questions and tabulated the results:

A *Is the content related in some way to travel and tourism?*

58% of the English hits were travel-related sites; 48% of the Arabic sites.

B *Does the site mention pilgrimage or* ziyaara?

22% of English hits mentioned pilgrimage; 26% of Arabic mentioned pilgrimage or *ziyaara*.

C *Does the site mention the Islamic significance of Jabal Haroun?*

20% of English hits and 50% of Arabic mentioned Jabal Haroun's Islamic significance.

D *Is the site strictly a religious, not travel-related site?*

10% of English and 12% of Arabic sites were strictly religious sites.

E *Is the site strictly an adventure travel site?*

36% of English sites and 2% of Arabic sites were strictly adventure travel sites.

Results A, B, and D are remarkably similar. Result C is unsurprising, since it would seem likely that Arabic speakers would remark more often on Islam. Result E was not surprising to anyone who has worked in Jordan tourism, but it supports what would otherwise be an anecdotal observation: evidently the Arab market is still marginal in the adventure travel niche. Like most things, the comparison is more interesting as we look more closely.

Thirteen websites in the Arabic-language search sites mention both travel/tourism and pilgrimage in some way. Two are actually in English (appearing also in the English-language search), and they don't refer specifically Muslim pilgrimage, or the *ziyaara* tradition at Jabal Haroun, but to an undefined sacrality. Three refer specifically to the traditional *ziyaara*—but only as an activity which took place in the past. Two refer to contemporary Muslims making a religiously motivated visit to Jabal Haroun: a history site that focuses primarily on old photographs (jordanhistory.com), and a question-and-answer page on a travel forum, in which the traveller asks for directions to the *maqaam* of the Prophet Haroun, indicating that it is a religiously motivated visit (the host provides directions without further comment).

Nine were commercial tourism sites (i.e. tourism providers or blogs intended to generate profit from tourism). (I defined a commercial travel/tourism site as one explicitly seeking to generate profit from the tourism industry—so commercially sponsored travel blogs, even if personal narratives, count as commercial travel/tourism sites, but articles in general-interest newspaper do not.) Of these, two are the English-language sites noted above, which mention an amorphous "sense of pilgrimage," without referring specifically to the *ziyaara* tradition or to Muslim religious tourism. A third is the traveller's question about *maqaamaat*, with no mention of *ziyaara*. The remaining six do not mention pilgrimage/*ziyaara* at all.

Of the top 50 hits for Jabal Haroun on English-language pages, 29 are travel/tourism-related. Of these 18 are purely adventure tourism sites, and 11 are commercial sites. Of the travel-related sites, 8 mention pilgrimage, and 4 of those are commercial tourism sites. There is, however, not a single reference outside scholarly articles to the local *ziyaara* tradition. Within the travel-related sites which refer to pilgrimage, the term is *in every case* used without reference to cultural context or a specific ritual tradition. We shall return to this point presently.

In short, it would seem that indeed the *mawsim al-ziyaara*, the seasonal pilgrimage to Jabal Haroun, has passed into history. To explore this intriguing result, let us return to 1985, the end of the traditional, communal *ziyaaraat* to Jabal Haroun.

———

The 1980s were a difficult transitional time for Jordan. By 1979 the regional balance of power was shifting dramatically following the communist coup in Afghanistan and the subsequent Soviet intervention, which burgeoned into the Soviet-Afghan War. Even more threatening to the Hashemite Kingdom of Jordan was the Iranian Revolution and the demise of the Shah, an ardent advocate of Westernisation, who had been a firm ally of Jordan's King Hussein. Jordan was also experiencing deep tensions with its neighbour, Syria, and in an effort to strengthen his regional position King Hussein allied himself closely with his other powerful neighbour, Saddam Hussein's Iraq. This alliance effected, however, a chill with the Saudis and the Gulf on whose generosity Jordan had depended for aid. Jordan was in deep and worsening debt, and Iraq infused the rentier state with over $400 million in less than twelve months between late 1980 and the end of 1981 (Robinson 1998; Metz 1989).

Meanwhile the influence of conservative Islam, including and perhaps especially the Salafi movement, was increasing in Jordan. The *Salafiyyin* are a literalist strand of Islam rooted in the teaching of Muhammad ibn al-Wahhab, the eighteenth-century theologian who inspired the state ideology of Ibn Sa`ud, the founder of the Kingdom of Saudi Arabia. The *Salafiyyin* claim an orthopraxy based exclusively on the *salaf*, the Muslims of the first three generations of Islam, as understood from the body of scripture known as the *hadith*. During the 1970s the quietist Salafi sheikh Muhammad Nasir al-Din al-Albani gained influence on the Jordanian Salafi movement, and in 1979, during a ruthless crackdown on Islamists, left Syria for Jordan, where he remained until his death in 1999 (Wiktorowicz 2000). As corps of mujahideen returned to Jordan from the Soviet-Afghan War, however, they brought waves of Salafi ideas tinged a more political and militant hue. The defection of Sheikh Mashhour Hassan bin Salmaan from the more politically enfranchised Muslim Brotherhood to the *Salafiyyin* in 1985 suggests the movement's rising influence, as well as widespread frustration with political engagement (Wiktorowicz 2000).

It was also an increasingly political Islam, especially amongst the Palestinian population (Wiktorowicz 2000), which by 2010 constituted nearly half of Jordan (Minorities at Risk Project (MAR) 2010). That percentage has been skewed since 2011 by the influx of between 656,000 and 1.4 million Syrian refugees (Hayden 2017; United Nations High Commissioner for Refugees (UNHCR) 2017). By 1989, when the regime held its first democratic election, the Islamists swept the vote (Utvik & Tonnesson 2008). Given the continuing failure of the Hashemite regime to address the Palestinian impasse via secular political strategies, and the fates of King Hussein's allies the Shah and Anwar Sadat at the hands of Islamists, the regime assumed a moderate and tolerant, but much more overtly Muslim, attitude. Increased religious programming on radio and television included conspicuous coverage of the King and Crown Prince attending Friday Prayers (Metz 1989). The construction of Amman's "official royal mosque," the King Abdullah Mosque adjacent to Parliament, was initiated in 1982 and completed in 1989 as part of the new Islamified landscape of the capital city (Shami 2007). This new Islamic posture was a studied one: an iconographic public reassurance of Hashemite piety. A regime-level nudge to the right in matters religious was intended to temper the popular sway in a much more conservative direction. While in some sense a concession to "fundamentalist" influences, the regime in fact made precise moves toward stronger control over Jordan's Muslim ethos.

In 1980, as part of the effort to reposition the regime as observant, if moderate and inclusive, King Hussein founded the Royal Academy for Islamic Civilization Research, Aal al-Bayt Institute (RABIIT) (2016a, 2016b). Its stated purpose is to "purify" Islamic culture of "external elements" and "misconceptions." While prima facie a call to infuse global culture with Islamic thought, teaching, and law, the eight primary aims of the Institute are woven throughout with the language of "modernity," "progress," "moderation," "tolerance," "dialogue," "rapprochement," and "cooperation." Its stated methods are the dissemination via the media of this moderate Islamic vision built through scholarship, education, publications, conferences, and *a review of the curricula of all educational institutions in Islamic countries* (italics mine) (The Royal Hashemite Court 2001). Not coincidentally, this approach is shared precisely by the Muslim Brotherhood, Salafi and Saudi ideologues (Yom & Sammour 2017), but to rather different ends. There is a meta-dialogue amongst regimes being conducted here. RABIIT is a thoroughly royal endeavour: its founder, King Hussein, delegated its administration to then Crown Prince Hassan, who was replaced by King Hussein's son Hamzeh, himself Crown Prince until replaced by the son of the current monarch. Today the President of RABIIT is Prince Ghazi bin Muhammad, of whom more shortly.

In 1986 the Dar al-Iftaa' ("Department of Fatwas") was formed under the aegis of the Ministry of Awqaf and Religious Affairs. A fatwa (pl. *iftaa'*) is an authoritative ruling on Shari'a law. Jordanian ministers are all appointed by the King and may be dismissed at the King's pleasure. The Dar al-Iftaa' home page explains delicately how, because of "new matters in the lives of citizens" the administration of the fatwa council was in 1986 removed from the authority of the religious mufti and transferred into the hands of the Chief Justice (General Iftaa' Department, Hashemite Kingdom of Jordan 2018). Jordan's Chief Justice is the president of the high Court of Cassation, and also appointed by the King (Metz 1989). Thus were all official authoritative thinking and ruling on matters Islamic gathered under the authority of the regime.

Meanwhile King Hussein himself was engaged in intense negotiations with Shimon Peres, then Israeli Foreign Affairs Minister, to solve the Palestinian-Israeli conflict. These negotiations were part of the precursory relationship which would eventually lead to the signing of the Jordan–Israel Peace Agreement in 1994 and what would come to be called "normalisation" of relations between Jordan and Israel. This ongoing relationship was a more or less open secret to all, it seems, but the Jordanian street (Scham & Lucas 2001). Peres and Hussein met several times in 1985. Throughout 1985 meetings between the two were documented. It is beyond the scope of this chapter to detail the relationship, but see Schanche (1985), Friedland (1985), Safire (1985), for a sampling. In 1987 the talks with Peres culminated in the Peres–Hussein London Agreement, which was scuttled by Likud. What is interesting for our purposes is Peres' conviction, later detailed in his 1993 manifesto *The New Middle East*, that economic development was the lynchpin of all other regional progress, and that tourism was the centrepiece and cash cow that would yield broad-spectrum economic benefits, especially jobs, in the short term, following normalisation (Hazbun 2002; Leslau 2006). This rhetoric was explicitly co-opted by King Hussein in speeches leading up to the Peace Treaty of 1994 (Hazbun 2002).

In 1985 Petra was designated a World Heritage Site (WHS) by the United Nations Educational, Scientific and Cultural Organisation (UNESCO). Jordanians, mostly members of the Bidoul tribe who had been living in the ancient tombs and monuments, were moved out of the ancient remains to a planned community now called Umm Sayhoun. Obviously a brand-new, planned village with infrastructure for 150 households, approximately 2,500 people, did not appear overnight in 1985. UNESCO states that the boundaries of the WHS are coterminous with "Petra National Park" (UNESCO 1985), which only existed as a proposal by USAID, first put forth in 1968 (USAID 1968). Aysar Akrawi (2012), longtime chair of Petra National Trust, notes in one article that the motivation of the Park proposal, on USAID's side, was tourism, not archaeological conservation. The Park idea persisted through the 1970s (UNESCO 1993): the plan to remove the Bidoul from their habitation within Petra's main city was floated in USAID's 1968 proposal, and planning for the relocation of the Bidoul began in the 1970s. The housing project was completed in 1982, but the Bidoul procrastinated moving out of Petra until 1984 (Tarawneh 2000). Petra Archaeological Park, as it was dubbed by UNESCO in 1985, was the centrepiece of a politically fraught, state-managed tourism strategy.

At the same time the tourism plans were cooking, there were backroom discussions proceeding toward normalisation with Israel, upon which was contingent a massive debt relief package from the United States (Scham & Lucas 2001). Furthermore, the promised economic growth, and especially job opportunities which would be spread so liberally across the population, were explicitly located in the tourism sector. Foreign aid investment in tourism and tourism infrastructure would, in the coming 30 years, reach into the hundreds of millions. Thus, King Hussein was compelled to walk a narrow line between appeasing a conservatively inclined citizenry and appeasing its very rich, Western benefactors. The direction Jordan would take aligned precisely with Peres' economic ideology, which taught that economic prosperity would weave anew the social and political fabric of the region. The regime positioned itself carefully at the intersection of Iran's new theocracy, its increasingly conservative population, the Wahhabi pseudo-fundamentalist Islam which undergirded Saudi Arabia, and the West, with which the regime had long identified, and on which, post-Peace, it would turn increasingly for foreign aid.

Jordan's worsening economic woes are commonly understood to have been the factor moving the populace toward more conservative Islam throughout the 1980s. The notion of *tajdid*, of Islamic "renewal," inspired at least in part by the rise of Imam Khomeini in Iran, gained currency as secular and state policies in the region failed and the general populace bowed under economic strain. While Salafism, Wahhabi Islam, and the spreading ethic of *tajdid* are distinct, they overlap and also share a general "fundamentalism," in the sense that all advocate a return to the dogma and praxis of a foundational community, though that community may be imagined rather differently by different groups. *Tajdid* teaches that the body of hadith scripture describes ideal Islamic praxis, and that *bid`a*, "innovation" in this practice is ethically and religiously wrong. One teaching shared by the entire spectrum is the condemnation of the tradition of *ziyaara* to the shrines of holy persons, whether these are tombs, memorials, or places in which supernatural events are believed to have occurred (Miettunen 2013; Nasarat 2013). Jabal Haroun, obviously, is just such a place.

The small, bright white shrine to Nabi Haroun is the one structure in the Petra Reserve that is visible from almost anywhere within a 20km radius—from the bottom of Wadi Araba to the highest points of the Jibal al-Shara. It is impossible to approach Petra from any direction without seeing it, almost eerily perched above the rest of the landscape. The journey to Petra, including the climb to Jabal Haroun, has long been a trope of near-mythic significance to Israelis (Stein 2002), finally made commonly feasible by the 1994 peace treaty. As noted above, the anticipated economic rewards of "peace" tourism were a keynote in King Hussein's efforts to sell normalisation to the Jordanian public. (A moving example of the Petra myth occurs in Amos Oz' beloved novel, *A Perfect Peace*.) While tourism did increase following the peace treaty (Hazbun 2002), revenue from Israeli tourism was paltry (Scham & Lucas 2001).

Even the surge in North American and European tourism, however, did not bring the broad-based economic benefits anticipated. Israeli tourists frequently came on day-trips, bringing their own food. North American and European tourists added a day or at the most two in Jordan onto Israeli-based "Holy Land" tours. Established elite tourism firms and investors benefited far more than independent entrepreneurs and local tourism providers (Hazbun 2002). But there was still hope: the Millennium was expected to bring waves of Christian pilgrims to the Holy Land, and Jordan rushed to compete for millennium tourism. Indeed, the baptism site at Maghtas, discovered by Prince Ghazi himself in 1994–1995, opened in 2000, just in time to compete with the West Bank site for millennium tourists and the Pope's historic visit. In fact, to find Jordan's holy sites on King Hussein's official website, the reader must link from "The Hashemites" >"Islam and the Hashemites"> "Holy sites in Jordan," which redirects to a page called "Touristic Sites." The page is divided into two topics: the Ancient Holy Land is the main title, with a subsection on "Islamic Holy Sites." The top section closes with an invitation to Millennium 2000 celebrations. The main image is Jabal Haroun.

In 1996 USAID funded a small RABIIT project of Hashemite Prince Ghazi bin Muhammad, a handsome "coffee table" book called the *Holy Sites of Jordan* (RABIIT 2016b). Keep in mind that RABIIT is the royal authority on matters religious, the voice of Hashemite *tajdid*. The *Holy Sites of Jordan* begins with a 1995 fatwa permitting *ziyaara* to graves and memorials (Muhammad 1999). Its final paragraph politely addresses Salafi and Wahhabi concerns. The same list appears on the RABIIT website. Along with the list on King Hussein's official website, these lists of *maqaamaat* carry a normative function. The holy places which are strictly Muslim are all memorials to historical figures and events from the foundational period of Islam. After these, the tomb of the Prophet Hud and a sacred tree commemorating a (Christian) prophecy of the young Muhammad's future are Muslim, and the remaining 20 are shared with Christianity, and of those 14 also with Judaism.

None of the dozens, perhaps hundreds, of purely Muslim sites venerated by local tribes, including the dozens examined with such care by Miettunen (2013), made the list. These are humble, mysterious sites, most often associated with a sheikh or tribal elder, and often associated with Sufi tradition (Miettunen 2013). The officially sanctioned sites have to be well-accepted Islamic historical sites more or less acceptable to the new conservatism in Jordanian Islam. "Correct," *sahih*, visitation does not include such activities as animal sacrifice, parading around behind a cross-shaped scarecrow, and singing songs of petition to some Umm Ghaith! (Dar al-Iftaa al-Misriyya 2018), much less burial facing the *maqaam*. Miettunen documents the popular shift in local attitudes toward *ziyaara* that is doubtless what I was hearing from my colleagues in 2005 and the years following: "these are wrong practices."

The normative list picks a delicate path between Islamic *tajdid* and the massive USAID funding that has poured into the Jordanian tourism sector for decades. I have argued elsewhere at length that explicit efforts were made in the late 1990s and early 2000s to efface Islam from the tourism landscape and route tourists away from contact with actual Muslims (Addison 2004). In 1985 the Bidoul were removed from their homes inside the ancient remains of Petra. The Millennium tourism surge was dampened by terror threats. Then came September 11 in the United States, temporarily decimating tourism world-wide and to Muslim countries in particular. In the wake of this letdown, USAID urged Jordan's policymakers, particularly in the tourism sector, to reduce the "perception of Jordan as a risk destination," to fight the "fear factor" (2004). The selection of officially sanctioned holy sites needed to be so unthreatening and inclusive that they are viable destinations for Western tourists—less from the perspective of the market itself than from the perspective of international donors pouring money into Jordan based on tourism's potential (Addison 2004).

The sites that "made the list" are emblems, on the one hand, of a tolerant, inclusive Jordan crafted to appeal to Western tourists. On the other, it is a list difficult for even a conservative Muslim to criticise: prophets are prophets, the companions of the Prophets are known from authoritative hadith, the battles took place, and they're known from Scripture—and it's all undergirded by a fatwa. Jabal Haroun is perfect: magnificently visible, sacred to the three Abrahamic traditions, set smack in the middle of a World Heritage Site. It only needed to be denatured of sketchy local traditions and the way cleared as much as possible of encounters with actual Muslims, *et voilà*—a tourist site. Given all of the foregoing, the fact that traditional *ziyaara* ended in 1985 seems hardly a coincidence.

In both English and Arabic, the virtual media of 2017 now hews to this line. To the Arab travel industry, the "visit" to Jabal Haroun has successfully been shorn of strange local practices. While 25 mention the Islamic significance of the site, in the few instances that

Plate 17.2 Jabal Haroun, Petra Region, Jordan

ziyaara is mentioned at all it is a curiosity of the past: a matter for scholars of history. Even the three travel-related sites which mention religiously motivated tourism strip Jabal Haroun of cultural context or detail: *people come to Jordan from all over the world for religious tourism; this shrine is located at the summit of Jabal Nabi Haroun.* That's all.

In the English-language media on Jabal Haroun the notion of pilgrimage itself has been universalised and homogenised. "Pilgrimage" is used again and again to lend a note of sacrality and solemnity to a hike, but the concept is unmoored from any technical ritual structure or reference to cultural context or tradition. In one case it is used as the title of a subsection which merely describes the physical hike. The confluence of trekking/challenge/ spirituality is certainly more related to the Romantic American nature writing of Henry David Thoreau and John Muir than anything remotely Muslim. Jabal Haroun has indeed become a fully sanitised Western tourist destination—an unthreatening, context-free adventure.

A note on transliteration of Arabic words

Names and loanwords commonly used in English (e.g. Jordan, wadi, sheikh) are not transliterated from Arabic, but written as they commonly appear in English. The definite article "ال" is written "al-", as it commonly appears in English.

Words not commonly known in English are transliterated as follows:

aa = ا	b = ب	t = ت	th = ث	j = ج
ḥ = ح	kh = خ	d = د	th̲ = ذ	r = ر
z = ز	s = س	sh = ش	s̲ = ص	dh̲ = ض
t̲ = ط	zh = ظ	` = ع	gh = غ	f = ف
q = ق	k = ك	l = ل	m = م	n = ن
h = ه	ou,w = و	i̲,y = ي	' = ء	

short vowels: a =' i =, u = '

ة is transliterated as "a" for fusha, "eh" for colloquial/dialect words

ٳ and ٱ are transliterated according to the short vowel they would carry

Many other subtleties are more difficult to transliterate, and probably not crucial to the argument.

References

Addison, E. (2004) 'The roads to ruins: Accessing Islamic heritage in Jordan.' In Y. Rowan and U. Baram (eds) *Marketing Heritage: Archaeology and the Consumption of the Past*. Walnut Creek, CA: Alta Mira Press, 229–247.

Addison, E. (2011) *Documenting Deforestation at Sadd al-Ahmar, Petra Region, Jordan 1924–2011*. Saarbruecken: Lambert Academic.

Akrawi, A. (2012) 'Forty-four years of management plans in Petra.' In D.C. Comer (ed.) *Tourism and Archaeological Heritage Management at Petra: Driver to Development or Destruction?* Springer Briefs in Archaeology, Vol 1. New York: Springer, 31–76.

American Planning Association (APA). (2012) '2012 national planning excellence awards: Pierre l'Enfant international planning award: Strategic master plan for Petra Region, Jordan'. [online] Available at: https://www.planning.org/awards/2012/petra.htm (accessed 1 March 2018).

Crawford, S. (1930) 'The attitude of the present day Arab to the Shrine of Mt.Hor'. In G.L. Robinson (ed.) *The Sarcophagus of an Ancient Civilization*. New York: Macmillan, 285–300.

Dar al-Iftaa al-Misriyya. (2018) 'What is the ruling of visiting graves and the grave of the Prophet in particular?' [online] Available at: http://eng.dar-alifta.org/foreign/ViewArticle.aspx?ID=146 (accessed 1 March 2018).

Fiema, Z.T. (2002) 'The Byzantine monastic/pilgrimage center of St. Aaron near Petra, Jordan', Arkeologipäivät 2002, 34–49.

Friedland, T.L. (1985) 'Peres and Hussein are said to reach accord on talks'. *New York Times*, 11 November. [online] Available at: www.nytimes.com/1985/11/11/world/peres-and-hussein-are-said-to-reach-accord-on-talks.html (accessed 1 March 2018).

General Iftaa' Department, Hashemite Kingdom of Jordan. (2018) 'About the general Iftaa' Deparment'. [online] Available at: http://aliftaa.jo/ShowContentEn.aspx?Id=74#.WpDGl2rwbIU (accessed 1 March 2018).

Hayden, S. (2017) 'Forced back to Syria? Jordan's unregistered refugees fear deportation'. *Reuters*, 21 February. [online] Available at: https://www.reuters.com/article/us-mideast-crisis-jordan-refugees/forced-back-to-syria-jordans-unregistered-refugees-fear-deportation-idUSKBN16100I (accessed 1 March 2018).

Hazbun, W. (2002) 'Mapping the landscape of the 'New Middle East': The politics of tourism development and the peace process in Jordan'. In G. Joffe (ed.) *Jordan in Transition, 1990–2000*. New York: Palgrave, 330–345.

Lahelma, A. and Fiema, Z.T. (2000) 'From goddess to prophet: 2000 years of continuity on the mountain of Aaron near Petra, Jordan', *Temenos*, 44, 191–222.

Leslau, O. (2006) 'The new Middle East: From the perspective of the old Middle East', *Middle East Review of International Affairs*, [online] 10 (3): 46–62. Available at: www.rubincenter.org/meria/articles/2006/september/leslau/4.pdf (accessed 1 March 2018).

Metz, H.C. (ed.) (1989) *Jordan: A Country Study*. Washington, DC: GPO for the Library of Congress. [online] Available at: http://countrystudies.us/jordan/(accessed 1 March 2018).

Miettunen, P. (2013) Our Ancestors Were Bedouin: Memory, Identity and Change: The Case of Holy Sites in Southern Jordan. PhD. University of Helsinki.

Minorities at Risk Project (MAR). (2010) 'Assessment for Palestinians in Jordan.' [online] Available at: www.mar.umd.edu/assessment.asp?groupId=66302 (accessed 1 March 2018).

Muhammad, G.B. (1999) *The Holy Sites of Jordan*. Amman, Jordan: Turab.

Musil, A. (1927) *The Manners and Customs of the Rwala Bedouins*. Prague: The American Geographical Society.

Nasarat, M. (2013) 'Mawsim al-Nabiy Haroun—`alayhu al-salaam—fiy al-batra: al-mawsim wa al-maqaam', *Jordan Journal for History and Archaeology*, [online] 7 (1): 110–152. Available at: https://journals.ju.edu.jo/JJHA/article/viewFile/5368/3441 (accessed 1 March 2018).

Robinson, G.E. (1998) 'Defensive democratization in Jordan', *International Journal of Middle East Studies*, [online] 30 (3): 387–410. www.jstor.org/stable/164267 (accessed 1 March 2018).

The Royal Aal al-Bayt Institute for Islamic Thought (RABIIT). (2016a) 'Law of the institute'. [online] Available at: www.aalalbayt.org/en/law.html (accessed 1 March 2018).

The Royal Aal al-Bayt Institute for Islamic Thought (RABIIT). (2016b) 'The Projects: The Committee of Turab'. [online] Available at: www.aalalbayt.org/en/projectsnewturab.html (accessed 1 March 2018).

The Royal Hashemite Court. (2001) 'Islam and the Hashemites'. [online] Available at www.kinghussein.gov.jo/islam_hashemites.html (accessed 1 March 2018).

Safire, W. (1985) 'King Hussein's double-cross'. *New York Times News Service*, 13 November. [online] Available at http://articles.chicagotribune.com/1985-11-13/news/8503180385_1_peres-plans-prime-minister-shimon-peres-israeli-leaders (accessed 1 March 2018).

Scham, P.L. and Lucas, R.E. (2001) '"Normalization" and "anti-normalization" in Jordan: The public debate', *Middle East Review of International Affairs*, [online] 5 (3): 54–70. Available at www.rubincenter.org/meria/2001/09/scham-lucas.pdf (accessed 1 March 2017).

Schanche, D.A. (1985) 'Peres offers to travel to Jordan for direct talks with Hussein'. *Los Angeles Times*, 21 February. [online] Available at: http://articles.latimes.com/1985-02-21/news/mn-626_1_direct-talks (accessed 1 March 2018).

Shami, S. (2007) 'Amman is not a city: Middle Eastern cities in question'. In A. Cinar and T Bender (eds) *Urban Imaginaries: Locating the Modern City*. Minneapolis: University of Minnesota Press, 208–235.

Stein, R.L. (2002) '"First contact" and other Israeli fictions: Tourism, globalization, and the Middle East peace process', *Public Culture*, 14 (3): 515–543.

Tarawneh, M. (2000) House Form and Cultural Identity: The Case of Bedouin Housing in Southern Jordan. Master's Thesis. McGill University.

United Nations Educational, Scientific and Cultural Organisation (UNESCO). (1985) 'World Heritage List: Petra. Report of the 9th Session of the Committee: Item 9 of the Provisional Agenda: Nominations to the World Heritage List'. [online] Available at: http://whc.unesco.org/archive/1985/sc-85-conf008-4e.pdf (accessed 1 March 2018).

United Nations Educational, Scientific and Cultural Organisation (UNESCO). (1993) 'A plan for safeguarding Petra and its surroundings'. In *World Heritage Newsletter*, Issue No. 2, June. [online] Available at: http://nabataea.net/ppark.html (accessed 1 March 2018).

United Nations High Commissioner for Refugees (UNHCR). (2017) 'Syria regional refugee response: Inter-agency information sharing portal—total persons of concern'. [online] Available at: http://data.unhcr.org/syrianrefugees/country.php?id=107 (accessed 1 March 2018).

USAID. (1968) *Master Plan for the Protection and Use of Petra National Park*. [pdf] Available at: http://pdf.usaid.gov/pdf_docs/pbaaa709.pdf (accessed 1 March 2018).

Utvik, B.O. and Tonnesson, T.H. (2008) *Islamist Movements in the Middle East: Challenging the Autocrats*. Report to Department of Culture Studies and Oriental Languages (IKOS): University of Oslo.

Wiktorowicz, Q. (2000) 'The Salafi Movement in Jordan', *International Journal of Middle East Studies*, 32 (2): 219–240.

Yom, S. and Sammour, K. (2017) 'Counterterrorism and youth radicalization in Jordan: Social and political dimensions', *Combatting Terrorism Center*, [online] 10 (4). Available at: https://ctc.usma.edu/counter terrorism-and-youth-radicalization-in-jordan-social-and-political-dimensions/(accessed 1 March 2018).

18

MUHARRAM IN IRAN

A religio-cultural festival

Saman Hassibi and Amir Sayadabdi

Introduction

Iran is the largest Shi'ite state in the modern world (Seyfi & Hall 2019), and home to one of the most significant Shia religious festivals that has been widely practised since the sixteenth century: Muharram festival. Although Muharram is a festival of mourning rather than of joy, it can nonetheless be considered a festival from a tourism point of view, for it is 'a celebration of a theme or special event for a limited period of time, held annually or less frequently to which the public is invited' (Smith 1990: 128). Moreover, it has the basic features of any other festivals for it showcases a great deal of the destination's intangible heritage, religious beliefs, local traditions, ethnic backgrounds, and cultural landscape (see, for example, Cudny, Korec & Rouba 2012).

Given the known and axiomatic income-generating impacts of festivals on localities (O'Sullivan & Jackson 2002), one would expect that the research on the impact and potential of festivals on Islamic tourism would be abundant. However, there is a notable lack of academic research with regards to the tourism impacts of Muharram and there are only a handful of researches that have dealt, albeit briefly, with the topic (see, for example, Khavarian, Zare & Mostofiolmamaleki 2014; Rezaei, Khavarian-Garmsir & Aliyan 2014; Khavarian-Garmsir, Stavros & Saraei 2017; Farahani, Rahmatpoor & Shabani 2014; Ghaderi, Ezzati & Hafezi Zadeh 2009). Therefore, this chapter shall attempt to call scholarly attention to Muharram festival in Iran by reviewing some of its most important aspects through the perspective of cultural and heritage tourism, particularly festival tourism.

Festivals

Festivals have long been used and devised as opportunities for social and commercial exchange often involving and focusing on travellers and observers (Arnold 2001; Robinson, Picard & Long 2004) and providing them with points of meaningful connectivity to the people and the place (Picard & Robinson 2006; Jaeger & Mykletun 2012). Yet, the status that festivals have occupied in the domestic and international tourism market is relatively recent, although it has become significant enough that 'festival tourism' is recognised as an important niche within the tourism industry (Cudny 2013).

Festivals are conceived of primarily in terms of their economic potential, numbers of visitors attracted, and revenues generated (e.g. Burgan & Mules 2001; Crompton 2006; Boo, Ko & Blazey 2007; Dwyer, Forsyth & Spurr 2006; Brannas & Nordstrom 2006), while some others have paid attention to issues of commodification, authenticity, and cultural identity (e.g. Delamere 2001; Fredline, Jago & Deery 2003; Small 2007; Whitford 2004). However, what most of these studies agree on is that encountering a festival, in any case or form, whether intentionally or spontaneously, provides tourists with the opportunity to interact with the locale and gives them a deeper insight into the culture, which will add to their overall experience. Therefore, in recent years, festivals have placed more focus upon special interest tourists, particularly cultural tourists for whom the exploration of authentic cultural tourism 'products' is a primary motivation for travel (Buch, Milne & Dickson 2011).

Festivals, just like any other type of event, come in a variety of shapes and sizes—centring on various aspects from sport and culture to agriculture and religion (O'Sullivan & Jackson 2002). As festivals can be viewed as means through which the cultural identities of place and communities can be constructed and expressed, they can also be seen as spaces within which the cultural tourist—who is in search of authentic engagement with the locals—can expect to achieve this goal. In this way, Muharram, as one of the largest festivals in Iran, brings about many opportunities for the development of tourism, particularly within the international sector.

Muharram as a festival

Muharram is the first month in the Islamic lunar calendar; its first ten days is the period for the most important mourning ceremony in Iran which commemorates the Battle of Karbala in AD 680. During this ten-day battle, Hossein—the grandson of Muhammad and the third Shi'i Imam—fought against the forces of the second Umayyad caliph, Yazid I, and eventually was killed on the tenth day of the month (known as *Ashura*). The event is of grave significance for Shi'a Muslims symbolising 'the moral dichotomy between worldly injustice and corruption on the one hand and God-centred justice, piety, sacrifice and perseverance on the other' and is also 'an important way of worshiping God in a spiritual or mystical way' (Aghaie 2007: 112).

Apart from its religious and symbolic significance, the commemoration of the event is also of historic value with the first public mourning ceremonies traced back to the tenth century in Baghdad (Chelkowski 1985). The ceremonies gained official recognition in Iran after the establishment of Shi'ism as the state religion of Iran in the early sixteenth century by the Safavid state (Aghaie 2007) which encouraged and sponsored the mourning rituals of Muharram, granting it patronage, thus developing its observance into an integral part of Iranian culture (Nakash 1993) that has continued to the present day.

From a tourism point of view, what distinguishes Muharram festival from most other festivals worldwide is that these festivals, unlike Muharram, are often created with the main purpose of drawing visitors and increasing revenue (O'Sullivan & Jackson 2002). This is even true about some heritage festivals and their 'cultural products' which are mostly dependent on the staging or re-creation of ethnic or cultural traditions (Chhabra, Healy & Sills 2003). Muharram festival, on the other hand, is for the most part community-based, and has never been promoted as an attraction by the official tourism channels of Iran. There have been some small, non-commercial organisations made up of local tourist guides who offered tours of Muharram ceremonies with the intention of promoting cultural and religious tourism in cities with large-scale events, but these tours were mostly shut down due to having little to no financial support from official channels that often view the presence of foreign tourists in 'sacred' events as a threat to the religious beliefs of the community. Therefore, the absence of any marketing or promotion for Muharram festival may have prevented Iranian tourism attracting some international tourists and their revenue. However, it has also given the festival, though quite unintentionally, a significant competitive advantage in terms of authenticity, for lack of commodification and commercialisation of indigenous culture can lead to the maintenance of authenticity (MacCannell 1976; Taylor 2001).

The significance of the role that festivals such as Muharram play within the experience of the traveller is its central feature that, similar to many international festivals, is 'the celebration or reaffirmation of community or culture' (Rolfe 1992: 7). Even with inevitable alterations that have occurred to the Muharram festival since its start in the sixteenth century, the festival remains one of the most authentic cultural events in Iran as it pays homage to its original historic concept (Taylor 2001). Today, the observance of Muharram has arguably become the largest festival in Iran that includes a number of unique rituals such as large, public processions (*dasteh*) and the re-enactment of the Battle of Karbala in the form of a play (*ta'ziyeh*). There is also a distinctive culinary scene that is rich in cultural and religious symbolism. Each of these can hold special appeal for tourists especially those seeking a deeper understanding of the local culture being visited.

While festivals can be key motivators and primary reasons for travelling to a destination, they can be an enriching experience also for travellers who have only stumbled upon them by chance (Picard & Robinson 2006). The latter seems to be the case for international tourists in Iran at least after the Iranian revolution (Ebadi 2017). There seems to be plenty of 'modern' international tourists who have described their 'coincidental' visit with the Muharram festival as 'an absolute privilege' (Fillis 2017) and one of the '10 reasons to visit Iran' (Yan 2016) while there also is a record of similar experiences in memoirs and travelogues of foreign diplomats, ambassadors, merchants, and missionaries of centuries ago (Matthee 2009). What these writings have in common in terms of observing festivals is that the spontaneous visitations of Muharram festival have often been described positively and as an added bonus to the experience of the foreign traveller of Iran. An examination of these accounts written by foreign travellers to Iran reveals that three aspects of the Muharram festival have often engaged tourists' attention and appealed to them as attractions, namely the processional aspects, the dramatic aspects, and the culinary aspects. These aspects are also the ones that gave the tourists a feeling of involvement in some uncommon communal activities, signifying a departure from their routines confirming the experience of authenticity (Wang 1999).

Processional aspects of Muharram festival

The processional aspect of the Muharram rites is perhaps the most visible one during the period. This ambulatory ritual (commonly known as *dasteh*) generally involves various attributes and objects symbolising the battle such as flags, banners, battle standards loaded with ex-votos, feathers, mirrors, lamps, lanterns, and candles. Some strong bearers carry these items on the front and are followed by often a large number of participants, some of which perform acts of self-mortification such as striking their chest rhythmically with their palms in time with the accompanying cymbals and drums.

Although some of the practised rituals in these processions are common in most parts of Iran, certain cities or regions have their own signature rituals and traditions, making them distinct and quite different from the others. For instance, the cities of Yazd and Ghazvin are, respectively, famous for their *nakhl*s and *tabagh*s, both of which are huge wooden structures—symbolising the Imam's coffin—that have to be carried by several hundred men in Muharram processions (Gaffary 1984). The city of Zanjan is known for having one of the largest religious processions in the world and the largest in the country, attended by around half a million people annually (Nazeri 2011), making it an item on Iran's national intangible cultural heritage list (Iranian Students' News Agency (ISNA) 2010). Lahijan, as another example, is renowned for its *karb-zani* traditions, during which a hand percussion instrument (*karb*) is played in a ritually rhythmic manner by the crowd in procession.

The processional aspects of Muharram festival and the rituals associated with them have been often a point of interest to the international tourist. For instance, Wharton and Swift (2013) describe the processions and the rituals as an unforgettable experience and 'one of the most interesting religious displays one can ever see'. Petrosyuk (2014) also notes that travelling to Iran during Muharram festival and getting to see these processions is 'a holiday you have not seen before [and one] you did not even imagine exists'. Visiting the processions has been, at times, even regarded as the sole motivating factor to re-visit the country as stated by Yomadic (2017):

> On the wall were some photos of different attractions, and one image in particular caught my eye. Wow. The scene in the photo was unlike anything I had ever seen. Countless people filling the city streets, congregating around a city … with everyone dressed in black. Truly, a sea of humanity. Although it was somewhat safe to assume it was taken nearby, I had to ask.
>
> 'Where was this photo taken?'
> 'Here! Zanjan! Ashura! Muharram!'
>
> Studying the image, I realised the photo was probably taken from our hotel window, and immediately made plans to come back and experience the image for myself.

In an increasingly globalised and culturally homogenised world, a festival—and generally a destination—needs to promote those aspects of culture that are most unique, authentic, and place-bound (Reisinger & Dimanche 2011). Not only are the large, ambulatory performances of Muharram in Iran culturally unique and potentially of interest to the international tourist, the different form and way of implementing the processions also establish local differences, providing tourists with the opportunity to visit the same event within multiple ethno-cultural contexts, therefore contributing to a deeper understanding of the diverse local culture, beliefs and tradition, thus influencing the tourist's depth of experience. In fact, sometimes these processions can be so different that, according to Grant (2010) who travelled to Iran during Muharram and observed the processions in three different cities, it is as if one was travelling from one country to another country within Iran.

Dramatic aspects of Muharram festival

The dramatic aspects of Muharram festival are most clearly seen within *ta'ziyeh* (literally meaning expressions of sympathy, mourning, and consolation) which is the re-enactment of events of Karbala and a form of ritual theatre formed and developed in Iran over a millennium. Performing *ta'ziyeh* is not limited to Muharram festival, but it is seen, in its strongest sense, during this period. The uniqueness of *ta'ziyeh* lies in the fact that it is 'the sole form of serious drama to have ever developed in the world of Islam' (Chelkowski 2009).

Though Islamic in appearance with its form and content derived from deep-rooted religious tradition, *ta'ziyeh* is 'strongly Persian' as it draws vital inspiration from the 'Persian political and cultural heritage' thus is an important part of Persian culture (Chelkowski 1997: 31). This form of passion play that combines poetry, music, song, and motion is believed to be derived partly from the ancient annual mourning processions and to be nourished by Iranian, rather than Islamic, traditions (Yarshater 1979).

As a form of cultural heritage, the main purpose of any re-enacted events is to 'present an aspect of a (located) culture's past to an audience over a specified period as an event' (Carnegie & McCabe 2008: 352). Such re-enactments, particularly when taking the form of a performance, would provide the tourist with a mediated experience of some kind; an experience of being in the past by creating a sense of 'being there' in the moment of trauma (Sturken 2011). In this sense, although *ta'ziyeh* can be thought of as a case in point, it is different with the 'usual' re-enacted event as known in tourism studies. From a tourism point of view, this difference lies in the fact that unlike the many cultural heritage re-enactment events that are staged within destinations to draw visitors and are intended for tourist consumption, *ta'ziyeh* has not been manipulated for extrinsic reasons (i.e. economic development or profit) or marketed as an attraction for the foreign tourist. In fact, it can be argued that *ta'ziyeh* is too localised an event or too 'personal' in nature with limited appeal to foreign tourists.

Nonetheless, throughout centuries, *ta'ziyeh* has been described by foreign travellers to Iran with a sense of admiration and appreciation. There are different accounts of the fascination Western travellers to Iran have felt upon visiting *ta'ziyeh* and its rituals from the early seventeenth century onward. In fact, *ta'ziyeh* was, at many occasions, regarded as the 'most interesting and most intriguing Shi'ite ritual for Westerners' (Chelkowski 2009): from the accounts given by Pietro Della Valle of the sixteenth and seventeenth centuries, Thomas Salmons and Matthias Van Goch of the eighteenth century and Eugène Flandin of the nineteenth century all of whom described *ta'ziyeh* as a captivating state of affairs and a phenomenon that is worth travelling miles for, to the contemporary times when Goytisolo (1997: 45) writes in his *De la Ceca a La Meca* that 'a few Westerners can see a *ta'ziyeh* and not be utterly moved by it'.

However, although *The Ritual Dramatic Art of Ta'ziyeh* was inscribed in 2010 on UNESCO's *Representative List of Intangible Cultural Heritage of Humanity*, no serious attempt has been done by Iranian tourism in terms of promoting *ta'ziyeh* as a cultural attraction. Therefore, there are not many accounts of tourists' interaction with this aspect of the festival in blogs and other sources, suggesting that *ta'ziyeh* has remained quite unknown to the 'modern' tourist when it can be a major attraction to the cultural tourist, not only because of its historical and cultural, but also due to its performative, theatrical, and dramatic significance that was praised by many, such as Peter Brook (1979: 52), who considered it as 'one of the strongest things … ever seen in theatre'; Jerzy Grotowski, who called it 'le theatre total' (cited in Chelkowski 2009); or Samuel G.W. Benjamin (1887: 382), who thought it an 'interesting exhibition of the dramatic genius of the Persian race'.

Culinary aspects of Muharram festival

The culinary aspects of Muharram festival present themselves mostly in an act of sharing votive foods and collective edible devotions. Such practice is rooted deeply in Iranian culture and had existed in the cultural practices of Zoroastrian antecedents (Gruber 2016). However, after Islam these practices and rituals gained a Shi'a Islamic tint and began to be dominated, more often than not, by mourning ceremonies commemorating the martyrdom of Imams (Kalinock 2003), and above all by Muharram festival.

During Muharram festival, cities of Iran are abuzz with the preparation and offering of copious supplies of free, votive food—collectively known as *nazri*—that are distributed by individuals and private benefactors to mourners as well as the public. Kiosks and food stalls are set up all over the country, serving a wide range of food and drinks from traditional beverages to elaborate Iranian dishes. In the capital alone, more than 17,000 mourning venues (*tekyeh* or *heyat*) and private houses offer *nazri* to the public every year (KhabarOnline 2016).

Witnessing such rites seems to have caught the interest of the foreign visitor who has often expressed, upon visiting such culinary scenes, feelings of admiration or wonder. For instance, Yomadic (2017) notes:

> They say there is no such thing as a free lunch. Well, that may apply in the West, but, I challenge you to name another place on the planet that leaves the doors to its homes open, unquestionably and without prejudice or judgment inviting any person that comes by—for a truly free lunch.

Not only was it eating such delicacies that added to the experience of travellers of Iran, but also participation in preparing and serving them was described as an 'incredible experience', giving the traveller a further insight into a rather complex food practice (Wharton & Swift 2013). In this sense, culinary aspects of Muharram can be viewed as having potential for culinary tourism as the tourist can, during Muharram festival, participate in the foodways of an 'other' in an exploratory manner, consuming, preparing, and presenting a food item that is considered to belong to a culinary system that is different from that of the tourist (Long 2013). *Nazri* food and rites can be viewed as 'non-food food festivals' that are events 'whose primary raison d'être is not directly food oriented, but where comestibles play a strong equal or secondary role in the celebration' (Timothy & Pena 2016: 156).

Culinary aspects of Muharram festival play a prominent, though not a primary, role that not only can nourish tourists and give them a chance to sample some of the offerings of Iranian cuisine abundantly and free, but also will connect them to the cultural heritage of the place. Just like any other food festivals, culinary aspects of Muharram have the potential to enhance the characteristics and principles of cultural heritage such as authenticity, protection/preservation, identity, community pride, and sense of place. Gastronomic heritage of Muharram festival can become—either singly or bundled with other practices—a strong tourism drawcard for many destinations as the consumption and sharing of food and participating in the same types of culinary activities as local residents provides an opportunity for tourists to engage in local intangible cultural experiences.

Arguably, *nazri* food and its associated rituals are not a means of generating revenues directly, as they are offered for free; however, they are an important part of tourist experience as they are offered in an extraordinary and non-daily context, bringing special meanings to food consumption and making food and the experience of its consumption a source of pleasure and enjoyment. The experience of Muharram food in its unique and unusual context has the potential to become one of the highlights, if not *the* highlight, of the international tourists' trip to Iran and provide them with a strong supporting touristic experience. Although for many tourists, especially the mass tourist, foods that are made with unfamiliar ingredients or served in strange ways may become a source of discomfort and dining chaos in destinations (Quan & Wang 2004), the cultural tourist of Iran oftentimes quests for food experiences that are beyond the boundaries of the routine and familiar (Sayadabdi & Hassibi

2019). For such tourists, even the act of satisfying a basic need, such as eating, may be motivated by a search for novelty and change; thus a novel experience such as consuming, preparing, and serving *nazri* food may become part of a tourist's total peak experience.

From a temporal point of view, for a food experience to become part of a tourist's peak experience, either the ingredients *or* the way(s) in which food is delivered need to be novel and enjoyable (Quan & Wang 2004). Typical Muharram votive food and drinks—such as rice dishes served with different stew-like saucy toppings of sacrificed meat and split pea (*gheymeh*); meat, herbs, and beans (*qormeh-sabzi*); saffron and barberry rice with chicken (*zereshk polow*); lentil pilaf with caramelised onion and minced meat topping (*adas polow*); basil seed sherbet (*tokhm sharbati*); herb-Sophia sherbet (*khakeshi*); and saffron sherbet, beside many others—are made with ingredients that not only are novel and exotic to taste, but also served in ways that are peculiar to the eyes of international, especially Western, tourists. The fact that a person can leave home and be fed for all the main meals and snacks throughout the days can make the food consumption a memorable, and thus a peak, experience. It is, in fact, such memorability of food consumption that is the key to making the eating of food during travel a peak experience, intensifying the total quality of the tourist experience in the destination.

Conclusion

Although the whole Muharram festival does not occur for commercial purposes, it is naive to only perpetuate its religious and symbolic values and ignore the revenue it generates and economic impact it has in different sectors and industries in Iran. So far, however, tourism, especially international tourism, has not been considered an avenue in which major revenue can be gained by systematically marketing Muharram festival to international or even domestic tourists. This might have been deliberate as the festival is thought to be too 'sacred' to market; however, it is also possible to consider it might be the result of mismanagement of tourism potentials. Apart from the income that can be gained by introducing the event to the potential market, Muharram festival can be a unique representation of the diversity of cultures within Iran.

Muharram festival and the rites associated with it can give the tourist the chance to directly experience a diverse past and present cultural landscape, performances, foods, and participatory activities. Tourists are often searching, not always successfully, for authenticity (Mac-Cannell 1973). Visiting a unique festival such as Muharram and participating in its rituals, even as an onlooker, enables international tourists to experience authentic cultural ambience *in situ* and give them the chance to meet local people, partake in something indigenous, and go through an authentic, rather than a staged or reconstructed, experience.

There is little information and few studies that would help planners determine whether or not Muharram is of any interest to international visitors. It is especially important to understand the motivations and perceptions of those who have, in the past, visited Muharram rites in Iran, as such information can be of use in the sustainable management of the cultural sites with respect to various factors such as the mission of those cultural attractions, understanding tourists' profiles, as well as public and private funding. Accounts by foreign travellers suggest that although visiting the processions of Muharram festival may not be, at the present, a motivating factor for many travellers—perhaps because tourists are unaware of it—if promoted under the right circumstances, it has the potential to become a motivator in the future. Similar processions in different parts of the world attract a considerable number of tourists to their destination of origin every year. The procession of Jesus del Gran Poder in Quito (Ecuador), Kumbh Mela in Prayag (India), the Procession of the Holy Blood in Bruges (Belgium), and Holy Week and Easter processions in various Christian-dominated countries are just a few examples of processions that have caught considerable attention as an instrument for fostering tourism for those regions; the processional rites of Muharram festival in Iran can be used in the same manner and is absolutely of the same potential.

Dramatic aspects of Muharram festival can also serve as an attraction as *ta'ziyeh* has never been mass-produced for the consumption of tourists, which makes it an authentic platform that is natural, unforced, and free of self-interest and commercial consideration, giving the tourists the chance to create their very own, meaningful connections and experiences through an un-staged authenticity. Moreover, culinary traditions and the abundance of food that is free of charge and available to all visitors, including tourists, although it may not generate straightforward revenue, it complements the whole travel experience and may be able to draw the attention of culinary tourists who may decide to travel to the country for this particular experience.

However, it should not be ignored that if a cultural attraction such as Muharram becomes too big and too exposed to the outside world, there is always the risk of commodification resulting in the attraction losing its authenticity and uniqueness. As the empirical findings of many cultural tourism studies show, commodification of culture may eventually result in transforming a traditional community, making them weaker and, in time, even disappear and become replaced by the emergence of a new culture. At such a point, a community's effort towards preserving the authenticity of a cultural experience may be impeded. Therefore, in promoting Muharram and its rites as cultural and religious attractions, it is vital to make a conscious effort to create a co-habitual or even complementary relationship between tourism and culture/religion, firstly to enhance the tourist experience and secondly to ensure that the cultural and religious integrity of the event and its associated belief systems are respected.

References

Aghaie, K.S. (2007) 'The passion of "Ashura in Shiite Islam"'. In V.J. Cornell (ed.) *Voices of Islam: Voices of the Spirit*. Westport,CT: Greenwood, 111–124.

Arnold, N. (2001) 'Festival tourism: Recognizing the challenges; linking multiple pathways between global villages of the new century'. In B. Faulkner, G. Moscardo and E. Laws (eds) *Tourism in the Twenty-first Century; Reflections on Experience*. London: Continuum, 130–162.

Benjamin, S.G.W. (1887) *Persia and the Persians*. London: John Murray.

Boo, S., Ko, D. and Blazey, M. (2007) 'An explanation of the influence of prior visitor experience and residence on festival expenditures', *Event Management*, 10 (2/3): 123–133.

Brannas, K. and Nordstrom, J. (2006) 'Tourist accommodation effects of festivals', *Tourism Economics*, 12 (2): 291–302.

Brook, P. (1979) 'Leaning on the moment: A conversation with Peter Brook', *Parabola*, 4 (2): 47–59.

Buch, T., Milne, S. and Dickson, G. (2011) 'Multiple stakeholder perspectives on cultural events: Auckland's Pasifika festival', *Journal of Hospitality Marketing & Management*, 20 (3–4): 311–328.

Burgan, B. and Mules, T. (2001) 'Reconciling cost–benefit and economic impact assessment for event tourism', *Tourism Economics*, 7 (4): 321–330.

Carnegie, E. and Mccabe, S. (2008) 'Re-enactment events and tourism: Meaning, authenticity and identity', *Current Issues in Tourism*, 11 (4): 349–368.

Chelkowski, P. (1985) 'Shia Muslim processional performances', *The Drama Review: TDR*, 29 (3): 18–30.

Chelkowski, P. (1997) 'Taziyeh: Indigenous avant-garde theatre of Iran', *Performing Arts Journal*, 2 (1): 31–40.

Chelkowski, P. (2009) 'Ta'zia', *Encyclopaedia Iranica*. [online] Available at: www.iranicaonline.org/articles/tazia (accessed 14 November 2017).

Chhabra, D., Healy, R. and Sills, E. (2003) 'Staged authenticity and heritage tourism', *Annals of Tourism Research*, 30 (3): 702–719.

Crompton, J. (2006) 'Economic impact studies: Instruments for political shenanigans?', *Journal of Travel Research*, 45 (1): 67–82.

Cudny, W. (2013) 'Festival tourism—the concept, key functions and dysfunctions in the context of tourism geography studies', *Geografický Časopis*, 65 (2): 105–118.

Cudny, W., Korec, P. and Rouba, R. (2012) 'Resident's perception of festivals—the case study of Łódź', *Slovak Sociological Review*, 44: 704–728.

Delamere, T. (2001) 'Development of a scale to measure resident attitudes toward the social impacts of community festivals: Part 2: Verification of the scale', *Event Management*, 7 (1): 25–38.

Dwyer, L., Forsyth, P. and Spurr, R. (2006) 'Assessing the economic impacts of events: A computable general equilibrium approach', *Journal of Travel Research*, 45 (1): 59–66.

Ebadi, M. (2017) 'Iran'. In L.L. Lowry (ed.) *The SAGE International Encyclopedia of Travel and Tourism*. Thousand Oaks, CA: Sage, 671–674.

Farahani, B., Rahmatpoor, T. and Shabani, M. (2014) 'The potentials of Tasoa and Ashura ceremonies in cultural tourism development', *International Journal of Cultural and Digital Tourism*, 1 (1): 28–39.

Fillis, C. (2017) *Witnessing Muharram in Tehran*. [Blog] Wild Frontiers. Available at: https://www.wildfrontierstravel.com/en_GB/community/blog/post/witnessing-muharram-in-tehran (accessed 1 December 2017).

Fredline, E., Jago, L. and Deery, M. (2003) 'The development of a generic scale to measure the social impacts of events', *Event Management*, 8 (1): 23–37.

Gaffary, F. (1984) 'Evolution of rituals and theatre in Iran', *Iranian Studies*, 17 (4): 361–389.

Ghaderi, E., Ezzati, E. and Hafezi Zadeh Sh, . (2009) 'Strategies to deploy Tasua and Ashura ceremonies as potentials for cultural–religious tourism in an inner suburb of Tehran', *Journal of Geographical Space*, 9 (28): 75–101.

Goytisolo, J. (1997) *De la Ceca a la Meca*. Madrid: Alfaguara.

Grant, A. (2010) *Muharram: A Holy Time in Iran*. [Blog] Travelling Two. Available at: http://travellingtwo.com/3122 (accessed 4 November 2017).

Gruber, C. (2016) 'Nazr necessities: Votive practices and objects in Iranian Muharram ceremonies'. In I. Weinryb (ed.) *Ex Voto: Votive Giving across Cultures*. Chicago: University of Chicago Press, 246–275.

Iranian Students' News Agency (ISNA). (2010) 'A look at the mourning ceremonies in the grand hosseyniyeh of Zanjan', *ISNA*, Tehran. [online] Available at: http://zanjan.isna.ir/Default.aspx?NSID=5&SSLID=46&NID=1820 (accessed 24 November 2017).

Jaeger, K. and Mykletun, R.J. (2012) 'The festivalscape of Finnmark'. In T.D. Andersson, D. Getz and R. J. Mykletun (eds) *Festival and Event Management in Nordic Countries*. Abingdon: Routledge, 157–178.

Kalinock, S. (2003) 'Supernatural intercession to earthly problems: Sofreh rituals among Shi'ite Muslim and Zoroastrian women in Iran'. In M. Strausberg (ed.) *Zoroastrian Rituals in Context*. Leiden: Brill, 531–546.

KhabarOnline. (2016) 'How many tekiyeh and hosseyniyeh does Tehran have?', *KhabarOnline*, Tehran. [online] Available at: https://www.khabaronline.ir/detail/587742/society/environment (accessed 29 November 2017).

Khavarian, A.R., Zare, M. and Mostofiolmamaleki, R. (2014) 'The ceremony of Tasua and Ashura as a tourism attraction in Iran: Case study of Taft city', *International Journal of Religious Tourism and Pilgrimage*, 2 (2): 90–102.

Khavarian-Garmsir, A.R., Stavros, J.M. and Saraei, H. (2017) 'Strategic planning for tourism development with a focus on Muharram ceremony using soar framework: A case study of Yazd province in Iran', *Event Management*, 21: 119–129.

Long, L.M. (2013) 'Culinary tourism'. In P.B. Thompson and D.M. Kaplan (eds) *Encyclopedia of Food and Agricultural Ethics*. New York: Springer, 452–458.

MacCannell, D. (1973) 'Staged authenticity: Arrangements of social space in tourist settings', *American Journal of Sociology*, 79 (3): 589–603.

MacCannell, D. (1976) *The Tourist: A New Theory of the Leisure Class*. Oakland, CA: University of California Press.

Matthee, R. (2009) 'The Safavids under western eyes: Seventeenth-century European travellers to Iran', *Journal of Early Modern History*, 13 (2): 137–171.

Nakash, Y. (1993) 'An attempt to trace the origin of the rituals of 'Āshūrā'', *Die Welt des Islams*, 33 (2): 161–181.

Nazeri, A. (2011) 'Muharram: A holy time in Iran', *Hotel Magazine*, 51: 9–10.

O'Sullivan, D. and Jackson, M.J. (2002) 'Festival tourism: A contributor to sustainable local economic development?', *Journal of Sustainable Tourism*, 10 (4): 325–342.

Petrosyuk, O. (2014) *A Holiday You Could Never Imagine: Ashura*. [Blog] WaveUp. Available at: http://waveuptravel.com/travel-photoblog/ashura-iran (accessed 2 December 2017).

Picard, D. and Robinson, M. (2006) 'Remaking worlds: Festivals, tourism and change'. In D. Picard and M. Robinson (eds) *Festivals, Tourism and Social Change: Remaking Worlds*. Bristol: Channel View, 1–31.

Quan, S. and Wang, N. (2004) 'Towards a structural model of the tourist experience: An illustration from food experiences in tourism', *Tourism Management*, 25 (3): 297–305.

Reisinger, Y. and Dimanche, F. (2011) *International Tourism*. Abingdon: Routledge.

Rezaei, M.R., Khavarian-Garmsir, A.R. and Aliyan, M. (2014) 'An analysis on structural planning of Shi'a ritual tourism with a focus on potential capacities of Muharram ceremonies: The case study of Taft city', *Journal of Planning and Development of Tourism*, 3 (8): 166–185.

Robinson, M., Picard, D. and Long, P. (2004) 'Festival tourism: Producing, translating, and consuming expressions of culture(s)', *Event Management*, 8 (4): 187–242.

Rolfe, H. (1992) *Arts Festivals in the UK*. London: Policy Studies Institute.

Sayadabdi, A. and Hassibi, S. (2019) 'Food tourism in Iran'. In S. Seyfi and C.M. Hall (eds) *Tourism in Iran: Challenges, Developments and Issues*. Abingdon: Routledge.

Seyfi, S. and Hall, C.M. (eds) (2019) *Tourism in Iran: Challenges, Developments and Issues*. Abingdon: Routledge.

Small, K. (2007) 'Social dimensions of community festivals: An application of factor analysis in the development of the social impact (SIP) scale', *Event Management*, 11 (1/2): 45–55.

Smith, S.L. (1990) *Dictionary of Concepts in Recreation and Leisure Studies*. Westport, CT: Greenwood.

Sturken, M. (2011) 'Pilgrimages, reenactment, and souvenirs: Modes of memory tourism'. In M. Hirsch and N. Miller (eds) *Rites of Return: Diaspora Poetics and the Politics of Memory*. New York: Columbia University Press, 280–294.

Taylor, J.P. (2001) 'Authenticity and sincerity in tourism', *Annals of Tourism Research*, 28 (1): 7–26.

Timothy, D.J. and Pena, M. (2016) 'Food festivals and heritage awareness'. In D.J. Timothy (ed.) *Heritage Cuisines: Traditions, Identities and Tourism*. Abingdon: Routledge, 148–165.

Wang, N. (1999) 'Rethinking authenticity in tourism experience', *Annals of Tourism Research*, 26 (2): 349–370.

Wharton, N. and Swift, D. (2013) *Ashura: A Month of Sadness & Self-Flagellation in Iran*. [Blog] Goats on the Road. Available at: https://www.goatsontheroad.com/ashura-month-sadness-self-flaggelation-iran (accessed 25 November 2017).

Whitford, M. (2004) 'Regional development through domestic and tourist event policies: Gold Coast and Brisbane, 1974–2003', *UNLV Journal of Hospitality, Tourism and Leisure Science*, 1: 1–24.

Yan, P. (2016) *10 Reasons to Visit Iran*. [Blog] Sassy Hong Kong. Available at: https://www.sassyhongkong.com/travel-visit-iran (accessed 26 November 2017).

Yarshater, E. (1979) 'Development of Persian drama in the context of cultural confrontation in Iran'. In P. Chelkowski (ed.) *Iran: Continuity and Variety*. New York: New York University Press, 21–38.

Yomadic (2017) *Sorry, But This is What Iran in 2017 is Really Like*. [Blog] Yomadic. Available at: https://yomadic.com/iran-tourism-2017 (accessed 5 December 2017).

PART IV

Emerging issues and relationships in certification

19

HALAL FOOD CERTIFICATION IN CHINA

Ning (Chris) Chen, Shanshan Qi, and C. Michael Hall

Introduction

Muslims have lived in China since the eighth century (Lipman 2011), and have developed a unique ethnic group in China known as the Hui (*Huízú* 回族) (Dillon 2013). The Hui, along with nine other ethnic groups with Muslim culture, including the Uyghyr, the Kazakh, the Kyrgyz, the Tajik, the Uzbek, the Tatar, the Dongxiang, the Salar, and the Baoan, form about 23 million of China's population in total (Sai & Fischer 2015). China is home to 10.6 million Hui people, the majority of whom are Chinese-speaking practitioners of Islam, though some may practise other religions (Gustafsson & Sai 2014). The Hui make up a large percentage of population in many provincial units, such as Ningxia Hui Autonomous Region (20.53 per cent), Gansu (11.89 per cent), Xinjiang (9.29 per cent), Henan (9.05 per cent), Qinghai (7.88 per cent), Yunnan (6.60 per cent), Hebei (5.39 per cent), and Shandong (5.06 per cent) (National Bureau of Statistics of China (NBSC) 2010).

Halal food in China can be traced back to more than 1,300 years ago in China's history. It has developed into a unique food culture in China, and was signified by two Chinese characters *qing zhen* (清真). *Qing zhen* food is widely welcomed by not only Muslims but also non-Muslims in China, for its ethnic cuisine and cooking methods. Almost every Chinese university has its own halal/*qing zhen* restaurant on its campus. There are 34 provincial units in China, with a population of 1.3 billion (NBSC 2010), and thus regulating and certificating halal food is rather a challenging job, not to mention the complex nature of halal food treatment at different stages of the food supply chain (Liu 2013). Various stakeholders that are involved in this complex process include different ethnic groups with Muslim culture, Islamic associations, central and local governments, Standing Committees of People's Congress, industrial and commercial bureaus, sanitary bureaus, and quarantine bureaus. More recently, halal food availability has also become significant for the country's tourism industry given the growth in arrivals from Islamic countries (Statistical, Economic and Social Research and Training Centre for Islamic Countries (SESRIC) 2017). After France, the USA and Spain, China is the fourth most popular destination for arrivals from the Organization of Islamic Cooperation (OIC) countries (SESRIC 2017). In addition, halal certification is also becoming increasingly important for tourism and trade initiatives, such as the UNWTO Silk Road Programme (SESRIC 2017) and China's Silk Road Economic Belt and Maritime Silk Road initiatives (Liu 2015; Yang, Dube & Huang 2016). Understanding the similarities and variations between different provincial units becomes the first task in comprehending the history, reality, and the future of halal food certification in China.

In China, the Ningxia Hui Autonomous Region (NHAR) is the only autonomous region for the Hui people, a Chinese ethnic group of adherents of Islam. The population of the Hui accounts for a big portion of the population of NHAR. NHAR was the first provincial unit in China to carry out regulations on halal/*qing zhen* certification and standardisation, and thus is a representative context for understanding regional halal food certification in China.

This chapter first briefly reviews the history of Muslim culture and halal food in China, and further summarises regulations on the halal food certification and standardisation in the 23 provinces, 4 municipalities directly under the central government, 5 autonomous regions, and 2 special administrative regions (SARs) of China. These regulations from different provincial units are compared in terms of a series of criteria, including legislative bodies, with or without standardised certificates or logos, etc. Specifically, NHAR, an autonomous region for Hui people, is studied on its halal food certification as a special case in the chapter. Via the summary of regional halal food regulation frameworks, this chapter depicts the status quo and studies the trend of halal food certification in China. The case study on NHAR further assists in illustrating the history and dynamics of halal food certification in China.

History of halal food in China

Muslim culture and the Hui in China

Since AD 651, the year that Islam was introduced to China in the Tang Dynasty (AD 618–907), Islam has spread into many regions of China (Chang 1987). Nowadays, most Muslim minorities reside in densely populated areas in north-west China, while the Hui reside nationwide (Sai & Fischer 2015; Hall & Page 2017). According to the sixth national census in 2010, China is home to about 23 million Muslims, out of which 10,586,087 are the Hui people (NBSC 2010). Table 19.1 illustrates the Muslim population in each ethnic group. The Hui population increased by 3.4 million in less than 30 years from 1982 to 2010 (Dillon 2013). Hui is the third-largest of China's minorities after the Zhuang (壮族) and Manchu (满族). The Hui have spread throughout China's provincial units, and the highest concentration is in NHAR, where 34.5 per cent of the population is Hui (Gustafsson & Sai 2014). The Hui are similar to the Han majority in physical appearance as well as in the use of language (Mandarin in general), but follow Islamic dietary laws consuming halal food only. The Hui in addition follow a religious dress code: "Hui women frequently wear headscarves and men wear white caps" (Gustafsson & Sai 2014: 973). The Hui used to marry only within their own ethnic group, but have become more open to intermarriage with other ethnic groups in recent years.

Halal/qing zhen food in China

Halal food has a long history in China, and it originated with Islam culture being introduced to China in the Tang Dynasty. He (2014) claims that the ideology of China's halal diet was founded by *Yūsuf Khāṣṣ Ḥājib Balasaġuni* (حاجب خاصّ يوسف) and *Mehmud Qeshqeri* in Kashgar, Xinjiang. According to He (2014) the principles of ancient Chinese halal diet cover aspects of habitus, food material, cooking methods, hygiene, regimen, and environment.

Table 19.1 Muslim population in China

Ethnic group	Total	Male	Female
Hui	10,586,087	5,373,741	5,212,346
Uyghyr	10,069,346	5,097,594	4,971,752
Kazakh	1,462,588	747,368	715,220
Dongxiang	621,500	317,490	304,010
Kyrgyz	186,708	94,645	92,063
Salar	130,607	66,281	64,326
Tajik	51,069	26,112	24,957
Uzbek	10,569	5,673	4,896
Baoan	20,074	10,016	10,058
Tatar	3,556	1,899	1,657
Muslim	23,142,104	11,740,819	11,401,285
Han	1,220,844,520	625,032,848	595,811,672
All	1,332,810,869	682,329,104	650,481,765

Source: NBSC, 2010.

Halal food is characterised by two Chinese characters *qing zhen* (清真), meaning the "Pure and True". These two characters are strongly associated with Hui identity (Yang & Li 2007). They have been used to distinguish restaurants, food shops, bakeries, ice-cream stands, candy wrappers, mosques, Islamic literary works, and can even be found on packages of incense produced in the Dachang Hui autonomous country east of Beijing (Gladney 1996). Although there are alternate terms including *haliale* (哈俩勒), *haliali* (哈俩里), and *hala* (哈拉), all of which are phonetic equivalents of the original Arabic term, the Hui people prefer *qing zhen* as an indication that the provider of the food or services is Muslim (Gillette 2000; Sai 2013, 2014).

Many Chinese Islamic scholars see *qing zhen* and halal as inseparable or transferrable. The relationship between *qing zhen* and halal has evolved historically through the engagement and interaction between Islamic, Chinese, and transnational cultural values, and accordingly *qing zhen* illustrates the outcome of the localisation and adaptation of Islamic food culture in Chinese culture, and food culture in particular. *Qing zhen* is "an ethnic term of Chinese-speaking people and its practical usage is linked to ethnic, religious and cultural understandings of Muslims" (Sai & Fischer 2015: 163). *Qing zhen* food is often considered as inseparable from Chinese cuisine, and is widely consumed by non-Muslims as an ethnic, local, and "clean" cuisine (Sai & Fischer 2015).

Halal/*qing zhen* food certification in China

Development of halal/*qing zhen* food certification in China

Halal certification and standardisation were not introduced to China until the late twentieth century. Prior to this, the two Chinese characters *qing zhen* (清真) were widely used to denote halal food, associated with "a water pot and a hat" (Sai & Fischer 2015: 161). "The water-pot signifies ceremonial cleanliness, and is a guarantee that no pork is used, while the hat indicates respect to customers" (Broomhall 1987: 224).

Different Islamic authorities in China and the People's Republic of China government's endeavours with respect to halal/*qing zhen* certification and standardisation are relatively recent. The politics and policies of *qing zhen* food regulation are not only affecting Muslim minorities such as the Hui, but are also influencing non-Muslim communities at different levels of their social lives. In principle, government regulation of *qing zhen* food in China was conducted under the aegis of ethnic policy (Sai 2014), as well as perceived concerns of both Muslim and non-Muslim communities over food safety.

Many provincial units have established their own regulations on *qing zhen* food certification and standardisation, and the legislative bodies include provincial or local governments, the Standing Committees of People's Congress, and regional Islamic associations. Different regulations further apply at four levels: provincial units, capital cities, prefecture-level cities, and county units. There is currently no national-level regulation on *qing zhen* food certification and standardisation in China, except general regulations to support all ethnic groups in the *Regulations on Urban Ethnic Work* carried out on 15 September 1993, as well as in the *Regulation on Religious Affairs* carried out on 30 November 2004 and revised on 14 June 2017 (State Council of the People's Republic of China (SCPRC) 2017). In this regulation, it is stated that *qing zhen* food manufacture and services should be protected and supported (The State Ethnic Affairs Commission of PRC (SEAC) 1993). In addition, there are no specially established regulation-enforcing departments at any level, and cases such as violations to these regulations are often dealt with by general functional departments, such as industrial and commercial bureaus, sanitary bureaus, and quarantine bureaus. The summary of *qing zhen* food certification in China is illustrated in Table 19.2, based on a review of all available documents on halal/*qing zhen* food certification from governments, Standing Committees of People's Congress, Islamic associations across all provincial units of China. Specifically, 30 halal food certification related documents were found from government websites, webpages of Islamic associations, legal document databases. These documents are from national to city levels, specifying regulations and guidelines of halal food certification in China.

Summary of qing zhen *food certification in China*

In summary, 24 out of 34 (70.6 per cent) provincial units have provincial-level regulations in place for *qing zhen* food certification and standardisation, and 4 (11.8 per cent) other provincial units have capital-city-level regulations (Guangdong, Hubei, Sichuan, and Guangxi). The provinces or municipalities directly under the central government or autonomous regions without regulations on *qing zhen* food certification and standardisation are: Fujian, Hainan, Taiwan, and Tibet. Neither Hong Kong nor Macau has any specific regulations with respect to supervising *qing zhen* food related business. The majority of these regulations were developed between 1995 and 2005, after the enactment of the *Regulations on Urban Ethnic Work* in 1993. Sixteen regulations were made by the Standing Committees of People's Congress at the provincial level, except that of Sichuan (made by the Standing Committees of Chengdu People's Congress). Nine regulations were written by relevant offices in the governments, and the Islamic associations released the other three. The majority of regulations specify the application of standardised logos (24 provincial units) and certificates (17 provincial units). However, contents vary to a great extent from province to province and many regulations lack details. For instance, very few regulations specify how long the period of certification is valid for. Table 19.3 illustrates the descriptive statistics summarising basic characteristics of these regulations.

Table 19.2 Qing zhen food certification in China

Provincial unit	Muslim population	Legislative body	Effective from	Level	Standard logo	Certificate and issuing body	Term	Coverage	Benefits[1]
Province									
Anhui	330,210	Islamic Association	6/1/2013	Provincial	Yes	Yes, by the association	1 year	Restaurant, manufacturing facility, equipment, package	No
Gansu	1,843,058	Standing Committees of People's Congress	1/3/2003	Provincial	Yes	Yes, by county government	Not specified	Restaurant, manufacturing facility, package	No
Guangdong	58,234	Government	10/6/2003	Capital city	Yes	Yes, by county government	Not specified	Restaurant, manufacturing facility	No
Guizhou	188,499	Islamic Association	1/1/2014	Provincial	Yes	Yes, by the association	3 years	Restaurant, manufacturing facility, equipment, package	No
Hebei	571,627	Standing Committees of People's Congress	1/5/2000	Provincial	Yes	Yes, by county government	1 year	Restaurant, manufacturing facility	Yes
Heilongjiang	104,275	Standing Committees of People's Congress	1/10/2000	Provincial	Yes	Yes, by county government	Not specified	Restaurant, manufacturing facility, equipment, package	Yes
Henan	966,239	Government	18/10/1997	Provincial	Yes	Yes, by county government	Not specified	Restaurant, package	No
Hubei	72,225	Standing Committees of People's Congress	04/12/1999	Capital city	Yes	No	Not specified	Restaurant, manufacturing facility, equipment, package	Yes
Hunan	104,463	Standing Committees of People's Congress	2/8/1997	Provincial	Yes	No	Not specified	Restaurant, manufacturing facility, equipment	No
Liaoning	138,165	Standing Committees of People's Congress	27/9/2012	Provincial	Yes	Yes, by provincial government	3 years	Restaurant, manufacturing facility	No
Jiangsu	11,657	Standing Committees of People's Congress	1/3/2006	Provincial	Yes	No	Not specified	Restaurant, manufacturing facility	Yes
Jiangxi	120,526	Standing Committees of People's Congress	1/3/2002	Provincial	No	No		Restaurant, manufacturing facility, equipment	Yes
Jilin	248,434	Standing Committees of People's Congress	1/11/2005	Provincial	Yes	Yes, by county government	Not specified	Restaurant, manufacturing facility, package	Yes

(Continued)

Table 19.2 (Cont).

Provincial unit	Muslim population	Legislative body	Effective from	Level	Standard logo	Certificate and issuing body	Term	Coverage	Benefits[1]
Qinghua	949,522	Standing Committees of People's Congress	31/03/2001	Provincial	Yes	No	Not specified	Package	No
Shaanxi	141,390	Government	14/11/1996	Provincial	No	No		Restaurant, manufacturing facility, package	No
Shandong	542,318	Government	1/1/2003	Provincial	No	No		Restaurant, package	No
Shanxi	60,740	Government	29/12/1997	Provincial	No	No		Restaurant, manufacturing facility, equipment	Yes
Sichuan	108,957	Standing Committees of People's Congress	1/5/2005	Capital city	Yes	Yes, by county government	1 year	Restaurant, manufacturing facility, equipment	No
Yunnan	701,000	Government	2013	Provincial	Yes	No		Restaurant, manufacturing facility	No
Zhejiang	48,769	Islamic Association	24/12/2013	Provincial	Yes	Yes, by the association	1 year	Restaurant, manufacturing facility, package	No
Municipalities directly under the Central Government									
Beijing	259,236	Government	1/4/1998	Municipality	Yes	Yes, by county government	1 year	Restaurant, manufacturing facility, shop	No
Chongqing	10,694	Standing Committees of People's Congress	1/6/2005	Municipality	Yes	Yes, by county government	Not specified	Restaurant, manufacturing facility, equipment, package	No
Shanghai	85,473	Standing Committees of People's Congress	1/1/2001	Municipality	Yes	No	Not specified	Restaurant, manufacturing facility, equipment	Yes
Tianjin	180,708	Government	20/04/1995	Municipality	Yes	Yes, by county government	Not specified	Restaurant, manufacturing facility	No

Autonomous Region

Guangxi	36,211	Standing Committees of People's Congress	20/10/2007	Capital city	Yes	Yes, by city government	Not specified	Restaurant, manufacturing facility, hotel	No
Inner Mongolia	223,394	Standing Committees of People's Congress	28/9/1998	Provincial	Yes	Yes, by county government	1 year	Restaurant, manufacturing facility	No
Ningxia	2,175,995	Government	25/12/1995	Provincial	Yes	Yes, by city government	Not specified	Restaurant, manufacturing facility	No
Xinjiang	12,709,593	Standing Committees of People's Congress	1/1/2005	Provincial	Yes	No	Not specified	Restaurant, shop, hotel, market, manufacturing facility	Yes

Note: 1 Benefits refers to the receipt of financial or policy support from government or associations after certification has been granted.

Table 19.3 Statistical overview of provincial unit halal regulations

Number of provincial units	34
Provincial units with regulations	28 (82.4%)
Provincial units without regulations	6 (17.6%)
Regulations at provincial level	24 (70.6%)
Regulations at capital level	4 (11.8%)
By the Standing Committees of People's Congress	16 (47.1%)
By the government	9 (26.5%)
By the Islamic association	3 (8.8%)
With standardised logo	24 (70.6%)
Without standardised logo	4 (11.8%)
With certificate	17 (50.0%)
Without certificate	11 (32.4%)
With policy support	9 (26.5%)
Without policy support	19 (55.9%)
Regulations specific to *qing zhen* food	25 (73.5%)
Regulations on general ethnic affairs	3 (8.8%)

The regulations on halal or *qing zhen* food can be defined into four streams (La 2008):

(1) The first stream of regulations defines halal or *qing zhen* food as food that is permissible or lawful in traditional Islamic law, i.e. religiously defined. One example of this type of definition of *qing zhen* food is in Gansu's regulation on *qing zhen* food certification:

> Qing zhen food in this regulation refers to all food produced, processed, transported, and sold that is lawful in Islamic law.

(2) The second stream of regulations defines *qing zhen* food from the ethnic perspective. Provinces such as NHAR, Xinjiang, Liaoning, and Henan follow this definition. For instance, the regulation from Shandong province defines *qing zhen* food as follows:

> Qing zhen food refers to the collection of food that is produced and processed in terms of the religious and cultural customs of the ethnic groups of the Hui, the Uyghyr, the Kazakh, the Kyrgyz, the Tajik, the Uzbek, the Tatar, the Dongxiang, the Salar and the Baoan.

(3) The third stream of regulations defines *qing zhen* food combining both religious and ethnic perspective such as Shanghai's regulations.

(4) The last stream of regulations is limited in clearly explaining what *qing zhen* food is, or does not have a clear definition at all.

Several provinces have no regulations specifically on halal food or the Muslim community, but rather use those regulating general ethnic matters for a wider audience. For instance, the titles of the regulations of Hubei, Jiangxi, and Chongqing are Regulations on Ethnic Affairs. These regulations do include items on *qing zhen* food but are limited in details.

Regulations on *qing zhen* food in different regions also vary greatly in terms such as requirements on ethnics, personnel, food processing, food supply, treatments of equipment, as well as *qing zhen* food practitioners' rights. For instance, *Nanning Qing Zhen Food Regulation* permits only Muslim owners to apply for *qing zhen* certificates, and requires *qing zhen* food appliances only when preparing *qing zhen* food. This regulation also entitles *qing zhen* food practitioners the rights of not serving customers with food not permissive or lawful in the definition of *qing zhen*. Regulation in Henan Province specifies that the ratio of Muslim to other staff in a *qing zhen* food manufacturing business should not be less than 15 per cent, that in a *qing zhen* food distribution company it should not be less than 20 per cent, and that in *qing zhen* restaurants it should not be less than 25 per cent. Other provinces such as Beijing, Inner Mongolia, Shaanxi, Shanxi, Tianjin, and Yunnan, also have similar requirements. Except for NHAR, the highest requirements for such ratios are in the regulation of the Inner Mongolia Autonomous Region where at least 40 per cent of the staff should be Muslims in *qing zhen* food processing companies.

The majority of regulations in China empower regional ethnic affairs departments or offices in the government issuing *qing zhen* logos and certificates. However, in many provinces and regions, it is the general commercial bureaus, rather than the ethnic affairs departments, that supervise and manage the halal market, as well as the law enforcement. A few other regulations entrust regional industrial and commercial offices with full authority for *qing zhen* food certification. This "issued-by-one-supervised-by-another" practice has both advantages and disadvantages. On the positive side, this practice avoids giving too much power to regional ethnic affairs departments that are often without specific expertise in market supervision. However, it is also the main cause for confusion in the market as general regional industrial and commercial offices work on all aspects of the market supervision, and often overlook the specific required practices of the *qing zhen* food sector (Zhang 2006).

Use of the Qing zhen *logo in China*

As can be seen in Table 19.2, standardised logos are available in 24 provincial units. However, none of these provincial-, city-, or county-level units releases its certified logo design to the public. Unfortunately, there are a huge number of certified and uncertified *qing zhen* logos across China, for a number of reasons. First, there is no national-level legislation or supervision on this matter and each region has its own regulation and design of *qing zhen* logo. Second, regulations from each provincial unit often lead to a lack of transparency in certifying *qing zhen* logos, as a result of which it is difficult for the public to distinguish certified logos from uncertified ones. Third, the use of *qing zhen* logos lacks supervision (La 2008), and usage of uncertified logos are generally not penalised. As discussed above, the "issued-by-one-supervised-by-another" therefore leads to chaos in the market with respect to logo use. Lastly, non-Muslim consumers in China are open to *qing zhen* food, motivating individual food manufacturing companies and restaurant owners to develop and use *qing zhen* logos. For example, Lanzhou Noodle Soup, also known as Lanzhou Lamian or Lanzhou Ramen (兰州拉面) is a famous *qing zhen* food made of stewed beef and noodles, created by the Hui people in Gansu area during the Tang Dynasty of China. There are numerous restaurants branding Lanzhou noodle soup almost everywhere in China. However, each of them has a different brand name and *qing zhen* logo. Figure 19.1 illustrates some examples of the variety of *qing zhen* logo usage in Lanzhou Noodle Soup restaurants. Different famous food brands in China also introduced a *qing zhen* version of their products and labelled these products with various *qing zhen* logos, such as milk brand Yili (伊利), cooking oil brand Luhua (鲁花), and the biscuit brand Oreo.

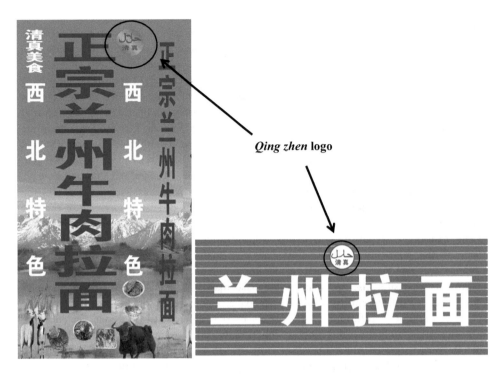

Figure 19.1 Different usage of *qing zhen* logos by Lanzhou Noodle Soup restaurants

The chaotic market circumstances of using a *qing zhen* logo have created opportunities for *qing zhen* food business owners and plays an important role in forming new marketing strategies. Niujie street (牛街) is a neighbourhood in Xicheng District in south-west Beijing, populated by the Hui people in majority, and is the home of a number of traditional Beijing-style *qing zhen* food shops. Due to the confusion surrounding *qing zhen* logo usage, the Niujie Qing Zhen Food Chamber of Commerce created and announced its collaborative *qing zhen* brand logo in December 2015, although it has not yet been recognised by the Beijing Hui community to date. Niujie *qing zhen* food practitioners create their own *qing zhen* logo as a brand, an identity, and also as a symbol to promote their historical *qing zhen* food heritage (as illustrated in Figure 19.2). However, the development of the logo was not a challenge by Niujie *qing zhen* food practitioners of the authority of the Beijing government in regulating *qing zhen* food, even though Beijing has its own *qing zhen* brand logo initiative. Instead, the district industrial and commercial office actually led the formation of the Niujie Qing Zhen Food Chamber of Commerce and provided great support for the design of this logo (China News 2015). From this perspective the logo becomes attached as much to local food promotion as it does to specific concerns over the halal status of foods.

Qing zhen *food without regulations*

There are several provincial units in China without regulations on *qing zhen* food certification and standardisation. For instance, in Fujian Province in southern China, there are few Muslims, hardly any *qing zhen* food shops, few *qing zhen*/halal restaurants, and no official halal standards. Sai (2014) studied an area in Fujian Province and found that, instead, the two

Figure 19.2 Niujie *qing zhen* food practitioners' own *qing zhen* brands

principles essential to halal matters were honesty and responsibility, factors associated with halal restaurants in other countries in which Muslims are in a minority (Wan Hassan & Hall 2003; Wan Hassan 2009). Sai's case study found that halal food (especially halal meat) shoppers secure the authenticity of halal food via two approaches: (1) to participate in animal slaughter to assure that the food process is permissible or lawful in traditional Islamic law; or (2) to obtain *qing zhen* food from a trustworthy personal contact. Generally, *qing zhen* restaurants display a self-made *qing zhen* logo or mark to indicate their identities. Sai found an interesting case when a Muslim owner sold his restaurant to a non-Muslim owner without removing his *qing zhen* logo. The imam visited the restaurant and convinced the new owner to remove the logo, after explaining the significance of *qing zhen* to Muslims. Interestingly, the public criticised the previous Muslim owner for being irresponsible and not removing the *qing zhen* logo before selling the restaurant.

Halal/*qing zhen* food certification in the Ningxia Hui Autonomous Region (NHAR)

Autonomous regions in China are first-level administrative divisions of China that are autonomous where ethnic minorities have more legislative rights. Out of the five autonomous regions, NHAR is the only autonomous region for the Hui people, a Chinese ethnic group that is composed predominantly of adherents of Islam. NHAR's ethnic legislation has been operating since 1954 (Li & Cai 1999). The population of the Hui people in NHAR is 2.17 million, accounting for 34.5 per cent of the population of NHAR. The *Regulation on Halal/qing zhen Food of Yinchuan* (the capital city of NHAR) was declared on 25 April 1992, and is the earliest and most detailed regulation on halal food certification and standardisation in China. It specifies processes in the manufacture, production, storage, sales, transportation, and other aspects of halal food business (Li & Cai 1999; Wang 2016).

On 1 January 2003, *NHAR Guidelines for Qing Zhen Food Certification* were introduced in NHAR. The guidelines were an updated version of the regulation developed in 1992. The *Qing zhen* logo was also updated by a new design. Figure 19.3 illustrates the introduced standard *qing zhen* food logo for NHAR. These guidelines have the strictest requirement on personnel in China, and require that all directors, procurement managers, storage managers, chefs, and at least 40 per cent of regular staff must be Muslims (Ningxia Hui Autonomous Region Government (NHARG) 2002). The guidelines empower both ethnic affairs departments and industrial and commercial departments in supervising and managing *qing zhen* food certification in a collaborative form. As of 2016, 20 institutions in 16 foreign countries and regions, including Malaysia, Australia, and New Zealand, had signed a mutual recognition agreement on halal food standards with Ningxia (Yang et al. 2016).

In 2013, five provinces in western China including NHAR, Gansu, Qinghai, Shaanxi, and Yunnan jointly founded the Regional *Qing Zhen* Food Certification Federation, and agreed to establish confederal guidelines entitled *Guidelines for Qing Zhen Food Certification*. This document equates *qing zhen* with halal, citing the Codex Alimentarius Commission's General Guidelines for using the term of 'halal' (Sai 2013). The new halal logos and certificates, issued by Islamic associations, incorporate not only *qing zhen* in Chinese characters, but also halal in English or Arabic in some instances, which may also reflect the growth in international tourism by Muslims (SESRIC 2017) as well as the desire to increase exports. "More and more halal productions, such as halal beef and mutton, dehydrated vegetables, dairy, sauces, and health care products, etc., have been successfully entered into the Middle East, Europe and the United States markets" (Yang et al. 2016: 2). The guidelines cover a population of 5.10 million Hui people (NBSC 2010). These guidelines were mainly developed based on *NHAR Guidelines for Qing Zhen Food Certification*, and specify in more detail the food materials not permitted in *qing zhen* food. Another three provincial units of China, Henan, Sichuan, and Tianjin, joined these guidelines in 2015, extending the coverage of these guidelines to a population of 6.34 million Hui people (NBSC 2010) as well as the export market.

Figure 19.3 NHAR standardised *qing zhen* food logo

A major initiative of these confederal guidelines was to push a "global assemblage" between China's *qing zhen* industries and halal industries in other countries, e.g. Malaysia (China Daily 2013). A standardisation and internationalisation of *qing zhen* food certification potentially enables a market transformation of China's *qing zhen* industry so as to connect to the global halal market, which may play an important role in China's initiative of the Silk Road Economic Belt and the 21st-Century Maritime Silk Road given the increased connectivity that this provides to major Islamic markets in the Middle East, South and South East Asia and North Africa (Liu 2015; Hall & Page 2017; Li 2018). This effort also reinforces regional government's commitment to ensuring the reliability and authority of *qing zhen* certification in China (Sai 2013). As of 2016, China's share of the international halal food trade was estimated at around 0.5 per cent (Yang et al. 2016) therefore highlighting the potential for Chinese halal food production in the future (Brose 2017, 2018). However, major barriers for development of Chinese halal exports are the certification process as well as halal logistics. According to Yang et al. (2016) their interviews with halal food producers and government agencies suggested that

> obtaining a halal certification in Ningxia is not very difficult for firms, but the effect of it on the export of products is unsatisfied. The survey result shows that companies have to apply for halal certification abroad because of lacking of standard mutual recognition, which virtually not only increased the operating costs, but also, more important, made the authentication process long and complex. Otherwise, understanding the foreign requirements, filling in the relevant formalities, and receiving the foreign certification test interview are also the greater challenges for the enterprises to face.
>
> *(Yang 2016: 3)*

Conclusions

China has a growing regulatory system for halal food that covers both production and supply to consumers, whether local or to the increasing numbers of Islamic tourists. However, its devolved nature and management structures creates substantial issues with respect to the authorised use of halal logos as well as their recognition in the marketplace. These issues are becoming of even greater concern given the interest of the Chinese government as well as some provincial governments, such as that of NHAR, in expanding halal exports, given the Chinese government's investment in new Silk Road initiatives as part of its international trade, tourism, and diplomacy strategy (Li 2018). In this China experiences some of the same problems with respect to halal certification, logistics, access, and end-consumer confidence in halal food markets as other non-Islamic countries (Abdul-Talib & Abd-Razak 2013).

As of late 2018, there is undoubtedly substantial contestation between different perspectives on halal certification and food in China. On one hand there is enthusiasm for the promotion of certification and production efforts given the potential of the international halal food market and the country' substantial investments in new transport infrastructure as part of Belt and Road initiatives. However, at the same time authorities in Xinjiang have launched a campaign against religious extremism, mainly focusing on preventing the generalisation of *qing zhen* concept beyond food domain, which might be interpreted differently by various stakeholders. This has been interpreted as a campaign against the spread of halal products (Kuo 2018). According to the state-owned *Global*

Times in an article about the new campaign in Urumqi, "A group of people in the society are calling for halal/*qing zhen* certification for almost all product rather than food only, such as *qing zhen* water, *qing zhen* paper, *qing zhen* toothpaste, *qing zhen* cosmetics, etc. This is what we see as a pan-halal tendency" (Ye 2016). The initiative has also spread to Gansu province, home to a large population of Hui Muslims, where officials shut down more than 700 shops selling "pan-halal products" in March 2018 (Kuo 2018). The Chinese case demonstrates that while there is enthusiasm to export halal products and therefore develop halal foods and logistics there are clear tensions between domestic and international policy positions and broader concerns over Islam in society and the potential challenges this has for the politics of food, heritage, and identity in China.

References

Abdul-Talib, A.N. and Abd-Razak, I.S. (2013) 'Cultivating export market oriented behaviour in Halal marketing: Addressing the issues and challenges in going global', *Journal of Islamic Marketing*, 4 (2): 187–197.

Broomhall, M. (1987) *Islam in China*. London: Darf Publishers.

Brose, M. (2017) 'Permitted and pure: Packaged halal snack food from Southwest China', *International Journal of Food Design*, 2 (2): 167–182.

Brose, M. (2018) 'China and transregional Halal circuits', *Review of Religion and Chinese Society*, 5 (2): 208–227.

Chang, H.Y. (1987) 'The Hui (Muslim) minority in China: An historical overview', *Institute of Muslim Minority Affairs Journal*, 8 (1): 62–78.

China Daily. (2013) 'Halal food helps Ningxia explore int'l market', *China Daily*, USA, 16 September. [online] Available at: http://usa.chinadaily.com.cn/food/2013-09/16/content_16972391.htm (accessed 15 September 2017).

China News. (2015) '牛街有了集体商标 "牛街清真食品"标识公布 [Niujie is introducing its collaborative "Niujie *Qing Zhen* Food" logo]', *China News*, Beijing, 8 December. [online] Available at: www.chinanews.com/cj/2015/12-08/7661645.shtml (accessed 15 August 2017).

Dillon, M. (2013) *China's Muslim Hui Community: Migration, Settlement and Sects*. London: Routledge.

Gillette, M.B. (2000) *Between Mecca and Beijing: Modernization and Consumption among Urban Chinese Muslims*. Stanford, CA: Stanford University Press.

Gladney, D.C. (1996) *Muslim Chinese: Ethnic Nationalism in the People's Republic. Harvard East Asian Monographs, 149*. 2nd ed. Cambridge, MA: Council on East Asian Studies, Harvard University.

Gustafsson, B. and Sai, D. (2014) 'Why is there no income gap between the Hui Muslim minority and the Han majority in rural Ningxia, China?', *China Quarterly*, 220: 968–987.

Hall, C.M. and Page, S.J. (2017) 'Tourism in East and North-East Asia: Introduction', in C.M. Hall and S. J. Page (eds) *The Routledge Handbook of Tourism in Asia*. Abingdon: Routledge, 301–308.

He, S. 何顺斌 (2014) 中国清真烹饪 *[Halal Food in China]*. Beijing: China Light Industry Press.

Kuo, L. (2018) 'Chinese authorities launch "anti-halal" crackdown in Xinjiang. Party officials also urged government officers to speak Mandarin at work and in public', *The Guardian*, 10 October. Available: https://www.theguardian.com/world/2018/oct/10/chinese-authorities-launch-anti-halal-crackdown-in-xinjiang

La, Y. 喇延真 (2008) '全国清真食品管理法规制定应注意的几个问题 [Some problems to be paid attention to in making the regulations of nation-wide Muslim food management]', *Journal of the Second Northwest University for Nationalities*, 82 (4): 125–127.

Li, F. (2018) 'The role of Islam in the development of the "Belt and Road" initiative', *Asian Journal of Middle Eastern and Islamic Studies*, 12 (1): 35–45.

Li, W. 李温 and Cai, W. 蔡伟 (1999) '宁夏民族立法建设五十年 [50 years of NHAR's ethnic legislation]', *Social Sciences in Ningxia*, 5: 26–30.

Lipman, J.N. (2011) *Familiar Strangers: A History of Muslims in Northwest China*. Seattle, WA: University of Washington Press.

Liu, J. 刘建功 (2013) '基于物联网的清真食品安全和清真认证可追溯系统研究 [Research on the tracibility system of *halal* identification and the safety of *halal* food based on the internet of things]', *Journal of Beifang University of Nationalities*, 6 (114): 56–59.

Liu, J. (2015) 'The research of Ningxia Hui Autonomous Region's *Halal* food Muslim supply chain in Silk Road Economic Belt'. In *International Conference on Social Science and Technology Education (ICSSTE 2015)*. [online] Sanya, China, 974–978. Available at: www.atlantis-press.com/php/download_paper .php?id=18910 (accessed 29 September 2017).

National Bureau of Statistics of China (NBSC). (2010) 'Tabulation of the 2010 population census of the People's Republic of China', *NBSC*, Beijing. [online] Available at: www.stats.gov.cn/tjsj/pcsj/rkpc/ 6rp/indexch.htm (accessed 2 August 2017).

Ningxia Hui Autonomous Region Government (NHARG). (2002) 'Guidelines for Qing Zhen Food Certification', NHARG, Yinchuan. [online] Available at: http://ningxia.mofcom.gov.cn/article/qzcy/ 201303/20130300072454.shtml (accessed 2 September 2017).

Sai, Y. (2013) 'Shoku no Halal wo Meguru Tayou na Koe to Jissen [Multiple voices and practices in halal food and eating]', *Waseda Asia Review*, 14: 82–85.

Sai, Y. (2014) 'Policy, practice, and perceptions of Qingzhen [Halal] in China', *Online Journal of Research in Islamic Studies*, 1 (2): 1–12.

Sai, Y. and Fischer, J. (2015) 'Muslim food consumption in China: Between Qingzhen and Halal1'. In F. Bergeaud-Blackler, J. Fischer and J. Lever (eds) *Halal Matters: Islam, Politics and Markets in Global Perspective*. London: Routledge, 160–174.

State Council of the People's Republic of China (SCPRC). (2017) '宗教事务条例 [Regulation on Religious Affairs]', *SCPRC*, Beijing. [online] Available at: www.gov.cn/zhengce/content/2017-09/ 07/content_5223282.htm (accessed 29 September 2017).

Statistical, Economic and Social Research and Training Centre for Islamic Countries (SESRIC) (2017) *International Tourism in the OIC Countries: Prospects and Challenges 2017*. Ankara: Organization of Islamic Cooperation, The Statistical, Economic and Social Research and Training Centre for Islamic Countries (SESRIC).

The State Ethnic Affairs Commission of PRC (SEAC). (1993) '城市民族工作条例 [Regulations on Urban Ethnic Work]', *SEAC*, Beijing. [online] Available at: www.seac.gov.cn/gjmw/zcfg/2004-07- 23/1168742761849065.htm (accessed 2 August 2017).

Wan Hassan, M. (2009) Halal Restaurants in New Zealand—Implications for the Hospitality and Tourism Industry. PhD Thesis, University of Otago.

Wan Hassan, M. and Hall, C.M. (2003) 'The demand for halal food among Muslim travelers in New Zealand', in C.M. Hall, E. Sharples, R. Mitchell, B. Cambourne and N. Macionis (eds) *Food Tourism Around the World: Development, Management and Markets*, Oxford: Butterworth-Heinemann, 81–101.

Wang, J. 汪景涛 (2016) '关于我国西北地区清真标识泛化问题的几点思考 [Study on the generalization of Muslim logo in northwest China]', *Journal of Hunan Police Academy*, 28 (6): 29–35.

Yang, H.J., Dube, F. and Huang, L.J. (2016). 'Research on the factors influencing halal food industry internationalization: A case study of Ningxia (China)'. *3rd International Conference on Economics and Management (ICEM 2016), DEStech Transactions on Economics, Business and Management*, DOI: 10.12783/ dtem/icem2016/4069

Yang, W. 杨文笔 & Li, H. 李华 (2007) '回族"清真文化"论 [Hui tribe "Islamic Culture" shallow discuss]', *Nationalities Research in Qinghai*, 18 (1): 100–104.

Ye, X.W. 叶小文(2016). 警惕宗教"泛化"后面的"极端化"[Watch out for the "extremism" behind pan-religious tendency] *The Global Times*, 7 May. Available: http://opinion.huanqiu.com/1152/2016-05/ 8873522.html

Zhang, Z. 张忠孝. (2006). '"清真食品" 定义和范围界定问题的探析 [Study on the definition of *qing zhen* food]', *Journal of Hui Muslim Minority Studies*, 1: 165–168.

20

FOOD CERTIFICATION

The relationships between organic and halal certification in Malaysian food retailing

Muhammad Azman Ibrahim, C. Michael Hall, and Paul W. Ballantine

Introduction

Food certification is a voluntary assurance quality scheme that is approved by a recognised accredited body (Albersmeier, Schulze & Spiller 2009). The purpose of standards and certification of food products is to demonstrate quality and to obtain the trust of consumers with whom producers do not have a direct relationship (Higgins, Dibden & Cocklin 2008). Aspects of the quality of food products or commodities that are sometime regulated and referred to in certification schemes include attributes such as safety, nutritional content, labelling, production processes, and/or branding (Watts & Goodman 1997; Busch & Bain 2004; Doherty & Campbell 2014). However, academic literature on the relationships between organic and halal certification in food retailing is limited, including in Malaysia. Previous studies have examined the perceptions of producers and consumers on food certification, in particular in relation to determinants such as socio-demographic characteristics and willingness to pay (WTP) for food safety and quality (Uggioni & Salay 2014; Probst Houedjofonon, Ayerakwa & Hass 2012). In addition, research has also been conducted on consumer awareness, trust, purchasing decisions, and WTP (Gerrard, Janssen, Smith, Hamm & Padel 2013; Essoussi & Zahaf 2009), and environmental and animal welfare (Golnaz, Zainalabidin, Mad Nasir & Eddie Chiew 2010).

According to Anders, Souza-Monteiro and Rouviere (2010), information asymmetries and uncertainty over product safety and quality is increasing in the global food retail sector. Information asymmetries occur when the processing of food products cannot be verified by the retailers or consumers of, for example, organic and halal products. Such products are considered as credence products (Darby & Karni 1973; Roe & Sheldon 2007). The credibility of food certification is important in reducing food product uncertainties and the overall cost of information asymmetries between producers and retailers in the food supply chain (Caswell 1998; Deaton 2004; Manning & Baines 2004; Anders et al. 2010). The credibility of food certification is also related to consumers' trust and coordination in the food supply chain that has become such a crucial element of modern food markets.

Organic principles

Food certification and labelling have become an important attribute in convincing consumers that the food they purchase is of good quality and safe to consume. This is particularly important for organic foods (Janssen & Hamm 2012). Depending on national food regulations and standards, organic foods can be labelled as organic products if they comply with the standards for organic production, processing, labelling, and control (Janssen & Hamm 2012).

Organic agriculture is a production system that sustains the health of soils, ecosystems, and people. The system is often further described by standards which govern labelling and claims for organic products (IFOAM—Organics International 2014). The word "organic" has been used in many different types of agricultural food products (Aarset et al. 2004). It has also led to the application of comprehensive principles that include the way people tend soils, water, plants, and animals in order to produce, prepare, and distribute food and other goods.

Halal principles

Halal is the term used in Islamic dietary laws in order to describe foods that are permitted or "permissible" for Muslims. While haram is the term used to describe foods that are considered forbidden or unlawful for Muslims to consume such as pork, alcohol, and meat that has not been slaughtered according to Islamic teachings (Rajagopal, Ramanan, Visvanathan & Satapathy 2011; Havinga 2010; Bonne, Vermeir & Verbeke 2009; Campbell, Murcott & Mackenzie 2010; Marzuki, Hall & Ballantine 2012; Regenstein, Chaudry & Regenstein 2003). The notions of wholesomeness, pure, and clean are known as "Halallan Toyyiban" and should surround the food supply chain with respect to the halal concept. If all the aspects do not meet the halal standard it will fall under the categories of haram and syubha (doubtful or suspect), that lie between the two extremes of halal and haram (Marzuki 2012).

For Islam, Muslim consumers need to follow a dietary prescription that is halal. Dietary laws that define foods that are "lawful" or permitted can be found in the Quran and in the Sunna. They prohibit the consumption of numerous products including alcohol, pork, blood, dead meat and meat that has not been slaughtered according to Islamic rulings (Bonne, Vermeir, Bergeaud-Blackler & Verbeke 2007; Marzuki et al. 2012; Manzouri 2013).

Organic certification in Malaysia

The Malaysian national government is responsible for regulations on all foods, drinks, and ingredients that have been locally manufactured or imported into Malaysia under the Food Act 1983 and the Food Regulations Act 1985. These regulations are to ensure that foods and drinks are protected from any illegal ingredients that can harm people's health or safety. These regulations are implemented by the Food Safety and Quality Division (FQSD) of the Ministry of Health of Malaysia. Organic products must have obtained organic certification in order to carry the government-approved logo SOM (Skim Organik Malaysia) and display it on packaging (Department of Agriculture Malaysia 2007; Stanton 2011).

Malaysian consumers appear increasingly aware and educated about the benefits and the importance of organic foods particularly in the context of potential contributions to health and wellness (Euromonitor 2013). The presence of more organic specialist retail stores as well as more space allocation to organic food products in leading hypermarkets and supermarkets may have increased consumers' awareness of organic food products as well (Euromonitor 2013). According to Terano, Yahya, Mohamed and Saimin (2014), Malaysian hypermarkets and supermarkets are becoming increasingly sophisticated in providing better service and products including the introduction of organic food products. Although Malaysian consumers are increasingly aware of organic products, previous studies have found that price is a major barrier in purchasing intention (Azam, Othman, Musa, Abdul Fatah & Awal 2012; Kai, Chen, Chuan, Seong & Kevin 2013). Other studies have noted that consumers with high incomes and preferences towards the perceived benefits of organic products are likely to have the highest intention to purchase (Voon, Sing & Agrawal 2011; Teng, Rezai, Mohamed & Shamsudin 2011).

There are also a growing number of quality guarantee schemes at national and international levels that offer higher food welfare and food quality, for example the Soil Association Certification is the biggest umbrella organisation for organic farming in the United Kingdom and provides the most common logo that can be found on British organic products (Baker, Thompson, Engelken & Huntley 2004; Gerrard et al. 2013; Janssen & Hamm 2012), including those exported to Malaysia. However, in the global context, the increasing number of organic brands, certification labels, and organic stores, among other features, does not appear to have increased consumers' trust in organic products (Hamzaoui-Essoussi, Sirieix & Zahaf 2013). Several studies have found that consumers are not convinced about purchasing more organic food because of the scepticism and uncertainty towards organic logos and certification schemes (Janssen & Hamm 2012; Aertsens, Verbeke, Mondelaers & Huylenbroeck 2009; Hughner, McDonagh, Prothero, Schultz & Stanton 2007; Padel, Röcklinsberg & Schmid 2009; Lea & Worsley 2005; Aarset et al. 2004). The number of organic products that are being imported from around the world and the accompanying plethora of organic logos is leading to confusion among Asian consumers. Dardak, Abidin and Ali (2009) revealed that more than 40 per cent of the respondents in their survey of Malaysian consumers did not recognise the Malaysian Organic Certification and more than 60 per cent had never heard about it especially those who were from outside Kuala Lumpur. Stanton (2011) also found that most Malaysian consumers tend to be confused between certified and non-certified organic food products.

Despite substantial research on consumer perceptions and behaviour in relation to organic food certification, the literature with respect to retailers' perception is extremely limited (Hamzaoui-Essoussi et al. 2013; Ellison, Duff, Wang & White 2016), especially in Malaysia. Essoussi and Zahaf (2008) emphasised that distribution, certification, and labelling are all related to consumer confidence and level of trust when consuming organic food products because consumers are more concerned on trusting the certification process. It is inadequate to focus on the wariness of consumers over guarantees of product quality/knowledge, labelling, certification, or pricing and communication strategies without also considering organic certification from the supply side. Clearly, retailers contribute at various scales and from diverse approaches to consumers' level of knowledge of, preferences for, and level of trust in organic products (Hamzaoui-Essoussi et al. 2013). Therefore, the absence of research on retailers and organic products appears to be a significant gap in knowledge of organic certification in the food system.

Halal certification in Malaysia

The influence of religion in shaping food choice depends on the religion itself and how adherents follow religious teachings (Bonne et al. 2009). In general, there is evidence showing that religion can influence the behaviour and attitude of consumers (Delener 1994; Kanekar & Merchant 2001; Pettinger, Holdsworth & Gerber 2004; Mashitoh, Rafida & Alina 2013;

Rezai, Mohamed, Shamsudin & Chiew 2009; Golnaz et al. 2010; Hasnah Hassan & Hamdan 2013), including food purchase intention (Aziz & Chok 2013; Lada, Tanakinjal & Amin 2009; Bonne et al. 2007). Many religions forbid certain foods and have specific requirements related to food that need to be followed, such as in the Islamic, Hindu, Buddhist, and Jewish faiths (Havinga 2010; Bonne et al. 2009; see also Chapter 2, this volume).

The halal food-processing industry in Malaysia has developed positively and the government is attempting to position the country as a global hub for halal produce. According to Said, Hassan, Musa and Rahman (2014), more than 300 certification bodies from outside Malaysia offer halal certification although Jabatan Kemajuan Islam Malaysia (JAKIM) only recognises 15 per cent of them. Malaysia's halal certification is accepted and recognised internationally as a result of the ISO compliance developed by the Department of Standards Malaysia. Moreover, halal certification in Malaysia not only focuses on poultry and meat but also covers other types of product such as cosmetics, pharmaceuticals, and toiletries (Aziz & Chok 2013). Therefore, food producers and manufacturers that want to obtain halal certification in Malaysia need to meet other food standards such as Hazard Analysis Critical Control Point (HACCP), Good Manufacturing Practices (GMP), Good Hygienic Practice (GHP), and ISO9000 (a family of quality management systems standards) (Aziz & Chok 2013).

All types of plants and plant products and their derivatives are halal except those that are poisonous, intoxicating, or hazardous to health. Similarly, all kinds of water and beverages are halal as drinks except those that are poisonous, intoxicating, or hazardous to health. All halal foods that are stored, transported, displayed, sold, and/or served shall be categorised and labelled halal and segregated at every stage in the supply chain (Manzouri 2013). Thus, it is important for companies that have halal certification to monitor their production and processing with Islamic compliance to meet the requirements of the Muslim market (Tieman 2011).

Halal is an important component of the food retail business (Regenstein et al. 2003). Most consumers and food industry are not aware of the range of foods that are under religious supervision. Food products cannot be visibly determined as to whether they are halal as this relates to credence attributes of products. Consumers often determine whether food products are halal by buying them from someone of known reputation, for example a Muslim butcher; seeking answers from a religious leader or organisation as to which food products are permitted; or buying foods with a halal label (Havinga 2010; Marzuki et al. 2012). However, reliance on local suppliers and religious leaders is often insufficient given the growth in the manufactured foods industry and the geographical distances between production and consumption as a result of the internationalisation of the food retail market. Consumers who currently seek halal food products are therefore often dependent on a certification or label that identifies a product as halal and that acts as a form of communication for consumers to trust (Havinga 2010). As a result, there are a growing number of halal labelled or certified food products in supermarkets around the world (Havinga 2010; Wilson & Liu 2010).

Halal certification is usually third-party certification that gives benefit to retailers and producers in terms of quality assurance to consumers and leads to worldwide acceptance of their products and services (Havinga 2010; Rajagopal et al. 2011). In addition, food certification such as halal is becoming increasingly important in order to enhance the competitiveness of retailers in the Islamic food market. Food products that have recognised halal certifications can also create opportunities for export markets (Hasnah Hassan & Hamdan 2013). Consumers can also view halal marks as a form of third-party endorsement by government and other key Islamic accreditation agencies. This certification provides a factual dimension assurance, quality warranty, or guarantee of the endorsed products and an evaluative opinion of the approval of the safety of the food for consumption (Hasnah Hassan & Hamdan 2013).

With respect to halal certification, major issues exist regarding third-party responsibility and authority for quality assessment and auditing. Internationally institutionalised quality reassurance systems are lacking and very few private and independent certification organisations are active in most European countries (Bonne & Verbeke 2008). Bonne and Verbeke (2008) stressed that trust in halal products is mainly based on personal confidence compared to institutional confidence. For example, the Belgian Muslim Executive (EMB), a representative institution for resident Muslims, has been charged with the introduction and execution of halal certification in Belgium. Yet, all Islamic requirements with halal certification in Belgium remain unclear, from breeding to retailing. Similarly, Campbell et al. (2010) found that consumers in France relied on their personal confidence in shopkeepers when buying halal meat.

Research method

Qualitative data were collected and analysed via semi-structured interviews conducted with participants that have experience and knowledge of food certification in Malaysia, and organic and halal certification in particular. Participants came from the public sector, private-sector organisations, and food retailers. On average they have been working in these organisations for more than three years. The purpose of the study was explained to participants and the author also informed them that the interview would be recorded with anonymity assured. A consent form was given to participants who agreed to participate in the interview session. The author then explained again what had been written in the consent form in order to ensure participants fully understood the purpose of the study and the contents of the consent form. Once participants gave their consent the interview commenced based on a series of questions prepared by the author.

Table 20.1 indicates the profile of participants including job position, organisation, and work experience. Interview participants were selected who represented different organisations with six participants from public organisations, three from private organisations, and three from food retail. There were 12 participants in total.

Table 20.1 Profile of participants

Participant	Job position	Organisation	Work experience (in years)
1	Director	Public	3
2	Assistant Officer	Public	6
3	Assistant Director	Public	8
4	Assistant Director	Public	6
5	Director	Private	16
6	Assistant Director	Public	4
7	Executive Officer	Public	3
8	Project Coordinator	Private	10
9	Chairperson	Private	12
10	Manager	Food Retail	6
11	General Manager	Food Retail	5
12	Senior Manager	Food Retail	10

The interview session initially covered the participants' understanding of organic and halal certification including its importance in a food supply chain context. The discussions then went more in-depth by covering the reliability and the implications of organic and halal certification on the organic and halal food products in the Malaysian market. Interviews were conducted in either Bahasa or English. All the interviews were recorded and transcribed. For the data extraction, the author analysed the data by reading all the transcripts and identifying any issues relating to this study. To ensure all the transcriptions have been check thoroughly, repeated readings were performed in order to avoid any miscoding. The data collected were extracted manually under thematic headings and afterwards were analysed by using thematic analysis. A list of coded categories was drawn up and three main categories were organised for thematic analysis. Two common themes were identified among the participants interviewed: organic and halal certification attributes that signify the organic and halal food products; and organic and halal certification issues. All the relevant keywords that were transcribed from the data were carefully selected and positioned under related categories.

Findings

The interview began on the topic of the definition of organic and halal and this led to a more detailed discussion on the concept, such as certification process, standards, benefits of organic and halal food products. Indeed, the majority of participants from public, private organisations, and food retail defined the basic meanings of organic and halal food according to their understanding.

> Organic food is related to the plants or green foods that being farmed without using any chemical substance. Organic food is produced naturally and there is no other chemical substance used during the process of planting. Biological control is frequently used together with the natural fertiliser that has no harm from any chemical substance. (Director of Quality Control, public organisation) (Translated from Bahasa)

> The concept of halal certification must be clean, pure and safe. As a certification body, these elements need to be meet in order to obtain halal certification. Any material of food products that can harmful consumers health will not be certified halal even the material is halal. (Assistant Director, public organisation) (Translated from Bahasa)

Credibility

The credibility of the product is very important especially for products that claim organic, Fair Trade, sustainable, or halal status. The information asymmetries of credence products are increasing and can lead to unnecessary or inappropriate behaviours in the food supply chain (Anders et al. 2010). From the interviews, the participants indicated that the purpose of food certification, such as organic and halal, is to differentiate between certified and non-certified products. In addition, organic and halal certification also ensures the credibility of the product as being of good quality and the consumers being able to trust such products when purchasing.

> The difference between organic and non-organic product can be determined by the logo itself. If they already have the organic certification, the product that they sell definitely has the logo or logo sticker of SOM (Skim Organik Malaysia). The logo contains the reference number of the certificate for the products. (Assistant Director, public organisation) (Translated from Bahasa)

Even the food products was 100 per cent safe, it is still not to be considered as halal if the food products does not meet halal principles. (Assistant Director, public organisation) (Translated from Bahasa)

Participants that are expert on halal certification commented that certification in Malaysia has positively impacted manufacturers' sales when their products carry halal certification. The participants explained that the majority of consumers in Malaysia are Muslim and that consumers tend to perceive halal certification as more credible compared to other products that are not halal certified even if the products claim organic status. In addition, one food retailing participant agreed that halal certification was a push factor for consumers to purchase products at retail outlets.

For me, it really helps. Why? We conducted a random survey with manufacturer to know the difference before and after they obtain halal certification. From the results, the manufacturer explained that there is a significant difference in sales after obtaining halal certification. Consumers everyday talk about halal product and halal premises. Therefore, we can see how the manufacturers and consumers demand halal product. It does not matter if the products can heal any diseases or declared as organic, [without halal status] consumers will be doubtful to consume it. (Assistant Director, public organisation) (Translated from Bahasa)

We have halal certification, as Muslim population in Malaysia is 66 per cent of total population. Although halal certification is a voluntary basis, the certification has become a compulsory to manufacturers including to our retail stores because halal certification is considered a push factor of consumers. So, the products need to have halal certification when listing in our retail stores. (Manager, food retail) (Translated from Bahasa)

Trust

Participants argued that products in food retailing need to have certification as it shows that the products have met the requirements of food standards. Most of the participants explained that organic and halal food certification are used not only to determine the quality and safety of the product but also to gain consumer trust.

Certification of course is something [that] is a sign of confidence to give to the customers because there have been many products who claim to be organic but without any certification. But again is still very subjective to say that those products are not organic just because they do not have a certification because they probably not going through the process of certification. So right now I think in Malaysia itself certified organic food or vegetables or for that matters it still very limited where else there are also some range of imported organic products from Australia, from New Zealand and so on. So those are bit of mixture of products that we can find in the market today. (General Manager, food retail)

The consumers are curious as to the authenticity of halal logo in Malaysia. Actually, the food products need to be halal certified before can use the halal logo. Then, the logo and labelling must displayed on the box along with safety features and each logo must have the reference number. (Assistant Director, public organisation) (Translated from Bahasa)

A majority of the participants suggested that large numbers of different organic and halal certifications in food retail can confuse consumers and affect their purchasing decisions.

> Sometimes, it does create a doubtful sense. We do import fresh organic products and these are repackaged by a company located in Malaysia. It means the product has been imported from the countries that declare it as organic. So, it does affect consumer buying decisions. Educated people probably know and understand about food certification but for local consumers, they will feel more confidence towards local product. To some extent the influence is based on consumer education. (Assistant Officer, public organisation) (Translated from Bahasa)

> I cannot deny that consumers are still confused with halal logo especially from abroad. However, we at JAKIM only recognise 73 certification bodies from abroad. We recognise these certification bodies based on their application and they need to be audited before we can recognise them as halal certification bodies. (Assistant Director, public organisation) (Translated from Bahasa)

Food safety and quality

Participants also agreed that food quality and safety can influence purchasing decisions. They pointed out that organic and halal certification can influence consumer decision-making if the product is perceived to have high quality and safety attributes. They stated that consumers are more concerned with the use of pesticides in supermarket food products than other safety dimensions.

> With organic certification, consumers that are safety-conscious are more confident towards organic products as they know the organic product is high quality. So they will definitely have confidence on the quality of organic product and understand how harmful the pesticide is and so forth. That is why they choose organic products compared to the others. (Assistant Director, public organisation) (Translated from Bahasa)

> Halal certification has huge influence on consumers' purchasing decision because they consider halal certification to be their main reference to purchase the food products. It is important for food products to carry halal certification even though the food products have other food certifications such as GMO [genetically modified organism] and GMP [Good Manufacturing Practice]. (Assistant Director, public organisation) (Translated from Bahasa)

Traceability

In order to maintain the reliability of the product, traceability is regarded as essential in organic and halal certification systems and has become one of the most important requirements for food certification programmes and monitoring of the food supply chain.

> The purpose of organic certification is to ensure the products or the outcome is originally organic and if anything happens, we can trace it back. It means that products can be traced. (Assistant Director, public organisation) (Translated from Bahasa)

It is for traceability. This helps consumers verify the halal status of food products by visit our website directory. (Assistant Director, public organisation) (Translated from Bahasa)

Misconduct and misused certification

During the interviews, the participants were asked whether there are any issues with organic and halal certification. The participants from public organisations explained there are several cases. In addition, participants from food retailers explained that the issues of misconduct and misuse were a concern to retailers and consumers.

I think it is a concern not only for retailer like us but also for consumers. They will not know which is genuine certification body and which is not. In the end, it creates confusion and it is also unfair for genuine suppliers because consumers are not sure who is the real supplier. So, I think that it has to be controlled by the government. (General Manager, food retail) (Translated from Bahasa)

The issue will occur as halal certification have been forged. It is not difficult for us to detect any forgery with Malaysian halal certification compared to other countries. However, we have a good relationship with the 73 Islamic certification bodies from abroad and if there any issues occurred regarding halal certification we can verify with them. (Assistant Director, public organisation) (Translated from Bahasa)

Consumers' lack of knowledge and awareness

On the consumer side, lack of knowledge and awareness became an issue or barrier with respect to organic and halal food products. The participants explained that the reason consumers have a lack of knowledge and awareness is because they tend not to read the label and some of them make many assumptions towards organic and halal certification.

They just buy it without asking about the certification and just because it is written organic. Some of the products are not organic but they do not read the label. They did not know that, and you will be surprised the people who sell it. They do not know that it is actually natural and not organic. For example, tin of oat milk, they say it is organic, the truth is the oat is organic but the rest is not organic. People think it is organic because it is in organic shop and sometime the manufacturers also put the word organic although it is not organic. So the awareness is not so much there. It is important to have the certification for dried goods and processed goods. (Project Organic Coordinator, private organisation)

At consumers' level, they do not understand the halal certification. As a result, they make many assumptions towards halal certification. It shows that consumers have a lack of knowledge. Similar to new manufacturers that also do not understand and are not well prepared to comply with halal procedures. (Assistant Director, public organisation) (Translated from Bahasa)

Discussion and conclusion

The importance of organic and halal certification on food product attributes is to indicate the safety and the quality of food products. It is important for food products that claim to be organic or halal to carry a valid certification to indicate the food products comply with the food standards. During the interview most of the participants agreed that carrying the organic and halal certification determined the quality and the safety of the organic and halal food products. This is also supported by Prabhakar, Sano and Srivastava (2010), who note that the implementation of food certification is applicable to a wide range of general food types by covering all aspects in the food supply chain system such as food production, processing, transportation, and retailing.

The concept of food certification is to protect consumers when purchasing the food products. In the case of organic food products certification not only exists to protect consumers but also to gain their trust and increase their confidence in the product. The interviews suggest that organic food certification helps gain consumer trust as well as convince them that organic food products meet the requirements of food standards. Voon et al. (2011) and Liang (2016), in their investigation of purchasing organic food products, reiterated the importance of organic certification in the context of trustworthiness as consumers or retailers cannot directly evaluate organic production.

This research suggests that having a credible organic and halal certification is important for trust in food products that focus on safety and quality. Participants from food retail believed that certification is a channel to reduce the information asymmetries of organic and halal food products. Liang (2016) claimed that the mechanisms of the quality assurance such as certification and labelling can reduce information asymmetry issues. Furthermore, interview participants believed that traceability is one of the purposes of organic and halal certification so as to be able to monitor the food supply chain. This is an increasingly important issue. Prabhakar et al. (2010) noted that food safety in Asian countries such as India, China, Korea, Bangladesh, Indonesia, and Thailand has become a significant issue due to the inappropriate use of chemical substances and pesticides in farming that results in adverse chemicals being found in food products.

In Malaysia, halal certification is considered to have a huge influence on consumers' behaviour because the majority of consumers in Malaysia are Muslim. This means that food products need to have halal certification even if the food product is organic. One of the participants from food retailing believed that one push factor of Malaysian consumers when buying organic and other food products is halal certification. This finding is supported by Marzuki (2012) who found Malaysian restaurant managers' expectations towards halal certification are very important to Muslim consumers as well as to non-Muslim consumer acceptance (see also Marzuki et al. 2012).

This research has found that there are several issues related to organic and halal certification in Malaysia. The findings of this study indicate some Malaysian producers claim their food products are organic without providing the certification and misuse the organic logo by putting it on food products that are not organic. Indeed, food retailers have expressed their concerns on the misconduct and misuse of organic certification and logo. Marzuki (2012) also noted some concerns of other respondents with respect to halal certification claims. These concerns may also be reflective of consumer anxiety over the sheer number of different organic and halal certifications.

Although both these food certifications focus on different food market segments they share similar values that can improve the assurance quality scheme system and increase the efficiency of food supply chain particularly in Malaysian food retailing. Technically, the purpose of halal and organic certification is to ensure the food safety and quality of food products but both of these food certifications have been perceived to have added value that not only focus on food safety but also on environmental and social issues including the relationship between the halal and organic concepts. For example, Izberk-Bilgin and Nakata (2016) also suggest that the halal concept is related to the issues of organic, fair trade, animal welfare, and ecological economics.

Based on the findings, organic food products and certification in Malaysia have several issues that need to be addressed in order to ensure the credibility of Malaysian organic certification and to increase the purchasing by Malaysian consumers of organic food products. As halal is also highly regarded by Malaysian consumers when making purchasing decisions Ali and Suleiman (2016) suggest that halal and organic can be combined and develop new brand labels, for example eco-halal, green-halal, and halal-organic. This could be a new initiative development of sustainable programmes as well as to stimulate the supply and demand for halal and organic food products in Malaysia food retailing. This is also supported by Rezai, Mohamed and Shamsudin's (2015) study on Malaysian food retailing that found that the environment has a strong relationship with halal food products and is also considered a vital segment for halal in relation to sustainable development in agriculture.

In conclusion, organic and halal certification are perceived to be important in Malaysian food retailing. The findings of this study have suggested that the government, producers, manufacturers, and food retailers need to take responsibility by working together in order to maintain the credibility of organic and halal certification as well as to increase the awareness and knowledge of consumers towards organic and halal certification. In addition, Malaysian enforcement measures need to be more efficient when monitoring food products that claim organic and halal status although there are more issues related to organic certification than halal certification. Most importantly, credible quality assurance schemes help give peace of mind to consumers when they are buying food products.

References

Aarset, B., Beckmann, S., Bigne, E., Beveridge, M., Bjorndal, T., Bunting, J., et al. (2004) 'The European consumers' understanding and perceptions of the "organic" food regime: The case of aquaculture', *British Food Journal*, 106 (2): 93–105.

Aertsens, J., Verbeke, W., Mondelaers, K. and Huylenbroeck, G.V. (2009) 'Personal determinants of organic food consumption: A review', *British Food Journal*, 111 (10): 1140–1167.

Albersmeier, F., Schulze, H. and Spiller, A. (2009) 'Evaluation and reliability of the organic certification system: Perceptions by farmers in Latin America', *Sustainable Development*, 17 (5): 311–324.

Ali, M.H. and Suleiman, N. (2016) 'Sustainable food production: Insights of Malaysian halal small and medium sized enterprises', *International Journal of Production Economics*, 181 (B): 303–314.

Anders, S., Souza-Monteiro, D. and Rouviere, E. (2010) 'Competition and credibility of private third-party certification in international food supply', *Journal of International Food & Agribusiness Marketing*, 22 (3–4): 328–341.

Azam, N.H.M., Othman, N., Musa, R., AbdulFatah, F. and Awal, A. (2012) 'Determinants of organic food purchase intention'. In 2012 *IEEE Symposium on Business, Engineering and Industrial Applications*. IEEE, 748–753.

Aziz, Y.A. and Chok, N.V. (2013) 'The role of halal awareness, halal certification, and marketing components in determining halal purchase intention among non-Muslims in Malaysia: A structural equation modeling approach', *Journal of International Food & Agribusiness Marketing*, 25 (1): 1–23.

Baker, S., Thompson, K.E., Engelken, J. and Huntley, K. (2004) 'Mapping the values driving organic food choice: Germany vs the UK', *European Journal of Marketing*, 38 (8): 995–1012.

Bonne, K., Vermeir, I., Bergeaud-Blackler, F. and Verbeke, W. (2007) 'Determinants of halal meat consumption in France', *British Food Journal*, 109 (5): 367–386.

Bonne, K. and Verbeke, W. (2008) 'Religious values informing halal meat production and the control and delivery of halal credence quality', *Agriculture and Human Values*, 25 (1): 35–47.

Bonne, K., Vermeir, I. and Verbeke, W. (2009) 'Impact of religion on halal meat consumption decision making in Belgium', *Journal of International Food & Agribusiness Marketing*, 21 (1): 5–26.

Busch, L. and Bain, C. (2004) 'New! Improved? The transformation of the global agrifood system', *Rural Sociology*, 69 (3): 321–346.

Campbell, H., Murcott, A. and MacKenzie, A. (2010) 'Kosher in New York City, halal in Aquitaine: Challenging the relationship between neoliberalism and food auditing', *Agriculture and Human Values*, 28 (1): 67–79.

Caswell, J.A. (1998) 'How labeling of safety and process attributes affects markets for food', *Agricultural and Resource Economic Review*, 27 (2): 151–158.

Darby, M.R. and Karni, E. (1973) 'Free competition and the optimal amount of fraud', *Journal of Law and Economics*, 16 (1): 67–88.

Dardak, R.A., Abidin, A.Z.Z. and Ali, A.K. (2009) 'Consumers' perceptions, consumption and preference on organic product: Malaysian perspective', *Economic and Technology Management Review*, 4: 95–107.

Deaton, B.J. (2004) 'A theoretical framework for examining the role of third-party certifiers', *Food Control*, 15 (8): 615–619.

Delener, N. (1994) 'Religious contrasts in consumer decision behaviour patterns: Their dimensions and marketing implications', *European Journal of Marketing*, 28 (5): 36–53.

Department of Agriculture Malaysia. (2007) *Standard Skim Organik Malaysia (SOM) Malaysian Organic Scheme*. Kuala Lumpur: Department of Agriculture Malaysia.

Doherty, E. and Campbell, D. (2014) 'Demand for safety and regional certification of food: Results from Great Britain and the Republic of Ireland', *British Food Journal*, 116 (4): 676–689.

Ellison, B., Duff, B.R., Wang, Z. and White, T.B. (2016) 'Putting the organic label in context: Examining the interactions between the organic label, product type, and retail outlet', *Food Quality and Preference*, 49: 140–150.

Essoussi, L.H. and Zahaf, M. (2008) 'Decision making process of community organic food consumers: An exploratory study', *Journal of Consumer Marketing*, 25 (2): 95–104.

Essoussi, L.H. and Zahaf, M. (2009) 'Exploring the decision-making process of Canadian organic food consumers: Motivations and trust issues', *Qualitative Market Research: An International Journal*, 12 (4): 443–459.

Euromonitor. (2013) *Organic Packaged Food in Malaysia*. [online] Available at: www.euromonitor.com /organic-packaged-food-in-malaysia/report

Gerrard, C., Janssen, M., Smith, L., Hamm, U. and Padel, S. (2013) 'UK consumer reactions to organic certification logos', *British Food Journal*, 115 (5): 727–742.

Golnaz, R., Zainalabidin, M., Mad Nasir, S. and Eddie Chiew, F.C. (2010) 'Non-Muslims' awareness of halal principles and related food products in Malaysia', *International Food Research Journal*, 17 (3): 667–674.

Hamzaoui-Essoussi, L., Sirieix, L. and Zahaf, M. (2013) 'Trust orientations in the organic food distribution channels: A comparative study of the Canadian and French markets', *Journal of Retailing and Consumer Services*, 20 (3): 292–301.

Hasnah Hassan, S. and Hamdan, H. (2013) 'Experience of non-Muslim consumers on halal as third party certification mark in Malaysia', *Asian Social Science*, 9 (15): 263–271.

Havinga, T. (2010) 'Regulating halal and Kosher foods: Different arrangments between state, industry and religous actors', *Erasmus Law Review*, 3 (4): 241–256.

Higgins, V., Dibden, J. and Cocklin, C. (2008) 'Building alternative agri-food networks: Certification, embeddedness and agri-environmental governance', *Journal of Rural Studies*, 24 (1): 15–27.

Hughner, R.S., McDonagh, P., Prothero, A., Shultz, C.J. and Stanton, J. (2007) 'Who are organic food consumers? A compilation and review of why people purchase organic food', *Consumer Behaviour*, 6 (2–3): 94–110.

IFOAM—Organics International. (2014) *The IFOAM Norms for Organic Production and Processing: Version 2014*. [online] Available at: https://www.ifoam.bio/en/ifoam-norms

Izberk-Bilgin, E. and Nakata, C.C. (2016) 'A new look at faith-based marketing: The global halal market', *Business Horizons*, 59 (3): 285–292.

Janssen, M. and Hamm, U. (2012) 'The mandatory EU logo for organic food: Consumer perceptions', *British Food Journal*, 114 (3): 335–352.

Kai, S.B., Chen, O.B., Chuan, C.S., Seong, L.C. and Kevin, L.L.T. (2013) 'Determinants of willingness to pay of organic products', *Middle-East Journal of Scientific Research*, 14 (9): 1171–1179.

Kanekar, S. and Merchant, S.M. (2001) 'Helping norms in relation to religious affiliation', *Journal of Social Psychology*, 141 (5): 617–626.

Lada, S., Tanakinjal, G.H. and Amin, H. (2009) 'Predicting intention to choose halal products using theory of reasoned action', *International Journal of Islamic and Middle Eastern Finance and Management*, 2 (1): 66–76.

Lea, E. and Worsley, T. (2005) 'Australians' organic food beliefs, demographics and values', *British Food Journal*, 107 (11): 855–869.

Liang, R.-D. (2016) 'Predicting intentions to purchase organic food: The moderating effects of organic food prices', *British Food Journal*, 118 (1): 183–199.

Manning, L. and Baines, R.N. (2004) 'Effective management of food safety and quality', *British Food Journal*, 106 (8): 598–606.

Manzouri, M. (2013) 'Lean supply chain practices in the halal food', *International Journal of Lean Six Sigma*, 4 (4): 389–408.

Marzuki, S.Z.S. (2012) Understanding Restaurant Managers' Expectations of Halal Certification in Malaysia. PhD. University of Canterbury.

Marzuki, S.Z.S., Hall, C.M. and Ballantine, P.W. (2012) 'Restaurant managers' perspectives on halal certification', *Journal of Islamic Marketing*, 3 (1): 47–58.

Mashitoh, A.S., Rafida, A.R.N. and Alina, A.R. (2013) 'Perception towards halal awareness and its correlation with halal certification among Muslims', *Middle-East Journal of Scientific Research*, 13: 1–4. DOI: 10.5829/idosi.mejsr.2013.16.s.10021

Padel, S., Röcklinsberg, H. and Schmid, O. (2009) 'The implementation of organic principles and values in the European Regulation for organic food', *Food Policy*, 34 (3): 245–251.

Pettinger, C., Holdsworth, M. and Gerber, M. (2004) 'Psycho-social influences on food choice in Southern France and Central England', *Appetite*, 42 (3): 307–316.

Prabhakar, S.V.R.K., Sano, D. and Srivastava, N. (2010) 'Food safety in the Asia-Pacific region: Current status, policy perspectives, and a way forward'. In *Sustainable Consumption and Production in the Asia-Pacific Region: Effective Responses in a Resource Constrained World*. Institute for Global Environmental Strategies: 215–238.

Probst, L., Houedjofonon, E., Ayerakwa, H.M. and Haas, R. (2012) 'Will they buy it? The potential for marketing organic vegetables in the food vending sector to strengthen vegetable safety: A choice experiment study in three West African cities', *Food Policy*, 37 (3): 296–308.

Rajagopal, S., Ramanan, S., Visvanathan, R. and Satapathy, S. (2011) 'Halal certification: implication for marketers in UAE', *Journal of Islamic Marketing*, 2 (2): 138–153.

Regenstein, J.M., Chaudry, M.M. and Regenstein, C.E. (2003) 'The Kosher and Halal food laws', *Comprehensive Reviews in Food Science and Food Safety*, 2 (3): 111–127.

Rezai, G., Mohamed, Z.A., Shamsudin, M.N. and Chiew, F.C. (2009) 'Concerns for halalness of halal-labelled food products among Muslim consumers in Malaysia: Evaluation of selected demographic factors', *Economic and Technology Management Review*, 4: 65–73.

Rezai, G., Mohamed, Z. and Shamsudin, M.N. (2015) 'Can halal be sustainable? Study on Malaysian consumers' perspective', *Journal of Food Products Marketing*, 21 (6): 654–666.

Roe, B. and Sheldon, I. (2007) 'Credence good labeling: The efficiency and distributional implications of several policy approaches', *American Journal of Agricultural Economics*, 89 (4): 1020–1033.

Said, M., Hassan, F., Musa, R. and Rahman, N.A. (2014) 'Assessing consumers' perception, knowledge and religiosity on Malaysia's halal food products', *Procedia—Social and Behavioral Sciences*, 130: 120–128.

Stanton, E.S. (2011) *Malaysia's markets for functional foods, nutraceuticals and organic foods: An introduction for Canadian producers and exporters*. Report for the Counsellor and Regional Agri-Food Trade Commissioner, Southeast Asia, and the High Commission of Canada in Malaysia. Ottawa: Agriculture and Agri-Food Canada.

Teng, P.K., Rezai, G., Mohamed, Z. and Shamsudin, M.N. (2011) 'Consumers' awareness and consumption intention towards green foods'. In *International Conference on Management (ICM 2011) Proceeding*, 917–926.

Terano, R., Yahya, R., Mohamed, Z. and Saimin, S.B. (2014) 'Consumers' shopping preferences for retail format choice between modern and traditional retails in Malaysia', *Journal of Food Products Marketing*, 20 (sup1): 179–192.

Tieman, M. (2011) 'The application of halal in supply chain management: In-depth interviews', *Journal of Islamic Marketing*, 2 (2): 186–195.

Uggioni, P.L. and Salay, E. (2014) 'Sociodemographic and knowledge influence on attitudes towards food safety certification in restaurants', *International Journal of Consumer Studies*, 38 (4): 318–325.

Voon, J.P., Sing, K. and Agrawal, A. (2011) 'Determinants of willingness to purchase organic food: An exploratory study using structural equation modeling', *International Food and Agribusiness Management Review*, 14 (2): 103–120.

Watts, M. J., and Goodman, D. (1997). 'Global appetite, local metabolism. Nature, culture and industry: *Fin de siècle* agro food systems'. In D. Goodman and M. Watts (eds) *Globalising Food: Agrarian Questions and Global Restructuring*. London: Routledge, 1–24.

Wilson, J.A. and Liu, J. (2010) 'Shaping the halal into a brand?' *Journal of Islamic Marketing*, 1 (2): 107–123.

21

HALAL LOGISTICS

Empowering competitive advantage and sustainability

Noorliza Karia, Muhammad Hasmi Abu Hassan Asaari, and Siti Asma' Mohd Rosdi

Introduction

Malaysia is a leader in the world's halal industry and is positioning itself as a leading global halal hub with an expected annual export of RM50 billion of halal products by 2020, equivalent to approximately 8.7 per cent of the country's GDP (The Borneo Post 2018). The Third Malaysian Industrial Master Plan (IMP3) 2006 to 2020 aims to further elevate Malaysia's role in halal logistics and business; and become the world-renowned halal hub for the production and trade in halal goods and services (Ministry of International Trade and Industry (MITI) 2006). According to the Malaysian Halal Industry Development Corporation (HDC) vice-president of Industry Development Hanisofian Alias

> Our halal exports stood at RM43 billion in 2017 and I am confident that we will be able to hit the RM50 billion mark by the end of 2020. Many non-Muslim countries have recognised the untapped potential in the halal market and are now racing to gain a footing, presenting a major business and export opportunity for us as Malaysia has always held the benchmark in halal production and certification.
>
> *(Borneo Post 2018)*

However, in order to meet such goals and to facilitate international trade in halal products the development of appropriate halal logistics strategies is essential (Karia & Asaari 2016a).

The growth of halal-oriented business has increased the pressure for halal logistics by which halal supply chains remain secure. Pressures on halal logistics service providers (HLSPs) has also increased because the supply chain and transport network has increasingly come to include non-Islamic majority countries and regions, such as the USA, United Kingdom, Europe, China, Japan, and Thailand, all of which want to increase their share of the global halal market (see Chapter 19, this volume, on China's export and trade initiatives). The fast-growing global halal markets are enormous (see Chapters 1 and 2, this volume) and only further increase the significant demand on advanced halal logistics services.

This chapter is divided into three main parts. First, a brief overview of the Malaysian halal industry and associated logistical issues. Second, a discussion of some of the key elements that need to be considered in halal logistics. Third, a case study of a Malaysian logistics company.

The Malaysian halal industry

In Malaysia, the halal industry is under the jurisdiction of the Malaysian Islamic Development Department (JAKIM), a government agency under the Religious Division of the Prime Minister's Department of Malaysia, and the Halal Industry Development Corporation (HDC) which is under the purview of the Ministry of International Trade and Industry (MITI). Malaysia was one of the first countries in the world to develop halal certification and processing procedures when, in 1974, the Research Centre for the Islamic Affairs Division in the Prime Minister's Office began to issue halal certification letters for products that meet the halal criteria. Since 2000 halal standards have been developed as part of a well-documented and systematic Halal Assurance System which included the introduction of a holistic standard for halal products through MS 1500: 2004 and the Malaysian Standard on Halal Food (MS 1500: 2009). This latter standard includes practical guidelines for the food industry on the preparation and handling of halal food (including nutrient enhancers). The standard sets the ground rules for halal food products and food businesses in Malaysia and is used by JAKIM as part of the basis for certification. Significantly from the perspective of Malaysia's halal hub strategy, Halal Malaysia (2018) states, "It is hoped that in the future, the Malaysian Standard (Government official document) will be promoted internationally and recognised by other countries or blocks such as America, Europe, China and members of ASEAN." JAKIM has been responsible for monitoring and regulating the halal industry in Malaysia since 2005 and its halal system programme is internationally recognised with over 50 halal agencies and bodies around the world having registered with it.

Halal logistics plays an essential role in halal manufacturing and halal tourism and the halal hotel industry. For instance, the granting of halal hotel certification (see Chapter 5, this volume). The Malaysian Ministry of Tourism has also set up the Islamic Tourism Council (ITC) to strengthen their aspiration to be an Islamic tourism hub and attract Muslim tourists especially from high-spending Muslim countries such as Saudi Arabia, Bahrain, Kuwait, Oman, and Qatar by developing the halal hotel industry and offering Muslim-friendly services in Malaysia.

Halal logistics

What does Allah want in logistics? Much halal literature highlights the significance of halal but is more concerned with what is halal (permissible) and toyiba (wholesome and good) in the food process, regulation, standards and product certification than understanding halal logistics and halal logistics service provision. Halal is not just the application of Shariah principles but also includes aspects of spiritual elements, behaviour, actions and decisions and values practised by the Prophet (PBUH). The ultimate goal of halal is being accepted by Allah. However, whichever definition or approach is used (see Chapter 2, this volume), the basic parameters of halal are constant: religious requirements, product/service excellence, competitiveness, well-being, and Allah's blessing (Karia & Asaari 2016c).

As a set of Islamic values, halal encompasses three main dimensions: (1) *Aqidah*—a strong faith and belief; (2) *Akhlak*—aspects of good behaviour, attitude, ethics, morality which influences acts and decisions; and (3) *Shariah*—Islamic law set by Allah SWT that determines acts, rules, manners, methods, and which provides a practical system for food, family, life and business/commercial transactions (Muamalat). Briefly, a strong Aqidah such as a good intention, vision, or mission is able to drive a person to be highly committed and responsible in action, decision, and achievement and have a positive effect on Akhlak. The term *Akhlak* refers to positive values of and in Islam; the visibility of positive acts and decisions; the practices of virtue, morality, manners; and an act of *ibadah* (worship, submission, and devotion to Allah, including as demonstrated in relation to others) in Islamic theology and philosophy (Ismail, Othman & Dakir 2011). Under Shariah humankind holds dearly to Allah SWT in fulfilling duties as a servant of God, as a person, with duties towards nature, environment, surroundings and life as whole (Kamali 2010; Din 1985).

The term 'halal service' refers to Islamic-related business values and practices embedded in products and/or services These can also include service innovations: a new service portfolio or wider services, a comprehensive way to improve service, or a new way of thinking about the process, practices, operations, and management (Karia & Asaari 2014). As framed by the Quran, the term 'halal service' also assumes accountable business practices and processes, meaning that the Shariah-compliant business operates and performs with justice, honesty, truthfulness, sincerity, timeliness, and discipline (Karia & Asaari 2016b). A halal business model can therefore incorporate strategic halal service or service innovation which empowers a firm's sustainable performance by maximising profits (economy), excellence of products/ services (quality), ensuring the well-being of humankind (society) and the planet (environment), and observing religious requirements as well as minimising cost or hardship, and ultimately the desire for Allah's blessing.

The term 'halal logistics' refers to Islamic-related business values and practices embedded in logistics systems such as an innovation in delivering halal products or services (Karia, Asaari, Mohamad & Kamaruddin 2015). Logistics is the movement and handling of materials, goods, or information from one point to another point. Therefore, halal logistics is an accountable logistics service, the Shariah-compliant logistics service/business that handles the movement of halal materials, halal goods, or information right from source of suppliers to the point of consumption, i.e. throughout the entire supply chain (Karia & Asaari 2014). The basic ingredients of the halal logistics system are constant: halal transportation, halal warehouse/storage, order processing, inventory, materials handling, and packaging. All halal aspects and Islamic-related business principles and values must be practised and performed right from the source of raw materials and flow into manufacturing till the finished products are distributed to the end user. For halal integrity to be ensured four key logistical functions need to be met: (1) a Halal Logistics Hub that provides secures halal storage for distribution from manufacturer to customer; (2) Halal Logistics Transportation with secure vehicles and equipment for halal products to avoid cross-contamination with haram products during transportation; (3) a Halal Logistics Route with a secure path from supplier to the customer; and (4) the provision of appropriate Halal Logistics Management that secures all managerial aspects of halal logistics, production, and distribution (Karia & Asaari 2014).

Halal logistics service provider (HLSP)

The term halal logistics service provider (HLSP) refers to the Shariah-compliant logistical firm that provides various types of halal logistics service such as halal transportation, halal warehouse, halal terminal, order processing, inventory, materials handling, and packaging. HLSPs are responsible for maintaining halal product/service integrity between production and end consumer and they support the halal integrity preservation among halal supply chain partners (procurement, manufacturer, retailer, supplier, and customer). The HLSP role is sizeable and is expanding rapidly with the growth in halal products and markets.

Halal logistics performance

Halal logistics performance has various dimensions. These include the extent of halal integrity preservation during the halal logistics processes and practices that depend on halal standards, halal regulations and government enforcement, contamination during delivery and storage or at the point of sale, issues of segregation (dedicated facilities in transportation, warehousing, and terminal), and issues of tractability and traceability. Economic performance is also a factor especially as some logistics service providers (LSPs) report halal operations use extra resources and have a relatively high cost (Karia & Asaari 2016a). Halal logistics may involve large initial capital expenditure or investment in halal logistics facilities and equipment, e.g. dedicated halal warehouse and vehicles (Talib, Hamid, Zulfakar & Chin 2015), and, for some products or markets, may not be cost-effective because of low consumer demand. Where this is the case it may weaken the likelihood of LSPs' initiation of or compliance with halal logistics standards.

Different constructs may be used for measuring logistics performance (Wilding & Juriado 2004) and it remains undecided which key performance indicators (KPIs) should be used for halal logistics performance measurement. However, the development of performance measurement systems based on non-financial indicators is becoming of increasing interest to both practitioners and academics. In the case of the service industry, output is also relatively intangible and difficult to quantify and may need to be evaluated on firm internal operations performance. Nevertheless, performance measurement systems need to be clearly defined for the operational strategy of organisations and measured by multiple performance indicators (Ray, Barney & Muhanna 2004). Logistics performance measurements such as cost, customer service, delivery, quality, flexibility, and innovation have been acknowledged by previous logistics scholars (Table 21.1). It is also often measured in terms of three categories of firm competitive advantages: (1) service advantage, (2) innovation/service variety advantage, and (3) cost (Lai, Li, Wang & Zhao 2008).

Green, Whitten and Inman (2008) defined logistics performance as the ability to deliver goods and services in the correct quantity and at the correct times as required by the customers. Halal logistics performance is therefore regarded as the HLSP's ability to deliver the right halal products and services in the right quantity, right condition, right place, right time, right customers, and right costs. The measurements for halal logistics performance refer

Table 21.1 Logistics performance measures

Measure	Examples
Cost	Operational costs, appropriate service costs/charges
Customer service	Dimensions of delivery, flexibility, and quality
Delivery	Timely and reliable delivery
Quality	Service level
Flexibility	Quick response to customer enquiries, claims, and complaints
Innovation	Value-added services offered

Source: After Brah and Lim, 2006; Lai et al., 2008.

to the indicators of halal work performance and/or the result achieved in halal logistics practices or processes. Halal logistics practices uphold the halal logistics performance indicators by maximising logistics performance while maintaining integrity and adhering strictly to Shariah-compliant logistics business/service. Halal logistics performance measurement can be operationalised into: (1) customer service, (2) innovation service, and (3) cost. The term 'customer service' is conceptualised into three dimensions:

(1) *delivery*—the efficient use of time from order to delivery: fast and reliable delivery,
(2) *quality*—service level: order accuracy, packing/shipping accuracy, damage free and,
(3) *flexibility*—quick response to customer enquiries, prompt follow-up of customer claims and complaints, to anticipate change, to adapt and to accommodate special or non-routine requests, and to handle unexpected events.

The term 'service innovation' refers to value-added service: additional service, unique/customised service, and the term 'cost' refers to operations costs: low service cost/charge, total logistics cost such as transportation cost, inventory and warehousing costs, and labour cost.

In summary, halal logistics practices are most likely to correlate with halal logistics performance comprised of multiple performance measurements such as customer service, service innovation, and cost. However, the effects of halal logistics practices are significant and will vary within and between performance indicators. Nevertheless, LSPs should be committed to halal logistics practices and their successful implementation.

Impact of halal

Value creation efforts such as environmental, industrial sustainability, green, lean, sustainable innovation, halal value creation, and shared value have increased attention as antecedents of sustainable performance and innovation (Yadav, Han & Rho 2016; Bocken, Short, Rana & Evans 2013; Karia & Asaari 2016a; Nidumolu, Prahalad & Rangaswami 2009). Firms may use several indicators to measure the extent to which their focus on positive value leads to improvements in sustainability (Bititci, Garengo, Dorfler & Nudurupati 2012; Reuter, Foerstl, Hartmann & Blome 2010; Nidumolu et al. 2009), cost reduction, revenues, and innovation (Nidumolu et al. 2009).

Karia and Asaari (2016a, 2016b) identified several antecedents for sustainable performance: product/service, profit, people, and planet. They described halal product/service in terms of firms producing product with quality, safety, purity, nutrients, wholesomeness and hygiene; and conducting services with principles of trust, dedication, honesty, timeliness, and discipline. Moreover competitiveness and positive outcomes of firms result from their positive products and/or services. In addition, halal product/service should induce employee commitment (perform jobs with sincerity and responsibly), employee well-being (well-trained employee performs excellent jobs), stakeholder interest, and social welfare.

Product/service

An important aspect of halal value is empowering firms to participate in their halal practices by offering halal services or producing halal products (Karia & Asaari 2016a, 2016c). The term 'halal product/service' refers to services with principles of trust, dedication, honesty, timeliness, and discipline; and/or products with quality, safety, purity, nutrients, wholesome;

and hygiene (security of product, product liability) that are contributing to the overall achievement of firm outcomes.

Profit

The term 'profit' refers to maximum benefits of halal for firms, right value for stakeholder, or firm or public interest. In a wider sense, 'profit' refers to the impact of halal on economic or operational performance, i.e. reduce production cost, save materials and energies, and increase competitiveness. Halal requires fully halal resources and capabilities (equipment, technology, and knowledge) which contribute more effectively to firm's growth and success and give positive effects on firm performance (Karia & Asaari 2016a). High levels of halal practices enhance profits, market share, product/service innovation, and maximise value for people and planet.

People

'People' refers to the impact of halal on employees, society, stakeholders, and the social value added. The successful implementation of halal should increase the likelihood that employees will be motivated to perform with sincerity, responsibility, commitment; and excel and be highly involved in their job. Halal also tends to enhance a good working environment, equal treatment, respect human rights, health and safety, and community well-being. Satisfied employees are also more likely to enhance firm competitive advantage in terms of customer service, service innovation, and cost (Karia & Wong 2013).

Planet

'Planet' refers to the impact of halal on the environmental and ethical values. Halal practices should promote green initiatives and encourage a safer environment. In Malaysia firms are encouraged to comply with the Shariah-compliant, Occupational Safety and Health and Environmental System Standard (ISO 14001) (Karia & Asaari 2016b, 2016c).

In summary, it is suggested that halal empowers 4P: products/services, profit, people, and planet. Firms that are highly committed to halal are more likely to provide high levels of service or practices; more effectively develop firm growth and success; and create an environment that elicits the best from employees and is safe.

Halal logistics achievement

Karia and Asaari (2016a) have been drawn to the question of what factors cause the success of a HLSP which can be emulated by other HLSPs and eventually become the ultimate success formula/model to other HLSPs. They suggest that halal value creation derives from a resource-based halal logistics (RBHL) approach and that an effective RBHL will enhance innovation capability and competitiveness. They summarise RBHL as being the right bundles of halal logistics, resources, and capabilities. In other words, the common and advanced physical, human capital (knowledge and skills), organisational, and relational resources are integrated to form the right RBHL. The right RBHL is leveraged to enable more cost-effective resource use and sustainability.

Halal value creation is the strategic importance of achieving the innovation capability of halal logistics practices and subsequently enhancing firm performance and competitiveness. Halal logistics practices produce positive effects on RBHL by employing fully halal logistics service capabilities. Consequently, emerging RBHLs are an important aspect of successfully implementing halal logistics practices in a firm that can contribute to its ability to launch successful halal goods and/or services, and to have positive effects on profits and market share. However, to do this means involving participation from supply chain partners. Strategic halal value creation therefore depends highly on the support of top management and/or leaders who see halal value creation as part of their strategic management responsibilities. Indeed, most successful halal logistics practices depend heavily on changing people's attitudes and activities and getting them involved in the process because the knowledge resources of staff and stakeholders are crucial to executing halal warehousing and halal transportation; utilising logistics technologies, and implementing other intangible resources such as relational resources (Karia & Asaari 2016a). Because halal logistics aims to create an environment that elicits the best from HLSPs, it is hoped that halal logistics will lead to maximising profits (economy), excellence in products/services (quality), ensuring the well-being of humankind (society) and the environment, observe religious requirements, as well as minimise cost or hardship and ultimately meet the desire for Allah's blessing.

Halal logistics practices

The term 'halal logistic practices' refers to a logistics integrated system that dominates Islamic-related business values and practices by providing fully halal logistics service capability. Karia and Asaari (2016a) note that halal logistics practices have been acknowledged to be slightly slow in the real-world setting of halal logistics. Although the significance of the halal industry has been acknowledged for decades, halal logistics practices are relatively new with respect to the delivery of halal products/service in Malaysia. The research thus emphasises the issues involved in implementing halal logistics in practice (what a LSP actually does to demonstrate its commitment to halal) rather than halal logistics ownership. The following case of an anonymous Malaysian logistics firm discusses the practical effect of halal logistics practices.

Case profile

ABC's vision is to offer the best value and highest possible service level and it aims to become Malaysia's main total logistics player in the industry especially on halal trade facilitation. As a JAKIM halal-certified logistics provider, ABC offers a full range of halal logistics services encompassing halal warehousing and halal transportation. In addition, it is expert in container haulage, warehousing, international freight forwarding, distribution, supply chain solutions and cold chain solutions, and has captured 70 per cent of the local market and 20 per cent of the ASEAN market; and has international networking in Asia, Europe, America, and Australia.

ABC has an experienced workforce of over 1,300 and a fleet exceeding 500 prime-movers, 3,100 trailers, and 4.5 million square feet storage facility. ABC has also invested extensively in information technology applications with the latest technology of logistics, packaging, transportation, and distribution using data warehouse, business performance management, user-interface, and business analytics tools.

Halal logistics implementation and halal logistics competency

The successful implementation of halal logistics depends heavily on resource-based halal logistics (RBHL). The emerging RBHL have been acquired by ABC to produce positive effects on its performance by improving innovation capability and profits and by enhancing competitive advantage. Figure 21.1 provides a SWOT (Strengths, Weakness, Opportunities and Threats) analysis that summarises corporate image, knowledge and skills; and innovative service providers as being the strengths of ABC that empowers it to take responsibility for halal logistics practices. Nevertheless, despite having external opportunities, ABC still has some weaknesses and threats that require it to be proactive with halal service provision in order to have a better position to meet the needs of halal global customers.

An important aspect of halal logistics practices is empowering ABC staff and stakeholders to participate more in the development of its halal logistics services. Halal logistics practices require maximum commitment of ABC. The high level of RBHL enhances successful halal logistics and service capabilities which is transformed into the benefit of profits for ABC and value for customers. ABC Company successfully offers halal logistics services in terms of:

* Halal storage and warehousing
* Halal transportation (containerised and conventional)
* Halal distribution
* Halal shipping
* Halal freighting for sea and air cargo
* Customs facilities
* Halal value-added services such as labelling and packaging
* Halal advisory services on certification.

Halal logistics practices produce positive effects on RBHL by improving ABC's commitment to halal logistics service capabilities. ABC focuses on halal in logistics and supply chain in practice (what ABC does to demonstrate its commitment to halal logistics practices). The practical effects of halal logistics practices are:

Strengths	*Weaknesses*
• Established brand name over decades • Committed, dedicated,and passionate on providing warehousing and distribution services by business member • The knowledge and skills demonstrated by the member • The creditworthiness of the business owner • R&D on the potential customersfor their business	• The lack of highly specialised warehousing and distribution expertise within the business. • The lack of funding to source highly specialised technology • The lack of a comprehensive marketing plan and strategy • The small workforce capacity for warehousingand distribution
Opportunities	*Threats*
• Government assistance • Economic opportunity (warehousing and distribution service) • Exporting products to ASEAN countries • ASEAN Free Trade Zone (AFTA)— avenues for leaner ship and development in the business • The growth in middle income groups as well as the increase in double income families • IncreaseinMuslim population	• Well-established competitors • Changes in the preferences and tastes and of consumers • Substitute services • New entrants • Different perception regardinghalal principles

Figure 21.1 ABC Strengths, Weakness, Opportunities, and Threats

- Inbound activities—only accept halal products for storage pick and pack service, stores consolidation and distribution.
- Import and export—set up in-house customs which allow customs clearance for import, export, and transshipment to be handled smoothly and in compliance to halal standards, guidelines, and regulations.
- Support functions—a specific call centre has been established in order to cater for halal inbound and halal outbound calls on questions, enquiries, escalations, complaints, and telemarketing.
- Standard practice—all processes in ABC must be halal guided, safe and secure.

The nature of halal logistics practices is reflected in the four main criteria that empower ABC to incorporate halal value creation in delivering halal products/services. The following describes details of each criteria.

Importance of halal certification

ABC has realised the vital importance of halal certification in increasing confidence in Muslim consumers and preserving halal integrity. It has experienced an increase in the number of consumers after obtaining a halal certification. ABC incorporates halal value creation in terms of being proactive in its services that provide halal logistics services for an increasing number of halal products and/or halal customer requirements.

Current trends indicate that Malaysian customers have moved towards increased halal food consumption. Demographic changes, such as an increase in female workers and a decline in home meal preparation, mean that ABC needs to focus on added-value products and services. Hence, ABC plays its role in increasing the amount of halal food items available in the market by delivering halal foods to consumers. As emphasised in interviews:

> Halal is used in every life of Muslim. But currently we have initiated all activities based on halal procedures. Halal logo is popular now among Muslim and even non-Muslim.

> Now Malaysia become one of the main player in halal logistics and begins to penetrate global market. Halal is crucial for our life even for health, safety and our daily needs.

Challenges in halal certification

ABC claimed that the Standard set by JAKIM is difficult to abide by and may not be cost-effective. The common challenges encountered are: (1) the criteria and requirement of JAKIM to be followed, and (2) various operational problems including product operations, inventory management, documentation, and goods storage between halal and non-halal goods. ABC claimed:

> Halal operations must follow certain criteria, we did not mix all goods between halal and non-halal goods.

> ABC is similar with other forwarders and logistics industry. We must follow requirements set by JAKIM. JAKIM more focuses on customer service, transportation, warehousing, freight forwarding and contract logistics.

In addition, there is still a lack of integration and communication between JAKIM, the Halal Industry Development Corporation (HDC), and logistics service providers. The transition from HDC to JAKIM made certification renewal process more complex and take longer. This implies that there is still no standard halal guideline and halal logistics competency model. The situation is also complicated by a shortage of halal logistics professionals that are halal experts or Shariah educated.

Strategies

ABC has proactively offered halal logistics services and, innovatively, has dedicated halal warehousing and halal transportation as part of its halal logistics practices. It complies with the halal segregation policy in warehouse and transportation. Halal warehousing refers to the physical segregation and separation of goods throughout warehouse processes: receiving, put away, storage, cross-docking, value-added logistics, order picking, and shipping. Halal transportation refers to the halal and non-halal goods not being mixed in a container, common transportation vehicle, or on handling equipment such as forklift, trolley, and pallet.

Being an innovative firm, ABC also employs logistics technologies for improving its halal services and halal integrity preservation.

> We use latest technologies to encounter any issues and solve it professionally. Internet web and networking is easy for customer to communicate with us. We have our own web which empowers a lot of information about our company background, strategies and customer service.

> We have customer satisfaction survey. We have 1 to 10 which 1 is least satisfied and 10 is most satisfy. The satisfaction score is usually ranked above 7.

Technology is a major variable that influences the development of many of ABC's services/products. ABC utilises the following technologies for the management of halal food supply chains:

- Wireless devices
- Intelligent scale
- Electronic shelf labelling
- Self-check-out machine
- Global Positioning System (GPS) Integrated Transportation System
- Radio Frequency Identification (RFID).

Support

The government agencies hold responsibility for protecting consumers from corrupt and ignorant certifiers and providers. They have undertaken initiatives for awareness and understanding of the importance of halal certification through formal education, training, conferences, and exhibitions. ABC emphasised that it has received government support and intervention in regards to halal certification.

> We are pleased to be able to achieve halal certification and gains government support whose encourage all industries to become halal. We have received tremendous support.

In addition, the firm indicates it needs more support and information being made available on halal business and practices especially halal logistics training.

In summary, ABC has faced some challenges to enhance its competitiveness to be a halal-certified leader in logistics. The challenges are:

To remain a halal-certified logistic service provider (LSP). ABC is facing challenges with customers' complaints. Every complaint is crucial and challenges ABC to prove its halal integrity that halal process is conducted throughout the manufacturing, inventory, stock, transportation, distribution, arrangement, and selling.

Business expansion. It is difficult to obtain new business partners or client base because all clients must first be halal-certified or at least have the halal product certification before seeking ABC services. This is a tedious process and not many clients want to embark on this, perhaps due to low awareness on halal concept. This perhaps could cause ABC to lose out on business opportunities.

No universal halal standard. Confusion, misunderstanding, and abuse in the halal audit and certification process has occurred internationally due to there being no universal halal standard. New regulations and/or agency requirements also prolong certification processes.

Market penetration. It is not easy to penetrate countries such as Saudi Arabia, Oman, Iran, and Iraq because each has its own halal logistics companies which are offering similar services. Malaysia's halal recognition is important but has little value in some international markets to stand as a competitive advantage.

Be most competitive. ABC needs to develop and sustain its competitive advantage by having strategic capabilities that are not easy to be imitated by their nearest competitors.

Conclusion

The chapter commences with an overview of the Malaysian halal logistics industry and reviews research on halal logistics studies from LSP perspectives. The terms 'halal service/ business', 'halal logistics', 'halal logistics service providers (HLSP)', and 'halal logistics performance' are framed by Shariah law. This chapter has explained the constructs of halal integrity preservation and halal logistics performance measurements. Novel features include the framework of halal impact, halal logistics achievement, and halal logistics practices. Halal thus potentially empowers sustainable performance antecedents by maximising profits (economy), excellence products/services (quality), ensuring the well-being of humankind (society) and the planet (environment), observing religious requirements, as well as minimising cost or hardship, and ultimately the desire for Allah's blessing. The resource-based halal logistics (RBHL) is an important aspect of successfully implementing halal logistics practices which produce positive effects on profits and market share by empowering halal service capability and by enhancing competitiveness. Overall, halal responsible firms, halal certification, and Shariah-compliance have become important strategies for business performance and sustainability.

Logistics service providers should focus more on the significant importance of halal towards competitive advantage and sustainability. Logistics providers should perceive halal value creation as a commitment, a responsible obligation towards business processes and practices, to safety in handling, warehousing and transportation, and meeting and satisfying customers' new needs and requirements. There is evidence that firms that proactively and innovatively initiate halal value creation in their halal services and/or halal logistics practices in turn enhance their service capabilities as well as profits for them and added value for customers.

Acknowledgement

This work was supported by the Research University Grant, Universiti Sains Malaysia [grant number [1001/PMGT/811216].

References

Bititci, U., Garengo, P., Dorfler, V. and Nudurupati, S. (2012) 'Performance measurement: Challenges for tomorrow', *International Journal of Management Reviews*, 14 (3): 305–327.

Bocken, N., Short, S., Rana, P. and Evans, S. (2013) 'A value mapping tool for sustainable business modelling', *Corporate Governance*, 13 (5): 482–497.

Brah, S.A. and Lim, H.Y. (2006) 'The effect of technology and TQM on the performance of logistics companies', *International Journal of Physical Distribution & Logistics Management*, 36 (3): 192–209.

Din, H. (1985) '*Manusia dan Islam*', Kuala Lumpur: Percetakan Watan Sdn. Bhd.

Green, J.K.W., Whitten, D. and Inman, R.A. (2008) 'The impact of logistics performance on organizational performance in a supply chain context', *Supply Chain Management: An International Journal*, 13 (4): 317–327.

Halal Industry Development Corporation (HDC). (2009) *Support Infrastructure—Halal Logistics*. [online] Available at: www.hdcglobal.com/portal/mainpage.php?module=Maklumat&kategori=49&id=242&papar=1&id2=4&menu=168 (accessed 8 June 2017).

Halal Malaysia (2018) *Halal Malaysia Official Portal. Malaysian Standard. Malaysian Standard on Halal Food (MS 1500:2009)*. [online] Available at: www.halal.gov.my/v4/index.php?data=bW9kdWxcy9uZXXdzOzs7Ow==&utama=panduan&ids=gp2 (accessed 2 January 2019).

Ismail, A.M., Othman, M.Y. and Dakir, J. (2011) 'The development of human behaviour: Islamic approach', *Journal Hadhari*, 3 (2): 103–116.

Kamali, M.H. (2010) 'The halal industry from a Shariah perspective', *Islam and Civilizational Renewal*, 1 (4): 595–612.

Karia, N. and Wong, C.Y. (2013) 'The impact of logistics resources on the performance of Malaysian logistics service providers', *Production Planning & Control*, 24 (7): 589–606.

Karia, N. and Asaari, M.H.A.H. (2014) 'Developing Halal logistics framework: An innovation approach'. In K.S. Soliman (ed.) *Vision 2020: Sustainable Growth, Economic Development, and Global Competitiveness*. Kuala Lumpur: International Business Information Management Association, 328–334.

Karia, N., Asaari, M.H.A.H., Mohamad, N. and Kamaruddin, S. (2015) 'Assessing Halal logistics competence: An Islamic-based and resource-based view'. In *2015 International Conference on Industrial Engineering and Operations Management (IEOM)*, 1–6. IEEE Conference Publications.

Karia, N. and Asaari, M.H.A.H. (2016a) 'Halal value creation: Its role in adding value and enabling logistics service', *Production Planning and Control*, 27 (9): 677–685.

Karia, N. and Asaari, M.H.A.H. (2016b) 'Halal business and sustainability: Strategies, resources and capabilities of Halal third-party logistics (3PLs)', *Progress in Industrial Ecology—An International Journal*, 10 (2/3): 286–300.

Karia, N. and Asaari, M.H.A.H. (2016c) 'Assessing innovation in Halal service: An Islamic-based view approach'. In S.K.A. Manan, F.A. Rahman and M. Sahri (eds) *Contemporary Issues and Development in the Global Halal Industry: Selected Papers from the International Halal Conference 2014*. Singapore: Springer Science + Business Media, 589–597.

Lai, F., Li, D., Wang, Q. and Zhao, X. (2008) 'The information technology capability of third-party logistics providers: A resource-based view and empirical evidence from China', *Journal of Supply Chain Management*, 44 (3): 22–38.

Ministry of International Trade and Industry (MITI). (2006) *Third Industrial Masterplan (IMP3) 2006–2020*. Malaysia: MITI.

Nidumolu, R., Prahalad, C.K. and Rangaswami, M.R. (2009) 'Why sustainability is now the key driver of innovation', *Harvard Business Review*, 87 (9): 57–64.

Ray, G., Barney, J.B. and Muhanna, W.A. (2004) 'Capabilities, business processes, and competitive advantage: Choosing the dependent variable in empirical tests of the resource-based view', *Strategic Management Journal*, 25 (1): 23–37.

Reuter, C., Foerstl, K., Hartmann, E. and Blome, C. (2010) 'Sustainable global supplier management: The role of dynamic capabilities in achieving competitive advantage', *Journal of Supply Chain Management*, 46 (2): 45–63.

Talib, M.S.A., Hamid, A.B.A., Zulfakar, M.H. and Chin, T.A. (2015) 'Barriers to Halal logistics operation: Views from Malaysian logistics experts', *International Journal of Logistics Systems and Management*, 22 (2): 193–209.

The Borneo Post (2018) 'HDC expects Malaysian halal exports to hit RM50 billion by 2020', *The Borneo Post*, 18 December. Available: www.theborneopost.com/2018/12/18/hdc-expects-malaysian-halal-exports-to-hit-rm50-billion-by-2020/

Wilding, R. and Juriado, R. (2004) 'Customer perceptions on logistics outsourcing in the European consumer goods industry', *International Journal of Physical Distribution & Logistics Management*, 34 (8): 628–644.

Yadav, P.L., Han, S.H. and Rho, J.J. (2016) 'Impact of environmental performance on firm value for sustainable investment: Evidence from large US firms', *Business Strategy and the Environment*, 25 (6): 402–420.

PART V

Issues and challenges

22

THE CHALLENGE OF THE *HALAL*/PORK BINARY FOR MUSLIM IMMIGRANTS IN SPAIN

Leela Riesz

Introduction: conflicting food cultures

Sancho greeted Ricote.... They stretched out on the ground ... they set out bread, salt, knives, nuts, pieces of cheese, and bare ham bones that could not be gnawed but could still be sucked. There was no lack of olives, dried without any brine but good-tasting and flavorful. What stood out the most on the field of that banquet, however, were six wineskins, for each of them took one out of his bag; even the good Ricote, transformed from a Morisco ... took out his wineskin, comparable in size to the other five. They began to eat with great pleasure, savoring each mouthful slowly, just a little of each thing. And then all at once, and all at the same time, they raised their arms and the wineskins into the air.

(Cervantes 2003: 812)

This scene from Cervantes' *Don Quijote* is commonly referenced by scholars interested in exploring the theme of the 'other,' the Muslim or *morisco* (Muslim convert to Christianity) in Cervantes' work. David Dominguez-Navarro claims that this shared meal between Sancho, a native Spaniard, and Ricote, a *morisco,* demonstrates the 'level of assimilation the Moriscos reached' (Dominguez-Navarro 2011: 289). Ricote, who has abandoned *halal* dietary practices, now has the ability to savour quintessentially Spanish cuisine such as 'ham bones and wineskins' that were once forbidden to him. Here, Ricote crosses a religious and cultural boundary through consumption of traditional Spanish food and drink. His newly adopted food practices signal his ability to integrate into Spanish society. This scene illustrates the tension between Spanish and Muslim foodways; thus the *halal*/pork binary, a concept that guides much of the following analysis, appears in Spain's most renowned work of literature. Olivia Remie Constable's (2013) 'Food and Meaning: Christian Understandings of Muslim Food and Food Ways in Spain, 1250–1550,' explores how, historically, food established boundaries between the Christian and Muslim communities. By the fifteenth century, in the context of rising anti-Islamic sentiment, pork was a symbol of Christianity while adherence to *halal* was a signal of one's Muslim status. In Spain's contemporary context, Muslims' avoidance of pork and alcohol and their patronage of *halal* food establishments are indications of their cultural and religious difference. What is more, their dependence on *halal* foodways and their adjustment to a new food environment are prominent features of their immigrant experience. Muslim immigrants' discussion of the difficulties around observing *halal* food practices, their negotiation of the forbidden versus the permissible, suggests that this food-mediated religious and cultural barrier continues to carry weight in contemporary Spain.

In Spain, Muslims' preoccupation around maintaining *halal* eating habits and a *halal*-conscious way of life is intensified owing to the omnipresence of pork products and dishes, forbidden food items. Today, Iberian ham is an emblem of Spanish national identity and it is common to find it displayed in Spanish restaurants and bars. This chapter looks closely at Muslim immigrants' dependence on the kebab industry as a means of maintaining *halal* eating practices in Spain. The desire to maintain a *halal* diet and the new pressures of the Spanish food system also influence restaurant owners' business decisions. Drawing on the voices of customers and restaurateurs, this chapter highlights their experiences engaging with and/or avoiding elements of Spanish food culture and explores how the negotiation of *halal* in Spain is connected to identity-forging in the new country. Such an analysis looks at the *halal* concept not only as a product in an emerging 'diasporic, religious market' (Bergeaud-Blackler, Fischer & Lever 2015: 13), but as a foodway and food behaviour that is measured against the mainstream food culture and thus raises questions of belonging. Finally, this chapter illustrates how in Spain, similar to other European nations, the *halal* concept has been drawn into food politics.

Background

According to various statistical sources, Muslims, both Spanish nationals and foreigners, constitute between 2.1 per cent and 3 per cent of Spain's total population of approximately 46.5 million (Govan 2016; Euro-Islam 2013; Frayer 2015a, b). Muslim immigrants constitute about 24 per cent of Spain's total immigrant population of 4.6 million (Femmine & Alameda 2017). Drawing on 2012 census data, Euro-Islam (2013) states that the total number of Muslims in Spain is 1.6 million of which 1.1 million are foreigners and approximately 465,000 are Spanish nationals. In other words, nearly 70 per cent of Muslims in Spain are immigrants while approximately 30 per cent are Spanish nationals. Euro-Islam (2013: 1) explains that 'in terms of national origin, the two main Muslim groups in Spain are the Spanish and the Moroccan, adding now the growing Pakistani group.' Of the total Muslim immigrant population, Moroccans make up nearly 50 per cent, and the remaining 20 per cent are of other nationalities (Euro-Islam 2013), such as Pakistani, Senegalese, and Algerian immigrants (Bravo 2014). Statistics from the National Institute of Statistics (Instituto Nacional de Estadística—INE) confirm that Moroccans form not only the largest Muslim community in Spain, but also constitute the largest overall immigrant group with a population of 747,872 as of January 2017 (Femmine & Alameda 2017; INE 2017). It should be noted that in his discussion of Islam in Spain, Fernando Bravo recognises the challenges of determining the precise Muslim population in Spain and argues that 'since statistics often do not distinguish population according to faith, we can only estimate quantity using national origin or national identity as a sign of religious adherence,' with an implied certain margin of error (Bravo 2014). Approximately 465,000 Muslims in Spain are Spanish nationals. Part of this figure includes Muslims of different nationalities who immigrated to Spain and have obtained Spanish nationality. Nevertheless, some portion of Muslim Spanish nationals are Spanish converts to Islam. Salman Al-Ansari's (2013) article on converts to Islam states that on average the Islamic Center in Madrid, Spain, sees 170 Spanish converts a year.

Owing to Morocco's historical ties and proximity to Spain, it is no surprise that Moroccans form the largest body of immigrants and the highest percentage of Muslims in Spain. However, in recent decades the Pakistani population has grown tremendously. As of January 2017, the Pakistani population had reached 80,000 (INE 2017). Pakistanis began arriving in the 1970s and family networks were established by the first wave to settle in Spain. In Almería, where ethnographic semi-structured interviews were carried out, the Pakistani population is predominantly male business owners. Both Moroccans and Pakistanis engage primarily in the Spanish commerce and services sector (International Markets Bureau 2011). The restaurateurs I spoke to arrived in Spain as early as 26 and as late as 6 years ago. In almost all cases, they had relatives who also immigrated to Europe. According to various restaurateurs, there are 23 kebab restaurants in Almería capital alone and Pakistanis tend to dominate the kebab industry in this region.

With the growth of the Muslim immigrant community in Spain, there has been a corresponding need for food establishments that observe *halal*. Similar to other European nations, Spain has seen the rapid development of a kebab industry, which has not only become popular street food, but offers *halal* meat, thereby meeting the religious and cultural needs of Muslim immigrants. There is scholarship that investigates *halal* food production, marketing, food establishments, and their significance in the lives of Muslim immigrants living elsewhere in Europe (Bonne & Vermeir 2007; Bonne & Verbeke 2008; Wright & Annes 2013). However, the case of Spain remains underexplored. As background to this investigation of the kebab industry's significance for Muslims, I trace its emergence in Europe. I also reference several studies that explore both the factors that compel many Muslims to observe *halal* food practices and the positive impact of *halal* fast-food restaurants, or 'halal environments' (Nasir & Pereira 2008). I then turn to the case of Spain and to my own ethnographic findings to investigate the dynamics that unfold around the concept of *halal*.

Development of the kebab industry in Europe

The kebab industry as we know it today is a product of the Turkish immigrant community's experience in Germany. Ayse Caglar's seminal essay, '*McDöner: Döner Kebap* and the Social Positioning Struggle of German Turks,' explores how the kebab became the iconic ethnic food of the Turkish community and uncovers the kebab's 'field of connotations … the social and political ideas projected onto it' (Caglar 2013: 220). According to Caglar (2013), with 140,000 Turkish migrants, Berlin is considered the largest 'Turkish city' outside of Turkey. Turkish migrants in the guest worker system opened up Turkish kebab stalls, with the first 'döner Imbiss' stand appearing in Berlin in 1975 (Caglar 2013).

As Turkish immigrants and other Muslim communities settled in countries such as Sweden and Belgium, the kebab industry eventually spread across Europe becoming part of the larger *halal* industry. John Lever and Mara Miele (2012: 1) refer to the *halal* industry as an emerging 'religious marketplace' that represents the 'supply side theory of religion.' As the kebab industry grows more popular, it is becoming a significant business niche as well as a food source for Muslim immigrant populations across Europe. France, home to the largest Muslim community in Europe, has one of the largest European national *halal* markets, estimated to be at 13 billion USD (Gorák-Sosnowska 2010). In their research on Muslims' dependence on the *halal* industry, Wilson and Liu (2010) cite the need for an increased availability of *halal* products as Muslim migration continues. In fact, Spain has seen the recent emergence of *halal* meat companies, such as Soyal, that distribute meat to kebab restaurants throughout the country (Vallarino & Ferrer 2017).

Defining *halal* and *haram*

Eating is considered ritualistic and a significant part of a person's worship of God under Islam. The concepts of *halal* (permissible) and *haram* (forbidden) are fundamental to the Islamic dietary code (Riaz & Chaudry 2003; see also Chapter 2, this volume). When it is difficult to determine whether a food item is permissible or forbidden, it is called *mashbuh*. As stated explicitly in the Qur'an, pork and its derivatives, blood, and carrion are forbidden. In their 2011 study on consumers' awareness and attitudes towards *halal* food in Pakistan, Salman and Siddiqui (2011) find that Muslims are confronted with a 'web of relationships' that influences their social and consumer behaviour. They argue that consuming non-*halal* food can lead to isolation from the Muslim community thereby affecting relationships with peers and family members (Salman & Siddiqui 2011). Recognition of the social import attached to *halal* in their countries of origin is essential to understanding Muslim immigrants' commitment to maintaining *halal* when living abroad.

The kebab industry and *halal* consciousness

During the summer of 2015, semi-structured interviews were carried out in Almería, a city of 190,000 in south-eastern Andalucía, Spain. This chapter focuses on interviews with three Pakistani kebab restaurateurs and four Moroccan customers as a means of investigating Muslims' dependence on the kebab industry in Spain, their preoccupation with maintaining *halal* eating practices, and the tensions between Spanish and Muslim foodways. Nadir, a Pakistani kebab restaurant owner, is 35 years old and has lived in Spain for 18 years. He owns three kebab restaurants and a franchise that sells *halal* meat to kebab restaurants throughout Andalucía. Nadir claims that the first Pakistani-owned kebab restaurant opened in Barcelona in 2011. Given the kebab industry's Turkish–German roots, Nadir's franchise originally sold a German brand of meat, but he currently sells a Spanish brand. Nadir claims that with the industry's rapid spread and tremendous popularity, there are now numerous factories in Spain that process and distribute *halal* meat. In Spain, it is now common to see menus for 'McDonor' or 'Doner Kebab' in young people's homes since the food is cheap and quick. Some restaurateurs told me that there are Turkish kebab owners in Almería, but the majority of these fast-food restaurants are Pakistani-owned. Nevertheless, Germany remains a cornerstone of the industry. For example, Nadir has travelled to Germany to attend instructive courses on kebab food production and restaurant procedures.

Mukhtar, the Pakistani owner of Alhambra Kebab, entered the kebab industry through pre-existing familial networks in Spain. Trained by his brother, Mukhtar learned how to work the machinery in the kebab restaurant. He comments, 'It's Turkish food, but Pakistanis are seen everywhere working in them.' Nadir similarly states that 'Pakistan is the community with the most kebabs after the Turkish.' In fact, Pakistanis in Almería have become associated with kebab restaurants to such an extent that one Moroccan woman I spoke to referred to them as 'Pakistani restaurants.'

Based on my interviews, frequent conversations with kebab restaurateurs, and partici-pant observation, it became evident that Pakistani immigrants' desire to maintain *halal* practices is a driving force behind their involvement in the kebab industry. Nadir explained that in a Pakistani or Indian restaurant it would be necessary to sell alcohol, whereas in kebab fast-food restaurants it is not. According to both Nadir and Mukhtar, non-Muslim customers are more willing to accept that alcohol is unavailable at such eateries. From a restaurateur's perspective, the obligation to keep *halal* practices in the workplace makes certain business endeavours challenging. Nadir says, 'If your own [cuisine] does not work in Spain, you have to pursue another path.' Kebab restaurants generally offer only *halal* meat—chicken and beef—making them the ideal non-contaminating workplace for Pakistani Muslims and preferred eating establishments for other Muslim immigrants in Spain. The kebab restaurants I visited in Spain were thus '*halal*' spaces that suited the religious and gustatory needs of owners, employees, and customers.

The kebab industry's ability to cater to the Muslim community's religious and gastronomic needs is a major factor of its success. Both Nadir and Mukhtar told me that 50 per cent of their customers are Spanish nationals and 50 per cent are Moroccan Muslim immigrants. Mukhtar added that Moroccans tend to come during the day, while Spaniards visit late at night. In fact, Mukhtar uses some Arabic phrases with his Moroccan customers and knows how to tell them that his meat is *halal*. Muhktar's decision to learn Arabic signals his recognition of a shared '*halal* consciousness' among Muslim immigrants of different origins (Hashim & Othman 2011).

Halal consciousness among customers

According to Nadir and his employee Hamal, a 28-year-old from Pakistan, Muslim customers always verify that the meat in their kebab restaurant is *halal*. Nadir says that although his restaurant has been open for three years, Moroccan customers continue to ask before they order because 'they do not trust that it is *halal*.' Hamal similarly contends that customers first ask, 'Excuse me, is this food *halal*?' at which point he assures them that everything in the restaurant is '100 percent *halal*.' Mukhtar similarly finds that Muslim tourists from France and Germany must be convinced that the restaurant's food is *halal* before ordering. All three restaurateurs witness customers' preoccupation around observing *halal* practices on a daily basis. This *halal* consciousness is evident in customers' wider shopping habits as well. One Moroccan customer explained to me that she buys *halal* meat from a shop which requires her to travel far outside her new neighbourhood. On another occasion, a Moroccan customer entered Nadir's kebab restaurant as he waited for the neighbouring *halal* meat shop to open. He explained that he wanted to buy meat and fermented milk, 'that many Arabs buy it.' These examples reveal how in Spain, an environment where *halal* food is not as easy to come by, some Muslim immigrants become concerned about their food purchases. For these customers, obtaining *halal* meat and other traditional foods remains a firmly established practice in Spain.

My conversation with Kadin, a customer at Alhambra Kebab, further illustrates Muslim immigrants' reliance on the kebab industry. Kadin, originally from Morocco, arrived in Spain by boat in 2003. Sitting and eating a dürüm beef kebab, he told me, 'We eat this or nothing.' He explained that his mother and sister, who normally cook Moroccan food at home, were visiting Morocco and that, 'Now I eat outside because my mother is away. We always eat our own food. It's important.' Thus, normally Kadin eats Moroccan dishes prepared by the women in his family. In their absence, he relies on kebab restaurants for *halal* meat options. Kadin's example demonstrates how the kebab fast-food industry enables many Muslims to eat in public while adhering to *halal* dietary law.

Furthermore, my discussions with Saru, Mukhtar's nephew, illustrate the challenge of living out one's Muslim identity from a consumer perspective. Saru told me, 'We do not eat out a lot at Spanish restaurants. It's pork and it's not *halal*.' We discussed the predominance of pork in Spain and I asked him if it is difficult to find adequate food. He explained, 'We have to look at the things in Mercadona supermarkets to see if there is any pork contained in them and to see if we can eat them … in Pakistan there is no pork.' Saru's comments exemplify that Spain is not as far along as other European countries such as France and Belgium, where *halal* products are more readily available at chain supermarkets (Bonne &Verbeke 2008). His account mirrors Roberta Giovine's (2013) findings that Muslims' difficulty maintaining *halal* eating practices in Italy greatly defines their experience as immigrants. Giovine recognises how Muslims' food needs shift from 'mainstream to minority' once they enter Europe. Saru's comments further reveal the boundaries set in place by conflicting Spanish and Muslim food cultures and how the *halal*/pork tension is now a salient reminder of his transition from one country to another.

Halal consciousness among restaurateurs

Not only must customers contend with the *halal*/pork binary, but Muslim restaurateurs sometimes encounter *haram* food and therefore exhibit a heightened *halal* consciousness in the workplace. Before coming to Almería, Hamal worked in a combined kebab pizzeria restaurant where Spanish customers often asked for Iberian ham toppings. He explained how 'normally Muslims cannot sell pizza with these ingredients,' but the need to cater to Spanish taste took precedence. According to Hamal, one solution was to ask the only non-Muslim employee to prepare orders containing ham. Muslim employees would ask, 'Hey look, could you please prepare this pizza?' This account exemplifies the negotiations that have to be made when labour, religion, food, and national taste intersect. While the owners in Hamal's previous job catered to Spanish taste by offering ham, this is not the case in Nadir's *halal* kebab shop. Nevertheless, Hamal finds that Spanish customers will ask if the restaurant offers ham along with kebabs. He recognises that the kebab restaurant is a space that deviates from the Spanish culinary norm. He makes it a point to explain: 'I don't say, "I don't like pork" and "It is prohibited in Islam."' Perhaps Hamal believes that sharing his views on pork consumption would be unprofessional, elicit negative responses, and signal his 'otherness.'

As previously discussed, kebab restaurants' embodiment of *halal* practices makes them an ideal work setting for Pakistani Muslim employees. However, a food industry in Spain that observes *halal* dietary restrictions brings with it the challenge of confronting tensions between Spanish and Muslim food cultures in determining which practices to uphold. In my first conversation with Nadir, he described the predicament of not being able to sell alcohol in his restaurant. Similarly, after spending time in Mukhtar's kebab restaurant, I observed several customers asking with surprise, 'You don't have beer?' This contrast between Spanish and Muslim customs regarding food led Nadir to remain in the fast-food industry and refrain from opening a South Asian restaurant. Nadir claimed that he is not bothered by this limitation, that 'this is all strictly business.' However, there is clearly an emotional element at work. He stated that if he ever sold alcohol in his business, it would hurt his parents back in Pakistan particularly because 'word gets out from the Pakistani community in Almería.' In his case, the need to abide by Islamic dietary law and honour family values needed to be weighed against his desire for business success. Nadir's account is also indicative of the power of the Pakistani community's 'web of relationships' (Salman & Siddiqui 2011: 642). Although he is far from home, the local Pakistani community is a reminder of his family's values and a connection to home, making it more difficult for him to deviate from firmly held practices.

While Nadir is not willing to sell alcohol in his restaurant, he expresses a personally flexible attitude towards disobeying some *halal* food practices. He explains that pork or pork fat cannot always be avoided, otherwise 'it would be impossible to eat in Spain.' While his friends and employees tend to rely on Pakistani food to avoid *haram* dishes, Nadir accepts the uncertainty that goes along with eating in non-*halal* restaurants. He differentiates himself from other Pakistanis unwilling to deviate from *halal* food practices. However, while Nadir demonstrates a modified *halal* adherence, he senses that he is a minority within the Pakistani community in Spain, especially when he attends social gatherings in people's homes. Nadir's case demonstrates the complexity of *halal* consciousness in business decisions and social interactions, in other words when negotiating public and private spheres.

Ultimately, the kebab restaurant's embodiment of *halal* food practices marks it as an alternative space, one that digresses from mainstream food culture. Magdalena Nowaczek-Walczak's Muslim restaurateur-interviewees in Poland found themselves in a similar predicament as Nadir and Mukhtar. They admitted that although they were aware that Polish customers 'would happily consume beer, they did not want to show support for a *haram* food item' (Nowaczek-Walczak 2011: 122). As an employee, Hamal identifies the conflicting experiences of Muslims and non-Muslims, noting that while Moroccan customers always ask whether food is *halal*, for Spaniards 'this is not a problem.' His comments reveal how foodways shed light on new cultural dynamics and imbalances that arise in a new country. Clearly, maintaining *halal* food practices is at the forefront of many Pakistani and Moroccan Muslims' minds and thus becomes a metaphor for maintaining a way of life that contrasts sharply from that of the majority population.

Halal wrapped up in food politics

For some interviewees, their newfound dependence on the *halal* kebab industry and concern around obtaining *halal* food items are reminders of their changed circumstances. What is more, interviewees such as Hamal perceive *halal* to be a marker of an alternative identity in the Spanish context. In several European nations and recently in Spain, *halal* food establishments and the concept of eating *halal* have come to represent the unwanted presence of Muslim immigrants, both construed as threats to national cohesion. Food imagery frequently enters political discourse, becoming a coded way to speak disparagingly about Muslim immigrant communities (Wright & Annes 2013). Owing to Spain's shorter history as a country of immigration, there is less literature on the subject. However, just as in neighbouring European countries, such dynamics are present in Spain and are evident in the media.

Spain's largest Muslim communities have settled in Andalucía and Catalonia, contributing to higher rates of Islamophobia in these regions (INE 2017). Lauren Frayer (2015a: 1) states that 'although Muslims account for about 3 per cent of Spain's population, they make up nearly 10 per cent of the people in the coastal Catalan provinces of Tarragona and neighboring Barcelona—the highest proportion in mainland Spain.' Recent news articles reveal rhetoric against the *halal* kebab industry on the part of the predominantly anti-immigrant, conservative Popular Party (PP). The kebab industry's ability to employ and serve Muslims, and its overall reminder of the changing demographics in Spain, has led to proposals for stricter laws aimed at preventing the industry's expansion. Thus, as previously seen in Norway and France, some Spanish politicians have begun to use the rapid growth of the kebab industry as justification for anti-immigrant policies (Thomas & Selimovic 2015; Wright & Annes 2013).

The authors of the *European Islamophobia Report* note that in Barcelona, during the 2015 election campaigns, the PP put forth slogans such as 'Do not let Raval [one of Barcelona's immigrant neighbourhoods] become an Islamic ghetto' (Bayrakli & Hafez 2016). In another neighbourhood, the party stated, 'Stop the proliferation of call shops, dollar stores and kebab restaurants … no to the great mosque of Cornellà' (Bayrakli & Hafez 2016). These slogans mark politicians' desire to limit the expression of Islam both in places of worship and in public food spaces (Bayrakli & Hafez 2016). Similarly, in 2015, a law was proposed in the Spanish municipality of Tarragona seeking to limit the formation of 'ghettos' by restricting the number of new kebab shops in the region. According to Frayer, under the proposed law, commercial licences would not be available for new kebab shops, dollar stores, or Internet cafes located within 500 yards of existing ones—overwhelmingly affecting Muslim business owners (Frayer 2015a, b). Alejandro Fernandez, a leader of the PP in Tarragona, insisted that such a law would 'protect traditional Spanish businesses from unfair competition.' Fernandez claimed that businesses such as kebab restaurants are seen as a threat to 'authentic and superior' Spanish food establishments. He further argued that 'the build-up of these kinds of businesses leads to an inferior quality of public space and a process of deterioration' (Frayer 2015b: 1). According to this viewpoint, the very presence of Muslim-owned businesses is seen as a detriment to Spanish society rather than a sign of newcomer economic contribution and increased consumer choice for nationals, immigrants, and tourists alike.

The anti-immigrant rhetoric underlying this proposed law is undeniable. Moreover, the lack of similar outcry over the many Peruvian, Mexican, Chilean, Argentinean, and Brazilian eateries in the region may also be indicative of the presence of anti-Muslim bias in Spanish politics. As previously noted, Muslim immigrants constitute only approximately 1.1 million of the total 4.6 million immigrants in Spain, and although certain areas of Catalonia have a higher proportion of Muslim immigrants, the overall immigrant population there remains non-Muslim (Femmine & Alameda 2017; INE 2017). Given this picture of immigration demographics, a focus on the supposed dangers of kebab restaurants is a clear indication of anti-Islamic sentiment.

By targeting their businesses and limiting access to *halal* food establishments, these conservative politicians hope to stifle Muslims' ability to thrive in Spain. Perhaps the most interesting element of this recent conflict is the reaction from kebab restaurant owners themselves. Nuari Benzawi, an Algerian immigrant, expressed his resentment towards the proposed Tarragona law. In a conversation with the *L.A. Times*, Benzawi declared the following: 'My tomatoes are Spanish. So are the potatoes I sell. Do I need to sell pork to be a traditional Spanish business? Do I need to sell wine?' (Frayer 2015b: 1). Benzawi understands that Muslim businesses are being stigmatised because they do not fit into the paradigm of Spanish food culture. He recognises the *halal*/pork binary and understands that because he does not sell items forbidden to his community his business is viewed as 'non-Spanish.' Drawing on food imagery, Benzawi is able to name the discrimination he experiences and in so doing highlights the connection between food and the question of national belonging in Spain.

Benzawi's statements echo conversations I had with restaurateurs in Almería regarding their restaurant practices. Nadir similarly grappled with the question of catering to Spanish taste, which would mean deviating from Islamic dietary law. Given that they are run by immigrants, use *halal* meat, and normally do not sell alcohol or pork, kebab restaurants do not conform to the idea of the traditional Spanish food establishment. In this politicised context, the kebab restaurant itself becomes a representation of the Muslim 'other.' Owing to manipulative political rhetoric, Islamophobic stances, and the existence of a *halal*/pork binary, the kebab restaurant can be cast as a space that runs counter to traditional Spanish values. While Spaniards, particularly youth, are also patrons of kebab restaurants, their decision is primarily economic and does not stem from a reliance on *halal* food. Thus, the image of the kebab eatery as a space of congregation for Muslims, a space decidedly 'non-Spanish,' is used to justify the conservative party's proposal to hinder Muslims' business success and limit their visibility in certain regions of Spain. It should be noted, however, that this 'kebab law' was ultimately not passed, which suggests that anti-*halal* rhetoric is not yet as pernicious in Spain as it is in France, where measures have been successfully enacted to eliminate *halal* food options from public food spaces.

Conclusion

This work underscores how the kebab industry in Southern Spain is serving the Muslim immigrant community by meeting its religious and cultural gustatory needs. The industry is sustained, in part, by Muslim immigrants' *halal* consciousness; interviews with restaurateurs and customers begin to shed light on new cultural dynamics taking place in the overall Spanish foodscape. The kebab restaurant in Spain offers a case study of supply and demand and identity-forging in the context of migration. The *halal* consciousness and *halal*/pork binary concepts are useful in tracing Muslim customers' and restaurateurs' negotiation of two divergent food cultures. Food purchasing and business decisions require Muslim immigrants to weigh their *halal* consciousness against the dominant food culture. Choosing when to adopt new food practices or maintain traditional ones is part of the process of place-making in a new context. This tension is readily apparent to Muslim immigrants. Some far-right politicians who detect this heightened dependence on *halal* seek to prevent its proliferation. The recent emergence of Spanish *halal* meat companies does suggest that *halal* is beginning to be incorporated into the Spanish economic market (Vallarino & Ferrer 2017). However, the question remains, to what extent can and will a *halal* consciousness become integrated and accepted in Spain as part of a more complex, more inclusive cultural image of itself? This study of modest dimensions signals the need for further explorations of the Spanish kebab industry, the emerging *halal* food market, Muslims' purchasing and consumer habits (including those of Spanish converts to Islam), and anti-*halal* rhetoric. Such investigations are critical to understanding the challenges of living out one's Muslim identity in contemporary Spain.

References

Al-Ansari, S. (2013) 'Islam in perspective: A journey through Islam: New Muslims in Spain', *Arab News*, 8 February. [online] Available at: www.arabnews.com/new-muslims-spain (accessed 29 September 2017).

Bayrakli, E. and Hafez, F. (eds) (2016) *European Islamophobia Report 2015*. [pdf] Washington, DC: SETA. Available at: www.islamophobiaeurope.com/wp-content/uploads/2017/03/SPAIN.pdf (accessed 25 September 2017).

Bergeaud-Blackler, F., Fischer J. and Lever, J. (eds) (2015) *Halal Matters: Islam, Politics and Markets in Global Perspective*. Abingdon: Routledge.

Bonne, K. and Vermeir, I. (2007) 'Determinants of Halal meat consumption in France,' *British Food Journal*, 109 (5): 367–386.

Bonne, K. and Verbeke, W. (2008) 'Muslim consumer trust in Halal meat status and control in Belgium,' *Meat Science*, 79 (1): 113–123.

Bravo, F. (2014) 'Islam in Spain: 800% population increase in mere 13 years'. *Muslim Statistics*, 11 April. [online] Available at: https://muslimstatistics.wordpress.com/2014/04/11/islam-in-spain-800-population-increase-in-mere-13-years/(accessed 7 October 2015).

Caglar, A.S. (2013) '*McDöner: Döner Kebap* and the social positioning struggle of German Turks'. In J. Costa and G. Bamossy (eds) *Marketing in a Multicultural World: Ethnicity, Nationalism and Cultural Identity*. Thousand Oaks, CA: Sage, 209–230.

Cervantes, M. de. (1605) *Don Quixote*. Translated by E. Grossman (2003). New York City: HarperCollins.

Constable, O.R. (2013) 'Food and meaning: Christian understandings of Muslim food and food ways in Spain, 1250–1550', *Viator*, 44 (3): 199–235.

Domínguez-Navarro, D. (2011) 'El mundo de la frontera: Cambio de religión y choque cultural de los personajes moriscos del Quijote'. In C. Strosetski (ed.) *Visiones y revisiones cervantinas Actas selectas del VII Congreso Internacional de la Asociación de Cervantistas*. Madrid: Ediciones del Centro de Estudios Cervantinos, 285–292.

Euro-Islam. (2013) *Demographic Study of the Muslim Population in Spain*, 17 February. [online] Available at: www.euro-islam.info/2013/02/28/demographic-study-of-the-muslim-population-in-spain/(accessed 5 October 2015).

Femmine L.D. and Alameda, D. (2017) 'La metamorfosis de España'. *El País*, 1 March [online] Available at: https://elpais.com/internacional/2017/02/27/actualidad/1488194732_820452.html

Frayer, L. (2015a) 'Spain's Muslim business owners feel squeezed by new zoning proposals'. *NPR*, 1 March. [online] Available at: www.npr.org/sections/parallels/2015/03/01/387481590/spains-muslim-business-owners-feel-squeezed-by-new-zoning-proposals (accessed 2 January 2017).

Frayer, L. (2015b) 'In Spain, proposed "kebab law" angers Muslim business owners.' *LA Times*, 5 May. [online] Available at: www.latimes.com/world/europe/la-fg-spain-muslims-20150505-story.html (accessed 2 January 2016).

Giovine, R. (2013) 'Children of Muslim migrants in Italian schools and the Halal meat issue'. *Proceedings in ARSA—Advanced Research in Scientific Areas,* [online] 1: 244–249. Available at: www.arsa-conf.com/archive/?vid=1&aid=2&kid=60201-81 (accessed 2 January 2016).

Górak-Sosnowska, K. (2010) 'Marketing Halal: From a religious duty into a global strategy', *Economic Papers*, 44: 125–135.

Govan, F. (2016) 'How the number of Muslims in Spain is far lower than people think'. *The Local Es*, 15 December. [online] Available at: https://www.thelocal.es/20161215/how-the-number-of-muslims-in-spain-is-far-lower-than-people-think (accessed 25 July 2017).

Hashim, A.H. and Othman, M.N. (2011) 'Halal food consumption: A comparative study between Arab Muslims and non Arab Muslims consumers in Malaysia'. In *Australian and New Zealand Marketing Academy (ANZMAC) Conference* [pdf] Perth, Australia, 28–30 November.

Instituto Nacional de Estadística (INE). (2017) *Población extranjera por comunidades y provincias, nacionalidad y sexo*. [online] Available at www.ine.es/jaxi/Tabla.htm?path=/t20/e245/p04/provi/l0/&file=0c caa002.px (accessed 19 September 2017).

International Markets Bureau. (2011) *Market Analysis Report: June 2011. Foodservice Profile Spain*. Canada: Agriculture and Agri-Food Canada.

Lever, J. and Miele, M. (2012) 'The growth of Halal meat markets in Europe: An exploration of the supply side theory of religion', *Journal of Rural Studies*, 28 (4): 528–537.

Nasir, K.M. and Pereira, A.B. (2008) 'Defensive dining: Notes on the public dining experiences in Singapore', *Contemporary Islam*, 2 (1): 61–73.

Nowaczek-Walczak, M. (2011) 'The world of kebab Arabs and gastronomy in Warsaw.' In K. Górak-Sosnowska (ed.) *Muslims in Poland and Eastern Europe: Widening the European Discourse on Islam*. Warsaw: University of Warsaw Faculty of Oriental Studies, 108–125.

Riaz, M.N. and Chaudry, M.M. (2003) *Halal Food Production*. New York: CRC Press.

Salman, F. and Siddiqui, K. (2011) 'An exploratory study for measuring consumers awareness and perceptions towards halal food in Pakistan', *Interdisciplinary Journal of Contemporary Research in Business*, 3 (2): 639–651.

Thomas, P. and Selimovic, A. (2015) 'Sharia on a plate? A critical discourse analysis of Halal food in two Norwegian newspapers', *Journal of Islamic Marketing*, 6 (3): 331–353.

Vallarino, A. and Ferrer, S. (2017) 'Los "reyes del kebab" producen carne para media España en un polígono de Alicante', *El Confidencial: Empresas*, 11 February. [online] Available at: https://www.elconfidencial.com/empresas/2017-02-11/reyes-del-kebab-alicante-alimentacion_1329734/(accessed 20 August 2017).

Wilson, J. and Liu, J. (2010) 'Shaping the Halal into a brand?', *Journal of Islamic Marketing*, 1 (2): 107–123.

Wright, W. and Annes, A. (2013) 'Halal on the menu?: Contested food politics and French identity in fast-food', *Journal of Rural Studies*, 32: 388–399.

23

MEANINGS IN EVERYDAY FOOD ENCOUNTERS FOR MUSLIMS IN AUSTRALIA

Kieran Hegarty

Introduction

Islam offers those faithful to the religion a range of prescriptions relating to the conduct of everyday life. Social scientific literature explores how these practices and norms change according to the social and cultural context in which they are practised (Fischler 1988; Mintz & Du Bois 2002). A growing body of this work focuses on Islamic dietary law and practices of consumption that are defined by the theological boundaries of *halal* (permissible) and *haram* (not permissible). In this chapter, I explore ways in which these religious ideas have been both increasingly commodified and politicised and how these dual forces impact practices of consumption for Muslims in Australia. To examine this, in-depth, semi-structured interviews were conducted with a diverse group of middle-class Muslims living in a large Australian city. These interviews explored subjective understandings of *halal*, locating *halal* food and drink in shops and restaurants, and acts of negotiation when *halal* requirements could not be taken for granted. The data reveal how Islamic food taboos result in Muslim identity becoming embedded in a range of 'intercultural' settings and offers rich descriptions of the intersubjective meanings generated in these encounters. Here I present the ways that my informants articulate and navigate different ideas surrounding consumption, to accommodate their specific understanding of living as a pious, moral Muslim whilst participating as citizens and consumers in different aspects of Australian life. In this way, I offer an insight into the politicisation and commodification of religious ideas in Australia and the impact this has on modern articulations of faith.

Political and commercial currency of *halal*: the Australian context

In the context of an increasingly globalised market, current systems of food production and distribution have significantly changed the way food is consumed and understood. In relation to *halal*, food and drink is now involved in a set of complex global processes far removed from religious authorities and consumers. In this context, *halal* certification has emerged as a key way for Muslims to ensure Islamic rules surrounding consumption are adhered to in contemporary capitalist societies (Fischer 2011). In Australia, the enhanced visibility of *halal* in the mainstream marketplace has recently resulted in a backlash from anti-Islam groups who have forged boycott campaigns, with varying success, against companies that have their products *halal*-certified (Mann 2014). These groups, activated and strengthened through social media (e.g. Boycott halal in Australia www.facebook.com/BH.Australia), have found a voice in the Australian political system through the recent election of several senators from the right-wing, anti-immigration, anti-Islam 'One Nation' Party. Paying attention to the consumptive practices of middle-class Muslims allows an empirical exploration of how Islamic practices and identities are interpreted, enacted, and reshaped within this specific context. My reading of data collected also offers an insight into how religious difference is defined and interpreted by non-Muslims in Australia by examining intercultural interactions involving food and drink. I discuss themes of belonging, inclusion and exclusion and how these processes are reflected and produced in these encounters with non-Muslims.

Islam, multiculturalism and everyday food-related encounters: an emergent field

The current place of Muslims in Australia is characterised by their emergent, yet uneven, interest from an economic and political perspective. Literature on political processes of multiculturalism can be seen to overlook the everyday lived reality of cultural difference in diverse cities and spaces (Wise & Velayutham 2009). In Australia, there is a growing literature from this perspective exploring interactions involving food (Wise 2011), however the experiences of Muslims and the negotiation of *halal* have been neglected until recently (Voloder 2015). Social scientific work on 'everyday multiculturalism' (Wise 2005, 2011) has begun to examine how Muslims navigate and negotiate the boundaries of *halal* and *haram* in everyday practices of consumption. Internationally, work among Muslims in the United Kingdom (Fischer 2005, 2010, 2011) and Singapore (Nasir & Pereira 2008; Marranci 2012) has offered an insight into the challenges and complexities of the lived experience of cultural diversity and difference in multicultural societies. Given that a politically hostile environment has seen symbols and practices specific to Islam treated with suspicion and scrutiny, exploring the dynamics of inclusion and exclusion through food-related encounters offers a novel way to articulate how belonging is forged through social interaction.

Research methods

A qualitative outlook and method allows the exploration of Muslim subjectivities and their experiences surrounding the consumption of food and drink in different aspects of Australian life. Specifically, in-depth interviews are used as they offer an effective way to explore individuals' interpretations of how specific religious ideas are reflected, translated, and challenged in everyday experiences of consumption. This approach presents an empirical challenge to widely circulating notions that deem Muslims to be bound by a set of religious prescriptions that confine and dominate the autonomy of the individual (Marranci 2004). The chosen methodology can offer specific insight into Göle's (2002: 174) assertion that contemporary Muslims 'blend into modern urban spaces, use global communication networks, engage in public debates, follow consumption patterns, learn market rules' and are active agents in shaping the social landscape in which they operate.

The interview participants, recruited using non-probability sampling methods, were eight individuals living in urban Australia who identified as Muslim. A broad inclusion criterion was used as the sample is designed to reflect the diversity of the Muslim experience in Australia. Like the broader Muslim population in Australia, the sample was heterogeneous with regard to background, ethnicity, and age. Many were born overseas—in localities as diverse as Pakistan, Kenya, Indonesia, and Turkey—before settling in Australia, whilst others had lived in Australia their entire lives. The majority of informants were based in Melbourne and one was based in Brisbane. Two males and six females were interviewed, who ranged in age from 22 to 49. Each informant was of a broadly 'middle-class' background, having attained or in the process of attaining tertiary education or professional employment. Throughout the collection, analysis, and presentation of interview data, the confidentiality of informants has been ensured through the use of pseudonyms.

'Negotiating and juggling' faith-based practices in everyday experiences

This chapter will discuss the way that these informants negotiate Islamic food taboos in broader multicultural Australian society. Particularly of interest are the social dynamics in everyday interactions between Muslims and non-Muslims involving food. Because food is at once so 'everyday, deeply embodied, and yet so symbolic of difference' (Wise 2011: 83), it offers an effective vehicle to how cultural difference is interpreted and negotiated in multicultural settings. Previous literature (Cesaro 2000; Gillette 2005; Nasir & Pereira 2008; Marranci 2012) has discussed how religious difference can become embedded in a range of situations because of Islamic food taboos, and how difference is interpreted and negotiated in the broader context of intergroup social relations. In Australia, despite a broad acceptance and valorisation of multiculturalism and cultural diversity at the societal level, a quarter of Australians hold negative attitudes towards Muslims (Markus 2014). Whilst useful, these statistics tell little about Muslim experiences in everyday intercultural interactions. I offer a qualitative perspective, exploring how middle-class, urban Muslims in Australia experience and interpret different quotidian food-related encounters with the wider non-Muslim population.

Informants' interactions with non-Muslims were reflected upon with an acute awareness of existing in Australia as a small religious minority. Australian society was variously defined as a 'secular environment', a 'Judeo-Christian society', and a 'Christian country'. Therefore, unlike findings from previous literature (Nasir & Pereira 2008; Marranci 2012), informants felt that *halal* food and other requirements attaining to Islamic practice were not something that could be taken-for-granted—nor expected—in every situation:

> It's always a juggling [process] … you know when you live in a society that isn't Muslim—and that's OK—you're always have to be negotiating and juggling and that's just the reality of living here. (Rachel)

Despite this, it was rare that informants felt that consuming *halal* (according to their religious subjectivities) was difficult. In fact, it was common for informants to outline convivial encounters with broader, non-Muslim society where their dietary needs were especially accounted for. This 'interactive culinary multiculturalism, based on the interaction between different cultural subjects' (Hage 1997: 114) is strikingly clear in the data. Therefore, I pay specific attention to the power relations and social dynamics present in these encounters and the various ways informants interpret, negotiate, and challenge them. Focusing on a range of quotidian, food-related experiences and their various interpretations offer an insight into the multilayered, multi-directional dynamics of inclusion and exclusion experienced by Muslims in Australia.

Constructions of conviviality and recognition in everyday interactivity

The degree to which the provision of *halal* was interpreted as 'respect', 'acceptance', or 'recognition' was dependent on the social distance between informants and the other in the encounter. Informants spoke of social situations where non-Muslim friends or family went to a particular effort to provide *halal* food for them. Rachel saw this as reflecting the mutual respect and acceptance of difference in her relations with others:

> It's uncanny how often our non-Muslim friends will have [our family] over and either they'll make vegetarian or they'll specifically go to the *halal* butcher on Sydney Rd or something. We're like 'you don't have to', [and they say] 'no, no, we want to' ... It's so lovely when people make the effort.

Mahnoor, whose friendship circle revolves around people from her 'really multicultural high school' where 'everyone was ridiculously accepting of each other' relayed similar stories. It was not uncommon for Mahnoor to be hosted by close friends who are 'like Asian ... Vietnamese, Cambodian ... and they use pork and that sort of stuff in their food', to have them cater for her needs. Once again, this was seen as 'a really amazing gesture of respect'.

These narratives, repeated across the spectrum of the sample, can be interpreted as acts of 'everyday recognition' (Wise 2011: 100). Whilst Taylor (1994) and Modood (2007) have promoted recognition of difference at a political level, these everyday encounters show how respect and inclusion are generated in practice through everyday interactions in multicultural settings. The acts of commensality outlined above show the ways in which difference is recognised and respected 'on the ground' in everyday situations, fostering positive relationships across religious and cultural boundaries.

However, the 'everyday' recognition generated in these convivial, inclusive encounters with non-Muslims was not perceived as one-directional. Rather, these experiences were interpreted as reflecting the 'mutual respect' and shared acceptance of different beliefs among those in the encounter. Mehmet saw social inclusion and cohesion as a multi-directional process whereby different beliefs and practices were recognised and respected. He saw this as reflecting a broader culture of respecting difference in Australia:

> If I invite you as my neighbour to a barbeque ... and I just have meat [that] is sourced from a halal butcher and I don't have any beer. But I've got say, Red Bull or something. Are you going to really care? You're going to say, 'Hey! I'm getting great food'. You know, there's different salads, different varieties of other food on the table. 'Who [are] [you] to complain? What do [you] care if there's not a pork sausage, so what if [you] don't have a beer?'

> You invite me over and you say, 'look, I couldn't source halal, but there is other stuff I will provide you', an alternative, at least you'll have something to eat, so you won't go hungry. Because that's what friends [and] neighbours do. You invited me, you hosted me, I invited you, I hosted you ... that's what builds trust, it builds relationships ... this is what enhances our society.

Mehmet's proverbial barbeque and his notion of fostering social cohesion through mutual respect in intercultural interaction contrasts with Marranci's (2012) and Nasir and Pereira's (2008) findings, where adherence to Islamic food taboos was actively adopted as a marker of group identity used to reinforce boundaries between Muslims and non-Muslims. In comparison, informants embraced a paradigm of personalised, privatised religious belief that was then negotiated within the broader multicultural milieu. Mahnoor sums this multi-directional process of social inclusion in her assertion that 'I would never impose my lifestyle on anyone else and I would hope no one would impose theirs on mine', using examples of 'homely' experiences of eating and socialising with friends to support this.

Tensions and ambivalence in culinary intercultural encounters

The encounters my informants spoke of reveal the dynamic ways that middle-class, urban Muslims in Australia articulate and negotiate their religious identity and practices in everyday interactions with non-Muslims. Ahmad, who migrated from Indonesia several years ago, maintains a pragmatic approach to *halal*. This approach allows him to participate in different aspects of social life in Australia, fostering relationships in a range of contexts:

> Once I joined friends from China, from Australia, they [drank] beer, I just [had] my coffee and we just [had] a chat … and I [smelt] the alcohol, OK, this is their thing and I did my thing. And we [had] no problem[s]. We just [had] a chat. It's not really a problem for me. Keeping the relationship, building up the friendship … for me that was more important.

Ahmad's narrative of balancing piety with conviviality in intercultural encounters suggests an unproblematic lived reality between non-Muslims and Muslims in Australia. However, despite treating adherence to *halal* requirements with pragmatism and flexibility, it is important to reflect on the tensions and ambiguities present in these encounters. Many informants registered a sense of discomfort surrounding the regular presence of alcohol in Australian social life:

> We've got a friend in a band and [if] they're playing in a pub, I feel very uncomfortable going in there, even if I'm not drinking, I feel really uneasy about going into a pub. I have though, in situations to support a friend, but I don't like it. I judge it on a case-by-case basis … how important to the friend is it that I'm there? If they won't care then it doesn't matter. Can I get out of this without causing offence? If it's really going to upset or offend someone then I try. (Rachel)

Rachel's rhetorical questions reveal the way that middle-class Muslims negotiate belonging and engagement in Australian life by balancing their beliefs and broader social identities. It does not suffice to simply say that Rachel will avoid particular spaces or situations because of her religious beliefs. Her shifting views on alcohol in different social contexts reveal the contextual and conditional nature of religious practice:

> [Alcohol] is a difficult one for me because I've got non-Muslim family and there's this tension between, they can legitimately say 'look, we're trying to accommodate you as much as we can, we go and buy halal meat for you. I'm not going to not have a glass of wine at lunch because you don't, I'm not asking you to drink it'. So in that situation I will at times, if I feel it is necessary, sit at a table with alcohol even though I would prefer not to. In the interests of trying to accommodate [others], for the greater good I guess.

These narratives show how eating and drinking can see religious difference becoming embedded in a range of social situations, and how intercultural encounters can become sites of risk, ambivalence, and anxiety. As Rachel's interpretations suggest, the level of discomfort felt in social encounters involving *haram* substances is dependent on the intersubjective meanings generated within the encounter. The everyday exchanges involving food and drink outlined by informants can be characterised as a 'moral-economy of place-sharing' with the 'people, objects and social relations' within them 'made and remade, understood and reunderstood' through social interaction (Wise 2011: 98).

Although Mehmet's confident assertion that 'living in Australia as a Muslim I couldn't cite one example where I felt excluded' speaks of an unproblematic lived reality between non-Muslims and Muslims, this is not always the case. Hage (1997) notes that a facile reading of intercultural encounters can overlook their complexity and the ways they reflect and reproduce intergroup power dynamics. In fact, several informants interpreted the growth of *halal*-certified items in mainstream retailers as a self-interested act to reap greater profits from Muslim consumers. Similarly, in everyday encounters with non-Muslims, recognition was interpreted differently according to the social distance and relations of power between individuals. For example, it was common for informants to outline experiences of having *halal* food provided for them in different institutional settings, including places of education, hospitals, schools, and workplaces. Hasina works in a professional capacity and recalled a business trip where she was hosted by a large external firm:

> I did the presentation and the lunch was served and they actually went and got halal [food] … and that was 'on them' [they paid for it]. And I thought, 'that was not necessary, but thank you'. You know, I'm a 'big girl' and I can adapt to situations.

This reveals how intercultural encounters are interpreted differently according to who is doing the consuming, in what kind of social setting, and with whom. In Hasina's anecdote, her identity as a Muslim was foregrounded as the corporate hosts made a visible effort to provide exclusively *halal* food. Her comments that she is a 'big girl' and 'can adapt to situations' captures the way in which the recognition of difference was interpreted with ambivalence, rather than simply a sign of mutual respect and conviviality. Similarly, Ahmad relayed a story of walking into a Chinese restaurant with his wife:

> The Chinese [shopkeeper was] surprised, they look[ed] at my wife wearing the hijab [and said] 'hello, do you know that this food is not halal?' And we were surprised, we [didn't] really care, if we could find chicken or beef [on the menu], that's fine for us!

Here, Ahmed's wife's visibility as a Muslim made the shopkeeper assume that they were not permitted to eat at the restaurant because of their religion. These encounters reveal the ways that attempts at showing respect and conviviality can instead be interpreted as exaggerated and abstracted from the daily lives of middle-class Muslims in Australia. Similarly, Aisha recalls being involved as a student representative in her first years in Australia and attending catered institutional board meetings:

> I remember that they had made an effort of having one plate that was all halal meat and it was labeled for me specifically [laughs]. But I remember the CEO of [the education institute] at the time was very upset that I had been excluded because of dietary requirements, and he basically asked the catering company that as long as

I was on the board ... every food that was served in each meeting would be halal. And I think that, for me, was the most significant gesture of welcoming me into that little group.

Although the CEO's provision of *halal* was in the best interests of Aisha and interpreted as 'a significant gesture of welcoming', it also signalled him as culturally sensitive and accepting of diversity, reasserting his position within the context of managing an international education institute. Aisha's narrative reflects Hage's (1997: 116–117) assertion that 'intercultural culinary interactivity' can be mutually experienced as 'homely' by both sides in the encounter. These experiences and their various interpretations show how multiculturalism can be both inhabited and appropriated as a form of cultural capital in everyday interactions between Muslims and non-Muslims involving food and drink.

Responses to challenges and hostility in everyday practices

Previous literature on Muslim dining practices (Marranci 2012; Nasir & Pereira 2008) overlooks individuals' agency to actively reflect on and challenge assumptions surrounding Muslims and Islamic religious practices through their everyday actions. My data registered that different ideas and discourses surrounding *halal* were actively reflected and translated through critical engagement and resistance in the mainstream market. Similarly, interactions with non-Muslims are also sites where informants act with agency to challenge both ignorance and negative assumptions of their religious practices and identities. Several informants saw common misconceptions that circulate about Islam and *halal* as a way to educate and inform others, actively building and strengthening understandings of both themselves and their religion. Aisha affirms that 'not a lot of people are very clear on [*halal*] and not a lot of people really think about it unless they have to'. Despite this, she challenges this perceived ignorance by actively developing the understandings of those around her:

My relationship with my non-Muslim colleagues and friends is that they've always been welcome to ask any questions, so over the years they've kept asking questions and I've been answering them and now some of them that have known me for a bit have a better understanding.

This method of engagement is shared by Hasina, who is always keen to 'deconstruct the hype' surrounding Islam and Muslims that she sees stemming from sustained negative media attention and widely circulating stereotypes. Mahnoor regularly experienced non-Muslims exhibiting curiosity towards Muslims and *halal* rather than unshakeable ignorance:

A lot of people are more so curious. If they don't know they'll ask to be informed, and I love that. Because then they know what [*halal*] is. So I'm always happy to answer questions for people if they're curious about it.

Informants' narratives of agency in everyday interactions with non-Muslims support Yasmeen's (2010) assertion that the processes of inclusion and exclusion are not one-directional and one-layered. Rather, they are marked by a sense of dynamism that plays out differently in different contexts. The diversity of meaning that is generated in intercultural interactions reveals the complexities present as social actors experience and negotiate cultural difference in a multicultural society, summed up by Wise (2011: 85) who notes:

In each setting—the spaces of consumption, the social rituals involved, the actual food consumed and the prevailing political and cultural 'winds'—all mediate how, and in what way, food matters in intercultural settings, and whether, and to what extent identities are traversed, ascribed, reinscribed or reworked.

Similarly, the data in this chapter suggest that social actors—both Muslim and non-Muslim—reflect on, translate, and challenge widely circulating ideas surrounding Muslims and Islamic religious practice through everyday practices of conviviality and commensality, generating new processes of belonging and social inclusion.

Despite the wide range of experiences given above outlining commensality and conviviality in everyday intercultural interactions, it must be noted that all but one informant noted the current political and media environment as imbued with hostility towards Muslims. Especially noted was the current furore over *halal* certification, variously described as constituting 'bigotry', 'hysteria', a 'moral panic', and 'idiotic boycott campaigns'. Despite the intensity with which this was felt, it was rare for informants to experience hostility in everyday encounters with non-Muslims involving food. Yasemin described it as 'frustrating' and 'upsetting', yet it was 'probably the least of [her] worries' living as a Muslim in Australia:

> If I were to look at all the issues affecting Muslims, it would certainly not be something that I'm passionate about, or that I would want to lobby for. I mean, I think I feel passionate about the hysteria associated with it today and the fact that you can go to [a major] shopping centre and in the [chain supermarket] they [will] have a huge sign that says 'kosher items' … you know if you were to go to a shopping centre that had a huge sign saying 'halal items', people would be taking to the streets. That aspect of it frustrates me and upsets me.

The degree in which Muslims were the focus of negative scrutiny in media and political discourse was inconsistent with both the broad societal acceptance of diversity in Australia and informants' everyday interactions with others. Apart from the occasional 'funny look' or experience of anti-Muslim sentiment online, only Aisha outlined an occasion where she had experienced hostility in relation to *halal* food:

> A couple of months ago I came home and in my mailbox I found pamphlets [that] were basically propaganda about halal and halal supporting Muslim terrorism and that kind of stuff. And the way that impacted me was it made me feel very unsafe in my home … because it's one thing to watch this stuff play out on the television and on the news [but] to find those pamphlets had been distributed in my mailbox and the mailboxes of my neighbours, it was too 'real' and it was very traumatic almost.

Despite this hostility, Aisha's response reveals how Muslims in Australia use methods of civic participation to resist widely circulating ideas and assumptions about Muslims and Islamic religious practices:

> I [wrote] to the Minister for Women Affairs [and the Minister for] Multicultural Affairs of my state, to express that, for a group to be openly targeting another group within the community … [it] is not OK.

Additionally, she has seen the incident and the generally hostile political environment as a way to 'have greater discussions' with non-Muslim colleagues and friends, educating and informing people about 'what *halal* is' and life as a Muslim more generally. These examples reveal the ways in which Muslims in Australia act with social and political agency to critique and resist negative assumptions towards Muslims, 'building new and more open social relations' (Jakubowicz 2007: 279) with wider Australian society in their everyday lives.

Joppke (2002: 252) has noted that despite a 'retreat of multiculturalism' from public policy in many culturally heterogeneous societies, 'implicit multiculturalism'—or the broad acceptance and valorisation of cultural difference at the societal level—is pervasive. The encounters surveyed and analysed in this chapter support this assertion by exploring how cultural difference is experienced and negotiated 'on the ground' in everyday encounters. This inclusivity is not one-directional and relies on mutual acceptance and recognition of difference. Additionally, belonging in Australian society is forged by middle-class Muslims through active engagement in acts of resistance and negotiation in everyday interactions with non-Muslims involving food and drink.

Exploring quotidian, intercultural encounters of commensality has allowed me to look beyond simplistic, uni-directional notions of 'exclusion' and 'discrimination' used to understand the experience of Muslims in Australia in a generally hostile social context (Poynting & Mason 2007). By actively and critically engaging in culinary intercultural encounters, middle-class Muslims reflect, translate, and challenge widely circulating ideas, discourses, and assumptions surrounding Muslims and Islamic religious practices in Australia.

References

Cesaro, M. (2000) 'Consuming identities: Food and resistance among the Uyghur in contemporary Xinjiang', *Inner Asia*, 2 (2): 225–238.

Fischer, J. (2005) 'Feeding secularism: Consuming halal among the Malays in London', *Diaspora: A Journal of Transnational Studies*, 14(2): 275–297.

Fischer, J. (2010) 'Halal sanitised: Health and science in a globalised religious market', *Tidsskrift for Islamforskning*, 4 (1): 24–47.

Fischer, J. (2011) *The Halal Frontier: Muslim Consumers in a Globalized Market*. New York: Palgrave Macmillan.

Fischler, C. (1988) 'Food, self and identity', *Social Science Information*, 27 (2): 275–292.

Gillette, M. (2005) 'Children's food and Islamic dietary restrictions in Xi'an'. In J. Watson and M. Caldwell (eds) *The Cultural Politics of Food and Eating: A Reader*. Malden: Blackwell, 106–121.

Göle, N. (2002) 'Islam in public: New visibilities and new imaginaries', *Public Culture*, 14 (1): 173–190.

Hage, G. (1997) 'At home in the entrails of the West: Multiculturalism, "ethnic food" and migrant home-building'. In L. Johnson, J. Langsworth and M. Symonds (eds) *Home/World: Space, Community and Marginality in Sydney's West*. Annandale: Pluto Press, 99–153.

Jakubowicz, A. (2007) 'Political Islam and the future of Australian multiculturalism', *National Identities*, 9 (3): 265–280.

Joppke, C. (2002) 'Multicultural citizenship'. In E. Isin and B. Turner (eds) *Handbook of Citizenship Studies*. London: Sage, 245–258.

Mann, A. (2014) 'Campaign to boycott *Halal* food gains momentum in Australia after yoghurt company ditches certification', *ABC News*, 21 November. [online] Available at: www.abc.net.au/news/2014-11-20/campaign-to-boycott-*halal*-food-gains-momentum-in-australia/5907844 (accessed 10 October 2017).

Markus, A. (2014) *Mapping Social Cohesion: The Scanlon Foundation Surveys*. Victoria: Monash University.

Marranci, G. (2004) 'Multiculturalism, Islam and the clash of civilisations theory: Rethinking Islamophobia', *Culture and Religion*, 5 (1): 105–117.

Marranci, G. (2012) 'Defensive or offensive dining? *Halal* dining practices among Malay Muslim Singaporeans and their effects on integration', *Australian Journal of Anthropology*, 23 (1): 84–100.

Mintz, S. and Du Bois, C. (2002) 'The anthropology of food and eating', *Annual Review of Anthropology*, 31 (1): 99–119.

Modood, T. (2007) *Multiculturalism: A Civic Idea*. Cambridge: Polity Press.

Nasir, K. and Pereira, A. (2008) 'Defensive dining: Notes on the public dining experiences in Singapore', *Contemporary Islam*, 2 (1): 61–73.

Poynting, S. and Mason, V. (2007) 'The resistible rise of Islamophobia: Anti-Muslim racism in the UK and Australia before 11 September 2001', *Journal of Sociology*, 43 (1): 61–86.

Taylor, C. (1994) *Multiculturalism: Examining the Politics of Recognition*. Princeton, NJ: Princeton University Press.

Voloder, L. (2015) 'The "mainstreaming" of halal: Muslim consumer-citizenship in Australia', *Journal of Muslim Minority Affairs*, 35 (2): 230–244.

Wise, A. (2005) 'Hope and belonging in a multicultural suburb', *Journal of Intercultural Studies*, 26 (1–2): 171–186.

Wise, A. (2011) 'Moving food: Gustatory commensality and disjuncture in everyday multiculturalism', *New Formations*, 74 (1): 82–107.

Wise, A. & Velayutham, S. (2009) *Everyday Multiculturalism*. Basingstoke: Palgrave Macmillan.

Yasmeen, S. (ed.) (2010) *Muslims in Australia: The Dynamics of Exclusion and Inclusion*. Carlton: Melbourne University Press.

24

HALAL CERTIFICATION UPROAR

The Muslim scapegoat as national safety valve

Ben Debney

Introduction

Halal food certification is a service provided by Islamic religious authorities to food manufacturers to certify that their processes and products meet the dietary and customary standards required by observant Muslims. Such processes consist of measures to guard against the presence of pork residues in manufacturing equipment, and the use of alcohol in cleaning processes—things considered 'haram' or forbidden. By its own testimony, the Australian Food and Industry Council considers third-party certification of this kind 'very common,' and groups halal food certification in with kosher food certification and the National Heart Foundation's 'Tick' logo (Australian Food and Grocery Council n.d.).

As a typical form of food certification, the halal variety also has comparable economic benefits, not least of which is its potential to open doors for local Australian foodstuff manufacturers to major export markets in predominantly Islamic countries, an industry the Australian Department of Agriculture valued at AUD$31.8 billion in 2012–2013 (Australian Government, Department of Agriculture 2014). The world's most populous Muslim nation, Indonesia, is not only one of Australia's regional neighbours but also the third largest destination for Australian food exports. In 2012–2013, their combined value was AUD$2.4 billion (Australian Food and Grocery Council n.d.). Of this, live animals and wheat, traditional Australian exports, were AUD$302 million and AUD$1.2 billion respectively. The value of manufactured foodstuffs was around AUD$900 million, coming second only to wheat (Australian Food and Grocery Council n.d.). The value of the export market for Australian manufactured foodstuffs is considerable; where Muslim countries such as Indonesia are concerned, halal food certification plays a vital part (Benns 2015).

Other issues associated with traditional Australian exports further highlight the importance and potential value of halal food certification. The live export trade, for example, continues despite protracted negative publicity due to its endemic animal cruelty; critics have cited the halal slaughter of sheep and cattle as a viable alternative. The replacement of the live-export trade with halal-certified meat exports represents a potential AUD$1.5 billion addition to the

Australian GDP—40,000 jobs in the meat industry alone (Animals Australia 2015). Meriting additional consideration is the fact that this figure only refers to one country, Indonesia. Total exports to all Muslim nations including the United Arab Emirates, Saudi Arabia, and Malaysia currently represent 16 per cent of total Australian food exports, or about AUD$5 billion. Proportionate increases in exports to these countries based on expansion of halal-certified meat exports suggest a potential overall increase in the total volume of Australian goods exports of at least AUD$1.49 billion (Australian Food and Grocery Council n.d.). Again this is only the figure for the meat industry; the total export figure of all halal-certified foods is potentially higher again.

The potential economic benefits to Australian industry from a more culturally sensitive engagement with Asia notwithstanding, halal food certification has come to be seen by some as evidence of subversion of 'the Australian way of life' at the hands of a permissive political correctness imposed on public discourse by willing dupes of creeping Sharia law, or extremist proponents of terrorism, or both. In one notable example, the Fleurieu Milk and Yoghurt Company was temporarily forced to drop a contract worth $50,000 to supply Emirates Airlines following aggressive social media campaigning (ABC News 2014, 2015). Within these discriminatory and increasingly extreme narratives, the 'Australian way of life' is necessarily defined in binary terms that exclude Islam as such, and racialise both in doing so, while those who invoke them insist unconvincingly that they are not racist. This chapter will examine such notions within the context of widening social inequality within Australian society and examine the extent to which scare mongering over halal certification plays in making scapegoats of Muslims in that context in particular.

Halal controversy

Opposition to halal food certification tends mostly to come in the form of various claims regarding the 'Islamification' of Australian society and the funding of terrorism. A good representative of such views is the website, *Halal Choices*, created and maintained by Kirralie Smith, a Pentecostal Christian whose prior claims to absolute truth deny the need for anything in the way of supporting evidence, and whose extremism draws on the most hateful aspects of the same kind of fundamentalist single-mindedness she claims to oppose in Islam. Like many who share her beliefs, Smith's approach is the logical equivalent of trying to establish the pretence that the Westboro Baptist Church are representative of all Christians:

> A woman's testimony is worth half of a man's. You need four male witnesses to prove rape. Underage children can be married. A non-Muslim's testimony is not equal to a Muslims. You can't criticise Islam, the Qur'an or Mohammed … Reports of young couples being maimed tortured and even slaughtered because they were together in the same house without a chaperone. Child brides. Beheaded journalists. 2000 massacred.
>
> *(Smith 2015)*

Commentary of this kind furthermore tends to promote the idea that massacres, beheadings, child brides, maiming, torturing and beheading, reactionary values, misogyny, and child abuse are unique to Islam. Mountains of evidence to the contrary notwithstanding (see for example, Cohn 1993; Ellerbe 1995), Halal Choices attempts to imitate the consumer portal *Choice* by purporting to provide the public with impartial information relating to food products bearing halal certification, while lacking anything of the latter's objectivity. Noting correctly that 'Halal simply means permitted or lawful' (Halal Choices 2011a), Halal Choices also claims incorrectly that Halal certification 'must comply with the religious ritual and observance of Sharia law' and that it is based on 'ritual sacrifice' (Halal Choices 2011a).

While the source of this notion of ritual sacrifice remains a mystery, the emotive language used conjures images of the Temple of Doom featured in the *Indiana Jones* movie franchise. Similar ideas appear via its claim that, 'all of the halal certification organisations are operating under sharia law and desire for sharia law to be accepted as a part of our mainstream society,' and that 'Money that is paid out in fees for halal certification is used to fund in part or whole the push for Sharia Law in Australia' (Halal Choices 2011b).

This latter claim is unique to the extent that Halal Choices does make an attempt to evidence it, which they do by quoting Siddiq Buckley, the secretary of the Australian Islamic Mission in Sydney:

> There are practical examples of [Sharia] here already. We have Muslim schools, mosques, funeral parlours, shops and businesses. We've got abattoirs, Islamic charities, Islamic financial institutions. There are so many things—halal meals served on airlines. This is all part of Sharia.
>
> *(Halal Choices 2011b)*

Halal Choices presents this quote as self-evident vindication, though it can just as easily be taken to mean that Islamic religious practice is evident in the variety of forms to which Buckley refers. More significantly, it can be taken as pointing out that Sharia is already present in Australian society, without any of the anticipated heinous consequences. Either way, the narrative from Halal Choices suggests that existence of Islamic communities of necessity signifies an expansionist plot, without any supporting evidence beyond the desire and will to believe. The fact that this quote is the only evidence Halal Choices bothers to present in support of its claims, coupled with the fact that it does so in such a way as to rely on the willingness of the audience to make connections that don't exist, reflects much about its attitude to facts.

Similar attitudes appear in a blog post from North Queensland Tory MP George Christensen entitled *Terror in the Tucker Box* (Hussein 2014). In this post, Christensen asks, 'Are groceries in Australian trolleys funding a push for Sharia law, supporting jihad groups or even backing terrorist activity?' (Christensen 2014), again without making any attempt to provide supporting evidence to demonstrate that his fears are grounded and that there is a tangible difference between them and scaremongering or panicked overreacting, claims that 'consumers are totally justified in calling for more information on halal certification because we need to know where the money's going' (Christensen 2014). In this instance the circular logic presumes guilt, needing to know where the money is going being a natural corollary of the reversal of the burden of proof, and thus suspicion on the basis of nothing other than sheer prejudice provides all the probable cause required for prior justification of the need for a campaign of scapegoating as a matter of definition (Kawakami, Dion & Dovidio 1998).

Christensen's own lack of respect for basic standards of evidence notwithstanding, he weighs in against 'the politically correct commentariat' who 'have gone into full outrage mode over their concerns, sneering at those worried about halal certification as unintelligent and racist'— though Christensen's own sneering at the 'politically correct commentariat' for their audacity in describing him as unintelligent and racist goes without comment, a fact that belies his playing the victim (see Bandura 1999). The circular logic upon which Christensen's attacks on the 'halal bandwagon' depend becomes even more obvious in a complaint about the purported propensity of the media to 'point to a bumper sticker displayed by some anti-halal activists—"Halal food funds terrorism"—as proof in itself that the anti-halal movement are extremists and not worthy of being taken seriously.' The rejoinder Christensen offers adds nothing new whatsoever to the debate. 'But, seriously,' he says, 'who knows where the money from halal certification is going?' (Christensen 2014).

South Australian Senator Cory Bernardi is another leader of the campaign against halal certification, having described it incorrectly on his own website as a 'religious tax' (Bernardi 2015). Bernardi, whose views on Muslims and Islam are so unpalatable even for conservatives that former Prime Minister Tony Abbott felt the need to distance himself from them, complains via his website that 'it's fair to say that there is a lack of clarity about where the facts end and the fiction begins in relation to halal certification' (Bernardi 2015). In and of itself, this comment is true enough— though Bernardi reveals himself to be the primary reason for that, proceeding directly to demonstrate why by systematically misrepresenting the nature of halal certification, claiming in the first place that 'halal certification schemes have been used to fund organisations linked to proscribed extremist organisations' (Bernardi 2015). In the second, Bernardi (2015) claims that 'we also know it has operated effectively as a religious tariff in order for Australian products to gain entry into certain markets.' In the third, he claims that products certified halal have been 'subject to ritual slaughter' (Bernardi 2015). All of these claims appear in one blog post, which perhaps unsurprisingly links back to Halal Choices. This is the sum total of attempts by Bernardi to substantiate his claims with anything approaching empirical evidence; as in the case of George Christensen, they are presented as self-evidently true on the basis of a prior assumption of superior insight— so superior that it need not be demonstrated. In any event it demonstrably is not, as Bernardi's own Senate inquiry later determined (Parliament of Australia 2015). This does not stop him from continuing to publish his disproven claims on his website, which features the slogan 'common sense lives here' in large red letters.

In contrast to Cory Bernardi's highly politicised interpretation of common sense, Andrew Bolt briefly sounds almost objective. 'Some of the attacks on halal certification are ugly,' (Bolt 2015) the Murdoch columnist concedes. 'No, there is no evidence this is cash for terrorism … No, a halal sticker on a bottle of no-alcohol beer is not the start of sharia law,' (Bolt 2015) he admits. 'And,' he notes finally, 'Muslims have every right to know which foods are prepared in accordance with their faith, just as Jews are entitled to know which foods are kosher' (Bolt 2015). As it turns out, Bolt's comparison of the Islamophobic targeting of halal certification and the anti-Semitic targeting of kosher methods of animal slaughter has more than a passing relevance. Julius Streicher, editor of the Nazi tabloid *Der Stürmer*, devoted the entire May 1934 issue to the subject in an attempt to establish a link between kosher methods of animal slaughter and purported Jewish habits of ritual murder (Judd 2007; Sax 2000). He accused German Jews of using ritual murder of Christians as a means of securing their blood for use in their own religious rituals under a headline reading, 'Jewish Murder Plan against Gentile Humanity Revealed' (Bytwerk 1998; Judd 2007). Bizarrely however, Bolt backtracks despite having just made this link, as if he was only doing so to try to establish the pretence of having a handle on both sides of the debate; repudiating everything he has just said, Bolt (2015) asserts in the face of patent evidence to the contrary that he himself has just established that 'the profit-taking and the secrecy over the funds raised are unacceptable' (Bolt 2015)— because scaremongering in the present over halal certification is comparable to historical scaremongering over kosher certification.

Its logical shortcomings notwithstanding, Cory Bernardi was able in 2015 to establish on the basis of the above trains of thought a Senate inquiry into third-party certification of foodstuffs, which as the ABC noted 'unleashed a torrent of hate' (ABC News 2014) in the form of 220 submissions containing what they describe as 'vicious attacks on Muslims and the Islamic faith' (Gartrell 2015). This inquiry concluded (Parliament of Australia 2015), having found 'insufficient evidence' that halal certification drives up food prices, that there is no imposition of religion on consumers because halal certification involves no religious rituals, and confirmation via the Australian Crime Commission of 'no direct link between halal certification in Australia and the funding of terrorism' (Brull 2015). As Charlie Pickering put it on *The Weekly*, 'the people who you pay to tell you if something is a terrorism, say this is not a terrorism' (cited in Chalmers 2015). *New Matilda* summarises this episode as the 'Little Halal Truther Campaign That Couldn't' (Brull 2015).

The national safety valve

Historian Frank Van Nuys describes institutionalised racism of the kind that became the impetus for the Bernardi-led 2015 Senate inquiry as a 'national safety valve'—one that has functioned historically to neutralise class antagonisms within capitalism (Van Nuys 2002). As Van Nuys (2002) points out, the utility of the 'national safety valve' derived in the main from its potential as a means of shifting the blame for the tensions produced by such things as increasing wealth inequality, and the ability of moneyed cliques to dominate the political process and turn it ever more to the service of their own vested interests, onto minorities too numerically weak to organise effective opposition.

The dynamics of the national safety valve are visible throughout Australian history, especially in terms of what Roediger (1991) refers to as 'the wages of whiteness.' This phenomenon references a comment by famed black abolitionist W.E.B. Du Bois regarding a 'public and psychological wage' paid to white majorities amongst subject classes (Roediger 1991). Such privileging of dominant ethnicities offset resistance to class rule through the age-old social engineering strategy of divide and conquer, favouring white workers ahead of their nonwhite counterparts with token privileges to encourage loyalty to class-based social hierarchy. As a means of shifting the blame for the injustices associated with the European colonisation of Australia, it was in the interests of the colonists to assume along with Daisy Bates that their fundamental role was to 'smooth the pillow of a dying race.'

In this respect, the racism that manifest as benevolent paternalism greased the wheels of land theft and genocide by enabling the racist myth that the inhabitants were racially inferior heathens and savages who needed saving from themselves and 'civilising'; white supremacy enabled the white invaders to morally disengage from their historical crime and reconstruct their theft of the land as a moral action carried out in the best interests of its victims. To this way of thinking, it was the fault of the original inhabitants for not having taken the land as property and cultivated it that entitled Europeans to apply their morality selectively (Davies, Nandy & Sardar 1993; Deckard 2009). Bringing civilisation to the Australian continent meant killing and enslaving the Indigenous inhabitants, usurping their sovereignty, destroying their culture and civilisation, stealing the land, and inventing a racist ideology to justify it by way of blaming the victims after the fact (Connor 2002; Pascoe 2014).

Historically speaking, however, appeals to whiteness through racism and xenophobia had not always been the foremost means of guaranteeing the stability of the class order. In the United States in the first half of the nineteenth century, westward expansion into frontier territory was represented as (and did indeed represent) a far more attractive proposition to many European settlers than protracted labour disputes in the East. As long as workers subject to the autocratic hierarchies inherent to capitalist relations of production still had other options and could retain their economic independence, the steam could be taken out of class conflict. As long as land was available this arrangement worked well enough, but westward expansion was ultimately finite. As the availability of frontier territory fell into decline towards the end of the nineteenth century, so too did its capacity to function as the 'national safety valve,' and a marked increase in labour struggles resulted (Van Nuys 2002; Brecher 2014).

The switch to racism was, in that sense, inevitable. If subject populations of black people, collectively subject historically to crimes against humanity such as the institution of chattel slavery, were poor, according to this mentality, it was because they were lazy and stupid. In such notions was a 'public and psychological wage' for every white worker, permitted credulity, negativity, hatefulness, slavishness, sanctimoniousness, and cruelty in the name of a pious moralistic vanity (Harris 1993). Similarly, in the case of what might be termed 'the wages of patriarchy,' and just as the minority of the opulent could pay a 'public and psychological wage' to the white working class, so too could they pay another to the male working class, regardless of ethnicity, thereby dividing it along the gender line as well as the colour one. The 'wages of patriarchy' paid to male workers in the idea that women were subordinate to men, served just as well as those of 'whiteness' to encourage an abusive relationship of emotional and psychological codependency and capture bonding within a system of class domination and exploitation.

Either form of 'public and psychological wage' or both in combination were often effective in neutralising constructive responses to class antagonism that, channelled into labour organising and social struggle, could have produced meaningful change. In this way did payment of the 'wages of privilege' provide a strategy for the political establishment to avoid accountability for its leading role in creating and exacerbating wealth inequality and all that encompassed in terms of social misery. By creating scapegoats out of the greatest victims and privileging various groups within the subject classes along multiple fault lines of gender, ethnicity, sexuality, and ability, amongst others, political classes ruling in the name of defending the minority of the opulent could, in the words of Cheryl Harris (1993: 1742), utilise the great national safety value in 'evading rather than confronting class exploitation.' It could provide a safe outlet for passions that otherwise threatened to undermine the stability of the class-based system and motivate slaves both owned and rented to revolt against their masters, while encouraging them to identify with them on the basis of superficial character-istics rather than their fellow workers on the basis of concrete material interests (Marx 1849).

Viewed from this perspective, the enduring value to societies riven by class tensions of an entire spectrum of prejudices that would eventually also come to take aim at Islam and halal food preparation is more apparent. The bribes for the white working class in the form of token privileges from the white ruling class are not and can never be enough to constitute their emancipation from the alienating character of a society divided into classes of haves and have-nots. Nevertheless, issues such as the continuing gap in living standards and life expectancy between Indigenous and European Australians can be explained away as personal shortcomings rather than the products of the historical legacy of dispossession, genocide, and oppression which also accounts in the intersection of privileges and oppressions for their own misery, alienation, and oppression— another example of blame-shifting that feeds into the collective vanity of Anglo-capitalism.

The national safety valve and authoritarian psychology

The willingness of the white working class to perpetuate the basic assumptions on which European settler colonialism was founded and is perpetrated, even when it meant colluding in their own exploitation and helping those responsible 'evade rather than confront class exploitation' is a question that has fascinated social psychologists for decades. In trying to come to terms with the dynamic of the 'national safety valve,' they have sought to understand not only what motivates some individuals to construct authoritarian systems, but what also motivates others to support them. In trying to develop a response to this question, Wilhelm Reich, a former student of Freud's in Germany and a practising psychoanalyst in Austria, prepared a number of treatments of the subject, most notable amongst which was *The Mass Psychology of Fascism* (Reich 1970).

Something of a mechanist, Reich (1970) argued that moralistic repression of all the personal drives towards individual assertion and self-fulfilment, be they physical or existential, diverted such energies instead into service of the totalitarian state. For the loyal subject of the Nazi state, Reich (1970) declared, the stereotype of the Jew provided a suitable scapegoat for its destruction of their individuality, and war a suitable outlet for otherwise frustrated energies (ideas adroitly conceptualised in the song *Wargasm* by US rock band L7). With these aspects of Nazi social engineering taken care of and the bread and circuses arranged to keep the peasants from revolting, Hitler was able to bring the entire nation of Germany behind a militaristic project that resulted comprehensively in its destruction.

More relevant today than the more mechanistic of Reich's theories was his observation that the dynamics driving the Nazi war machine were anything but limited to Germany in the 1930s. They were, on the contrary, he argued, a dangerously acute example of psychological and emotional tendencies far more pervasive in individual human subjectivity. 'Fascism', Reich (1970: ix) wrote,

> is the only politically organized expression of the average human character structure … In this characteristic sense, 'fascism' is the basic emotional attitude of man in authoritarian society, with its machine civilization and its mechanistic-mystical view of life.

There was, in other words, a little bit of Hitler in all of us— various attempts to portray the Nazi leader as somehow something other than human, as opposed to someone who was in reality all too human, notwithstanding.

Another German, Erich Fromm, reached similar conclusions. A student of Jung, Fromm (2001) took a far less mechanistic approach to studying authoritarian psychology. He argued in books such as *The Fear of Freedom* (2001) that the power of totalitarian regimes derived in the main, not so much from the repression of personal physical drives, but from the inculcation and development of a relationship of emotional attachment to and dependence on authority. Many, Fromm (2001) found, had essentially the same kind of relationship with the state and with religious hierarchies that they had with abusive codependents in the personal sphere—a kind of capture-bonding or 'Stockholm Syndrome,' in essence. 'Frequently, and not only in the popular usage, sadomasochism is confounded with love' (Fromm 2001), he observed.

> Masochistic phenomena, especially, are looked upon as expressions of love. An attitude of complete self-denial for the sake of another person and the surrender of one's own rights and claims to another person have been praised as examples of 'great love'. It seems that there is no better proof for 'love' than sacrifice and the readiness to give oneself up for the sake of the beloved person. Actually, in these

cases, 'love' is essentially a masochistic yearning and rooted in the symbiotic need of the person involved.

(Fromm 2001)

This was as true where love of the fatherland and the spiritual father was concerned as in the case of dysfunctional personal relationships. Not only were these kinds of codependent political relationships ruinous of happiness, well-being, and the capacity of people to function effectively as individuals, Fromm (2001) argued, but they were also destructive of their ability to function outside of them. The longer they lasted, the harder it was to leave; subjective dynamics of this have in more recent times been studied in the form, on the one hand, of prison institutionalisation, and on the other, in anthropological studies of slave psychology. In his summary of the nature of prison institutionalisation, Craig Haney (2003) notes that

> in the course of becoming institutionalized, a transformation begins. Persons gradually become more accustomed to the restrictions that institutional life imposes. The various psychological mechanisms that must be employed to adjust (and, in some harsh and dangerous correctional environments, to survive) become increasingly 'natural,' second nature, and, to a degree, internalized ... The process of institu- tionalization is facilitated in cases in which persons enter institutional settings at an early age, before they have formed the ability and expectation to control their own life choices. Because there is less tension between the demands of the institution and the autonomy of a mature adult, institutionalization proceeds more quickly and less problematically with at least some younger inmates. Moreover, younger inmates have little in the way of already developed independent judgment, so they have little if anything to revert to or rely upon if and when the institutional structure is removed. And the longer someone remains in an institution, the greater the likelihood that the process will transform them.

Along similar lines, Wyatt-Brown (1988) noted of slave psychology that 'Internalization of the master's values was often so complete that slaves ignored opportunities to escape.'

> Josiah Henson, a slave who eventually escaped to freedom, lamented that in his youth he, like other country blacks, had long assumed the legitimacy of his own bondage. Moving his property prior to a sheriff's sale, his master had assigned Henson to guide some eighteen slaves from Virginia to Kentucky. 'My pride was aroused in view of the importance of my responsibility, and heart and soul I became identified with my master's project of running off his negroes.' Even though they floated past the wharves of Cincinnati, where crowds of free blacks urged them to flee, Henson suppressed excited talk of freedom. As he sadly recalled, he 'had a sentiment of honor on the subject'. Accustomed to obedience and 'too degraded and ignorant of the advantages of liberty to know what they were forfeiting', the crew heeded his orders, and the barge journeyed southward.

(Wyatt-Brown 1988: 1237)

In both cases, the result was repressed, dogmatic, rigid, and inflexible personalities, people who were fearful of their own shadow, paralysed by terror in the face of meaningful freedom. For them, real freedom was tantamount to rejection or abandonment from their codependent idol, and no less painful a prospect. Nevertheless, and despite its patent dysfunctionality, this condition also had its uses insofar as 'the more the drive toward life is thwarted, the stronger is the drive toward destruction; the more life is realized, the less is the strength of destructiveness' (Fromm 2001: 207). The fact that 'destructiveness is the outcome of unlived life' was a potential source of all sorts of energy for someone who knew how to channel it.

For political manipulators who stood to gain from taking advantage of the capture bonding potentialities associated with authoritarian psychology, the logical move was to encourage them as much as possible; but they were missing a way to 'hook' potential victims. This was the point at which they discovered the utility of appeals to whiteness, arguably the basis of racism and the value of the national safety valve historically and in the present day. In geographically isolated Australia, the appeal to whiteness historically speaking took the form of xenophobia and a bellicose nativist movement demanding assimilation into a white Christian monoculture. In this instance, the right to invade the Australian subcontinent and impose an alien culture on the locals is reserved exclusively for white Europeans, a fact that serves to account for the cognitive dissonance surrounding the campaign against halal certification in that respect in particular.

Whiteness and moral panic

Hall, Critcher, Jefferson, Clarke and Roberts (2013) argue that misinformation campaigns of the kind developed around halal certification are indicative of the dynamics associated with moral panics, or episodes when society is overwhelmed by fears of one or another 'existential threat' to its existence (Cohen 2011). Relying for justification on prior attachment to prejudice to give weight to overblown fears and the irrational attitudes of attachment to authority to encourage cognitive biases (Kawakami et al. 1998; Bess 2016), these campaigns against immigrants act 'as a perverse legitimation of inexpressible fear and anguish ... What is taking place is only secondarily an expression of prejudice' (Seabrook 1973: 57).

> It is first and foremost a therapeutic psychodrama in which the emotional release of the protagonists takes precedence over what is actually being said. It is an expression of their pain and powerlessness confronted by the decay and dereliction, not only of their familiar environment, but of their own lives too—an expression for which our society provides no outlet. Certainly it is something more complex and deep-rooted than what the metropolitan liberal evasively and easily dismisses as prejudice.
>
> *(Hall et al. 2013: 158).*

In this sense, the anti-halal campaign in particular, in addition to being a particularly demonstrative example of the absurd extremes of Islamophobic prejudice, is also indicative of what sociologists call the 'production of deviance,' the core principle behind moral panic (Cohen 2011; Oplinger 1990). Deviance being subjective, and what is regarded as deviant socially is a result of who has the power to define the meaning of the term and impose that definition on public discourse, not of any attribute of anyone thus labelled. Therapeutic psychodrama cum production of deviance over halal certification demonises Muslims for existing and aims to polarise public opinion in the interests of establishing a pretext for ideologically driven scapegoating and persecution. Muslims are blamed for things like high food prices and the unresponsiveness of purportedly democratic governments, real problems created by a neoliberal economic regime that serves the wealthy and powerful at the expense of the rest of us, but for which the former do not find it convenient to be accountable.

As is typical of moral panics, the perceived problem of halal food certification is linked to xenophobic fears of creeping Sharia law—a textbook example of 'convergence' or 'stereotype priming' (Blair & Banaji, 1996; Sassenberg & Moskowitz 2005), another moral panic-associated phenomenon, the wedge issue becomes an ideological justification for bigotry via the whiteness-based binary between 'Islam' and 'the Australian way of life.' Blair and Banaji (1996: 1158) find that 'automatic processes may be involved in stereotyping is disturbing because such processes reveal the potential to perpetuate prejudice and discrimination independently of more controlled and intentional forms of stereotyping.'

> For example, because people may be either unaware of the automatic influences on their behavior or believe that they have adequately adjusted for those influences, they may misattribute their (stereotypic) response to more obvious or seemingly justifiable causes, *such as attributes of the target.*
> *(Blair & Banaji 1996: 1159 [emphasis added]).*

Such is a classic form of deviance production, the building block of moral panics. In a similar vein, the Murdoch press in particular does this by using emotive language ('evil,' 'vile,' 'menacing,' 'wicked') to demonise Muslims and turn them into deviants for propaganda purposes, using the mechanism of 'convergence' to link 'folk devils' to perceived threats to a racially charged status quo and build momentum behind a scare campaign (Morgan & Poynting 2016: 258). Journalist Neil Doyle, whom the UK *Sun* described as a 'terrorism expert,' primes readers to accept further stereotyping by scaring them with language such as the following: 'Abu Hamza [an Egyptian imam imprisoned in the United States on terrorism charges] might be out of action but in many ways, he's already completed his mission ... there's a jihad army in this country and that's thanks to Hamza and others like him' (quoted in Morgan & Poynting 2016: 266).

The anti-halal campaign performs the same role, linking food labelling to economic aid for 'terrorism' amongst a population already on edge. The degeneration of popular fears into moral panic reflects the deployment of whiteness narratives associated with the national safety valve on the one hand, and the dynamics of capture bonding associated with those narratives, themselves born of authoritarian psychology, on the other. The resulting power relationship is not substantially different from a standover racket. On the one hand, the population is told a threat to their safety exists. On the other, the violent ideology of racism and white supremacism menaces anyone who dares to challenge its fundamental precepts, which being rooted in authoritarianism are incapable of tolerating doubt or free discussion, while offering 'protection' to those who accept them unquestioningly. Rather than freeing themselves from fear, they become permanent prisoners of it.

Conclusion

Australia, like the rest of the world, faces increasingly dire social, economic, and environmental crises as varied as the widening gap between rich and poor and its damaging effects on Australian democracy, trade agreements like the Trans-Pacific Partnership, our victimisation of refugees, the ever-increasing threat of runaway climate change, and the bleeding sore of race relations in Australia stemming from white invasion. In the face of these issues, scapegoating by opinion makers in government and the corporate media derails rational and dispassionate public debate, and imposes a false binary between the Australian way of life and Islam, as noted above.

This strategy invariably racialises both and undermines democratic norms. Ironically enough, people who buy into this false binary and the bizarre conspiracy theories associated with it, almost uniformly fail to notice all the support they give to extremists like the

Wahhabist Saudi Royal Family every time they fill up their car at the petrol station (Butt 2015). Such facts only draw into relief the pettiness and vindictiveness of the reaction to halal food certification, demonstrating not only the resounding ignorance informing the campaign but also its terminal hypocrisy. The need of its defenders to make use of the 'national safety valve' to defend their way of life only reveals in the latter the abandonment of reason, respect for the rights of others, and democratic values of pluralism and freedom of conscience in defence of class privilege.

Furthermore, and no less significantly, it also highlights the specifically Australian context for the authoritarian dynamics underwriting the anti-halal campaign—what is generally referred to as 'dog-whistling.' The prevalence of this kind of capture-bonding politics seems more appropriate for Australia of the penal colony period; if Australia as a penal colony was essentially an open-air prison, and the early convicts were subject to the same authoritarian dynamics of brutalisation, institutionalisation, and emotional dependence on authority, then this would seem to account at least in part for the virulence of racism as expressed in things such as the anti-halal campaign. Merely federating and declaring a democracy does not make such dynamics go away, any more than it does the crimes that accompanied European colonisation. On the contrary, the existence of the campaign against halal certification as a national safety valve and a public and psychological wage to the white working class, suggests that, as a populace, we are institutionalised, yet it also suggests that the bars of the penal colony remain—the only real difference being that they have migrated into our heads. The greatest difference between past and present prisons, where the white working class is concerned in particular, is the amount of space, as it were, between the bars.

If all of this follows, the great irony of the scare campaign against halal certification as a manifestation of the 'national safety valve,' and as an expression of capture bonding and authoritarian mass psychology expressed in the language of moral panic, derives from its great potential to do damage to growth industries that might be a source of employment for many of those who respond to the politics of scapegoating. By giving in to the politics of scapegoating and crisis leverage, those who embrace the anti-halal scare campaign and others like it bring about themselves the damaging outcomes they are told will happen if halal certification is allowed to go ahead. Having so much at stake demonstrates something of the danger posed by the baseless conspiracy theories promoted by the likes of Smith, Christensen, Bernardi, and others of their ilk. Their scaremongering over halal food certification, deployed as national safety valves using the dark arts of capture bonding and stereotype priming, ultimately benefits only them insofar as it serves their privilege, while their underprivileged supporters amongst the general population are forced to bear the consequences of social injustice, the victims of all of the above in Muslim Australia doubly so.

References

ABC News. (2014) 'Fleurieu Milk and Yoghurt Company loses $50,000 Emirates deal after bowing to pressure to drop halal certification'. 9 November. [online] Available at: www.abc.net.au/news/2014-11-09/company-drops-halal-certification-due-to-social-media-pressure/5877584 (accessed 24 June 2016).
ABC News. (2015) 'Halal certification secures Emirates deal for Fleurieu Milk and Yoghurt Company after social media campaign'. 22 May. [online] Available at: www.abc.net.au/news/2015-05-21/halal-certification-fleurieu-milk-yoghurt-emirates-deal/6488322 (accessed 24 June 2016).
Animals Australia. (2015) 'Halal meat exports—A viable alternative'. [online] Available at: www.banliveex port.com/facts/halal.php (accessed 12 May 2016).

Australian Food and Grocery Council. (n.d.) 'Halal certification. Some facts about halal certification'. [online] Available at: https://www.afgc.org.au/about-afgc/prioritiesandpolicies/halal-certification/ (accessed 12 May 2016).

Australian Government, Department of Agriculture. (2014) *Australian Food Statistics 2012–13*. [pdf] Available at: www.agriculture.gov.au/SiteCollectionDocuments/ag-food/publications/food-stats/australian-food-statistics-2012-13.pdf (accessed 12 May 2016).

Bandura, A. (1999) 'Moral disengagement in the perpetration of inhumanities', *Personality and Social Psychology Review*, 3 (3): 193–209.

Benns, M. (2015) 'Halal certification in Australia is big business and worth millions to certifiers'. *Herald Sun*, 16 August. [online] Available at: www.heraldsun.com.au/news/halal-certification-in-australia-is-big-business-and-worth-millions-to-certifiers/news-story/621b3f642d22f78a884a365c007e8def (accessed 12 May 2016).

Bernardi, C. (2015) *Getting to the Bottom of the Halal Certification Racket*. [Blog] 25 March. Available at: www.corybernardi.com/getting_to_the_bottom_of_the_halal_certification_racket (accessed 22 June 2016).

Bess, G. (2016) 'How racial bias influenced Stanford swimmer's rape case'. *Vice*, 7 June. [online] Available at: https://broadly.vice.com/en_us/article/brock-turner-rape-case-sentencing-racial-bias (accessed 21 June 2016).

Blair, I.V. and Banaji, M.R. (1996) 'Automatic and controlled processes in stereotype priming', *Journal of Personality and Social Psychology*, 70 (6): 1142–1163.

Bolt, A. (2015) 'Hidden profits from halal certificates should be exposed and stopped'. *Herald Sun*, 21 April. [online] Available at www.heraldsun.com.au/news/opinion/andrew-bolt/hidden-profits-from-halal-certificates-should-be-exposed-and-stopped/news-story/f9df7dd8000bf33ff15d410992e21502 (accessed 22 June 2016).

Bolt, A. (2016) 'The yammering of the silenced'. *Herald Sun*, 7 August. [online] Available at: http://blogs.news.com.au/heraldsun/andrewbolt/index.php/heraldsun/comments/shout_of_the_silenced/ (accessed 22 June 2016).

Brecher, J. (2014) *Strike! Revised, Expanded and Updated Edition*. Oakland, CA: PM Press.

Brull, M. (2015) 'Cory Bernardi and the little halal truther campaign that couldn't'. *New Matilda*, 3 December. [online] Available at: https://newmatilda.com/2015/12/03/cory-bernardi-and-the-little-halal-truther-campaign-that-couldnt/ (accessed 22 June 2016).

Butt, Y. (2015) 'How Saudi Wahhabism is the fountainhead of Islamist terrorism'. *The World Post*, 22 March. [online] Available at: https://www.huffingtonpost.com/dr-yousaf-butt-/saudi-wahhabism-islam-terrorism_b_6501916.html (accessed 8 May 2016).

Bytwerk, R. (1998) 'Caricatures from Der Stürmer: 1933–1945'. *German Propaganda Archive, Calvin College*. [online] Available at http://research.calvin.edu/german-propaganda-archive/sturmer.htm (accessed 22 June 2016).

Chalmers, M. (2014) 'Welcome to the strange logic of Kirralie Smith, anti-halal truther'. *New Matilda*, 21 November. [online] Available at: https://newmatilda.com/2014/11/21/welcome-strange-logic-kirralie-smith-anti-halal-truther/ (accessed 21 June 2016).

Chalmers, M. (2015) 'WATCH: Charlie Pickering takes on Cory Bernardi and halal truthers'. *New Matilda*, 20 May. [online] Available at: https://newmatilda.com/2015/05/20/watch-charlie-pickering-takes-cory-bernardi-and-halal-truthers/ (accessed 23 June 2016).

Christensen, G. (2014) *Terror in the Tucker Box*. [Blog] Available at: www.georgechristensen.com.au/terror-in-the-tucker-box/ (accessed 12 May 2016).

Cohen, S. (2011) *Folk Devils and Moral Panics*. London: Routledge.

Cohn, N.R.C. (1993) *Europe's Inner Demons: The Demonization of Christians in Medieval Christendom* (2nd ed.). London: Pimlico Books.

Connor, J. (2002) *The Australian Frontier Wars, 1788–1838*. Sydney: UNSW Press.

Davies, M.W., Nandy, A. and Sardar, Z. (1993) *Barbaric Others: A Manifesto on Western Racism*. London: Pluto Press.

Deckard, S. (2009) *Paradise Discourse, Imperialism, and Globalization: Exploiting Eden*. London: Routledge.

Ellerbe, H. (1995) *The Dark Side of Christian History*. Windermere, FL: Morningstar & Lark.

Fromm, E. (2001) *The Fear of Freedom*. London: Routledge Classics.

Gartrell, A. (2015) 'Cory Bernardi's anti-halal crusade unleashes torrent of hate'. *Sydney Morning Herald*, 20 June. [online] Available at: www.smh.com.au/federal-politics/political-news/cory-bernardis-antihalal-crusade-unleashes-torrent-of-hate-20150620-ght0l8.html (accessed 22 June 2016).

Halal Choices. (2011a) 'What is Halal?' [online] Available at: www.halalchoices.com.au/what_is_halal.html (accessed 12 May 2016).

Halal Choices. (2011b) 'What is Sharia Law?' [online] Available at: www.halalchoices.com.au/what_is_sharia.html, (accessed 12 May 2016).

Hall, S., Critcher, C., Jefferson, T., Clarke, J. and Roberts, B. (2013) *Policing the Crisis: Mugging, the State and Law & Order*. London: Palgrave Macmillan.

Haney, C. (2003) 'Psychological impact of incarceration: Implications for postprison adjustment'. In J. Travis and M. Waul (eds) *From Prisoners Once Removed: The Impact of Incarceration and Reentry on Children, Families, and Communities*. National Criminal Justice Reference Service: 33–66. [online] Available at: https://www.ncjrs.gov/App/Publications/abstract.aspx?ID=205852 (accessed 21 February 2016).

Harris, C.I. (1993) 'Whiteness as property', *Harvard Law Review*, 106 (8): 1707–1791.

Hussein, S. (2014) 'The inglorious charge of the anti-halal brigade'. *ABC Religion and Ethics*, 27 November. [online] Available at: www.abc.net.au/religion/articles/2014/11/27/4137397.htm (accessed 12 May 2016).

Judd, R. (2007) *Contested Rituals: Circumcision, Kosher Butchering, and Jewish Political Life in Germany, 1843–1933*. Ithaca, NY: Cornell University Press.

Kawakami, K., Dion, K.L. and Dovidio, J.F. (1998) 'Racial prejudice and stereotype activation', *Personality and Social Psychology Bulletin*, 24 (4): 407–416.

Marx, K. (1849) 'Wage labour and capital'. *Marxist Internet Archive*. [online] Available at http://marxists.anu.edu.au/archive/marx/works/download/doc/wage-labour-capital.doc {accessed 16 January 2017).

Morgan, G. and Poynting, S. (eds) (2016) *Global Islamophobia: Muslims and Moral Panic in the West*. London: Routledge.

Oplinger, J. (1990) *The Politics of Demonology: The European Witchcraze and the Mass Production of Deviance*. London: Associated University Press.

Parliament of Australia. (2015) *Report: Third Party Certification of Food*, 1 December. Canberra: Senate, Parliament of Australia. [online] Available at: www.aph.gov.au/Parliamentary_Business/Committees/Senate/Economics/Food_Cert_Schemes/Report (accessed 22 June 2016).

Pascoe, B. (2014) *Dark Emu: Black Seeds*. Broome, WA: Magabala.

Reich, W. (1970) *The Mass Psychology of Fascism*. London: Macmillan.

Roediger, D. (1991) *The Wages of Whiteness*. New York: Verso.

Sassenberg, K. and Moskowitz, G.B. (2005) 'Don't stereotype, think different! Overcoming automatic stereotype activation by mindset priming', *Journal of Experimental Social Psychology*, 41 (5): 506–514.

Sax, B. (2000) *Animals in the Third Reich: Pets, Scapegoats, and the Holocaust*. London: A & C Black.

Seabrook, J. (1973) *The Unprivileged: A Hundred Years of Family Life and Tradition in a Working-Class Street*. Harmondsworth: Penguin Books.

Smith, K. (2015) 'Halal is Sharia law!'. *Pickering Post*, 15 January. [online] Available at: http://pickeringpost.com/story/halal-is-sharia-law-/4408 (accessed 3 January 2019)

Van Nuys, F. (2002) *Americanizing the West: Race, Immigrants and Citizenship 1890–1930*. Lawrence: University of Kansas Press.

Wyatt-Brown, B. (1988) 'The mask of obedience: Male slave psychology in the Old South', *American Historical Review*, 93 (5): 1228–1252.

25

COMMODIFIED RELIGION

The keys to halal food?

Deniz Parlak

Introduction

In recent years, the production and consumption of halal food has been portrayed as a necessity for the Islamic market and serves as a good example for showing the changing perception of religion in capitalist societies. Halal food, which is promoted for its being used in all aspects of everyday life, is defined as: "a product that does not include anything against Islamic rules, which is prepared–processed–transported via proper devices and means in accordance with Islamic rules, and which is not directly in touch with anything except for the proper conditions through preparation–procession–transportation and storing" (CODEX Alimentarius, International Food Standards 1997: 1). The 'halal' field is not be limited to the food industry and ranges in all fields from food to cosmetics and health to cleaning products in terms of its preparation–procession–storing rules. The production or the consumption of halal food, which can be alternatively framed in terms of daily life or the political–economical field or belief, brings with it a meaningful discussion that reveals the broader functions of religion under the guise of belief. The size of the halal food and beverage market was estimated by Thomson Reuters and DinarStandard (2016) in the *State of the Global Islamic Economy Report 2016/17*, as totalling $1.17 trillion and it is expected that the market will reach $1.9 trillion by 2021. According to the report, the halal food market accounts for 16.6 per cent of the global Muslim market (Thomson Reuters & DinarStandard 2016: 30). In addition, Turkey has become a significant actor in this sector after the Turkish Standards Institution entered the world halal food market in 2011.

In a relatively short period, halal food, whose source is a religious commitment, became a commodity in the food market. This example shows us that the sacred is not necessarily attributed just to the religious anymore, and the sacred actually wraps itself in new forms. Indeed, it is necessary to manifest the political–economical motives behind this transformation of religion. In this context, this chapter aims to examine how 'halal' has been commodified in today's modern world, although it has had a religious meaning for 1,400 years. It is also presumed that both the certification organisations which debate about religious and secular approaches to the halal food industry, along with the companies which have already had halal certification, have used the functions of halal food to raise capital in Turkey and develop a branding process around halal. To support these arguments, this chapter will briefly discuss how 'halal' has been turned into a brand

and a market and the implications of this change of meaning of 'halal' in this Muslim economy. In terms of methodology, this study is based on in-depth interviews undertaken with two large certification institutes and 25 companies which have already received the halal certificate from the certification institutes of Turkey. These companies were selected because of their dominant positions in Turkey's halal food market. Fieldwork was carried out in Istanbul and Ankara. The first phase consisted of in-depth interviews with all large certification institutes and some managers. The second phase was completed with complementary interviews with all relevant institutions and companies. Overall, this chapter aims to contribute to our understanding of commodification of halal food through the Turkish experience.

Welcome to the field of the 'halal': changing from a religious duty to brandisation

Religion, which is in a symbiotic relationship with capitalism, has taken on new forms while building capital in its ambition to make money. The religion which turned out to be 'meta' in the capitalist world is 'halal food,' which is now valued at $2 trillion depending on the level of consumption of the Muslim population. If the 'halal' that is written on the products of the food, cosmetics, and industrial cleaning sector is interpreted as something solely in terms of being a 'sacred' concept or as a 'religious duty,' it could only be thought of as naive.

The halal food which is borne out of the global market exists as a result of the Islamist manner of "being away from the prohibited" which has taken over as a duty. As in other religions, prohibited foods are also presented in Islam. While in Judaism prohibitions on the intermingling of meat with milk exist, in Islam, foods like pork and alcohol are completely prohibited. In Islam, these kinds of prohibitions are mentioned in the Qur'an, and they are extended with the sayings of the Prophet Mohammed. Concordantly, the emphasis on 'halal' in verses and hadiths of the Qur'an is considered to be the origin of 'halal food.'

The word 'halal' is an Arabic word which means 'lawful' or 'permissible.' In the terminology of religion, 'halal' refers to religiously permitted and 'haram' refers to religiously prohibited. Drawing the legitimate fields of 'halal' and 'haram' is attributed to God. Only God and His Prophet can define what is halal and what is haram. The Qur'an includes many detailed explanations about halal and haram. It is possible to say that halal is not only related to the food itself but is also related to the products which have been in touch with something 'haram.' Thus, the halal certificate covers many products of different industries, such as the food, cosmetics, pharmaceutical, and cleaning sectors (Fischer 2005). Halal food can be similar to other foods, but its form, production process, content, and manner of production are defined by and must conform to Islamic rules (Abdul, Ismail, Hashim & Johari 2009). Hence, the food additives are classified not only as 'haram' and 'halal' but also as 'healthy' and 'unhealthy.'

The concept of halal, which is considered to be a religious obligation, is a multidimensional concept. The insufficiency of the religious knowledge that is entirely open to interpretation is increasing due to improvements in new technology. The 'halal label' originating in the verses of the Qur'an on the exported products that are transported from one Muslim location to another is proof of the rise of the worldliness of this halal concept once again. The halal, which has lost the sacred, is becoming a symbol of the commodities of specific brands. The certification of halal products, which have a significant market share, bears witness to the competition of companies trying to obtain certifications and also to competition between the companies that have received certifications for raising their export share. Furthermore, such a loss of sacredness is also contributed to by the many publications about halal food and its certification. All this attests to the fact that halal food is being seen as just another part of branding.

Halal food as a market

The main reason why halal food is being given more attention is the increasing population rate of Muslims. It is reported that there were 1.6 billion cultural and religious believers of Islam according to the data of the Pew Research Center's Forum on Religion and Public Life in 2011. This number is equal to 23 per cent of the world population (Pew Research Center 2011). The current Muslim population density and the predictions that this population will increase in the near future pave the way for the growth of a halal market which can satisfy the demands for halal food by Muslim society. There are several reasons which affect the emergence of the demands for halal food that are seen as a religious duty for believers. But, why now? Why are Muslim people demanding to consume halal products nowadays in spite of the fact that halal is the religious obligation which has been known for centuries? The production of halal food has taken place as part of the new market-seeking behaviour of the global neoliberal economy. In the context of neoliberalism, capitalist 'modern' societies have followed more expansionist policies and these policies have overlapped with globalisation. The development of halal food products can therefore be correlated with the rise of such concepts as globalisation, multiculturalism, the emphasis on religious and cultural identities, migrations, ethno-cultural practices, and the spread of international norms besides the broad impact of tourism and its impact upon cultural commodification in local economies (Adams 2011). Hence, the rise of halal food's production depends on the penetration of new capitalist markets.

If we think of the 1.6 billion population of Muslim people as potential consumers of halal food, it is not difficult to assume that the halal food market is one of the most significant ethnic food market in the world (Adams 2011). Consequently, halal food has come to be increasingly framed as a profitable element in a capitalist world rather than being a sacred element. Therefore, it was inevitable that the halal food sector became a battlefield for those who want a share in this market. *JWT*, a global advertising company, defined the halal food market as "young, large and becoming bigger," implying precisely this battlefield (Power & Shadiah 2009).

The 'Islamic Market,' which was created to help construct the new industry in the fields of media, advertising, management and consumption, became increasingly popular within the context of commodified cultural forms and fields. "The identity of Muslims is structured in the fields of memories, novels, daily journals, newspapers, television channels and also in the religious training centers, halal markets, restaurants, holiday centers, and exurbs by means of the practices of trading and consumption" (Gökarıksel & McLarney 2010: 1–2). Halal food, which has increased in significance so much in past 20 years, is considered to be under this effect too. Hence, halal food is a unique invention of late neoliberal capitalism.

As halal also means healthy, besides its religious dimension, it encourages non-Muslim religious consumers who notice hygiene and food safety to also buy the products with the halal certificate. Many of the company executives in the halal market indicate that there are non-Muslim people in their customer profile. The Dutch company Marhaba, which produces chocolate and cookies, declares that 25 per cent of their customers are non-Muslims and most of the people who are interested in their products are moved not only by religious ethics but also food safety (Power & Shadiah 2009). According to Alserhan (2010), "as the awareness of halal labels among Christian and Jewish consumers increased, the demands for them also increased." In parallel with this view, the manager of the brand Al Islami Foods, which took the best halal food prize of The Superbrands Council of United Arab Emirates, in 2010 stated that "halal is a philosophy for our company. The wellbeing and health of our customers are our priority, and we never classify our customers as halal entrepreneurs" (Mansoor 2010).

What we therefore now see is that people buy halal food not because it is sacred but instead because it is related to such concepts as 'pure,' 'clean,' 'hygienic,' 'proper,' and 'healthy.' Concerns over food poisoning and food security have resulted in the creation of food security and quality systems (Rahman, Ahmad, Mohamad & Ismail 2011). Such systems and concerns are therefore both a contributor to the high demand for halal food as well as a consequence. Thus, there is a cause and effect relationship between halal food and consumption habits.

The adventure of halal food in Turkey

Halal food, which is a focus of the Muslim population in 112 countries, is also an important issue for Turkey, where most of the population is Muslim. In Turkey, since the Justice and Development Party (AKP) came to government in 2002, the desire to be involved in the halal food market has increased. During this period, Islam has infiltrated firstly local administration, then national governing bodies, and, finally, the Turkish economy. It is true to say that Islamic thought, which was restrained in the period of modernisation, has now made its presence felt in all fields of life, and therefore religion has become intertwined with capitalism. While Islamists were "rejecting modernism, they were [becoming] modern" and likewise while "Islamists were rejecting capitalism they [became] capitalist." That is to say that *homo economicus* became *homo islamicus economicus* (Yıldız 1995). Nonetheless, this development certainly is not one-dimensional. One field of society which cannot be thought of as separate from another is economics, as it is an incontrovertible truth that it is always concerning itself with other fields. It is not possible to expect that there is no visible change in the lifestyles of the Islamists who were acquainted with money and power. When Islamist societies embraced capitalism and modernism, they became acquainted with 'the sacred' concepts of consumption, fashion, and profit. As they benefited from being a newly emerging bourgeoisie, capitalism itself is now considered as a belief.

The AKP, which existed in the political arena on its own for 15 years, changed the religious perception into a 'modern' perspective, and this caused the social structure to be re-coded. This process, which is constructed by cultural and religious codes, is borne within class conflicts. In this period, as the integration into a capitalist economy gained speed, the halal food market became a relevant field for Turkey as well. However, there is one element which distinguishes it from other countries and makes it unique. In Turkey the Muslim population is quite dense, but Turkey also wishes to be a kind of representative of the whole industry towards the West that is already the leader in the halal industry. In addition, Turkey wishes to be president of a certification institution that covers other Muslim countries and to be a part of the Organisation of Islamic Cooperation (known as Organisation of the Islamic Conference until June 2011) (OIC) integrated with other Islamic countries. Turkey would therefore like to have one hand in Islamic countries and have the other in the West, which has most of the share in the market, as part of Turkey's attempt to be the owner of the industry.

The halal food certification process started in Turkey in 2005 with the foundation of the Association for the Inspection and Certification of Food and Supplies (GIMDES) which is religiously oriented and also considers halal as a religious theme. But the profit of the halal market shows that GIMDES has a structure that cannot be left alone as is the case for other countries. One should not think that GIMDES does not make a profit because it has religious emphasis. However, after 2011, the Turkish Standards Institution (TSE) also started certifying and in this way halal became 'national.' This is because the TSE is a public institute dependent on the Ministry of Industry and Commerce which standardises all kind of goods and manufacturing and also standardises systems and services. Many foundations large and small have now started becoming involved in the certification process. In addition to certification institutions, the number of institutions and organisations that await certification is also quickly increasing. The number of companies that are certified by GIMDES is approaching 325 in 12 years, and in six years the number of the companies who applied to TSE was 385.

Religious approach to halal certification: GIMDES

In 12 years GIMDES has given Halal Food Certificates to almost 325 companies and has organised various international conferences since it was founded. The institution defines itself as: "a non-governmental organization that is founded to conduct research and certify halal and healthy products which are the main elements of healthy living in our country" (GIMDES n.d. 14). Although halal food is defined as "the main element of healthy living," it is actually defined more like a religious duty. The emphasis made by the head of the institution Hüseyin Kâmi Büyüközer while he was explaining the halal food system makes this fact clear:

> The halal food system must rely on a religious source above all. It is not an artefact. The Qur'an or the Hadiths must be our guides. A halal product should not be defined as haram in the verses and hadiths. Besides religious knowledge, "halal" also means hygiene and health but it must not be unhealthy. For example, alcohol is haram, even if it is hygienic because it is unhealthy. For instance, if there is a wine stain on our hand, we cannot perform the ritual prayers of Islam. We have to refer to the religious sources to call something halal. If it the criterion of what is haram is made by mortals, it cannot be a halal system. It has to be wholly religious. (Büyüközer, personal communication)

Turner (1994) established two tendencies which belong to Islam in the modern world. First is a tendency to form a global Islamic system, and the second is the reaction of consumerism against the birth of the West and Islamic fundamentalism. Büyüközer emphasises that GIMDES was founded to stop European dominance of halal, which is seen as exploiting religion and as being responsible for social pollution. He further claims that "it is necessary to live our religion as it is," thereby supporting the validity of Turner's (1994) argument. At the same time, Büyüközer says in one of his interviews that their entering into the halal food industry is a reaction to the condition that the industry, which is controlled by non-Muslims and makes human beings 'prisoners,' is developing extremely fast and modifying our food (The Brandage 2011).

Religion, which pulled away from the otherworldly realm and had a new appearance, has offered a place in the market, and it has become commercialised. Turkey's position in this market aims at the same economic goals, as illustrated by the claims of the president of GIMDES, who explains that they are in the market for religious purposes.

> The Halal market has 2 to 2.5 trillion worth of market share. Our association is studying this. Only the food part of halal products has around 900 billion to 1 trillion dollars in market share. Turkey should get a significant share in this market. Turkey's

share in the market is potentially around 40 to 50 billion dollars. The companies, which are certified by *GIMDES,* imported products and they earned more than 4 billion dollars in 2011. It is religiously mistaken if we leave this profit to the West, which is exploiting our religion. Up to now, non-Muslim capitalists took advantage of it. Western civilisation does not want us to become conscious. (Büyüközer, personal communication)

After defining that the halal market is profitable, it was necessary to attribute the entrepreneur to a religious ground in order to benefit from this profit. Furthermore, Western involvement in halal was necessarily attributed to a "religious mistake" rather than being attributed to capital loss, showing that there is a necessity for basing the existence of the entrepreneur on religious grounds. This language, which is an expression of Islamic bourgeoisie, is actually a tool to imply that the capital is obtained with a religious responsibility. Despite entirely Islamic expressions, GIMDES sees the newly joined actors of the halal market as being institutions that are trying to obtain a share in the market rather than as being non-governmental organisations that are trying to fulfil their religious duties and responsibilities. Büyüközer says that he is surprised when observing that halal food is suddenly a focus of interest now with many associations that emerged after GIMDES.

National intervention in halal market: TSE

When the Turkish Standards Institution entered the halal product industry as a national element, it was a religious entity that became governmental. TSE, as the only authorised body on the national level in the worldly religious domain, became quite powerful. Above all, within the Organisation of the Islamic Conference, two groups were founded under the presidency of TSE: "The Group of Islamic Countries Standardization Specialists" and "The Comity of Coordination." These groups conducted studies and founded The Standards and Metrology Institute for the Islamic Countries (SMIIC) (Tuğ & Özdemir 2009). The institute prepared the rough draft for the standards in the light of their studies; however, as there was a condition stating that the halal standard would become operative only if it is issued in a directive by the assemblies of the member states, it was not until 2011 that this standard became operational. However, TSE is the only national institution that has accepted SMIIC's OIC SMIIC-1 standard, in order for it to become functional in the market and secure its position.

The interview with Necla Solak, TSE Food Industry Information Manager, showed that there is a clear difference between the points of view of GIMDES and TSE about the process.

It is not possible to say that there was a direct reason to enter the standardisation process … Factors like the internet, mass communication, and the media gave information to people about consumption, and so these people want to see "halal standard" on the products. It is also addressed to a particular type of consumer. The halal food label is essential for trade because this certification makes things easier. Exporting companies convey this demand to us. Besides other factors, customers push these firms to obtain the certification. (Solak, personal communication)

These statements support the notion that halal food is being constructed as a trade bloc and that the reason why companies apply for a halal certificate is to make trade easier. Therefore, a national organisation that serves a domain which is traditionally 'unworldly' shows us that religion has become worldly and commercialised by means of halal food and not unworldly anymore.

The most important stated reason for halal food is the increase in demand for food safety. The Information Manager laid stress on food safety, saying that "OIC-SMIIC 1 is based not only on religious knowledge but also on technical expertise.' Therefore, food safety is also standardised according to 'halal' criteria. The basis is actually 'food safety.' She says that the main aim why they obtained this certificate is to certify themselves for food safety and hygiene even though they do not export their products. She adds that the Halal Food Certificate is not so different from the ISO 22000 food safety certificate, which is not focused on halal criteria but rather on objective criteria.

The argument that the global market 'needs' halal food is also supported by what Food Industry Information Manager Necla Solak has to say. Solak explains:

> If there is a demand for halal food, then we need to satisfy this demand because we export in the end. The Ministry of Agriculture was specifying the products from non-Muslim countries with signs like "no pork included". However, these countries now ask how they can contribute to the halal food industry. For, the market is gradually growing, and countries would like to remove obstacles which can decrease their commerce. If a country's export is decreasing, then they need to get certified. Actually, it is necessary for making trade easier. (Solak, personal communication)

The element which stirred the competition in the commercial halal food market is the fact that there is no single worldwide standard, and there are religious issues which are open to discussion (see also Chapter 2, this volume). Therefore, both the institutions that can certify and the companies that obtained the certificate give voice to a worldwide standard. Consequently, SMIIC's remarks about the process gained importance on account of its cooperation with the Organisation of Islamic Cooperation (OIC) in forming the OIC-SMIIC 1 standard.

The concept of halal, which has left the unworldly realm and become a product logo has now also become a standardising certification. What makes the competitive field unequal is the worldwide equivocal nature of the standard on halal food. The companies that want to obtain the certificate must fulfil the requirements of the country they are applying for, and this promotes the ambiguity of the Islamic rules. Countries can certify using whatever criteria they want, and so what one country requires another might prohibit. As of 2018 the OIC-SMIIC 1 standard, had been approved by 31 member countries out of 57 in OIC. Two specialists of the SMIIC unit, Yasin Zülfikaroğlu and Çağrı Cankurtaran, highlight the trade dimension.

> We—as SMIIC—made an effort to make it as a standard, and we are still making an effort. The concept is a standard, and we aim to remove obstacles in between countries. … The origin of halal food is a commercial concern and necessity. For example, when Jagler was exporting to Iran, it faced obstacles, and so it obtained the halal certificate from Iran. Therefore, we move according to the logic of the standard. (Zülfükaroğlu & Cankurtaran, personal communication)

To put halal products under standards reinforces the notion that it is a symbolic form of food management in a neoliberal age. Interestingly, the specialists of SMIIC are concerned with the fact that if this standard is not completed soon, the Europeans will become more active in the process.

> CEN—*Comité Européen de Normalisation*—is a big standard organisation in Europe, and this organisation has just begun working on the halal food standard. They are

better than us and more organised, so if we do not hurry up, they will extend their standard to the whole world, and we will end up buying their standards as we do for other standards as well. Someone in the 57 Islamic countries will go and buy their standard. (Zülfükaroğlu & Cankurtaran, personal communication)

Halal food: opening the gate to capital by the companies

The concerns of SMIIC specialists with respect to standardisation issues are widely recognised. For example, in the Ideal Ratings *Socially Acceptable Market Investments (SAMI) Halal Food Index Series,* it was pointed out that the domination of non-Muslim countries of the halal food market is tied in with the fact that Islamic countries cannot come up with a universal standard (Ideal Ratings 2011). This deficiency is depicted in the internal Islamic market too. The general manager of Aytaç Gıda Yatırım San. ve Tic. A.Ş., which certifies companies by TSE, indicates that there is a demand in the internal market to solve this common problem by determining a single standard:

> What we want most is a common halal standard on which all of the Islamic countries agree on. This standard should be inspected by all of the countries' religious institutions and also by institutions similar to *TSE.* The one common valid standard in the world will remove all of the questions in customers' minds. In [non-Muslim] foreign countries, institutions can certify according to this standard, or they can ask a company from a Muslim country to do it. (Demirhan, personal communication)

While consumers in Turkey still ignore the concept of halal food, there is an ambiguity originating in the problem of a common standard worldwide for the entrepreneurs. In spite of this uncertainty, determining the reasons why companies remain in this market will help us to define the problem. Besides the competition created between certification institutes on account of the halal food system, the issues originating in the diversity of standards affect the companies that obtained the certificate. Almost all of the company executives in the interviews that were undertaken spoke about this problem. When we look primarily at the problem at the level of the companies that export their products, it is apparent that the halal food certificate is a necessity for the opening to the international market so that they can increase their sales.

Serhat Demirhan, the general manager of Aytaç R&D, which was founded in 1995 and considered to be the second biggest company in meat and meat products in Turkey, thinks that it is necessary to obtain this certificate, because their factory in Belgium has important exporting sources, and they do not want to face a problem with importing their products unless they have the certificate. The quality control manager of Sultan Et, which was certificated by TSE, Yurdaer Şahin, explained that even though they are smaller than Aytaç, the certificate became a necessary condition for them to remain competitive. The export manager of Seyidoğlu Gıda, which is certified by GIMDES, pointed out that getting certified is essential both for increasing brand value and for increasing international trade. Zeynep İlkbahar, the then Director of Technical Operations of Aromsa, which is also certified by GIMDES, stated that they entered into the halal food system because of customer demands in the Middle East (İlkbahar, personal communication; Şahin, personal communication; The Brandage 2011).

The company's differences in import/export activities, along with the size of their market share, are factors that affect their reasons for being in the halal food market. On the one hand, the ones that export and have relatively more significant market share pay more attention to the international market rather than to domestic market. On the other hand, the ones who produce for local markets define their primary motivation as being consumer safety. Aytaç, whose market share is 10 per cent, explains that the reason why they are in the market is the demand of customers abroad. However, Özlem Et, which was certificated by TSE, and whose market share is 4 per cent and is only active within the domestic market, explains that they are in the market because they would like to be one of the safe companies in the market; especially given that meat is imported from other countries. Demir, who is a quality control manager, stated that importance is given to customer satisfaction and to being a certified company in terms of food safety (Demir, personal communication).

The quality assurance officer of Sultan Et, Yurdaer Şahin, said that while they were obtaining the certificate, their target group was conservative customers who are sensitive about halal food (Şahin, personal communication). However, the interviewed officer of Doygun Gıda, certified by TSE, Handan Dönmez, defines their target group as everyone who has consumer awareness (Dönmez, personal communication). Similar to Doygun Gıda, Ender Abalıoğlu, the food sales marketing group leader of Lezita, which is certified by GIMDES, and has been in the market since 1969, states that "they target large masses who care about food safety, quality, and healthy consumption" (Yılmaz, personal communication).

The impression we got from all the representatives of the companies was that there is a widespread lack of consumer awareness on halal certification. The general opinion about its cause is that there is so much information out there that people cease to pay attention to it, and also that consumers were not encouraged to buy halal food. The fact that there is not a well-formed consumer mass towards halal food disturbs the companies. The officer of Seyidoğlu, certified by GIMDES, thinks that 80 per cent of customers are not aware of halal food. Similarly, the chemical engineer of Nafia Gıda, certified by GIMDES, Emre Peköz, complains about the fact that halal food is only known roughly as a product which does not contain pork or alcohol. The general manager of Lamis Organic, also certified by GIMDES, Leyla Abu Ahmad, thinks similarly to the other representatives and also states that consumers do not have an optimal awareness (The Brandage 2011). In the interview with Aytaç, Serhat Demirhan says that in Turkey there is no established customer awareness. Furthermore, he noted that in some of the religious sects, this kind of awareness is established, and he thinks that these religious sects' sensitivity influences the halal food system.

Conclusion

The halal food industry showed us that religion is in touch with capitalism in every structure. Although superficially the main concern with halal food is religious, it turned out to be a market and economic concern, because companies would like to have an increased market share of the volume of the global halal food industry. This study's area of investigation was Turkey, and we see that Turkey is trying to find a place for itself in the world, and in regard of its current foreign policy, it seems that Turkey is trying to be the centre of the Middle East. It seems inevitable that Turkey wants to be the lead actor in the halal food market whose volume is so great. We also identified the close contact between Islam and capitalism nowadays in Turkey under AKP's governance, and there are several changes in practices that have occurred in parallel to this relationship. The construction of 'halal food' is therefore a reflected image of this period in the economy. Although TSE, GIMDES, SMIIC, and the companies separate their approaches on halal food as being religious or secular, their common point is that halal food represents commercial profit.

Consequently, halal food is an example of a commodity like all others in the world. Halal came out of personal prerogative and became a representative of an area where the religious person comes to life in a food industry. The concept of halal, which is immanent to the unworldly realm, has altered so much that it is perceived to be only a label on products, as if it does not have another meaning anymore. Halal, which is taken from an individual's personal choice, is now considered to be an object of consumption. This study is conducted on the grounds of this change, and we see that the legitimacy of modernisation making religion more worldly and the legitimacy of the ambition to make more profit have become materialised in halal food.

References

Abdul, M., Ismail, H., Hashim, H. and Johari, J. (2009) 'Consumer decision making process in shopping for halal food in Malaysia', *China–USA Business Review*, 8 (9): 40–47.

Adams, I.A. (2011) 'Globalization: Explaining the dynamics and challenges of the halal food surge', *Intellectual Discourse*, 19 (1): 123–145.

Alserhan, B.A. (2010) 'Islamic branding: A conceptualization of related terms', *Brand Management*, 18 (1): 34–49.

CODEX Alimentarius, International Food Standards. (1997) 'General guidelines for use of the term "halal"'. *Food and Agricultural Organization of the United Nations and the World Health Organization*. [online] Available at: www.fao.org/docrep/005/Y2770E/y2770e08.htm (accessed 22 September 2017).

Fischer, J. (2005) 'Feeding secularism: Consuming halal among the Malays in London', *Diaspora*, 12 (2/3): 275–297.

GIMDES (n.d.) *Faaliyet Kitabı (Introduction Book)*. Istanbul: GIMDES.

Gökarıksel, B. and McLarney, E. (2010) 'Introduction: Muslim women, consumer capitalism and the Islamic culture industry', *Journal of Middle East Women's Studies*, 6 (3): 1–19.

Ideal Ratings (2011) *SAMI Halal Food Index*, 28 February, San Francisco: Ideal Ratings. Available: www.idealratings.com/solutions/sami-halal-food-index-series.

Mansoor, Z. (2010) 'Al Islami Foods—taking "halal" to new heights', *DinarStandard, Rabi Al-Thani*, June, 1431 (32).

Pew Research Center. (2011) 'The future of the global Muslim population', *The Pew Forum on Religion and Public Life*, 27 January. [online] Available at: www.pewforum.org/The-Future-of-the-Global-Muslim-Population.aspx (accessed 13 August 2017).

Power, C. and Shadiah, A. (2009) 'Buying Muslim', *Time International*, 25 May, 173 (20): 37–40.

Rahman, AH., Ahmad, W.I.W., Mohamad, M.Y. and Ismail, Z. (2011) 'Knowledge on halal food amongst food industry entrepreneurs in Malaysia', *Asian Social Science*, 7 (12): 216–222.

The Brandage. (2011) 'Helal Markalama' [Halal Branding], *The Brandage*, 34: 66–82.

Thomson Reuters and DinarStandard. (2016) *State of the Global Islamic Economy Report 2016/17*, [pdf] Available at: https://ceif.iba.edu.pk/pdf/ThomsonReuters-stateoftheGlobalIslamicEconomyReport201617.pdf (accessed on 3 September 2017).

Tuğ, S. and Özdemir, Ö. (2009) 'Helal Sertifikası'nın Dünyadaki ve Türkiye'deki Gelişimi', in İslam Fıkhı Açısından Helal Gıda (VI. İslam Hukuku ABD Koordinasyon Toplantısı) Sempozyumu, Bursa.

Turner, B. (1994) *Orientalism, Postmodernism and Globalism*. London: Routledge.

Yıldız, Y.G. (1995) 'Din ve Siyaset (Religion and Power)', *Kopuş*, 3: 20–23.

PART VI

Emerging and future issues

26

EMERGING AND FUTURE ISSUES IN HALAL HOSPITALITY AND ISLAMIC TOURISM

C. Michael Hall and Girish Prayag

Introduction

This book has covered a range of issues with respect to halal hospitality and Islamic tourism. In so doing it points to current areas of interest in such research and also points the way to research gaps and new areas of research opportunities. This chapter provides some observations of emerging and ongoing issues in halal hospitality and Islamic tourism and is divided into five main areas: definitions, seeing Islamic pilgrimage as extending beyond the hajj, better understanding the Muslim traveller, gaining deeper insights into tourism products and destinations from Islamic perspectives along with the impacts of tourism, and reflexivity and commodification. The last section provides distinct challenges to researchers with respect to their positionality and the nature and manner of their own research journey.

Definitions

Numerous chapters in this book, along with many other papers (e.g. Henderson 2009; Aziz, Rahman, Hassan & Hamid 2015; Razzaq, Hall & Prayag 2016; Khan & Callanan 2017; Boğan & Sarıışık 2018; Vargas-Sánchez & Moral-Moral 2018), have noted the lack of agreement over definitions as to what constitutes halal and Islamic tourism and hospitality. Definitions are clearly important for policy and regulatory practice as well as delineating the scope of a field of study. As a result they can also assist with answering the significant question as to whether halal tourism is 'really halal?' (El-Gohary 2016) and the interpretation of Islamic teachings for insights as to travel and how to respond to visitors and the other with appropriate hospitality (Siddiqui 2015).

Khan and Callanan (2017) provided an excellent outline of the issues of definition in their paper on the "Halalification" of tourism in which they found no clear difference between the various terms (e.g. halal, Muslim friendly, Islamic, Sharia) that were used in their content analysis of popular UK media, UK-based tour operators' websites, and tourism strategies of destinations popular with Muslim tourists. They argued that the lack of a clear and consistent use of terminology may have implications for market development and particularly issues of consumer trust. Such inconsistency, they noted, also applied to the lack of standardisation of halal certification, an issue which is a substantial concern of many of the chapters in this volume. Indeed, Khan and Callanan (2017) also wondered as to whether halal values were in danger of being commodified in the absence of a universal agreed criterion for halal certification.

It seems unlikely that there will be general agreement on definitions of the different types of Islamic tourism, in much the same way as differences in general over definitions of key concepts in many areas of tourism. However, the lack of agreed definitions arguably is not surprising given that the relative spatial spread of research on Islam and tourism remains relatively limited and has not yet encompassed all of the different schools of Sharia thought that exist within Islam, the different expressions of Islam in different countries, nor even the different types of mobility and tourism. For example, in the case of the latter there is surprisingly little discussion of business travel, student travel, and visiting friends and relatives (VFR), while event and health tourism related research are only slowly starting to diversify in terms of study locations. Indeed, the wider role of Islam in national and regional diasporas is a significant factor for tourist flows that has not yet been incorporated into studies of Islamic tourism and halal hospitality.

Beyond the hajj

One area that has obviously been of considerable interest to scholars as a form of religious mobility is the hajj. This has been investigated from a number of different perspectives (Peters 1996; Ockey 2011; Bianchi 2013), not least of which is from the field of travel medicine (Alzeer et al. 1998; Aguilera et al. 2002; Benkouiten et al. 2013; Shafi et al. 2016; Al-Tawfiq, Gautret & Memish, 2017; Ahmed, Ebrahim & Memish 2018; Alfelali et al. 2018; Benkouiten et al. 2018). However, there are clearly substantial opportunities for understanding not only visits to the holy cities outside of the hajj as part of umrah (Hassan, Zainal & Mohamed 2015; Almuhrzi & Alsawafi 2017; Alsumairi & Tsui 2017; Gannon et al. 2017; Lochrie et al. 2018), but also how the hajj intersects with other travel and destination opportunities (Moufahim 2013; Akbulut & Ekin 2018). The latter is becoming increasingly important for Saudi Arabia as it seeks to diversify its economy by promoting a wider range of tourism and leisure opportunities for both domestic and international visitors (Sherbini et al. 2016; Euchi, Omri & Al-Tit 2018). In addition, there is a need to better understand the role of pilgrimage as a form of travel behaviour in general within Islam (Bhardwaj 1998; van Doorn-Harder & de Jong 2001; Haq & Wong 2010; Zamani-Farahani & Henderson 2010; Reader 2013; Laksana 2014; Cohen & Cohen 2015; Nassar, Mostafa & Reisinger 2015; Abdi 2017; Lochrie et al. 2018; Moufahim & Lichrou 2019) and the ways in which different schools of Islamic thought interpret the role and function of pilgrimage. Such concerns are clearly important as, from some interpretations, all travel by Muslims, who are keeping faith with The Prophet's words, could be regarded as a form of pilgrimage given that they are extolled to look at and understand all of Allah's creation. The notion of pilgrimage in Islam therefore needs to be understood in a more nuanced fashion than is sometimes the case to appreciate the different varieties of Islamic pilgrimage, that exist in its broadest sense (Ebadi 2014), and the implications that it has for travel behaviours and their interpretation.

Better understanding the Muslim traveller

Even though there has been a rapid expansion in research on Muslim travellers it is clear that there are many areas that require further attention (Oktadiana, Pearce & Chon 2016). Perhaps foremost amongst these is broadening the range of markets in which research is conducted. Indeed, the Muslim consumer segment is under-researched in comparison to all the other major consumer groups, while as Alserhan and Alserhan (2012) also observe, its significance is greater than the other identified billion-member market segments because:

1 the Muslim consumer group is not limited to one country, but instead exists in economically feasible numbers in the majority of the countries in the world.
2 the Muslim population is relatively young, which will have major implications for consumption patterns and consumer lifestyles.
3 the growth of halal and shariah-compliant regulations in the marketing system will substantially shape consumption practices and the trajectories they will take.

Studies of the Muslim market can also draw on the developing literature on Islamic marketing (Alserhan 2010, 2011; Alserhan, Althawadi & Boulanouar 2016; Bouzenita & Boulanouar 2016). Of particular value, for example, is the need to utilise appropriate research strategies when dealing with women and when the researcher is a woman (Boulanouar, Aitken, Boulanouar & Todd 2017). Similarly, there is a need for more nuanced approaches to understanding dress and verbal and non-verbal communication in both the research process and from the perspective of better appreciating Muslim behaviours in general in tourism as part of service delivery processes (Koc 2018; Akhtar, Sun, Ahmad & Akhtar 2019).

Tourism products and destinations, and the impacts of tourism

Most of the research on Islamic tourism has tended to focus on lodging and restaurants/food as elements of the tourism system that are immediately recognisable for issues of halal hospitality. However, the range of tourism products and the different stages of the travel process clearly indicate the potential application of Sharia to their marketing and management (Mohsin, Ramli & Alkhulayfi 2016). One area on which much work is needed is the transport system that tourists use, especially with respect to the design and use of public transport and rail services, including associated infrastructure (Hall, Le-Klähn & Ram 2017). There is also little research undertaken on shariah-compliant airlines, such as Iran Air, Royal Brunei Airlines and Saudi Arabian Airlines, as well as dual-service (halal and non-halal services) carriers from Islamic states, and the overall availability of halal services and food on international carriers (Idris & Wahab 2018; Latiff et al. 2019). The types of analyses undertaken on lodging with respect to food, dress codes, entertainment, could easily be undertaken on airlines, along with the extent to which halal hospitality is integrated into marketing and communication strategies. In addition, there are opportunities to examine airport terminals and associated infrastructure with respect to their Shariah compliance (Arif, Gupta & Williams 2013; Gupta, Arif & Richardson 2014; Abdul Rahman, Mohammad, Abdul Rahim & Mohd Noh 2018). Similarly, key activities such as tourist shopping, sightseeing, and special-interest tourism also deserve closer attention with respect to Muslim-relevant product design. Indeed, heritage is positioned as a major tourism element in a number of Islamic countries but it is also clear that there are substantial tensions over conservation practices as well as the effects of commodification (Seyfi & Hall 2018, 2019).

There is also an emerging body of work on the promotion of halal by destinations and businesses (Razzaq, Hall & Prayag 2016; Yousaf & Xiucheng 2018), and the extent to which it meets the reality of what is offered (Alserhan et al. 2018). Such issues raise questions not only about the ethical aspects of service offerings but also the extent to which businesses find themselves "forced" into stating that they offer particular services so as to meet pressures from government and religious stakeholders. In addition, there is a need for further work on locations that explicitly promote themselves as halal or Islamic tourism destinations and the extent to which this may affect other markets (Qaddahat, Attaalla & Hussein 2017). Indeed, a statement made in many papers on halal and tourism is the extent to which halal and Sharia provides a point of strategic advantage and differentiation. This may well be so depending on the market for particular products, however empirical evidence to support such claims is often lacking and closer and more critical analyses are required.

There is substantial evidence in the tourism literature with respect to the negative impacts of tourism. However, there is, so far, little discussion of the potential effects of Islamic tourism. Although pilgrimage and religious events are often marked by a great sense of community there is little assessment of the social impact of leisure travel by Muslims. There is also a substantial gap with respect to Islamic understandings of the role of tourism and travel in climate change and other harmful effects on the environment, what might otherwise be regarded as haram, and the personal and state perception of such damage and responses to it. As Islam (2012) noted the Qur'an provides a firm basis for environmental critique and action within an Islamic Environmental Paradigm (IEP):

> The Qur'an guarantees equal rights to other creatures living in the planet to exist and thrive. Not only is that, in IEP human beings are expected to protect the environment since no other creature is able to perform this task. Humans are the only being who have been "entrusted" with the responsibility of looking after the earth. This trusteeship is seen by IEP to be so onerous and burdensome that no other creature would "accept" it.
>
> *(Islam 2012: 77)*

Similarly, the environmental impacts of the halal supply chain need to be considered beyond porcine contamination (Lubis, Mohd-Naim, Alizul & Ahmed 2016), along with a greater focus on the environmental dimensions of halal food growing (Rezai, Mohamed & Shamsudin 2015).

Reflexivity and commodification

The final research issue is that of the reflexivity of researchers on Islamic tourism. There is often a lack of critique in the presentation of notions of halal and Islamic tourism and the governments that promote it. Of course, this may arise, at least in part, from different value and cultural bases with respect to the relative rights and responsibilities of individuals versus the state. Furthermore, in reading work on halal the operation of institutional factors and pressures to favour certain initiatives also needs to be considered. At times, some of the contextualisation of halal, especially in conference papers and open access journals, almost takes the form of attempts to prove the piety of the author rather than critically assess halal matters. There is also often insufficient criticism of poor halal certification procedures, the (lack of or partial) enforcement of halal by responsible government agencies, and the large gap that may exist between what business and enterprises say they do and what actually happens. Such lack of criticism or a willingness to discuss negative aspects of halal or Islamic tourism may be because of not wanting to appear to be critical of either Islam or one's country. However, it may also be that a somewhat unbalanced portrayal of research topics and subjects is presented.

In addition, there is often limited reflection available on the research process and how this is part of a personal and spiritual journey, particularly if you are considering notions of halal and haram and trying to understand the path you take and the relationships with others. This means, for example, ensuring that research and publications are ethically sound and that full acknowledgement is given of others' work and research. Researchers in Islam must not only adhere to university and publisher requirements for ethical publishing but, most importantly, the Qur'an and the hadith if their findings are to be given due weight and consideration. Such reflexivity is an important part of qualitative research but can also greatly assist in understanding a researcher's positionality in any research situation including the impact of one's work (Wan Hassan 2011). This last point is extremely important with respect to halal certification and Islamic tourism because of the issues that are raised about the commodification of the religious experience and the sacred (Tumbat & Belk 2010; Reader 2013; Redden 2016). For example, Sandıkcı (2018) notes how the development of the concept of the Muslim consumer is linked to the growing influence of neoliberalism and the expansion of market logic into the religious sphere—of which the development of halal certification and halal standards are the clearest examples.

Researchers are both placed within and contribute to the intersections between Islam, consumption, and the market and, as Sandıkcı (2018) observes, the conceptualisations of Muslims along with their food and lifestyles have changed in relation to market dynamics and broader socio-political and economic structures (also see Armanios & Ergene 2018). However, within tourism and hospitality there appears inadequate appreciation of this. While the development of halal certification schemes, standards, and promotion can be justified as contributing to improved levels of consumer trust in a globalised marketplace we can simultaneously argue that such developments also are used for the achievement of narrow political agendas, private commercial and economic interests, trade protectionism and competitiveness, and the exclusion of others (Fischer 2011, 2016; Bergeaud-Blackler, Fischer & Lever 2015). Just as profoundly, the focus on physical markers of "halalness" that can be marketised has meant that the intangible nature of our spirituality and our inclusive hospitality to the other are either ignored or not considered in enough detail. The full implications of the marketisation of halal and Islamic tourism need to be much more considered and thoughtful rather than rushing to take advantage of the Islamic dollar. In other words researchers may need to reframe Islamic consumers as people and the market as a community, complete with all its differences and disagreements while still maintaining a sense of common identity. In so doing, and in thinking about the future of halal hospitality and tourism research, we should follow the history of the holy Prophet Muhammad (PBOH) and reflect on how not to succumb to temptation by taking what may seem to be easier paths.

References

Abdi, M. R. (2017)·'Flock with God, ally with money: Ziarah Wali as generator of local economy', *Nizham Journal of Islamic Studies*, 5 (2): 1–14.

Abdul Rahman, N. A., Mohammad, M. F., Abdul Rahim, S. and Mohd Noh, H. (2018) 'Implementing air cargo halal warehouse: Insight from Malaysia', *Journal of Islamic Marketing*, 9 (3): 462–483.

Aguilera, J. F., Perrocheau, A., Meffre, C., Hahné, S. and W135 Working Group. (2002) 'Outbreak of serogroup W135 meningococcal disease after the Hajj pilgrimage, Europe, 2000', *Emerging Infectious Diseases*, 8 (8): 761.

Ahmed, Q. A., Ebrahim, S. and Memish, Z. A. (2018) 'From Hajj services to mass gathering medicine: Saudi Arabia formalizes a novel discipline', *Travel Medicine and Infectious Disease*, DOI: 10.1016/j.tmaid.2018.07.007.

Akbulut, O. and Ekin, Y. (2018) 'Reflections of Hajj and Umrah pilgrimage on religious stores in Mugla-Turkey', *International Journal of Religious Tourism and Pilgrimage*, 6 (3): 4.

Akhtar, N., Sun, J., Ahmad, W. and Akhtar, M. N. (2019) 'The effect of non-verbal messages on Muslim tourists' interaction adaptation: A case study of Halal restaurants in China', *Journal of Destination Marketing & Management*, 11: 10–22.

Alfelali, M., Barasheed, O., Badahdah, A. M., Bokhary, H., Azeem, M. I., Habeebullah, T., et al., on behalf of the Hajj Research Team (2018) 'Influenza vaccination among Saudi Hajj pilgrims: Revealing the uptake and vaccination barriers', *Vaccine*, 36 (16): 2112–2118.

Almuhrzi, H. M. and Alsawafi, A. M. (2017) 'Muslim perspectives on spiritual and religious travel beyond Hajj: Toward understanding motivations for Umrah travel in Oman', *Tourism Management Perspectives*, 24: 235–242.

Alserhan, B. A. (2010) 'Islamic marketing: The birth of a new social science', *Journal of Islamic Marketing*, 1 (1), https://doi.org/10.1108/jima.2010.43201aaa.001.

Alserhan, B. (2011) *The Principles of Islamic Marketing*. London: Routledge.

Alserhan, B. A. and Alserhan, Z. A. (2012) 'Researching Muslim consumers: Do they represent the fourth-billion consumer segment?', *Journal of Islamic Marketing*, 3 (2): 121–138.

Alserhan, B. A., Althawadi, O. M. and Boulanouar, A. W. (2016) 'Theories of Islamic marketing', *International Journal of Islamic Marketing and Branding*, 1 (4): 297–304.

Alserhan, B. A., Wood, B. P., Rutter, R., Halkias, D., Terzi, H. and Al Serhan, O. (2018). 'The transparency of Islamic hotels: "Nice Islam" and the "self-orientalizing" of Muslims?', *International Journal of Tourism Research*, https://doi.org/10.1002/jtr.2197.

Alsumairi, M. and Tsui, K. W. H. (2017) 'A case study: The impact of low-cost carriers on inbound tourism of Saudi Arabia', *Journal of Air Transport Management*, 62: 129–145.

Al-Tawfiq, J. A., Gautret, P. and Memish, Z. A. (2017) 'Expected immunizations and health protection for Hajj and Umrah 2018: An overview', *Travel Medicine and Infectious Disease*, 19: 2–7.

Alzeer, A., Mashlah, A., Fakim, N., Al-Sugair, N., Al-Hedaithy, M., Al-Majed, S. and Jamjoom, G. (1998) 'Tuberculosis is the commonest cause of pneumonia requiring hospitalization during Hajj (pilgrimage to Makkah)', *Journal of Infection*, 36 (3): 303–306.

Arif, M., Gupta, A. and Williams, A. (2013) 'Customer service in the aviation industry: An exploratory analysis of UAE airports', *Journal of Air Transport Management*, 32: 1–7.

Armanios, F. and Ergene, B. (2018) *Halal Food: A History*. New York: Oxford University Press.

Aziz, Y. A., Rahman, A. A., Hassan, H. and Hamid, S. H. (2015) 'Exploring the Islamic and halal tourism definition', in S. A. Jamal, S. M. Radzi, N. Sumarjan, C.T. Chik, and M. F. S. Bakhtiar (eds) *Innovation and Best Practices in Hospitality and Tourism Research, Hospitality and Tourism 2015: Proceedings of HTC, Melaka, Malaysia, 2–3 November 2015*, Leiden: CRC Press/ Belkema, 139–150.

Benkouiten, S., Charrel, R., Belhouchat, K., Drali, T., Salez, N., Nougairede, A., et al. (2013) 'Circulation of respiratory viruses among pilgrims during the 2012 Hajj pilgrimage', *Clinical Infectious Diseases*, 57 (7): 992–1000.

Benkouiten, S., Al-Tawfiq, J. A., Memish, Z. A., Albarrak, A. and Gautret, P. (2018) 'Clinical respiratory infections and pneumonia during the Hajj pilgrimage: A systematic review', *Travel Medicine and Infectious Disease*, https://doi.org/10.1016/j.tmaid.2018.12.002.

Bergeaud-Blackler, F., Fischer, J. and Lever, J. (eds) (2015) *Halal Matters: Islam, Politics and Markets in Global Perspective*. Abingdon: Routledge.

Bhardwaj, S. (1998) 'Non-hajj pilgrimage in Islam: A neglected dimension of religious circulation', *Journal of Cultural Geography*, 17 (2): 69–87.

Bianchi, R. (2013) *Islamic Globalization: Pilgrimage, Capitalism, Democracy, and Diplomacy*. Singapore: World Scientific.

Boğan, E. and Sarıışık, M. (2018) 'Halal tourism: conceptual and practical challenges', *Journal of Islamic Marketing*, https://doi.org/10.1108/JIMA-06-2017-0066.

Boulanouar, A. W., Aitken, R., Boulanouar, Z. and Todd, S. J. (2017) 'Imperatives for research designs with Muslim women', *Marketing Intelligence & Planning*, 35 (1): 2–17.

Bouzenita, A. and Boulanouar, A. W. (2016) 'Maslow's hierarchy of needs: An Islamic critique', *Intellectual Discourse*, 24 (1): 59. Available from http://journals.iium.edu.my/intdiscourse/index.php/islam/article/view/749

Cohen, E. and Cohen, S. A. (2015) 'A mobilities approach to tourism from emerging world regions', *Current Issues in Tourism*, 18 (1): 11–43.

Ebadi, M. (2014) 'Typologies of the visitors at Khaled Nabi shrine, Iran: Tourists or pilgrims?', *International Journal of Culture, Tourism and Hospitality Research*, 8 (3): 310–321.

El-Gohary, H. (2016) 'Halal tourism, is it really Halal?' *Tourism Management Perspectives*, 19: 124–130.

Euchi, J., Omri, A. and Al-Tit, A. (2018) 'The pillars of economic diversification in Saudi Arabia', *World Review of Science, Technology and Sustainable Development*, 14 (4): 330–343.

Fischer, J. (2011) *The Halal Frontier: Muslim Consumers in a Globalised Market*. New York: Palgrave Macmillan.

Fischer, J. (2016) 'Manufacturing halal in Malaysia', *Contemporary Islam*, 10 (1): 35–52.

Gannon, M. J., Baxter, I. W., Collinson, E., Curran, R., Farrington, T., Glasgow, S., et al. (2017) 'Travelling for Umrah: destination attributes, destination image, and post-travel intentions', *Service Industries Journal*, 37 (7–8): 448–465.

Gupta, A., Arif, M. and Richardson, P. A. (2014) 'Assessing customer service in airports—models from the UAE', *International Journal of Aviation, Aeronautics, and Aerospace*, 1 (2): 3, https://doi.org/10.15394/ijaaa.2014.1007

Hall, C. M., Le-Klähn, D. T. and Ram, Y. (2017) *Tourism, Public Transport and Sustainable Mobility*. Bristol: Channelview.

Haq, F. and Wong, H.Y. (2010) 'Is spiritual tourism a new strategy for marketing Islam?', *Journal of Islamic Marketing*, 1 (2): 136–148.

Hassan, S. H., Zainal, S. R. M. and Mohamed, O. (2015) 'Determinants of destination knowledge acquisition in religious tourism: Perspective of Umrah travelers', *International Journal of Marketing Studies*, 7 (3): 84.

Henderson, J. C. (2009) 'Islamic tourism reviewed', *Tourism Recreation Research*, 34 (2): 207–211.

Idris, J. and Wahab, N. A. (2018) 'Shariah-compliant airlines in Malaysia: An initial review'. In *Proceedings of the 3rd International Halal Conference (INHAC 2016)*. Singapore: Springer, 135–362.

Islam, M. S. (2012) 'Old philosophy, new movement: The rise of the Islamic ecological paradigm in the discourse of environmentalism', *Nature and Culture*, 7 (1): 72–94.

Khan, F. and Callanan, M. (2017) 'The "Halalification" of tourism', *Journal of Islamic Marketing*, 8 (4): 558–577.

Koc, E. (2018) 'Service failures and recovery in hospitality and tourism: A review of literature and recommendations for future research', *Journal of Hospitality Marketing & Management*, https://doi.org/10.1080/19368623.2019.1537139.

Laksana, A. B. (2014) *Muslim and Catholic Pilgrimage Practice: Explorations through Java*. Cheltenham: Ashgate.

Latiff, Z. A. A., Masril, M. V., Vintisen, R., Baki, M. Z. and Muhamad, N. (2019) 'Consumers' intention towards halal food in low-cost airlines in Kelantan, Malaysia', *Journal of Contemporary Research in Social Sciences*, 1 (1): 82–86.

Lochrie, S., Baxter, I. W., Collinson, E., Curran, R., Gannon, M. J., Taheri, B., et al. (2018) 'Self-expression and play: Can religious tourism be hedonistic?', *Tourism Recreation Research*, https://doi.org/10.1080/02508281.2018.1545825.

Lubis, H. N., Mohd-Naim, N. F., Alizul, N. N. and Ahmed, M. U. (2016) 'From market to food plate: Current trusted technology and innovations in halal food analysis', *Trends in Food Science & Technology*, 58: 55–68.

Mohsin, A., Ramli, N. and Alkhulayfi, B. A. (2016) 'Halal tourism: Emerging opportunities', *Tourism Management Perspectives*, 19: 137–143.

Moufahim, M. (2013) 'Religious gift giving: An ethnographic account of a Muslim pilgrimage', *Marketing Theory*, 13 (4): 421–441.

Moufahim, M. and Lichrou, M. (2019) 'Pilgrimage, consumption and rituals: Spiritual authenticity in a Shia Muslim pilgrimage', *Tourism Management*, 70: 322–332.

Nassar, M. A., Mostafa, M. M. and Reisinger, Y. (2015) 'Factors influencing travel to Islamic destinations: An empirical analysis of Kuwaiti nationals', *International Journal of Culture, Tourism and Hospitality Research*, 9 (1): 36–53.

Ockey, J. (2011) 'Individual imaginings: The religio-nationalist pilgrimages of Haji Sulong Abdulkadir al-Fatani', *Journal of Southeast Asian Studies*, 42 (1): 89–119.

Oktadiana, H., Pearce, P. L. and Chon, K. (2016) 'Muslim travellers' needs: What don't we know?', *Tourism Management Perspectives*, 20: 124–130.

Peters, F. E. (1996) *The Hajj: The Muslim Pilgrimage to Mecca and the Holy Places*. Princeton, NJ: Princeton University Press.

Qaddahat, R., Attaalla, F. and Hussein, M. M. (2017) 'Halal tourism: Evaluating opportunities and challenges in the Middle East: Jordan and Egypt', *International Journal of Heritage, Tourism, and Hospitality*, 10 (2/2).

Razzaq, S., Hall, C. M., & Prayag, G. (2016) 'The capacity of New Zealand to accommodate the halal tourism market—Or not', *Tourism Management Perspectives*, 18: 92–97.

Reader, I. (2013) *Pilgrimage in the Marketplace*. New York: Routledge.

Redden, G. (2016) 'Revisiting the spiritual supermarket: Does the commodification of spirituality necessarily devalue it?', *Culture and Religion*, 17 (2): 231–249.

Rezai, G., Mohamed, Z. and Shamsudin, M. N. (2015) 'Can halal be sustainable? Study on Malaysian consumers' perspective', *Journal of Food Products Marketing*, 21 (6): 654–666.

Sandıkcı, Ö. (2018) 'Religion and the marketplace: Constructing the "new" Muslim consumer', *Religion*, 1–21.

Seyfi, S. and Hall, C.M. (2018) 'Managing World Heritage site stakeholders: A grounded theory paradigm model approach', *Journal of Heritage Tourism*, DOI: 10.1080/1743873X.2018.1527340.

Seyfi, S. and Hall, C.M. (eds) (2019) *Tourism in Iran: Challenges, Development and Issues*. Abingdon: Routledge

Shafi, S., Dar, O., Khan, M., Khan, M., Azhar, E. I., McCloskey, B., et al. (2016) 'The annual Hajj pilgrimage—minimizing the risk of ill health in pilgrims from Europe and opportunity for driving the best prevention and health promotion guidelines', *International Journal of Infectious Diseases*, 47: 79–82.

Sherbini, A., Aziz, Y. A., Sidin, S. M. and Yusof, R. N. R. (2016) 'Income diversification for future stable economy in Saudi Arabia: An overview of tourism industry', *International Journal of Economics, Commerce and Management*, 6 (11): 173–189.

Siddiqui, M. (2015) *Hospitality and Islam: Welcoming in God's Name*. New Haven, CT: Yale University Press.

Tumbat, G. and Belk, R. W. (2010) 'Marketplace tensions in extraordinary experiences', *Journal of Consumer Research*, 38 (1): 42–61.

van Doorn-Harder, N. and de Jong, K. (2001) 'The pilgrimage to Tembayat: Tradition and revival in Indonesian Islam', *The Muslim World*, 91 (3–4): 325–354.

Vargas-Sánchez, A. and Moral-Moral, M. (2018) 'Halal tourism: State of the art', *Tourism Review*, https://doi.org/10.1108/TR-01-2018-0015.

Wan Hassan, M. (2011) 'Studying halal restaurants in New Zealand: Experiences and perspectives of a Muslim female researcher', in C. M. Hall (ed.) *Fieldwork in Tourism: Methods, Issues and Reflections*. London: Routledge, 112–126.

Yousaf, S. and Xiucheng, F. (2018) 'Halal culinary and tourism marketing strategies on government websites: A preliminary analysis', *Tourism Management*, 68: 423–443.

Zamani-Farahani, H. and Henderson, J. C. (2010) 'Islamic tourism and managing tourism development in Islamic societies: The cases of Iran and Saudi Arabia', *International Journal of Tourism Research*, 12 (1): 79–89.

INDEX